AMERICAN PAINTING

History and Interpretation

AMERICAN PAINTING

History and Interpretation

BY

VIRGIL BARKER

BONANZA BOOKS

ACKNOWLEDGEMENTS

American Philosophical Society and Mr. Charles Coleman Sellers: for quotations from Mr. Sellers' *Charles Willson Peale* (2 vols.). Copyright, 1939, by Charles Coleman Sellers.

Brandt & Brandt: for quotation from *Sonnets* by Edna St. Vincent Millay. Copyright, 1920, 1948, by Edna St. Vincent Millay.

Doubleday & Company, Inc.: for quotation from *The Seven Seas* by Rudyard Kipling. Copyright, 1896, by Rudyard Kipling, reprinted by permission of Mrs. George Bambridge and Doubleday & Company, Inc.

Dover Publications, Inc.: for quotation from *Shaker Furniture* by Edward Deming Andrews and Faith Andrews. Copyright, 1937, by Edward Deming Andrews.

Mrs. Alice G. Dow: for material reproduced in *Arts and Crafts in New England,* compiled by George Francis Dow. Copyright, 1927, by The Wayside Press.

Essex Institute: for quotations from the *Diary* of William Bentley.

Mr. Charles E. Goodspeed: for advertisements reproduced in his and Frank W. Bayley's edition of Dunlap's *History . . . of the Arts of Design.* Copyright, 1918, by C. E. Goodspeed & Company.

Harvard University Press: for quotation from *Three Centuries of Harvard* by Samuel Eliot Morison. Copyright, 1936, by the President and Fellows of Harvard College.

Houghton Mifflin Company: for quotation from *The Tale of Genji* by Lady Murasaki (translated by Arthur Waley).

Magazine of Art: for a portion of my article "Santos and Signs" (April 1943).

Massachusetts Historical Society: for quotations from *The Smibert-Moffatt Letters* and *The Copley-Pelham Letters.*

Mrs. Richard W. Millar: for material reproduced in *Nancy Shippen, Her Journal Book,* compiled and edited by Ethel Armes. Published 1935, by J. B. Lippincott Co., copyright, 1935, by Ethel Armes and Lloyd P. Shippen.

The New-York Historical Society: for newspaper material reprinted in *Notes on American Artists* compiled by William Kelby, and in *The Arts and Crafts in New York* compiled by Rita S. Gottesman.

Dr. J. Hall Pleasants: for quotations about Francis Guy.

Simon and Schuster, Inc.: for quotation from *Trader Horn.* Copyright, 1927, by Ethelreda Lewis.

William E. Rudge's Sons and Mr. Avrahm Yarmolinsky: for quotation from Paul Svinin given in *Picturesque United States of America, 1811–1812.* Copyright, 1929, by R. T. H. Halsey.

University of Pennsylvania Press: for quotation from *One Man In His Time* edited by Maud and Otis Skinner. Copyright, 1938, by the University of Pennsylvania Press.

The Valentine Museum: for newspaper material about Fisher reproduced in notes deposited with The Frick Art Reference Library.

The Walpole Society: for advertisements reproduced in *The Arts and Crafts in Philadelphia, Maryland, and South Carolina* collected by Alfred Coxe Prime (2 series), Copyright, 1929, by The Walpole Society.

Further bibliographical details on these sources will be found in the notes.

This edition is published by Bonanza Books, a division of Crown Publishers, Inc., by special arrangement with the Macmillan Company. (B)

Preface

Samuel Isham's *History of American Painting* is a permanent landmark in its field; it was the first book on the subject to combine an orderly time sequence, logical groupings, and a consistently applied standard of professional criticism. In the forty-five years since it was first printed, the ideas of criticism have changed so markedly that they can yield a new interpretation; the amount of knowledge has increased so strikingly that it both suggests more complex groupings than his and requires a more precise organization of them in order to clarify the transit of history. But any attempt to survey the field as a whole can never be a last word on the subject; it can only be, for its own time, a helpful first word.

The additions to factual information since Isham wrote have indeed been so immense that this attempt to re-tell the history of American painting omits his third, or Cosmopolitan, time division, leaving it and its successor, the Contemporary period, to receive their duly detailed treatment in some other book. Retaining Isham's characterizing adjectives, Colonial and Provincial, this book supplies each with three divisions which correspond to changes of climate in American culture. Certain painters with whom this book concludes lived and worked beyond the end of the Provincial period, which may be most conveniently dated as 1880; but in both spirit and craft they developed their provincial inheritance more than they participated in the technique and attitude of the somewhat younger cosmopolitans.

Of course, the whole device of periods and subdivisions is only an artifice of narrative for the historian who must describe change. As Mr. Edgar P. Richardson has put it with irrefutable simplicity: "There are no periods except in books." However, since they are necessary there, they should be made as distinct as the facts may warrant. When the books are shut, the human mind will blur and merge all periods quite as effectively as history itself.

Though only one name appears as author on the title page, this book is the work of two. My wife, Ida Ogden Barker, shared in the long search for the paintings through the better part of ten years: five trips through the East from Florida to Maine, a prolonged trip from Detroit and St. Paul to New Orleans, and one to California. In this way all the pictures, with less than a dozen exceptions, have been examined together; on every important painter and many minor ones, stylistic notes have been made by both, working independently, and any differences clarified in conversation. Factual research in books and articles has been the work of V. B., and he also wrote a first draft of the text; subsequent revision has been so complex that every paragraph is now a joint production.

The idea of the book began to take shape during the years of working on *The Arts Magazine* under the prophetic leadership of Mr. Forbes Watson. An incentive to proceed with it was a commission from the late Mrs. Juliana Force, Director of the Whitney Museum of American Art, to write *A Critical Introduction to American Painting*. A general indebtedness through twenty years is acknowledged to that invaluable storehouse for the student of art history, the Frick Art Reference Library; and we wish to express our appreciation for the courtesies extended by Miss Ethelwyn Manning, Mrs. Henry W. Howell, Jr., and the staff. We are grateful to Mrs. A. Travers Elwell for comments in the course of typing the manuscript. The generosity with which private owners made pictures and records accessible to us was memorable; and in this we received important aid from the late Hon. Alexander Wilbourne Weddell, of Richmond, and Miss Sarah Henderson, of New Orleans. We wish also to record our thanks to our friends: Dr. Bowman Foster Ashe, President of the University of Miami, Coral Gables, Florida; Miss Alice M. O'Brien, St. Paul, Minnesota; Mr. Jay Darling, Des Moines, Iowa; Mr. and Mrs. C. Robert Morse, New York City; Mr. Lloyd Goodrich, Associate Director of the Whitney Museum of American Art, New York City; Mr. Holger Cahill, New York City; and Mr. Cecil Scott, Associate Editor, The Macmillan Company, New York City.

Table of Contents

PERIOD TWO: THE PROVINCIAL

DIVISION FOUR: The Federal Era—1790 to 1830

DIVISION SIX: Aftermath of the Civil War—1860 to 1880

DIVISION SEVEN: National Culmination

List of Plates

In choosing the illustrations the dual aim has been to emphasize the more important painters and at the same time to achieve a rounded representation of American painting as a whole. Subsidiary to that, preference has been given to pictures in collections generally accessible to the public. All the paintings are in oil on canvas unless otherwise specified. Dimensions are given in inches, with height first and width second.

PERIOD ONE: THE COLONIAL

DIVISION ONE: Colonial Beginnings—to 1725

DIVISION SEVEN: National Culmination

PERIOD ONE
THE COLONIAL

DIVISION ONE
Colonial Beginnings—
to 1725

1. Exploration, conquest, and settlement

The first pictures by Europeans in the Americas were the work of a few explorers who, being amateur artists, made their own crude drawings; slightly later explorers brought along professional artists who set down their records in water color. Those productions were all taken back to Europe as visual reports of the discoveries, and many of them were reproduced in engraving to accompany the printed reports by which Europeans were incited to further exploration and conquest. Neither the pictures nor their makers participated in the actual transplantation of painting to the new world because in any time and place the life of an art or a craft requires the presence of a third factor. Painters can make a living only where people want their paintings. Artist, work, and audience must all be present to form the whole called art.

This threefold requirement was early fulfilled in Mexico and Peru because there the Spaniards chanced upon nations that had accumulated reserves of wealth and created great arts. In both countries workmen were so skilled that they could readily adapt European techniques and even adopt European concepts; in both countries splendid hybrids of art were developed which derive their vitality as much from native talent as from European styles. In both, furthermore, the masses, which included the artisans, were already in subjection to native conquerors, so that the Spaniards found governmental and social structures well adjusted to their own formula for conquest: exploitation by a ruling class.

Contrastingly, the Spanish-controlled regions now within the boundaries of the United States remained distant and imperfectly civilized frontiers where sparse populations had no need of technically advanced arts. Out of Florida to Spain went some manuscript illustrations in routine reports by the Catholic missionaries and the government officials; in that militarized province a remarkable fort could be erected, but the life of the other arts was meager and uncertain. The Spanish interregnum in Louisiana left a bequest of massive buildings, to which the French later added their own lighter touches, yet scarcely a trace of painting. In Texas and in California also, though a few religious pictures were made by natives under the tutelage of the friars, the

3

artistic legacy of the Spaniards was mainly architectural. In New Mexico, however, where the capital Santa Fe was founded a few years before the English
put ashore at Jamestown, there was a considerable amount of technically
humble but religiously expressive art.

The paintings, called retablos to distinguish them from the carved bultos,
stood on the mission altars and hung in the homes, to watch the meditation of
an hour or to receive a momentary prayer. The religion embodied in them
permeated life so completely that their makers were effective members of the
community, uncrippled by the self-consciousness which derives from doing
something not generally understood. Some of them worked with a degree of
artisan skill deserving to be called professional, while others remained amateur;
and of both sorts, some worked wholly in their own settlements while perhaps
more sought out their markets as itinerants.

Both the content and the technique of the retablos were as suited to the life
around them as the adobe churches and homes. In them and all other crafts the
irregularities of handwork had the same vitality for the eye and mind; and the
retablos in particular, despite their customary smallness, exhale a truly primitive
largeness of feeling. The unconscious boldness of their linear consistency com-
pensates for the absence of the third dimension; their artistic character is more
pictographic than pictorial. Their color range is sharply limited by the sources
of the pigments—earths and vegetables and imported indigo; and this limitation is a fitting parallel to the somber spiritual life which was in such marked
contrast to the radiant immensity of that high country. Since the pictures were
the religious expression of ideas that were more communal than personal, they
remain appropriately anonymous for the most part; but the names of a few
painters are known and intensive study is now permitting some instances of
stylistic identification. In general, repetition in both handling and theme makes
it difficult or impossible to assign dates to specific examples, but the better ones
seem usually to be also the older ones. Their esthetic quality was not singled
out as a separate experience until after the twentieth-century re-discovery of
primitive art the world over; and long before that occurred these New Mexican
retablos had become an anachronism incapable of survival into a culture increasingly antipathetic.

In the more easterly regions controlled by the French the two governmental
centers were very far apart—Quebec on the St. Lawrence and New Orleans on
the Mississippi. Communication was possible, though perhaps more slowly than
by sea, along a far-flung chain of forts protecting traders and missionaries
through the middle of the continent. Such posts do not produce schools of
painting; and in neither city, while it was French-ruled, was there any really
intensive patronage of that art. In Canada, at least, some altar-paintings were

made both by priest-painters coming over from France and by a few local work-men whom they taught. Their approximations to the sophisticated work of the mother country do not now carry the conviction felt in the more awkward but more intense retablos just discussed. The French long handicapped them-selves by the belief that they, too, were here to exploit the natives on the Spanish pattern; yet nowhere did they find the dense and permanent popula-tions which such a program required for its success. Not until the English had demonstrated the superiority of colonizing did the French decide to change, and then it was too late for them to achieve continental domination.

It was the different concept of the English which enabled them to transform the same conditions into advantages. The two competing ideas and their con-trasting results were clearly described as early as 1754 by the Marquis Duquesne in his farewell address to the Iroquois:

Are you ignorant of the difference between the King of England and the King of France? Go, see the forts that our King has established, and you will see that you can still hunt under their very walls. They have been placed for your advantage in places which you frequent. The English, on the contrary, are no sooner in possession of a place than the game is driven away. The forest falls before them as they ad-vance, and the soil is laid bare so that you can scarce find the wherewithal to erect a shelter for the night.

The French wished the Amerinds to remain as they were because they could thus be more easily controlled; the English wanted the Amerinds out of the way because they hindered the extension of settlement.

It was mistakenly arrogant in all of the invading Europeans to stigmatize the state of these eastern Amerinds as barbarism. It was especially unjust in the English because their own settlements encroached upon stabilized Amerind communities and because only the temporary good will they met with per-mitted them to acquire the skills of native woodcraft and agriculture by which their own stability was assured. For the Europeans such skills were clear and permanent gain, serving them for generations along a continually advancing frontier. But the firearms which they sporadically tried to keep from the Amer-inds and the firewater which they more freely bestowed were both shockingly destructive in their effects upon the Amerinds' long-established equilibrium in their environment. Yet no retrospective moral indignation can alter the fact that there was an unbridgeable gap between the two stages of culture.

As recognized in the speech of Duquesne, the Amerinds east of the Missis-sippi were forest dwellers, and their possessions were practically confined to the single category of perishable utilitarian objects. Unlike the natives of Mexico and Peru, their craft skills were not of a kind to permit artistic grafting. Their rudimentary drawing and coloring in particular were limited to temporary body decorations and to pictographs; on that basis they could make no use of the painting brought in by Europeans. Grandfather's portrait, so bracing to a family's pride on a living room wall, was an impossible encumbrance in a wigwam.

The new-world swarming of the English on a scale unmatched by other Europeans was caused by conditions at home which were then unique in that part of the world. Across the Channel only Holland was crowded with people, and they were so busy with trade that relatively few wanted to leave; the rest of the continent was depleted by the scourge of war. But in England there was a large surplus population cast adrift by the economic readjustments of a changing order; there were many who desired to escape from religious persecutions; and there were also merchant companies ready to finance emigration in the hope of profits.

Any transplantation of civilization is first of all affected by its participants' ideas of what civilization is; it therefore becomes important to note the kind of English who emigrated. Those who chose to come here were—in an approximate order of decreasing number and increasing rank—laborers, farmers, tradesmen, artisans, clergymen, country squires, and a very few younger sons of "gentle" birth. With no opportunity to choose, a fair number of jailbirds were shipped here. If the men did not bring wives and children with them, they quickly acquired families and thus made permanent their commitment to the new world; and people so committed to winning their living by personal labor would be qualitatively modified by new-world conditions much sooner and in the end much more profoundly than soldiers and administrators coming out in the hope of a quick wealth which would enable them to go back to Europe. Even the sometimes appalling decimations of disease did not prevent the rapid growth of the English colonies, and the system of charter by which they were initiated permitted them to devise governmental and economic structures freer from remote control than those of New France and New Spain. In this way the sheer numbers of the English combined with their ways of life to make them dominant in economics and politics, in language and in literature, and in the other arts as well.

At first there were considerable differences among the English from colony to colony, but they were to prove culturally less significant than English homogeneity in relation to the variety of other national groups who had come here—some of them independently, others with the help of the English colonizing agencies desirous of filling up the land. As with all other water fronts, those in the colonies resounded with a jumble of languages from the first; and about a score of European countries contributed to the permanent population before the colonial period closed. By no means all of these diverse stocks demonstrably affected painting here; but wherever it can be discerned, every such effect has some meaning in the amalgamations and mutations which enter into every phase of American history. Yet even before the colonies joined themselves into a nation the differences, not merely between the various English but also between the English and the non-English stocks, had become less important, so far as concerned the art of painting, than the uniformity of taste and style determined by conditions common to the country from Maine to Georgia.

2. Protestantism and art

Cultural uniformity in the colonies was achieved relatively quickly in large measure because in England and the north of Europe, before ever embarking for North America, the settlers-to-be had developed one fundamental likeness: a likeness which, perhaps even more than the new environment itself, was to influence the formation of colonial taste. In religion they were Protestants.

Lutheranism was imported by the Swedes along the Delaware. Very few among the Swiss and Germans of the middle region were Lutheran; most of them were Christian radicals of varying beliefs who had been persecuted in Europe by Lutheran and Catholic alike. The Dutch, the Scotch, the Scotch-Irish, the few Swiss in the south, and the more numerous French scattered through the coastal towns were all Calvinist. The Puritans of Massachusetts were purifiers of an Established Church they did not wish to destroy, but the Pilgrims who preceded them were separatists in a still older tradition. The first dominant organizing group in Pennsylvania were Quaker in belief; throughout the southerly regions the great majority of the settlers held to the more easy-going faith of an unchanged English Established Church. Whether exacting or tolerant in matters of dogma and conduct, this Protestant temper common to the nationally diverse colonials meant that they came together in the new world with an attitude toward arts and crafts different from that of the Catholics.

The Catholic position was that men and women could be persuaded to the divine through the senses and that the sensuous appeal of the arts would be most effectively employed in conveying religious teachings and evoking religious emotions. This stand had not been adopted without opposition, for hatred of images gave rise to schisms even in the early stages of Christianity; the strain of asceticism is in human nature, and to this day there are esthetic puritans among the Catholics. Moreover, the Catholic church was not the only active religious group during the Middle Ages; human nature being what it is, the orthodoxy of any age implies the co-existence of non-orthodoxy. The medieval church was strong through its very struggle against different ideas, and not even during its time of greatest ascendancy was dissent extirpated.

Heresy in fact took forms as authentically medieval as Catholicism itself; long before Luther and Calvin there had been Waldo and Wyclif and Huss. Their followers, being from the less privileged classes, were motivated by an inex-

8

tricable mingling of desires to purify the doctrine of the church and to strip it of its material wealth. But the church maintained its use of art with sufficient success to produce the buildings and carvings and pictures which were for almost a thousand years the greatest glories of European civilization. By the time of settlement here, of course, such loftily religious art was far in the past, and images then being installed in Catholic churches were in general so theatrical that they could be rejected by tastes far from puritanical. The Catholic theory, however, remained unimpaired by the inferiority of current production; it could still function vitally in the humble retablos of the American Southwest.

The Protestants, rejecting priestly and saintly mediation between a man and his Deity, affirmed that their proper relationship was a private matter. This at once wiped out all need for religious visual art. Representations of sacred stories for the eye became distractions for the mind. The Protestant would not have his religion profaned by human forms in carvings or in paintings on walls or windows; he wanted the clear white light of divinity shining directly upon his individual soul. By thus stripping away almost all ritual and all the slow accretions of art, the Protestant seemed to gain for himself an intensified devotion; but he also thereby limited himself and, even more unfortunately, his descendants to the arts of worldly usefulness. Protestantism in religion produces utilitarianism in art.

Since the English were to become dominant here, the state of painting among them at home may be indicated more precisely. The Wars of the Roses from 1455 to 1485, though dynastic rather than religious in character, had been so devastating in their effects on all crafts that these had to be renewed from the continent. The renewal of specifically religious art was prevented by the churchly separation enforced by Henry the Eighth, who not only expropriated the holdings of the monastic orders but also commenced the spoliation of the chief religious centers throughout the land. Such defacements, after the interval of Catholic Mary, were resumed under Elizabeth; there is in existence a picture painted in 1567 which shows a government commission presiding over the destruction of the art works in the cathedral at Canterbury. For iconoclasm to have reached the point of defacing, under official auspices, the central shrine of England indicates the extent to which the secular idea had triumphed.

The painting of professional quality which was fostered through these reigns was exclusively portraiture; and the mass of portraiture, in the times of its greatest popularity, has never attained the highest rank of art. As an early nineteenth-century writer neatly phrased it, the portrait ". . . recommends itself to the personal vanity and the household affections of all mankind . . ." In England before the eighteenth century, success even in portraiture was largely confined to the foreigners who took advantage of the English fondness for continental fashions: a fondness which paid little attention to artistic quality and cared only for a craft displaying the new nobility and merchant class with specious richness of effect. Only in the miniature portrait, a development out of the medieval manuscript illumination in which Englishmen had shown striking ability, did the native-born English exhibit any outstanding talent.

So nearly complete a canalization of painting into a single non-religious branch had never before occurred in Christian Europe, and its consequences were bound to prove severe in any colony dominated by English taste as well as ruled by English law. In colonial American churches paintings were remarkable for their rarity; and since the colonial period constitutes one-half of our national history, so pronounced a lack is still operative in its effects. In the experience of Americans generally the dissociation between painting and religion has been so complete that the art has been emptied of the most powerful emotions possible in either the private or the communal life: a void which is still to be replenished for the democratic audience of today.

3. Early Virginia

Chronologically the first permanent English colony (1607), Virginia was slow to attain the conditions in which painting could be practised there. Too few of those who were earliest concerned with the Virginian venture were willing to scale down their dreams of sudden riches to the blunt common sense of Captain John Smith's "Nothing is to be got thence except by labour." Economic stability was further delayed by preconceived ideas of Company officials who remained in England, and it was contrary to their plans that the colony managed to establish itself on the basis of tobacco as the single exportable crop. It was this crop which caused the spread of indentured servants—a hundred thousand of them—self-sold to labor for their masters four or five years in the hope of freedom and farms.

The relatively small number who managed to realize that hope did not thereby become able to acquire possessions on the scale needed to give life to a localized art; on the contrary, it would be difficult to exaggerate the coarse living and rude belongings of the thinly distributed population. So long as such freedmen formed the character-giving element in the colony even portraiture was apparently unknown; not until the appearance of large-scale landowners using slave labor did that branch of painting develop as one among several crafts contributing to elegance of living and family prestige.

Mature colonial society in Virginia, including its attitude toward painting, was affected to a remarkable degree by an influx of royalist refugees from Cromwell and his Parliament. The colony's loyalty to the two Charleses, beheaded father and restored son, was such as to earn for it the still cherished title of His Majesty's Old Dominion. With the restoration most of the exiles returned to England, but their stay of fifteen years and the continuing influence of the few who remained were sufficient to set a definite pattern of life for later generations of plantation-owners. The economic basis for that pattern has been described in the observation that for southerners ". . . waste is a principle . . .": two centuries of accelerating exploitation on a continental scale have established a far wider applicability for the epigram, but the South's quick adoption of slavery permitted the earliest manifestation in the colonies of lavish living. Existence there was more genial than in New England, more elegant than in New York, and more careless than in Pennsylvania; and even a cautious historian must grant it at least the semi-cavalier glamor of candle-lit banquets and dances, of spirited horse races and fox hunts, of reckless gambling and gay theatricals.

The royalists brought with them more wealth and personal property than the original colonists had brought, and among their possessions were some family likenesses. If they did not actually introduce the idea of the social function of portraiture, the sojourners certainly implanted in Virginians generally the belief that the most desirable portrait was one from a London studio; and so effective was this guidance in taste that there occurred one extreme instance of a written description sent over in lieu of the sitter. The portrait sent back must have depicted the momentary last word in fashionable costume, and its ostensible subject could have conferred a belated degree of similarity upon the picture by copying as closely as possible both clothes and posture. As for likeness and character, those not unimportant elements were then subordinated, particularly by the most popular painters in England, to a species of standardized craft.

This is most convincingly shown by the wearying monotony of the portraits themselves, but there is competent recorded testimony to the same effect; the poet Alexander Pope, for example, though a friend of the court painter, Sir Godfrey Kneller, likened his practice of portraiture to the making of a Kidderminster carpet. During the one visit usually required of a sitter, Kneller would himself make a crayon sketch—sometimes fourteen in one day—or would paint the head directly on the canvas. The work would then pass under the hands of studio assistants who each in succession added his assigned bit: hat or wig, coat or buttons, laces or ruffles. This overly specialized piecework was often very deft in achieving flattery and glitter, but on its own social level of luxury it was as much of a trade as was sign painting on its level of usefulness; each was a commercial job which a particular buying public wanted.

The Virginians who wished to visit England to be portraitized found it relatively easy through the direct traffic of the tobacco boats. Even so, pictures in Virginia wearing English attributions are too numerous. The London-painted portrait indeed rivals the English-made brick as a prime tradition; it is still, in specific cases, re-affirmed in the face of probability because it is natural for descendants to prefer thinking that their ancestors were depicted in metropolitan studios crowded with courtly patrons instead of by less capable itinerants visiting incipient manorial estates.

Frequently, also—and not only in Virginia but in every colony—family identifications have slipped backward a generation or two. Thus, in Virginia, examples said to be of seventeenth-century subjects show them wearing eighteenth-century clothes. Though legend yet prevails there in respect to the early portraits, legend must sooner or later give place to history. Winnowing out the obvious errors will still leave authentic seventeenth-century works, and among these some may prove to possess the momentous cultural significance of being local products instead of imports.

4. The first century in Massachusetts

It was direct practicality in Captain John Smith to specify the correct means of making Virginia into a successful colony, but there was prescience in his words of 1616 comparing New England with other parts of the world:

> . . . mine owne eyes that have seene a great part of those Cities and their King-domes, as well as it, can find no advantage they have in nature, but this. They are beautified by long labour and diligence of industrious people and Art. This is onely as God made it, when he created the worlde. Therefore I conclude, if the heart and intralls of those Regions were sought; if their Land were cultured, planted, and manured by men of industrie, iugdment, and experience; what hope is there, or what nede they doubt, having those advantages of the Sea, but it might equalize any of those famous Kingdoms, in all commodities, pleasures, and conditions? . . .

That last sentence may be grammatically cloudy, but as an idea it is clear enough; and though as idea it must then have seemed fantastic to many, the event has shown Smith's vision of the future to have been as shrewdly accurate as his estimate of his own present. For in comparison with any colony planted then or since, New England can certainly hold its own in both material and cultural accomplishment.

Painting in particular was apparently practised there earlier than in Virginia; even so, it was part not of the newness but of the oldness. The painters who transplanted their craft to Massachusetts re-established its old-world serviceable-ness even as the people themselves continued the old-world pattern of their living. It was a pattern of villages expanding into towns and cities; the result-ing compactness and density of population favored that specialization of skills by which the crafts best thrive. A silversmith, a joiner, and even a certain kind of painter could make a living in late seventeenth-century Boston because the town is the artisan's natural market. And since the New Englanders came not as chance conglomerations of individuals but as functioning communities, they managed, somewhat sooner than settlers in other regions, to get beyond trans-planting toward creating a culture.

The English in Massachusetts, both Pilgrim and Puritan, chose to live on a frontier, yet they were not frontier people; nor were the things they made after the first year or so frontier substitutes. From a combination of religious persecu-tion and a severe ideal of personal conduct, the settlers were sufficiently stern in character before they sighted the not-so-rockbound coast of their destiny, but they had not stripped themselves of beautiful possessions. They came from the provincial towns and the countryside of England, where medieval craftsmanship was still alive; and among the people of the Bay especially there were workmen in full possession of several forms of craft. In the things of greatest usefulness such as house-building and furniture-making, which were subjected to the greatest pressure toward modification from the new living conditions and the greatest stimulation toward experiment from new materials, there occurred stylistic developments which deserve to be called creative. Although the painter's craft did not manifest such originality so quickly, the fact that it was wanted at all is significant enough.

New England towns needed signs as much as English ones, and New Englanders desired portraits as naturally as they wanted the houses in which the portraits were hung. The "First Comers" to Plymouth (1620) were a special case. It is highly improbable that they had been accustomed to pictures in England; they certainly came away from their twelve-year stay in Holland uncontaminated by either the Dutch geniality of temperament or the Dutch fondness for painting. Seemingly they did not bring the legendary furniture with them on the *Mayflower,* and in their part of Massachusetts they apparently made no room on their walls for even portraits until Boston had set them the example. But the leaders, at least, of the "Great Migration" (1630) had owned portraits in their English homes; thence they brought to Boston some which were later transformed into public memorials, as Cotton Mather describes:

. . . And know, that as the picture of this their governour [John Winthrop] was, after his death, hung up with honour in the State-house of his country, so the wisdom, courage, and holy zeal of his life, were an example well-worthy to be copied by all that shall succeed him in government.

Effigies of Bradstreet and Endicott and Belcher were also placed alongside Winthrop, where they were seen long afterward by John Adams in his youth, to be recalled in his old age with mistaken scorn. As early as 1720 pictures were being offered in advertisements as "fit for any Gentleman's Dining-room or Stair-case," and the inescapable inference is that they were bought for their subject interest and for their attractiveness as home decorations.

These few details about painting, when joined to what is known about the other crafts practised in Boston, should suffice to contradict the bogeyman of the art-hating Puritan; this figment of fancy seems to be largely a phantasmal throwback from a later nineteenth century in revolt against its parents' genteelness. To be sure, a few individuals in early New England rejected the very idea of depicting any human worm of the dust and regarded all counterfeit presentments as sins against one of the commandments. Cotton Mather tells of two such ministers with seeming admiration, but Mather himself did not emulate that degree of saintliness. If Mather and the majority of ministers had been convinced that portraits were indeed vanities in the eyes of a jealous god, they could doubtless have made that view prevail for their time. They constituted a theocracy as powerful, within its geographical boundaries, as any the world has seen. Communities which, under their leadership, expelled schismatics and tortured Quakers and harried some poor women to death as witches might easily have secured an obliteration of even secular human images. Yet that attitude got into the record only because it was exceptional.

The determining evidence on this point of course consists of the portraits actually painted in New England during its first century. Those that survive the most skeptical scrutiny prove that the Puritans, far from suppressing that pragmatic branch of painting, patronized it quite actively. Any seeming poverty in the results, in quality or in quantity, can be traced not to community antagonism but simply to the conditions affecting small communities in a wilderness. Yet even under such conditions portraiture was so vigorously supported through the second half-century of New England history that it was ready to rise into greatness for the mercantile society which succeeded the theocratic one.

5. The artisan painter

William Johnes: act. 1634
John Gibbs: ?–1725
Thomas Child: c. 1678–1706

Naturally there is no contemporaneous narrative of how painting was brought over. People finding it difficult to stay alive would not stop to disentangle that minute thread in the complex warp-and-woof of a transplanted civilization. Some individuals kept diaries and some composed formal histories that are immensely informative as to the general conditions in which the painter had to work; more specific are the relatively few references to painters scattered through a variety of documents: church records, government ledgers, wills, inventories of estates, marriage registers, and the like. Their value depends largely upon how typical they may be; the exception remains only the exception, and the essential material of history is the usual. The most crabbedly illegible day-to-day account book of a seventeenth-century painter would possess truly scriptural authority, but no such manuscript is now known. There may never have been any. Accordingly a description of an early painter's round of making a living must be a compilation of details and deductions from many sources.

In a ship register of 1634, it is said, one Margaret Johnes is listed as on her way to join her husband "Will. Johnes late of Sandwich, now of New England, painter." The significance then of that last word almost certainly had to do with utilitarian craft. Early in the eighteenth century the word once designates John Gibbs and at least three times identifies Thomas Child; and about these two it is further known that they were painter-stainers, men who painted everything from houses to heraldic devices. Gibbs enters history as dying in 1725, but nothing is known about his living. On the other hand, about Thomas Child enough is known to let him illustrate in some detail the professional equipment and activities of the artisan painter.

The facts of his career were mostly uncovered as the result of something which later turned out to be not a fact, and the circumstances are worth recounting in an aside for the light they throw on the uncertainties hampering all investigations into the earliest painting done in this country. During a recent decade Child had a slight degree of artistic personality through the wide acceptance of a portrait attributed to him. When first publicly exhibited, it bore an exceptionally legible signature which later failed to meet the scientific tests nowadays applied to old pictures. The corroboratory inscription on the back has become fainter than it was a few years ago and is therefore now "regarded with some hesitation"—so runs the verdict in the understatement characteristic of scholarly condemnation. In addition, the pedigree supplied with the portrait has not been confirmed by independent investigation; it is even doubtful that the person named as its last owner by inheritance ever existed. The brief appearance of this picture in the record affords an apt instance of the general law ruling historical investigations phrased by Bill Nye when he wrote: "This story was foundered on facts." Child has therefore lost his faint stylistic individuality, but the short biography which can be formed out of information excavated from widely separated sources is more securely founded.

He served as apprentice to a member of the London Company of Painter-Stainers from 1671 to 1679, when he was admitted a member of the Company itself. Those dates can be filled in with a description of the usual such apprentice's experience. He would live in his master's house continuously on call while being taught all the phases of the craft "mystery," as trade secrets were then termed. That instruction comprised refining the oil and grinding the colors, making the brushes and cleaning them at the end of each day's work, priming panels and canvases for the master's own use. Later would come learning how to paint houses and stain furniture, how to devise trade signs, how to draw decorative figures and landscapes. The latter pictures would be conventionalized copies of shop products rather than direct renderings of the model or of actual scenes. There might be a certain amount of study from life in learning how to paint portraits; but by no means all of the artisan apprentices received such training; even for those who did, portraiture in England then was not likely to afford a professional career. For already in London, just as in the continental cities, portraiture was monopolized by specialists, and those who wanted to become portraitists would at once begin their specialized studio training. When Child was ready, by license of the guild, to set up in business for himself, he was not an artist in the present meaning of that word but only the painter-stainer specified in the guild name, equipped to make his living by humdrum ways of applying paint for utilitarian purposes.

The first mention of Child on this side of the ocean is the registration of his marriage in April of 1688. It is not known whether he brought with him or later imported the guild coat of arms, beautifully carved in high relief, which still exists [The Bostonian Society, Boston]; but here it was joined with another less well carved section, and together they served as the sign for his shop. Under the rules of the guild he was not entitled to use its insignia for that purpose, but other members in England itself were then guilty of the same infraction. The purchase of Child's combined house and shop is recorded, and also his purchase and subsequent sale of an interest in other real estate. The earliest citation of professional work done by him is an entry in the records of King's Chapel of his painting its window frames in 1689. On two later occasions he also painted its window shutters and its hourglass.

Child is said to have executed the decorations worn by the horses that pulled the mourning-coach in the funeral of Colonel Samuel Shrimpton in 1698. Judge Samuel Sewall noted them in his diary: "Scutcheon on their sides and Deaths heads on the foreheads." The Judge made similar notations more than a dozen times, for he was a genuine Puritan and enjoyed funerals. Puritans may have frowned on many of the minor elegancies which maintained the crafts in general, but they did not deny themselves every extravagance; and their most approved form of extravagance was funeralizing. Where the wilderness was so close, where the aborigines were soon more ferocious than the wild animals, where human associations were in consequence pathetically precious, it was natural to lavish a difficult superfluity upon laying away the dead. Another symbol of the Shrimpton family's bereavement was the hatchment, a panel of lozenge shape bearing the family arms on a black ground. During the mourning period, generally a year in length, it was displayed outside the dwelling; afterward it was either taken inside or deposited in the church. Such regalia were only one manifestation of an insistence on social rank which was usual among the colonists entitled to it, but from the first they had to be relatively well-to-do in order to make it effective. What with such painted emblems of mourning, the gravestone to follow, sometimes memorial rings willed to friends, and possibly a mortuary portrait, a dead Puritan might make more work for these various kinds of craftsmen than he would ever have thought of doing while alive.

From executing painting jobs for others Child went on to process painting materials for them to use. It is not likely that Child was faced with lack of enough work to keep him going; even a town of less than ten thousand would offer many opportunities to an all-round artisan. Yet he must have seen a chance for additional income where many homemakers would do their own painting, just as they would make their own furniture, until they were better able to pay professionals. At any rate, in 1700 Child imported a stone trough about twelve feet long, together with a suitably large ball of stone which was rolled back and forth in it by hand to crush the pigment and mix it with the oil. This paint mill had a capacity of about two barrels. At some later time the trough was broken, and thirty-one years after Child's death a three-foot fragment of it was set up as "The Boston Stone." Thus inscribed and also dated, and now surmounted by the stone ball, it stands today in the city's shopping section.

The records of the Boston Selectmen for the year 1702 supply a detailed description of a particular commission executed by Child. That governing body

. . . ordered that Mr. Thomas Child do the following work abt. the Latten Schoolmasters House vizt. finish the Gate and prime the fence, finish the Out side work of the House. And to prime the Inside worke of the Same, and to be paid what is reasonable for the Said work.

The Selectmen were taking exceptional care of the house in having it painted on the outside; and with only the priming ordered for the fence and the inside, they may have been counting on the schoolmaster himself to complete it in his spare time. That individual then was the Ezekiel Cheever who was already locally famous as an intellectual drillmaster, yet the esteem in which he was held as a teacher would not have freed him from the necessity of physical labor.

Four years later Child, a few weeks before his death, presented his bill of thirty pounds to the provincial council for priming and painting twenty carriages for the new cannon at Castle William. The painter's death is recorded by Judge Sewall in his diary on November 10th, 1706; to the bare notation the Judge added a very curious quatrain:

> Tom Child had often painted Death,
>   But never to the Life, before:
> Doing it now, he's out of Breath;
>   He paints it once, and paints no more.

The punning conceit of that memorial rhyme exemplifies one element in Puritan literature generally, prominent in the most ambitious prose and verse alike. For the Puritan mind, an elaborate pun in a sermon often had the force of a knock-down argument, and it is quite probable that Judge Sewall regarded his quatrain as a genuinely poetic fancy. Yet punning is a permanent streak in human nature, and his little jingle may now fairly be called childish. The importance of those lines for the painter's biography is not lessened by their obscurity, since they have a bearing on the question of whether Child actually painted portraits.

In the interpretation of them one argument takes the words "painted Death" in the narrowly figurative sense of referring only to the mourning decorations. Another suggests that Child executed only portraits after death. It may now seem more than a little ghoulish to make a picture with the look of life when working from a corpse, but in New England then it was done fairly often.

Aside from the few who were antagonistic to portraiture, there were more who were neglectful or indifferent; and in such cases a bereaved family might well consider a mortuary likeness better than none. After all, though, if Child painted dead people he almost certainly painted living ones too.

But it was not portraiture that earned him his living in seventeenth-century Boston. Nowhere in the colonies then was any craftsman wanted except those who could do things of immediate benefit: carpenters to build houses, joiners to fashion furniture, smiths to work metals. If any painters were to thrive here by their painting, they had to be able—or at least willing—to paint anything. The manual and technical comprehensiveness exemplified in Thomas Child would be the decisive factor in making him a successful member of the civil community wherein justification was by works, even as in the smaller religious group which controlled the larger justification was by faith.

The guild training made Child and his kind independent of shops selling commercially prepared materials; that in turn made them more adaptable to the miscellany of current needs. The guild technique, however lacking in subtlety and sophistication, was sound as far as it went; its scattered transplantations to the coastal towns during the first century were to be fundamentally important as the sources not only of executed works but also of such technical knowledge as was transmitted to native-born craftsmen. Until well into the nineteenth century this was often achieved by means of legal apprenticeship on the English model, just as in silversmithing and cabinetmaking, in medicine and the law; and an apprentice artisan painter completing his term would usually come out a reasonably well trained professional carrying on a long-lived technical tradition.

Thus the artisan painters coming here before 1725 played a much more significant part in American painting than all the portraits and other pictures brought over. Indeed, the craft they and their successors practised continued far beyond the time when professional portraitists began to transplant their more specialized skill. It was the very quantity and extensiveness of the work by the artisans functioning on the fundamental level of usefulness which in time made it possible for artists in paint to make pictures which were spiritually expressive.

6. The amateur painter

Joseph Allen: ?–1728

Only a little less prominent from the beginning than the guild-trained artisan was the amateur. His works sometimes suggest a partial training in the guild technique; they more often indicate simple self-teaching, with no more help than somebody else's pictures to study. He did not originate in the colonies, but conditions here accelerated and intensified his operations. In pioneering there was such a frequent need for the jack-at-a-pinch that inevitably he became a Jack-of-all-trades.

The amateur was certainly practising here before 1684, but he happens to be so fully described in a letter of that year that some of it is worth quoting for its applicability to earlier as well as to later men. The letter was written by the Reverend Nathaniel Mather in Dublin to his brother, the Reverend Increase Mather, in Boston; it concerned the bearer, Joseph Allen:

. . . hee [Allen] was bound prentise to an ironmonger, but hath so strong a naturall byass to ingenious handicrafts that hee is thereby mastered, & indeed so wholy carryed, that hee cannot thrive at buying & selling, but excells in those other things, & thence hath acquired good skill in watchmaking, clockmaking, graving, limning, [&] that by his owne ingenuity & industry chiefly, for he served an apprentiship faythfully to another trade. His design in comeing to New England is that hee bee under a necessity of earning his bread by practising his sk[ill] in some of those things.

With the warrant of Mather's words Allen can surely be credited with that love of practical processes which is so important a motive in amateurs every-where, together with the lively curiosity and many-sided interests which mark the tinkerer.

The rapidity of settlement here and its subsequent extension westward gave such exceptional opportunities to this sort of person that for a considerable time he could be cited as the typical American. As late as the mid-nineteenth century Emerson would be praising the ". . . sturdy lad from New Hampshire or Vermont, who in turn tries all the professions . . ." Such lads even tinkered with the arts, and several of them together started off American sculpture with nicely countryfied European accents just about the time Emerson was thinking his agreeable thoughts. Many more of them chose the more accessible medium of paint; but in painting especially, perhaps, did the amateur character of their efforts limit their expressive capacity. In painting, as in any other craft capable of becoming an art, the amateurs and their works are only makeshifts when judged by the demands of a fully developed civilization.

That verdict, however, should not minimize their actual importance in the history of painting in this country. It is true that the amateurs diluted professional standards: at first those of the artisans and later those of the specialists. In its earliest phase the process may be taken as part of the general colonial assimilation of all the crafts and professions; toward the end of the seventeenth century here it can be traced in education, in writing, in the ministry, and in medicine. In those activities subsidence proved temporary, a preliminary to better things. The important thing was that in all of the crafts and professions the native-born took over. In its nineteenth-century phase the activity of amateurs in painting may perhaps be best understood as part of the general democratization of culture. The important thing then was that a large number of people participated and the largest possible audience was reached.

Without that, even the more specialized and sophisticated developments would not have had their degree of life.

There are few matters on which we can lay down definite laws in relation to outbursts of artistic energy, but the law which we can infer from observation with the least element of doubt is that an essential condition of such an outburst is the pre-existence of a continuous and strong tradition of common art.

The nearest American equivalent to such a tradition has been the artisan work, with its extension upward into the lower ranks of professionalism and its extension downward into a widespread amateurism. And this amateurism, despite all its inadequacies, in retrospect offers frequent compensations of spirit through its many delightful manifestations of naïvety.

7. The signs

All the early men, whatever their training or preferences, would be as likely as Child to undertake any painting chore they could get. They might from time to time be called upon to refurbish a few sedan chairs and coaches after hard usage on the unpaved streets. As early as 1646 Governor Winthrop was, to his great satisfaction, being carried about by four lackeys in a sedan chair captured from a Spanish galleon. The last Dutch governor of New Netherland had a coach; and in all the British colonies coaches were necessary to the representatives of the Crown for maintaining the degree of stateliness proper to their office. Well before 1700 even private coaches were being used in all the principal coast towns. In Boston, the largest, a prominent minister acquired one in 1669. Almost twenty years later an extremist voiced disapproval of such worldliness; but by then that was only croakingly antiquated prejudice in a city where already a hackney coach was for hire. Whoever owned such vehicles, they were bright with variegated colors setting off body and wheels and trim; on their doors there might be a decorative fanciful scene or at least the semi-pictorialism of a coat of arms.

However, the greatest degree of pictorialism within the usual working experience of the artisan painter was on the signs. In the seaboard settlements they displayed their crude gayety before all the tree stumps could be cleared out of the garden lots; they were easily the most colorful feature of townscapes in which externally painted houses were rare. Ordinary wear and tear probably caused the first sign to disappear even before Thomas Child ever got to Boston, and it is as certain as any unrecorded fact can be that during his two American decades he devised replacements for many that went into woodpiles for kindling. He probably carved as well as lettered the section added to the guild coat of arms to form his own sign. That section is the only existing American-made sign certainly from the seventeenth century; and in fact, from the entire two hundred years of their functioning, relatively few examples survive for the reason that they were so common they were not thought of as historically interesting until their day was done. Nevertheless, as a branch of "painting in general" they were so important that they must be discussed first—another case of history made out of something missing. Quantitatively those trade emblems bulked so large that the very name of sign painter could serve for all the artisans until near the middle of the nineteenth century.

The signs that enter into this account of one American art were drawn and painted on wood panels, but there were other kinds: wood carvings or painted plaster models or metalwork or stuffed animals' heads. The most strikingly different American contribution to the craft in general was indeed not pictorial but sculptural—the tobacco-store Indian; but the coloring applied, usually both neat and gaudy, was often more important than the modeling.

Every tavern had a sign, every tradesman's and artisan's shop; and at a later date, when shopkeepers could also advertise in newspapers, they frequently described or illustrated their signs. In some businesses there was at first a connection of idea between them and their signs, as when a boot indicated a shoemaker or a wheat sheaf denoted a baker; but very soon there were more shops in the same line of business than there were appropriate symbols. Accordingly the signs became more and more arbitrary, and one of *The Great Trees* served a chemist or an elaborate *Blue Glove & Brazen Head* served a simple butter-seller. *The Blue Hand* could logically symbolize a dyeing establishment, but perhaps only an owner's whim could associate *The Three Nuns* with a dry-goods shop. A Philadelphia carpenter of 1751 claimed usefulness for the whole of life by his comprehensive *Cradle & Coffin*, but in Boston another man was then using *The Spectacles* to designate neither an oculist's office nor an optician's shop but a place where prints were sold. Also on record is the curious instance of a sign-concept passing over from one business to another; a Boston tavern of 1712 was appropriately identified by a *Bunch of Grapes*, but the same visual symbol was on a dry-goods store in Providence in 1766 and on a candlemaker's shop in Newport in 1773.

The arbitrary choice of an emblem could be in itself a more effective form of advertising through the scope which it permitted to the artisan's inventiveness. The function of a sign was to attract attention; and the best way of doing that was for it to be entertaining, striking, amusing, lovely—in some way easy to look at and likely to cause talk. Yet success in this latter aim was not always advantageous. A tavern in Philadelphia using the name of *The Quiet Woman* displayed on its sign a woman with her head cut off and lying at her feet; that caused not only talk but indignation enough to get it removed. Another inn repeated a well known English precedent in using the sign of *A Man Making His Way Through the World* as a sort of visual pun; it showed a globe with a man's head and shoulders emerging like a hatching chick. What might have been the pictorialism of *Aesop in the Shades* rouses wonder even now.

This increase of fancifulness in the later signs has been called a degeneration from the earlier purity, and the better craftsmanship accompanying the more picturesque manifestations has been stigmatized as flamboyant decadence. This view seems unnecessarily severe; and perhaps the very language of the condemnation may be inappropriate to such humble material. Apparently popular taste welcomed the so-called corruptions, and it would be difficult to impugn the verdict of the audience to which that species of painting was addressed. The development also had a consequence which was important for the art of painting as a whole: in proportion as the later signs came near to being full-fledged pictures did they incite painting ambitions in youths who became more-than-respectable professionals.

Signs appeared in the smaller settlements, too, and even in the country, because some painters, along with other craftsmen and hawkers of small merchandise, became seasonal or permanent itinerants. As workers with little or no capital, dependent on temporary employment, nomad artisans were in the next-to-bottom layer of society; below them were only indentured servants and slaves. Although some of the roamers must have been wanderers by temperament, most of them, with their stock of brushes and colors, were perhaps driven to the road by being less capable craftsmen. The farther inland they went, the more likely their sub-artistic skill was to astonish people; and where the inland settlers had little or no money to spare for paintings, the itinerant could still eat and sleep his way along by making things which passed for pictures.

Although a farmer's wife would probably get more satisfaction from looking at the herbs suspended from her kitchen rafters, she might also relish a tiny landscape painted on a chair back; the country innkeeper would be glad to get a new sign; a few villagers might be persuaded into commissioning portraits. Whatever his degree of skill, the sign painter went very nearly everywhere. His appearance anywhere effectively reminded those who lived away from the older settlements that there was such a thing as painting.

Merely to paint a barn necessitates a choice by somebody between one color and another, between different shades of the same color; such a preference is elementary, to be sure, but it is esthetic so far as it goes. With the signs, pleasure in making and looking at pictures begins to be conscious. Fortunately human beings are so compounded that any work is done better when the element of play has scope. The nature of paint in particular invites its user to do something extra; with it, the most practical end can be more satisfactorily achieved by some flourish of embellishment. In the absence of the profounder emotion of worship, this one of delight in visual attractiveness can be sufficient to give life to the art; and although this life flickered but feebly in American colonial signs, it yet was not extinct.

Worship was of course both the source and goal of the retablos, and the exclusively secular character of the signs only dramatized the Protestantism of the people by and for whom they were made. Yet the contemporaneous signs and retablos possessed important traits in common despite the fact that makers and audience in each region remained unaware of those in the other. Both signs and retablos were symbols painted on wood panels; the outlines were drawn boldly and were sometimes emphasized by incision. In general the signs displayed a neatness of effect which may have come from the semi-mechanical nature of the craft, whereas the calligraphic drawing in the retablos had much to do with their greater degree of emotionalism. In the signs not only were the color areas somewhat larger but they were also more even in texture, with thicker pigment; this was another consequence of the guild training even where it was learned at second or third hand.

Moreover, the symbolism of both signs and retablos was addressed to the widest possible audience at the time. Although the signs appealed only to the shallow emotions of curiosity and amusement and pleasure in anecdote, they pervaded the entire community life because they supplied information. They were necessary for people who could not read; in colonial days they were most necessary where there were the most people—so necessary that in some places they were required by law. When increased literacy had begun to make them superfluous, the law again took a hand and gradually legislated them out of existence in the towns as dangers to life and limb.

Yet it was their long-lived usefulness which gave the craft out of which they came a continuity underlying the sudden stylistic changes of more sophisticated techniques. Conveying information is of course the lowest level of pictorial usefulness, and the moral of that as concerns this country is that esthetic responsiveness had to be re-grown on this bedrock. For this reason the pictorial deterioration from the pure functionalism of the earlier signs can be interpreted as a benefit to the mass of Americans; for in their experience through more than a century, just as for the English populace through an even longer period, the nearest thing to a gallery of pictures was to be found on the streets.

8. Portraits by artisans and amateurs

Anon.: *John Endecott, c. 1665*
John Foster: 1648–1681
Anon.: ? *Thomas Thacher, ?*
  William Stoughton, c. 1700
  Mrs. Anne Pollard, 1721
  Mrs. Elizabeth Wensley, c. 1675

The first portrait painted in this country will never be known. Just as the first sign was at some time worn out, just as the first silver was later reworked into more fashionable shapes, just as the first table or chair was promptly discarded as soon as something better could be bought, so several factors made the life of the first portrait highly precarious. Fires were frequent, in individual homes and through large sections of the towns; there was a rapid deterioration in badly executed work; miscellaneous accidents of falls and holes and ill judged cleaning played a part; and later there was an unknown amount of deliberate destruction by descendants who happened to dislike what they considered old daubs. With so many hazards against survival, therefore, behind any first now known for any colony must loom the vague shape of an actual first tantalizingly unknowable.

An extreme illustration of the mistreatment befalling many early colonial portraits is documented by stories about the existing effigy of *Governor John Endecott* [c. 1665: privately owned], so famous that twenty-three copies are known to have been made. Shortly after the Revolution, it is said, a negro slave scrubbed the canvas with soap and sand, with results that must have been disastrous. In 1796 the zealous antiquarian, William Bentley, recorded in his diary that "The face is the only part, which is not entirely gone." In 1801 he found the canvas being used as a fire screen and wrote: "The old picture grows dimmer by the smoak." During one restoration the right side of the face was filled out with putty—a piece of technical stupidity extraordinary in even a mid-nineteenth-century hack painter. There is also another story about the face being re-painted from a descendant's countenance; but that is perhaps less fantastic than the vandalism just mentioned, for the English countenance that made the Yankee face is a very persistent thing.

Despite so many factors militating against historical certainty, there was,

27

early in the present century, something like a race among a small group of
antiquarians eager to discover the first visiting artist or the first native-born
painter, and among a still smaller group of collectors to own the first discoverable
painting. This competition was of immense value in bringing to light many
biographical facts and some authentic examples, but it further confused the
general situation by some indefensible claims and very questionable pictures.
These have been motivated by prestige and profit both, and in the long absence
of a sufficiently exacting criticism it has been relatively easy to juggle an old
English or continental portrait into a colonial product. Several such transmogri-
fications have been reproduced in histories of painting and of the period in
general; there they do make accounts of the early years vivid, and to the layman's eyes they look solidly historical.

However, scholar and connoisseur and antiquary and scientist have begun
checking over the whole body of colonial painting with a minute examination
of legends and documents, analyses of workmanship and technical influences,
microscopic inspection and microphotographs of surfaces, shadowgraphs of
what is hidden under the surfaces, chemical tests of age for pigment and canvas
or panel, debates over esthetic quality. Under such a variety of attacks more
pictures than that once attributed to Child are foundering on the facts. To be
sure, it is possible to take a more liberal attitude, such as was suggested in another
connection by the Breakfast-Table Autocrat: "All generous minds have a horror
of what are commonly called 'facts' . . ." This brand of generosity it is which has
already been practised by dealers and collectors to a point where a sober historian's job is needlessly difficult.

For the historian in any field must make sure that his ascertainable facts
and his necessary general ideas do not contradict one another; he is fortunate
indeed when they dovetail conveniently into a convincing whole. The historian
of American painting in particular, compelled to begin with this general situation, may at least risk the affirmation that portraits were for a considerable time
the by-products of artisans without specialized training or of amateurs mostly
busy with other activities. These were the two kinds of workmen who were in
the colonies long before any portrait specialist; in the conditions existing then
it would be natural for them to take on portraiture as just one more among the
many jobs to be done.

How early that might occur must remain in some degree a matter of opinion.
The roughness of the few buildings collected around the first meetinghouse of
Boston and the general unkemptness of the village on its exposed peninsula do
not seem sufficient by themselves to rule out the possibility that William Johnes
or some other unknown artisan about then set the precedent for the general
workman venturing into the territory of the specialist. But insofar as external

conditions may be considered significant, they were certainly more favorable twenty years later; a description of 1654 runs in part:

. . . this City-like Towne is crowded on the Sea-bankes, and wharfed out with great industry and cost, the buildings beautifull and large, some fairely set forth with Brick, Tile, Stone, and Slate, and orderly places with comly streets, whose continuall inlargement presages some sumptuous City. . . . the streets are full of Girles and Boys sporting up and downe, with a continued concourse of people. . . .

The writer of another description, published twenty years later still, seems, from his phrasing, to have been familiar with his predecessor's; but he intensifies the note of cheerful prosperity with details about handsome buildings and fair shops on streets paved with pebble stone, crowded meetinghouses, two constant fairs, gardens and orchards on the south side, and the

small, but pleasant Common where the gallants a little before Sunset walk with their Marmalet-madams, as we do in Morefields, &c till the nine o'clock Bell rings them home to their respective habitations, when presently the Constables walk their rounds to see good order kept, and to take up loose people.

Published in 1674, those words were written about the Boston of four years earlier: the very year in which were executed the first portraits that can now be certainly dated. Between that year and 1725 a fairly large number were painted in and around Boston which display all the mental and technical characteristics to be expected in work by artisans and amateurs who often had the courage to attempt likenesses but less often had the ability to achieve them.

Among the earliest acceptable portraits in New England one of the most interesting groups consists of three or four which appear to be from the hand of John Foster. As a person he is quite as nearly the ideal embodiment of the amateur as Joseph Allen, and part of Foster's funeral elegy is for this reason even more interesting than the letter about Allen.

> His Curious works had you but Seen
> You would have thought Him to have been
> By some Strange Metempsychosis
> A new reviv'd Archimedes;
> At least you would have judg'd that he
> A rare Apelles would Soon be.
>   Add to those things I have been hinting
> His skill in that rare Art of PRINTING:
> His accurate Geography,
> And Astronomick Poetry;
> And you will Say, 'twere pitty He
> Should die without an Elegie.

This indifferently poetical hinting can be made quite precise by the facts of Foster's brief life.

He established the first printing press in Boston and issued six almanacs for which he made his own astronomical calculations. From the press he published his life of the Reverend Richard Mather, who had baptized him; to this biography he prefixed a portrait of Mather which is the first known woodcut made in this country. One copy of this bears a note in the handwriting of a personal friend of Foster to the effect that Foster cut it. This woodcut was in all probability made from the now almost ruined portrait in oil [American Antiquarian Society, Worcester, Mass.]; and the conclusion that he painted the portrait is justified by the fact that the inventory of his estate lists "colours" along with "cutts" to the value of fifteen shillings. The use in that elegy of the descriptive term "a rare Apelles" is strongly confirmatory of his being a painter; that is a conventional seventeenth-century literary ornament, but it is precise in that it refers exclusively to painters. As one of them, accordingly, Foster safely emerges from anonymity by a chain of inferences.

In the almost obliterated Mather portrait a technical trait or two can be dimly made out which can be more clearly seen in the *John Davenport* [1670: Yale University Art Gallery]; and this in turn gives similar leads to the portrait now called *John Wheelwright* [1677: plate 1]. In these works the erratic handling of the pigment and the blundering corrections revealed by shadowgraphs betray ignorance of the medium and extreme uncertainty in Foster's mind. Even the casual eye can see that the painting is spotty and the drawing is feeble; and the pinched discomfort experienced in looking at these portraits of ministers is an emotional effect directly from the painfully incompetent craft rather than from the characters of the individuals portrayed. In both technique and perceptiveness Foster is a complete fumbler. And although this involves a drop in skill from the level of the guild artisan, it is at least a re-beginning in one art that is necessary to any rounded civilization.

Where Foster was uncertain of everything, another painter, still anonymous, was at least sure of how to apply his pigment. The portrait he painted is now called by the name of the *Reverend Thomas Thacher* [Old South Association, Boston]; but it may some day prove to be of someone else rather later in date. Its painter used a relatively thick impasto and built it up into the hard smoothness which would best resist exposure to the weather; of course he knew that the portrait would remain indoors, but he had to follow his sign painter's technical habit because he knew no other. In still another anonymous portrait —that of *William Stoughton* [c. 1700: Harvard University]—the mark of the artisan is seen not only in the rigid figure and the stiffly extended hand but also in the attempted accuracy of Stoughton Hall in the background. Yet

1. JOHN WHEELWRIGHT (?) *by* JOHN FOSTER

Owned by The Commonwealth of Massachusetts. Photograph from Worcester Art Museum.

neither of those workmen had that degree of talent in picturemaking which would have enabled him to get beyond his rough record of a sitter and devise a pattern for visual pleasure.

A striking achievement of this sort appears a little later in the *Mrs. Anne Pollard* [1721: plate 2]. This man's artisan training becomes most obvious, perhaps, in the monotony of texture; his capacity for artistry becomes almost startlingly clear in the complex interplay of repeating and opposing triangles through costume and features. By this conscious arrangement he earned the artist's reward of not only pleasing the eye but also convincing the mind. By insisting upon his pattern he raised his factual record of age and shrewdness into an independent pictorial life.

This transformation of craftsmanship into artistry is not only mysterious in itself; its mystery is often intensified by the circumstances in which it occurs. Almost half a century earlier in New England still another workman had achieved the same miracle, though in a more gracious version, with *Mrs. Elizabeth Wensley* [c. 1675: Pilgrim Hall, Plymouth, Mass.]. Few things could so well indicate the comparatively recent change in taste as the fact that this painting, which seemed to the historian Samuel Isham merely one of a whole class "without artistic interest," should now possess esthetic value for those who have come beyond naturalism in search of qualities properly pictorial. The eyes of both painter and layman have served a long slavery to appearances; they are now coming into what seems to be a new freedom by responding to design. Something seems to have happened to the surface of the *Mrs. Wensley,* but the surviving color scheme of browns and brickish reds has its own considerable charm. The anatomically inaccurate hands have a languid elegance, the expression a gentle melancholy, which, whether or not they are a valid interpretation of the subject's actual character, endow her with present individuality. But the means by which this interpretation comes alive is the animated decorative beauty of the pattern of interrupted diagonals and flattened curves devised out of the elaborate costume and conventionalized flowers.

Whatever may be their degrees of skill in craft or grasp on character, these portraits exhibit traits which make them as medieval as the houses in which they first hung. In those houses the sharp-edged massiveness of the chairs and cupboards made tangible the moral weightiness of their owners; the sometimes rough and sometimes subtle severity of the portraits made visible the same people's angularity of mind. The likenesses, if that is what they are, display a formula of placing the figure at an oblique angle on the canvas and of keeping the eyes turned toward the spectator. The most striking trait of all is the linear effect; hands and bodies and backgrounds are all rendered in the same plane. The treatment of contours ranges all the way from the arbitrary

hardness of the *Thacher* to the equally arbitrary delicacies of the *Mrs. Wensley,*
but the contours always enclose flat areas with little or no hint of any naturalistic third dimension. One and all the portraits are limning in the strictest
medieval sense of that word.

The examples attributed to Foster, together with the *Thacher* and the
Stoughton, may be taken as representative of the average product. They afford a base line—an incurable punner would add, a very base line—by which
to estimate the subsequent improvements in craft. The mass of art in every age
is mediocre, and the history of how art plays its part in any civilization must
rely upon a few typical examples to illustrate the quantitative product from
which it is selected. Yet the proper interpretation of any time's artistic achievement must emphasize what rises out of that mediocrity into esthetic worth and
spiritual greatness. The qualitative is always exceptional, but its very quality
cannot be adequately comprehended except in relief against its quantitative
background. Individual mediocrities die and mass mediocrities change, but
their place is taken by more—always more and more. The mediocre is permanent through repetition; only the exceptional in art achieves the intrinsic worth,
and sometimes the uniqueness, by which it earns its individual permanence in
the memory of men.

2. MRS. ANNE POLLARD *by* UNKNOWN PAINTER
Courtesy of Massachusetts Historical Society.

9. The Master of the Freakes

Anon.: *John Freake; Mrs. Freake and Baby Mary*.

This painter is at present not a person with a factual biography, but he has left a clear artistic autobiography. Name and narrative, if research ever uncovers them, will be less important than the quality of mind discernible in this pair of portraits. *John Freake* and *Mrs. Freake and Baby Mary* [both 1674: privately owned] evidence in their maker an altogether remarkable talent; despite the rigid placement of the figures, a linear grace controls both; and despite some difficulty in getting likenesses, a human graciousness animates both. Especially in her portrait, the painter manifested extraordinary artistry in arranging the resonant colors so that their pattern only emphasizes the spiritual dignity of this woman's somewhat shy and self-conscious pride in motherhood.

His artisan craft is evident in the way he applies pigment; he lays on clean-edged areas of solid color with substantial impasto. Quite as significantly, he places everything in one plane; in the picture of mother and child, hands and chair back, knee in the foreground and curtain in the background, are all about equally near the eye, just as the details of a sign swinging in the wind would be. Any sign painter at that time, even if he could perceive atmosphere in our naturalistic way, would find it only a distraction from his inherited convention of flat treatment; and in these portraits the painter did not attempt what his training had not taught him to look for. But within the limits of two dimensions he attains a clarity of pattern which, in spite of some awkward drawing, is large in feeling and lively in effect. The very crackle of the paint after two hundred and fifty years attests the soundness of his skill; the marks of age are such as could develop only on a technically healthy product.

This soundness of surface has been strikingly emphasized by the discovery of certain changes which he made in the course of his work. Unlike John Foster, whose mental fumbling can be sensed at first glance, this man is such a good craftsman that he can eradicate misjudgements. They are still successfully hidden from the eye and can be read only in shadowgraphs out of the laboratory. It is of course these alterations which certify his non-professionalism in the art of portraiture, as distinct from his professionalism in the craft of sign painting. What he could not conceal, and accordingly very sensibly did not try to cover up, is the difficulty he had with hands. With them he was faced by the necessity of drawing something specific in nature which is not adequately provided for in any shop formula; the result falls short because the sign painter's flatness of treatment is a denial of the essential character of hands. Yet this workman betrays no uneasiness as to his own technique; he drew wrongly, but he did not draw waveringly, as Foster did. Everything that can be treated as pattern—clothes in silhouette, the delicate filigree of lace, the almost unshadowed features—was patiently drawn; what needs physical substantiality, a rendering of inner structure, was muffed.

The changes revealed by the shadowgraphs of the mother-and-child portrait are not so much corrections of errors as improvements in both design and interpretation; and an examination of them can give an understanding of this artisan-artist's essentially creative mind. Baby Mary's right hand at first held something, handkerchief or glove, and the mother's left arm originally did not reach across so that their hands almost touch. Nor was the child's left arm originally extended in the charming gesture now seen. These alterations dramatize in human terms the bond between mother and daughter; quite as importantly they develop a strong rhythm of horizontals for unifying the details in the area of major interest.

Because this workman was so little at ease in the problems of portraiture, it would be unwise to speak too positively about what went on in his mind. It is a pleasant fancy that the baby might actually have dropped the glove and reached out to steady herself even as the mother reached across to catch her. In that case it was certainly the mark of a fresh and sensitive nature in the painter for him to perceive the human and pictorial gains and to incorporate them into the picture. If he had not the help of accident, if he made the changes out of his own thinking about how to improve his pattern, he gave all the more imposing proof of innate creativeness. Whatever may have been the part played by external chance, all these changes were intentional; nothing was foreseen in the manner of a portraitist with a studio formula, but through trial and error a skilful craftsman developed a concept of pictorial and human charm.

Then, there is the further element of color. Even the darkened areas of the *Mr. Freake* preserve something of their strong harmony of brown and red-brown; lace and muslin and silver buttons and light flesh tones still vibrate with contrasting delicacy. The companion portrait of *Mrs. Freake and Baby Mary* startles with its purposeful and satisfying richness; the mother wears a red skirt with gold and white embroidery, an olive-green overskirt and bodice, a black bracelet placed next to black and red ribbons dangling from her sleeves. The baby wears a yellow dress with matching cap. Both mother and daughter are overlaid with lovely cream-white in lace and apron and pinafore. More light flesh tones and pale yellow hair complete the charming brightness and contagious gayety of this unquestionably esthetic intention.

This artisan craft and amateur drawing and artistic delight in color were put to work depicting human beings. Since the painter had nothing of the special professionalism of the portraitist, the expressions of his sitters approach immobility. Yet Mrs. Freake seems only waiting for one to turn away before relaxing into her own individuality, and Mr. Freake only in part suppresses his jocundity of spirit. Of him it is related that he was the first "gentleman" in New England to entertain his friends in a tavern; that memory of him curiously suits the charm of the portrait. Even in the flatness of his visual existence he seems to be taking a deep breath; he expands in the enjoyment of being alive and handsomely dressed, in happy unawareness that about six months later he is to die a victim of a harbor explosion.

In this way analysis can marshal evidence that the painter under discussion possessed the basic requirement for esthetic and spiritual greatness: an experiencing mind in love with his medium. The naturalistic awkwardness pervading his work was but the result of a limited technical inheritance; although it impaired his ease of expression, it did not stifle his perceptiveness. The handicaps under which he worked did not prevent him from standing supreme among the painters of the first century in all the colonies. With only an artisan's professional equipment, he was creatively stimulated into something close to greatness by the unfamiliar problems of portraiture and the scope they afforded to his personal inventiveness.

10. Portraits of children

Anon.: *Margaret Gibbs; Robert Gibbs; Henry Gibbs,* all 1670
Alice Mason; David, Joanna, and Abigail Mason, both 1670

Certain child portraits are, in their medieval flatness and decorative treatment, stylistically allied to the Freake pair. Superficial similarities like lace and sleeve-ribbons are likely details of current costume; to establish identical authorship would require strong similarities of technique. While some of this may exist in drawing, especially in the face of *Margaret Gibbs* [1670: plate 3], the pigment throughout the child portraits has a somewhat thinner impasto. Perhaps more importantly, shadowgraphs show no alterations of design in these earlier works such as exist beneath the surface in the Freakes. The man who depicted Margaret also painted her two brothers [1670: privately owned], but probably another artisan portraitized little *Alice Mason* [1670: Adams Memorial, Quincy, Mass.] and three other Mason children as a group [1670: privately owned].

Although each face has its own degree of individuality, all these portraits have in common a flatness in the treatment of costume which prevailed in England almost until the advent of Van Dyck. This in turn derived to a considerable extent from contemporaneous Dutch practice; indeed, Dutch painters themselves were largely responsible for its popularity in England among the newly enriched and newly ennobled classes under Henry the Eighth and Elizabeth. It is of course quite possible that the painter or painters of these American examples brought that manner direct from England; but it is worth pointing out how some artisan here could have picked up this manner through being lucky enough to see a couple of De Peyster child portraits which had been done in Holland and brought to New Netherland in 1646.

The medieval flatness of these child portraits in New England is simply the most striking element in a general stylistic recipe. The light and dark squares need not imply marble flooring there at that time; they are probably just part of the painting formula. On the other hand, the costumes do not appear to be studio properties conferred by painters upon their sitters indiscriminately; not only is there the variety of detail which usually occurs with a fashion but there is also a consistent exactness in depicting that variety of detail which implies a specific dress in each instance. Nor does the costliness of these clothes

3. MARGARET GIBBS   *by* UNKNOWN PAINTER

Courtesy of Mrs. Alexander Quarrier Smith.   Photograph from Worcester Art Museum.

make any historical difficulty. The Puritans as a group did not raise the moral scruples which caused the original Quakers to adopt the badge of plainness. In the very year that the three Gibbs children were painted their father was erecting "by the shore" of Boston's east end a business building at a cost of almost three thousand pounds. Their rich array, as well as their portraits, came out of an admirable parental love; and the existence of such pictures should modify the long-prevalent idea that the New England child was the hapless prisoner of Puritan jailers.

Doubtless these very boys and girls, along with the rest of their generation, were made to memorize that portion of Wigglesworth's *Day of Doom* wherein Jehovah consigns unbaptized infants with shockingly inappropriate tenderness to "the easiest room in hell." The more lurid fates incurred by heathens and by sinners were relished by maturer minds because parents, and their children too, were safely past baptism into the security of sectarian dogma. The thrill of damnation so vividly depicted in the tom-tom beat of Wigglesworth's rough rhymes was vicarious, and it did not interfere with worldly prosperity or with family affection.

It may be further assumed that not even the Gibbs and Mason children, well-to-do as their parents evidently were, escaped their fair share of the household labor. Their respective mothers might not have to work as hard as poorer men's wives, but even rich men's wives had plenty to do, for in colonial America the home had to be practically as self-sufficient as in ancient Greece. The women's tasks were numerous and complicated: cleaning and cooking, sewing, churning, spinning, weaving, making candles and soap and bullets and brooms. There is tragedy as well as humor in *The Tired Woman's Epitaph*:

> "Don't mourn for me now, don't mourn for me never—
> I'm goin' to do nothin' for ever and ever."

In that variety of daily work much could be forwarded if not fully executed by the children—at least when under supervision. That is one reason why children were then an asset; they were actually a means to economic security for the family as a group. The children's share was genuine work in the home, not something brought back from school for doing at home; it was probably the most important factor in forming the well known New England character —reputed to be strong.

Religious sternness and moral severity were certainly present in living to an extent not known today, but their excessive predominance in the printed matter of the time quite as certainly gave rise to a distorted interpretation in minds unable to discern behind print the less rigid and more complex realities of human relationships. Moreover, not all the books and pamphlets were theological blood-

and-thunder. Cotton Mather's numerous hysterical pages paralleled the hysteria of the witch-hunts, but a few poems of personal affection by Anne Bradstreet can re-establish in later minds the basic sanity of New England society. Judge Samuel Sewall was the Puritan Pepys in more respects than the factual fulness of his diary; on Sewall's social level Boston afforded few or no opportunities for gallantry such as Pepys enjoyed in London, but neither Boston nor Puritanism could keep Sewall from being, like Pepys, the average sensual man, at once contemptible and lovable.

11. Anticipations of studio technique

Anon.: *John Woodbridge,* c. 1690
  Mrs. James Pierpont, 1711
Thomas Smith: act. 1680–1690
J. Cooper: act. 1714–1718

All the foregoing portraits, even when as late as 1721, are medieval in mind and guild-derived in technique. Yet overlapping them in time, and partially anticipating a style which was to be more fully transplanted after 1725, portraits in a different manner were executed; and this manner was appropriate to the increasing secularism and cosmopolitanism of growing Boston.

For although the town remained largely theocratic in tone until the death of Cotton Mather in 1728, it was at the same time altering culturally in response to a shift from an economy of agriculture to one of commerce. In 1680 Jasper Danckaerts, a traveler up from New Netherland, recorded how, at sundown on Saturday, a general change of countenance occurred to suit the sabbath day; and then he added:

. . . Nevertheless you discover little difference between this and other places. Drinking and fighting occur there not less than elsewhere; and as to truth and true godliness, you must not expect more of them than of others . . .

The difficulty is, now as then, for an outsider to be moderate in opinion about moral and cultural traits when confronted by the obviously exaggerated assurance of superiority in those respects which radiates from the typical Bostonian in every generation. But as for noisy debaucheries, they are perhaps more fairly chargeable to less characteristic elements; ten years earlier Josselyn had stressed how Boston was already ". . . very populous, much frequented by strangers . . ."

It was therefore only suitable that Boston limners should begin to show some awareness, however feeble, of a way of making portraits more modish than the medieval way. One workman, for example, who was about on the level of Foster in his self-taught clumsiness, attempted to depict *John Wood-bridge* [c. 1690: privately owned]. As with Foster's efforts, no feeling of form in space is conveyed by this thin and timid layer of pigment; there is no substance enclosed or suggested by this pinched and unsure drawing; even the flesh color is only an approximation. The subject might be any age from thirty to sixty; the painter could not clearly say. Nor could the painter of the *Mrs. James Pierpont* [1711: privately owned] tell much more about her as a person, but he handled pigment with greater awareness of its physical character and he used shadow to secure some spatial projection in the features. His management of that necessary element in all optical naturalism was, however, only slightly better than that in the *Thacher* of thirty-five years earlier.

The artisan portraying *Mrs. Pierpont* and the amateur portraying *Mr. Woodbridge* displayed similar inadequacies: poor placing, woodenness of pose emphasized by badly articulated necks, inadequate textures and evasive studio generalizations for clothes. In actual achievement, therefore, these two portraits embodied little or no advance over the work of the medievally minded workmen here; about all they did was to show how even the artisan and the amateur were becoming aware of a different portrait formula. The amateur gives a very faint foreshadowing of more animated design; the artisan manifests in a barely discernible degree another kind of dexterity in manipulating pigment.

One participant in this transition has a name and one date in addition to a few portraits. The records of Harvard College in 1680 note a payment of four guineas to one Thomas Smith "for drawing Dr. Ames effigies pr Order of Corporation." A biography requires more facts; as with the Master of the Freakes, what is worth knowing about this painter must be deciphered from the works. One among them is a *Self-Portrait* [c. 1690: plate 4], and what it says in visual terms is confirmed and supplemented by a set of rhymes transcribed on the painted paper held down by the skull-like object under his right hand:

> Why why should I the World be minding
> therein a World of Evils Finding.
> > Then Farwell World: Farwell thy Jarres
> > thy Joies thy Toies thy Wiles thy Warrs
> Truth Sounds Retreat: I am not *forye*.
> > The Eternall Drawes to him my heart
> > By Faith (which can thy Force Subvert)
> To Crowne me (after Grace) with Glory.

Even if Smith is only quoting those lines, they are appropriate to the face seen above them; but the initials appended probably mean that Smith himself composed them. They are certainly awkward enough for an amateur Puritan poet—in Milton's words, true "scrannel pipes." The crabbed condensation of the phrases and the roughness of the rhymes are as robustly Puritan as the sentiments they express. The fine "Truth Sounds Retreat" is an idea which

4. SELF–PORTRAIT *by* THOMAS SMITH
Courtesy of Worcester Art Museum.

was to be re-voiced more than a century and a half later by Ralph Waldo Emerson, who remained a Puritan even in his personal transformation of the Puritan virtues:

It is time to be old,
To take in sail.

Contempt for that sentiment can be felt only by inexperienced natures; on the ears of the mature it sounds with warning comfort. The other two elderly men whom Smith depicted also comprehend the significance of the painter's rhymed valedictory: *Captain George Curwin* [c. 1680: Essex Institute, Salem, Mass.] and *Major Thomas Savage* [1689: privately owned]. All three are aware of life in a similar way. From the security of personal reserve they look out on the world patiently, appraisingly, perhaps even a little warily. Bearing the stamp of practical success, they are becoming more content to watch, as sure of their position in this world as of their salvation in the next.

As these subjects are astutely aware of life, so is the painter aware of the world with a naturalistic vision different from that to be seen in the unconfused single picture plane of the medieval-minded. If traces of optical naturalism seem doubtfully present in some of the sign painters' work, such as Thacher's face and Stoughton's figure, the unclearness of the results is most satisfactorily explained by saying that the habit of two-dimensional thinking inhibited the vision of the workmen. Smith's perceptiveness of appearances seems greater than his capacity for realizing them in paint; though his renderings are incomplete and inconsistent, the intention is plain. Both Savage and Smith in their portraits have a solidity which is three-dimensional at least to the point of bas-relief, even though the space supposedly around the figures is not given visual existence. The naval engagement depicted in the *Self-Portrait* is not now identifiable; but more important, in view of the painter's intention, is the naturalistic failure to correlate exterior distance and interior nearness in values. A parallel inconsistency exists between the delicately brushed hair and the unconsidered tassel and curtain at the upper right. At the lower left, in contrast, the painter not only takes minute pains with the handwriting of the poem but also aims for some texture in the paper and carefully differentiates the change in values as it bends over the table edge. Yet as for that insistent *memento-mori*, Smith did not draw it from an actual skull; if he was thinking of anything he had seen, it could only have been some stonemason's rough gravestone symbol. Despite inadequate results, though, Smith was by and large intending to make a visual report of appearances.

Optical faithfulness was to be the goal of the studio-trained for two hundred and fifty years in this country; and in New England, Smith may be said to have begun the process of subjecting the painter's eye and hand to imitative images. But by the time he had made his slight naturalistic advance, the earlier two-dimensional technique of the artisans was so well established that it retained its own technical characteristics even when the artisans began trying to acquire a fashionableness of manner foreign to their shop training.

The faint beginnings in Boston of this tendency were greatly exceeded by a certain J. Cooper who scattered his flamboyant efforts across New England. The brush strokes weave a coarse latticework of the broad lines characteristic of shop practice; but perhaps the strongest indication of a sign painter at work is the way in which the pigment, though spread on canvas, appears laid on a surface with the hardness of wood. The seemingly superior skill with which Cooper has arranged his surplusage of detail is probably due to his having used prints for source material; but whatever indications of three dimensions there may have been in the prints, Cooper has reduced them to two with such technical consistency as to command admiration. Perhaps the use of prints also accounts for the lack of specific likeness in the faces; the features are so stylized that they seem at times to escape altogether from the name of portrait. In the *Eighteenth-Century Gentleman* [plate 5], the second fully signed example thus far discovered, the relative richness and variety of color afford the most personal note in this artisan's un-Puritanical striving toward Renaissance animation.

5. EIGHTEENTH–CENTURY GENTLEMAN   *by* J. COOPER
Courtesy of The New-York Historical Society, New York City.

12. The Central Colonies

Henri Couturier: ?–1684
Anon.: *Nicholas William Stuyvesant,*
    1666
   David Provoost; Mrs. David Provoost,
    c. 1700
Evert Duyckinck the First: 1621–1702

Gerardus Duyckinck the Second (?):
   ?–1756
Evert Duyckinck the Third: 1677–1727
Gerret Duyckinck: 1660–1710
Hudson Valley Master: act. 1717–1730
Christopher Witt: c. 1675–1765

From the erection of the first permanent houses of New Amsterdam in 1628 to conquest by the English in 1664 there was time for only one generation of the Dutch to come to maturity. Even that short time was full of difficulties: badly planned immigration, much neglect and some misrule from home, even a little preliminary skirmish of conquest against the Swedes along the Delaware. Yet enough Netherlanders came over to the new-world trading center to put a lasting stamp upon the whole colony and eventually to contribute some distinctive manners and ideas to the cultural composite of the entire central region of the Atlantic Coast.

So far as concerns painting particularly, the most striking thing about the Dutch, in contrast to the English north and south of them, is the profusion of pictures in their homes. Certain eighteenth-century travelers noted it because they had not experienced it elsewhere. There is also still earlier evidence in estate inventories, which sometimes specify the pictures room by room: the Great Chamber, the Fore Room, the Withdrawing Room. A half-dozen titles in one inventory is not unusual; Jonas Bronck left eleven pictures, Cornelius Steenwyck left thirty-nine, and Doctor De Lange left sixty-two. Still more remarkable was a collection of seventy-four left by Captain Giles Shelley; they were probably acquired as loot, for he had been a pirate; yet even a pirate can like pictures—especially after he retires from piracy.

The probable reason for so many pictures in New Netherland was a unique situation in the mother country. In Holland there was then in progress the first wholesale patronage of painting under approximately democratic conditions; a prosperous middle class with a liking for pictures made painting easy as a craft because current taste was not exacting, but difficult as a career because there was so much competition. Hundreds of workmen were engaged in manufacturing thousands of works, and whole families engaged in the business at once; pictures were so cheap that every middle-class home could have them in every room.

Such examples all through New Netherland up to Fort Orange, as Albany was then named, were of course importations and therefore merit only a brief comment in a history of American painting. But they do indicate among the Dutch a very active pleasure in pictures; and this is emphasized by the variety of subject-matter. In Dr. De Lange's home were landscapes (*Evening: Break of Day*), anecdotes (*A Cobbler: Country People Frolic*), still-lifes (*Flower Pot: Bunch of Grapes with Pomegranate*), seapieces (*Sea-Strand*), portraits (*My Lord Spelman: Mr. De Lange*), decorations (*Coat of Arms*), and scriptural scenes (*Abraham and Hagar*).

Yet the presence of Dutch pictures in New Netherland did not lead to any immediate patronage of local painters, even the portraitists, on a scale more liberal than in New England. A certain Henri Couturier painted portraits of Governor Peter Stuyvesant and his sons before 1663, but no existing portrait can yet be convincingly assigned to Couturier. In fact not one existing pic-ture is generally acceptable to students of the period as having been done before the English took over the colony. Apparently not until then did the Dutch themselves prosper sufficiently to give out many painting commissions.

Nicholas William Stuyvesant had himself depicted [1666: New-York Historical Society, New York] in a ludicrously disproportioned but spiritedly designed equestrian portrait. The hypothesis of two workmen putting their hands to this seems the simplest way of accounting for the hobbyhorse effect underneath the large face whose expression, or lack of it, remains placidly unaware of the precariously prancing animal below. A pair of portraits of members of the Provoost family may be taken as typical of a fairly large group of still anonymous works done in New York around the turn of the century. This pair were for a time dated from 1685, but now, because of costume details, from fifteen years or so later; they are probably of *David Provoost* and *Mrs. Provoost* [New-York Historical Society, New York]. They and the others run along an even level of moderate workshop competence which seems higher than that of the equestrian Stuyvesant only because these run-of-the-mill bust portraits never dare as much in design.

A fair quantity of biographical facts has accumulated around Evert Duyckinck the First. He is described in some records as a limner, and some portraits have been attributed to him; but the attribution first made has, like that made to Child, foundered on facts. Along with that key picture the subsequent attributions have slithered away; and Duyckinck, like Child, now stands in moderate biographical definiteness but bereft of even the slight artistic individuality which was his for a time. Yet there are plenty of anonymous portraits

6. MRS. GERRET DUYCKINCK *by* GERRET DUYCKINCK
Courtesy of The New-York Historical Society, New York City.

out of which Duyckinck the limner may possibly still be satisfactorily constituted.

His main occupation was manufacturing glass, but he exhibits the same
versatility found among workers in the other colonies at the time. In the documents he is variously called a glazier, a burner of glass, a painter of glass, a
stainer of glass, a painter, and a limner. In 1679 he and his son Gerret installed colored glass windows in the new church of the Labadist Fathers of
Long Island. Much earlier he had engraved coats of arms on the windowpanes
of the Stadt Huys; they were of course devices for making governmental
authority visibly impressive, like painting similar decorations on a governor's
coach, but there may have been some extra pleasure in looking at them with
the light shining through. Duyckinck also engraved private coats of arms on
the windowpanes of the Reformed Church; and he had to go to law to get
his pay for some of these.

For painting in general, one of Duyckinck's tasks was to put coats of arms
on the leather fire-buckets which, passed from hand to hand along human
chains, were then the only organized manner of fighting fires. The buckets on
which he worked were owned by the city, though there was no fire department
like that developed in the nineteenth century; such buckets, along with lad-
ders, were required by law to be ready in private homes when citizens were
called out to put down a blaze. The coats of arms or initials on the buckets
served as a means of identification after the hubbub and confusion were past.
In New Amsterdam, as everywhere else in the colonies, such humble tasks
were regarded as any painter's routine business.

This first Duyckinck is further notable for founding a veritable dynasty of
artisans who either combined glazing with painting or almost succeeded in
becoming portrait specialists. As late as 1746 a Gerardus Duyckinck was advertising a continuance of his father's business: "Limning, Painting, Varnishing, Japanning, Gilding, Glasing and Silvering of Looking-Glasses, all done
in the best Manner." This was probably a great-grandson; and a grandson also
painted, Evert Duyckinck the Third. The painting son of the founder was
Gerret Duyckinck, whose portraits of himself and *Mrs. Gerret Duyckinck*
[plate 6] have sufficient stylistic character to be a nucleus for further attributions. Over fattening jowls and sullen mouth his eyes are supercilious and a
little suspicious; hers look out with pained tolerance from a face that has not
lost quite all of its piquant curves.

To account for all this, it is reasonable, even necessary, to suppose a continuous training down four generations: a family workshop maintained by the
usual artisan miscellany of jobs in which ordinary painting and portrait painting were just two among many. Directories and city records have yielded the

names of about half a dozen more artisans from the decade ending in 1726, and the appearance of a couple of non-Dutch names in that short list may be interpreted as the natural result of English rule. At the time one Christian Lodowick was writing: "Our chiefest unhappiness here is too great a mixture of nations." That is only his way of saying that in New York, as distinct from New Amsterdam, the Dutch were not as important as they had been.

But up the Hudson Valley Dutch tenants were still the most numerous element and the Dutch landowners, called patroons, were economically the most powerful class. The homes of the patroons were being filled with portraits about as rapidly as were the homes of city-dwellers. The De Peyster family, for example, had brought over family portraits in the middle sixteenhundreds and had since then been supplementing them with locally painted ones. Dominie Nicholas Van Rensselaer in Albany owned thirteen pictures; no contemporaneous Puritan or Anglican minister is known to have had even half that number. During the childhood of John Jay Chapman the old house on the Jay farm at Bedford was full of portraits, by both early unknown and later famous known painters; but antedating them all was the portrait originally known as "The Patroon." By the time Chapman and his cousins were spending their summers there, it had been so often re-painted that no one knew whether the Patroon was sitting or standing; so the children dubbed him "The Sliding Poltroon."

No poltroonery but rather an ungainly courage marks the work of a Hudson Valley itinerant who inscribed the ages of his subjects on a series of portraits around 1720. He was one among several limners at work in that region then and a little later, but his manner is so positive and so appropriate to both time and place that in this book he is called the Hudson Valley Master. His mind was vigorous and his hand attained a coarse facility. His placing of the figures was distantly derived from studio practice, probably by way of reproductive prints; from the same source came the ill articulated gestures which he gave them. Postures and gestures both, however, are rigid; in grotesque contradiction to that trait are the painter's energy in covering his large areas with pigment, and particularly his slashing brush strokes with the high lights. He seems to be painting by main force. "It's dogged as does it."

In this artisan's portrait of *Thomas Van Alstyne* [1721: plate 7] he made naturalistic inaccuracy itself serve his concept. The lines are too emphatic; the shapes are too flat; the color is too monotonous. The artistic illiteracy of this limning affirms in visual terms more vivid than words the rude energy of people hewing fortunes out of a wilderness. The derivative stylism suggests the cultural sophistication to which both painter and patrons aspired; the actual execution directly expresses the countryfied approximation they achieved. Their

7. THOMAS VAN ALSTYNE   *by* HUDSON VALLEY MASTER
Courtesy of The New-York Historical Society, New York City.

middle-class economic security was far from being the aristocracy fancied in their descendants' retrospective wish fulfilment. Better than all such make-believe is the painter's rustic swagger by which he showed himself and his patrons both as they wished to be and as they were.

About a ten-mile crow flight southwest from New York City, in New Jersey at Perth Amboy, Scottish John Watson was established from the year 1714; and somewhat earlier Swedish Gustavus Hesselius had landed among his countrymen a little further south. Certainly both men had completed pictures before 1725; but because the greater part of both painters' American careers follows that date, a stylistic discussion of their work can be more conveniently made later.

Pennsylvania as a colony and Philadelphia as a city were ethnically perhaps the most mixed of all at their start, but that was mainly because both were late in starting. The Holy Experiment, so long as it was true to its idea, developed no taste for pictorial art even in portrait form; Quakers of a later time were sufficiently influenced by their fellow citizens to have their portraits done and to that extent they became, if not renegades, at least compromisers with worldliness. But before such Quakers were won over, portraiture had been begun by people of other sects.

Christopher Witt came to Pennsylvania in 1704 as a member of the small religious group with the strange title of "Society of the Woman of the Wilderness," to which no women were admitted. The leader of this sect was the famous Johannes Kelpius, and his followers were unusual in their general education as well as in their adoption of his pietistic form of mysticism. Kelpius died in 1708, and the community broke up; but some time during the four years that Witt was a member of it he painted a portrait of the leader. In its tentative technique and its equally tentative rendering of personality it is as amateur as the work of Foster in Boston. The amateurism of Witt himself is further indicated by his various occupations in Germantown after 1708: astrologist, conjurer, herbalist, naturalist, and physician. Whether he continued painting through these activities is not stated.

13. The South

Justus Engelhardt Kühn: ?–1717
Anon.: *Jaquelin Family Portraits; Brodnax Family Portraits*, c. 1722
Mrs. Henrietta Johnston: ?–1728/9
Mrs. Elizabeth Le Serrurier: act. 1684–1717
Isaac Mazyck: 1661–1736

Below Philadelphia a different economic organization was developed by 1725; although it was controlled by a class similar in social type and cultural taste to its northern counterparts, it produced a very different pattern of living. Through Maryland and Virginia stretched the slave-worked plantations centered around great houses where the owners lived for most of the time. Once a year planter-families did customarily leave their relative isolation to participate in a round of races and dances and dinners, and for a few weeks the villages of Annapolis and Williamsburg became crowded and gay while law courts and legislatures were in session. People at the time were probably too busy to sit to painters; but they could hear about and sometimes inspect the work of men who might later visit them in the country in order to paint them in the homes where the portraits would hang.

In Annapolis, for example, throughout most of the second decade of the eighteenth century, would-be patrons could make such arrangements with Justus Engelhardt Kühn. Six bust portraits [all c. 1710: all privately owned] afford a good idea of his average product. He differentiated the countenances of his sitters, but in other respects he practised a formula. The placing in the ovals, real or feigned, is little varied; neckcloths on three of the four men, arrangements of lace and hair on all three women, exhibit similarities which seem to owe as much to Kühn as to current fashion. The further peculiarity of all three women wearing practically identical brooches and pearl strands makes it even more likely that the painter was conferring on his sitters a recipe fashionableness which went beyond their actual possessions.

This easy means to splendor is startlingly illustrated in the semi-royal settings which Kühn puts into two large-scale portraits of children: *Henry Darnall the Third* [c. 1710: Maryland Historical Society, Baltimore] and his sister *Eleanor Darnall* [plate 8]. Here again the faces are somewhat individualized; and the meticulousness of detail in costumes, so different from the casual

8. ELEANOR DARNALL *by* JUSTUS ENGELHARDT KÜHN

Courtesy of Maryland Historical Society.   Photograph from The Frick Art Reference Library.

generalizing of the bust portraits, indicates that the painter was rendering specific costumes. But the vistaed grandeurs of gardens and distant palaces are
most probably, in their diagrammatic perspective and thinness of pigment,
adaptations from prints or book illustrations of the time. In relation to actuality they could hardly be even the most sanguine anticipations of things-hoped-
for in eighteenth-century Maryland; they seem rather engagingly frank visual
fictions for adding interest to large canvases.

A record in Virginia somewhat earlier than Kühn permits the inference of
a painter being there. In 1698 William Fitzhugh wrote to London ordering
certain supplies "to set up a painter." A quarter of a century later some still
existent portraits were painted in Jamestown—of two families, Jaquelin and
Brodnax, but in a manner so similar as to suggest the same hand at work.
This manner, moreover, has such unmistakable likenesses to the manners of
the Hudson Valley Master and J. Cooper that it seems equally logical to think
of this workman also as an artisan undertaking to "set up" the Virginians in
currently fashionable costumes derived from prints. What those Virginians
would have had, if they could, was something straight out of the studio of
Kneller; what they got was something not much nearer to his formula than
Jamestown was to London. Young *Edward Jaquelin the Second* [c. 1722; plate 9]
presents a countenance forceful enough to compete effectively with dog and
bird, with his own white-trimmed red suit and blue robe which flies off
flamboyantly, not because any wind is blowing it but because the painter wants
it to fill up space. He, like his northerly contemporaries, cared little for naturalistic vision; but his coarsely slashing brush stroke achieves a consistent and
appropriately rustic approximation to a sophistication distant both in space
and in spirit.

In contrast to this artisan's boldness was the timid refinement of a lady artist
who had begun a little earlier to use pastel in Charleston. Mrs. Henrietta
Johnston was the wife of the rector of Saint Philip's, whose small salary and
ill-health made it necessary for her to seek portrait commissions. In 1725, nine
years after his death, she journeyed as far as New York, seemingly for work.

She is at present not only the first recorded woman to work in the colonies
but also the first painter, man or woman, known to have used pastel. She was
certainly exceptional, therefore, but she was not in any sense a freak. To be
sure, women painters had not been exactly plentiful even in Europe; but from
Marguerite, the sister of the Van Eycks, through Sofonisba Anguisciola at work
a hundred years before Mrs. Johnston, to the latter's own time, there had been
a number sufficiently large for them all to escape that charge. In England the
records of Stuart times contain a half-dozen names of women painters before
1700, and Mrs. Johnston had several European and English contemporaries,

among whom Rosalba Carriera was the most famous. Indeed, Mrs. Johnston may not have been alone even in Charleston; family tradition claims that Mrs. Elizabeth Le Serrurier, who lived there from 1684 to about 1717, painted portraits.

In Mrs. Johnston's work there is a feminine sensitiveness which, because it lacks intensity, can be praised only by straining good will; and that sensitiveness is further blunted by technical weaknesses. Mouths are imprecise, with little observation of the modulations between mouth and nose; a heavy line does duty for an upper eyelid, a high-bridged nose is tightly attached to brows, and the heads are vaguely put together. It is all feminine enough, but simply as an uncertain repetition of a partly learned formula. It seems even possible that she was attracted to pastel in the first place by the leeway it permits to indecision of mind and tentativeness of touch, because the medium itself has a larger margin of tolerance for weak handling than either oil or water color. Perhaps even more important with Mrs. Johnston was the novelty of the medium then as an attraction to patrons.

It was fitting that a socially acceptable amateur practising a fashionable medium should appear in Charleston. That settlement was the great exception in the southern region, and quickly became as much a "city-like Towne" as any northern one. Endowed with a community pattern and a unique architectural consistency by group settlement from Barbados, it was the single port of outlet and intake for a large region of plantations. The malarial climate of the back country kept the planters' families in town for a good part of the year; and life there took on a gay distinction notable in the new world—notable enough to entice some cultured Europeans to make it a permanent home. Its liveliness and intelligence may have been somewhat superficial, but they were remarkable enough to be repeatedly mentioned in the annals of travelers as well as in the reminiscences of native Charlestonians.

The practice of painting as a decorative occupation for leisure hours was to recur many times in the city's history. Almost at once even a gentleman, along with Mrs. Le Serrurier, took up portraiture for pleasure; he was her son-in-law Isaac Mazyck, who had been depicted in miniature before he came to Charleston. Both of these society amateurs were French; it is not recorded of any English immigrant of the same social level that he or she was an amateur painter. Yet the French lady and gentleman were to have plenty of later emulators among the American-born of English stock.

9. EDWARD JAQUELIN THE SECOND *by* UNKNOWN PAINTER
Courtesy of the Ambler Family and Virginia Museum of Fine Arts.

14. Indications of a broadening taste

William Burgis: act. 1715–1731
Anon.: *Decorations in the Clark-Frankland House,* c. 1715
Nehemiah Partridge: act. 1713
John Watson: 1685–1768 (decorations)
Gustavus Hesselius: 1682–1755 (religious and mythological pictures)

The overwhelming predominance of the portrait among the examples actually surviving from the first century is already clear. Although there was from the first a wide variety of subject-matter in the signs, they remained too exclusively utilitarian for them to be preserved as pictures. The pleasure obtained by the contemporaneous audience from the panel paintings inside the taverns may have been closer to the pictorial awareness of later times, but little can be inferred one way or the other from available documentation.

Almost certainly it was along this level that American interest in landscape began. Aside from the occasional descriptive intention to be discerned in portrait background views, such as those behind William Stoughton and Major Savage, there is evidence in a few topographical prints which probably derive from original drawings by William Burgis. One of New York dates from about 1717, that of Boston harbor from about 1723, and that of Harvard College from 1726. In the records Burgis is variously called draftsman, painter, innholder, taverner, gentleman; it has been conjectured that this last title, asserted by himself, was a piece of presumption in some way associated with his disappearance, despite which his wife was unable to secure a divorce in 1736. The aim in Burgis' work was descriptive, just as in the drawings and engravings connected with the explorers; but his prints were perhaps primarily addressed to an American public.

One painting with this literalistic aim can be dated before 1725—ten years before, in fact. It purports to depict the front of the Clark-Frankland house in Boston; and it is indeed no more than a front, since its draftsmanship suggests nothing behind the shallow wall of window-pierced brick. This charmless crudity was nevertheless the overmantel panel in the parlor of that costly house itself, and in the same room with it were eleven larger panels of a quite different character.

Three of those which remain are tall and narrow panels with rather small figures set in varied landscapes; in the skyey portions are identifiable coats of arms in boldly intentioned but poorly rendered relief. [One of these three is in the Maine Historical Society, Portland; the other two are privately owned.] A similar fourth one is now lost. Another surviving example is the *Landscape Panel* [c. 1715: plate 10]; the sky in it rises over a steeply composed view of mountain and mansion, cliff and stream, before which two men dramatize some unclear event. Six other similar panels have disappeared through the years since the destruction of the house. In the existing uprights the human incidents are so definitely subordinated to the scenery that the pictures cannot be classified as anecdote; and the landscapes, further, are treated in such a generalized way that they are best described as fanciful decorations.

But all, in striking contrast to the horizontal overmantel of the building itself, exhibit a decided degree of facility; they have left the medievalism of a sign painter's awkwardness far behind and made a stylistic leap to the very end of the Renaissance. They are so fluently even though coarsely rococo, so completely caught up with the current fashion of London, that they make credible the story that the house's owner imported a workman straight from that capital. They might, however, have been executed in London and shipped over ready for installation; even so, they can be taken to embody the specific desires of the owner because of the family connections seemingly symbolized by the coats of arms. Yet the appearance of this startling splendor in still puritanic Boston would seem to have behind it a motivation more complex than worldly display: a motive complex enough to contain a good deal of that delight which, irrespective of the artistic quality of the objects involved, may properly be called esthetic.

There is of course a much greater likelihood that this esthetic motive would occur in the mind of a workman; there is even a probability that it actually did occur before 1725. The inventory of the painter Kühn's estate, for instance, specifies "14 pictures & Landskips." No doubt the latter remained in the estate because nobody would buy them; and if the ornate wish fulfilments inserted behind the Darnall children dependably indicate the technical characteristics of Kühn's landscapes, they must have been thin in conception and meager in execution. It is indeed a curious thing that for all the time that the older spelling of "landskip" continued in use here, the pictures themselves should have skipped so much of the specific detail which a later taste came to ask as a means to recognizability. But Kühn's patrons probably would not have declined to buy his landscapes on the ground that they were not well enough done; their reason, if they had any, would more likely have been that they could not justify themselves in purchasing any painting not a portrait. Therefore the most significant thing is that Kühn painted them—maybe in a hope of selling them, but surely for his own pleasure.

10. LANDSCAPE PANEL *by* UNKNOWN PAINTER
Courtesy of Maine Historical Society.

As early as 1715 there is a record of something like a landscape on view in Boston. In March of that year, one Nehemiah Partridge, who had two years earlier offered to do japanning and to sell paints, announced

The Italian Matchean, or Moving Picture, wherein are to be seen, Wind Mills and Water Mills moving round, Ships sayling on the Sea, and several curious Figures, very delightful to behold. . . .

That description suggests some kind of mechanical toy rather than the painted scenery called moving pictures in the early nineteenth century, and probably contemporaneous curiosity about it constituted a beginning of an interest in machinery rather than in art. Yet the appearance in this connection of the word "delightful" may without undue forcing be understood as foretelling something of later importance. Mechanical and artistic interests were often inextricably blended in the American audience, and individual Americans frequently united a talent for painting and a talent for invention.

Through these same years, probably, John Watson in Perth Amboy was ornamenting the shutters of his painting-room with "the heads of sages, heroes, and kings," "personages in antique costumes, and the men with beards and helmets, or crowns." When, more than a century later, William Dunlap began to write the first history of the arts in this country, he opened his narrative with his childhood memories of Watson's decorations.

An extension of subject interest which, among Protestant colonists, seems more daring than landscape was the commission given by a church in Maryland to Gustavus Hesselius for an altar-painting of *The Last Supper;* it was perhaps the beginning of the slow dissipation of distrust for imagery in churches. Two other pictures by Hesselius, since they descended in the family, probably indicate a quite personal taste for more fanciful subjects than his patrons possessed. *A Bacchanalian Revel* [privately owned] and its companion piece, which is apparently on the theme of *Bacchus and Ariadne* [Detroit Institute], look like youthful works when his mind was still brimming with the academic exercises of the art schools of his native Sweden.

These facts concerning painting which are now mostly lost are few enough to find in the history of a hundred years, but their very meagerness makes them the more important. Painting has played a somewhat larger part in American life than can be satisfactorily indicated by surviving examples alone, and the obscure beginnings of esthetic consciousness and broadening taste are as much a matter of cultural history as the preservation of a relatively large number of portraits for family and personal reasons.

15. Retrospect from the year 1725

The sum of the first century of painting in this country was the establishment of an all-round craft along the healthily useful level of the artisan and the amateur. The actual works remaining are as modest in their esthetic character as would naturally be expected along that level. Their predominant awkwardness, their mixture of belated medievalism and halting fashionableness, were appropriate to the society then transplanted into frontier conditions.

No overtone of apology is involved in pointing out that most of the surviving pictures are from the years of general cultural subsidence which preceded the colonial culmination, that the craftsmen coming to the colonies were less skilful than those who could prosper in the mother country, and that in England at the time painting itself was in a period of doldrums. Rather there can be the contrasting overtone of congratulation that the societal life brought over was in itself complete enough to need the craft of painting in its humblest function.

Indeed, the historian might justify the view that even portraiture, though matter-of-fact in its own nature, constituted then and there a breakaway from the bonds of strict utilitarianism in painting. Building and furniture and metalwork and weaving were all more important in the difficult conditions of colonization; in them portraits could legitimately be called superfluities. Nevertheless, the many that remain are by no means all that were executed; and though, in esthetic terms, most of them are poor daubs, a few manifest esthetic intention and achieve the communication of art. The Master of the Freakes certainly did both of those things; and like all other artists, he did them in obedience to the needs of his own nature. That it should have happened so early in our history in unfavorable circumstances is one of those fortunate accidents which reward historical students and later appreciators even more than the people among whom it occurs.

This expressiveness is also quite as authentically American as the technical crudity of the average picture then; and culturally it is far more important. Making the word "American" thus retroactive is not unhistorical; the thing must exist before the name. Americanism at any given time is what Americans then are. Nor is there any inherent improbability about the occurrence even so early of a local accent in painting; it had already happened in the people, and it was even then happening in the crafts. The half-timbered house had here received an exterior sheathing of shingle and clapboard clearly stamping it as of New England rather than of Old England; the mass and weight of oak furniture were being supplanted by the delicacy of form and openness of construction made possible by lighter woods. Likewise, the Freake Master's personal variation within the medieval manner is as vital a localism as those more utilitarian adaptations; and his resolute grappling with the deeper problems of painting and of portraiture may be taken as the earliest appearance of a trait that recurs down the generations. This craftsman's rectitude communicates the conviction of reality, which is more lastingly significant than what is commonly called realism precisely because it requires a greater measure of creativeness. Whenever and wherever it occurs, it radiates spiritual reassurance across the uncertainties of history.

PERIOD ONE
THE COLONIAL

DIVISION TWO
Colonial Culmination—
1725 to 1775

16. The emergence of an upper class

From the beginnings of colonization there had of course been a small but growing upper class composed of officials and those who through luck or ability were gaining wealth and influence. But by 1725 this group was so clearly established economically and stratified socially that it could advance beyond the tentative patronage previously practised and play a definitive role in the development of arts and crafts.

The economic base of this group varied from colony to colony: the planter class of the South being matched by the landed patroons of New York; the New Englanders controlling extensive fisheries or shipbuilding or lumbering; the leading merchants dominating all of the coastal cities. By and large they were alike in origin, rising into prosperity from below; the universal new-world necessity of owner-management made them alike in human type; their position in relation to the enlarging mass of the population favored intermarriage on a class basis, together with the acquisition of identical manners and similar tastes. It was therefore natural that a distinct colonial culture should appear in the economically privileged group, from Maine through the Carolinas, and that their possessions should be stamped with a consistent style.

The stylistic change accompanying the change in society was extreme; if a contrast be drawn between two dates only a century apart, which is not very long in any national life, it now seems startling. In 1670 Philadelphia and Charleston were not in existence; the houses of Boston and New York and the plantation homes of Virginia, though they exhibited obvious differences to the eye, yet had one thing in common: each had in its own structure the possibility of addition and adaptation to the changing needs of a growing family. In 1770 all medieval irregularity of aspect had been supplanted by a trim elegance of homes paper-planned in advance from imported handbooks of fashionable architecture, often animated by round-arched windows and occasionally by doorways with broken pediments.

Although perhaps the truth is always wrenched a little when compressed into an aphorism, one by Louis Sullivan probably contains as much truth as any aphorism: "What people are within, the buildings express without." It would permit the interpretation of the quickly attained colonial uniformity in architecture as a parallel to the class change in clothes from homespun to satin, and of each of these as the expression of faith in the permanence of prosperity. The demand for furniture and silver was such that fine craftsmen worked all up and down the coast; and in these appurtenances of good living the change of style was most dramatic of all: from medieval rectangularity of structure over to a perhaps excessive curvilinear rococo.

These Americans were unawares repeating a process observed in France a century earlier by La Rochefoucauld: "In order to establish themselves in the world, men do all they can to appear established there." Here too, the effort to translate this desire into actuality was a creative element in society during the brief half-century of colonial culmination in that it enabled craftsmen in general to function vitally in bringing a culture to birth; and the works left by those craftsmen remain as the most direct and delightful means of our own imaginative comprehension of one phase of our complex inheritance.

Far earlier than the French aphorist, six hundred and fifty years earlier, in fact, and in then unknown Japan, Lady Murasaki had written down another observation applicable to both the France of Molière and the America of Franklin. "I have often noticed that people of quite common origin who have risen in the world can in a very short time achieve a perfect imitation of aristocratic importance. . . ." The success of the Americans was sufficient to warrant a tacit agreement among themselves to forget their own middle-class character and to think of themselves as a securely based aristocracy.

17. A conscious taste in painting

Nathaniel Emmons: 1703–1740
John Mare: act. 1760–1770

Part of the Americans' effort to appear established was their acquisition of portraits on a much more liberal scale than during the preceding period. In the absence of banks, handsome silver on a mahogany sideboard would give its owner economic reassurance as well as visual pleasure; and freshly painted likenesses hung on the paneled walls of withdrawing rooms would speak to the families even more strongly of their own social position. These things, and the homes in which they were placed, confirmed the people in the conviction of their own reality, which is the necessary preliminary to convincing others.

The technical soundness and esthetic worth of the pictures remained almost entirely the responsibility of the individual craftsman, with the inevitable result that they varied widely according to the personal factors of his training and mental capacity. The comprehension of his patrons for the product did not often rise to the level of esthetic awareness; those patrons very clearly illustrated the mental pattern of all societal groups newly coming into culture as well as into money.

Fairly compendious evidence as to eighteenth-century taste is contained in the obituary notice of Nathaniel Emmons. That his work remains somewhat nebulous does not in any way impair the initial documentation of certain long-lived traits in all American appreciation of painting. The notice appeared in the *Boston News Letter* for May 29th, 1740:

He was universally own'd to be the greatest master of various sorts of Painting that ever was born in this country. And his excellent works were the pure effect of his own Genius, without ever receiving any Instruction from others. Some of his pieces are such admirable Imitations of Nature, both in faces, Rivers, Banks and Rural Scenes, that the pleased Eye cannot easily leave them; and some of his Imitations of the Works of Art are so exquisite, that though we know they are only Paints, yet they deceive the sharpest Sight whyle it is nearly looking on them, and will preserve his memory till age or some unhappy accident or other destroy them. He was sober and modest; minded accuracy more than Profit.

In relation to the actual circumstances, the adverb "universally" resounds somewhat stridently even when proper allowance is made for obituary license. Better than the encomiums lavished upon Cotton Mather, this affords a very parochial instance of exaggerated community consciousness. After all, through his writings, Mather's name was known as far away as London; but it may be doubted if the painter's name was known even as widely as the subscription list of the *News Letter* itself before his death brought that about. Though Boston has perhaps been pre-eminent in its assumption of superiority all through American history, it has also had some competition in that respect; but even Philadelphia and Charleston have fallen short of Boston's glacial calmness which kept it unaware of its own arrogance.

Emmons' obituary next makes the claim of autogenesis for the painter. Something like that had been claimed for Joseph Allen sixty years earlier in the private letter he brought with him, but here it appears full-blown in print. Already, in this country, a special prestige was collecting around the self-made man in every line of activity; among the painters from this time on it will become almost a point of honor to insist upon having been self-taught. It will almost immediately recur with Feke and Badger, with Copley and with West; thus it becomes a professional tradition before the nation itself is formed; and after this event, along with nationalism in every other phase of culture, it becomes the painters' version of the Log-Cabin-to-White-House saga. Long before, Vasari had used the fable to waken wonder at Giotto; it became distinctively American only in its extent and virulence. This was possible, even appropriate, in a country where wealth and power were presumed to be (and sometimes really were) attainable by one's own efforts. With many painters, asserting this claim of self-teaching has been an unconscious obeisance to the spirit of the age or a conscious means of ingratiating themselves with customers; but some have put such extreme emphasis on this idea that they seem to be making an aggressive apology for unacknowledged shortcomings in their own work.

The idea connected with Emmons which is significantly most emphasized is probably as old as the craft of painting: the art of it consists of imitation pushed to the point of optical deception. That has certainly been the initial attitude of the layman in looking at pictures ever since his reactions have been recorded. Even Greek writers on painting make considerable use of it; but then, of course, in the total mass of writing about art, intelligence has been somewhat rare. In the enjoyment of art, pleasure in attempted visual deception is permanent; it has certainly been prominent many times over in American experience.

However, what constitutes illusionism in this craft is highly variable with the time and the individual concerned. The Amerind who, almost a century earlier, had thought that a portrait was Governor Winthrop in the flesh would perhaps have received a sneer from the writer of the obituary; to us, what that writer accepted as ultimate in illusionism would probably seem only more obituary license. What he meant by "Imitations of Works of Art" is obscure, but they might have been something on the order of monochrome renderings of supposed carvings or even panels painted to counterfeit grained marble; such tricks are known to have been asked of colonial painters a little later by people newly well-to-do.

Twenty-four years after Emmons' death, Thomas Ainslee in Quebec wrote to Copley about how his own baby son in distant Scotland had looked at his portrait by Copley and ". . . sprung to it, roared, and schriched, and attempted gripping the hand, but when he could not catch hold of it, . . . he stamp'd and scolded . . ." Ainslee then assured Copley that the sort of skill which gave rise to so remarkable a circumstance would certainly bring him much patronage if he would visit Quebec. In Newport before 1775 there was the story of a negro slave bowing before Samuel King's portrait of his master displayed in a shop window; and as if to dramatize the universality of the admiration for verisimilitude, there came out of Philadelphia a little later the story of President Washington bowing to the elder Peale's double portrait of two younger Peales. In this last anecdote occurs the first trace of deprecation for what a few people were coming to regard as a trick: Washington was excused as having been preoccupied at the moment with affairs of state.

But the general idea continued strong throughout the nineteenth century, and toward the end it even became for a time the defining characteristic in the work of a highly successful group of craftsmen. The recent revival of interest in this late-century manifestation has overlooked one known colonial instance of an equal skill. John Mare, in depicting *John Keteltas* [1767: privately owned], put a fly on the frilled cuff of the sleeve. For certain minds it is still a temptation to try brushing the insect away; and if such an impulse is a tribute to artistic quality, Mare should be acknowledged as a master. His technical feat is amazing even to the sophisticated eye; and admiration for this type of craft may continue to be confused with esthetic pleasure so long as painting continues under the necessity of winning a new audience with each new generation.

The audience for painting in the mid-eighteenth century displayed one further trait which was to persist through the next, but which was at that earlier time taken over from England itself. The idea is succinctly given in the very last sentence about Emmons: he possessed the virtues associated with thrift. This praise of sobriety and industry in artists, often with the strong implication that they are adequate substitutes for talent and genius, occurred frequently in shop-keeping England. It appeared even in the writing of the ostentatiously unmercantile Horace Walpole, and it had a great deal to do with the success of the American West in both the Italian and the British capitals of culture. Reading Dunlap's account of the artists whom he knew before 1830, one comes to welcome the faintest whiff of the laziness or insobriety or rascality which incurs his now pleasantly priggish censure. And with Tuckerman, whose book appeared soon after the Civil War, sober diligence is impossibly inflated into creativeness; genteel dullards in paint become illumined with the halo of greatness.

Thus the Emmons obituary throws forward a revealing light upon a century and a half of taste among Americans who will have something like the power of life and death over the art of painting.

18. Specialists into New England

Peter Pelham: 1697–1751
John Smibert: 1688–1751

The emergence around 1725 of a portrait-purchasing class had its natural consequence of attracting from Europe men whose craft had been acquired not in the shops of the guild but in the studios of specialists. It is sometimes impossible to discover a recorded reason in a particular instance; but somehow or other, and in good time, word got about Britain and even the continent that portraits were wanted in the American colonies, and men who thought they could supply them began coming across the ocean. Those who did so had to be youthfully optimistic or in nearly desperate need of work for them to make so fateful a voyage. "Dukes don't emigrate"—nor do the princes of painting. When Van Dyck and Lely and Kneller went to England for patronage they left better men than themselves on the continent; and those who ventured so much further, to these colonies, left better men than themselves in command of the markets at home. But here, of course, any specialist from Europe would become important, no matter how obscure he might have remained at home; a full transplanting of civilization required the specialist as well as the artisan.

Peter Pelham was a competent engraver in mezzotint, and just why he quit a seemingly prosperous career in London remains unknown. But the first thing he did after reaching Boston in 1726 shows a shrewd estimate of the local situation; he made a portrait of the region's intellectual leader, Cotton Mather, and from it made the first known American mezzotint engraving [1727]. If he hoped that this initial effort would open the way to a prosperous career here, he met with disappointment, for through the next twenty years he engraved very few known plates; only in the last five years of his life was he really active as an engraver, issuing nine mezzotint portraits in that time. Six of these bear his name as their painter also; but his work in oil has not yet been stylistically clarified.

However, as a person and as a cultural influence Pelham was nothing less than a landmark in the development of Boston from one phase into a distinctly different phase. In 1734, about eight years after his arrival, he gave occasion for a long and censorious communication to the *Boston Gazette,* whose editor

85

printed it with a brief word of approval from himself: a protest against the Monthly Assemblies for music and dancing which Pelham was advertising by handbills distributed on the streets.

I could not read this Advertisement without being startled and concern'd at the Birth of so formidable a Monster in this part of the World; and I began to consider what could give encouragement to so Licentious and Expensive a Divertion, in a Town famous for its Decency and Good Order. . . .

　　When we look back upon the Transactions of our Fore-Fathers, and read the Wonderful Story of their godly Zeal, their pious Resolution, and their Publick Virtues; how should we blush and lament our present Corruption of Manners, and Decay of Religious & Civil Discipline? . . . But this their Posterity are too delicate to follow their sober Rules, and wise Maxims, and crying out for Musick, Balls and Assemblies, like Children for their Bells and Rattles. . . .

　　In vain will our Legislature provide wholsome Laws to suppress this Epidemical profaneness. In vain will our Ministers preach Charity, Moderation and Humility, to an Audience, whose thoughts are ingaged in Scenes of Splendour and Magnificence, and whose Time and Money are consumed in Dress and Dancing. . . .

And why in vain? He gives answer that the appeal of such vanities to the women is so strong that no man can restrain his wife and daughters from attending when other men do not keep theirs at home.

　　Pelham's assemblies were one among several activities by which he supported a growing family. His other efforts were less dangerous to community morals: straight schooling for children in reading and writing and arithmetic, needlework and drawing and painting on glass. Members of the Pelham family were musical; a concert was advertised as early as 1731. Within the next year or two a notable European musician, Karl Theodor Pachelbel, visited Boston; and when he left for Newport and points south, Pelham's eldest son accompanied him. This son re-appeared in Boston in 1743, and his advertisements claimed nine years of training in preparation for giving lessons on the harpsichord and in psalmody. This son went south again in 1749, and settled down for forty years as organist of Bruton Church in Williamsburg, Virginia, serving also as town jailer; on one occasion he conducted a performance of *The Beggar's Opera*. These details about the son do not concern Boston directly, but they do imply a great deal about the general cultivation of the household into which young Copley was to move when his mother became the third Mrs. Pelham. A home full of music and dancing, of painting and drawing and mezzotint engraving, must have been not only a busy one but also one which appeared rather pagan to puritanic minds. Yet Pelham and his family could not have changed Boston's manners unaided; a new generation of Boston-born was welcoming the pleasurable dissipations they provided. That letter of protest was a vigorous affirmation of a still strong conservatism, but its real meaning was that theocratic puritanism was fast giving ground before the inevitable worldliness of a commercial society.

That society's favorite portrait painter was John Smibert. His life before his coming here with Dean Berkeley in 1729 is full of picturesque details which have been emphasized many times from Dunlap on, but only some of them have any bearing upon his American career. Commencing as a house painter in his native Scotland, he moved on to London, where he decorated coaches and copied "old masters" for the dealers; in England then many who considered themselves to be connoisseurs collected such copies of old masterpieces rather than risk their own judgement in buying original pictures by living painters. If less sophisticated buyers could be persuaded to believe that such copies were genuine "old masters," their only remedy, then as now, was to charge it off to their own education in the ways of a fashionably cultured circle. Smibert prospered and attended an art academy; eventually he spent three years in Italy making copies for himself and acquiring both prints and plaster casts.

When the Dean persuaded him to come to the new world as Professor of Drawing and Painting and Architecture in a college that never materialized, Smibert brought all this professional equipment with him; he therefore became famous by owning a collection as well as by being a painter. His copies and prints were the only means that many Americans had of forming any idea of great painting; and not until they went to Europe did such native painters as Copley and Trumbull and Allston learn how superior were the originals to Smibert's copies.

In his original portraiture Smibert often shows himself possessed of a vigorous even if monotonous mind. His best productions are animated in arrangement even where placing and gesture fulfil a formula. The figures are stiff without being quite wooden; they are usually substantial to a degree not known in earlier New England work, but the surrounding space closes in somewhat oppressively. Where views open out, oftenest to the spectator's right, they preserve the studio characteristic of being a back-drop, looking as if they were copied from other paintings. The drawing of hands is more assured than any previous workman's here, but in its mannerized elongation it is far from being correct or varied. Other details in figure construction are also exceedingly repetitious: heavy-lidded eyes, turned-up mouths, swollen necks, fattily inexpressive jaws and chins. And as for the expression, that key to character, genuinely observed individuality is with Smibert practically confined to the countenances of the elderly.

On the other hand, Smibert did like to handle paint. His small brush strokes followed contours and sometimes blended into long lines with some liveliness. Though he treated clothes with less care than they deserved, he was definitely interested in approximating textures and in emphasizing somewhat arbitrary patterns of sweeping highlights. Above all else he was fond of loading his brush with white and sometimes achieved minute effects of considerable charm in that pigment.

The rather complicated and still impressive *Bishop Berkeley, Family, and Friends* [1729: Yale University Art Gallery] which initiated Smibert's American work was followed by nothing so ambitious. The most complicated design achieved by him for any American patron belongs to his first years in Boston, *Three Gentlemen* [c. 1730: plate 11]. The difficulty of three heads in a row near the top of the canvas was overcome by a handsome dramatization of the hands, skilfully enough achieved for it to seem appropriate to the formality of a group portrait. It is worth mentioning that Daniel Oliver, the one to the spectator's left, was never in this country and that Smibert used a miniature sent over from England as his source in enlarging this subject to the size of the other brothers. The predominance of dark areas in clothes and table and background does not prevent this from being a cheerful picture, for faces and hands together hold the attention, and the ripples of white that everywhere lead up to the faces are interestingly spaced across the darks. But this pictorial success led to no more such opportunities for Smibert. Indeed, despite the relative wealth of the Bostonian whom he married, Smibert, like Pelham, had to increase his income by activities outside of painting. He kept an art shop, selling supplies at both retail and wholesale; and he went so far as to offer for sale his collection of prints after the great masters made "for his own private use and improvement." Such necessities on his part probably were not caused by any actual indifference in the community; some individuals might even strain their pocketbooks a little to be depicted by one who conferred luster upon Boston—for that was the sentiment of those who relished the breath of European air he had brought.

There was a local poet there to say so at once. Soon after Smibert reached Boston he held an exhibition of his pictures, and the Reverend Mather Byles produced a set of rhymes which were reprinted in distant London. With a nod to the "barb'rous Desert" that existed here before Boston, the writer then cast a somewhat imperious look upon that city's own past:

> An hundred Journeys now the Earth has run
> In annual circles round the central Sun,
> Since the first Ship th' unpolished Letters bore
> Thro' the wide Ocean, to the barb'rous shore.
>
> .   .   .   .   .
>
> Solid, and grave, and plain the Country stood,
> Inelegant, and rigorously good.
>
> .   .   ‘   .   .
>
> Till the great Year the finish'd Period brought,
> A *Smibert* painted and a —— wrote.

11. THREE GENTLEMEN *by* JOHN SMIBERT   *Courtesy of Mr. Andrew Oliver.*

Next follows a mixture of references to specific pictures: his copies of Rubens and "th' *Italian* master," female portraits concealed under classic names, and identifiable portraits of men—Sewall "in hoary majesty," Byfield "fixt in strong thought," and "studious *Mascarene* asserts his Arms." Then the couplets begin to swell with something of a Popean elegance:

> Landskips how gay! arise in ev'ry Light,
> And fresh Creations rush upon the Sight.
> Thro' fairy Scenes the roving Fancy strays,
> Lost in the endless visionary Maze.
>   Still, wondrous Artist, let thy Pencil flow,
> Still warm with Life, thy blended Colours glow,
> Raise the ripe Blush, bid the quick Eye-balls roll,
> And call forth every Passion of the Soul.
> Let thy soft Shades in mimic Figures play,
> Steal on the Heart, and call the mind away.

Upon Smibert's death twenty-one years later, the language was only prose:

. . . well known for many fine Pictures he has done here, and celebrated in Italy, as well as Britain, for a good Painter, by the best Judges. As a Member of Society, he was a valuable Gentleman of a happy Temper, great Humanity and Friendship, a kind Husband, tender Father, and steady Friend. . . .

The coldly ceremonial reference to Smibert's painting may have been partly owing to his having had eye trouble and therefore executing no commissions for several years before his death; but the absence of expressed delight is a disappointingly negative verdict upon a whole life's work.

19. Specialists into the Central Colonies

Anon.: *De Peyster Child Portraits; Van Cortlandt Child Portraits*
Lawrence Kilburn: 1720–1775
John Watson: 1685–1768
Gustavus Hesselius: 1682–1755
William Williams: c. 1710–c. 1790

Through the second quarter of the eighteenth century Boston experienced the stylistic transformation registered in its portraiture as part of a cultural change from theocracy to mercantilism. New York had been mercantile from the first, so that during this time of colonial flowering the cultural alteration there was simply the more complete subordination of Dutch tradition to fashionable preferences derived from the English element in the population. Such a change could not occur overnight, for even in their eager adaptation to prosperity under the English the Dutch were tenacious of their ways of living. In individuals an artistic taste may be immediately responsive to the pressure of fashion, but in communities the process requires time.

Yet plenty of portraits were painted. A trio of De Peyster life-size child portraits [New-York Historical Society, New York] and their parallels, the Van Cortlandt children [two of these in the Brooklyn Museum] form the most striking group. Their formula was not at all the closed-in medieval one of a column-like figure isolated against a rather meaningless dark tone doing duty for an interior: the formula followed with the Gibbs children in Boston before 1700. Rather was it a more elaborate and more substantial variant of that used after 1700 in Kühn's Darnall pair. Each child in the two sets of cousins stands full-length in an elaborate setting of architecture and landscape which is more substantially painted than in Kühn's manner but is no more convincing than his as to the physical existence of such settings here before 1750; an extra complication of design in the New York portraits is the introduction into each of some animal—sheep or dog or deer—which may or may not have been an actual pet but which in each case enhances the visual charm and the general effect of artifice. The general recipe seems no more specifically English than specifically Dutch; it seems to be the current cosmopolitanism of the whole European continent. From the many smaller-scale portraits executed in New York between 1725 and 1750, other groups can already be formed on the basis of technical similarities which indicate definite but different workmen; and further documentary research may still uncover some painters' names for them. But no such group is at present sufficiently large or of sufficient esthetic consequence to suggest any single figure outstanding there as Smibert in contemporaneous Boston or as Theüs in Charleston through the following quarter-century.

From Denmark by way of London came Lawrence Kilburn, whose activities can be traced through a series of advertisements over twenty years: advertisements which spell his name in five different ways. The very first of these, in the *New York Gazette* for July 8th, 1754, by emphasizing the word "limner," showed that Kilburn himself wished to be considered a specialist instead of an artisan; it also struck the note of anxious fashionableness which was a sort of leitmotiv through the entire period in every colony. Gentlemen and ladies were informed that

. . . he don't doubt of pleasing them in taking a true Likeness, and finishing the Drapery in a proper Manner, as also in the Choice of Attitudes, suitable to each Person's Age and Sex. . . .

Two portraits of *James Beekman* and *Mrs. Beekman,* both signed and dated 1761 [privately owned], give ground for assigning to Kilburn two more couples: the *Garret Abeel* and *Mrs. Abeel* and the *Gerardus Duyckinck* and *Mrs. Duyckinck* [all four in the New-York Historical Society, New York]. There is throughout a bland smoothness of finish which involves an absence of vitality. The countenances differ, but none has personal distinction; such hands as appear are treated fussily and have no character. The best drawing and painting occur in the accessories of costume and ornament, yet that best constitutes no more than a general obviousness. The half-dozen advertisements which succeed that first one record how Kilburn, in order to live, fell back upon giving instruction and upon doing other kinds of painting: miniatures, landscapes, fans, flowers, and "sundry curious pieces." And before very long he did as Smibert did in Boston: sold painting supplies for commercial work as well as for portraiture.

Like Smibert in Boston, John Watson in Perth Amboy was part of the transplantation of the studio stylism by portrait specialists. Like Smibert, Watson was from Edinburgh; but he came to the colonies fifteen years earlier. Like Smibert, Watson had started as a house and sign painter. Like Smibert, Watson had a collection of copies and of pictures other than his own; but apparently Watson did not bring the bulk of his until 1730, when he made a trip back to Edinburgh to collect an inheritance.

In Perth Amboy Watson was near enough to New York to paint there at will; one list in his notebook consists of about a half-dozen portraits done there in 1726, and missing pages probably had more such information. However, the most voluminous details in that source book concern not painting but the variety of merchandise which Watson sold to others through the years: dry goods in general, clothes and buttons and hats and handkerchiefs, necklaces and cutlery, medicines and powder flasks. Add to all this the various known deals in real estate, his probable business involvement in the very ferry upon which he traveled back and forth, and the money-lending stressed by Dunlap: out of that emerges a life in which portrait painting was presumably not the major source of income. Even so, the present excessive scarcity of generally accepted originals by Watson may have been caused by the destruction of his painting-room during the Revolution and by the forgetfulness of his sitters' descendants.

The dozen little portrait heads now known [some in the New-York Historical Society, New York] are studio notes, as if in preparation for larger versions or by way of keeping his hand in practice during slack times. They all exhibit a uniform placing in their vellum ovals, a rigidity of posture, and a repetitious tendency to smirk which compose the formula of a mind little interested in those variations of character which should be a fundamental concern of a genuine portraitist. Another dozen of such drawings show unknown people or ideal subjects. The *King Stephen,* which is for a change rectangular in shape, is a moderately sensitive copy from some better original; the *Hercules* displays the typical copyist's unperceptive exaggeration of muscular contortions out of all proportion to the physical effort actually visible. It is true that the little curlicued strokes betray his failure to examine his sitters with sufficient exactness, but they do evidence his pleasure in making the strokes themselves. The human monotony involved in practising a portrait recipe does not debar the practitioner from delight in the process.

A wood panel with the painted head of *Caligula* in a feigned oval [privately owned] may well be one of the actual window shutters for Watson's painting-room which Dunlap recalled so vividly sixty years after the Revolution. If this can be taken as representative of Watson's work in oil, it is possible to say that he was fairly well at home in the medium. There is still, as in the drawings, an erratic modeling of form due to insufficient observation of nature; but there is also a painterly rendering of light-and-dark in general. The use of several vivid shades of red might imply that Watson himself was shrewdly aware of the publicity value of gay color in those prominent decorations; shutters like that would advertise him as well as signs could do and still not lower his painting-room to the level of a tavern. More clearly and more importantly, this colorism and this pictorial play beyond professional commissions indicate that Watson had in him some of that delight in the physical responsiveness of paint which is the basic reason both for making pictures and for looking at them.

Two years earlier than Watson, Gustavus Hesselius came to Delaware and soon removed to near-by Philadelphia. He was a minor figure in the general

12. TISHCOHAN   *by* GUSTAVUS HESSELIUS
Courtesy of The Historical Society of Pennsylvania.

exodus from Sweden during the years when the wars conducted by Charles XII made things economically difficult for artists; the somewhat older and better known Michael Dahl in London was another such emigrant. Hesselius went to Philadelphia with a commendatory letter from William Penn himself, and that must have served him well in securing such patronage as was possible among its few thousand inhabitants. After seven years he found it advisable to go into Maryland for a residence there of about fifteen years; he thus initiated a cultural orientation of Maryland toward the Middle Region which was to strengthen through several generations.

Probably it was Hesselius' activities in Maryland which did most to justify one couplet in an unknown rhymester's obituary tribute to George Calvert in the *Maryland Gazette,* March 8–15, 1734:

> Secure the Artist gives his Rule the Praise
> And dates his thriving Trade from Calvert's Days.

Whatever degree of success may deserve that adjective "thriving" of course depends upon environmental conditions, but in this case a fair amount of poetic license may be suspected, since in that very year Hesselius returned permanently to Philadelphia. Much clearer is the cultural significance of joining the concepts of "Artist" and "Trade"; exactly half a century after the arrival of Joseph Allen in Massachusetts, a poet in Maryland was thinking of the painter in the same way as the preacher Mathers in Dublin and Boston thought of Allen. Moreover, that idea corresponded to the economic fact; for the first known work by Hesselius on his return to Philadelphia was to paint most of the interior of the new State House, afterward to be called Independence Hall.

In 1740 he was in partnership with an avowed artisan, as shown by an advertisement in the *Pennsylvania Gazette* for December 11th:

PAINTING done in the best MANNER, by Gustavus Hesselius, from Stockholm, and John Winter, from London, viz. Coats of Arms drawn on Coaches, Chaises, &C, or any other kind of Ornaments, Landskips, Signs, Shew-boards, Ship and House Painting, Gilding of all Sorts, Writing in Gold or Colour, old Pictures clean'd and mended, &C

This list of painting jobs is so complete that it seems to leave nothing over for that final "et cetera"; the only thing missing is precisely portraiture. Yet Hesselius was painting some portraits through these latter years—and at least two more religious pictures. One was the altarpiece in the new Christ Church which was mentioned by a traveler in 1744; a *Crucifixion* was seen in Saint Mary's Roman Catholic church by John Adams, who wrote his wife about the "blood stains trickling down, the mob of Roman soldiers, the darkness, etc." Hesselius' work in organ-building and spinet-making may have marked a shift of his own interests away from painting; by this time his son John was ready to fulfil portrait commissions.

In the father's portrait work four examples are of major stylistic and psychological consequence: those of himself and wife and those of two Amerind chiefs which were commissioned by John Penn in 1735 [all in the Pennsylvania Historical Society, Philadelphia]. In the pair of Amerinds the veracity of expression caught by Hesselius is such that both subjects might be foreseeing the shameful trick played upon them two years later in the acquisition of their tribe's valuable land holdings; Lapowinsa's eyes smoulder with intense suspicion, while those of *Tishcohan* [1735: plate 12] somewhat hold back the condemnation foreshadowed by the wry grimness of his massive mouth. Mrs. Hesselius is shown in middle age as frank and even lovable; the square face of the painter himself is rather somber, with a hint of danger to others in the thrust of jaw and set of mouth. The general stylistic character of this work is not somber, but it is certainly sober, and therefore in striking contrast to the intentions shown in Watson's little studies. Something close to bluntness inheres in the angularity of these bent arms and broadened bodies; the effect falls short of forcefulness by reason of thin pigment and uncertain modeling. The rendering of depth and of textures is confused and inadequate; yet the unpretentious directness and dominating dignity are quietly reassuring. Even though this painting was emotionally appropriate to the Quaker strain in Philadelphia, its principal cause can probably be found only in the accident of Hesselius' early training; for a likely source exists in the relative austerity of David von Krafft, court painter at the time Hesselius left Sweden.

But about ten years before Hesselius died there was room in growing Philadelphia for quite another taste which was fed, and may have been introduced there, by the work of William Williams. His earliest known appearance there was as the teacher of nine-year-old Benjamin West, who first saw a portrait in Williams' studio and who probably caught from Williams a fondness for the castellated buildings that appear in his boyhood paintings. Williams also lent West the books of Fresnoy and Richardson, which prepared the boy's mind only too well for the teaching he was soon to receive in Rome. Williams painted the scenery for the first theater to open in Philadelphia; and in 1763, after a trip to the West Indies, he was back there under his sign of Hogarth's Head, prepared to do "painting in general," and conducting "an Evening School for the Instruction of Polite Youth, in the different branches of Drawing, and to sound the Hautboy, German and common Flutes. . . ."

Six years later Williams was in New York, under another sign of Rembrandt's head; it may have been easier for him to paint a new sign than to bring the old

13. DEBORAH HALL *by* WILLIAM WILLIAMS
Courtesy of Brooklyn Museum.

one along, but it may also be guessed that the names differed more than the likenesses. Williams' works are relatively ambitious in size and design; three of them are in fact of the kind called conversation pieces in England. In more general terms these are figures in landscapes, with the added element of intended portraiture. The coarse fluency that Williams displayed in approximating to his prototypes is technically allied to scene-painting. The background garden in the *Deborah Hall* [1766: plate 13] is more substantially painted than in any portrait by Kühn [plate 8], but it has the same remoteness from colonial actualities. In this and other pictures by Williams the restlessness of rococo is emphatically present, but the frequent refinement and subtlety of its sophisticated practitioners in Europe are absent. Again, as so often in American history, the very technical inadequacies manifested a certain degree of expressive capacity for a way of living which itself displayed parallel inadequacies when compared with the old-world pattern it was attempting to emulate.

20. Specialists into the South

Charles Bridges: act. 1735–1740
Jeremiah Theüs: 1719–1774

Through the half-century of colonial culmination a small group of plantation families in Virginia came closest to matching the life and culture of courtly circles in England. The Virginians who participated in this emulation were few in relation to the total population, and the whole group was small enough to share in the cultural luster of a few remarkable individuals among them. The reason stands clear in the direct tobacco trade and the access to England it permitted. Moreover, the isolation of the plantations resulted in the use of resident tutors for education; and the inadequacies of this system almost necessitated an English finish to the education of at least the sons. Occasional advertisements in the *Virginia Gazette* between 1736 and 1775 hint at sentimental episodes such as could flutter briefly into life at some masked balls. More than one friend of Evelyn Byrd, among the women as well as the men, could have written the memorial acrostic upon her name published on December 9th, 1737. Her father kept his diaries in a species of secret writing, and found that a means of being frank with himself beyond the habit of diarists; once he read *The Beggar's Opera* aloud to a lady friend—could that have been in preparation for the Williamsburg performance of it conducted by the junior Peter Pelham? And as for music, it is recorded by a northern youth engaged as tutor that Robert Carter the Third, at Nomini Hall, having "a nice well judging Ear," owned a half-dozen different instruments and played them all;

. . . His main Studies are *Law & Music,* the latter of which seems to be his darling Amusement— It seems to nourish, as well as entertain his mind! . . .

He captivated his hearer by using the harmonica for an air called "Water parted from the sea."

It was no coincidence that such a sparkling group of colonials should be visually recorded by Charles Bridges, a craftsman in possession of the most courtly formula among all the painters who visited the South. It probably was the result of his having known some of the colonials in England; and the Virginian of most service to him seems to have been the influential Colonel Byrd

14. MANN PAGE THE SECOND (?)   *by* (?) CHARLES BRIDGES
Courtesy of The College of William and Mary in Virginia.

just mentioned. That colonel wrote a letter to his fellow colonel, Alexander Spotswood, at his plantation on the Rapidan:

The person who has the honour to wait upon you with this letter is a man of Good Family, but either by the frowns of Fortune or his own mismanagement, is obliged to seek his Bread a little of the latest in a strange land. His name is Bridges and his Profession Painting, and if you have any employment for him in that way he will be proud of obeying your command.

He has drawn my children and several others in this neighbourhood, and tho' he has not the Master Hand of a Lilly or a Kneller, yet had he lived so long ago as when places were given to the most deserving, he might have pretended to be Sergeant Painter of Virginia. . . .

The meaning of that peculiar phrase "a little of the latest" is that Bridges was already about eighty when that letter was written; and aside from the specific mention of his "Good Family," if his painting permits any sound inference as to his person (a thing that is sometimes possible), he was a welcome adornment to Virginian dinners. He was probably as much to the manner born as they were to their manors.

He, like all other pre-Revolutionary visiting painters, used a formula; and his formula is so close to that of Kneller that he may himself well have been a product of the latter's portrait manufactory. The learner in that studio acquired a knowledge which was from the first more specialized in kind than that of the guild: of colors and canvases, of set poses and fashionable costumes, how to make complete copies and how to bring portraits far enough along to receive the master's finishing touches. This training did not, any more than that of the artisan, confer any power of vision on those who did not possess it; that is indeed beyond the scope of any method of training to do—then or now or ever. For the routine student, the acquisition of the specialized craft of portraiture remained a routine matter; and when such a workman got out on his own, he was content to supply a standardized article for a socially classified market.

So it was with Bridges—at least after he reached Virginia. The canvases are well filled with all the lively details of rococo stateliness; in the costumes, which are as prominent as the faces, the folds of stiff materials are large and shallow; though they do not always satisfactorily follow the form beneath, they rise and fall, approach and recede, with considerable animation. Hands, that sure test of competence, are not noticeably individualized; but they are modeled with firmness. The color has variety from canvas to canvas, and real unity upon each one taken alone. In the matter of personality, the formula is more evident in the women than in the men. Typical are the *Maria Taylor Byrd* [Metropolitan Museum, New York] and the *Mann Page the Second* [plate 14]. The ladies' features are unnaturally similar, especially in the areas of nose and brow, and each head is tilted on the same neck and shoulders; only in the well rendered eyes is there some slight variation of individuality. But to his men Bridges gave greater substance of physical structure and mental difference; apparently he could relish their forcefulness as well as their clothes, and felt no obligation to flatter them.

Bridges' work in Virginia was not confined to portraiture. In the order book of Caroline County for October, 1740, there is a notation of sixteen hundred pounds of tobacco to be sold for money "to pay Charles Bridges for drawing the King's Arms for use of the County Court." This omnipresent colonial necessity for even the specialists to turn a hand to every kind of painting is even more strikingly recorded in the case of Jeremiah Theüs, for forty years resident in Charleston. His announcement in the *South Carolina Gazette* for August 30th, 1740, is about as comprehensive as any elsewhere:

. . . all gentlemen and Ladies may have their pictures drawn, likewise Landscapes of all sizes, Crests and Coats of Arms for Coaches and Chaises. Likewise for the convenience of those who live in the country he is willing to wait on them at their respective plantations.

In 1744 he advertised an evening school in drawing. Apparently it was entirely from such professional activities that Theüs amassed the "handsome fortune" that he left; so he probably painted even more pictures than are now attributed to him. But by no means all of these attributions are justified, and some of the justified ones have been seriously marred by ill judged nineteenth-century "restoration."

Theüs shared fully in the taste of his time and the intention of his fellow professionals in the matter of fashionableness; but his general technical skill and his portrait formula both fell short of the opulence of Bridges. The training that can be inferred from the Charleston portraits seems clearly French in source, but those portraits also seem to retain a certain prim rusticity which has frequently appeared in the painting of Switzerland, where Theüs was born. Probably this failure to acquire a full metropolitan fluency before leaving the continent is the main cause of what has been well called the "pouter-pigeon pose" such as can be seen in the *Elizabeth Rothmaler* [1757: plate 15]. He usually avoided any difficulty with hands by slipping them into waistcoats or cutting them off completely with the feigned ovals of his canvases.

However, such limitations are not completely negative in their significance, for even they play a part in the frequent attractiveness of individual examples. Some of these from the seventeen-fifties have their pigment sensitively laid on, with some loveliness in delicate shadows on flesh and white materials. The result is generally rather hard, what with the rigid solidity of the figures and the

15. ELIZABETH ROTHMALER *by* JEREMIAH THEÜS
Courtesy of Brooklyn Museum.

high-lighted brilliance of the accessories. All this was deprecated by Dunlap, who relied upon the miniaturist Charles Fraser for his verdict; they censured Theüs because ". . . he had not the art to give grace and picturesque effect . . ." But the grace and picturesqueness of Dunlap's time were too often gracility and saccharinity; and now it seems a more than modest merit in Theüs that "His pictures were as stiff and formal as the originals . . ."

21. The spread of foreign fashion

Joseph Blackburn: act. 1752–1763
John Wollaston: act. 1749–1767
Cosmo John Alexander: 1724–1773

Two more British painters who came to the colonies near the middle of the
eighteenth century achieved each a considerable amount of work: Blackburn
in a few towns of New England and Wollaston in a leisurely expedition from
New York to Charleston. Neither, apparently, played any important part in the
development of portraiture in Great Britain; so that, despite their not becoming
American residents after the manner of Theüs and Pelham, their positions in
the general history of painting are determined by what they accomplished here.
They also, like the elder Hesselius and the elder Smibert, contributed to the development of American painting by discernibly affecting certain native-born
craftsmen.

Joseph Blackburn practised with somewhat inhibited skill a rococo habit of
design which was a novelty in New England at the time. The glossy hardness
of his pigment is mitigated by a daintiness in drawing; yet this very trait, pleasing enough on occasion, makes even his largest figures appear smaller than life.
His further shortcomings as a designer are clearly revealed in the two group
portraits now known. In these he had opportunities for full rococo pattern to fit
the picture shape, but to it his organizing power was not equal. In *The Winslow
Family* [1755: plate 16] the figures are awkwardly aligned in one plane across
the canvas; the verticals are so stiffly repetitive that they interfere with his
sprightly treatment of costume. For all that they are within one frame, the
figures remain virtually separated in arrangement as well as separated emotionally
by self-conscious posing. The single verticals of other portraits, though monotonously placed, do not overpower the gay artificiality of broken curves fluttering
off into mid-air.

This predominant artificiality was recognized at the time, as shown by a delightful letter which reads in part:

Dear Chaney:
 . . . Have you set for your Pickture. is the mouth placed in proper order. do your
eyes roll about.
 Tel Mr blackburn that Mifs Lucy is in love with his Picktures wonders what

16. THE WINSLOW FAMILY *by* JOSEPH BLACKBURN *Courtesy of Museum of Fine Arts, Boston.*

buſineſs he has to make such extreme fine lace and Satten beſides taking so exact a likeneſs. . . . from Yours and Your Lady's

Afft Friend
Mary Ruſsell

The redeeming mischievousness of Miss Mary's remarks about mouth and eyes contrasts with Miss Lucy's adoration of the fashionable splendor conferred by the painter on the ladies generally. This instance of admitted pleasure, and the survival of almost a hundred portraits from the years of Blackburn's activity, afford evidence of how far society in New England had come toward worldliness and fashion.

The technical means by which Blackburn succeeded add up to a strongly marked and strongly limited formula. That is only to say that the formula was less a record of living people and actual appearances than a mold of fashion into which the patrons were glad to be fitted. The ladies whom he depicted probably did not possess the profusion of too similar jewelry he puts on them; they would not, without coaching, have imprisoned themselves in the few poses of his repertory. More importantly, they could not have presented to him the repetitious "furniture faces" which he built up with invisible brush strokes into hard contours. In the countenances of Blackburn's men there is a little variety, especially when, past their youth, they are seated with letters in hand or books at elbow; even then, however, a preoccupation with keeping their legs in place makes them oblivious of these accessories. Men on their feet stand or gesture with the dancing-master triviality which is the painter's own transmogrification of them.

But irrespective of what they actually were, enough members of New England society wanted to look like that for Blackburn to experience a prosperity here which he probably could not have had at home. The arching skirts and billowing trimmings below the ladies' faces are stiff with their own soft-tin substance. Dresses, laces, pearls, elegantly varied hands and insipid faces are all enameled into glossiness and relieved against perfunctory backdrops; and this uniform emphasis on foreground textures results in a truly monotonous restlessness. From the golden regalness of Rubens and the silvery splendor of Van Dyck, portraiture has here dwindled into a minuscule courtliness.

A more expansive but coarser formula of elegance brought a parallel popularity at the same time to John Wollaston, who is often identified as the Younger because his father in England also painted. It is not certain if Charles Willson Peale was referring to the father when he wrote that the son ". . . had some instruction from a noted drapery painter in London . . ."; but that is a prosaically accurate summation of a mediocre painter. Peale's implied ranking came with the second thoughts of a later generation; the first thoughts of those who saw Wollaston pass were romantically different. Francis Hopkinson's panegyric is worth quoting for the way in which the artificiality of the verses matches that of the pictures.

> To you fam'd *Wollaston!* these strains belong,
> And be your praise the subject of my song:
> When your soft pencil bids the canvas shine
> With mimic life, with elegance divine,
> Th' enraptured muse, fond to partake thy fire,
> With equal sweetness strives to sweep the lyre;
> With equal justice fain would paint your praise,
> And by your name immortalize her lays.
>   Ofttimes with wonder and delight I stand,
> To view th' amazing conduct of your hand,
> At first unlabour'd sketches lightly trace
> The glim'ring outlines of a human face;
> Then by degrees the liquid life o'erflows
> Each rising feature—the rich canvas glows
> With heightened charms—the forehead rises fair;
> The glossy ringlets twine the nut-brown hair;
> The sparkling eyes give meaning to the whole,
> And seem to speak the dictates of a soul.
> The lucid lips in rosy sweetness drest,
> The well-turn'd neck and the luxuriant breast,
> The silk that richly flows with graceful air—
> All tell the hand of *Wollaston* was there.

These rhymes unwind from out the same verse-machinery as those to Smibert already quoted, and both pieces of versification may be accused of the typically colonial exaggeration which somewhat desperately craves to become fashionably cultured. Colonials are always too credulous of what they see and sing—but then it is always wonderful to see something that seems good enough to sing about.

Wollaston's progress can be traced from New York to Charleston in a few records but for the most part in the increasingly mannerized canvases with which he flatters or slanders, depending on the point of view, the mercantile and planter societies along the way. Until he was identified by name he was frequently called "the almond-eyed artist": a phrase which twistedly applied to him what he imposed on his sitters. Hardly less noticeable was the sharp slant of the features down to a central perpendicular line—a trick which makes New Yorkers and Philadelphians and Virginians impossibly akin, though there was plenty of intermarrying on the top economic level. By the time Wollaston reached Virginia he seemed to be having almost conscious fun with his sitters' fingers by making them bonelessly elegant. In and near New York he made his subjects puttily ponderous, but from Philadelphia on he puffed out the older ones with fat

17. THE CHILDREN OF WARNER LEWIS   *by* JOHN WOLLASTON
Courtesy of The College of William and Mary in Virginia.

to where they appeared uncomfortable not merely in their clothes but in their skins. And all along the way his silks and satins shone with the smug obstreperousness beloved by the newly rich. A more ingratiating aspect of his formula was developed in a few portraits of children, such as *The Children of Warner Lewis* [c. 1756: plate 17]; to such examples may be applied with no ambiguity Robert Sully's verdict of "a very pretty taste."

The earlier work seems better so far as likeness goes, but with Wollaston at any time that probably never went very far. If likeness be disregarded, as apparently the sitters themselves were willing for it to be, the later work is better in fluency and mannerism. Along with a more pronounced reliance on formula there came an easier manipulation of pigment and a more frequent effort to achieve elaborate design. It was as if recipes for faces and hands freed him from the annoyance of studying any sitter's personality and left him able to indulge a more elaborate elegance and a slightly greater variety of color in the clothes. As the portraitist weakened the painter became gayer. His London background naturally helped him to put all this across; and if some of his sitters may have felt that he was distorting their countenances inhumanly, they may also have had a compensatory sense of emulating the world of fashion across the ocean.

Another traceable influence was by Cosmo John Alexander, a Scotsman who affected American painting, though only slightly, through his association with Gilbert Stuart. Alexander's activity in the colonies lasted only about six years, and may not have been continuous; that was hardly enough to make him a formative part of American painting as a whole. Only the fact that he accepted Stuart as a pupil, even taking the boy home to Edinburgh in 1772, enabled him to exert any influence at all. His large portrait of *Alexander Grant* [1770: Stonington Historical Society, Stonington, Conn.] glitters with intended fashionableness; its square-built countenance and hard outlines were fully taken over by fifteen-year-old Stuart; but that mannerism was left behind as soon as Stuart secured better instruction.

22. A native-born talent

Robert Feke: ?1705–?1750

When it came the turn of the native-born to take over portraiture, they were necessarily aware, in varying degrees, both of the fashionable formulas brought in by the foreign-born and of the colonial patrons' liking for such flattery. It was only natural that the native-born should admire the formulas and seek to master them for the satisfaction of the same audience. Yet they were more importantly to strike the note of nativism in one of two ways and sometimes in both together: negatively, in technical awkwardness, and positively, in some personal inventiveness. Both ways at once were emphatically manifested in Robert Feke.

For him there was no public panegyric like that addressed to Smibert or Wollaston, not even an obituary like that of Emmons; but one observant traveler privately set down a brief description of him. Doctor Alexander Hamilton, in his remarkable diary of a tour through the colonies north from his home in Annapolis, wrote that his Newport friend, Doctor Moffatt, on July 16th, 1744,

. . . led me a course through the town . . . [and] . . . carried me to one Feake, a painter, the most extraordinary genius ever I knew, for he does pictures tolerably well by the force of genius, having never had any teaching. . . . This man had exactly the phiz of a painter, having a long pale face, sharp nose, large eyes,—with which he looked upon you steadfastly,—and long curled black hair, a delicate white hand, and long fingers.

It was fortunate that Feke so strikingly embodied what seems to be something like a preconception in Hamilton, since it resulted in so vivid an equivalent in words to both of Feke's self-portraits; but a wider experience might have kept Hamilton from even faintly implying that every painter should look like his idea of one. Feke's own "delicate white hand" is visible only in the later self-portrait, and it was painted in long after his death; but he gave that sort of hand so uniformly to his sitters that it became a gratuitous monotony of anatomy. Nor is it likely that all of his sitters had eyes which so uniformly repeated his own. Those delicately done cheeks and eye-sockets, those carefully drawn mouths with full lips, that angle of placing the head and figure—all combine with hands and eyes into a general mannerism which is kept interesting today more by its use of pigment than by its interpretation of people.

In estimating Feke's technique, it seems significant that the idea of self-teaching should again appear only four years after the death of Emmons. Any would-be artist struggling against difficulties is naturally more conscious of the intensity of his own efforts than he is of what other men or other men's works are teaching him. The point he is likely to overlook is that, however much he may feel himself to be groping his way on his own, he is actually receiving guidance. As Renoir was to say a century later, nature does not make the painter, but pictures. The visible forms and colors of the world may make a youth want to paint them, but at the outset of his efforts painting is learned only from paintings and by painting. To be sure, what the beginner learns from pictures (or from teachers) he applies to nature in his subsequent study of it; and if he has sufficient personal sensitiveness, that study will play its part in his developing personal vision and an appropriate style. But for several thousand years now the start of every painter who has done anything worth looking at twice has been the work and teaching of his predecessors.

Therefore the meaning of these recurrent American claims to being self-made painters is simply that those making them did not participate in any formal and prolonged teacher-pupil relationship. Sometimes it may mean, even more narrowly, that there was no legal apprenticeship. Either way, the broad claim relies for its validity upon a perhaps undue degree of literalism. Practically every native-born workman had chances, however sporadic, to watch some older man at work and therewith to receive words of counsel, however casual. They copied other pictures and imported prints; and at least the later ones consulted books from England. Of course, this is professionally inadequate in proportion as it is unsatisfactory to the student himself; but it is a process of learning, and of learning from others. Another thing which enables American painters to put the emphasis where they did is the probability that not one among them ever fully realized that, even in the formal training they missed, it is always necessary for the pupil to transcend or depart from his teacher through his own capacity for pictorial experience.

The precise occasions when Feke was able to see pictures and meet painters are at present largely conjectural; but almost everything about him is conjectural except the succession of dated portraits. There are enough of them to content the historian of painting, who is not the same as the biographer of a painter and who accordingly feels no obligation to choose between conflicting suppositions exclusively biographical in nature. Moreover, the known times and places of Feke's portraits make almost inevitable some personal contact with Gustavus Hesselius and John Smibert. Feke's early treatment of arms and the angle at which he sets the heads are possibly from the Swedish painter; his fondness for exploring textures and his use of loaded whites are perhaps from the Scotsman. In the opinion of some, his later work requires the intervention of a European stay; it might have occurred, but always his own kind of visual sensitiveness has to be kept in mind: which makes it possible to contend that he could do what he did with only what he could learn here.

For that sensitiveness gave him a responsiveness to pigment, an awareness of its sensuous appeal, and a consciousness of its coloristic possibilities which were extraordinary at that time. Only a little less striking, in relation to contemporaneous work, was Feke's way of emphasizing form. Often anatomically incorrect, it was present from the first and toward the end even assertive. Though Feke made mistakes in the unseen structure of the human body, he was never vague about what he could see. Each person, man or woman, is uncomfortably inflexible; but that seems also to have an essential share in the general impression of latent energy. Substantiality of form, however, is with Feke distinctly subordinate to the visual sensuousness of beautifully colored textures; occasionally an embroidered coat or a brocaded skirt is keyed so high that it may seem to protrude from the bordering frame. This then unprecedented splendor of translating the visible into paint was not enough to make Feke great, but it pulled him through to distinction.

Both the modeling and the colorism were important contributions to the general resources of painting at that time. The taste of the time channeled his painting into portraiture; and though Feke's delight in pigment is necessary to beautiful painting, it is of no help for probing personalities. The absence of variety in this fundamental of portraiture denies the interpretation of individual or class pride to these repetitive substitutes for people; the explanation is more likely the simpler one that Feke himself never wearied of his new-found ability to model soberly rich or dramatically gleaming textures over figures which, though they lack naturalistic articulation, yet present to the eye a substantiality without precedent in colonial painting.

But at the end of his career he achieved, in the *General Samuel Waldo* [plate 18], a picture, if not a portrait, of splendor in its iridescent color. It alone might tempt that speculation over a might-have-been which the historian avoids from the low motive of caution which is usually elevated into an admirable conscientiousness. The remarkable landscape behind General Waldo would alone almost justify an oversubtilization of the verdict just pronounced: even if Feke's work is not intrinsically great, Feke himself had greatness in him.

18. GENERAL SAMUEL WALDO *by* ROBERT FEKE
Courtesy of Bowdoin College Museum of Fine Arts.

23. More native-born

BOSTON

Joseph Badger: 1708–1765
Thomas Johnston: 1708–1767
John Greenwood: 1727–1792
Nathaniel Smibert: 1734–1756

PHILADELPHIA

James Claypoole: 1720–c. 1796
John Meng: 1734–1754
John Hesselius: 1728–1778

Following Emmons and Feke there came a fair-sized group of more native-born who went far toward taking over the business of portraiture: an effort which has a collective historical importance even though the careers of several among them were cut short. John Greenwood left the country at twenty-five, never to return. Nathaniel, John Smibert's son, and John Meng died young. James Claypoole seems to have given most of his energies to business and office-holding; possibly, also, the major part of his painting was utilitarian and therefore went the way of all job-work. But Joseph Badger in Boston and Gustavus Hesselius' son John, ranging from Philadelphia to Virginia, were active through relatively long periods of time and left behind them large groups of portraits.

Joseph Badger started as a house painter and glazier; he ventured into portraiture about five years before the failure of the elder Smibert's eyesight. It is reasonable to infer that the latter circumstance had something to do with the increasing prominence of the people who submitted themselves to Badger's coarse manner of painting. With continued practice he did improve through the seventy-five or more works now identified as his, but he never displayed either Smibert's fluent brushwork or Feke's startling purity of color. It might be contended that those very qualities in the better painters' works conferred a degree of grace, if not of glamor, upon a society more appropriately recorded in the laborious awkwardness of the artisan; but this, of course, is among the intangibles of interpretation about which differences of opinion may be permanent.

At any rate, though Badger's sitters look important enough as people, they seem to have assumed significance for the occasion. They seem insufficiently accustomed to worldly importance, including its consequence of portraiture; they do not take it for granted in the way that Copley's sitters began to do just when Badger's life was closing. With Badger there is no definite information about any formal teaching, but there are many indications of learning by means of prints and other men's paintings. He used standard studio practice in pose and placing, though he rarely gave his subjects sufficient head-room on their canvases. From his source material he copied a water view or a clump of trees in brushwork which confesses this secondary derivation; probably from the objects themselves he attempted a high-backed chair or a table with inkpot and book. These details remained disparate, not fused into a coherent concept of the picture-space. Even the colors remained atmospherically unrelated, their erratic intensities still further confusing the logic of recession from the eye. This is why a black-and-white reproduction sometimes rouses expectations which are disappointed by a sight of the original.

These faults described in general terms are specific enough in two of Badger's most ambitious efforts: the *Cornelius Waldo* [1750: plate 19] and the *Captain John Larrabee* of about ten years later [Worcester Art Museum]. The absence of accessories in the *Mrs. John Edwards* [Museum of Fine Arts, Boston], midway between these two in time, both accentuates and refines her austerity. If Badger himself ever keenly experienced the conscious pleasure in handling paint which is written so plainly across the work of Feke, he came nearest to making it visible in a few full-lengths of children. Little *Jeremiah Belknap* [c. 1758: Cleveland Museum of Art] is an uncomfortably miniature adult, but younger *James Badger* [1760: Metropolitan Museum, New York] has the face of a real child above his doll-like figure and harshly modeled costume. Yet old or young, male or female, the bodies of Badger's subjects are poorly articulated; and their uniformly dome-crowned features are pastily and puttily grayed by his dullish color.

John Greenwood left this country in 1752 before he had developed a steadiness of manner in portraiture. In his fifteenth and sixteenth years he was apprentice to Thomas Johnston, who not only painted some portraits but also japanned furniture and built organs, executed and published engravings, and apparently portioned out his various skills among some of his eleven children for continuation. One engraving made and published by Johnston was from a lost drawing by Greenwood of *Yale College* [1749]; and Greenwood himself, during his brief time with Johnston, engraved two bookplates and painted some funeral decorations. Five years later, however, Greenwood made a mezzotint reproduction of a painting by himself. He was painting portraits in his sixteenth year, which would be while he was still with Johnston or immediately thereafter; but the approximately two dozen examples now assigned to his American years show marked variations of manner which indicate either some other teacher besides Johnston or self-teaching by lurches from one influence to another. Some of his later inconsistencies seem at times to contradict the general improvement of a decade. Yet even the inconsistencies testify to an alert and active mind, so that his leaving may be counted as a more than quantitative loss to colonial painting in general.

19. CORNELIUS WALDO *by* JOSEPH BADGER
Courtesy of Worcester Art Museum.

Greenwood seems to have had from the first some skill in placing the figure; the general gains he makes over his beginnings are in the elimination of heavy shadows, increased fluency in values and textures, better expression in the at times laboriously rendered eyes. But to the end the faces may show bad proportions and the figures without exception remain inflexible. The *Greenwood-Lee Family* [c. 1747: privately owned] was, for one of his limited experience, a recklessly ambitious undertaking which came surprisingly near to success. He was acquainted with the group paintings by Feke and Smibert, but all he owes to them is some interest in texture and a habit of monotonous construction in head and features; even in these respects he is so far behind them that he doesn't owe them much. Yet he remarkably differs from them in the character of his design as a whole—so much so that derivation from a print may be inferred; but wherever he got it, his arrangement of sleeves and hands, of ruffles and necks keeps the eye swinging around and about until weariness sets in because there is nowhere any point of rest, psychological or visual. In the seemingly later *Mrs. Nathaniel Cunningham* [privately owned] he built up the exaggeratedly spreading dress-mass by broadly diagrammatic lines which give a highly inaccurate account of the sitter's proportions; and the impression here of careless fluency and robust awkwardness in combination may stand for Greenwood's work as a whole.

Upon leaving Massachusetts Greenwood made a stay of six years in Surinam, where he is said to have painted an anecdotal picture which will be mentioned later. His subsequent activities in Holland and London have nothing to do with painting in America; unlike West and Copley, neither his work nor his personality was projected back upon the American scene. Yet before leaving Boston he had briefly but strongly influenced young Copley and in 1770 he wrote Copley from London to commission a portrait of the re-married Mrs. Greenwood, his mother. Five years later, after some fresh personal contact between the two painters in London, Copley wrote Greenwood from Rome a letter containing a profoundly revelatory autobiographical remark.

Smibert's painting son Nathaniel, being recurrently ill with tuberculosis, could not complete a large body of work. The best among the portraits now known, that of *Ezra Stiles* [Yale University Art Gallery], shows a weakly drawn hand, fair textures, and some perception of character as it is concentrated in the eyes. Dark eyeballs with dotted high lights and pronounced lines along the lids produce a mild intensity which is re-enforced by a rather arbitrary shadow down one side of the face but is weakened by an inadequately modeled mouth. All that the portrait indicates is the possibility of its painter becoming a straightforward recorder of the less spectacular aspects of colonial society in New England.

It is therefore fitting that the two obituaries should give little attention to his painting activities; it is also significant that one of them uses the word "business" to describe the father's activities, to which the son succeeded. The notice then proceeds with fifty lush lines of praise for his lovableness and goodness and religiousness. The other notice follows the same pattern, and part of it reads as follows:

. . . He was a young Gentleman possessed of all those amiable Qualifications that endear or sweeten Life: From his Cradle, he wore the Marks of unaffected Virtue and Goodness; and thro' the whole Course of his Life, exhibited the most unexceptionable Pattern of filial Piety: . . . his Manners were Soft and engaging; his Friendship sincere; his affections Kind; and his Conversation lovely: . . . Happy they that have called him Son! Happy the Youth that shall copy his Example!

This anticipated by a century a tone of writing and an attitude toward life associated with Victorianism in culture; every quality here praised fits into a pattern of behavior most profitable to a static society, and the marked emphasis upon dutifulness only illustrates what happens when the elders have the writing of obituary tributes.

In Philadelphia, which was perhaps the neatest among colonial cities and was surrounded by "villas, gardens and luxuriant orchards," several wealthy gentlemen were forming collections of pictures attributed to European painters so important that in 1771 Copley made an excursion from New York in order to see them. Yet the earliest native painters there were finding their own unplentiful commissions confined to portraits and signs. James Claypoole practised "all the different branches of the painting business," but he is among the small crowd of colonial painters who are still without authenticated works to give them a degree of stylistic being. A few examples by the short-lived John Meng show him to have been a very assimilative student of Gustavus Hesselius; he combined in his person the misfortunes of parental opposition to a painting career and of early death from yellow fever.

No completer contrast to Meng could be found than his fellow Philadelphian John Hesselius. The latter's painter-father must have begun teaching him early; the mixed manners of certain large-scale portraits in Virginia suggest that the son began working on the same picture with his father before he was competent to do so; but a portraitist traveling from plantation to plantation would naturally enough adopt this means of shortening his absence from home and at the same time bringing his son and intended successor into favorable notice. A few examples by the son alone, executed through the early seventeen-fifties, display an assimilation of the father's habit of portraiture; the youthful workman's disjointedness in figure construction becomes less noticeable, though hands still are not properly articulated with arms, and his render-

20. CHARLES CALVERT   *by* JOHN HESSELIUS
Courtesy of Baltimore Museum of Art.

ing of shadows becomes both softer and more varied. However, within three years following the father's death the son had abandoned that sober manner to take over the showy manner of Wollaston. In view of the youthful Benjamin West's parallel attempt and of Hopkinson's extravagant praise for Wollaston, the younger Hesselius' technical shift may have been a response to the pressure of fashionable taste: a taste which he himself shared to the full.

Justification for the latter inference lies in the consistency with which he adhered to this mannerism for the rest of his painting career. John Hesselius maintained, with little modification, the Wollastonian concept of the canvas as a whole; yet within that marked limitation his form gained in solidity and his backgrounds in definiteness, his contours increased in variety and acquired greater delicacy of recession into shadow. To the end he retained the Wollastonian habits of arranging features in diagonals, of slanting the heads sharply back from the chins, and of harmonizing his sometimes high-keyed color areas with pervasive browns. All these characteristics can be seen at their best in the now well known rococo elaborations of the *Charles Calvert* [1761: plate 20]. The *Mrs. Richard Galloway, Jr.* [1764: Metropolitan Museum, New York], which was long mistakenly attributed to the father, almost but not quite escapes from Wollaston's influence; even though it falls short of the personal accent of Feke, and much more of Copley's mastery, the picture achieves substance of both physical and mental being and extracts a coloristic resonance from a relatively simple chord of browns and whites.

Claypoole, as already pointed out, remains in that form of near anonymity which consists of being a name with some biographical facts attached, but with no known paintings to give him artistic existence. The younger Smibert and Meng left too few examples to tell anything significant about their minds. Greenwood's erratic energy might well have taken him on into an importantly personal accomplishment in painting had he remained in this country where he would have had little or no outlet for that miscellany of business activities which in London kept down the quantity of his production. As for Badger and the younger Hesselius, their work makes it clear that in the forefront of their conscious minds was a desire to make their sitters pose with elegance and shine with fashion; their failure to succeed came from the lesser intensity of their own minds. Neither one showed Copley's capacity for a personal exploration of certain aspects of nature; neither one showed even Feke's capacity for making paint itself into an adventurous discovery. For the very reason that both were without the inner pressure to transcend the formula of fashion, both failed to master fully the formula itself.

24. A native-born genius

John Singleton Copley: 1738–1815 (work to 1774)
Henry Pelham: 1749–1806

Where Feke had manifested a painting talent, Copley displayed an artistic genius: the only native-born of the colonial period who did. It was the insistent taste of his American patrons which channeled his genius so narrowly into portraiture, as it had already channeled the talent of Feke; and where Feke had shown himself to be less than a portraitist in his preoccupation with texture and color, Copley showed himself to be much more than a portraitist in both technical development and greatness of mind.

With Copley there was a notable recurrence of the claim of self-teaching which had such long-continued psychological and cultural importance in the history of painting here. With Copley it resulted in a controversy sharp and intensive enough to affect historians and biographers through three generations. Copley's work can now be seen clear of all that; but the idea itself, as it recurred in his case, may receive glancing illumination from another idea which was then current as advice by Poor Richard. Like many other sayings thus circulated by Franklin, this was just a re-minting of something much older: "Learn of the skilful; he that teaches himself hath a fool for a master." As practical counsel, it was well suited to a country where artisans and their products were fundamentally important for civilization, for anyone best learns a craft from another's instruction; but so far as concerned the artistry to which Copley from the first aspired, it was wide of the mark.

In painting, Poor Richard's common sense is valid only for the permanent pupil. Where the painter reaches the point of transforming his craft into artistry, self-teaching becomes his only way of working. Even the arch-academician, Sir Joshua Reynolds himself, was soon to say: ". . . Few have been taught to any purpose who have not been their own teachers. . . ." Although it was unfortunate that Copley found no better men to learn from than those who worked in Boston, he would have had to go beyond his teachers in any place or time in order to achieve individual expressiveness.

One significant thing about Copley's student period was its brevity—only about five years; the frequent instances in later years of his taking backgrounds or costumes from prints somewhat impaired but did not prevent the originality of his personal development. Another significant thing about the preparatory years was the variety of the sources he drew upon. Since he used several kinds of prints from the beginning, it would be easy to assume that they were the major source for everything because prints were then the handiest form of picture and the universal study material for painters; but Copley also certainly had access to the original paintings and the copies brought here by Smibert. From one or another of such sources he got his ideas for drawings of battle scenes, paintings of mythological subjects, landscapes for portrait backgrounds, and the derivative anatomical drawings which had to suffice him in the absence of an art school with a life class. The earliest oil portraits and a single mezzotint engraving show further that he was conscientiously emulating various technical details in the work of Pelham and Smibert, Feke and Badger and Greenwood, and—most influential of all as well as last in time—Blackburn. Tracing these evidences in specific pictures would assume considerable importance in any full-scale separate treatment of Copley; in the biographically telescoped manner necessitated by a general history they need be mentioned only to point up the fact that his heights of achievement rise with historic and stylistic naturalness from the foothills of his predecessors and contemporaries.

For an estimate of Copley's skill in depicting people, later times of course cannot have recourse to one test on which some of his own patrons strongly relied: face-to-face comparison between the image and the person. Copley in private letters named that as a fault in them, but not so much for their applying it as for their applying that only. He strove for likeness as earnestly as they desired it; he also achieved much more which they did not have the wit to perceive, and their failure gave him the feeling of being artistically stranded in the shallows of their incomprehension. It was part of his bad luck, at which he complained freely and sometimes strongly. However, it was also part of his good luck, which he seems never to have recognized. For the very literalism of his patrons' idea of likeness enabled him to record many faces among them with an exceptional degree of objective accuracy. Yet his uncompromising faithfulness in that respect was frequently surrounded with the elaborate make-believe of setting which Copley and his patrons together thought was necessary to the stateliness of colonials emulating homeland fashions.

Copley's first major success with rendering character in a face came with the portrait of an old lady. The basis for it is to be found in a human situation of frequent occurrence; the elder proves to be intelligent enough to perceive the younger as a person capable of intelligence. In this way forceful old ladies are frequently able to put boyish beginners in life at ease in their company. It seems to have happened to Copley when he was about twenty; the lady, *Mrs.*

Michael Gill [c. 1759: privately owned in England], who was four times his age, did not so much sit self-consciously for a portrait as watch with shrewd kindliness the behavior of a young man who forgot himself in what he was doing. The network of minute wrinkles across the still plump face, the attentive sidewise inclination of the head, the steady gaze, the easy stillness of the body—all these registered not only the character of the old lady but also the concentration and laboriousness of an artist who was already capable of fathoming the psychological inwardness of external signs. Four years later Copley was at ease in technique and human approach together; he recorded sixty-four-year-old *Mrs. Nathaniel Appleton* [1763: Harvard University] with even more substantiality precisely because he had in the interval taught himself a lighter touch and a more fluid handling for attaining the same precision.

Although partial successes had occurred earlier with men of several ages, a man equal to Mrs. Gill came a little later. *Epes Sargent* [c. 1760: privately owned] is monumental in mind and body and pose all three; with him Copley commenced a series of two dozen male portraits in half as many years which, standing out among more than a hundred others by him, deserve to be called magisterial in their authority. Even more impressive than Epes Sargent is *Jacob Fowle* [c. 1763: plate 21], which has the same technical ease noted in the portrait of Mrs. Appleton; and these two men by Copley, if placed beside two by Thomas Smith three-quarters of a century earlier, would vivify the New Englanders' change to worldliness without loss of forcefulness and with considerable gain in mellowness from material well-being.

From 1763, indeed, Copley seems on occasions to have been equal to anything in the perception and recording of character in either men or women of all degrees of maturity, and even in one boy of fifteen. In the finest works of his American period Copley was intent upon delineating a solidly constructed figure in space, but he achieved a more massive triumph in the uniqueness of the person inhabiting the figure. It was this which caused John Adams in 1817 to write about Copley's portraits in general that ". . . you can scarcely help discoursing with them, asking questions and receiving answers." Adams used words such as less sophisticated people might have used about wax-work figures, but in a time inadequately equipped with a vocabulary of criticism and appreciation those words were a natural way of responding to Copley's profound power of characterization. The individualities of his sitters are so convincing on canvas that it is easy to credit them as existing in life, but it is possible to claim that Copley unconsciously gave them a more intense existence in their portraits; for the strength of his mind can be established independently of his subjects by examining the whole body of his American work in two further aspects.

21. JACOB FOWLE *by* JOHN SINGLETON COPLEY
Courtesy of Corcoran Gallery of Art, Washington, D.C.

The first of these consists of the extraordinary thoroughness, in relation to his colonially limited opportunities, with which he acquired every painting medium he could use in the Boston portrait market. In his stepfather's craft of mezzotint he issued only one known plate, the *William Welsteed* of 1753; and in the light of his rapidly developing interest in color, it may be conjectured that the limited black-and-white of print-making had most to do with his abandonment of it. Within the five years of his preparatory period he achieved full control of the oil medium, as documented by dated works; a now unlocated miniature of 1753 might show a parallel in this medium also, for the technical quality of the first known example, the *Deborah Scollay* [c. 1762: Worcester Art Museum], certifies earlier work of considerable skill.

A pastel of 1758 likewise indicates earlier practice of this medium, and several more between it and 1763 show him continuing to gain; but he was not content with what he could do, and late in 1762 he drafted a letter to the famous Swiss pastelist, Liotard, asking for the best crayons and instructions for using them. Whether Liotard ever replied remains of no consequence; Copley's manner in pastel was clearly defined before he wrote his letter and his subsequent pastel work manifests only its logical stylistic consequences. The pastels are not uniformly successful, but the best of them display striking brilliance and vivacity of color; and practically all of them are marked by an overly emphatic handling which is perhaps traceable to his positive handling of oil. A provincial mind will sometimes push things a little too far from a fear of being insufficiently clear; though sophistication is no cure for provincialism, and is often a very poor substitute, one virtue in sophistication can be tact—in handling an art medium as well as in human association.

No similar disparities are found in the few miniatures which are by general agreement given to Copley, but this judgement may even yet be upset by the discovery of an indisputable instance of inferior workmanship. The quality of the two signed examples has discouraged the wide acceptance of any less good; but it cannot be safely contended either that Copley did no more miniatures than are now known or that all of them were as exceptional as the *Self-Portrait* [1765: privately owned]. Fortunately plenty of Bostonians were ready to pay the necessarily higher fees for oil portraits which were ambitious enough in scale to give Copley scope for much more than a likeness; and the complex pictorial successes of these suffice to prove that Copley's mind could never have been content with the limited likeness-making of the other slighter mediums. It cannot be claimed that Copley definitely quit using these at any specific date in his American period, but he certainly tapered off his miniature and pastel production after 1767. Yet his skill in them did not diminish, and his latest works in both were about the finest: the miniature of *Mrs. Samuel Cary*

[1772: privately owned] and the pastel of the second *Mrs. Joseph Barrell* [c. 1771: privately owned].

It is in connection with work in miniature that there occurs the topic of Copley as a teacher. Putting to one side the slight help he extended to Charles Willson Peale and John Trumbull, Copley's only pupil was his half-brother, Henry Pelham, almost twelve years younger than himself. Several miniatures by Pelham are both fine in their own right and surprisingly different from Copley's. The latter's are small even for miniatures, and their remarkably luminous and high-keyed colors were applied in microscopic touches; young Pelham's are somewhat larger (though still not large) and their usually darker colors were put on with visible brush strokes which achieve a bulkier modeling. Such clear and strong stylistic differentiation so early in the pupil's lifetime, coupled with intrinsic fineness of technique, is evidence of Copley's capacity as a teacher; and it is psychologically sound to infer that Copley's own work was improved by the carefulness of the instruction he gave. For this instruction was in oil, too, and a few sentences in letters which passed between the half-brothers indicate that Pelham painted on some of Copley's later American canvases.

Copley's technique in oil presents two main traits: a reliance upon line as his principal means of rendering form and a use of color for conscious visual delight. A chronological study of the American portraits would show an uneven development of both phases through the first decade and a fairly steady mastery of them through the second; their union into outstanding successes was complicated by Copley's difficulties in reconciling these two aims with some of the conventions of British-school portraiture which he understood less well. The failures and partial successes could be analyzed and correlated into a revealing artistic biography, but it is of course only the better pictures which fully define Copley's individuality as a painter.

The line with which Copley began working does no more than define an edge on the flat surface of the canvas; to give the volume of a figure, he attempted variations of value which are not subtle enough to render the full thickness of bodies or to show them occupying their due amount of space. By 1760 Copley's line and values together not only established a pattern across the canvas but also created solidity in the figure and sufficient depth in space to give the figure room. When he retained an unspecific darkish tone for background, no contradictory element of vision now presents itself, even though many such portraits have gone too dark in background to retain their original unity of effect. But when Copley introduced elaborations of architecture or landscape behind the figures, his control of space weakened or vanished, and the eye is brought up short by the inadequate studio convention. This very

defect of itself testifies to the dependence of Copley's mind on actuality before him; in taking such imaginary settings from prints he left their inconsistency unconcealed, and whether he did so consciously or unconsciously does
not impair the honesty of the result.

Apparently Copley, in common with his fellow colonial painters, did not
habitually make preparatory studies for his portraits, whether in drawing or in
color; and this probably has much to do with the impression frequently made
by his three-quarter lengths of seated men that he commenced working so far
below the upper edges of those canvases that he did not leave himself room
enough for complete anatomical consistency in the lower portions. But it is
also possible that working directly upon each canvas from the beginning was
the main reason for one of the most remarkable features of Copley's altogether
remarkable technique: his exactitude in drawing with the brush. All of the
earlier productions, in their dogged wrestling with the difficulty of seeing more
than he can put down, suggest that the youth was thinking of line and color
as separate problems; but by 1760 his brush had begun to follow the contours
of everything and thus to render shape and hue and location in space by a
continuous application of pigment. From the climactic year of 1765 the major
works all exemplify a precision in this method which would seem admirable in
any place or period of painting and which, in eighteenth-century America from
one who had never been many miles from Boston, was nothing less than
astounding. Lace and embroidery, flowers and fruit, papers and inkstands—
all such details, when seen from a few feet away, solicit the examination of
"nearly looking" from anyone with a mind to it; but the actual examination
reveals no hard minuteness of uniform emphasis but rather the lightest and
most tactful touching of brush to canvas. Copley had learned to think in paint.

No less remarkable was his deliberate cultivation of a personal sense of
color composition. From current prints he could of course learn nothing about
color, and the verbal descriptions in handbooks of painting were no more helpful than they are today. For ideas about color, Copley had available a very
few portraits by secondary Europeans and more by Smibert and Feke and
Blackburn; and he developed a colorism far beyond theirs in complexity and
richness. But the virtues in Copley's color were conditioned throughout his
American period by one peculiarity of handling which, for several later generations, hampered painters and laymen alike in comprehending his full degree
of greatness. Copley did not avail himself of the effect of atmosphere in unifying colors into color, in modifying separate hues by light and air into a dominant harmony. Probably he had already adopted the habit, which he is known
to have practised later, of matching the colors on his palette with the tints of
each sitter's face before starting work on the canvas. If he did this close to

the sitter and then stepped back the usual distance to paint, he would thereby eliminate the slight veil of atmosphere between: and this would well account for the too intense and somewhat airless local colors actually observable in the pictures today. But the nearly complete absence of atmosphere from in front of the figures only emphasizes the purposiveness with which the colors are ordered through the contrasts of different ones or through the gradations of one or two at a time.

Mrs. George Watson and George Watson [1765 and 1768: privately owned], although painted three years apart, were posed as pendants; in colors the two portraits seem radically different to the casual eye. Hers is high in key with red and white, his is lower with brown and gold; the only colors they have in common—and that without being exactly the same—are vague browns around the figures and the greens of his foreground tablecloth and her background curtain. Yet the two are mates in color because the contrasting schemes are pitched at matching intensities. In the Mrs. Daniel Sargent [1763: privately owned; on loan at the Corcoran Gallery, Washington] a strong and relatively simple chord was sounded with a series of greens in dress and falling water set off by the transparent whites of lace and the tinted alabaster of flesh. In the Mrs. Ezekiel Goldthwait [c. 1770: Museum of Fine Arts, Boston] there occurred the deliberate multiplication of technical difficulties which Henry James was to specify as one mark of an authentic artist; here Copley used flesh color, both white and black lace topping a plum-colored dress, backed by a brilliant blue chair with an edging of bright brass tacks, and in the foreground a mirror-like mahogany table-top supporting a basket of apples and peaches done in vivid greens and reds and yellows. The colonial limits of Copley's experience kept him from achieving here the subtly rich Venetian harmonics of colorism, but his provincial rawness of tone nevertheless demonstrated a true painter's attempt to secure what he himself called the "flowery luxsuriance" which, about a year later in Philadelphia, was to give him such delight in a copy from Titian.

So brief a discussion of Copley's rendering of personality and acquisition of technique can of course take note of only the broader aspects and must stop far short of the unusually complete account of his development which could be written in the form of a documented year-by-year discussion. Inextricably intertwined with that would be another strand concerning the development of Copley the artist; that is to say, the mind which, in the course of improving the craft, achieved an important statement about life. Concerning Copley the artist all that can be attempted in a general history is to describe the characteristic which is of central importance.

From the first Copley had the intention of becoming a painter in what

22. MRS. THOMAS BOYLSTON   *by* JOHN SINGLETON COPLEY
Courtesy of Harvard University.   Photograph from The Fogg Museum of Art.

then seemed to everyone the completest way of all: a painter of history. Since American conditions confined him to the single phase of portraiture while he remained here, he chafed at the narrow-mindedness of his patrons and felt himself defeated. Yet his will was so firm, his mind was itself so comprehensive, his capacity for experience was so vital that even before going to London he had attained an amazingly complete mastery over every kind of object which could be studied in the studio. To regard this limitation as a censurable error of choice in Copley would be to take insufficient account of the conditions in which he lived; if he never showed curiosity about landscape under naturalistic illumination, neither did any American predecessor or contemporary so far as now known; and within the studio Copley painted so well that he became the first in point of time among the half-dozen painters of major rank in the three hundred and fifty years of American history. For him the painting-room was no limitation; by his thoroughness and tenacity and intensity he enlarged it into a mental exploration of the visible.

For an effective measure of the pictorial adventuresomeness of Copley's mind an examination of his rendering of still-life alone might suffice. It may be true that no picture of still-life is by common consent among the hundred "best" in the world—a device for rough and ready judgements which may be valuable in summarizing the taste of an era—but the handling of still-life as a part of more complex pictorial themes always tells a great deal about the painter's idiosyncrasy. For example, the early portrait which was long called *Peter Pelham* [?1753: privately owned], but which cannot be Copley's stepfather, conclusively evidences by its still-life that even from boyhood Copley was interested in much more than portraiture. Spread out on the table below an impassive face are several engraver's tools; supposedly they appertain to the sitter, but they have a curious effect of emotional detachment because of the rigid arrangement into which Copley has forced them as a means of achieving the shallow foreground depth by linear emphasis. A very moderate success in differentiating values aided the effect a little, but the colors were set down in harshly solid areas which failed to cohere. For shadow in a blue coat, Copley simply deepened the shade of blue; he made the metal graving tools a dead black, with highlights in white. Yet even with inadequate color he showed his emotional pleasure in pigment and with blunt drawing manifested an intellectual delight in shape; and he joined both satisfactions into a conscious imposition of order upon a group of objects. Fifteen years later, with the engraver and silversmith *Paul Revere* [? after 1765: Museum of Fine Arts, Boston], Copley almost captured the secret of eliciting a purposeful design out of an accident; Copley nearly succeeded in making the pose look like a natural pause in the sitter's everyday shop-work and he fully succeeded in merging the graving tools into a design while leaving them their casual look of being ready to the sitter's hand. Copley has here also learned to model surfaces with subtlety and variety without sacrificing strength in the form as a whole, to modulate edges from flat lines into rounded contours, and to observe how not only polished surfaces but also flesh and white cloth reflect adjoining colors. When Copley first began to look at things in front of him, they were just so much "dead nature" (a transliteration of *nature morte* which is both accurate and untruthful); a decade later he could perceive in objects no less still than the earlier ones a life of color and form which rivals in vividness the livingness of a human face.

Flowers, of course, are alive in their own right, and so are fruits in their degree; from Copley these things received all the vividness which fine drawing and unlabored brushwork can give, but they usually also received a waxen gloss inappropriate to them all except the dramatic lilies. Copley had more success with the metal inkwells and crisp papers appertaining to the genially domineering merchants of Boston; and indeed he had nothing less than a passion for metallic glitter in elaborate embroidery and damask hangings and fine furniture—a passion which came to its American climax in the *Colonel Jeremiah Lee* [1769: privately owned]. Perhaps a hand, too, becomes still-life when considered by itself; but fairly often Copley gave it an amazing amount of character—and a character which corresponded to that in the face above. Probably Copley directed *Epes Sargent* to place his right hand at the very center of the fine design, and he then rendered it with the care needed for so prominent a detail; this hand retains its strength of structure underneath the puffiness of age and re-enforces the quiescent power of the features. Some years later Copley used the same motive in depicting *Richard Dana* [? after 1765: privately owned]; but this softer-fleshed hand is self-consciously oratorical, and may have needed no prompting from the painter to dramatize itself. Better still is the magnificent hand of *Jacob Fowle*, which so surely and quietly affirms a significance superior to the blaze of gold and scarlet in the coat on one side and the brown and silver birch trunk on the other.

In the otherwise splendid *Mrs. Thomas Boylston* [1766: plate 22] the hands are without expression; they are excellently placed in the design, but only the shadow in which they lie keeps them from injuring the general effect. The serene strength in her features keeps chair and clothes properly subordinated as no more than a triangular base for the central beauty of her countenance. As for the background curtain and tassel and pillar, they are only print-derived symbols of position and wealth which Copley thought he was professionally obligated to supply. He felt no such compulsion with *Nathaniel Hurd* [? after 1765: plate 23], and with a minimum of shapes he constructed a design of

23. NATHANIEL HURD *by* JOHN SINGLETON COPLEY
Courtesy of The Cleveland Museum of Art [The John Huntington Collection].

monumental ease to match the massive personality of the man. Here the hands are assigned a most important part both in basing the visual pyramid and in expressing character; these hands are a portrait in themselves. Copley thus for once achieved a design which seems so accidental that the calculation of its inevitability remains hidden; and at the same time he passed on to nature the credit of the colorism which he so carefully and so intricately mingled throughout. Character and design, drawing and color, were here unified into one of the major examples of portraiture in America.

In at least one hundred portraits through his American maturity, Copley painted both hands of each sitter, whereas in only about twenty-five did he give one hand alone; but the best proof of his interest in hands is qualitative—the high proportion of times when the hands not only function in the design but also do something appropriate to the sitter and the occasion. This is particularly notable through a succession of decoratively assured ladies who hold flowers or carry a parasol or simply let their hands relax in the unaccustomed idleness of the studio. And to make an end of hands, there is the one that holds the fine gold chain in *The Boy with the Squirrel* [c. 1765: plate 24]. This older title is better than to name the boy as Henry Pelham, because the picture definitely transcends the bounds of portraiture. Free from the need to please a patron, Copley composed a picture into which he put nothing he didn't see, and everything he did put into it he chose for the beauty it would yield him in the painting. In depicting his half-brother Copley caught the charm of boyhood in general; hands and glass of water, gold chain and squirrel, distributed across the complex reflections in the table-top, sing the painter's praise of a world in which form and color join in the "flowery luxsuriance" which is the fundamental reason why most painters have painted. Here Copley's intellect penetrated the structure of things and his emotion responded sensuously to their colors and textures. With complete belief his whole mind entered into the things which he proceeded to re-create on canvas; and the appreciator can with similarly complete credence enter into his re-creation.

In the long established terminology of art criticism, Copley's way of rendering appearances is usually described as objective; this implies an activity predominantly intellectual and consisting largely of close observation. But consider the single detail of the squirrel in this picture of Copley's which, sent over to London nine years before he went there himself, was praised by West and Reynolds and admired by exhibition visitors. The first perception of the creature in all its minute particularity was necessarily an act of good eyesight; such a convincing statement in paint of the original perception involved the further activity discriminated as conception, and that act of the mind is much too complex to be narrowed down to the operation of sight alone. What is called the objectivity of Copley's work consists in the close correspondence of the resulting image to appearance, but that very result is attained by the mind's reshaping of the eye's perception.

This dominant element in Copley's work of visual similitude to nature expresses an attitude of which later times become acutely conscious by the contrast of their own extreme subjectivity. Through these later periods imagination in painting has been usually considered the prerogative of the introspectives, with their increasingly wilful departures from a supposed norm of appearances. Yet conformity to that norm can itself be imaginative, for it all depends upon how intense and comprehensive and convincing the painting itself may be.

To understand any painter, it is necessary to answer the question: where lies reality for him? Copley credited every object and every person with independent existence; and the whole power of his mind was turned to reconstituting them with exactitude in paint. The fact that he frequently did this in designs with an organic unity which came not from nature but from his own conceptual power in pictorial terms infused even his exceptional degree of objectivity with the tinge of imagination; and the pictures of his American period in which this control is most strongly exerted—almost concealed in the *Nathaniel Hurd* and more easily discerned in *The Boy with the Squirrel*—have achieved the permanence of art.

24. THE BOY WITH THE SQUIRREL *by* JOHN SINGLETON COPLEY
Anonymous loan to Museum of Fine Arts, Boston.

25. *Important stylistic beginnings*

Charles Willson Peale: 1741–1827 (work before 1767)
John Trumbull: 1756–1843 (work before 1780)
Ralph Earl: 1751–1801 (work before 1778)
Gilbert Stuart: 1755–1828 (work before 1775)
Matthew Pratt: 1734–1805 (work before 1764)
Benjamin West: 1738–1820 (work before 1760)

On Monday, July 15th, 1765, Charles Willson Peale, seeking temporary safety in Massachusetts from his Maryland creditors and political enemies, visited the painting-room which Smibert had used and which was still being run as an art shop; there Peale saw what he thought were better pictures than he had seen in Annapolis and Philadelphia, but nobody told him about Copley then at work on near-by Beacon Hill. Peale went on to Newburyport, where he painted some portraits and made a landscape drawing; only after his return to Boston did he learn of Copley and visit him in his studio. Whatever of his current work Copley may have shown Peale was important, for it was about this time that he had in hand such masterpieces as the *Mrs. George Watson* and *The Boy with the Squirrel*. Peale has recorded how Copley was helpful with advice and lent the picture of a candle-lit head for copying.

From so brief a contact little perceptible influence could normally be expected, but Peale was far enough advanced in his art to grasp a good deal very quickly. Through boyhood he had made drawings, including one from an uncle's corpse at the request of his grandmother; after learning and leaving the trade of saddlery, he had conducted a sign-painting shop and painted portraits and studied a two-volume *Handmaid of the Arts;* he had also received instructions from John Hesselius—all that before the journey to Boston. The portraits of *James Arbuckle* and *Mrs. Arbuckle* [1766: privately owned], executed in Virginia between his return from Boston and his departure for London in December, remained stylistically closer to Hesselius than to Copley; but in all probability Peale's lifelong preference for linear emphasis in his work was much strengthened by his talks with Copley and the sight of whatever pictures Copley had shown.

A few years later Copley was visited by a Connecticut youth not yet sixteen, John Trumbull, on his way to Harvard under the compulsion of his father although he himself wanted only to learn painting from Copley. At college Trumbull read Hogarth's *Analysis of Beauty,* studied a *Handbook of Perspective,* and copied whatever interesting prints and paintings he could find. With these copies he sought advice from Copley, and for at least one received commendation which he remembered all his life. On his return home he kept at his painting, only to be interrupted by the outbreak of war. He saw brief service under Washington and could doubtless have played a somewhat important role throughout the war if he had not allowed personal pique to rush him into resigning his commission. Out of the army, he rented what had been Smibert's painting-room, with its important contents still in place, and for a time painted more industriously than ever. Copley was then in England, of course, but his Boston portraits remained in all their freshness; inevitably Trumbull's work embodies what he could teach himself by looking at the work of one who seemed to him a master.

Among the sixty-eight works of several kinds which Trumbull completed before he first went abroad in 1780, two are particularly interesting. *The Family of Jonathan Trumbull* [1777: plate 25] makes use of the reflecting table-top which had become so prominent in Copley's work through his last American years. Without copying any specific Copley now known, he intelligently followed the precedents Copley set in this compositional motive; the seated father and mother, however, seem shortened in body as though fitted by force into the canvas; the child standing at the right has not been subjected to a like compression. Clothes and features are modeled by strong contrasts of light and shadow, just as Copley often rendered them; but the edges of everything are harder and the drawing blunter in effect than in any mature Copley. The earnest self-consciousness of these villagers sitting to Trumbull makes an unconscious record of the young painter's own strained intentness upon self-teaching. A more direct expression of the same thing is in his *Self-Portrait* [1777: privately owned], in which the fixed stare of the strongly lighted face distracts attention from the compactly designed figure. Copley's provincial baroque was extremely sophisticated in comparison with Trumbull's countryfied approximation; this beginner's efforts, just as Copley's own a quarter-century earlier, were stamped with the artisan inheritance that environed all American painters for more than two hundred years.

A portrait of *Roger Sherman* [c. 1777: plate 26] by another Connecticut painter, Ralph Earl, may at first glance appear even more countryfied in general effect than Trumbull's self-portrait. Though Earl had no known personal contact with Copley, he correctly thought that he was working in Copley's manner. Before doing the Sherman portrait, Earl had attempted something quite different. He and Amos Doolittle, as members of the Connecticut militia,

25. THE FAMILY OF JONATHAN TRUMBULL *by* JOHN TRUMBULL *Courtesy of Yale University Art Gallery.*

were in Lexington a few weeks after the famous battle; what they saw and heard fired them into a joint enterprise of historical picturemaking. Earl provided the paintings which served as sources for four engravings by Doolittle published in December of 1775. The source painting for the second in the series—*A View of the Town of Concord* [privately owned]—has been discovered; it is described as much superior to the engraving, being high-keyed and colorful and having the striking peculiarity of a quarter-inch band of bright yellow for a border around its four sides. The greater intrinsic importance of the *Roger Sherman,* and the reason for dating it later, consists in the painter's effort to draw the figure so that the contour lines establish not merely its edges but also its construction and its volume. The results here seem superficially more awkward than Trumbull's mainly because the figure is seen full-length and in greater depth. Though portions are inaccurately rendered, no detail in the highly complex visual problem is shirked; the result conveys not only strength of character in sitter but also resolution of mind in the painter. Even after going to England Earl painted young *William Carpenter* and his sister *Mary Carpenter* [both 1779: Worcester Art Museum] with such effective re-affirmation of linear probity that they are as fully American in quality as anything he ever did.

The earliest work by Gilbert Stuart is accounted for without any direct influence from Copley, but in boyhood Stuart got from Cosmo Alexander a definiteness of line and a hardness of pigment which kept both teacher and pupil safely within the general colonial manner. Stuart is said to have had some earlier instruction from Samuel King; but King's surviving works place him later than Alexander and no technical connections are discernible between them and Stuart's early portraits in oils. In relation to contemporaneous fashion in Great Britain, Alexander's own work was provincial; Stuart's was therefore quite unlike what he was shortly to find in London. There he too, like Ralph Earl, briefly re-affirmed his colonial inheritance; his portrait of *Dr. Benjamin Waterhouse* [1776: Redwood Library, Newport] was simply a more concentrated statement of the substance in his earlier *Alexander Redwood* [c. 1774: Redwood Library, Newport]. However, the earlier prosaic pomposity, with a comic overtone of which both sitter and painter remained unaware, was replaced by intimacy of feeling; the earlier extrovert obviousness of treatment was supplanted by a richness of handling which seemed to forebode subjectivity in the work to follow.

Matthew Pratt in Philadelphia was oldest among these colonial beginners, but discussion of his work comes later in the record because his early pictures are too few and uncertain. His most recent biographer assigns only two oil portraits to the first part of his career and takes away two miniatures previously attributed. Yet Pratt seems to have had seven or eight years of professional work between completing his apprenticeship under his uncle Claypoole and going to London in 1764; and Dunlap affirmed that for at least part of that time Pratt had plenty of commissions.

In the opinion of Dunlap, Benjamin West was one of the great artists of all time; it was accordingly natural for him to seek out the portraits which West had painted in America before leaving in 1760, never to return. Dunlap's difficulty in discovering some was caused by the general neglect which followed the disappearance of West's reputation, but all his life Dunlap struggled loyally to revive that reputation and erase that neglect; it therefore seems surprising at first to read Dunlap's admission that West's American portraits, when found, proved to be not worth the search. The surprise may disappear when we remember that both West and Dunlap regarded portraiture as an inferior branch of painting, and that inferiority of skill in that inferior branch was for them entirely defensible in any master of history painting. A different attitude prevails now, of course, and everything which West did here has interest simply for its having been done here. Its intrinsic importance is very small, but it does possess significance in that it confirms some of the generalizations already noted concerning work by the native-born in colonial times and it throws some light upon the talent which gave West his tremendous success in Europe.

And West did have talent. Like most others among American colonials, he was highly assimilative. A seapiece and a landscape are print-derived; some among the eighteen portraits are clearly indebted to Feke and Gustavus Hesselius and Wollaston. The most nearly personalized American portrait by West is the *Thomas Mifflin* [c. 1758: Pennsylvania Historical Society, Philadelphia]; it departed far from Wollaston in the prominent blues, but little in drawing. At the same time, and at the same age, Copley was much further beyond Blackburn into the maturely personal draftsmanship and assured modeling of his *Elizabeth Oliver* [Massachusetts Historical Society, Boston]. This parallel suggests that West's facility lacked the transforming capacity requisite to artistic greatness.

The same general impression is made by most of the drawings by West in a small sketchbook [Pennsylvania Historical Society, Philadelphia]. Some of these are working details like a hand or a bit of costume; others are apparently studies of poses and clothes in preparation for portraits; but a few go beyond such studio exercises to record individualities with considerable effect. Among these few, three or four convey the model's character by the pose or gait of the entire figure, and do so with an intensity that borders upon caricature. The human oddity named Sammy Worral glances out resentfully as he strolls past, the

26. ROGER SHERMAN *by* RALPH EARL
Courtesy of Yale University Art Gallery.

crooked stick under his arm as carelessly eccentric as his disorderly hair and his breeches unbuttoned at his knee. A figure of fashion said to be Francis Hopkinson bends with rococo elegance over a chair back to hear something being said by a lady whose action in turning around is well caught. In these vivid characterizations the strokes rapidly note the fleeting gestures; they pause to make more definite a construction line, a few such accents pulling the figure into full coherency; they apply to the ribbed paper a few touches of tone which suggest volume—and a human being comes to life with a vividness never attained in West's oil portraits of the time. What happened to the keen-eyed observer within the young American?

He was smothered by the very assimilativeness seen in his American oils. Going to Rome at the moment when that youthfully normal trait was working most effectively, West directed his facility to taking over the pictorial formulas of the eclectics. He had also been prepared for this by William Williams with the painting handbooks of Fresnoy and Richardson, and by Provost William Smith at the College of Philadelphia, who filled his mind with ancient history and subjects out of Plutarch. Even the plaudits he was to win in Rome were preceded by public tributes in Philadelphia. In February of 1758 the *American Magazine* printed some rhyming praise of the young painter and for good measure threw in some editorial eulogy:

. . . so extraordinary a genius . . . without the assistance of any master has acquired such a delicacy and correctness of expression. . . .

In October of the same year the same periodical printed Francis Hopkinson's lines to Wollaston which have been quoted; they were there followed by something like a postscript:

> Nor let the muse forget thy name O WEST,
> Lov'd youth, with virtue as by nature blest!
> Of such the radiance of thy *early Morn,*
> What bright effulgence must thy *Noon* adorn?
> Hail sacred *Genius!* may'st thou ever tread,
> The pleasing paths your *Wollaston* has led,
> Let his first precepts all your works refine,
> Copy each grace, and learn like him to shine.
> So shall some future muse her sweeter lays,
> Swell with your name, and give *you* all *his* praise.

In relation to the actual pictures West executed in and around Philadelphia, the praise of Smith and Hopkinson was as parochial as Boston's eulogy of Emmons eighteen years earlier; and its sincerity as well as its extravagance would seem sufficient to satisfy an old man's memories of his youth. But toward the end

West devised even greater marvels of prophetic events for his childhood which form no part of history; the stories which he allowed his biographer to print are for the later historian largely a problem in psychological interpretation of self doting age.

Both Smith and Hopkinson lived long enough to hear all about West's effulgent noon, for he was so soon famous that within five years of his departure a print seller in Philadelphia found it good business to put the painter's head on his sign. No wonder that all the other beginning painters discussed in this section were drawn to West in London as filings to a magnet, or that they were only the forerunners of many more.

26. More artisans and amateurs

William Faris: 1728–1804
Bernard Wilton: act. 1760
Benjamin Blyth: 1746–after 1787
Cosmo Medici: act. 1772
George Mason: act. 1768
John Durand: act. 1767–1782

Alexander Gordon: 1692–1754
Francis Hopkinson: 1727–1791
Peter Precour: act. 1732/3
John and Hamilton Stevenson: act. 1774
James Smither: act. 1769

Where the six painters just discussed transcended their awkward beginnings, many artisans never did. The reasons would vary, of course; some might not receive enough patronage to rouse them into development, some might be incapable of it no matter how numerous their commissions, and some would simply be too busy about other things. A man of the latter sort was William Faris living at Annapolis; in the variety of his activities he surpassed Joseph Allen and perhaps even equaled his younger fellow townsman, Charles Willson Peale. "Silversmith, watch maker, clock maker, designer, portrait painter, chair maker, cabinet maker, tulip grower, tavern keeper, dentist, diarist par excellence and gossip"—so runs the summation of his life. This catalog of skills is as miscellaneous as the contents of a colonial shop, where the shopper had choice among red leather chairs, Flanders bed ticks, cinnamon, New England hops, "beavour" hats, silk stockings, rod iron for nails, whale oil and whalebone, and "sundry other goods." Perhaps the shopper might also have found bladders of pigment there; by 1774 paints and oil and glass were no longer the specialty of painters selling supplies on the side but were being advertised even by drugstores. That detail alone suggests how the artisans were increasing in number to take care of increasing business.

The years of colonial culmination were the heyday of coaches, private as well as official, and the lines of communication between towns became passable for public conveyances. Those newly made were more splendid than the earlier ones, giving artisan painters more scope for their skill. As for the signs, they even enlarged their domination of the townscapes; occasionally, as surviving stories show, they played a part in amusing or significant local legends. There was, for instance, the sign for the tavern of Nathaniel Ames in Dedham which, about the year 1748, got him into trouble with the General Court of Massachusetts because he used it to deride that body for a verdict rendered against him. An

Englishman, Bernard Wilton, at work in Philadelphia in 1760, devised a sign for the Bull's Head Tavern which was long attributed to Benjamin West. In what was then distant Winchester, Virginia, two stores had signs—one of a spinning wheel and one of an umbrella. There, too, among the artisans was listed a maker of painted chairs. In Charleston, as early as 1735, an artisan had trained two negro slaves whom his widow hired out by the day or by the job.

As in the preceding period, the artisans found their main support in utilitarian work, but both pictures and advertisements indicate that increased demand gave them more opportunities to venture into portraiture. A number of pastel portraits by Benjamin Blyth in Massachusetts and a couple of oil portraits by the curiously named Cosmo Medici in Virginia show how low the workmen could decline in skill and still get work. Medici, who left a somewhat cloudy record in the Revolutionary War, may have been an amateur making a likeness for a friend; his suspicions about individual character are too faint to compensate for the repulsive handling of pigment. Blyth left enough work to show that portraiture was important in his total effort, but his poor drawing and his uncertainty in the medium raise a wonder why people sat to him at all. The antiquarian Bentley explained that Blyth and another man, Cole, were "the only persons who undertook at that time" and said that their livings came "from the money of the privateermen."

In the absence of identified examples it is not known how good or how bad were the pastels of George Mason, but his advertisement in the *Boston Chronicle* for June 7th, 1768, has a documentary interest:

George Mason, Limner, begs leave to inform the public (with a view of more constant employ) he now draws faces in crayon for two guineas each, glass and frame included. As the above mentioned terms are extremely moderate, he flatters himself with meeting some encouragement especially as he professes to let no picture go out of his hands but what is a real likeness. . . .

His price was exactly half of what Copley was getting three years earlier; and in that light Mason's plaintive self-encouragement in the face of poor patronage sounds a little like whistling in the dark.

John Durand had high ambitions to paint history, but his now identifiable work reveals him as only a portrait artisan. His people are painfully stiff in their efforts to be gracious and graceful, and he renders them almost as flatly as if they had been sliced through for pasting on the canvases. If put beside Copley's work done in New York, Durand's production there must have seemed crude even to casual eyes. Going from New York into Virginia, he made no advance in rendering the third dimension, but he modified the coarsely linear emphasis of his northern work and gained considerably in modulation of color. It is this color which charms even now, with generally pale harmonies which come into a deeper intensity of hue in the formalized nosegay held in boneless hands.

> Hard and dry, it must be confessed,
> Flat as a rose that has long been pressed;
> Yet in her cheeks the hues are bright,
> Dainty colors of red and white.

Those are the rhymes of Doctor Holmes about a Massachusetts artisan; but Robert Sully, writing to Dunlap about Durand's work in Virginia, used the very words "hard and dry." And when Sully goes on to credit Durand with securing strong likenesses, it may have been because they seemed so to one who himself practised the dullish discretion of flattery which prevailed in his own day among the second-raters.

Socially quite above such artisans there developed into new prominence the society amateur who had been foreshadowed by Mrs. Le Serrurier and her son-in-law. It was indeed appropriate that in Charleston the first notable foreign-born gentleman-amateur found conditions so attractive that he made it his permanent home; and for that reason alone he deserves a paragraph despite the present lack of works from his hand. Alexander Gordon came to Charleston in August of 1743 as secretary to Governor James Glenn; in the remaining eleven years of his life (to the month exactly) he was one of the most ornamental members of a notably ornamental society. As an antiquary his reputation had been established before he left Scotland by his *Itinerarium Septentrionale*, an account of his journeys of research over the continent of Europe. In Charleston, Gordon participated in the musical life of the city to such an extent that he was known as "Singin' Sandy." His will bequeathed two portraits by himself to their respective subjects and to his son a self-portrait, "together with all and sundry other Pictures, Paintings, Views and Representations by me painted, drawn and represented." As legal phraseology that is satisfying, and it may give the impression that Gordon was a more prolific painter than he actually was; but it is tantalizing to get only that inadequate glimpse of the "artist, antiquary, author, musician, teacher of languages and politician." Yet even that much is sufficient to show his significance as a transplantation to the new world of an important old-world phenomenon, the eighteenth-century dilettante; and the sanction of his example must have made it easier for other Charlestonians to venture upon some portrait sketches or some "prospects" in water color.

An American parallel to Gordon did come along a generation later in the person of Philadelphia-born Francis Hopkinson. His previously quoted rhymes addressed to Wollaston and West testify to his interest in painting. He also worked a little in pastel, performed and composed music, signed the Declaration of Independence, wrote some essays and some poetry much better than the quoted examples. Nor did all these activities interfere with his more important career as an astute and learned judge. His actual practice of painting was almost confined to the amusingly egotistical channel of making copies from other men's portraits of himself. At least one of his songs—"My Days Have Been So Wondrous Fair"—still sounds on the ear with fragile grace. The set in which the song was one was dedicated to President Washington, and about the offering Hopkinson wrote

. . . that it is such as a Lover, not a Master, of the Arts can furnish. I am neither a profess'd poet, nor a profess'd Musician; and yet venture to appear in these characters united. . . .

The attractively worded distinction between the amateur and the professional was to acquire even greater significance on Hopkinson's social level through subsequent years.

In his own generation the recognition of Hopkinson's genuine ability in writing and in music was certainly impaired by the accident of his bodily appearance. John Adams wrote:

He is one of your pretty, little curious, ingenious men. His head is not bigger than a large apple. I have not met with anything in natural history more amusing and entertaining than his personal appearance, yet he is genteel and well-bred, and is very social.

The Adams family were to require three more generations for one among them to attain a full recognition of the spiritual importance of the arts, and even in that belated recognition Henry Adams was to be in advance of most Americans of his time. For the colonial Adams, all the bright and bustling dilettantism of Hopkinson only confirmed a Yankee tendency to regard all the arts as dispensable decorations. The important things were politics and business, and for a man in the midst of such affairs to display more than a distant respect for the arts would be to show himself lacking in earnestness.

The general concept of artistic amateurism as nothing more than a graceful adornment had the ultimate consequence in the nineteenth century that artistic accomplishments on the society level were almost confined to the girls and women; but even during the half-century of colonial culmination this concept was perceptibly strengthened. An announcement in the *South Carolina Gazette* for March 7th, 1732/3, reads in part:

Peter Precour, Master of Arts, is arrived in the Province but a Small Time and willing to acquaint the Publick that he will teach the French Latin Tongues: and his Spouse Mounts and paints Fans and learn to Draw. . . .

The degree which this gentleman claimed referred to bookish learning alone; it certainly conferred on him no mastery of English, whatever may have been the case with French and Latin; perhaps more significant is the superficiality of the so-called arts professed by his spouse.

In the same paper forty-one years later, on November 18th, 1774, a much lengthier advertisement sufficiently establishes the still more elaborate triviality of art among the privileged:

. . . John and Hamilton Stevenson, Limners, who propose to teach the Principles and Practice of this beautiful Art [drawing and painting] in all its various branches, after the Manner they are taught in the Roman schools, viz: Portrait, Landscape, Flowers, Birds, Figures and Drawing from the Bust and Statue in a Stile never before taught in this Province; Painting from the Life in Crayons, and in Miniature on ivory; Painting in Silk, Sattin, &c. Fan painting, together with the Art of working Designs in Hair upon Ivory, &c.

They continue to paint as usual . . . History and Portrait, Large and in miniature for Rings, Bracelets, Family and Conversation pieces; Designs of every kind executed in Hair; and in Hair and Colours, a manner never before attempted: Also Sewing with Hair upon Silk for Bracelets, a method which preserves the Hair and Work to the latest ages.

Some of the bracelets which they believed would last so long may be still unidentifiably cherished among Charleston heirlooms; but it is open to doubt on the ground that the Stevensons' wide-ranging claims were, even by the standards of their own day, inconsistent with thoroughness. For the principal significance of their advertisement is the note of anxious fashionableness in soliciting the patronage of females who have both spare time and ornamentally cultural ambitions.

Appeals on behalf of the visual arts were also directed at young men specifically, and in them too can be traced the same increase in superficiality of idea. Here, for example, are the words of Benjamin Franklin in 1749:

. . . Drawing is a kind of universal language, understood by all nations. A man may often express his ideas, even to his own countrymen, more clearly with a lead pencil or bit of chalk than with his tongue. . . . Drawing is no less useful to the mechanic than to a gentleman. . . . By a little skill of this kind a workman may perfect his own idea of the thing to be done before he begins to work; and show a draft for the encouragement and satisfaction of his employer.

Characteristic of Franklin's serenely practical mind are his way of letting the idea carry its own conviction and his slanting it toward the sort of youth he thinks of most importance then and there.

Twenty years later, in the *Pennsylvania Chronicle* for January 16th, 1769,

James Smither printed an advertisement which, in its shift of emphasis and its increase of verbiage, stands in dramatic contrast:

Drawing is a most ingenious, interesting and elegant art, and the study of it ought to be encouraged in every youth, who discovers a peculiar genius towards the practice thereof; its utility being so extensive, that there are few arts or professions in which it is not serviceable.

All designs and models are executed by it—Engineers, Architects, and a multitude of professions, have frequent occasion to practice it; in most stations it is useful, from the general who commands an army, to the mechanic who supports himself by handicraft. A young gentleman possessed of an accomplishment so exceedingly desirable, both for amusement and use, is qualified to take a sketch of a fine building—a beautiful prospect of any curious production of art, or of any uncommon and striking appearance in nature, especially to persons of leisure and fortune, it affords a most pleasing entertainment, and enables them to construct and improve plans to their own taste, and judge of designs, &c. with propriety. Of all others this art has the greatest number of admirers, and no wonder, since in a kind of universal language, or living history understood by all mankind, it represents to our view the forms of innumerable objects, which we should be otherwise deprived of, and helps us to the knowledge of many of the works of nature and art, by a silent communication. . . .

The pretentiousness of the advertisement is a more important quality than the grammatical confusion, and it is as representative of one continuing phase of American culture as today's advertising persuasions to self-improvement.

The same James Smither engraved a business card for a cabinet-maker which goes even beyond verbal ornateness into an almost surrealist profusion of inconsistently proportioned pieces of furniture and architectural fragments. His engraving skill was such that he was employed by the Colony of Pennsylvania to make the plates for its paper money; and that made it all the easier for him to counterfeit the currency during the British occupation of Philadelphia. Such pliability, to give it no worse a name, is merely a more serious manifestation of the hollowness that rings through the sham philosophy of his advertisement; and this also sounds in obvious harmony with the education already being given to the young ladies of the leisured class in many private academies.

Their education was hardly more than a superficial polish applied in a hurry: a posture, a gait, a few recipes, a smattering of facts, and a set of correct opinions. Nancy Shippen's mother, born Alice Lee of Stratford, was voicing the hopes of many mothers when she wrote to her daughter:

. . . Needlework is a most important branch of a female education, & tell me how you have improved your head and sholders, in making a curtsy, in going out or coming into a room, in giving & receiving, holding your knife & fork, walking &

seting. These things contribute so much to a good appearance that they are of great consequence. . . .

It was with such training in manners that art kept company in Mrs. Shippen's mind, for on another occasion she urged:

Why don't you write to me and tell me how you improve your work, in writing and drawing, in your address, in holding yourself & in the Graces? . . .

In a curriculum like that, lessons in drawing would not advance much further than copying or adapting prints after the works of others; a few touches of water color would brighten up those derivative patterns with a more personal note, but even they would probably follow the rules inculcated by the instructor. Somewhat more difficult would be painting on glass or low-relief modeling in wax. But another process of decorative picturemaking which exacted a lesser degree of skill was papyrotamia: cutting out designs in stiff paper and mounting them on a black paper background. The general conception of art as a pleasant occupation for idle hours was only the cultural veneering which is always one mark of a society on the make.

Yet there was never any telling when chance amateurism would strike fire and flare up into the most admirable professionalism. John Trumbull's older sister returned home from boarding school in Boston where she had made some drawings, together with two heads and a landscape in oil; it was the sight of these pictures which started him drawing at the age of five and sent him on against parental opposition to studying under West and earning the praise of David and Goethe.

27. The further broadening of taste

In view of the long excessive predominance of the life-size bust portrait in oil, the extension of portraiture into the pastel and the miniature constituted a broadening of taste in the portrait-buying class. Not only did both occur as experimentation on the part of the artist, but both mediums offered to the public the fillip of novelty necessary to fashion. The miniature in particular, besides possessing the fascination of all minute objects and the delight inherent in trinkets, by its usually oval shape gave a welcome change from "the monotony of the rectangle," which was then as noticeable in the oil portrait as it was in architecture.

Since those two mediums of portraiture were to prove especially dependent upon fashionable patronage, it was altogether appropriate that they should have first manifested themselves in what was probably, through the earlier part of the eighteenth century, the most fashionable city in the colonies: Charleston. Its being the first to afford a market for pastel is clearly established both by records and by the surviving works of Mrs. Johnston; as to its primacy in buying miniatures, that rests upon a reasonably well founded stylistic attribution of one miniature to Jeremiah Theüs. In New Jersey, Watson's portraits and ideal heads on vellum are only small-scale drawings, not true miniatures. But in Philadelphia there is one such work to be found in the *Self-Portrait* at eighteen by Benjamin West [privately owned]; there is also one other Philadelphia example given to Matthew Pratt on stylistic grounds. Among all the colonials, however, only Copley brought both mediums into a high state of excellence, and he was drawn away from their smaller perfections into the more ambitious scale permitted by oil. Under his tutelage his half-brother, Henry Pelham, briefly continued a brilliance of technique in the miniature. Several advertisements ranging from Georgia through the Middle Colonies rest their case for commissioning miniatures upon the trinket concept; not until the nineteenth century would the "portrait in little" achieve sufficient popularity to ensure technical standards both fine and widespread.

The full-length portrait on the scale of life was somewhat exceptional throughout the colonies, but apparently the only reason was the natural one of higher cost. Group portraits on that same scale were quite rare—perhaps not alone for their still greater cost but also because few houses could yield sufficient wall space. The less formal group portrait called the conversation piece, although room could easily be found for its characteristic small scale, met with a vaguer but stronger hindrance from the state of colonial culture. The formal life-size group rightly aims at a decided degree of stateliness, or at least of dignity, in terms of both its human participants and its visual organization; it is essentially the physical and social impressiveness of scale which makes it desired by every newly formed privileged class even when, as was the case in colonial America, the actual results are artistically immature. The informality of the conversation piece requires in both painter and patron a familiarity with wealth and position so well established that they can be taken for granted. The people themselves must be enough at ease in their setting for them to escape pomposity by being shown in a seeming accident of ordinary life; even the design in which they are caught should have its care for balance effectively disguised by the appearance of casualness. The work of William Williams evidences some awareness of this "visual eavesdropping"; but the effective practice of this branch of portraiture requires in the painter and his subjects, and even in a somewhat larger audience, a degree of sophistication which did not exist in colonial America.

However, the most effective broadening of taste among Americans need not be looked for in what are, after all, the minor phases of newly introduced medium and subtilizing attitude. With every large-scale audience broadening most naturally occurs in the domain of subject-matter; and the painters of greatest consequence have usually managed to avail themselves of this element in the total thing called art while at the same time developing their own more professional interests of techniques and interpretations.

The most natural extension of the picture content beyond the limits of the portrait consists in the anecdote, which goes only a little beyond the conversation piece by subordinating or eliminating the element of portraiture. What is achieved thereby is a casual human situation amenable to any kind of painting temperament, from reporting appearances through adventurous technical experimentation to imaginative vision. Nothing like this can rightly be looked for in colonial American painting; but there is clear documentation for the beginnings of the type and there are a few examples remaining which in their technical character further illustrate the quantitative dominance of the artisan-amateur work.

Anecdotal paintings were executed in Boston—probably by Emmons before 1740, certainly by Badger in 1757 or earlier. The relative abundance of anecdotes of Dutch origin in New York has been noted; when young West went there from Philadelphia in 1759 he saw one of a monk praying before a lighted lamp which incited him to a parallel technical experiment with a man reading by candlelight. Copley, before he came to New York in 1771, had sold to King's College (now Columbia University) a *Nun with Candle*; the low price he set upon his picture was for the express purpose of helping to start an art gallery there. No doubt Copley's experiment had also been suggested to him by something he had seen, painting or print. For the basic truism about the whole art of painting is that pictures breed pictures; in some periods they breed so prolifically and repetitively that the painters through whom this occurs seem to be only passive instruments of an impersonal process. In colonial America, however, the extension of pictorial subject-matter beyond the bounds of portraiture was an event of cultural significance even when it was a copy or an adaptation of another picture. Gilbert Stuart in youth was in this respect as un-typical as he was to be in other matters when mature; he turned straight to direct observation for his picture of two dogs. Henry Warren, who was a bird of passage in Williamsburg in 1769, advertised for visitors to see his "night pieces," and closed his announcement with a couplet of naïve persuasion which causes a little extra regret for the disappearance of the pictures:

> If you're pleased then sure you'll recommend
> Your humble servant to a tasty friend.

A kind which may be called the anecdotal picture of specific occasion was made by some amateurs for the pleasures of memory among groups of friends. Doctor Alexander Hamilton, whose travel diary has been drawn upon for his remarks about Feke, left behind him still another record—a sort of minute book of the feastings and frolics of the Tuesday Club of Annapolis [1749]. There are three volumes in duplicate, and both copies are profusely interspersed with Doctor Hamilton's sketches illustrating the events there recorded. Though very amateurish in execution, they are full of shrewd observation, varied characterization, and a warming sense of frank amusement at human oddities. An even more vigorous relish for even more riotous conduct is visible in an oil painting attributed to John Greenwood; the *Sea-Captains Carousing* [City Art Museum, St. Louis] are New Englanders, but the incident took place in Surinam, where Greenwood is supposed to have painted it after leaving this country. New Englanders' high jinks away from home certainly present a point of considerable psychological interest for any commentator on their life and character; even more interesting for the commentator on painting is the animated pictorial experimentalism which accompanied this flare-up of unpuritanical conduct. The technical inadequacies and inconsistencies are here even more noticeable than in Greenwood's other work; but they are more than compensated by a plucky attempt upon complex problems of artificial illumination falling across twenty-two figures drunk or sober, asleep or dancing or playing cards. In New England Greenwood could have been technically daring only with other subjects.

Some delightfully painted still-lifes in Copley's more ambitious portraits could be esthetically satisfying as independent pictures, but only one existing example of still-life done for its own sake can now be cited from before 1775. It is still in the Connecticut home where it was painted about 1769 by Winthrop Chandler, who is one of the most interesting workmen in the period of Revolutionary Transition. Chandler's row of painted books is now quite dim with age, yet it seems clearly addressed to the prevalent interest in illusionism; in that respect it falls far short of Mare's amazing fly because Chandler's technique is that of a partly-trained artisan.

The *Boston News Letter* for May 15th, 1760, carried the following appeal:

Lost at the late Fire, Two small Pictures of dead Game in their proper Colours, the one representing a Hare hanging by the hind Feet imboweled; the other a Lark falling, in plain gilt Frames and glaz'd. Whosoever has them it's desired they would inform the Printer, that the owner may send for them.

Those may of course have been imported pictures, like the still-lifes by Snyders and Vander Moulen [sic] offered for sale in New York in 1771, along with landscapes by Bachhousen and Brughel [sic]. But the Stevensons in Charleston [1774] named flowers and birds among the kinds of painting they could teach; and in the same year a decorator in Baltimore, Samuel Rusbatch, included still-life subjects among the many he was prepared to put on walls and ceilings. Thirty years earlier Kilburn in New York had also specified flowers among his subjects. Yet all such examples, if executed, could have been no more than random precursors of the extensive practice which was to come in the nineteenth century.

A rather different situation obtained in the much broader field which is unsatisfactorily called history painting. In all the colonies among both artists and the relatively few picture buyers there existed a general conception of this species as the very crown and glory of the whole art. It was an idea spread here very effectively by the many imported books on painting. The youthful attempts of West were derived from books as well as prints, and so were copies or adaptations of history subjects by Feke and Copley. Yet no census of all known attempts at history painting could set forth either the glamour or the complexity of the book-derived idea; the most adequate expression of it is to be found in the *New York Journal* for November 26th, 1768, where, among the advertisements, appears a miniature treatise inserted by John Durand while he was there painting portraits.

The Subscriber having from his infancy endeavored to qualify himself in the art of historical painting, humbly hopes for that encouragement from the gentlemen and ladies of this city and province, that so elegant and entertaining an art has always obtained from the people of the most improved minds and best taste and judgment, in all polite nations in every age. And tho' he is sensible that to excel (in this branch of painting especially) requires a more ample fund of universal and accurate knowledge than he can pretend to in geometry, geography, perspective, anatomy, expression of the passions, ancient and modern history, &c., &c., yet he hopes, from the good nature and indulgence of the gentlemen and ladies who employ him, that his humble attempts in which his best endeavours will not be wanting, will meet with acceptance, and give satisfaction; and he proposes to work at as cheap rates as any person in America.

To such gentlemen and ladies as have thought but little upon this subject and might only regard painting as a superfluous ornament, I would just observe, that history painting, besides being extremely ornamental has many important uses. It presents to our view some of the most interesting scenes recorded in antient or modern history, gives us more lively and perfect ideas of the things represented, than we could receive from a historical account of them, and frequently reveals to our memory a long train of events with which those representations were connected. They show us a proper expression of the passions excited by every event, and have an effect, the very same in kind (but stronger) that a fine historical description of the same passage would have upon a judicious reader. Men who have distinguished themselves for the good of their country and mankind may be set before our eyes as examples, and to give us their silent lessons—and besides, every judicious friend and visitant shares, with us in the advantage and improvement, and increases its value to ourselves.

The breathlessness is Durand's own, no doubt, but the ideas which he rushes together pell-mell were those of all European "cognoscenti" from Rome to

London. The advertisement is in fact an inadequate re-wording of some among the opening ideas in Jonathan Richardson's *Essay on the Theory of Painting* [London, 1715]. Yet what good fortune could such ideas meet with in colonies then so distant from Europe, so much less populated, so much poorer? The first paragraph, indeed, in its servile and self-distrustful tone, seems to despair of convincing anybody to the point of buying "histories," no matter how enlightening and improving they may admittedly be. And in the New York of that day, even if they were commissioned, where could they have been placed? Even if placed in a few of the larger homes, what could they intimately and personally say to people mainly intent upon comfort, however much they might talk about culture? It might be well enough for a few rich men to make room for some religious and mythological paintings acquired through the accidents of privateering; but such pictures were outside the experience of colonial Americans generally; and as the political tension with Great Britain increased, their concern with anything historical was more and more monopolized by current events.

It was therefore natural for history to manifest itself pictorially in the parsimonious but colonially normal form of prints. Seemingly the first was *The Battle of Lake George* [1755], an episode of the conflict between the English and the French in America. Samuel Blodgett, a participant who drew it in preparation for the engraving, produced one of those map-and-view combinations of inconsistent perspectives which savor more of the diagram than the picture. A second engraving of it was made the following year in London for the English public because it visually described novel methods of fighting. More conventionally pictorial was Henry Dawkins' print of *The Paxton Expedition* [1764], but here also the difficulties of perspective were too much for the craftsman. These two prints were the meager beginning of pictorial reporting in America, and as such had about them nothing of the associated ideas of high art which haloed Durand's advertisement.

As the troubles presaging the Revolution began to spread, such prints became more than reporting; they turned into effective propaganda. It was this element in Paul Revere's technically crude print of *The Boston Massacre* [1770] which put money into his pocket; but it was young Henry Pelham who made the original drawing and protested to Revere that

. . . after being at the great Trouble and Expence of making a design paying for paper, printing &c., [I] find myself in the most ungenerous Manner deprived, not only of any Advantage, but even of the expence I have been at, as truly as if you had plundered me on the highway. . . .

Bernard Romans' line engraving of *The Battle of Charlestown* was issued in Philadelphia not long after the event itself [1775], and a reduced copy of it by Robert Aitken served as an illustration in the *Pennsylvania Magazine* for September of that year. Only three months later Amos Doolittle published his set of four prints after the pictures by Ralph Earl which have been mentioned. During the war years and immediately thereafter the number of such prints increased; but there will be no need to discuss historical prints after this point because later there was an ambitious development of the historical subject as a separate branch of painting proper. These prints initiated pictorial history here; just as the topographical views of William Burgis in the preceding period initiated a taste for landscape.

One actual painting [privately owned] surviving from near the middle of the eighteenth century combines factual and symbolic intentions in a very unsymmetrical composition. The right-hand portion shows *A Conference of Ministers* at the Portsmouth home of the Reverend John Lowell; the left-hand portion shows a symbolic landscape which may have been intended to confer upon the event some lofty or hidden significance. This portion, however, evidences confusion in both symbolic idea and physical vision; the historical portion has something of the anecdotal spirit associated with conversation pieces. Because the whole is heavily executed, clumsy to the point of incapacity, its anonymous maker must have been a not very well trained artisan venturing beyond his depth; the confused symbolism may come from preacher Lowell, who apparently commissioned the picture, but the visual incapacity is the painter's own.

A history picture which more fittingly illustrates the elegant concept of Durand's advertisement is *The Continence of Scipio* [Bowdoin College Museum]; the execution is by Smibert but design and color are out of Poussin—one of those copies which formed part of the first collection of art in America. Another painting of this type attributable to Smibert is a *Hector and Andromache* [Museum of Fine Arts, Boston]; since no definite source has yet been found for this design, it may be one of his own ideas—at least in good part; a slight indication in favor of this supposition lies in the degree of particularity discernible in the faces, which seems to constitute a minor departure from the statue-derived facial masks of European examples.

Among younger men at work here, others besides John Durand had ambitious ideas. For West and Copley in particular, history painting was the great road to imaginative compositions. The literary and moralistic content which has since bored so many unresponsive minds was then the means of setting free whatever imagination the painter might have; and even when he did not have imagination, history painting could enable him to explore more important pictorial qualities than he found feasible in portraiture. The fact that the concept here played so large a part in the thinking of the painters well in advance of technically competent examples of it justifies a closer description of the several sorts of picture comprehended in the eighteenth-century use of the term.

A history picture was the inspiring delineation of a subject elevated above ordinary life: some secular event sanctified by time or portentous meaning, any occurrence from the Bible conceived in that same secular spirit but with its gravity intensified into solemnity. The essential thing was that the narrative content of the picture should suggest lofty moralizings upon human destiny. The technical procedure consisted largely of following rules put together out of the practice of the masters by eclectic minds; either in the condensed generalities of Fresnoy or in the speciously precise wordiness of Richardson, the verbal formulas were difficult to translate into acts of picturemaking in a country where that type of picture was rare. From the Earl of Shaftesbury's *Characteristics* [1714] Feke copied in paint the engraved frontispiece made from the painting which had been executed in fulfilment of the author's ideas about *The Judgment of Hercules;* maybe Feke thought the engraving did actually convey all the philosophy and psychology which the earl packed into his directions to his painter, but both are missing for those who look at the print without the encumbering text. The boy West, stimulated by having similar ideas read to him and probably also by prints, painted some history pictures now known only by their titles: *The Death of Socrates* and *The Trial of Susannah.* In Baltimore during 1752 the general practitioner A. Pooley specified "altarpieces" among the kinds of picture he could paint. Even in Boston a few such pictures were privately owned, and it is said that some paintings of ostensibly religious cherubs by Smibert adorned the chancel of the Trinity Church that burned in 1872.

Perhaps the most curious instance of religious painting in colonial America is afforded by John Valentine Haidt, who as a child in Germany had shown enough artistic precociousness to receive some state aid which was not continued long enough for him to become fluent in the correct academic manner. However, he managed a stay in Italy by working at his hereditary craft of goldsmithing; thus he got to know pictures by late Renaissance men, some of whose mannerisms are vaguely and crudely echoed in his American pictures. He became a religious enthusiast, and in 1754 was sent out to the Moravian settlement at Bethlehem, Pennsylvania, by Count Zinzendorf. Haidt wanted most of all to preach, and made missionary trips into New England and Maryland. But much if not most of his time was given to painting. His portraits are locally most valued today because they document the personalities of the sect's early days; but his religious paintings have a larger importance in being at least quantitatively unique in that time. Five are preserved in Bethlehem and fourteen in Nazareth; all except one are standard subjects out of the Bible, and eight of the Nazareth paintings depict, as a series, important episodes in the life of

Jesus. The color scheme of these is described as markedly limited, dominated by reds which tend toward subdued scarlets.

A third kind of subject which the eighteenth century included under the general term of history painting was from pagan mythology. Such a theme seems out of place in Boston then, but young Copley, copying or adapting prints or paintings, executed a *Galatea* [c. 1754: Museum of Fine Arts, Boston] and a *Mars, Venus, and Vulcan* [1754; ownership unknown]. Smibert's collection suggests itself as the source of these works. Though they are not much in themselves, they indicate how soon Copley's painting hopes went beyond the bounds of portraiture. And even as derivative pictures they illustrate how mythology possessed, for certain temperaments, one advantage. The absence of the moralism of secular history and the solemnity of religious history left the way open for whatever power of fancy might inhere in the painter's mind. From a combination of environmental pressure toward the practical and a prevailing temperamental bias toward the prosaic, conscious playfulness in any painting was not to be effectively manifested in this country for a long time. But in the mythological subject the possibility was present from the middle of the eighteenth century.

The topographical prints of the preceding period were followed up in this one by more, with a few among them giving evidence of increased awareness of picturesque detail; it was with such slightly more conscious art that Bishop Roberts in Charleston and Christian Remick in Boston reiterated Burgis' harbor views. The landscape paintings mentioned as part of Kühn's estate had their successors in similar items listed after the death of Theüs and Smibert; and landscapes were stressed in the Emmons obituary. The apparent loss of all these examples is particularly unfortunate because only the originals could tell whether the painters were examining nature or repeating the studio generalizations which served as back drops in some of the portraits. It is rarely possible to surmise even an intention to be specific in any such view, and nowhere is there any close observation of its component forms of tree trunk or grass texture or water surface to match the frequent precision of embroidery or still-life. Theüs' biographer refers to having seen one landscape and says that it did not "evince any special ability"; the eye of the eighteen-nineties cannot be trusted to have recognized qualities which would seem important today, but that testimony, for what it may be worth, points toward the studio recipe. More positive indications of the same tendency are contained in Smibert's own words in a letter of 1749:

My eyes has been some time failing me but I'm still heart whol and hath been diverting myself with some things in the landskip way which you know I always liked.

That is a pleasant enough trait of character in any painter, but the emotional pressure in the words seems hardly sufficient to have produced landscapes of intrinsic esthetic interest.

Sometimes landscape painting was professed by one who claimed a better-than-artisan training, such as Alexander Stewart [1769] in Philadelphia, lately a pupil at the Glasgow Academy and of M. De la Cour at Edinburgh; but Stewart was careful to specify a willingness to accept jobs of cleaning and mending pictures. About the only surviving pre-Revolutionary landscape that gives any evidence of technical suavity—and it is very slight indeed—is a faint drawing of *Purgatory, Newport* [1768: Library Company, Philadelphia] by Pierre Eugène du Simitière; not only is his execution timid in itself but the distance from which he views the low shore line also lowers its interest almost to the topographical level. This French-born man of many interests was a very active person in his day; his important collection of Revolutionary documents still exists in Philadelphia, where he also for a time conducted his two-room American Museum, semi-scientific and semi-historical, which may have incited the elder Peale to surpass it a little later.

Landscape drawings both cruder and more lively were inserted by young Albertina Ten Broeck into the genealogical record of her family compiled before the Revolution. But the known examples of that time which have the status of independent pictures are practically all in oil on panels originally built in as overmantel decorations; and all are explicable only as the efforts of artisans trying to render specific scenes and unconsciously evading the major difficulties of unfamiliar technical problems. Two examples from Massachusetts are the *View of Holyoke* [c. 1760: National Museum, Washington] and the *Ipswich Harbor* [before 1776: Ipswich Historical Society]. Both of them are still anonymous, but a group of six landscape panels in Massachusetts and Connecticut have been convincingly attributed to Winthrop Chandler, who has been mentioned for his early still-life. Possibly three of them were done before the Revolution, while the others may be later in date; but one and all they show the topographical interest of contemporaneous prints and the emphatic balance of pattern inculcated by the recipes of the guild.

Chandler's landscapes, since they were on inset panels, might be narrowly defined as interior decoration; but they seem to have been intended as pictures in the completest sense he could conceive. Strict decoration, as then understood, generally manifested itself in more elementary ways. There was, for instance, a series of painted rooms in the Woodbridge house in Salem, Massachusetts, done by John Holliman; "the beauty of this man's coloring" was such that it was visited by the antiquarian Bentley almost seventy-five years later. Holliman was a stonecutter by trade, and from Bentley's description his painting seems clearly non-pictorial; its attractiveness consisted only in using variegated black and white and variegated white and red. In Salem, at least, it would be stigmatized as extravagance; just prior to the Revolution one man remarked to another about a friend of theirs: "Well! Archer has set a fine example of expense—he has laid one of his rooms in oil."

Elsewhere even more ambitious decorations would not incur such censure. An advertisement in the *Maryland Gazette* for January 6th, 1774, suggests that people there could be more free with their money.

To the Ladies and Gentlemen, Samuel Rusbatch, late pupil to Robert Maberly, Esq., coach and herald painter; and varnisher to their majesties and the royal family; proposeth (under the direction of Joseph Horatio Anderson, architect in Annapolis) to carry on all the various branches of coach and herald painting, varnishing and guilding; as well plain as in the most decorated taste. Also painting in fresco, cire-obscuro, decorated ceilings for halls, vestibules, and saloons, either in festoons of fruits, flowers, figures, or trophies. Carved ornaments in deception, guilding and burnishing in the neatest manner, as well house-painting in distemper as dead whites, as in the common colours, &c. . . .

Almost exactly eight years earlier, on January 21st, 1766, the *South Carolina Gazette* printed the notice that Mr. Warwell had arrived from London with the intention of settling in Charleston,

. . . he paints History Pieces, Altar Pieces, Landscapes, Sea Pieces, Flowers, Fruit, Heraldry, Coaches, Window blinds, chimney blinds, Skreens, Gilding. Pictures copied, cleaned or mended. Rooms painted in Oil or Water in a new Taste. Deceptive Temples, Triumphal arches, Obelisks, Statues, &c., for Groves or Gardens.

Within eighteen months he was dead: his widow was asking a settlement of accounts and seeking opportunities to mend china. It is doubtful if even the free-spending Charlestonians saw fit to avail themselves of all his skills, but gardens ornamented with those deceptions fast weathering into shabbiness would have been something to see.

In other parts of the country artisan painters were engaged in less ambitious schemes, such as stenciling repeating patterns on walls or floors or simply pasting up the square sheets of the newly imported and soon fashionable

. . . stained paper for rooms, in the Gothic and Chinese Taste; beautiful Painted Landscapes. . . .

But two instances of ambitious house decoration worthy of the unfortunate Mr. Warwell are still preserved.

One is a carved and paneled room [American Wing, Metropolitan Museum, New York] removed from "Marmion," a colonial plantation mansion in Virginia. Woodwork and decorations were installed in the eighteenth century, although the house was older. Five main panels are decorated with varied arrangements of fruits and flowers in baskets and in one cornucopia; below these are dados with painted garlands of leaves imposed upon a ground of brown mottled in imitation of veined marble. All this painting is in colors which remain predominantly light enough in tone to establish a mood of moderate gayety. In such a strong contrast of heavily handled pigment as to suggest a different man at work, perhaps at a slightly later date, are four pictorial panels which irregularly intersperse the others: a small horizontal *Storm at Sea* over the door, a rather large and almost square *Landscape with Windmill and Figures* over the fireplace, and two larger matching uprights of anecdotal subjects. Possibly the human actions depicted in the last two had some meaning for those who lived in the house; if so, it seems irrecoverable now. In strictly pictorial terms there is little pleasure in this elaborate room; but it is historically eloquent testimony to a vanished mode of living and vividly documents that phase of Virginian society which came nearest to being "cavalier."

In Portsmouth, New Hampshire, the stately Warner house contains a series of wall paintings, "several hundred square feet" in area, covering the entire stairway end of the central hall from first to second story. They were discovered under four layers of wallpaper in the eighteen-sixties; and unlike the panels from "Marmion," their varied story content is fairly clear. One scene is straight anecdote: an eagle snatching a chicken in spite of an attacking dog in the presence of a woman spinning. Another is straight secular history: Sir William Pepperell on horseback at the siege of Louisburg in 1745—this design apparently taken from a cast-iron fireback of the time. A third is straight religious history: Abraham about to sacrifice Isaac with a dramatic sweep of his sword and being halted by an angel gesturing out of a satisfactorily substantial cloud. The fourth is a formally balanced design surrounding a large window: a painted canopy over the window extends into painted draperies which lead the eye on either side to the figure of a well known Amerind chief, both figures being adapted from (probably prints of) portraits by Simon Verelst in London [1709–1710]. All this was visual splendor indeed even for the house of a merchant rich enough to marry the daughter of a lieutenant-governor; but it may have actually been installed by his son-in-law, whose own importance was sufficient to cause the house to be called by his name instead of by that of his father-in-law who built it.

28. The beginning of West's influence

Abraham Delanoy the Younger: c. 1740–c. 1790
Matthew Pratt: 1734–1805 (work from 1768 to 1775)
Charles Willson Peale: 1741–1827 (work from 1769 to 1776)
Henry Benbridge: 1744–?1812

The younger Abraham Delanoy was the first painter on record who tried to capitalize upon having been a pupil of West in London; several unfavorable circumstances combined to keep him from attaining high professional rank. Among these factors the most important was his own mediocrity of technical competence; at least the *Benjamin West* [1766: New-York Historical Society, New York], which he executed in London, exhibits no distinguished, hardly even any distinctive, handling. In passages of modeling which should have presented no particular difficulty Delanoy resorted to an evasiveness which reveals his inability to render form. Since it was after Delanoy's return that New Yorkers paid Copley higher prices than the Bostonians had to pay, it would seem that they wanted better work than Delanoy could give. For a living he fell back on the usual device of a shop; and among his miscellaneous goods, imported food and drink predominated over supplies for writing and sewing. Dunlap's first attempt in oil was done as a favor to Delanoy, who was still painting signs when he could get orders for them, although he was a sick man, already old at fifty. His share in the transmission of influence from West was little more than the accident of beginning it.

Probably Matthew Pratt had preceded Delanoy to London and West; along with West's own father, Pratt had accompanied his relation, Miss Shewell, on her way to marry West in 1764. Four years older than West, Pratt nevertheless studied under him for two and one-half years and then worked independently in Bristol for eighteen months longer before returning home. The pictures he is known to have brought back with him afford a curiously comprehensive forecast of the ways in which West's influence upon American painting was to be effectively manifested through later pupils.

Portraits there were, of course; and though it was not portraiture which either West or his pupils wished to be pre-eminent in this country, that branch of painting was, through the earlier London years, the mainstay of West himself.

The portraits of Delanoy and Pratt had in common a general blandness of aspect which points to their common source; but Pratt was superior in his grasp upon form and in his personal colorism which occasionally, in cool and subtle blues and greens, rose to distinction. The *Self-Portrait* [c. 1765: Pennsylvania Academy, Philadelphia] is alone sufficient to waken admiration for his painting and affection for his personality; it sets down a sensitive mind that has enough humor to escape the pomposity of egotism and enough reticence to choose quiet and dignity for himself as well as for his work. This is exactly the individual whom Charles Willson Peale described as "a mild and friendly man, not ambitious to distinguish himself." Any unaggressive individual with a taste for simply watching American life must have then seemed quite as odd as he does today; yet such a mind's function in civilization must always be estimated by values less obvious than those of ambition and career.

The pictures other than portraits which Pratt brought back with him show that West inculcated on his colonial pupils the same ideas about the supremacy of history painting which his later pupils would attempt to promulgate throughout the new nation. In London Pratt had copied mythological subjects by Guido Reni and by West; he even copied a copy by West of a Correggio—a religious subject, this. Probably more interesting to present-day taste and perhaps historically influential upon subsequent American work was the now lost *Still-life* which Pratt exhibited in London in 1765; this or a similar picture Pratt advertised for sale in Williamsburg in 1773. But still existing is *The American School* [1765: plate 27], which tells more about Pratt's mind than the copies or the portraits and in so doing points up the serious loss to American painting when the only outlet that contemporaneous taste permitted to his authentic talent for design proved to be sign painting.

Not that the picture of West and his students in the studio is a masterpiece, but to the coloristic charm and restrained treatment which are so attractive in some of the portraits it adds a partially achieved intention of making a picture out of the space that contains the figures. West stands at the left commenting upon a drawing being shown him by Pratt, who is seated; across to the right another pupil, still unidentified, is seated so that his profile is strongly relieved by the nearly blank canvas alongside; and in the center background are two additional and more youthful pupils. The remarkable thing about all this is not what they are doing, though they are intelligibly unified in this respect; nor is it their likenesses in the sense of portraiture, though they were recognizable enough to those who knew them. The remarkable thing is the way in which everything else is clearly subordinated to a purely pictorial problem; every line and every modification of tone jointly converge, and with a pretty well managed regularity of recession, upon the head most distant from the eye. The legs are visually assertive, both because of the current fashion of knee-breeches and light-colored stockings and because they all direct the eye up to the level where depth is most emphasized. This also determines the awkward pose of West and the way in which the student seated opposite holds his brushes. In the central depth of the picture the acute angle of vision established by the brushes is joined by the graceful shallow curve of the row of heads receding from the left. It was apparently the necessity of keeping his own head in place along this all important curve that caused Pratt to make his own torso too long; but there is also a total inconsistency of scale between his figure and the others. The least successful part of the whole picture is the handling of the right-hand stretch of wall, but there is a compensating sureness in the control exerted over the lines of the table at the center. The boyish figure serving as the focal point for everything else, though the lower part of his bent arm is incorrectly drawn, is otherwise rendered with technical mastery sufficient to hold the eye as a satisfactory goal for the elaborately organized design. The provincial imperfections of the painting matter very little in comparison to the rare thoughtfulness of mind from which the picture came.

The thoughtfulness in Pratt was not accompanied by the intellectual power manifested in Copley; he did not feel compelled to push ahead from this ambitious beginning in defiance of the lack of a market for such attempts. From his known character it is doubtful that he thought of himself as tragically defeated by circumstances, but it is surely one of the tragedies of American painting that circumstances repressed a talent which even at the outset was so individual and genial. For its own time, this ambitious picture was a history piece. Yet it has no allegorical, or mythological, or religious theme. It is not an actual event of consequence to mankind in general which the authentic grand style demands. The likenesses seem to be consciously slighted; the element of portraiture is in fact so minimized that the picture cannot be termed a conversation piece—and another reason for refusing this description is its obviously formal, not to say stiff, arrangement. Pratt's mind was at work with singular directness and simplicity upon the complex problem of rendering a series of forms in space. Its failure to disguise the problem with a more fluent naturalistic accuracy is far less important than the occurrence of so abstract a concept in the mind of an American painter. Pratt found his occasion in what lay nearest at hand; his imaginativeness consisted in imposing upon that casual material a visually interesting formal organization. It escapes the usual labels because it comes so near to being purely pictorial.

Pratt brought *The American School* home with him in 1768, and in April of the following year the *Virginia Gazette* recorded the arrival there of another history piece which, in its total contrast, marked the other extreme of West's

27. THE AMERICAN SCHOOL *by* MATTHEW PRATT *Courtesy of The Metropolitan Museum of Art.*

range of influence. It was Charles Willson Peale's large combination of portrait and allegory wherein the British defender of the American colonies, William Pitt, draped in a Roman toga, was officiating at the altar of liberty. Standing in front of a vaguely Roman column, he pointed across the altar-flame toward a vaguely French statue; some distance behind was the recognizable palace of Whitehall, intended as a reminder of Charles the First's execution for repressing liberty. From Peale's explanation printed to accompany his own mezzotint reproduction the complex symbolism may be learned item by item; and it is essentially an American speech upon the current political situation which remains outlined in the words and does not speak out in visual terms from the painting or the print. Both the unpictorial ideas and the futile gigantism of their attempted embodiment were even more prominent in West's teaching than the everyday subject and contemporaneous costume in Pratt's earlier production.

Peale made his original picture eight feet high; he also made a replica only slightly smaller, with a few minor changes; and he further executed the reproductive plate nearly two feet high—all toward the end of his two-year stay with West. Throughout that time he had shown himself a miracle of industry by improving his oil and miniature technique and by acquiring other crafts: engraving in mezzotint (as noted), painting in water color on paper, modeling (presumably in clay), and making casts in plaster. For practice work he had made the inevitable copies of other men's history pieces; he had also both copied portraits and painted them from life to support himself through his studies.

Upon his return home by the middle of 1769 Peale kept right on with the busyness which characterized his entire life. Since his prints did not sell very fast, he sought portrait work on trips both southward and northward from Annapolis. The most famous picture of these years was an official effigy rather than a portrait—the *George Washington* [1772: Washington and Lee University] showing the subject in militia uniform. The rigid and uninteresting countenance does not adequately dominate the blue and scarlet coat, the prominent sash of plum color, and the gleam of metal buttons, silver gorget, and gold braid. For a group portrait done in Maryland, Peale was not paid as promptly as he would have liked, and he resorted to the curious device of threatening to publish and then publishing the delinquent's name in the *Maryland Gazette;* the following week, September 22nd, 1774, the debtor replied in a similar advertisement: "YES, YOU SHALL BE PAID; BUT NOT BEFORE YOU HAVE LEARNED TO BE LESS INSOLENT." Another curious incident of this period was his depiction of his wife mourning over a baby lying dead before her—a very satisfactory piece of painting but a picture which his wife naturally could not well endure; he therefore kept it in the studio covered by a curtain, but always showed it on request. The dilatory debtor may have been displeased with his picture, for its composition is not a success; but there was apparently entire approval at Mount Vernon, where that first of the many Peale portraits of Washington hung for twenty-seven years.

And the busy painter was certainly giving satisfaction generally in his many commissions. Like Smibert and Wollaston before him, he received poetic tributes in print. In the *Maryland Gazette* for April 18th, 1771, appeared four stanzas in praise of a portrait by Peale of his own wife; the last stanza was:

> Give me, depictur'd warm from Life
> Each soft Emotion of the mind;
> Give me the Mother and the Wife,
> As here in beauteous Arria join'd.

Both the different meter and the altered sentiment suggest the change that was actually going on in life from the somewhat stilted provincial courtliness of the eighteenth century to the bourgeois homeliness of the nineteenth; and the pronunciation indicated by properly rhyming the final word is an amusing reminder of how artificial at times cultural propriety can be. An almost comic reiteration of that came about seven months later in the same paper in a tribute to the portrait of an actress, Miss Sarah Hallman:

> In this, Oh Peale, both excellancies join;
> Venetian colors and the Greek design.

The intention behind such public testimonials was gratifying, no doubt, but for enough paying patrons Peale had to keep traveling; and in Philadelphia he found such substantial encouragement that eventually, in 1776, he settled there permanently. From that city in 1772 he wrote a friend:

My reputation is greatly increased by a Number of New Yorkers haveing been here, who have given me the character of being the best painter of America—that I paint more certain and handsomer Likenesses than Copley. What more could I wish? I am glad I can please. But, Sir, how far short of that excellence of some painters, infinately below that perfection that even portrait Painting may be carried to. My enthusiastac mind forms some Idea of it, but I have not the Execution, have not the abilitys, nor am I a Master of Drawing. What little I do is by mear imitation of what is before me. Perhaps I have a good eye, that is all, and not half the application that I now think is necessary. A good painter of either portrait or History, must be well acquainted with the Greesian and Roman Statues, to be able to draw them at pleasure by memory, and account for every beauty, must know the original cause of beauty in all he sees. These are some of the requisites of a good painter. These are more than I shall ever have time or opportunity to know, but as I have variety of Characters to paint I must as Rembrandt did make these my Anticks [antiques], and improve myself as well as I can while I am providing for my support.

The ideas there set down about what a good painter must know and do are straight out of West as well as the accepted handbooks of the time. But not from West or anyone else did Peale have to learn that likable humility or that resolute will to adjust himself ungrudgingly to circumstances; those traits were consistently manifested throughout a long life by a man of remarkable goodness.

Delanoy, Pratt and this first of the Peales constituted the pre-Revolutionary group of West's pupils; their bringing back his teaching to this country did not do very much to spread his ideas among other painters, for the reason that work and association both were so seriously impaired by wartime conditions. Perhaps, also, since they were West's own exact contemporaries, their main indebtedness to West was technical rather than mental; complete belief in the artistic gospel according to West waited upon pupils young enough to be disciples.

Another American-born painter, Henry Benbridge, came back in 1770 after six years abroad; and though he never studied under West, he was indoctrinated with the same ideas and equipped with the same technique through having studied with West's own teachers in Italy—Antony Raphael Mengs and Pompeo Girolamo Batoni. In Philadelphia his mother and step-father had encouraged his fondness for painting, and when about seventeen he had painted their entire home—rooms and halls, even the ceilings—with life-sized figures copied and adapted from prints, including those after Raphael's cartoons. In Italy he became acquainted with prominent English visitors, was amusingly caricatured by the famous Thomas Patch, and was selected by the already well known James Boswell to visit the island of Corsica and paint his friend General Pascal Paoli. As a result of that commission Benbridge received considerable notice in London, and for a time had so much work that he debated staying there for his career. But back he came, to experience the same hindrances as the others through troubled times; and in the circumstances, as he journeyed back and forth between Philadelphia and Charleston, he was successful. At least he was able to execute a few ambitiously designed groups in addition to the usual bust portraits. Most of his work has fallen into poor condition; even that fails to obliterate his solid draftsmanship, though it does make it difficult to form a satisfactory general judgement on his color. Fraser, the Charleston miniaturist, censured his shadows for being opaque; but it is an indication of his competence that he could use shadows so effectively in clarifying his design in the groups. Such pictures by him are more interesting when on a scale much smaller than life; *The Saltar Family* [1781: privately owned] affords one of the best instances of what the historian-critic Tuckerman called "a singularly formal aspect," which now assumes the aspect of pictorial organization—something more important than likeness. Benbridge's mind was thoroughly academic, and less than first-rate of the kind; but at that stage in the development of American painting it was so desirable for the training of younger men that the thwarting of it by external circumstances was unfortunate for more than himself. He had few pupils, Thomas Sully being one for a very short while, and his long obscurity has been undeserved.

29. Retrospect from the year 1775

Holt and Gains: act. 1772
John Winter: act. 1771

The most significant development in painting through this wonderful half-century of colonial culmination was clearly the stamp put upon it by the emergence of a privileged class at the top of society; the taste of that class was consciously exerted in accordance with its own conception of fashionable taste in England. In response, there came to the colonies a group of studio-trained specialists who, though varying widely in their individual degrees of skill, persuaded their American patrons that they could supply them with the most fashionable manner in portraiture. However, not enough of the foreign-born specialists came to satisfy the quantitative needs of the wealthy; in consequence it was often necessary to call upon men whose training on the artisan level prevented them from making portraits technically as sophisticated as those of the others. The initial training of the native-born came sometimes from the studio men and sometimes from the artisans; the average of innate capacity in the native-born kept the bulk of their work upon the technical level of artisan and amateur craft. The exceptions were as striking in quality as they were few in number: Pratt, with his subtle tastefulness; Feke, with his talent; and Copley, with his genius.

The prevailing preference of the well-to-do for incoming foreigners and for such natives as could best ape the foreigners' manners was only an American repetition of a long-established European habit. Fashionable Flemings in the sixteenth century and fashionable French in the seventeenth preferred Italians or Italian-trained natives of their respective countries; the Spanish court drew in the Italians at one time and at another the Flemings; and English portrait buyers had, ever since the days of Henry the Eighth, exalted Germans and Flemings and Italians and French—painters of any nationality except their own. With the American colonials, as in the earlier instances, it was less a matter of esthetic discrimination than a simple desire to consolidate a newly won position, social or cultural or both together. It was the specific business of the foreigner to confer an air, even a glamour, above and beyond the day-by-day circumstances of living. If that air required the unreality of being depicted in too costly clothes and unowned jewelry, it did not amount to outright self-deception; the patron accepted such things, and the painter included them, as part of professional good manners.

There is, however, another aspect to this general use of formula which presents a question more intimately involving the painter's professional conscience. A half dozen or more of the pre-Revolutionary portraitists, visitors and natives both, occasionally indulged themselves in such thorough-going repetitions from canvas to canvas that, except for the heads, they were literally replicas. If this had occurred every time, as it did sometimes, several years apart and in different places, it might now appear to have been a species of dishonesty. But it also occurred in circumstances where the portrait buyers themselves must have known about it at the time; it can therefore be interpreted as at least an occasionally acceptable procedure. There was British precedent for this, too. Walpole says that when J. B. Medina went to Scotland "He took with him a number of bodies and postures to which he painted heads." It is also known that in this country after the Revolution the practice was for two generations fairly widespread among itinerants. With English precedent and with American consequences, therefore, it seems fairly certain that some among the painters of the period confronted would-be patrons with prepared canvases from which the purchaser chose the dummy he or she wanted posterity to believe in. They and their families and their friends were all aware that what they bought was a fiction agreed upon; and though the fiction involved obvious irrealities, its social value at the time was quite real. By way of comment on such an open, even genial, habit of agreeing to falsify, a later student of life and art can only quote Samuel Butler: "I don't mind lying, but I hate inaccuracy."

However extensive the inaccuracies of colonial portraiture, one thing the painters were unable to lie about was the middle-class character of the subjects. There exists in every generation, of course, something often called a natural aristocracy of intelligence, which is simply a way of describing the mental ability of the individual; and though colonial Americans displayed it in plenty, it would be silly to confuse that with the long-standing European definition of aristocracy by birth and breeding. Neither Franklin, as one instance of outstanding mental capacity, nor Copley, as another, was an aristocrat in origin or in achieved position; and while they could doubtless have had considerable success in England had they been born there, they had one great advantage in the newly forming American society that their abilities could win for them a place of influence more nearly commensurate with their actual worth.

Yet every middle-class society has large areas of philistinism; and just as colonial portraiture in general was philistine in its emulation of portraiture executed for a different class under different conditions, so other colonial activities made the same incorrect emphasis in cultural matters. The theme of cultural independence awoke in the American consciousness along with that of political freedom, and quickly came to a head in the commencement address at Yale in 1770 by a precocious scholar and rhymer, John Trumbull, the younger cousin of the painter. After claiming that Americans excel in natural genius, though few are free to devote themselves to study, he noted a widespread middle degree of knowledge corresponding to the prevalent middle degree of prosperity. He next advanced to the only ground then possible for anyone searching for some native quality in literature—prophecy; and with colonial inevitability he conceived of future writers as doing again what had been done.

> This land her Steele and Addison shall view,
> The former glories equall'd by the new;
> Some future Shakespeare charm the rising age,
> And hold in magic chains the list'ning stage;
> Another Watts shall string the heav'nly lyre,
> And other Muses other bards inspire.

This is a very handy and comprehensive instance of the labeling which was one persistent symptom of the cultural colonialism consequent upon being colonies in fact. As such it was as fully American in character as any other trait produced by the interaction of inheritance and environment. For the time being, the narrower thing which may be called nativism was, in literature, nothing but a hope—something to talk about. Usually there must be a great deal of talk to stimulate people to the point of acting, and on this theme the talk began a good half-century before Emerson was able to announce the approaching end of colonial discipleship. Meanwhile, a strong new-world nativism had already been achieved in portraiture, along with the conscious repetition of old-world fashion; but the present-day natural tendency to find a special value for national identity in the nativism should not obliterate the historical and cultural validity of colonialism.

It was in a fashionably imitative spirit that picture collecting was begun here—collecting defined as not the accumulation of family portraits but the purchase of pictures for their own sake or for the sake of the famous names attached to them. The already-formed collections brought over by Smibert and Watson were a different matter; Smibert's was mainly professional equipment for the teaching that never materialized, and Watson's was part of the windfall of an inheritance. The second William Byrd had a taste for more than family portraits, and, in addition to some of these by Kneller and Bridges, he put upon the walls at Westover canvases bearing the names of Titian and Rubens; but they must have been hardly more than mementoes of his years in England, for he did not continue collecting such paintings through his years

in Virginia. Some Bostonians purchased copies by Smibert, and probably copies
by others; the most interesting item of this sort is mentioned in a letter to
Copley from the rector of King's Chapel, Boston, in which the minister argues
that a painting he owns is, contrary to Copley's opinion, a genuine Leonardo.
In New York, by the late seventeen-seventies, the old Duch paintings were
already unfashionable; they were being rescued from garrets there and offered
for sale in Philadelphia. And as early as 1772 paintings recognized as dubious
at the time were being offered to collectors; someone unknown inserted an
advertisement in the *New York Journal* for January 9th ridiculing a collection
of pictures supposedly imported from England by one Holt and strongly implying a hoax in which "your neighbor Gains" had a hand. Just six months earlier
in Philadelphia John Winter had once more offered his artisan skill as he had
done when associated with Gustavus Hesselius in 1740; but in 1771 he also
offered for sale a portrait of Mary Queen of Scots copied from Holbein, landscapes in the manner of Poussin, and six small landscapes as originals by Zuc-
carelli, a well known Italian at work in London.

Philadelphia was indeed a center of collecting as it was of versifying. By
1771 the pictures in the houses of the rich were of sufficient repute for Copley
to make an excursion from New York to see them; in a letter to his half-brother,
he described only two in any detail, but he promised a full account (with a
sketch of one) on his return. These and other references mention that Doctor
John Morgan had an original Angelica Kauffman and several copies; that Chief
Justice Allen had notable copies after Titian and Annibale Carracci, and that
his supposedly original Murillo had been captured from a Spanish vessel in the
seventeen-forties. No doubt oil copies were better than engravings as a second-
hand experience of the old masters, but the taste that sanctioned those copies
tolerated nothing but portraits from living Americans. The American painters
who got to see the copies were properly grateful, but such collections did no
more for their support than the couplets of Thomas Godfrey's *Court of Fancy*
[1762], in which he personified Painting.

> At her creative touch gay fictions glow,
> Bright Tulips bloom, and op'ning Roses blow.
> The canvas see, what pleasing prospects rise!
> What varying Beauty strikes our wond'ring eyes!
> Chill'd Winter's wastes, or Spring's delightful green,
> Hot Summer's pride, or Autumn's yellow scene;
> Here lawns are spread, there tow'ring forests wave,
> The heights we fear, or wish the cooling lave.

Though this could have been put together from a knowledge merely bookish,
it may have owed something to Dutch originals; quartets of the seasons were

so common that a set of them might well have found their way to Philadelphia and would there have been accessible to Godfrey as another protégé of Provost Smith, along with Francis Hopkinson and Benjamin West.

But only by such special persons, beyond the owners and their friends, could the paintings be seen—originals, copies, or portraits; for most Americans who liked paintings, esthetic experience was still confined to the streets and taverns. From the vantage point of today that seems to be inadequate nourishment; but it is humanly probable that even such thin pictorial diet gave a pleasure which, however far short it fell of the self-consciousness almost inseparable from our present awareness of art, was yet conscious. But thoughts about that aspect of colonial life must be almost as speculative as the thoughts of colonial Americans were about our own time—and they did occasionally venture so far into what was their future. From the 1758 almanac of Nathaniel Ames comes the following:

O! Ye unborn Inhabitants of America! Should this Page escape its destin'd Conflagration at the Year's end, and these Alphabetical Letters remain legible, when your Eyes behold the Sun after he has rolled the Seasons round for two or three Centuries more, you will know that in Anno Domini 1758, we dream'd of your Times.

PERIOD ONE
THE COLONIAL

DIVISION THREE
Revolutionary Transition—
1775 to 1790

30. The disruption of the upper class

Thomas Spence Duché: 1763–1790
Mather Brown: 1761–1831

The Revolutionary Transition interrupted all the arts and crafts. Motivated by the spirit and aims of the Revolution itself, some writers could go on writing; some could even write better under the pressure of current passions than before or afterward. But people would not begin building fine houses while such houses were frequently looted or destroyed. The craftsmen themselves, too, were likely to be off fighting in the army. Even the established art of portraiture would decline through a time when few were tranquil enough to sit and when many who had inherited portraits perforce left them behind in seeking their own safety. The division of loyalties caused by the Revolution cut deepest and most disastrously through the very class that had given life to portraiture, and that seemed likeliest to extend their patronage to other forms of painting.

Among the painters themselves the question of which side to take did not often rise to the level of moral or even political conviction. In a professional position too valuable to be risked, West remained on good terms with both sides. Copley, despite Tory connections, could share the revolutionaries' ideas up to a certain point; but what they were doing blasted his American career, and left no place but London adequate to the maturity of his art and the ambitiousness of his aim. Almost the only painter who was royalist from conviction was Copley's half-brother, Henry Pelham; and though his leaving may be counted as a loss to American painting, it was no gain for British painting, since he made no outstanding contribution there before his accidental death by drowning. A few more American-born painters avoided the Revolution by staying in London primarily for personal convenience.

Young Thomas Spence Duché was taken there by his minister-father, who was to prove a double turncoat later on; after a brief pupilage under West the youth showed sufficient promise before his early death for him to be remembered as one of the might-have-beens on the edge of history. His obituary in *The Times* (London) for April 2nd, 1790, may be quoted as a partial prophecy of a development in British painting in which later Americans were to be prominent:

The death of Mr. Duché is the more to be regretted, because from the elegance and correctness of his mind he attached himself chiefly to moral and sentimental compositions, subjects hitherto little handled by artists of the English school, and which, if treated with ability, could not fail to promote the best purposes of painting.

Had he lived, young Duché could have accompanied his father upon that ignoble return to Philadelphia and thus become an American for the record rather than the British school-man.

Mather Brown made himself even more completely part of British painting through a half-century of careless living and fluctuating workmanship. His was a semi-Bohemian career on the fringes of worldly greatness which no second-rate talent could have managed in this country; here such painters inevitably declined into the shabby makeshifts which incurred the censure of anxiously respectable Dunlap. Brown made no secret of the fact that his motive for staying in London was to avoid army service.

Gilbert Stuart too, it seems clear without documentation, liked things better where there was no fighting to be done. But Stuart's independent painting career even in England did not begin until the war was over, and the outstanding achievements of Americans in painting through the Revolutionary years were those of West and Copley. It is worth emphasizing that although the scene was London and although their work had even stronger effects upon European painting than upon painting in the United States, both Copley and West thought of themselves and were thought of by everybody else as Americans.

31. Benjamin West in London

Benjamin West: 1738–1820 (work after 1760)

Like many other youths with artistic talent, West could absorb influences rapidly. In Philadelphia, he had temporarily imitated Wollaston; but Wollaston's formula was too limited to take any youngster very far, and if West had remained here he would have been compelled to teach himself. This possibility of another authentically colonial mind developing in painting vanished when West went to Rome at the age of twenty-two. Rome was the artistic capital of Europe at the time, swarming with religious pilgrims and culture-seeking tourists. It was in Rome that the entire academic tradition, inherited through five generations since the death of the Carracci, was then concentrated; and the current godlets of painting were Antony Raphael Mengs and Pompeo Girolamo Batoni. Italian Batoni's influence was exerted mainly through direct teaching of pupils; German Mengs was even more important as a theoretician, and in a sense he became the academic ultimate through his compendious codification of the "laws" of painting. What no Roman would have admitted was that the only living Italians in whom the art of painting was still alive were in Venice; Tiepolo was to die within the decade, but Guardi was to stay on until near the close of the century. West was already too solemn by nature and inelastic in temperament to respond to their seeming frivolity in paint; and in his lifetime of practising the "sublime" West remained too trivial in mind ever to recognize the superior artistic seriousness of their brilliance and grace.

In Rome, West was the boy wonder from the new world, just as in Philadelphia he had been the boy wonder from the country. His initial success came from his likeable naïvety; Roman sophisticates could condescend with unalloyed pleasure to such remarks as that about the *Apollo Belvedere*—"How like a Mohawk warrior!" But the "young savage" maintained the interest in him by his capacity for absorbing academic precepts in double-quick time. Though Meng's formulations of the rules were not yet in print, young West in Rome had them straight from the teacher. They were systematized under several headings: drawing, chiaroscuro, color, composition, drapery, harmony; these elements of picturemaking were then described in the treatments they received from the greatest masters: Raphael, Correggio, Titian, and the Ancients. In this complex exposition the possible variations were so numerous that they left the student free to do almost anything he might wish, so long as he combined pictorial quotations. How mechanical the process was may be illustrated by just one of the rules: if the outer side of the right hand is shown, the inner side of the left must also be shown. This was simply one rule among many which were collectively concerned with the general and really important problem of securing variety in the whole; the evil lay in the minuteness with which it reduced the pictorial proprieties to a conformity entirely external.

Another evil followed: that the "connoisseurs" then current could pronounce by the book upon such minutiae of conformity. Even before West left this country the original mind of Lawrence Sterne had perceived the silliness of such "bobs and trinkets of criticism"; and in satirizing the connoisseur Sterne needed only to squeeze a little water out of the verbosities of the handbooks.

. . . 'Tis a melancholy daub! my lord; not one principle of the *pyramid* in any one group!— and what a price!— for there is nothing of the colouring of *Titian*— the expression of *Rubens*— the grace of *Raphael*— the purity of *Dominichino*— the *corregiescity* of *Corregio*— the learning of *Poussin*— the airs of *Guido*— the taste of the *Carrachis*—of the grand contour of *Angelo.* . . .

It was indeed a canting criticism thus to pelt the living with the names of the dead, but worse would be a canting art that claimed it could actually combine those qualities into pictorial unity.

Yet that is what West quite promptly set out to do and what he quite sincerely to the end believed he had done. The completeness with which he passed on to others the eclecticism he practised is indicated more vividly than anywhere else in a letter he wrote to Copley in 1773 about what should be studied in Italy:

. . . The works of the Antient Statuarys are the great original whare in the various charectors of nature are finely represented, from the soundest principles of Philosophi. What they have done in Statuary, Raphael, seems to have acquiered in painting. In him you see the fine fancey in the arraignment of his figures into groops, and those groops into a whole with that propriety and fitness to his subject, Joynd to a trouth of charector and expression, that was never surpass'd before nor sence. Michal Angilo in the knowledge and graundor of the Human figure has surpass'd all artists. his figures have the apearance of a new creation, form'd by the strength of his great amagination. in him you find all that is great in design. Corragio [surpassed even those] in the relieaf of his figures by the management of the clear obscure. The prodigious management in foreshortning of figures seen in the air, The greacefull smiles and turnes of heads, The magickcal uniteing of his Tints, The incensable blending of lights into Shades, and the beautyfull affect over the whole arrising from thoss pices of management, is what charmes the eye of every beholder. Titian gave the Human figure that trouth of colour which surpass'd all other painters. . . .

As counsel about what to look at, that has considerable validity for any student in Italy; the good or the harm it may do depends upon how the student uses what he learns. West's own mind was not only assimilative but remarkably tenacious as well; his memory, aided by a large collection of copies and prints and (in time) originals, became an anthology of poses and groupings upon which he could effortlessly draw in devising an endless series of enormous tableaux of subjects out of all history, sacred and profane.

Upon his arrival in England it was precisely this readiness which earned his initial favor with George the Third and which kept him in royal favor until the eclipse of the king's mind almost forty years later. It was the Archbishop of York who introduced West to the king; and when the king read aloud to West a passage from Livy as a subject which would make a fine picture, West responded at once with a sketch for *The Departure of Regulus from Rome.* By the completion of the picture, West and the king were firm friends; the king gave him a pension, paid him extra for many paintings, and left West free to accept other commissions as he saw fit. It was this royal favor which, in Dunlap's undemocratic words, "placed Benjamin West on the throne of English art." It was this alone which gave West both money and fame in a London where, with an equal personal devotion to the idea of history painting, John Hamilton Mortimer had failed, Henry Fuseli was not succeeding, and Benjamin Robert Haydon would later commit suicide. This was the natural consequence of the fact that the king almost alone had at his disposal sufficient wall space for placing such canvas epics—West's own nature prevented them from being epic canvases. George the Third wished to re-introduce pictures as churchly adornments; fearful of offending Protestant precedent, he consulted some dignitaries of the Church of England, who collectively assured him that no laws or usages would be violated provided His Majesty confined them to his own chapel. West obliged with designs for thirty-six pictures dealing with *The Progress of Revealed Religion,* half from the Old Testament and half from the New. Twenty-eight were executed before the king's insanity gave the queen her chance to cancel the project; and by then West had received nearly twenty-two thousand pounds on that one commission alone. On another occasion the king had the idea of decorating Saint George's Hall at Windsor with a series about Edward the Third; the eight large paintings for this location were completed by West and put in place. But all of these are gone; the Prince Regent, even before he began to reign as George the Fourth, disposed of them in derision.

The execution of such projects alone, to say nothing of the other commissions which West undertook, required a manufacturing plant, and that is just the establishment over which West presided. In theory it was a workshop or atelier on the Renaissance model: an organization which could be vitalized only by a first-rate mind like Verrocchio or Rubens. West's facility for synthetic quotation allowed his own sketches to come easily; these were then enlarged by student assistants; and at the last the Master placidly and industriously applied his "finishing" touches to the plaster-cast edges and the robes of harsh blues and greens and reds that almost never commingled into harmonious tone. The king's white elephants have vanished, but their progeny remains: *Christ Healing the Sick* [c. 1811: Pennsylvania Hospital, Philadelphia] and *Christ Rejected* [1814: Pennsylvania Academy, Philadelphia]. The popular plaudits for these monstrosities of moralism were re-enforced by pamphlets which expounded their narrative and symbolical complications and designated the emotions which should be felt for this or for that. Such aids to the audience's intellects and emotions were rendered necessary by West's central dogma itself: ". . . the true use of painting resides in assisting the reason to arrive at certain moral inferences by furnishing a probable view of the effects of motives and passions." The pamphlet for *Christ Healing the Sick* runs to fourteen pages of close print; one composed for *Christ Rejected* runs to thirteen, and also uses a diagram which does not correspond to the design of the picture but gives a schematic view of the proper emotions—Caiaphas being "The strongest paroxysm of Envy & Rage" and so on through the cast of characters.

The artistic fatality consequent upon all this can be more compactly demonstrated by one more citation. A picture by West now lost survives as one of a group of outline engravings by Henry Moses, published as a book in London in 1811—*Caesar's Regret While Reading the Life of Alexander*. The Dictator-Consul is shown, not actually reading, but in the company of two men; and the text explains that Caesar, bald from libertinism and voluptuousness, is expressing regret at wasting his youth while Alexander during the same span of life was conquering the world. This instance of West's conception of a "probable view" is truthfully described; but as Boileau wrote, "There are times when truth seems hardly probable." Once people had taken their profit from such verbal instructions, the canvases ascended into the limbo of pictorial illegibility from which there is "no resurrection in the minds of men."

In view of the fact that West all his life followed the academic rules of composition and coloring and drawing, it seems at first glance curious that Joel Barlow's *Vision of Columbus* should have praised him for going beyond the rules.

> See, West with glowing life the canvass warms,
> His sovereign hand creates impassion'd forms,
> Spurns the cold critic rules, to seize the heart,
> And boldly bursts the former bounds of art.

There is no irony here, and Barlow was not just a literary man misunderstanding painting. The whole age thought that a synthetic re-arrangement of familiar pictorial elements could be in itself a piece of imaginative daring. It was the prevalence of this conception which permitted Francis Hopkinson's few lines of praise for West to be prophetic. The praise swelled from Philadelphia to Rome, from Rome to London, from London through the occident. When the king's mind went into eclipse, the middle-class masses took his place; and when their paid admissions began to dwindle, West himself was safe in an old man's self-delusions. Thirteen years before West died Joseph Farington, whose diaries instead of his paintings have proved to be his real legacy, was noting how West publicly claimed to have started the British Institution: ". . . To such lengths does West's self-love carry Him,—to expose Himself to be confuted by many." Beginning with Dunlap, many writers have found fault with John Galt's biography of West for its fantastic stories, but one and all have failed to grant that Galt was nothing but an amanuensis for West. West was the fabulist, and the fact that he believed the fables was reason enough for Galt to record them. But the reputation built up to that preposterous climax was bound to collapse; and the collapse was swift. William Hazlitt, whose recognition for the genuine in life and literature and art was inevitably accompanied by an intolerance for sham, was the first mind of consequence to point out the technical commonplaceness and spiritual emptiness of West's most admired works. It was Hazlitt who had the wit to say that West was great only "by the acre"; and even while the *Christ Rejected* was attracting its greatest crowds, Hazlitt spoke out clear and true. He rejected it. Byron's phrase, "dotard West," which was printed in Philadelphia fifteen years before it was printed in London, had in it all the careless savagery of brilliant youth. And in 1827 the British sophisticate, Mrs. Basil Hall, affirming the newest London opinions in Philadelphia, found the *Christ Healing the Sick* appropriate to its location but in itself just another of West's "disagreeable daubs."

A general judgement based upon the whole of West's work must be a general censure. It is to be remembered that West, with the help of three generations of students whose training consisted largely of hack work around the premises, put out more than three thousand canvases, and that a shockingly large proportion of them were gigantic factory products. This quantitative aspect of West's work was naturally a reason for praise from those who were already disposed to praise. Dunlap records the calculation that for a simultaneous exhibition of the lot, "a gallery would be necessary four hundred feet long, fifty broad, and forty high"; and this was later translated by someone else into the more dramatic form of "a wall ten feet high, and three quarters of a mile long." In so large a production there are likely to be exceptions undeserving of censure; but if by actual count there should be a fairly large number of pictures for which good words could be spoken, that would still not invalidate the adverse verdict upon the body of work which West himself relied on to maintain his fame after death. Even among the larger pictures, however, not all were as dull as the majority, and among the preparatory sketches a higher proportion give evidence of the talent which was sporadically operating at the heart of the picture factory.

West's portraiture need not be taken seriously. To a visitor he once said: "I seldom paint portraits, and when I do, I neither please myself nor my employers." He was certainly wrong on the first point, and probably wrong on the second too. Actually he painted a great many portraits, and some of the unpretentious examples were attractively composed, but he never once penetrated below the surface to a sitter's individuality. About his portraiture there was a bland superficiality which even today is often found acceptable simply because few ask more of a portrait; its very omnipresence makes analysis futile and denunciation idle. The group portraits on the scale of life were likely to show West's worst deficiencies; being obliged to arrange actual people in front of him usually impaired his composition and he often resorted to poses and actions of ridiculous pseudo-elegance. Yet West was probably wrong in saying that he did not please his employers; why should so many have come to him for portraits? His statement is best understood as a corollary of his belief in the superiority of history painting; it was a way of saying that to be a good portraitist would be unbecoming in anyone accustomed to the "sublime."

When West's thoughts were not self-consciously grand, he could throw off—for he was an exceptionally rapid worker—sketches or small-scale pictures which are attractive in their freshness of feeling and direct execution. *Etruria* [1791: Cleveland Museum of Art], which seems to be a first idea for something larger, is of the eighteenth century in the artificiality of its idyllism; the girls spinning and weaving are not engaged in industries but in leisurely pleasures, and the most prominent lady is putting the finishing touches to a vase with no more conviction than if she were Marie Antoinette milking a cow. But the figures are well grouped and roomily spaced within the oval shape; the whole makes a pleasant decoration for a tolerant taste. But the pervasive commonplaceness of this timid rococo becomes deadly clear when compared with the genuine thing in West's contemporary, Fragonard. A more full-bodied quality can be seen in the *General Kosciusko* [1797: Allen Memorial Art Museum, Oberlin], where the hero, reclining on a window seat amid encircling furniture and heavy drapes, dramatizes a Byronic romanticism fifteen years before *Childe Harold* burst upon the world. Because this was hastily executed, some of its drawing is poorly done, but for that same reason it is consistently spirited

28. PENN'S TREATY WITH THE INDIANS *by* BENJAMIN WEST *Courtesy of The Pennsylvania Academy of the Fine Arts.*

and for West singularly coherent in design. Unfortunately it was not the example of such works which West's pupils followed out in their own; they took their cues from the more ambitious works whose range of treatment can be illustrated by two specific examples.

Penn's Treaty with the Indians [c. 1771: plate 28] is a specially successful instance of how West could stage a secular event with strict obedience to all the rules for historical composition. He made full use of the Amerinds to introduce the neo-classic figure in the guise of seemingly factual accuracy; as he had called Apollo a Mohawk, so now he disposes his Mohawks as if they were Roman statues. The seamen's colorful jackets and the Quakers' cloaks and long coats avoid stressing the contemporaneous note in costume which was said to have annoyed conservative adherents of the "grand style." Only the matter-of-fact paunchiness in the central figure of William Penn does not comply with the exactions of the school concept as to dignity and elevation above the casualness of life. At the same time West was exhibiting *The Death of Wolfe* [1771: National Gallery, Ottawa, Canada], which was long supposed to have been the painter's particular triumph in originality and to have freed the "grand style" from its bondage to the Roman toga. That is another of the biographical fables which have disintegrated under recent investigations; but the story was spread about early enough for it to have influenced some latecomers in history painting. The sources for pictorial quotation in this picture have been variously named as Raphael and Van Dyck and Rembrandt and Fuseli; but its inferiority consists in the fact that compliance with the rules was obviously the only thing with which West was actually concerned. It was West's own shallowness of mind which inflated the drama into melodrama and thinned out the sentiment to sentimentality. In *Penn's Treaty* the factualism of the incident suited his prosaic spirit, and he did not feel obligated to an emotionalism which he could assume only as an actor assumes a part. More precisely, the theme allowed West to compose in visually static terms.

Death on the Pale Horse [1817: plate 29] was in several ways a fitting climax to a career during which West was invested with the sovereignty of history painting almost as formally as he had been with the Presidency of the Royal Academy upon the death of Reynolds in 1791. The one year in thirty-one during which a rebellion in the membership kept West out of that position might have been taken to foretell his deposition from his earlier eminence. This climactic picture exists in several versions, at least three previous ones being known. The elaborate oil study [1802: Philadelphia Museum], which was exhibited at the Paris Salon of 1802, is the best in execution and also the most unified in effect; its evident derivation from Rubens hardly lessens the surprise at West's being for once so stirred by anything that he could maintain a consistent animation of brushwork through such a torrent of forms in motion. The final version was enlarged by West's son, Raphael, and such touches as a man of seventy-nine could have added probably did not erase the younger man's handiwork. Yet this was the version that awed the multitudes. Just three years after West's death the American portraitist Chester Harding, in the midst of his professional success in England, visited the pictures still being shown in the house and studio. His diary is amusing in the passage where he seems to say that he did not expect the paintings to equal his expectations; but from this example of the "awfully sublime" he shrank back in unfeigned horror—a form of enjoyment to which the cultivated were especially partial. The handbook to the pictures, which Harding surely read, stressed that the operative element in the picture was ". . . the terrible sublime and its various modifications, until lost in the opposite extremes of pity and terror. . . ." Another sentence was: "The principle of destruction is exemplified through every part of the subject . . .": and it is certainly true that the coherence of the earlier version has been destroyed. What had been a dynamic movement of mass has here been dis-unified, so that the violent gestures are only frozen poses; arms and legs, which had been the light-catching froth on the torrent, have here become separately elocutionary. Pictorially this is as rhetorical as the verbalisms of the catalog.

As Reynolds expounded, so West exemplified, the "grand style"; and both of its contrasting phases in West's work—the static classicism and the theatrical romanticism—have been considered to be influential upon the France of David and the France of Delacroix. The circulation of engravings after his paintings certainly counted for something in a time when prints still played a definite role in artistic study, and maybe his actual pictures in the Salon of 1802 arrested the eyes of some younger men. But the absence of all inner vitality from the uniform and steady output of West's picture industry, together with the failure of his direct pupils to maintain history painting as a major form of expression, would seem to eliminate West as a directly creative factor in anything. His pictures were weather vanes that indicated the wind currents in the climate of painting.

A history of painting can be only tangentially concerned with the private character of the painters, but the poorness of most of West's pictures should not be allowed to obscure the fact that as a man he did innumerable kind things. His goodness seems to have been mainly sustained by his serene belief that he was the greatest artist in the world; and though that made his kindliness appear maddeningly implacable to small natures, it did not impair the effectiveness of his help to many young painters. Much sooner than Hazlitt, Gilbert Stuart was aware of West's inferiority as a painter and yet through

29. DEATH ON THE PALE HORSE *by* BENJAMIN WEST *Courtesy of The Pennsylvania Academy of the Fine arts.*

fifty years Stuart was quick to defend the goodness of the man; that is sufficient, for Stuart was a good judge of painting and a profound judge of human beings. And if the historian of painting is compelled to diminish the fame of the painter, it may be remembered that the man had his fill of it alive and does not need it now.

32. John Singleton Copley in London

John Singleton Copley: 1738–1815 (work after 1774)

When Copley arrived in England for a short stay on the way to Rome he was thirty-six; within the limitations of a provincial technique he was a mature master, and within them he had manifested greatness of mind. Intellectually and emotionally he was in a state of intense excitement at the prospect of seeing the lands which were the home of art, of coming face to face with paintings by the old masters, and of giving scope to his own creativeness in history painting. A letter to his wife noted the majesty of London, the surpassing beauty of the country, with its fields of grain safe from trespass and the neatness of every humble home; at a loss before Canterbury Cathedral, he described it as "curious." In setting out for Rome he secured a traveling companion who was acquainted with foreign languages; they proved to be un-congenial, and each has left vividly phrased expressions of the other's un-pleasant aspects—all of them true. Copley, however, was intent upon things that were much more important to a painter: sensuous responses of every sort to the world and to art. To his half-brother he wrote there was "something in the Air of France that accilerates or quickens the Circulation of the fluids of the Human Body"; mentioning Gluck's *Orpheus* at the opera, he said ". . . tho a strainger to the Language, the Musick Charmed me." From Rome eight months later he wrote to John Greenwood in London the most revealing thing of all: ". . . there is a kind of luxury in *seeing,* as well as in eating and drinking, and the more we indulge, the less are we to be restrained." Evidently he was finding in Italy a climax to the "flowery luxsuriance" which he had so presciently divined in mere copies of Titian when in Philadelphia. In mind and body, therefore, the provincially mature Copley was still young enough to assimilate new experience; probably his very anxiety about his family, who had remained in Boston and were facing street riots and lootings he had not ex-pected when he left, helped to keep him alert to the complex old-world life and the glut of pictures in its galleries. His first paintings in Rome were to show both how exhilarated he was and how well he managed to keep his head.

He had of course been emotionally prepared for Raphael by the tributes of all the handbooks, but such intellectual preparation as he could have got from

copies and engravings was necessarily inadequate. His first academic but vigorous exercise in history painting was a religious subject: *The Ascension* [1775:
Museum of Fine Arts, Boston]; and it embodies the most important pictorial
lesson which Raphael taught him. The design is out of the old master's *Trans-
figuration,* considerably modified; the visual base line of disciples and angels
is not very interestingly grouped and there are errors of proportion in some
figures, but there are also well painted passages. The figure in air is self-conscious about the feat of levitation, but is in design handsomely related to the
row below. The lovely distant landscape across the center was derived from
pictures, too, although it is safe enough to assume that Copley was as responsive
to classic clarity of the Italian country as he was to the neat domesticity of the
English. From Raphael he also learned a simpler treatment of form which was
to reach full effectiveness in later work; but most important of all was his assimilation of Raphael's management of space, by which he succeeded in giving to a
complex design on a canvas only a little larger than that of his usual bust portrait an easy largeness of feeling until then unknown in his work on a similar
scale. The significance of the picture, then, is not in spite of its derivation from
other pictures but because of it; it shows that Copley, after a stage in which his
painting habits were strongly fixed, was still capable of expansion in mind and
flexibility in technique. It proved that his lifelong ambition to achieve the grand
manner could be realized.

The other principal work done in Rome was twice as high and three times
as long: a double portrait of *Mr. and Mrs. Ralph Izard* [1775: Museum of Fine
Arts, Boston]. They are seated opposite each other, and on the table between
them stands a statuette from which she has made the drawing he holds in
his hand; behind and above him are a large Greek vase and the base of a
column, while above and behind her hangs a heavy drapery with complicated
folds, and between column and curtain is a distant view of the Colosseum;
his chair, her sofa, and the massive table are more elaborate and more insistent
than in Copley's usual Boston product. In short, this double portrait is an intensification of all his provincial ideas about stateliness in portraiture; it would
seem that he took the gleam and glitter of Roman accessories as warrant for a
materialistic grandiosity "beyond the dreams of avarice." However, in the
colonial portraits his rendering of the physical substance of visual splendor was
confined to such fragments as he could study in actual objects—a chair or a
piece of damask; in them the occasionally ambitious architectural settings are
all insubstantial because derivative. The Izards are completely environed by
actual objects, and when confronted with them in however great a number
Copley could give them all their due in weight and texture and relationship in
space. Copley's mastery of portraiture could still keep ostentation subordinated

to the personal attractiveness of the sitters; the gaudiness of all this detail came simply from the intensity of Copley's sensuous response to the "luxury of seeing"—and as such it was a painter's proper reaction. If it meant being vulgar, what of that? It was the intensity that counted, that enabled his mind to permeate and inform all this gross matter. The Izard portrait is of course no major creation, but it establishes Copley's capacity to do even better what he had been doing all along; and for what was ahead of him in London, that was quite as important as the assimilation of new qualities.

By the end of 1775 Copley was re-united with his family in London; but his mother had thought herself too poorly to risk the ocean voyage, and a son born to Mrs. Copley after her husband's departure was left with Mrs. Pelham. The child soon died, but Mrs. Pelham lived some years longer without ever rejoining her famous son. In 1776 Copley was elected an Associate of the Royal Academy; two years later at its annual exhibition he showed the most original design of his entire career as a fitting prologue to his election as a full Academician in 1779. *Watson and the Shark* [1778: plate 30] exists in several versions, since both preliminary studies and replicas were painted; the one here reproduced is the best in the relationships maintained between the central mass of figures and the surrounding space. In this picture Copley harmoniously blended his colonial materialism, his Roman self-schooling, and a new element brought up from a greater depth within himself than he had ever before sounded. Even Tristram Shandy's "canting critic" must have granted that here was the "principle" of the pyramid; Copley could have found it laid down in one of the rules by Mengs: "Every group must form a pyramid and at the same time be as rounded as possible in its relief." But for this vitalization of a compositional idea he more likely drew upon his personal experience of Raphael's pictures; the actions depicted are so energetic that the superior strength of the containing shape may pass unnoticed. Its base lies across the entire lower part of the picture, composed of the struggling man and the attacking shark. Naturalistic inaccuracies of detail in the shark are pictorially insignificant against its surpassing embodiment of imminent danger, and in this effect the seemingly human character of the shark's eye plays a large part. Naturalistic errors can be found in the man as well, but the white body straining to get above the green water responds to the danger with antiphonal desperation. From this convulsiveness the pyramid ascends with diminishing agitation to the calming outstretched arm of the standing Negro, and even the violent gesture of the man wielding the harpoon is mastered by the emphatic straightness of his weapon. Copley's comprehension of the grand style had at last become imaginative by being fused into his lifelong sense of the actual, and it was this imaginativeness which contributed a new greatness to the result.

30. WATSON AND THE SHARK *by* JOHN SINGLETON COPLEY *Courtesy of Museum of Fine Arts, Boston.*

This is as good a point as any to bring in the inescapable comparison with West—historically inescapable because of the antagonism which existed in life, first unacknowledged and then open; critically inescapable because it is always necessary to discriminate between the imitation and the genuine. Copley's genuineness, up to the time of his artistic disintegration which set in during his middle fifties, originated in the thoroughness and consistency with which he strengthened his most grandiose attempts by continual reference back to the physical matter of which people and things are made and to which he had always given his uttermost belief. The more ambitious a picture by West might be, the fuller it was of pictorial quotation; the more ambitious a picture by Copley might be, the more scope there was for some fresh perception drawn from his direct study of nature. The romanticism of *Watson and the Shark*, for example, has a convincingness which West never could achieve; everything that went into the Copley has been first extracted by Copley's mind from actual colors and textures and forms; only his mode of composition is drawn primarily from pictures. Having made that normal start in his early years, and renewed it on reaching Europe, Copley went beyond it by a continually renewed contact with the world that exists before and after pictures. This alone evidenced a strength of mind far greater than any painting by West ever displayed, and it gave this particular picture a monumentality that West never once attained. This picture also was spread everywhere by engraving, and in an estimate of influence which can never be verified by a census it may be guessed that its impact upon minds good enough to become good painters was stronger than that of any engraving after West.

When the following generation of British historians and critics began to revise the lifetime reputations of West and Copley, they were not ready to discriminate. Allan Cunningham said that Copley ". . . shared with West the reproach of want of natural warmth—and uniting much stateliness with little passion." He missed the point about Copley. Copley did lack natural warmth and he did stress stateliness, but his passion escaped notice because it was withdrawn from the human element in his portraits and history pieces alike, from personality and from situation, and concentrated more and more upon the pictorial embodiment. One of the best illustrations is *The Death of Chatham* [1791: National Gallery, London], in which the formally grouped convocation of peers in their robes of state, something that did not occur, frame the collapse of William Pitt, something which did. There is no convincingness about either element; Pitt's dramatics are as theatrical as the care of the peers for advantageous self-display—and both came from the painter. But the painter's real passion was expended upon the material splendor of costume and most of all upon his means of unifying the whole with a dramatization of light and shadow. And here again Copley shows some imaginativeness, in this instance of a narrowly technical character; and in the general transfer of his passion from the content of a picture to its execution he more clearly than ever demonstrated the baroque quality of a mind which had been present from the first. *The Death of Major Pierson* [1783: National Gallery, London] carried still further his concern with chiaroscuro by a more complicated distribution across the canvas, and emphasized still further his baroque quality by an access of agitated gesture throughout.

From a mood of melodramatic danger Copley swung over to the joyous baroque of the *Three Daughters of George the Third* [1785: Buckingham Palace, London]. Two girls and a baby sister, three dogs, two highly colored parrots, and a grapevine are all engaged in a visual dance of motions and of colors. The portraitist and Academician, John Hoppner, printed public ridicule in *The Morning Post,* chiding Copley for what he called "confusion"—everything "striving for pre-eminence and opposing with hostile force all attempts of our wearied eyes to find repose." There were also stories about the rebellion of the girls themselves against the tedium and the strain to which the painter subjected them. Tedium and strain, labor and boredom, may have happened at times for everybody concerned—possibly even for Copley; but there is none in the painting. To be sure, anyone today, by "nearly looking," can recognize the care that went into every clear-edged leaf and the pains with which every texture was differentiated; but for all that, it gives the gay mood and triumphant assurance of a painting mind that is experiencing the felicity of finding a full expression for the intensity of his sensuous response to matter.

1785 was also the year of the family's establishment in a handsome home off Hanover Square, and in this year there died two of the children who appear in the stately group of *The Copley Family* [plate 31]. The picture had probably been begun earlier, and the deaths may well have been one reason why its completion was postponed. As a design, however, it shows Copley near his best; the only serious failure is one in values, by which the landscape reverts to the old backdrop effect with the added inconsistency that the excessively blue water seems about to pour over the edge of the sofa into the room. Here again appears the "principle" of the pyramid, though here it is somewhat confined by the indoor setting and by the fact that not all of the space occupied by the figures is accounted for. But the face of Copley's father-in-law has all the magisterial convincingness of the best colonial work, and the festoon of the children and their mother contains some painting of flesh and dresses of amazing brilliance. But the mental distance which Copley had come in art was greater than the physical distance from Boston to London, and can be measured even by details of still-life. It was the whole way from the

31. THE COPLEY FAMILY *by* JOHN SINGLETON COPLEY *Courtesy of National Gallery of Art [Copley-Amory Collection: Loan], Washington, D.C.*

painfully harsh and admirably dogged engraving tools in the so-called *Peter Pelham* to the spirited delicacy and assured freedom of the doll placed with such careful carelessness in the fold of a curtain at one corner of *The Copley Family*. Above all the others, but in the background, stands the maker of the pictures—at ease, the eyes exerting their power of penetration, the ironical half-smile on the lips softening slightly the disdain in the nostril. It is the countenance that both concealed and revealed a great mind: a mind which had massively enlarged a parochial craft into a comprehensive art; then, before its eclipse, had created works ranging from released exuberance to restrained intensity. In the best of them there still exists a power which has yet to be adequately interpreted.

33. Transition artisans and amateurs

Ignatius Shnydore: act. 1788
Matthew Pratt: 1734–1805 (work after 1775)
John Mason Furness: 1768–1804
Samuel King: 1749–1819
Winthrop Chandler: 1747–1790 (work after 1775)

The return of peace in this country meant everywhere a refurbishing of business and tavern signs as part of the general flurry of artisan activities directed toward freshening everything up. During the year 1788 Ignatius Shnydore in New York, desirous of becoming a citizen, announced that he was no longer painting scenery but was applying himself to ships and houses, coaches and signs, and to rooms "in the Italian mode, on canvas."

The most obvious change that overtook signs was in subject-matter. Kings and queens were replaced by Washingtons and Lafayettes over the entire country, and the general note of patriotism was heavily stressed. Doubtless this wholesale alteration made many new signs necessary, but some tavern keepers tried to retain their old signs under new names. Thus one sign which had been known before the Revolution as *The Golden Lion* was thereafter called *The Yellow Cat*.

This story concerns Philadelphia, where a law of 1770 had restricted the use of signs to the taverns. Maybe the restriction had something to do with the fact that there is in existence a larger body of information about tavern signs there than anywhere else in this country. Maybe, also, the restriction had something to do with the seeming fact that the tavern signs there were better made than before; three which were in place by 1785 were still functioning over eighty years later. And for some reason the tavern signs of Philadelphia from then on became intensively pictorial.

The individual most prominent in this development was the well known portraitist, Matthew Pratt. The signs are lost, but Pratt's son has left some information about several done after 1785 and has even preserved two or three of the painter's own rhymes. One quatrain accompanied the picture of a full pack of hounds with riders following which Pratt painted for Brown's Tavern:

> Our Hounds are good, and horses too,
> The Buck is quite run down,
> Call off the hounds, and let them blow,
> Whilst we regale with "Brown."

Pratt's free-swinging sign for the Lebanon Garden had a picture on each side: *Neptune with Triton Attendants* on one and on the other a marine, *Still Calm*. The *Game-Cock* seems to have been the most admired of all for artistic quality until Woodside impaired its effectiveness with his re-touching; but the one most often mentioned was the *Federal Convention of 1788*, which served as a sidewalk history picture until 1814. Neagle wrote to Dunlap how Pratt's signs stirred in himself the desire to become a painter and tells how they were ". . . broad in effect and loaded with colour. . . ." In more general terms, Pratt was raising signs to the level of the studio artistry and endowing them with the painterly qualities of full-fledged pictorialism.

It thus seems safe to infer that Pratt's signs had much of the compositional skill of *The American School* [plate 27] and perhaps even some of the charm of his portraits. Yet even the latter were not all approved by contemporaneous opinion, as shown by a paragraph in the *New York Daily Advertiser* for April 22nd, 1788.

American Anecdote. —As the facetious and satiric Col. D—r was one day viewing the paintings in Pratt's exhibition-room at New York, he observed the portrait of the beautiful Miss Achmuty, under which were written some verses by her impassioned admirer, Major Montcrief. The portrait was rather indifferently executed, and the poetry scarcely rose to mediocrity; upon which he took out his pencil, and wrote the following lines at the foot of the canvas:

> To paint or praise thy charms how vain the hope,
> Pratt is no Titian, nor Montcrief a Pope.

By flying so high for his comparisons the Colonel weakened the effect of his barbed couplet, and Pratt at least was safe from any deep wound in his own innate modesty. It is recorded that in the presence of some of Copley's work done in New York Pratt said that he himself couldn't do as well. That was true, because he lacked the Bostonian's intellectual grasp upon both technique and human character; and his saying so is a memorable detail concerning a very attractive personality. But it does not follow that his portraiture was poor. Certainly his pre-Revolutionary work was sensitive and occasionally lovely; and among the dozen post-Revolutionary examples attributed to him by his latest biographer are several which, if they are eventually accepted by other scholars, will only confirm the admiration for which there is already adequate reason.

Largely because of Dunlap's chronicle, Pratt's portraiture was long shadowed
by the reputation which his signs achieved with a public to whom his portraits
were inaccessible. Pratt was an outstanding success in making signs function
properly in attracting attention and causing comment; and so long as they
remained in place, they were standards by which the work of other men
was judged. No doubt the general public of that day, as in any day, was initially interested in the subjects; yet the record is clear on the point that it was
not subject alone which gave Pratt his popular esteem. That would not have
developed to the extent it did unless the subjects had been beautifully executed. In other words, good if not superlative craftsmanship was at length beginning to count in enabling subject-matter to register strongly upon the popular consciousness. Thus the "corruption" of signs by a notable degree of pictorialism did much to waken the public to what it recognized as beauty.
Though Pratt's signs have disappeared, Pratt the sign painter—and for the
very reason that he was more than a sign painter—made himself a vital even
if now untraceable factor in the development of the American capacity for
pictorial experience.

Pratt stands alone in the history of American painting in being a mind of
sensitiveness and artistry who exerted a beneficial effect downward through
a utilitarian form of picturemaking. While he was doing that, others were repeating the older pattern of artisan minds attempting to work upward into
artistry at least as far as portraiture. There was, for example, John Mason
Furness in Boston, who engraved bookplates with the tools inherited from his
uncle Nathaniel Hurd, the silversmith, and who was occupying Smibert's
painting-room in 1785. His advertisement in the *Columbian Centinel* for
May 11th of that year continues:

. . . and as he is a native of Boston he hopes for the same encouragement that is
given to foreigners, provided his Paintings are as well executed.

One look at his somewhat frightening effigy of *John Vinal* [Brooklyn Museum]
settles the matter so far as concerns the known foreigners. It seems hardly likely
that even a Bostonian was then using that word for other Americans tres-
passing into the home of codfish and culture; and if Furness meant Europeans,
any comparisons made now must, in the absence of information about any
Europeans competing with Furness in life, go back to the earlier men. And
Furness cannot compete with Blackburn, say, on Blackburn's own terms of
technique. In the *Vinal*, for instance, the textures are dry, the modeling is
brittle, and the color is somewhat harsh. But for all its erratic handling and
its incomplete control of the picture-space, it yet has a forcefulness and homely
honesty which are more welcome than Blackburn's sleek and mincing ele-

gance. In all technical matters the advantage is with Blackburn; Furness' advantage is entirely one of spirit, of attitude, of authenticity for his time and place.

The Newport painter Samuel King had received artisan training in Boston. The occasion when a negro slave mistook a portrait by King for its living subject has been mentioned; whether that or any similar event caused King to attempt portraiture professionally is not known. Apparently he did not make his entire living by it, for he also followed his father's craft of fashioning nautical instruments. Probably not all of his work has yet been identified, and one or two examples present amusingly inconsistent treatments of features and costumes; it has been suggested that for these he called upon another to execute the figures. He is known to have been the first teacher of the miniaturists, Malbone and Ann Hall, and of the more important painters Stuart and Allston. The mere listing of these names is enough to suggest that King had nothing to give them beyond the most elementary instruction; all that these four could have had in common, as regards King, would be the kindliness that is naturally felt toward one who gives the first glimpse of art. The mixed and mediocre quality of King's own work, as it is now known, leaves him a figure whose precise position can be clarified only by a connoissership more sensitive than the work itself seems to deserve.

What King needs, in fact, is what has been so satisfactorily done with Winthrop Chandler. His still-life and the landscapes dating from before 1775 have been mentioned; the landscapes done after that date and a typographically inaccurate *Battle of Bunker Hill* [c. 1777: privately owned] involved no change of manner. Neither was there any fundamental alteration of manner in the portraits; but from 1785 through 1788 he described himself as a limner, and for one with the artisan training indicated by the whole body of his work, the psychological significance of the self-conferred change of title must have been considerable. He had quit thinking of himself as a general workman and was claiming a definite degree of specialism. In the still meager documents available there is no evidence that Chandler was here putting on any social airs; on the contrary, he painted houses in Worcester at the very time he called himself a limner. But his obituary in the Worcester *Spy* for August 17th, 1790, seems to echo Chandler's own ideas about his lot:

. . . a man whose native genius has been serviceable to the community in which he resided. By profession he was a house painter; but many good likenesses on canvas show he could guide the pencil of a limner. . . . The world was not his enemy; but as is too common, his genius was not matured on the besom of encouragement. Embarrassment, like strong weeds in a garden of delicate flowers, checked his usefulness and disheartened the man. Peace to his manes.

Chandler, the country talent, yearning for the greater patronage and understanding that he might find elsewhere—in Boston, maybe: Copley, the colonial genius, chafing at Boston's lack of comprehension for his real desires as a painter and longing for the patronage and understanding that he might find in London: the human pattern recurs from generation to generation. Maybe even Van Dyck at the Court of Charles the First fancied that he might have had more scope in Flanders or in Rome for the pictures he most wanted to paint.

Some among Chandler's portraits, both early and late, display a fundamentally vigorous interest in design. Because of the technical limitations of such training as he was able to get, he fell short of his aim—so far short that the very word "design" might justly be replaced by "pattern." However, it seems as if he were consciously advancing upon the third dimension in his ambitious works. The *Mrs. Ebenezer Devotion* [1770: Brookline Historical Society, Brookline, Mass.] is boldly decorative in the arbitrary handling of skirt and curtain; their repeating ripples are, however, wholly linear across the surface; not a line leads back from the eye into depth, and apparently Chandler has not yet perceived atmospheric modifications of form and color. The *Mrs. William Glysson and Daughter Bethia* [c. 1780: privately owned] shows he has begun to see in a more naturalistic way without being able to set it all down; he conveys a somewhat vague sensation of roominess around the figures, but he cannot yet construct the figures in three dimensions and give them a definite position in space. Here he still relies upon a two-dimensional pattern in the costumes for his major pictorial effect.

In similarly ambitious portraits of men Chandler had ample opportunity to wrestle with figure construction if he had been able to realize it three-dimensionally; but he does not get beyond heavily handled edges enclosing flat areas of color. Longer life and more work might only have intensified the dawning indecision discernible in the *Mrs. Glysson and Daughter* and thus disintegrated the lively even if awkward decorativeness which remains Chandler's most memorable characteristic. He may not have been satisfied with his time, but his pictures are the most interesting products of the New England country mind in the rougher stage just before the idyllic ruralism of Ralph Earl's maturity.

34. *Fractur*

Another form of painting which lasted for almost a century throughout a large part of Pennsylvania was fractur. Its character and function fit it easily into all the other artisan and amateur work in this country, but certain special factors set it apart from other manifestations.

For one thing, the people whom it served kept themselves apart from the rest of Americans; and the survival of fractur itself actually depended upon the maintenance of relative isolation. For another, in contrast to sign painting and the freer kinds of picturemaking allied with it, fractur was closely allied with the genuine folk art of Europe; even when transplanted to America it remained but one among several homogeneous crafts—pottery, ironwork, furniture, and others—which, during their similarly conditioned continuance here, retained their folk characteristics. A third peculiarity was that the great mass of it was calligraphically decorative, strictly subordinated to some more important purpose, literally on the margin of documents as well as on the margin of fully pictorial concepts.

Fractur consisted of the lettering and the border ornamentation of birth and baptismal and marriage certificates, of Bible verses and moral maxims for hanging on the wall. Letters and outlines were drawn with a quill pen; the colors of vegetable origin were applied in flourishes and washes by brushes which were usually made of cat's hair; sometimes the whole design was overlaid with a glaze of red cherry gum. It was a craft taught by schoolmasters, each of whom made his own teaching model; and many of them made yearly rounds along regular routes to bring family records up to date. As a craft it was essentially a survival of medieval illumination, considerably narrowed in scope, and gradually dying out through the increasing use of printed forms with blanks left for filling in.

The semi-pictorialism of the decorative motives which intertwined with or framed the words was identical with that on the pottery and the painted chests. They were strongly conventionalized flowers and birds and heraldic animals, with an occasional angelic figure, each one handed down traditionally as a unit of pattern and thus capable of infinitely variable combination with other such units at the desire of the craftsman. The major elements were recognizably derived from Near Eastern sources: peacock and tulip and pomegranate: apparently from the circumstance that the Germans in Europe who first used them lived along the overland trade routes between Northern Europe and Persia, and thus had the patterns on exotic bowls and jars and textiles to draw from in brightening up their own possessions. In taking over the designs, the earlier Germans also gave some of the motives different meanings; perhaps they never knew that to the Persians the tulip suggested earthly love, and thus they may never have been aware of how great a change was involved in their making it symbolize the heavenly city. Nevertheless, even those ideas kept fractur on the margin of religion, too; the religious elements were left in the realm of traditional association and never embodied in an imagery immediately visual like that of the retablos in New Mexico.

Unlike the people in that region, the Pennsylvania Germans were not physically remote from the rapidly developing culture of the English-speaking region along the Atlantic; and in the face of increasing pressure they had to maintain their language, their customs, and their crafts with an increasingly conscious resistance. Everything considered, their persistence and success were remarkable; but the necessity of negation made cultural death inevitable in the long run. The products of industrialism undersold the ironwork and the pottery; the execution of fractur work coarsened and its colorfulness diminished. The technique was itself so static that even portraiture proved uncongenial as subject-matter; there occurred a small amount of picturemaking freed from dependence upon the words or document or motto, but as soon as its later practitioners began to show some interest in the naturalistic appearance of people or landscape the technique revealed its inadequacy to such demands.

35. Anticipations of later developments

Joseph Wright: 1756–1793
Robert Edge Pine: 1730–1788
Mr. Mack: act. 1785
William Verstille: 1755–1803
John Ramage: c. 1748–1802

Joseph Dunkerley: act. 1784–1787
Robert Fulton: 1765–1815
Anon.: *The Eidophusikon*, 1788
Alexandre Marie Quesnay de Beaure-
paire: act. 1777–1788

The hundred thousand people who left voluntarily or were expelled through the fifteen years of Revolutionary Transition called themselves loyalists; the outcome of history was such that a more accurate title is royalists. The life of loyalty as a principle sometimes requires such a radical change in its object that in its new manifestations it wears at first the aspect of rebellion; and such a change was irrevocably achieved here between 1775 and 1790. So early as 1774 Patrick Henry had said: "I am not a Virginian, but an American." Yet at that moment only Franklin was already an American in his superiority to sectionalism, and the Revolution itself produced only one more in George Washington. But from 1790 on Americans increased in numbers because their loyalty could be centered upon an effective government.

If the Revolution kept Mather Brown in England, it brought back to this country Joseph Wright in 1783. He had been taken to London by his mother, Patience Wright, who modeled portraits in wax, and he had there been trained under West. However, by the time he arrived in America Wright had developed a delicacy of line and a subtlety of modeling in faces which cannot be found in West's own portrait work. Wright repeated his portraits of Benjamin Franklin and George Washington, each one several times; and it may be regretted that in painting the latter he did not choose to give at least a three-quarter view instead of a profile, for the habitual closeness and sensitiveness of his observation would have carried an extra weight of authenticity. The *John Jay* [1786: New-York Historical Society, New York] is a particularly successful character study which emphasizes the loss to American portraiture when Wright died of yellow fever just ten years after his return. One example, a pleasantly rococo conversation piece of *Self and Family* [c. 1793: Pennsylvania Academy, Philadelphia], is weak in the drawing of more difficult details such as hands; but it also indicates some talent for gayety and charm in design—and that would have been a specially welcome lightening influence in the prevailingly sober portraiture of the following period.

Once more, if the Revolution sent youthful Duché to England, its success brought to Philadelphia a fairly well known English painter, Robert Edge Pine. He had long been an enthusiast for liberty, and his eclipse by West as a history painter in London caused him to welcome an offer in 1782 from a rich Philadelphia merchant making it possible for him to come back two years later to stay; the merchant, Robert Morris, went so far as to build a studio for Pine with the hope that the Englishman would take business away from the politically radical Charles Willson Peale. Pine, by bringing with him a full-sized cast of the *Venus de' Medici,* caused the first important American flurry of moralistic uneasiness over the nude in art. Pine's solution was to keep the figure in its case and show it by appointment; discreetly separating ladies and gentlemen for their visits, Pine satisfied both individual curiosity and community decorum. His main purpose in removing to this country was, however, never fulfilled; he intended to paint the events of the Revolution, but he found no support for his project from either the government or individuals. All he achieved was a partly executed *Continental Congress Voting Independence* [Independence Hall], which was completed after his death by Edward Savage.

In order to support his family Pine fell back upon the only branch of painting then capable of extracting money from Americans: portraiture. Apparently for the first time in this country, he made use of a device for reducing the cost of large-scale groups; on small pieces of canvas he painted heads which were afterwards pasted on the full-sized canvas, that being finished up by his daughter. This practice was by no means rare in England; one painter in London made a business of completing such composite canvases for other men who brought back collections of heads from the provinces. Pine, however, according to Rembrandt Peale, got into trouble through giving his heads wrong identities. An example like the *Mrs. Reid As a Sultana* [Metropolitan Museum, New York] displays an academic sophistication in its richly colored impasto which must have seemed exotic to American painters then even as the picturesque costumes of the sitter and her turbaned blackamoor attendant seemed exotic to American businessmen and their wives. The absence of inconsistent handling in this example surely means that Pine painted it all, and the Reynolds-like color suggests that Pine could have become a helpful influence on art here if his career had not been cut short by death. When the pictures he left were auctioned off, a number were taken to Boston for Bowen's Columbian Museum and there, before the establishment burned, they gave young Washington Allston some of his earliest ideas about color.

Pine's way of speeding up group portraiture foreshadowed still other devices by incoming foreigners for reducing costs; and another prophetic activity through those years was a spread of miniature painting indicating its later popularity. Yet for the time being some miniaturists did not find patronage plentiful. Early in 1785 one Mr. Mack, in Philadelphia, was asking four guineas; but later in March he cut his price in half and added a little persuasion to his advertisement:

. . . And as his character as an artist depends on the good or ill opinion his works may deserve, he shall by no means require any reward for, or suffer a picture to go out of his hands, that is not (to the satisfaction of his generous employer) a striking likeness, and elegantly painted.

William Verstille made the same promise, and his noticeable mannerism of giving his sitters piercing black eyes raises some doubt that his likenesses were exact. Very soon this reassurance in the advertisements was reduced to the straight commercial formula: "No likeness, no pay."

Irish John Ramage painted perhaps the most attractive ivories through these transitional years, some of them having George Washington for subject despite the painter's strongly royalist sympathies; complications of wives and debt prevented him from remaining permanently in this country. Another fine craftsman was Joseph Dunkerley, who worked a few years in Boston and left miniatures which have been attributed to Copley. Charles Willson Peale executed good miniatures, but stopped for a time in an effort to make more business for his brother James. And possibly from one of the Peales Robert Fulton in Philadelphia learned to execute miniatures, to add to his painting of signs and other things; in the three years ending just about the time of Mr. Mack's advertisements Fulton earned enough to buy his mother a farm and set himself up for a trip to London and West. Success with painting continued, but Fulton was drawn away into other activities. He introduced the spectacle of the panorama to Paris and engaged in a series of inventions which culminated in a commercially successful steamboat. He used part of his wealth to buy the paintings of other men, but the few portraits he did after his return to this country in 1806 have little significance for American painting; in his union of interests, however, he was typical of a sizable group among whom the painter-inventor Morse was to be the most important.

The landscape with mechanically moved details which had appeared in Boston received a seemingly more elaborate successor in Williamsburg; the *Virginia Gazette* for August 29th, 1788, carried the following anxiously apologetic announcement:

EIDOPHUSIKON OR MOVING PICTURES—The Artist who has the above exhibition on hand has taken pains (as health has permitted) to render them particularly striking to those who shall become his auditors. At the same time he is obldged to inform those patronizers of his exhibition he cannot get it ready as soon as he proposed, and is sorry for a retrogradation of his last advertisement, but shall certainly inform his subscribers and the public in general, of the first evening's performance, which will be early in the following week, as he has completed his paintings and machinery, and has only the space of time above mentioned to see their motions and movements completed in a manner that he flatters himself will not only delight the eye but his recitals and songs will charm the ear.

With the change of one letter, this becomes *Eidophusicon*, which was the name for a play-spectacle elaborately staged by Dunlap during his theatrical career, and the appeal of all these devices was obviously to the same taste for mechanics and substitute travel which reached a climax with the moving panoramas of the Mississippi river fifty years later.

Even before the war was over ambitious plans were being drawn for an institution in which the fine arts were to be quite as important as the languages and the sciences. Chevalier Alexandre Marie Quesnay de Beaurepaire, a French soldier who lost his health while fighting against the British here, was fired into leading the project by his friend John Page of Rosewell, in Virginia. Its American headquarters were to be in Richmond, with branches in northern cities; and in Richmond a building was actually erected. About a dozen "schools" were to be manned by professors from Europe, links were to be forged with existing institutions there, and a press was to be maintained in Paris. One actual publication was issued in 1788, a *Memoir and Prospectus,* just as a professor of chemistry and natural history was about to leave France for America; but the French Revolution put a stop to all that. Between the inception of the project in 1778 and the dedication of the building in 1786, Quesnay traveled through the country raising funds; and it was probably he who, in 1780, conducted an academy in Philadelphia for instruction in the arts of fortification and painting. In 1784 several elaborate advertisements from M. Quesnay appeared in New York papers proposing an academy of the polite arts with instructors from Europe; something must also have been actually undertaken—maybe assemblies for music or dancing on the order of Pelham's in Boston—for in the *New York Packet* for December 30th appeared another advertisement:

We are requested to give notice to the public that should any person presume to introduce, at any time, into company at the Academy of Polite Arts, any woman of ill-fame, proper plans are concocted by Mr. Quesnay's friends to disgrace such person, and prosecute the perpetrator. As Mr. Quesnay means to preserve the strictest order and decorum in the Academy, he suspects none but his enemies will endeavour to disgrace it.

The difference between the dilemmas confronting Pelham and Quesnay marks some of the changes that were taking place in the larger cities of America. This relatively insignificant appearance of a question of morals in connection with culture and the curiosity about Pine's *Venus de' Medici* foreshadowed circumstances which were frequently to upset Dunlap's anxious concern that art and artists should become respectable.

PERIOD TWO
THE PROVINCIAL

DIVISION FOUR
The Federal Era—
1790 to 1830

36. The new nation

Recalling once again the persuasively worded generalization by Louis Sullivan that "What people are within, the buildings express without," its application to the Federal Era of American history is perhaps exceptionally rewarding. For the period displays a marked stylistic consistency in architecture; through all the states of the newly formed nation it was a time of classic revivals.

There were modifications of manner within the general style not only in the United States as a whole as contrasted with Europe but also within the United States from region to region. McIntire and Bulfinch in New England were distinguishable from a certain French accent to be discerned in New York City; and both were distinct from the rather more severe formality of the Roman-derived variant initiated farther south by Thomas Jefferson. But none of these desirable and even semi-creative differences impaired the harmony of general agreement throughout the nation among architects and patrons as to the appropriateness and the clearly ordered loveliness of their provincially accented classicism.

The style therefore possessed the vitality that comes from unclouded choice: a choice, moreover, which was exercised on the basis of an already steadied taste and by way of positive development toward greater suitability rather than negative dislike of the old. It was, further, a choice which involved the whole existence of the people who made it, satisfying their spiritual aspirations as well as their practical needs. After the disruption of war and the long lapse into disrepair, they wished a visible neatness, even dignity, in the setting of their lives which would not only immediately embody but also perhaps make permanent for their descendants the serenity which they thought was essential to civilized living.

The classic revival here was even more significant. It may be interpreted as a phase—though not the only one, surely the most ingratiating—of the entire nation's initial awareness of dawning unity. The exhilarating achievement of that unity in government against great odds of selfish interests was at least parallel, if not directly expressed, in the visible coherency of the buildings, private and public both, from 1790 to 1830.

To be sure, it is needful to recall that this new and deep collective aspiration toward order achieved its results in the midst of conditions which were disorderly to the point of wildness. In that imaginary bird's-eye view to which im-

portant larger aspects may be revealed, no seaboard state yet displayed the continuous clean-edged and contour-fitting pattern which marks man's full and
intelligent agricultural development of his environment. Such areas, where
they existed, were only intermittent spots or thin fringes of relative neatness
along miles upon miles of land unsubdued by man. No eastern city was completely organized for healthy living. In good weather the usually straight streets
of rather box-like buildings might present an appearance of almost monotonous
cheerfulness; but the dust rose with every passing vehicle and every gust of
wind, the odors of offal and garbage inadequately taken care of by the scavenging goats and pigs implied a threat of epidemics throughout the months of heat.
It was indeed the customary summer exodus from the towns of all who could
manage it which established the custom of elections in November, when the
chill of autumn had presumably made things safe again.

Quite as important then, and later on even more so, was wild nature west of
the Alleghenies, seemingly infinite in extent, by its scale subduing for a time
the individuals and the small groups who ventured into it, shaping their character into something like its own roughness and by deprivation, short or prolonged, affecting profoundly their tastes in all the arts and crafts. Even those
in the east who never ventured one step toward the physical frontier were increasingly aware of its existence, its allure, and the certainty of its altering the
national life and mind. Where the colonials had looked east over the ocean for
spiritual sustenance, more and more citizens of the new nation began to watch
the west, many with hopes of wealth and power but many others who wished
to feel secure in culture with contempt and fear.

Meanwhile the social and intellectual leaders, together with those who still
accepted that leadership, brought into existence the homes and banks and
churches and government buildings which, without ever attaining grandeur,
were satisfyingly balanced in plan and occasionally mildly imposing in appearance. If the great majority of the pictures hung inside them were less interesting
than the accompanying furniture and silver, that was owing not so much to
the monotony of the human countenance as to the necessity of an exceptional
talent in the painter if he was to succeed in capturing individuality. Perhaps,
too, there was then more to it; for at the very outset of the period, and ever
more notably as it drew to an end, some of the books and pictures and many
of the people took on a timid propriety: that blight of genteelness which consists in covering an inner emptiness with a merely external correctness.

Blight though it be, the process is unavoidable in all wholesale extensions of
culture; and if there were any objectively accurate method of measuring such
processes on a nationwide scale, what occurred in the United States might be
revealed as not appreciably worse than parallel developments in Europe. Yet

visiting Europeans poured their scorn into print upon what passed for culture and art in the United States. No doubt almost all they wrote about deserved that scorn and more; but as coming from foreigners it might appear misplaced. If they had sought out the corresponding groups in their own societies, they could have profitably used their energy at home. The wordiness and the intensity of their faultfinding with Americans were fairly accurate gauges of how formidably the new nation almost at once loomed up before uneasy Europe. Within specific arts—music or painting—the separate peaks of personal achievement above the level of the average did not erupt here to the heights they did in Germany or in France; the United States was to produce no Wagner and no Delacroix. Yet the spread of art into the experience of the masses through the nineteenth century demonstrated the essential unity of occidental civilization on both sides of the Atlantic.

Of course, neither Americans nor Europeans then saw things in that light, and the natural reaction of Americans generally to such rough handling from visitors was simply stubbornness and hard feelings. The youthful confidence in the cultural greatness of the nation-to-be which had been expressed in the commencement address of a young poet at Yale was followed by a president of Princeton with the invention of the word "Americanism" to designate linguistic differences already so marked as to require labeling. Then came Noah Webster's elaborate exploration of the existing extent of Americanism and his energetic program for extending the concept from language into literature and all of life. Even before 1790 he had taken a commanding tone:

America must be as independent in *literature* as she is in *politics*, as famous for *arts* as for *arms*.

The italics may be only Webster's way of putting a platform manner into a private letter, where they are as much out of place as the raised voice in conversation; but Webster was never less than crusadingly intense. He was always fanatic in his preaching of Americanism in everything, yet he somehow retained enough Yankee caution to stay out of the quagmires and quicksands of mere patrioteering.

It was unfortunate but perhaps inevitable that few among the earlier American advocates of Americanism kept their heads as well as Webster. There was, for instance, Doctor Samuel Latham Mitchill at Columbia University who thought it so needful for young American minds to remain free from the contamination of Europe that he revised Mother Goose. His way of eliminating the political wickedness of royalty was to write:

> And when the pie was opened, the birds they were songless;
> Wasn't that a pretty dish to set before the Congress?

Another collegiate luminary, Samuel L. Knapp, remained superior to so puerile a program; but in lecturing on American literature in 1829 he lapsed for one moment into a confusion of mind which was long quite common among over-zealous Americanizers.

What are the Tibers and Scamanders measured by the Missouri and the Amazon? Or what the loveliness of Ilyssus or Avon by the Connecticut or the Potomack?

Attempting to maintain the concept of Americanism with that kind of emotional nourishment would be cultural imbecility; yet such errors about Americanism itself have not been confined to Americans. In becoming eloquent over Smibert's venture into the wilds of the new world, Horace Walpole was betrayed into the implication that the geographically vast would logically condense into the artistically great. And wasn't it at least possible for some of Queen Victoria's subjects, if not for the Queen herself, to think, while watching Banvard's Mississippi panorama, the "longest painting in the world," that its length had something to do with its rank as art?

Cultural self-consciousness on a national scale was indeed cried up so intensively that it seemed to bring with it an increased awareness of the very sectional differences which it was intended to minimize. Such differences of interest were clear as yet only in the field of economics, but they were beginning to emerge into politics. In the tenth issue of *The Federalist* (1787–1788) Madison wrote:

A landed interest, a manufacturing interest, a mercantile interest, a moneyed interest, with many lesser interests, grow up of necessity in civilized nations, and divide them into different classes, actuated by different sentiments and views.

It was in part this clear-sightedness in the leaders of the Constitutional Convention that brought about the creation of a document so conciliatory to all interests that it could in the end be adopted and made to work. That, of course, did not eliminate or perhaps even minimize the conflict of interests; it only provided a framework of organization within which they could accommodate themselves to one another without disaster to the country as a whole. The factor which accelerated the development of clashing interests to the point where the national organization was subjected to the extreme test of civil war was the long-continued coincidence between the economic groups which Madison specified and the geographical regions where each was the strongest—even the sole—controlling power.

This foreshadowing of the general situation within which the art of painting was to be practised in the Federal Era is noted because in the end it had profound effects on that art as upon the other arts. Yet for the time being—that is to say: for the period now being discussed—painting did not seem to be affected by the struggle of interests that was already shaping up. Art-buying groups all through the nation remained harmonious in taste along social levels which were determined by degrees of wealth. In short, the source of wealth then did not matter; economic security tended to result in the same attitude toward culture in general and painting in particular all across the coastwise strip of states. A family might draw its income from a Carolina rice plantation, or from one of the new textile mills of Massachusetts, or from an import-export business in New York; they were all agreed upon what sort of pictures to admire and buy—when they were aware of pictures at all. As Emerson observed in *Representative Men,* "men resemble their contemporaries even more than their progenitors." This tendency is in fact what brings into being a mind common to a group or an age, and nowhere is it stronger in effect than in the patronage of painting. There the influence of fashion operates with intensity, almost as thoroughly as in costume. Taste in painting is especially liable to conform to the often mysterious orthodoxy promulgated by those who buy pictures in order to show themselves possessed of taste.

This taste along the top economic level was not yet ready to go beyond the portrait in any really active degree; other forms of painting were to wait until the very close of the period to receive enough patronage to give their practitioners a living. A little earlier there had been a stir of popular interest in the attempts of some among West's pupils to propagate here his ambitious concept of the historical picture, but it was not sustained long enough to afford a permanent career to any of those who attempted it and more than one among them met with both professional disappointment and financial disaster. Meanwhile those who were buying any kind of picture from the studios, whether here or abroad, were agreed that the painter's business was still to record the human countenance. What had been through the years of revolutionary uncertainty a trickle of patronage now swelled quickly into a flood; but the inability or unwillingness of the buyers to pay for the ambitious forms of the life-size group and the full-length scaled the mass of work down to the monotonous repetition of head and shoulders.

This omnipresence of portraiture struck some contemporaneous minds as stupid; two such opinions, although unrepresentative of the age in general, are worth quoting because they do, in their very contradiction of the prevalent taste, afford vivid historical testimony to the strength of the taste itself.

A minor official in the Russian diplomatic service, Paul Svinin, being a respectable amateur in water color, indulged himself in something like traveler's gossip in a series of anecdotal pictures. Svinin also wrote letters, and in one of them somewhat dryly noted that the Americans had a weakness for bequeathing their likenesses to posterity.

For that reason, portrait painters are consistently in demand and are very well paid. The most wretched paint-slinger receives no less than $20 for a bust portrait, and some men get as much as $100.

On the whole he was entirely right in assuming that not only the liveliness but the life of painting, if it is to be anything more than an immediate drudgery for the painters and an ultimate weariness for the patrons, requires the presence in it of much more than the human countenance.

Opposition to portraiture on more thoughtful grounds had already been voiced twenty years earlier by the American politician-poet whom Washington called "that rascal Freneau." Freneau was one of those eighteenth-century Americans who had been more or less persuaded by the high perfectionist hopes of Europeans romantically expecting a new humanity to develop in the new world. In one of his journalistic essays attributed to "Tomo-Cheeki," Freneau made his Amerind philosopher note how American men and women were then ". . . fond to distraction of their own images."

Wherever we pass through these streets and narrow ways, we are not only gratified with a sight of the originals, but we see the copies also, in profuse abundance, suspended by way of a sign from the houses; fixed over the doors as an invitation to come in; or attached to glass-windows as an article of sale. This is the sort of vanity or folly, that gives disgust to my heart. . . . Can the great white men do nothing for their country but the little people must be compelled to become minutely acquainted with the width of their faces; the length of their noses, the rotundity of their cheeks, the depression of their chins, or the elevation of their foreheads? . . . O Vanity! I find thee existing here in every shape, and under every guise.

Just as an occasional Puritan minister a century and a quarter before had based his abhorrence of portraiture on the religious conviction that he was a worm of the dust, so did Freneau base his scorn of portraiture on the philosophical awareness that each individual is no more than a grain in the sand dunes of humanity. But agreement with that would not come from people whose faces were bright with the expectation of wealth, and who were busy all their years making their expectations come true through a dozen changes of occupation.

37. A returning master

Gilbert Stuart: 1775–1828 (work after 1775)

But the intensifying dominance of the portrait, against which so few voices were raised, at least forwarded the career of Gilbert Stuart, who in the absence of other people's egotism, would probably not have painted at all, so tyrannous was his desire to probe human character. Just the same, certain technical traits in his work through fifty years suggest with equal convincingness that pigment was the only possible medium of expression for his mind; his painterly brush-work and atmospheric colorism outsoared the relatively harsh draftsmanship and opaque pigment of his contemporaries and successors. But Stuart was an exceptionally inclusive example of the proverbial bundle of contradictions, and no biographer has yet proved psychologically adequate to the large store of anecdote which might be magnetized by a kindred mind into the living presentation of a profound and complex spirit.

Stuart achieved his greatness by not only confining his effort to portraiture but also by further narrowing it down to a particular kind of portraiture. Professor Mather has put it that ". . . while Gilbert Stuart was not quite a great portrait painter, he was one of the greatest of face-painters . . ."; and as Professor Mather qualifies and enlarges that combined semi-paradox and semi-epigram it becomes an effective characterization of Stuart's peculiar quality. He made his choice in obedience to an instinct, but he persisted in it with singular clearheadedness. To persist was often difficult because, even though dependent upon the contemporaneous taste for portraiture, he would not concern himself with putting into portraits much which that taste demanded. His compromises were few, and his frequent rudeness and occasional savagery toward people who thought themselves important tend to obscure his obstinate loyalty to what was for him a vital idea.

Even while young in London, Stuart took a stand indicative of his subsequent conduct in the United States. His words have come down through the painter John Neagle as a remembrance of what he was told by Stuart in extreme old age. Though they are therefore hardly a verbatim transcript and though the account of the accompanying circumstances may contain errors of detail, the statement is trustworthy as an expression of Stuart's consistent belief and practice. About 1780 Stuart was among a talkative group of fellow students; one after another was proposing to imitate this or that great painter of the past, but Stuart dissented:

. . . I will not follow any master. I wish to find out what nature is for myself, and see her with *my own eyes.* This appears to me the true road to excellence. Nature may be seen through different mediums. Rembrandt saw with different eyes than Raphael, yet they are both excellent, but for dissimilar qualities. They had nothing in common, but both followed nature. Neither followed in the steps of a master. I will do, in that, as they did, and only study nature. . . .

By the word "mediums" Stuart seems to have intended what might better be called temperaments, or mental attitudes which condition visual perception. In such company at that age, Stuart was a keen-minded provincial stripping away the major artificialities of an academic cosmopolitanism; his own different kind of cosmopolitanism was still in the future.

Yet in two things he was wrong: historically in regard to Raphael and biographically in regard to himself. Even as a provincial and still a student, he should probably have known about Raphael's indebtedness to Perugino; he cannot fairly be asked to have known how he would later school himself by imitation of living painters before attaining his own distinct "medium" for seeing nature.

Maybe his youthful confidence in being able to go his own way at once came from his awareness of how fast he was already getting beyond the hard mannerism of his teachers. His *Self-Portrait in the Rubens Hat* [1778: Redwood Library, Newport] is much ahead of his first and second teachers, Samuel King and Cosmo Alexander, in both technique and psychological perception. In that year Stuart was working in London under his third teacher, West; but the portrait shows a romantic use of light and dark and an intensity of introspection which owe nothing to West unless by way of conscious reaction. All his hack work for the King's favorite painter doubtless taught Stuart a great deal about painting, but as a portraitist he excelled West while he was still a studio assistant; the *Dr. John Fothergill* [1781: Pennsylvania Academy, Philadelphia], done from memory a year after the doctor's death, records a unique human being with delicate precision. While still working for West, Stuart openly ridiculed some of the master's unthinking short cuts in brushwork; and all of the master's lofty "principles" for history pictures, familiar to the young man through his having executed two such designs by West for a London church, were ignored by Stuart as unsuited to his own painting purposes.

Even before leaving West, Stuart commenced his search for style through emulation of the stylists; the *James Ward* [1779: Minneapolis Institute] suggests that he studied Van Dyck and at the same time was taking long looks at Gainsborough. But it was during the following decade, the first half of it practising independently in London and the other half in Dublin, that Stuart most clearly showed in specific examples how thoughtfully he was assimilating the manner of both Gainsborough and Reynolds. If the *Sir Joshua Reynolds* [1784: National Gallery, Washington] were the only painting showing the influence of its subject, it could be taken as an instance of deliberate homage from one artist to another; but late in the Dublin period also there was the *Admiral Peter Rainier* [c. 1793: Museum of Fine Arts, Boston] as evidence of Stuart's occasional need to remind himself of that volumed baroque which was the best phase of Reynolds' uneven output.

It was Gainsborough, however, from whom Stuart learned most, and his choice of the master of subtle colorism for closest study is proof of his own intelligence as well as of some temperamental affinity. The portrait which Stuart exhibited in the Royal Academy of 1782 as *A Gentleman Skating* [privately owned in England] was actually attributed to Gainsborough when it was shown there almost a hundred years later [1878]. But two works after 1782 tell more about the selectivity to which Stuart subjected even the master whom he most admired. In the *James Heath* [c. 1785: Wadsworth Atheneum, Hartford] the indebtedness is extensive; about all there is here to mark a mind different from Gainsborough's is a moderately greater degree of linear emphasis. In the *Marchioness of Dufferin* [c. 1792: Museum of Fine Arts, Boston] the relation to Gainsborough is no longer that of pupil to master but that of kinship on approximately equal terms; the opalescence infusing the swift exactitude of values by which the form is constructed establishes the technical maturity of a great colorist. Not here visible is a Raeburn-like ruddiness which was to come into much of Stuart's American work as a sort of memory infusing his most impressively personal style. Again the inescapable conditions of artistic development compelled a would-be painter to learn from the work of other painters before he could reach the point of transmuting nature—in this case, human nature—into pictures which were fully his own in both technique and vision.

The mastery which Stuart brought back to the unified nation which he had left as separate colonies was in more ways than one a novelty here. He had come beyond all colonialism of accent in the management of paint; within his self-set limitation to face-painting, his style was already highly personalized. On a later occasion, when asked why he didn't make a habit of signing his works, he replied: "I mark them all over." Most important of all, perhaps, certainly in strongest contrast to all colonial painters, Stuart had banished line as the dominant factor in picturemaking and replaced it with a painterly colorism hitherto unknown in this country. In addition, after his return he developed further technical refinements which were not overtaken by others for half a century after his death.

Within a few months after his arrival in New York Stuart painted a portrait which is not only remarkable in the whole range of his own work but which is also capable of keeping company with the work of the great portraitists of Europe. *Mrs Richard Yates* [c. 1793: plate 32], even if her portrait had never been painted, would surely have been remembered by all who knew her in life; but did even they perceive in her what is now plain to everyone through the accident of a genius's having been commissioned to depict her? Almost never afterwards was Stuart to attempt gesture as a means of expressing character; but Mrs. Yates' hands join with her turning head and her lifting eyelids to arrest the same fleeting moment of time. The gesture itself, as part of the hardly interrupted act of sewing, belongs to neither hand by itself but requires both together; the gesture's own clarity joins with the equally clear articulation of physical structure in the hands themselves to say the same thing about Mrs. Yates' character that is said by her features. She is as positive as she is watchful, as reticent as she is tolerant, as keen in apprehension as she is elegant in dress. Stuart comprehended all this at the instant of her speculative glance; he kept both vision and conception vivid through a pellucidly roseate notation of both. Here Stuart manifested his genius for consummate spontaneity and penetrating interpretation. This superb directness in painting had its psychological origin much earlier in the effect of an American environment upon his innately distinguished mind. The brilliance of the craft was the result of that mind's acquisitions in London. Thus Stuart, back in an America that was still provincial, showed himself so easy in his authentic cosmopolitanism that he could be "at home in his own country."

The point just raised, whether Mrs. Yates' family and friends perceived her in the way Stuart did, can be enlarged to ask whether, in Stuart's work generally, there is not more of himself than of his subjects. This question recurs in some form with every important portrait painter and receives an answer which necessarily differs with the artist involved. For example, human variety is notable in portraits by Copley—largely because of his severely objective presentation and his own seeming preoccupation with technical problems of picturemaking. In the case of Stuart a hurried look at the large number of his portraits together might well give an impression of sameness in the people; but any such effect would be due entirely to the superficial monotony of his formula. This formula of placing figures and of slighting clothes and carelessly misstating proportions was nothing but a wilful master's device for reducing to a minimum the amount of thought exacted by pictorial organization. Stuart did not want to be bothered with even seeming to evolve a fresh arrangement for each portrait. For him a

32. MRS. RICHARD YATES *by* GILBERT STUART
Courtesy of National Gallery of Art [Mellon Collection], Washington, D.C.

new face was the only important thing—provided it had humanity in it. If it was dull or insipid, he might paint it for money, and no good would come of it; but if it so much as hinted at that mystery of personality which was Stuart's genuine passion through fifty years of painting, then he could respond with the equal mystery of his thin veil of pigment which fixes human uniqueness into relative immortality. His psychological success with paint is a fair enough substitute for his refusal to encounter the pictorial difficulties of fine design. A relish for human beings is as legitimate in painting as in literature, and those who can respond to it when it occurs will find the next thing to "God's foison, God's plenty" in Stuart's thousand repetitions of the human face.

The result of this pictorial narrowness joined with psychological depth was that Stuart's few divagations into the official type of portrait with elaborate settings on the scale of life never got beyond a cold and only approximate correctness in following the rules of European formalism. When he forsook human intimacy he could only parody the sort of picture at which he mocked when it was painted by others. But the life-size bust portrait, which Stuart was content to repeat for thirty-five years, certainly best suited the pocketbooks of most Americans then. If they wanted more detail more minutely executed than he thought fit, he readily and often derided their presumption. On one occasion a buyer sent back a portrait to have the costume improved, and Stuart threatened to paste some actual fabric on the canvas in rebuke; he left clothes, he said, to the tailor. His mixed character had in it other traits even less admirable: frequent refusals to complete portraits for which he had accepted at least part payment, extravagance in living and heavy drinking coupled with cruelty toward his family, and (to taper off with something milder) a slavery to snuff. The emphasis placed upon his patriotism in returning to the United States for the express purpose of depicting the Father of his Country was an effective smoke screen for his flight from debtors' prison; and when he died he left his women-folk in bitter poverty. In the light of all that, their neglect of his grave becomes more understandable; their genteel care to perfume the taint of his birth in a snuff mill with hints of connection with the royal house of Stuart and their attempted whitewashing of his conduct take on an air of pathos.

Professor Mather has perceptively observed that Stuart's ability to read the character of others probably owes much to the defects in his own; and that probably means further that in the secrecy of his own mind Stuart had faced his own defects and come to some sort of working acceptance of them through the hours when he could not forget them in sleep and drink and painting-plus-conversation. At some point in his life he had stripped away pretense with himself; and even if that didn't make it easy for him to live with himself, it gave him a kind of divination for what the human countenance revealed. His very concept of portraiture itself came out of his impatience with the unnecessary and his laziness in doing what others expected. His own character thus displayed some parallels to the mixed and unfinished aspects of the American scene in which he played so brilliant a role.

Eight years in Philadelphia and near-by Germantown, until the United States government moved to Washington, and about two years there, were full of work and of the episodes which went into the stories. In 1805 he settled in Boston for his final phase: America's first master to be acknowledged as an "old master" while alive. There was appropriateness in this setting for his maturest work; where the irregularities of his character suited the country at large, the minor scale and classic restraint of his art suited the Boston of Bulfinch. Few families there for whom Copley had painted retained their wealth and position into the time of Stuart; they had been supplanted by a new merchant class whose Yankee shrewdness of character kept them from aping any distant aristocracy. It was these people who created the city so prominent in the republic, relegating the colonial city to a memory, so that Boston is culturally younger than she likes to think. Stuart's shrewdness as a portraitist matched theirs as merchants, but he also stood ready to credit them pictorially with every hint of intelligence above money-making which their faces might possess.

Whenever he was confronted with innate superiority he could match it by his own appreciation; the result could therefore be a masterpiece of serene refinement such as the *Mrs. Timothy Pickering* [c. 1816: privately owned], where a characteristic piece of carelessness in the hand seems insignificant, so authoritative is the spiritual beauty of the features. Equally authoritative, and conveying the force of a much more assertive personality, is the *Admiral Sir Isaac Coffin* [c. 1810: plate 33], wherein the flesh itself is radiant; this indeed has a vitality of light-drenched color not to be seen again in American painting until after the importation of the full impressionist method late in the century.

To Stuart in Boston came younger painters seeking guidance in technique, not merely from near by but from as far away as Kentucky. He never took anyone as a formal pupil; only young Vanderlyn had been allowed in Stuart's studio for a few months in Philadelphia. Apparently no student was ever turned away from his Boston studio; his generosity to them all and his freedom from petty professional jealousy resulted in a surge of sorrowful gratitude all over this country when he died. Unquestionably he adapted his advice to the capacity of its recipient—much or little, elementary or advanced; but it was always advice which assumed previous practice by the other person. Kentucky Jouett, perhaps because he came from farthest away and felt the most need of it, kept the fullest record of what Stuart told him: invaluable for light upon Stuart's practice, but

33. ADMIRAL SIR ISAAC COFFIN *by* GILBERT STUART
Courtesy of Mr. William Amory.   Photograph from The Frick Art Reference Library.

no complete system of technical instruction—and not intended to be that. For the dominant idea in all the help that Stuart so freely gave was the idea on which he had based his own professional career: the only effective teaching is self-teaching. With Stuart, however, this had none of the aggressive or opportunistic overtones noted in other American-born painters; with him it was simply an inescapable condition of being a painter, something to be accepted and acted upon, whether with difficulty or with ease. He knew he could do nothing to change the inherent mental quality of anybody else, and accordingly he left all seekers largely to their own capacity for perceptiveness. All that they could assimilate was theirs for the taking—from listening to his talk or from watching him at work.

It seems almost like watching Stuart at work to examine some pictures that he left unfinished. There is, for example, the *Mrs. Perez Morton* [c. 1802: Worcester Art Museum], beside which the two other portraits of her which Stuart completed are quite commonplace; whether from Stuart or from her, the uncompleted version possesses the poetry so conspicuously absent from her own rhymes. The dozen or more partially executed examples are incomplete only in the most superficial sense, for Stuart always went straight for the essentials of character. Brush strokes so economical and purposeful that there always appear to be more of them than is actually the case, pigment so thin that it seems hardly more than a stain, and then (depending upon how far along Stuart brought the work before quitting) transparent touches building up vibrant tones and velvety textures. Perhaps the most wonderful instance of this extraordinary ease in the immediate capture of essentials is the *Nathaniel Bowditch* [1827: privately owned]. Not often does it happen that an artist, at the very end of a long career, manages to sum it all up in a work so characteristic and so satisfying—supremely characteristic in containing not one stroke more than his own interest demanded, supremely satisfying in not needing one stroke more to convey both the mind that informs the features and the mind that made the record.

In the portraits where Stuart, in deference to the expectations of his patrons, kept at work after he had set down all that really interested him, there is a very great unevenness in the results; the failure of his interest was sometimes so sudden and complete that the pictures suggest an ineradicable amateurism at the heart of his technical mastery. But his failures are not deductible from his successes; his successes cannot be impaired. In the final Boston years Stuart's hand developed a noticeable tremble which would have defeated a less brilliant technician. One observer described how intelligently the painter overcame that handicap by deliberated sudden charges of the loaded brush upon the canvas which he thereupon left untormented. Another wrote:

. . . Stuart, with shaking hand, would poise the brush above his work, and then stabbing it suddenly, get the touch he desired. . . .

It may be conjectured that the coloristic brilliancy maintained and even enhanced to the end actually owed something to Stuart's triumph over his physical infirmity. Whatever were his shortcomings in association with others, this triumph is a dramatic example of the artist's professional morality: the functioning of the will where it counts for artistic creation.

38. An influx of foreigners

Signior Rossetti: act. 1797
M. du Snaw: act. 1794
Geslain the Younger: act. 1796
Belzons: act. 1792
Joseph Perovani and Jacint Cocchi: act. 1795
Archibald Robertson: 1765–1835
Alexander Robertson: 1768–1841
Martin: act. 1797–1808

Weaver: act. 1797
Woolley: act. 1797
John Roberts: 1768–1803
Francis Martin Drexel: 1792–1863
Pietro Ancora: act. 1800–1820
James Sharples: c. 1751–1811
Charles Balthazar Julien Fevret de Saint-Mémin: 1770–1852

As a returning native Stuart was alone in his eminence, nor was any incoming foreigner his equal in mind or in art. Yet the new nation magnetized painters from every country in Europe that had any. Italy, Switzerland, Austria, Germany, Denmark, and Sweden were each represented by a few painter-immigrants. But the representatives of all these countries were outnumbered by the Frenchmen. For one Signior Rossetti in Charleston, there were Monsieur du Snaw from Santo Domingo, Geslain the Younger, who claimed to be a pupil of David, and other Frenchmen. Philadelphia, as the seat of the national government, attracted a high proportion of the newcomers; among these were more Italians, but they, too, found themselves a minority beside the French.

Violent political upsets in France and its colonies, accompanied by large-scale executions, sent refugees here in great numbers. Fifteen hundred from Santo Domingo into Baltimore during one month of 1791 was an extreme instance in a total that has been estimated at twenty-five thousand. Very few of them had been professional painters at home, but it would seem that very many of them had the usual French amateur acquaintance with water color and pastel (and also music) as ornamental diversions. There were dozens of men like Belzons who, in Dunlap's genteel circumlocution,

. . . employed that skill, which had been attained as a source of amusement, or an elegant accomplishment in France, to the purpose of gaining a reputable subsistence in a foreign country for himself and family.

Almost none of these refugees made any important contribution of actual pictures to art here, but an incalculable influence was exerted by them, principally upon the ladies of America, through drawing lessons and the opinions of polite society picked up in conversation.

As for painting by professionals, the major influences on technique and taste still came from Great Britain; England, Scotland, and Ireland sent over the men who demonstrably strengthened American preferences in portraiture and more importantly helped to extend American taste into landscape. For some reason or other these men did not often advertise; perhaps they could get plenty of work without advertising.

Perhaps, also, it was still true, as it seems to have been before the Revolution, that the elaboration of an advertisement was in itself an indication of little work. At any rate most foreigners were content with simple announcements, adding only a phrase or two of self-commendation. Very few spread themselves as largely as did two Italians in the *Federal Gazette* of Philadelphia for September 19th, 1795:

Perovani, Joseph and Jacint Cocchi, of the republic of Venice, Painters, have the honour to inform the public, that they arrived in this respectable city about two months ago. During a residence of several years in the city of Rome, they have given specimens of their arts and talents in that city, as well as in several other cities of Italy, having been employed by Princes as well as private persons. Having understood that taste for the fine arts is rapidly increasing in these happy States, they resolved to quit Italy, and to try to satisfy the respectable citizens of America, by their productions. The kinds of painting they excel in, are as follows, *viz.* The first (Mr. Perovani) paints all kinds of Historical Pieces, Pourtraits of all sizes, and Landscapes, as well in oil color as in fresco; the other Mr. Cocchi, all kinds of Perspective, Paintings and Ornaments; and both are able to paint any Theatre, Chambers, Departments, with Platfonds in figures, and ornamented in the Italian taste: a small specimen whereof they have given in one of the saloons in the house of the Spanish Minister here. The one of them likewise is a compleat architect, not only able to furnish the draft in the most compleat stile, but likewise to superintend the execution thereof. They may be found by enquiring at No. 87, Second Street, North.

It is difficult to imagine any branch of "the painting business" not mentioned there that could be wanted in a city which, though a capital, was still small and provincial according to European standards. So strong a whiff of "a certain condescension in foreigners" rises from this attempt to ingratiate themselves with respectable citizens, that it raises doubts about the effectiveness of the approach; and it may be further wondered why, if the skills matched the claims, the workmen had to come so far in search of work. But in 1796, for Washington's birthday, Perovani announced an exhibition at the Temple of Minerva of a statue of the Goddess engaged in contemplating a bust of the President.

Another advertisement which had appeared in New York in 1792 appears better judged in its equally obvious flattery.

Painting and Drawing at the Columbian Academy, No. 89 William Street, New York. Archibald Robertson, Limner, Duly and sensibly impressed by the encouragement the citizens of New York have bestowed upon his efforts to establish an Academy for the Arts of Painting and Drawing in this City, begs leave to inform the public that his brother, Mr. Alexander Robertson, has lately arrived from the Royal Academy of Painting, London, where he has been under the tuition of the most celebrated artists.

They, therefore, by joint and unremitting attention to their pupils, hope to merit a continuation of the encouragement which Archibald Robertson has for twelve months experienced, and the public may depend that no pains or expense will be spared to make their Academy useful to citizens of this State and to the United States in general.

Following that come details about hours and classes and subjects, all so elastic that it amounts almost to saying that anybody can be instructed in anything at any time anywhere. In tone, this seems not much of an advance over the colonial finishing school, but the Robertson brothers actually achieved something important. Both left works—miniatures and little views in water colors—which are attractive and modestly meritorious in technique. Their school gave about the best instruction available in New York during the first quarter of the nineteenth century; such promising talents as Ann Hall, the miniaturist, and John Vanderlyn there received the instruction which brought them beyond their uncertain beginnings. Of the brothers, Archibald published a book on drawing and Alexander became secretary of the American Academy of Fine Arts in 1816.

The names of some among these foreign-born painters flocking to the United States have been preserved mainly because their characters or their works gave opportunities for Dunlap's verbal bludgeoning—Martin, "a most wretched pretender to crayon painting"; the intemperate Weaver doing small portraits in oil on tin "hard as the tin and as cutting in the outline"; Woolley, "the Woolley painter"; and perhaps the most intriguing of all, John Roberts. During his ten years here he showed himself to be the same kind of person as Joseph Allen and John Foster a century earlier, but surpassed his prototypes in range of interests and probably in actual talent. He could work in crayon, paint miniatures, and design pictures; but he was more active as an engraver. In this craft he devised better tools and a new mode of stippling which permitted a greater degree of the finish which was then so much admired. Especially interesting, in relation to what was soon to become a very important strand of development on the borders of painting, was Roberts' consuming interest in invention for its own sake; he would work at art only to get money for his experiments. He made a printing press and devised an original stove, a bellows for forging, improvements in the manufacture of eyeglasses, and an organ on a new principle. He performed not only on that instrument but also on the piano, clarinet, and flute; he was a founder of the Euterpean Society and led the orchestra as its first violinist. He was a good mathematician and devised an original system of algebra. Dunlap says that Roberts' death, supposedly from apoplexy, was more likely from alcohol; he then explains Roberts' intemperance by the state of culture in New York.

. . . The low estimation in which artists were held at that period in our cities, where trade is the source of wealth, and wealth the fountain of honor, were both cause and effect in respect to that conduct I have been obliged to record . . .

Dunlap had an immoral fondness for drawing morals which were lacking in charitableness; but in here extending his censure from the individual to society he was being certainly kinder and perhaps wiser than usual.

Other newcomers managed to make the necessary adjustments. As an example there was Francis Martin Drexel, an Austrian who had begun an artistic career in Italy at the age of eleven and who came to Philadelphia in 1817. Through almost a decade there he painted and gave drawing lessons, but in 1826 he set out on the first of two extensive trips in South America, where he had some success for a time selling portraits of Simon Bolivar. Back in this country by 1837, he opened a brokerage office in Louisville, Kentucky, and moved his business to Philadelphia in the following year. A few group portraits, which almost cross the line into anecdote, and a couple of religious pieces, ranging from 1818 to 1835, give the impression of a talent which had come to a stand in picturemaking; promising compositional ideas seem stalled by inadequate drawing of their component figures. Whatever the reason, Drexel turned from painting to business and founded the fortune out of which came Drexel Institute and other benefactions. As another example of adjustment to a mercantile way of living there was Pietro Ancora, an Italian who had commenced teaching art in Philadelphia in 1800 and who gave Neagle his first lessons; he turned to importing European paintings for sale. Sporadic shipments had been brought in before 1819, but Ancora is credited with establishing in that year the first business firm to engage regularly in such activity. It is not possible now to guess how good or how bad Ancora's importations may have been, but later ones by New York dealers played a definitely injurious part affecting American painters through the mid-century.

An Englishman who had considerable family assistance in portraiture was James Sharples. Two sons by previous marriages, together with his third wife and their daughter and son—all shared at one time or another in the quantity production of small portrait heads in pastel. Nine years of group effort in two visits (1793 to 1801 and 1809 to 1811), with relatively little work remaining in England, would seem sufficient reason for counting them as American portrait-makers; when here, they were all itinerants together, and there is one specially likable detail in their collective biography—after experiencing a run-away stagecoach, Sharples devised an original conveyance to transport the lot of them from place to place. Sharples was by temperament so at home in this country that he tinkered with attempted inventions to the detriment of his finances. The family also used a machine at the beginning of each portrait: the physiognotrace, which outlined a shadow profile in five minutes or less. Their use of pastel was not in the usual form of crayons of different colors and shades; they kept powdered pigments in glass cups and applied them to the profiles with applicators (seemingly not actual brushes) of camel's hair. The result was a surface of notably greater softness than could be secured with prepared cray-ons; and it was accompanied by generally darker color effects than those of the masters of the medium. The Sharples showed no artistic or interpretive mastery; from beginning to end their profile-making was a craft, and the mechanical accuracy of the initial outline was never upset by any searching after character which is the true portraitist's unassailable advantage. For likenesses in which the sitter faced the painter, and for which therefore the profile machine was useless, Sharples charged more and almost always produced more attractive pictures. He was so fortunate as to be favored with sittings by President and Mrs. Washington in 1796, and through subsequent years every member of the family made copies of his originals—and even copies of copies.

Another itinerant whose work is more interesting, although it too started with the physiognotrace profile, was Charles Balthazar Julien Fevret de Saint-Mémin. Of all refugees from the French Revolution he made the most striking contribu-tion to portraiture in this country. His portraiture was not actually painting; the starting point was in every instance the machine-made profile and he used only charcoal and chalks with which to fill in the outline. His touch was more light and varied than that of any among the Sharples; his first drawing was also on the scale of life. This combination of scale and touch enabled him to secure much greater liveliness of detail and perhaps gave him somewhat broader scope for observation of individuality. However, he too worked rapidly in the groove of a semi-mechanistic formula; and in view of that, the sense of moderate variety which his work leaves in the memory testifies to considerable skill of hand and keenness of mind.

Saint-Mémin would make only the portrait drawing where the purchaser wanted it alone, but his great skill as a salesman of his own work lay in per-suading eight hundred Americans to order a dozen prints from an engraved plate which he would make from the drawing. For this he used another machine, the pantograph, which would trace on the metal a much reduced circular copy (about two inches in diameter) of the original. In this business for the first two years he had an associate, a fellow refugee by the name of Valnuit; but for at least a dozen additional years of United States travel Saint-Mémin performed both processes himself. The precision of the craft which produced the small engravings gave to the result an attractiveness akin, though distantly, to that of certain Renaissance portrait medals; and to study the most nearly complete collection [Corcoran Gallery, Washington] can give the pleasant but entirely erroneous impression that Americans of the Federal Era were as gracefully neo-classic *à la Français* as the stairway and cupola of the New York City Hall.

Even more exclusively than is the case with the Sharples, Saint-Mémin's portrait-making was confined to the United States; he went back to France in 1815 to thirty-five years as a museum curator. The cultural significance for this country of Saint-Mémin and the Sharples together is that by mechanical speed-ups to production they put portraiture within reach of many who would otherwise have remained unrecorded. The repetitiousness which was an essential part of the process was in itself not uncongenial to American likings, and the mixture of art and mechanics in a single craft helped rather than hindered the success of these wide-ranging itinerants. In all this they set an effective precedent which was to be followed by native-born itinerants in the nineteenth century until the time when the inexpensive portrait became the monopoly of the daguerreotype.

39. The popularity of the miniature

FOREIGN-BORN

Walter Robertson: ?–1802
Robert Field: c. 1770–1819
Jean Pierre Henri Elouis: 1755–1840
Edward Miles: 1752–1828
M. Maras: act. 1800

NATIVE-BORN

Joseph Wood: c. 1778–c. 1832
Nathaniel Rogers: 1788–1844

Sarah Goodridge: 1788–1853
Anson Dickinson: 1779–1852
Daniel Dickinson: 1785–after 1840
Samuel H. Dearborn: act. 1807–1810
Benjamin Trott: c. 1790–c. 1841
James Peale: 1749–1831
Charles Fraser: 1782–1860 (work to 1830)
Edward Greene Malbone: 1777–1807

In miniature painting on ivory about the only feasible device for increasing output and lowering prices is the collaboration of workmen each of whom can work exceptionally fast upon certain details. Such an arrangement was described in the advertisement of two unnamed men in the Philadelphia *Aurora* for May 13th, 1797:

. . . One of the artists will circumscribe his whole care and attention to the head; and the other who excels in Draperies &c. will confine himself to that department. . . .

Since sittings were to be taken by only one of the artists, the chances are that the "Draperies &c." were somewhat imprecise as a record of the sitter's actual clothes. In the true miniature no mechanical speed-ups on the order of the physiognotrace and pantograph could be used, and therefore the price for good or fine work was greater than for the small portraits of the Sharples and Saint-Mémin. However, other visitors from Great Britain and France played a prominent part in extending the popularity of this "portraiture in little" far more widely than at any earlier time. For even fine miniatures were still less expensive than work of comparable quality upon the scale of life in oil; and this fact, coupled with the contagiousness of fashion which always operates in art patronage, occasioned not only an influx of foreign-born but also the appearance of native-born specialists of superior skill.

The miniaturist Walter Robertson was Irish and no kin to the Scotch Robertson brothers who manned the art school; he came here in 1793 on the same boat with Gilbert Stuart. Stuart later quarreled with Robertson over some miniature copies the latter made from Stuart's oils; but Robertson's original work during his rather short stay in this country was the envy of fellow professionals, with Dunlap both censuring it for artifice and praising it for charm. Dunlap's censure was directed at the uniformity of color for all ages and both sexes; but he did not describe the technical peculiarity of making the long brush strokes follow the contours which was Robertson's means of modeling heads. English Robert Field made a longer stay here, divided between the four or five major cities; his modeling also was pronounced, and to it he joined a stronger sense of individuality than Robertson's, but his technique was more mixed. He used contour brush strokes in the features, but in the backgrounds short and repetitious strokes which enlivened the textures; in color he habitually tended to darkish brown shades modified by reddish tints which failed in richness of effect and he often put transparent and solid pigment on the same ivory.

As for the French-trained miniaturists, the most interesting was Jean Pierre Henri Elouis, who very sensibly adjusted himself to conditions here by calling himself Henry Elouis. He was something of a traveler before coming here in 1791, and the fifteen years that passed before his return to France were interrupted by a five-year jaunt to Mexico and South America in the company of the famous scientist, von Humboldt. Charles Willson Peale wrote that Elouis painted "in the new stile" without going into particulars; perhaps what seemed new was the mannerism of short and relatively broad brush strokes in lively color giving a decided brilliance to the whole. It is said that Elouis gave instruction to Washington's stepdaughter, Nelly Custis, much as young ladies of lesser social prominence were given lessons by the lesser known Frenchmen previously mentioned. And while all of that did something to spread a general interest in painting, its actual contribution to American culture can only be guessed, not accurately assessed.

The three foregoing foreign-born miniaturists were only birds of passage here. Elouis went homing to France; Field died in Jamaica, and Walter Robertson in far-off India. The little-known Edward Miles died here after twenty years in Philadelphia, during which time he did more teaching than painting; and in that city he may have seemed a mildly romantic figure through having painted at the court of the Emperor Paul of Russia. An even stronger note of exoticism rises from Dunlap's brief condemnation of the miniatures of a certain M. Maras when he adds that from New York Maras went on to Constantinople and became painter to the Sultan. There were numerous other unillustrious obscure to paint the hundreds of miniatures many gentlemen used to adorn their snuffboxes and many more ladies wore on chains or mounted in brooches and bracelets and rings.

The popularity of the miniature soon reached the point where even the average American-trained practitioners had plenty of work. Nathaniel Rogers, for example, whose drawing and coloring and character interpretation all three were indifferent, was patronized by the fashionable in New York after Joseph Wood, his teacher and his superior in craft, moved on to Philadelphia. In Boston and its vicinity Sarah Goodridge executed satisfactory miniatures, which became better after some instruction from Gilbert Stuart. The Dickinson brothers, Anson and Daniel, found plenty of purchasers, although Dunlap pounced on the former with a preachment about his wandering and irregular life being no credit to the profession. Samuel H. Dearborn, securing some charm in his uncertain craftsmanship, circulated through Kentucky. But among the habitual travelers the man capable of the best work was Benjamin Trott; his traveling, indeed, was of a kind to give him the name not of itinerant but of peripatetic, and seems to have been caused as much as anything by his own quarrelsome nature. The uneven quality of his known miniatures makes it impossible to describe a consistent style, but the best among them are among the best of the time. The variability of his technique came partly from his own experimentation and partly from his occasional enthusiasms about the practice of other men, during which his own became imitative; Dunlap put much emphasis upon Trott's time-wasting efforts to discover what he mistakenly thought was the chemical secret of Walter Robertson's work.

James Peale did not do as many different things outside of painting as his older brother, Charles Willson, did, but he made all kinds of pictures: oil portraits, conversation pieces, anecdotes, history pieces both factual and mythological, landscapes and still-lifes. This readiness to tackle any type of subject is a merit in a painter, but the intrinsic merit of the results of course depends upon other factors: the quality of his mind to begin with, the intensity of his involvement in the subject, and the adequacy of his technique to both the subject and the mind. In scope and skill James Peale certainly supplied all the proof that is possible for his brother's contention that anyone could paint; yet there, precisely, was the trouble. James Peale's mind was, in a way of speaking, just any mind. It proved good enough for technical competence and good enough for inclusiveness of subject, but not good enough for intensity in either respect. His most interesting paintings were still-lifes, although even there he was surpassed by his nephew Raphaelle. His best accomplishment was his work in miniature; and in this branch, although Malbone developed a richer color and Fraser a more delicate draftsmanship, James Peale was technically more varied than either and even more robust in the interpretation of character. The variety involved inequalities and the robustness meant some loss in refinement; but a lesser man like Peale, along with a major figure like Stuart, is entitled to be ranked according to his successes; and in the miniature, perhaps even more than in the oil portrait, a vital personality in the painter remains interesting longer than a technique without that human essential.

Charles Fraser executed some miniatures during the lifetime of his older friend Malbone which naturally show the influence of the latter's superior technique. About the time Malbone died, Fraser turned aside from painting to earn a competency as a lawyer; and when this was accomplished he quit the law to become a professional miniaturist for the rest of his long life. The change occurred in 1818; in the twelve years then remaining for the Federal Era, Fraser did much work, but almost all of his stylistically mature work was done after 1830.

By common consent at his death and continuous acquiescence since then, Edward Greene Malbone has been ranked as the foremost among American miniaturists. There is of course no denying the technical mastery of his touch or the frequent richness of his color effects; but it is possible, as suggested in connection with James Peale, to prefer the work of other men for other qualities. For the small body of Malbone's work—his early death from tuberculosis reduced his painting years to only twelve—can be cloying. Anyone for whom that happens to be true need not look further than Allston's often-quoted praise for the reason: "He had the happy talent . . . of elevating the character without impairing the likeness . . . and no woman ever lost any beauty from his hand. . . ." From another point of view the talent so described was neither more nor less than the time-hallowed one for professional flattery which is the stock in trade of a certain type of portraitist. Sitters liked it from Malbone, just as they liked it from Blackburn; and such patrons sometimes receive, as they did from Malbone, a craft so remarkable in its own right that, for some tastes, it suffices.

Malbone's achievement was indeed a triumph of specialism in technique, but its very brilliance emphasizes the limitations of that branch of painting in which it occurred. The miniature cannot do more than give pleasure by its craft and by the subject's beauty or character. An unknown writer quoted by Dunlap with approval baldly compared the miniature to the sonnet; a generation later Tuckerman in his effusive way altered the image to that of the lyric. Both were wrong, because the miniature, unlike either literary form, by its character definitely prevents the expression of strong emotions or major concepts. There is no room in the miniature for the language of design by which great pictures are made. As a likeness it may be precious to generations of descendants; as both a likeness and an example of fine workmanship it may be interesting to anybody. Even so it is never more than a memento; and in the occasional attempts to escape the limits of portraiture into "fancy" subjects like cherubs or symbolical ladies it falls to the level of a trinket.

40. *Portraiture in the oil medium*

BOSTON

John Johnston: 1758–1818
Christian Gullager: 1759–1826
Henry Sargent: 1770–1845
James Frothingham: 1786–1864

CONNECTICUT

Ralph Earl: 1751–1801 (portraiture after 1785)

NEW YORK

John Wesley Jarvis: 1780–1839
Samuel Lovett Waldo: 1783–1861
William Jewett: 1795–1874

PHILADELPHIA

John Eckstein: c. 1750–c. 1817
Charles Willson Peale: 1741–1827 (portraiture after 1790)
Jacob Eichholtz: 1776–1842
Thomas Sully: 1783–1872 (work before 1830)

WASHINGTON

Charles Bird King: 1785–1868

THE OLD SOUTH

James Warrell: act. 1799–1822
John B. Martin: 1797–1857
Phillippe Abraham Peticolas: 1760–1843
Edward F. Peticolas: 1793–?
James Earl: 1761–1796

THE COTTON SOUTH

Ralph Eleazer Whitesides Earl: ?–1837
Nathan Negus: 1801–1825
Eliab Metcalf: 1785–1834
José de Salazar: act. 1792–1801

THE OLD WEST

Matthew Harris Jouett: 1787–1827
John Grimes: 1799–1837

The general pressure of the buying public toward lesser cost was the main cause of the development of the smaller forms of portraiture and the various technical shortcuts in them. These manifestations, however, did not mean that there was any slackening in the production of the life-sized bust in oil. On the contrary, this type increased in popularity, with the results that its practitioners became more numerous than ever and began to exploit more than one device for turning out work more rapidly and reducing prices. In consequence, this type predominated through the Federal Era to such a degree that anything more ambitious, and therefore more complicated in design, may now appear momentarily better than it is simply because it affords relief from the monotony of half-bodies facing half left or half right.

The social fact recorded by portraiture in all mediums and sizes was the appearance of a newly rising middle class. From its painters the women expected (or at least received) a superficial flattery; the men asked (or at least received) little more than a prosaic record of the repellent male costume which accom-

panied the commercialism of the nineteenth century. The increasingly obvious
uniformity in the people portraitized was accompanied by a parallel increase
of uniformity in technical practice; and both processes were favored by the
rapidly increasing ease of communication and travel. A half-century earlier the
journeyman painter was certain to be an artisan, and almost certain to be one
of lesser skill; now even the better-grade specialists made seasonal trips to
distant cities.

No painter in the cities where Stuart had worked could escape taking up
some attitude in regard to his manner and influence. Practically all recognized
his superior artistry, and so widely was his work received by even laymen of a
certain cultivation as the standard by which to judge, that very few professionals cared to find fault with him. On the other hand, not many painters made
really serious efforts to take over his intensely personal technique; they could
rarely rise to its subtlety and refinement, and never to its economical directness and brilliant finality of touch. Accordingly, the effect of Stuart's technique
upon other American painters was limited by their own receptivity; and not
even those whom he helped in personal contacts were equal to making his practice the basis of a nationwide stylistic development.

When Stuart reached Boston in 1805 he found John Johnston active there.
Johnston was a son of that artisan who had taught John Greenwood in the
seventeen-forties; the son was only fifteen when his father died, and his further
training was as an apprentice to another artisan. His training completed, Johnston painted houses; then he saw service in the Revolutionary War; and after
that he resumed painting, but on the higher level of portraiture. His skill
varied from canvas to canvas, but always—as in the *Judge Samuel Davis* [pri-
vately owned]—he used the blockish modeling normal to artisans; facial planes
of nose and chin were squarely accented, and highlights were sparingly applied.
His color at its best kept close to dominant browns, but is nonetheless pleasing
for that. Three years older than Stuart, Johnston gave no sign of altering his
established technical habits after Stuart's arrival.

Nor did any effect from Stuart appear in the work of Christian Gullager,
whose personal history had been in strong contrast to that of Johnston, but
whose painting exhibited a curious technical likeness to the general artisan
manner which Johnston embodied. Gullager was a Dane appearing in this
country supposedly after a stay in the Virgin Islands, where his uncle was
governor; and the professionally important thing about him is the report that
his youthful artistic talent had secured him a government scholarship for three
years of work in Paris under David. A portrait such as that of *Colonel John
May* [1789: American Antiquarian Society, Worcester] has a good deal in
it to confirm the report: a crisp touch and a measure of sophistication in

managing detail. But these merits were accompanied by some uncertain drawing and a treatment of important edges which indicates impatience with the
difficulties of achieving substantial form. Gullager worked in Boston for the
earlier part of his thirty-five years in this country, but he left behind him in
New York the story of a discharge from scene painting for carelessness and
laziness; his rivalry in Philadelphia with the sign-painting firm of Rutter and
Company was recorded in advertisements and remembered by Jarvis. Thus a
good deal of utilitarian practice could have brought Gullager's technique into
line with that of the shops; at any rate, his stay in Paris did not give him the
full degree of superiority to the home-trained workman which might be reasonably expected.

Henry Sargent seems never to have staked his all upon painting; though
he did a good deal from time to time, he was as much a military man as he
was a painter. He and Stuart were congenial in temperament, and Sargent's
portraits certainly display an occasionally strong degree of derivativeness; but
the portraits, even though they constitute the bulk of his remaining work, are
consistent only in their mediocrity; Sargent is both more interesting and more
significant for his work in anecdotal and historical painting.

Mediocrity is also present in the greater part of the work left by James
Frothingham; but a few marked exceptions owe their degree of distinction entirely to Stuart's coaching, which was in this instance especially generous.
Frothingham had come into portrait work from the then usual artisan level
by the then usual method of self-teaching through copying prints and reading books; and a few details of his earlier procedures contribute an exceptional
vividness to the general picture of American country boys becoming painters.
Ignorant of how to manage the palette, Frothingham arranged his colors in a
row of thimbles; unsure of how to apply his color to canvas, he followed a rigid
routine of finishing detail by detail: beginning with forehead and eyes, going
on to the other features and the hair, then setting down draperies and therewith arriving at the background. Such work turned out for low prices gave
him a living by the time he was twenty; shortly afterward, on the advice of
one who knew both him and Stuart, he began taking portraits to the famous
man for criticism, and did not earn praise until he brought in his sixth attempt. In portraits where he elaborated the settings in an effort after extra dignity, such the *Edward Augustus Holyoke* [c. 1821: Essex Institute, Salem,
Mass.], he was likely to be baffled by the difficulties of achieving complete
visual consistency. But where he contented himself with the usual head and
shoulders he occasionally, though rarely, approached distinction; one example
of this is his *Abraham Garland Randall* [High Museum, Atlanta]. His moderately fluent technical average has no particular personal accent.

With Ralph Earl, the emphatic affirmation of his New England accent noted in the pictures first painted in England was followed, during his six or seven years there, by its serious impairment with no compensating gains in mastering the current British style. However, not long after his return in 1785 he righted himself by what appears to have been the deliberate sloughing of a partially acquired manner. He renewed the blunt positiveness of his drawing and the emphatic solidity of his color areas. Most striking of all, Earl resumed the essential character of his earlier habit in the conscious manipulation of light-and-dark for constructing his idea of the human figure; and this idea retained its colonial archaism until it went to pieces a short while before his death. But because the full-length figure was so often successfully integrated with a consistently arbitrary treatment of complex surroundings, the adaptable eye can readily accept Earl's pictorial equivalent of nature.

Through including large chunks of a sitter's immediate environment Earl sometimes escaped the penalty of his usually inadequate perception of character; in this way he often made interesting pictures out of people who, in his renderings and without their accessories, would make little or no impression on the mind. Thus it is, for instance, that the entire arrangement around the overly bland face of *Colonel William Taylor* [1790: plate 34] achieved meaning. The Colonel is seated before his own sketch of the landscape which is seen out the window beyond him: he holds his maulstick not for use in his sketching but as directed by Earl in order to make an enlivening diagonal in the composition. Taylor also makes a slight turn toward his portraitist which is kept stiff by his concern to maintain the interesting placement of his arms; he is as fully aware as Earl himself of the design into which he is arranged.

Earl repeatedly used the landscape motive in his pictures; though he did so in more than one way, he most often framed it as a window view. Almost always it is handled with sufficient arbitrariness to keep it technically consistent with the interior. The quite distant view in the *Chief-Justice and Mrs. Oliver Ellsworth* [1792: Wadsworth Atheneum, Hartford] is rendered with an insistence which makes every detail as emphatic as the pattern of the foreground carpet; in this respect it vividly illustrates Earl's habit of depicting not what is naturalistically seen at a given moment but what is cumulatively known. In doing this he answered to what was already a well developed and perhaps now permanent trait in the American mind; a generation later than Earl the French observer, Alexis de Tocqueville, pointed to it when he wrote that Americans ". . . like to discern the object which engages their attention with extreme clearness . . ." A further detail about the window view in the Ellsworth portrait is that the house there seen is the house in which the couple are seated; like so much else in Earl's paintings, this is not self-explanatory in strictly visual

34. COLONEL WILLIAM TAYLOR *by* RALPH EARL
Courtesy of Albright Art Gallery, Buffalo, N.Y.

terms but a piece of non-pictorial information which nevertheless contributes something of importance to the total effect. An essentially surrealist idea is successfully recorded as an objective fact.

In his conduct John Wesley Jarvis was a singularly perfect example of the irresponsible Bohemianism that Dunlap deplored and feared, but in his character he was so winning and amusing that Dunlap along with other men relished the continuous spectacle of his character and conduct in combination. Jarvis' geniality was the main means of his securing so many commissions and his conviviality was the main reason for his indifferent success with most of them. His whole life was roistering and romantic, with some imaginativeness within its external shabbiness. Even his boyhood in Philadelphia, as much of it as he could manage being spent in doing chores for Bohemian sign painters, is picturesque in his own words set down in Dunlap. It is a pity that his fanciful spirit not only never got into his pictures but also never so much as colored his conception of painting. With him it was always a trade in which the aim was simply to turn out a quantity of work and turn it out fast.

His apprenticeship had been in engraving, which of course taught him something about drawing; with that and the little knowledge of paint he had picked up from sign-makers (and maybe from Pratt), he changed over to portraiture because he saw some pastels so bad that he knew he could do better. An early and prosperous partnership with Joseph Wood in making profiles and miniatures lasted about five years. For a brief period in the New York years Thomas Sully, then on the margin of poverty, worked for Jarvis; thereafter Jarvis made trips away—to Baltimore, to Charleston, and for several seasons in succession to New Orleans—but always returned to headquarters in New York. A Louisiana stay was marked by a great spurt of prosperity largely because he then had Henry Inman for apprentice; together they could produce six oils in a week. Collaboration like this seemed necessary to Jarvis' impetuous and impatient nature, but it resulted in inconsistent canvases. Costumes and accessories were more often than not as careless as Stuart's worst without the compensation of individuality in the faces. In these, which were Jarvis' own part in all joint productions, the paint was usually laid on reasonably well, but his command of character interpretation was erratic. He and his helpers left a large quantity of unsatisfactory portraits among which even the examples of relative distinction do not attain a quality sufficient to make them stand out from the mass of contemporaneous work.

A better co-ordinated collaboration was continued through many years by two painters more evenly matched: Samuel Lovett Waldo and William Jewett. When Waldo worked alone the result could be at the same time brilliant and solid; when the two of them worked together on the same canvas the brilliance disappeared, and though the solidity remained it seemed of less consequence. The most convenient illustration of this is found in two portraits of *John Trumbull* [Yale University Art Gallery]: the later version by the firm depicts an unusual face above a pair of shoulders which afford a satisfactory visual foundation but nothing more; the earlier version by Waldo depicts a head of remarkable distinction, and the imperious expression is re-enforced by a tensely held body where the very brush strokes help to convey the sitter's energy. The joint production of this most prolonged of all American painting partnerships remained as sound as it was steady; it easily commands respect as craft without ever arousing enthusiasm as art. The respect may be ungrudging, but the absence of the enthusiasm means that such painting stays in the record simply because it happened. It remains a portion of that part of the past which is spiritually unusable by later times.

Since culture and politics united to make Philadelphia a genuinely national capital for the opening years of the Federal Era, it was the gathering-place for the portrait specialists who were already beginning to draw a line between themselves and the artisans. The difference was in many cases real enough, but in retrospect it seems a typically nineteenth-century mistake to deny the more important identity of professional interest. Thomas Sully, for example, reported to Dunlap that John Eckstein was a drudge; and the record does indeed seem to bear out that opinion. Advertising himself as "formerly historical painter and statuary to the King of Prussia," he professed several kinds of painting and in 1812 exhibited a model for a proposed equestrian statue of George Washington in Roman costume. His few known engravings in stipple are not very good, but a few portraits in oil display the artisan-like modeling which appeared crude to Sully and Dunlap and now seems meritoriously forthright.

Forthrightness seems also the right word for the average portrait work of Charles Willson Peale, whose painting and other activities had much to do with making and keeping Philadelphia a vigorous center of cultural influence for his lifetime. He had settled there in 1776, only to have to find another haven for his family while he was away fighting and the British occupied the city. When the war was past, he made many excursions north into New York state and south into Maryland, but each time he rounded back to Philadelphia with some money from portrait work or some specimens for his museum. He did much painting for the museum, but his inclusion in it of natural history and invention interfered with his painting for long periods. Yet through all his desistings and resumings he was wholly consistent in character. The very fact of his not being a painter exclusively was what preserved him and his family through years when painting alone supported no one here. A soldier who served under him in the army said of Peale: "He fit and painted, painted and fit." Afterwards, too, he did many other things, but he always came back to painting—doing good work up to almost his eighty-fifth year.

So long a life-span of course did something to make possible a large quantity of painting despite his other activities; but the main reason for his productiveness was the unique way in which he combined the untemperamental craft attitude of the shop with the facility in executing a formula then more often practised in the studio. He had a firm belief, pragmatically confirmed by his own experience, that anybody could learn to paint. In this belief he urged instruction and careers upon brother, nephews and nieces, daughters and sons; upon nine of his children he practised the psychological ruse of naming them for famous painters of Europe. It speaks well for human nature that only two out of the nine became lifelong professionals.

In keeping with his ultrademocratic idea about the practice of painting, Peale's concept of portraiture was wholly literal; yet at the same time his mechanical turn of mind and his habit of haste often impaired the very accuracy which can be the virtue of a literalness which takes sufficient pains. He early began to take advantage of the fact that prominent men were much in Philadelphia to make two small portrait heads of every such person who would consent: one for the sitter and one for the museum. Apparently Peale had in mind something like a National Portrait Gallery; but the uniformity of his presentation, though it probably satisfied his own desire for neatness and regularity, must have repelled rather than invited curiosity. Enough of the originals have been re-assembled in Independence Hall to repel now, at least, even when the doubtful examples and the late copies are deducted from the total. Row upon row of heads, seen at the same distance and from the same angle of vision, appear all the more monotonous for the repetitious way in which too many of them approach the egg in shape. On the other hand, by concentrating attention upon the features, it becomes possible to realize how shrewd an eye Peale had for character when it existed. Apparently he could not confer it upon anyone; he was too innocently extrovert for that. But confront him with a face of any strength, and he would record it with a technical directness which also expressed the candor of his own mind.

So strongly predisposed to the matter of fact, Peale was not at home in the more ambitious form of official portraiture which borders upon history painting. When the Pennsylvania legislature in the midst of war commissioned such a portrait of General Washington, the painter misjudged what would be appropriate. *Washington Before Trenton* [1778–1779: Pennsylvania Academy, Philadelphia] is a puzzle to the understanding now—but less for its failure to achieve either dignity or informality than for its seeming attempt to embody both qualities at once. The oversize standing figure is ridiculous as well

as unsteady in posture, just a farmer trying to seem at ease among the paraphernalia of war. The pictorial catastrophe is so complete that it is in a way
reassuring that Peale never knew it but went on making replicas and variants
to the number of nineteen.

In other commissions where he could remain his hearty and unconstrained
everyday self Peale was frequently interesting in his design as well as admirable
in his rendering of character. The *Richard Tilghman* [1790: privately owned]
may be cited as an example in which character is the more important factor,
and the *Charles Petit* [1792: Worcester Art Museum] as one in which design has more significance. However, Peale was never the man to narrow his
interest down to one element at the expense of others; he might fail totally, as
in the *Washington Before Trenton,* or he might succeed delightfully, as in
The Children of Benjamin Stoddart [1789: privately owned]; but at both
extremes and at all stages in between he brought to bear upon every picture
all he knew about painting. He had a faith in his own competence which was
frequently justified by works. Yet as his own life and the Federal Era together
drew toward their close he became more and more plainly a survivor from an
earlier time working with an increasingly antiquated technique. In it not only
was the color subordinated to line, but the line itself developed relatively
little subtlety through the years. It could be bold and sweeping; it could even
convey volume and weight. But the figures it outlined remained inflexible,
perhaps a little archaic, when put alongside the current production of younger
men.

Peale's work was better in its kind than much in the newer way of painting;
the difficulty was that even good work in the older manner was no longer favored by fashion. Take Jacob Eichholtz as an example. The usual Peale is now
seen as a much sounder performance in all essentials of portraiture than the
usual Eichholtz, but not many portrait buyers then thought so. Possibly the
younger man might have become better than he did if he had continued his
development in a direct line out of sign painting from which he started; in
that case he would have found himself allied to Eckstein and Peale. But a
visit to Lancaster by Sully started Eichholtz upon an attempt to acquire the
different manner derived from British studio practice; he further followed
Sully's advice in seeking out Stuart in Boston. But Sully and Stuart together
could not pull him above mediocrity and keep him there; no more often than
Frothingham did Eichholtz lift himself above a spiritless technical average.
His financial success in a time of keen competition shows what his contemporaries thought; and at a testimonial dinner which was tendered upon his
return from Philadelphia to Lancaster, Eichholtz was toasted with: "The
skill of the artist is only equalled by the moral excellence of the man."

Those traits were also manifested in a much more conspicuous way by Eichholtz's mentor, Thomas Sully. Dunlap's opening words about him are appropriate to both the period and the man who

. . . has long stood at the head of his profession as a portrait painter, and whose designs, in fancy subjects, all partake of the elegant correctness of his character. . . .

Although Dunlap wrote at almost the half-way point of Sully's career, his words fit the whole with the effectiveness of an epitaph. Nevertheless, there was also a measure of difference between Sully's work before and after 1830 by which each phase suited its own setting with its own shading of significance.

Since his earliest pictures are unknown, it is not possible now to study the actual stages in Sully's development toward his full-blown Britishism of manner, but the opinion may be hazarded that he early manifested a talent for quick assimilation which made it possible for him to be a self-teaching eclectic. After his beginnings in company with his boyhood friend in Charleston, Charles Fraser, fifteen years elapsed during which in six cities Sully received smatterings of help from eight or more professionals. To Stuart he always felt particularly grateful, and in London West earned from him the same lasting sentiment. The advice West gave him was shrewdly calculated to help him overcome his weakness in construction, but the brushwork and colorism which Sully brought back were not those of the seventy-year-old history-painter; they were straight out of the Royal Academy schools and the practice of Beechey and Lawrence.

Within two years after his return Sully had painted two ambitious canvases with an ease of brushwork and a sureness of figure construction and a consistent substance all through such as he never afterward joined together so convincingly. The *George Frederick Cooke As Richard the Third* [after 1811: Pennsylvania Academy, Philadelphia] is both solid and splendid in its dramatic light-and-dark. The figure of *Samuel Coates* [1812: plate 35] is about as solid as that of the actor, but the tall desk and the window embrasure look a little less so in the sparkling daylight which here appears as direct illumination in an American interior for probably the first time. Here also Sully's remarkable fluency enabled him to exert control over the picture-space and also, in adding what was then an unusual amount of space overhead, to keep it interestingly modulated in tone. A while before 1830 some portraits gave unmistakable portents of a habit which became more noticeable after that date: the habit of transmogrifying handsome women into pretty females. But in the main this first half of Sully's career contributed an important strain of technique and feeling to the American blend; even if it was an artificial importation into the still somewhat rustic Federal Era and even if it lacked the technical uniqueness and frequently profound perception which raised Stuart above his age, Sully's early romanticism was robust enough to stay sound today.

Cities south of Philadelphia had their resident portraitists who received varying degrees of local support, but that was often definitely lessened by the incursions of better known workmen from outside. At Washington the principal artist-in-residence from 1816 on was Charles Bird King, who earned a harsh word from Dunlap for not helping with autobiographical information; the impression left from other references to him is that King succeeded less by his painting skill than by a bachelor's pleasant manner when dining out. Political turnovers with every election kept Washington society continuously changing, so that there were few professional fixtures like King; but one noticeable result of the city's increasing importance was to emphasize the Potomac as the dividing line between North and South. Earlier there had been nothing so definite, but rather a vague region of gradual change somewhere between Philadelphia and Richmond. Now it became clearer with every decade that crossing the river into Virginia meant entering a climate of opinion much more sharply different than the climate of air and temperature.

It was principally that cultural intangible which gave significance to the appearance in Richmond of a few settled painters in addition to its one or two seasonal visitors. The itinerants of colonial times, from the Anon. of 1722 in Jamestown to John Durand a half century later, could leave little tradition where there were few workmen to carry on; and as a new town, Richmond repeated the pattern of older ones in that its first resident painters combined other activities with their painting. James Warrell was a dancing master who, having broken a leg, offered portrait work after 1812; he founded the Virginia Museum in 1817 with some plaster casts of classic statues and executed some history pieces that have disappeared. John B. Martin worked in stipple engraving and lithography from 1822; at least one small portrait by him is technically attractive—the *Major James Gibbon* [Virginia Historical Society, Richmond]—but others range from poor to bad. A French refugee with a family showed up in 1805; he was Phillippe Abraham Peticolas who had come to the United States from Santo Domingo in 1790. He kept a store and painted miniatures. Four sons mixed miniature painting, music teaching and store keeping in Richmond and other places; the best painter among them seems to have been the second son, Edward F. Peticolas, who had the initial advantage of some lessons from Sully.

Charleston of course had had its resident painters from the beginning; for a short while, as the Federal Era opened, some charming work was done there by James Earl, the younger brother of Ralph. James had spent a longer time in England, and it is said that his going to Charleston was accidental, his ship

35. SAMUEL COATES *by* THOMAS SULLY
Courtesy of The Pennsylvania Hospital.

having been blown off its course; evidently he was welcomed, for he was kept busy there until he died of yellow fever. About fifteen works have been attributed to him, one of the most interesting being the double portrait of *Elizabeth Paine and Her Aunt* [Rhode Island School of Design, Providence]. He was more fluent than his brother, and achieved a greater degree of unity in both design and tone. That does not make him more interesting, for the rougher authenticity of Ralph now has a greater power of command over the mind; but James did something attractively personal in giving to a few canvases a wine-dark gleam.

Ralph Earl's English-born son, Ralph Eleazer Whitesides Earl, became identified with the newer South which was coming into existence west of the coastal states. Passing his boyhood with his father in Connecticut, he returned to England in 1809, where he studied with West; after several months in Paris he returned here in 1815 and in 1818 married a niece of Mrs. Andrew Jackson. His wife soon died, but he stayed on as a member of the Jackson domestic establishment until his death, and he is buried at The Hermitage. His sobriquet of "Portrait Painter to the King" suggests an anomalous semi-feudal relationship between him and the frontier would-be aristocrat whose rowdy followers wrecked the furnishings of the White House in celebrating the political victory of the common man. Doubtless a personal warmth of feeling between Jackson and Earl does them credit as human beings, but in a Tennessee which was still a frontier there is a curious unreality about a pet painter functioning as a household retainer. It may have had publicity value, for Earl turned out many portraits of Jackson—all bad.

The really prosperous South which began to flourish in the Federal Era was the land of cotton all through the Lower Mississippi Valley. It was exploited into its amazingly quick wealth mainly by men coming straight west from the Old South along the Atlantic coast; and it was to factories far away that they sold the product of their own brand of agricultural industrialism known as slave labor. Natchez and Mobile were certainly settlements, but they were far from being cities like those in the east; only later did they reach the point of supporting locally resident painters whose work can be found there today. Even the itinerants were few at first, and some of them were on a search for health in which work was only incidental. The search for health then almost always meant for a climate to arrest tuberculosis; and this was why a young Massachusetts painter, Nathan Negus, landed at Savannah late in 1820. In a series of removes through two and a half years he reached Mobile; during the next two years he lost his fight against the disease, returned to Boston, and reached home again four days before he died. Eliab Metcalf lived fifteen years longer, but that only meant more years spent in a hunt for the proper

climate. He was making a stay of three years in New Orleans just before
Negus reached Mobile; later he sought out various Caribbean lands, and spent
his last eight years in an equilibrium of summers in New York and winters in
Havana. These two and others in the record were wholly or largely dependent
upon selling their work as they traveled, which is why most of them went
like Metcalf to New Orleans, where an interest in pictures already existed.
In that respect New Orleans was fast becoming notable, but in a way which
has a very special and somewhat complex cultural significance.

After the Louisiana Purchase in 1802 the place rapidly changed from a town
into a city. The tremendous increase of down-river commerce brought with it
a prosperity till then unknown, of which an ample share went to the Creoles
of French and Spanish descent; but it also brought with it the American "in-
vaders," whom the Creoles disliked. Despite the absence of significant intellectual life in the whole region throughout the checkered century of French
and Spanish colonial rule, the Creoles adopted an attitude of cultural superiority to the Americans; and the use of the French language was long locally
regarded as the necessary mark of good birth. As profits piled up from sugar
and cotton some of them were spent on the arts and crafts; and in that patronage, too, through the mid-century the note of protest against the Americans
became tangible. But before 1830 the Creoles did not distinguish themselves
for any really lavish patronage of their own kind in painting; it was too soon for
good painters from France to seek work there and also too soon for any Creole-
born to seek professional training in Paris. An occasional French name is listed
as a painter in the directories, generally for work in miniature; and a number
of portraits in oil have been identified as by José de Salazar. One of them is
said to be in the Roman Catholic Cathedral at St. Louis; whether that means
that the painter himself was there is not certain. But several portraits in Philadelphia have caused a surmise that he might have traveled that far north. His
work has the technical feebleness usual in the earlier colonial efforts. Yet in the
newer New Orleans accumulating around the colonial kernel portraits were
much in demand, and to get that trade painters like Metcalf and Jarvis paid
their visits; and in the eighteen-twenties Audubon on his bird explorations
earned his way by painting portraits and teaching the children on certain plantations near St. Francisville.

Far up the Mississippi and the Ohio, whence the flatboats came, was the
region which in time acquired the identifying name of the Old West—in 1830
still new enough, indeed, and raw enough to incur the famous scorn of Mrs.
Trollope, but already supporting its own portraitists and soon a native-born
professional architect. A year before Mrs. Trollope arrived in Cincinnati an
Academy of Art was functioning in which Hiram Powers, later famous as a

sculptor, received his first lessons. Marietta, like Cincinnati, was an outpost of the East; and only fourteen miles down the river Herman Blennerhassett had built, on his own island before 1800, a stately home fitted with furniture and paintings from Europe and had called in a painter to decorate his ceilings. But within a decade all this splendor was destroyed in consequence of his becoming involved with the traitorous activities of Aaron Burr. About 1820 Chester Harding painted "near a hundred heads" in Paris, Kentucky, at twenty-five dollars each; in 1818 John Neagle had tried his luck in Lexington, only to find Jouett living there; Neagle therefore went on down the river to New Orleans, where Jouett also was to make winter sojourns. Not only Kentucky and Ohio but the whole Mississippi Valley was in those years a colonial empire for the eastern states, and the people who first appointed themselves the guardians of western culture were excessively colonial in their efforts to hasten the transplantation of eastern standards and fashions. As Wren had sketched the first idea for the first building at William and Mary, so Bulfinch did for Kenyon College. But the eastward-looking westerners were not to alter the nation's politics and economics and culture; that was rather to be done by the spiritual descendants of the earlier westerners who ironically flattered Heaven by calling it "a Kaintuck of a place." It was the Kaintucks with whom the Creoles frightened their children—the Kaintucks who boasted they were part horse, part alligator, and part snapping turtle. Like a great deal more of the oral literature of the frontier, it has a rough imaginative vigor, but it is not what passes for culture; it may have considerable value for a later culture, but as the direct embodiment of an actual state of mind it is a wild philistinism. Before the art of painting in particular the Kaintuck mind in its purity was helpless when it was not antagonistic.

This mind appears in the remark made by the father of Matthew Harris Jouett: "I sent Matthew to college to make a gentleman of him, and he has turned out to be nothing but a damned sign-painter." On the other hand there was a later statement from an art professor in Cincinnati: "Rembrandt is next to God, and Jouett is next to Rembrandt." The two sentences about the same man present a neat contrast between attitudes which just about match each other in the ignorance displayed and in the harm they do. Either extreme as applied to the moderate competence of Jouett's work shows a serious incapacity for forming opinion, but the judgement each incurs is very different. The father's was simply original sin in its cultural aspect, the normal inheritance of human beings in American civilization; the professor's was mortal sin in esthetic terms because, though lacking in judgement, it pretended to speak from completeness of pictorial experience. One attitude would expose the unwanted bantling of art to the elements; the other would nurse it into prodigies of immaturity. Operating at the same time, they can together make art almost impossible of attainment.

Jouett himself was of course unaware of such issues shadowing his portrait work; he shared the mid-western haste to hurry up culture. At the start of his brief twelve years of professional practice he spent four months with Stuart in Boston; and though he made the most adequate record in words of what Stuart said, he never succeeded in practising Stuart's advice as well as Frothingham at the time or as Neagle a little later. What he did do upon returning to Kentucky was to double his prices from twenty-five to fifty dollars. He also took into his studio as pupil an art-struck waif, John Grimes; and the fact that the pupil soon became an assistant probably had something to do with the inconsistencies to be found through the more than three hundred portraits bearing the name of Jouett. An occasional example rises to an unpretentious technical straightforwardness which allows the subject to count in human terms without interference from the flaws of carelessness and unperceptiveness.

Many hundreds of portraits were painted by the men discussed in this section; many hundreds more were done by other painters who rang the changes upon the manners practised by these typical few. Attentive examination of so much ordinary work is at best a very mixed experience which suggests that several factors need consideration in order to reach a correct estimate. The right comment on the subjects of these portraits was made much later in another connection by Abraham Lincoln: "The Lord prefers common-looking people. That is the reason he makes so many of them." As a fact of life that is to be accepted—and accepted as soon as possible. But as a fact in the craft of painting, acceptance is more difficult; there it requires the usually delayed attitude which in a philosophical context is called stoicism. So many commonplace countenances perpetuated in so much commonplace painting must be noted by the historian as the quantitative phenomenon it was. Its major significance for the interpreter is the circumstance that all but a small fraction of it lacks both technical and spiritual distinction.

That points straight to the painters themselves. Copley in the generation of Americans just before them and Stuart in their own were proof enough that the portraitist who is capable of distinction in his art sets down distinctive people. Whether he perceives what actually exists in them or attributes his own nature to them may be a matter for metaphysical debate; it seems not debatable that artistically important portraiture is not commonplace. Perhaps it would be natural for commonplace people to prefer the same quality in their painters; but it is at least possible that the commonplaceness of the painter is the real reason why the people seem so in the portraits. Certainly all the people and all the painters who imagined that painting could be legitimately narrowed down to portraiture knew almost nothing about art. The life of painting as an art required a nation's release from the tyranny of the human countenance, and the pleasantest part of the historian's task is to seek out tangible evidence for the development of other forms of painting.

41. *Forms strengthened by the foreign-born*

STILL-LIFE

Cornelius de Beet: act. 1812
James Cox: 1751–1834

HISTORY

Denis A. Volozon: act. 1811–1820
Adolf Ulrik Wertmüller: 1751–1811

ANECDOTE

Charles Catton: 1756–1819
John Lewis Krimmel: 1789–1821

TOPOGRAPHICAL VIEWS

William Russell Birch: 1755–1834
Joshua Shaw: 1776–1860
William Guy Wall: 1782–1864
John Rubens Smith: 1775–1849

William James Bennett: 1787–1844
(work to 1830)

PANORAMA AND SCENE
PAINTING

William Winstanley: ?–after 1806
Cotton Milbourne: act. 1794
John Joseph Holland: c. 1776–?
James Coyle: 1798–1828
Michele Felice Corné: c. 1765–1845

LANDSCAPE

William Groombridge: 1748–1811
John James Barralet: 1747–1815
George Beck: 1750–1812
Francis Guy: 1760–1820

In the Federal Era trained foreigners practised, with varying degrees of success, several kinds of painting beyond the confines of portraiture. Again records contain information about more pictures actually painted than have been preserved. For example, Dunlap mentions still-life as well as landscape being painted in Baltimore by Cornelius de Beet in 1812; but his work is not now known despite the date's being almost two decades after examples of both types had been exhibited in the first exhibition of the Columbianum Association. Just one year earlier than the exhibition, in 1794, James Cox arrived in Philadelphia from London, where he had been a colorer of prints for Boydell; he may have brought still-life pictures with him and he probably began painting them at once. For that subject-matter was already a stand-by in teaching, and as a teacher Cox was a fashionable success; he must have been intelligent, too, since he used his money to collect more than five thousand books on art which he bequeathed to the Library Company of Philadelphia. Denis A. Volozon sent several kinds of paintings to various Philadelphia exhibitions, and it is particularly regrettable that nothing is now known about his history pictures except their titles, for they anticipate the academic stock in trade of the entire nineteenth century in Europe even more than in this country: *Homer Singing*

His Poems, Angelica and Medor, The Death of Cleopatra, Rinaldo and Armida.

In some of these subjects there was an opportunity to paint the nude if the painter wished, and Volozon as a Frenchman may have been puzzled by a strong American prejudice against it. At present there is no information that Volozon himself risked censure in that respect, but he must certainly have been aware of the experience a few years earlier of the Swedish-born internationalist, Adolf Ulrik Wertmüller. The latter's career had for thirty years kept him busy over the greater part of Europe, but especially at the French court, where he had painted a state portrait of Marie Antoinette and her children in 1785. After such associations, the French Revolution put him in some danger and he also lost a large investment in French bonds; so he sought a haven here. He stayed from 1794 to 1797: then he went to Stockholm, but in 1800 came back here—to marry and live out his last decade. In the United States he painted portraits, beginning with a *George Washington* [1795: Metropolitan Museum, New York], but it was a picture he brought with him which affected American taste near the beginning of the century-long contest over the nude in art. His mythological *Danaë* [National Museum, Stockholm, Sweden] got him into the same kind of financially profitable trouble that Pine had experienced with his cast of the *Venus de' Medici.*

From the time that Wertmüller exhibited his picture in 1787 it had been admired in Paris and elsewhere in Europe; and it was natural that he should want to show it here. In this he had the help of Rembrandt Peale, who incurred the disapproval of his father by devising a scheme of illumination which dramatized the nudity of the figure; there was disapproval also from some Amerind chiefs who turned their backs at the sight. Even after Wertmüller's death the picture continued to be an occasion for scandal among those who thought themselves in charge of American morals as well as American culture. In 1814 Jarvis in New York was making money from it and its continued exhibition caused the *Analectic Magazine* in 1815 to say that ". . . both in subject and in style of execution it offends against pure taste and the morality of art." That is not the way in which the condemnation would be phrased today, but even from today's different point of view it can be understood how the *Danaë* gave offense to many Americans around 1805.

The European academic training of that day stressed drawing as the major factor in the making of pictures, and Wertmüller was a quite competent draftsman of the time. His line, however, lacked the sensitivity necessary to great drawing; it was not content to be clear but was assertive in the way characteristic of little minds. It was essentially this trait which further betrayed Wertmüller into crossing the boundary which separates good from bad taste. The boundary probably shifts from one age to another, and it can never be exactly located or described in any verbal formula; it can only be empirically tested in particular cases. In the case of Wertmüller's *Danaë* the deciding factor seems to be that to the hard draftsmanship he joined a hard glossiness of pigment surface which strongly vulgarized the whole. It was historically accidental and culturally unfortunate that the nude in painting was initially exemplified here in work by an insensitive mind.

About the same time the far less controversial type of picture called the anecdote was being produced on the level of studio professionalism by other foreign-born. An Englishman named Charles Catton, who came here in 1801, painted a theatrical drop-scene of Shakespeare characters in New York twelve years later; that was as definitely historical in subject as any easel picture, and other pictures by Catton were both easel paintings and anecdotal in character. Dunlap mentioned one of animals in a landscape owned by the Quaker sectarian, Elias Hicks; and it seems permissible to speculate that this was one source for the well known *Peaceable Kingdom* paintings, in about two dozen examples, by his preacher-painter cousin, Edward Hicks. Catton's last work, one of Noah "ushering" all the animals into the ark, was copied by Charles Willson Peale for his museum; that, too, might have been seen by Hicks the painter. Catton had the background of both artisan and studio training; his father was an English heraldic painter of importance in his day and Catton himself while still in England had been good enough with animals for him to paint the horse in a royal portrait by Beechey. His obituary says that in his later years he "seldom exercised his pencil, except to gratify personal friendship, or enliven the dull monotony of a rural winter life."

The most influential painting of anecdote was done by John Lewis Krimmel, whose accidental death by drowning at thirty-two doubtless deprived this country of many more pleasant pictures. Dunlap says that Krimmel, after executing a few small portraits, schooled himself in the anecdote by copying in oil a print of Wilkie's *Blind Fiddler*. Krimmel's own *Country Wedding* [c. 1814: Pennsylvania Academy, Philadelphia] partly bears that out, for the figures have a very English look; yet the meticulous handling of the complicated still-life at the edges of the picture suggests that Krimmel's technique had been thoroughly acquired before he left his native Germany. Painters with a different technique deprecated Krimmel's minuteness of vision and excessively small brushes; but the results pleased many laymen because it suited the American preference for positiveness in everything. A few small water colors of outdoor crowds have a pleasant sparkle which approximates to an effect of light; but the animation simply overlies a quite static grouping of the people. To these his oil painting of *The Artist and His Family* [c. 1820: National Gallery,

Washington] offers a strong contrast; the ten human beings, the black poodle and the doll, are steadied almost to immobility, but the whole picture into which they enter is visually vivacious. Large areas of color and clear-edged forms are organized into a design in which every shape and gesture leads the eye into the next, so that the activity of the lines strongly overcomes the studied poses.

The arrival of a number of engravers from Great Britain, together with some painters whose specialty lay in readying pictures for engraving, resulted in a sudden increase of views—both as individual prints and (a novelty here) in sets. William Russell Birch issued a group of twenty-eight plates [1799–1800] after his own drawings of Philadelphia scenes; he followed that in 1808 with a set depicting the country homes of certain rich men. He was a reasonably competent workman with a semi-mechanical formula, turning out prints which satisfied a factual curiosity in a matter-of-fact way. He had greater competence in the altogether different craft of the miniature in enamel. Two later landscape sets of greater artistic value than those by Birch were reproduced in aquatint by John Hill; one was *Picturesque Views of American Scenery* [1819] after originals by Joshua Shaw and the other was *The Hudson River Portfolio* [1828] after originals by William Guy Wall. In Shaw's set the American land was not yet tamed by man; in Wall's, nature had been strongly stamped by man's control, though the calm expanses of the river determined the dominant composite impression. Other men united in themselves both crafts, at times composing their own pictures for translating into prints and at times simply reproducing the pictures of others. Among these John Rubens Smith was important not only for his work but also for his influence upon many pupils and the books he published on drawing and anatomy. William James Bennett was another who both engraved and painted, and his originals in water color were considered sufficiently distinguished to gain him membership in the National Academy of Design and direction of its art school until his temperamental unfitness was demonstrated.

Like the pastel portraits by the Sharples, these aquatints and water colors never hint at anything subjective. To be sure, many of the people who first looked at the prints seem to have read emotions into them, for their appearance on the market was in a time when the associated ideas of the romantic and the picturesque were making a considerable stir. Landscape prints were frequently featured as illustrations in magazines which professed cultural guidance, and there they were a part of the self-conscious nativism beginning to permeate all such activities. The *New York Magazine* for June, 1794, called attention to its frontispiece, *A View of Minisink, New Jersey*, with an editorial note:

. . . an elegant rural proſpect from a part of our country, which affords as many novel and romantic ſcenes as a lover of the charm of nature can any where meet with, or as the moſt enthuſiaſtic artiſt could poſſibly deſire. . . .

Both the illustration and the text exemplify a sentiment in the most popular of the then recent plays, Royall Tyler's *The Contrast;* there the elegant urban hero, Colonel Manly, speaks of

. . . a laudable partiality, which ignorant, untravelled men entertain for everything that belongs to their native country. I call it laudable;—it injures no one; adds to their own happiness; and, where extended, becomes the noble principle of pa-triotism. . . .

Yet even patriotism must have more to feed on than such "novel and romantic ſcenes" in both picture and drama; the only real novelty was the editorial use of the word "romantic" as a label with which to claim the attention of fashion.

To a later taste the many prints and the relatively few surviving originals seem anemic, but every generation is entitled to its own pictures—or to none, if it does not want any. The rising middle class of the Federal Era naturally enough liked cheerful and pretty things, but they did not yet feel like paying much for them. In the newly fashionable landscape prints they were content with neatly presented information about the unknown or an equally neat re-minder of the familiar. However, the predetermination to make and own merely pleasant pictures exacted a price. A preference for grace and charm in art amounts to a refusal of tragic intensity, and upon that refusal there follows spiritual inadequacy to artistic greatness.

Less than a decade after its invention the novelty of the panorama was intro-duced to Americans. Dunlap says that the first one here was shown in New York, 1795, that it was of London, and that it was executed by an English-man, William Winstanley, after a set of prints which had in turn been de-rived from the panorama made by its inventor, Robert Barker. Dunlap regarded this use of prints as theft, and told other stories to Winstanley's discredit. Four landscapes by him which survive were purchased by Washington for Mount Vernon, where two of them now are, the other two being owned by the Smith-sonian Institution in Washington. Their weak drawing and inadequate model-ing suggest that similar defects were present in his panorama; if so, they may have been the cause of its apparently short duration.

For the spirit and aim of the panorama were essentially the same as those of the topographical prints. Instead of confronting the spectator with a few inches of landscape on a miniature scale, a complete panorama surrounded him with many feet of it; as he stood at the center under the shadow of an umbrella-like covering, his eyes could travel around the whole horizon of the picture.

If he had viewed the actuality there described in paint, he could have the pleasure of recognition and frequently the further pleasure of discovering incorrect details; if he had not been to the spot, he usually came away with a good substitute for the traveler's gratification. But this was possible only by means of verisimilitude sufficient to permit the slow examination which people in general at all times think they most enjoy.

There is no way of knowing how minute an execution was asked in the allied craft of stage scenery, but its early practitioners coming here from England found themselves very welcome in all the principal cities except Boston. Cotton Milbourne in Philadelphia won praise late in 1794 for painting three local scenes for *The Elopement*. John Joseph Holland's skill in the scene painting obtained him pupils in New York, and at least one of them turned to panoramas later; Holland's own water-color landscapes were much admired. James Coyle's scenery for *The Lady of the Lake* and *The Flying Dutchman* was also admired in the middle eighteen-twenties, and he was among the founding members of the National Academy of Design. It may be presumed that Coyle treated his subjects in a spirit different from that of the factually informative panorama; perhaps the memorableness of his work came from its imaginativeness.

Another foreigner showed some very long landscape views which were called panoramas in Salem, Massachusetts: he was Michele Felice Corné, who came here in 1799 at the invitation of the famous merchant, Elias Hasket Derby. This painter's *Siege of Tripoli*, of 1807, was ten feet high and sixty feet long. In 1809 the antiquarian Bentley was disgusted to find *The Bay of Naples* "only a copy of the common plates . . ." with the topical addition of the famous warship *Constitution* to stimulate interest. In an existing wall decoration called *The Bay of Naples* Corné may have repeated the essential part of the so-called panorama; this decoration remains in the Sullivan-Dorr House in Providence, Rhode Island [1812–1815]. It alone is eight by twenty feet in size, yet it covers only one wall among many; other pictures complete the parlor, fill the hall, and extend up the staircase. They are all done in water color directly on the plaster, and may therefore be called fresco even though not in the method of the Renaissance. The work is technically careless in places and hasty in execution throughout, but its varied and derivative motives gain considerable spiritedness from the coarse and sometimes slashing stroke of a fast worker. There is an operatic romanticism in this panorama-like anthology of Italian coast, ruins that might be farther north, a couple of vaguely English countryscapes, and a palm tree sheltering a hunter who shoots at a fantastic bird; and the air of fantasy is only enriched by the addition of a heavy-snowed bucolic scene which foretells Currier and Ives. Using other techniques, Corné decorated other houses around New England, some of which have been destroyed. He painted portraits of sea captains in Salem, and what passed for portraits of their vessels; he also executed a series of naval battles during the War of 1812, which may be judged by pictorially tiresome examples which are preserved at the Naval Academy, Annapolis. He is reputed to have been a social ornament of Newport for the last twenty years of his life; he certainly needed a talent of some sort to put across his flashily inadequate pictures. But historically he did much to enliven a region where the portrait had long throttled other forms of painting.

The technique of William Groombridge was as thin as that of Winstanley, but he manifested a more ingratiating decorativeness which was fortunately joined to a somewhat stronger observation. In consequence his *Fairmount and the Schuylkill River* [1800: Historical Society of Pennsylvania, Philadelphia] and his earlier *Washington Heights* [1793: Jumel Mansion, New York] combined a reasonable degree of localization with a pleasant echo of the current British manner. John James Barralet, who worked mostly at designing and engraving topographical prints, left one landscape in oil. *The Market Street Permanent Bridge* [1812: Historical Society of Pennsylvania, Philadelphia], which is more dryly precise than Groombridge in noting a particular view. In Dunlap's book Barralet makes a vivid episode with his personal dirtiness and professional deviousness; but this painting is as straightforward and neat as any contemporaneous print.

Among all the foreign-trained who came here in the Federal Era, George Beck had the most substantial and the best mastered landscape style; the quality of his practice in Great Britain is indicated by a list of thirteen paintings and two groups of drawings exhibited there through four years at the Society of Artists and the Royal Academy. George Washington purchased two pictures by him of *Falls of the Potomac* [1796–1797: Mount Vernon, Virginia]; Washington's thorough and thoughtful mind, as he lived with these two pictures and the four by Winstanley, doubtless perceived how Beck's superiority in craft enabled him to render the rocks with a strength sufficient to withstand the turbulent rush and falling weight of water. Beck's ability to construct the forms of rock and tree, to give the solidity of earth, and even (though less well) to modulate values toward a distant horizon appears most clearly in the *Baltimore from Howard's Park* [1796: Maryland Historical Society, Baltimore]; it derives from better painters, but in drawing upon them for these technical traits it also echoes their grave and spacious minds.

Only six originals executed here by Beck have so far been identified, but more are on record: nine exhibited in Philadelphia, an unknown number owned in Kentucky, where he lived his last eight years, and six "drawings" of American scenes reproduced by aquatint in London. It seems reasonable to think that Thomas Doughty's trees and foliage owe something to Beck's sound traditionalism and further that both trees and light effects in various Baltimore views by Francis Guy shortly after 1800 are similarly indebted to Beck's view done six years earlier.

Guy's pictures were stigmatized by a Baltimore woman journalist in 1809 as ". . . only a sort of Mosaic, drawn from compositions well known and even engraved, of several celebrated painters . . ."; she was railing at Baltimore, "the Siberia of the arts," for favoring Guy with more patronage than Groombridge. In 1811 a Philadelphia newspaper writer renewed the charge of derivativeness in connection with some of Guy's paintings recently exhibited there. To this Guy replied in a Baltimore paper offering five hundred dollars to anyone who could show that a single picture of his was copied from any other pictorial source. He may have been safe with that particular wording; at least all of his known paintings are manifestly taken from specific scenes in nature. Rembrandt Peale described Guy's early device of beginning a picture by drawing its outline in chalk on a strip of black gauze set up before the actual scene; this piece of mechanics must have been useful in several ways—reducing labor to some extent, achieving a certain literal accuracy, and gradually confirming a habit of composition which he could use without any difficulty of fresh thought. Just the same, people kept charging him with plagiarism; four years after his death, John Neal, an American writing for *Blackwood's* in Edinburgh, said that Guy stole ". . . very judiciously; almost always from the same source—Claude . . ." Whether the indebtedness was as exclusive as that or more complex, as charged by the Baltimore lady, could be better determined if more than nineteen of his nearly three hundred and seventy-five pictures were available for study. Guy was no roamer—he stayed in Baltimore for about twenty years before going to Brooklyn for his last three; but in him were large streaks of the picaresque rapscallion hero. Such a character turned painter would take his own where he found it:

> An' what he thought 'e might require,
> 'E went an' took—the same as me!

So Kipling wrote of Homer; and for Guy, in his own small way, the justification would be the same.

Whatever he took from others he turned to personal use; and he did this either despite marked craft deficiencies or because of them. As had occurred several times among colonial portraitists, Guy's technical awkwardness prevented him from slavishly reproducing what he saw. But this negative conditioning factor would have been worth no more to Guy than anyone else except for a more important positive factor. His eye and mind were both fixed intently upon what was before him; the mechanics of setting down some scenes only stimulated his mind. Once the ground plan or pattern was outlined, he exerted himself to note values and edges with care; and if the resulting shapes usually lack volume, the picture-surface as a whole is nevertheless built up with satisfactory impasto. This characteristic is noticeable in his first known American work, *Tontine's Coffee House* [c. 1797: New-York Historical Society, New York], and in a pair of spacious country scenes, one of which is *Pennington Mills, View Downstream* [1804: plate 36]. It is the impasto, together with changes in size, that preserves from monotony Guy's trick of paired figures which he so often repeats through nine or ten views of Baltimore and near-by estates. And impasto remains important in the most important one among the group of four Brooklyn views which at present close the list of Guy's works: *Brooklyn in Winter* [1817–1820: Brooklyn Museum].

Hundreds of European painters had taken snowy streets between snow-covered buildings for their theme: a subject inherently so pictorial that only an extraordinarily poor painter could succeed in failing with it. No doubt the idea was suggested to Guy by some painting or print, but he looked at it freshly. The hard lines present particular houses; posture and gesture and gait in the little silhouetted figures are visually so specific that no key of names is needed to confirm a conviction of their being recognizable to those who knew them in life; it is even possible to believe that the half-dozen dogs could have been recorded by name if someone had thought of it in time. This picture is the climax of a tendency in Guy which had been his source of strength all along and which enabled him to fit so well into his American environment despite his not coming here until he was thirty-five. Selling more than three hundred landscapes and sea battles to Americans of the Federal Era is evidence enough of popularity—evidence perhaps all the stronger for his frequent use of raffling as his sales device. The taste he satisfied seems more admirable than the taste which preferred Groombridge's more slavish school pieces. It may be that Guy's kind of Americans were willing to take his cruder craft because with it he took a firmer hold upon the things which they knew to be their own. And besides, whatever may have been the case with Groombridge's pictures, Guy's were cheap.

36. PENNINGTON MILLS, VIEW DOWNSTREAM *by* FRANCIS GUY *Courtesy of The Peabody Institute, Baltimore. Photograph from Walters Art Gallery.*

42. Forms developed by the native-born

ANECDOTE
Bass Otis: 1784–1861
David Claypoole Johnston: 1799–1865
Henry Sargent: 1770–1845

PANORAMA
John Trumbull: 1756–1843
Edward Savage: 1761–1817
John Vanderlyn: 1776–1852

LANDSCAPE
Charles Fraser: 1782–1860
Ralph Earl: 1751–1801
Alvan Fisher: 1792–1863
William Dunlap: 1766–1839

STILL-LIFE
John Johnston: 1758–1818
Henry Smith Mount: 1802–1841
Asa Park: act. 1800–1820
Charles Bird King: 1785–1862
James Peale: 1749–1831
Raphaelle Peale: 1774–1825

Among the foreign-born considered in the preceding section Krimmel, Guy, and the print-makers apparently succeeded in maintaining themselves by their craft. With the native-born now to be considered, their very variable painting incomes derived from portraiture; yet they all, though to different extents, turned aside from that sure thing to experiment with other branches of painting which interested them as much or more. They thus paid a price of their own for departing from the norm of American taste in their day, but thus they prepared the way for later painters to make a living by pictures which were not portraits. Although the landscapes and anecdotes and still-lifes by these earlier men did not reward their makers with money, the pictures themselves frequently reward examination today by their artistic merits.

Interesting examples are fewest in the anecdotal type, and examples by known workmen remain quite isolated from the rest of their work. The dullish average portraiture of Bass Otis has its single remaining exception in his *Village Forge* [1819: Pennsylvania Academy, Philadelphia]. When the picture was fresh it may have shown some effort after variety of treatment in the large expanse of shadow through its upper part, but Otis seems not to have known enough about paint to make permanent his own picturesque intention. Yet he had a way of convincing some of his contemporaries with accuracy of detail, for a Boston story about him says that, in his business of making mortuary portraits from a quick sketch or even a verbal description, he would borrow the deceased person's clothes and paint them so "like" that the facial resemblance proved acceptable too. Perhaps Otis' execution of the first lithographs known to have been done in this country will do more than anything else to keep him in the historical record. The engraver, David Claypoole Johnston, extended his rather adolescent kind of humor into anecdotal water colors which ask a considerable degree of indulgence for both the satire and the technique.

Two anecdotal pictures by a painter of the Federal Era which do not ask that relaxation are Henry Sargent's *The Tea Party* [plate 37] and *The Dinner Party* [Museum of Fine Arts, Boston]. All they require is adjustment to a hard and dry pigment surface and a restricted range of color, which are quite minor shortcomings in pictures so full of pleasure then in the doing of them and now in the looking at them. The shortcomings were not so much personal faults of judgement in Sargent as technical traits prevalent in his time; yet they did prevent him from developing fully his complex visual problems of cross lights, half lights, and reflected lights. On the other hand, there is the surprising courage of his trying to paint such subjects at all and the originality then and there of his emphasizing a purely pictorial appeal to the point wherein individuals took a distinctly second place. His degree of success came from his thoughtful management of space, his well planned dominants of lights and darks, his consistency of drawing even where it is not equal to finesse of detail, his intelligently arbitrary gradation of shadows, and his carefully gauged transitions of tone.

The failure of Sargent's craftsmanship to achieve naturalistic nuance in figure construction points toward one reason for the slowness of American painters generally in mastering the visual anecdote. Portrait painting as then practised, almost entirely by formula and mostly on the scale of what was then elegantly termed the "busto," was inadequate training for the multiple problems of the anecdote. Compositions of several or many figures in which the formal staging of history painting is given up for the appearance of everyday casualness are just that much more difficult to carry off. Probably another cause of delay in anecdotal painting was the normal human slowness to perceive the artistic possibilities of the ordinary, which affected literature as well as painting in this country.

Landscape did not have to wait as long as anecdote for attention from the native-born. Well before his artistic ambitions had arrived at his preference for miniature, Charles Fraser was making water-color sketches in and around Charleston which have been preserved in the little sketchbook he carried about with him from his fourteenth to his twenty-fourth years, 1796 to 1806. The earliest ones have the thin drawing and timid washes of color natural to a boy who was emulating topographical prints; the latest ones show the improvement consequent upon practice and even some advance toward interpreting a scene

37. THE TEA PARTY   *by* HENRY SARGENT
Courtesy of Museum of Fine Arts, Boston.

in terms of mood, but they afford no ground for thinking that an important landscape artist was lost when Fraser turned miniaturist.

But Ralph Earl, with less portrait work and more landscape, would perhaps have become more important than he is. Even in his first known picture of the Revolutionary episode at Concord his concern with the landscape seems to have been stronger than his concern with the event; and very soon after his return from England he showed himself fascinated by the small and distant views which he put into many of the portraits. They were painted sharp and clear, with that extra degree of positiveness so relished by the American taste in general; and a few of them could be successfully extracted to form independent pictures. In 1791, with *Mrs. Mosely and Son* [Yale University Art Gallery], he ventured to make the entire background of landscape on a large scale; and while the background offers much of interest as an experiment, the picture as a whole suffers through his failure to give a satisfactory transition of light from the figures to the landscape. Somewhat later Earl reached the point of omitting the portrait element entirely and making a few pictures out of unmixed landscape motives.

They achieved a degree of particularity absent from previous efforts and from all contemporaneous attempts except those of Francis Guy. Earl did not secure this specific quality by closely observing the time of day; he did not trouble himself at all about the changeable light of the open air. He attained his exactness by noting a series of shapes—trees, a rounded hill, a field, or the mass of a distant grove; the illumination of the shapes was equally exact in gradation of values, resulting in a satisfactory sense of depth, but controlled by a light that seems arbitrary and unchanging. Earl painted no scene as it appeared to the physical eye at a given moment; he rendered it as re-created by the mind out of a knowledge accumulated through repeated examination.

Thus Earl's precision was obtained by a method the very opposite of the later one of impressionism, which relied upon wholly visual and fleeting effects; but even more curious, perhaps, was the further seeming contradiction presented by his habit in composition. The formal balance of component shapes is most evident in the well known *Looking East from Denny Hill* [1801: plate 38], but the influence of the general concept is in other examples too. This concept, with the long horizontal shape which determined it, was probably adopted by Earl from the artisan overmantels which he had seen in homes and taverns of Connecticut and Massachusetts. It was but the final phase of his continual reaffirmation of artistic vigor out of the local craft traditions. In all his pictures he was saying what Whitman later put into words:

What is commonest, cheapest, nearest, easiest, is Me.

Earl's mind was in a good sense countrified, with a homely bluntness unconsciously expressed in prevailingly blockish forms. Without imaginative heights
or emotional depths, his landscapes are attractively direct in manner and substantial in feeling.

The name of Alvan Fisher early appeared among the painters of landscape
and also of anecdote. Examples of the latter include portraits of famous race
horses, claimed as the first of the type to be painted here; examples of landscape
now known are more interesting for a pleasantly idyllic quality that informs the
moderately competent craft. The turning point of Fisher's career was a trip to
Europe beginning in 1825, and the subsequent *Sugar-Loaf Mountain* [1827:
privately owned] went beyond his earlier work in technical skill and romantic
feeling; but thenceforth, too, he was just one among the many who made up
the mid-century average. There is a shade more of importance in relation to the
time in his pictures of Niagara done in the early eighteen-twenties for the same
patron who commissioned the horse portraits; as these were primarily factual
reports like most human portraits then, so Fisher's early landscapes were essentially topographical reports of a famous piece of scenery.

Niagara was indeed a natural subject for every painter who had in mind
either popular interest or the charm of the picturesque for its own sake. The
latter motive animated William Dunlap; in the short episode of his varied career
during which he served as militia paymaster he enlivened his travels with "A
little amateur painting in water-color [which] shows the innocent and quiet
mind." The more practical motive caused John Trumbull, not long after 1800,
to make two elaborately detailed topographical studies [New-York Historical
Society, New York] with the idea of getting the panorama's inventor to use
them for an exhibition work in London—an idea which was never carried out.
Two later pictures by Trumbull [1808: Wadsworth Atheneum, Hartford]
gave a slightly more romantic interpretation of segments of scenery better suited
to easel painting.

Through the early years of its popularity as a subject, Niagara was more often
treated factually than poetically, and it is a little strange that before 1830 the
most poetic version of the scene should have been done by the man most
strongly identified with the dominantly factual intentions of the panorama,
John Vanderlyn. The technical distinction of his various preparatory studies
is obvious, but the poetry of the large final version [1826: Senate House
Museum, Kingston, N.Y.] would be almost hidden by the severely restrained
handling if it were not for the blasted tree boldly effecting pictorial contrast and
dramatic emotion.

Vanderlyn's own work in panorama was, however, chronologically belated. A

38. LOOKING EAST FROM DENNY HILL *by* RALPH EARL *Courtesy of Worcester Art Museum.*

panorama by the native-born Edward Savage was shown in Philadelphia in the same year that the foreign-born Winstanley opened his in New York; Savage's subject was London, too, whence he had recently returned from study under West, and a newspaper reported that it was "in a circle and looks like reality." Both Savage and Winstanley may have been preceded a short while by somebody in Boston, for meticulous Bentley noted on February 4, 1795: ". . . at Boston I saw the PANORAMA, a catch penny shew, but not without its merit in an Infant Country. It encourages better attempts. . . ." And Charles Willson Peale is said to have made preparatory drawings for a panorama as early as 1788, from the top of the Maryland State House, with the aid of a pantograph.

Vanderlyn's purpose to establish a panorama here was formed in Europe, where he had seen the success of Barker's in London and Robert Fulton's in Paris. He thought that "the magic deceptions of the art" would be even more successful in the United States for having no competition from public galleries of painting and for needing "no study or cultivated taste" as a preliminary to the "instruction and mental gratification" thus obtainable. In 1817, two years after Vanderlyn's return, the city of New York got around to authorizing a building for his panorama; but the enterprise was handicapped before ever opening for business since the actual costs ran to more than half as much again as the estimates. It is somewhat speculative, but there may have been a less tangible but no less effective handicap in a mistaken approach which probably originated with Vanderlyn himself. His advance opinion about the American public in one of the quoted phrases was amplified, with an extra note of condescension, by the *National Advocate* for April 21, 1818, in announcing the commencement of work on the Rotunda:

. . . Although it was not to have been expected that Mr. Vanderlyn would have left the higher department of historical painting, in which he is so eminent, to devote his time to the more humble, though more profitable pursuit of painting cities and landscapes—yet, in a new country, taste for the arts must be graduated according to the scale of intellect and education, and where only the scientific connoisseur would admire his Marius and Ariadne, hundreds will flock to his panorama to visit Paris, Rome, and Naples. . . .

To spread the idea that visiting the panorama was in itself evidence of an uncultivated taste would seem to be a poor way of attracting patronage. However, in rooms adjoining that for the panorama itself there always were to be seen the historical paintings which had made Vanderlyn famous in Europe. As the main attractions, a succession of famous cities followed one upon the other; and there were also some famous Napoleonic battles, two of them being recent enough to count almost as current events in panorama reporting. Yet financial difficulties accumulated, the trouble being that interest in each panorama waned well before a change was made. Throughout the years of dwindling interest Vanderlyn did other things in an effort to get out of debt: built panoramas in New Orleans and Havana and—painted portraits. But in 1829 the city took possession of the property for other uses.

Vanderlyn retired to Kingston, his birthplace, and took with him his own panorama of Versailles with which the nine-year life of his panorama effort had begun. Portions of it are still there—enough by which to estimate the painter's craft and guess at the general impression it made when new. Technically the whole must have been quite extraordinary in the detailed consistency with which it managed a pictorial equivalent for a three-dimensional actuality, in the precision of the building façades and of the scale adopted for the intervening paved stretches spotted with scattered figures. The use of strong shadows along the fountain edges and clipped hedges resulted in striking effects of relief; but the dominant device was an altogether remarkable accuracy of values. Vanderlyn was aiming at illusionism and perhaps he came as near to achieving it as can reasonably be expected.

It is a permanent human desire to make experience in some way permanent, and one expression of this desire is to ask in painting for a definiteness in excess of what is seen in nature; the particular kind of definiteness which intends visual deception is simply this general need pushed to an extreme literalism. It would seem that if any subject-matter could yield visual finality it would be still-life; and this concept has strongly affected the American practice of still-life since its beginning. Yet even in its initial appearance the results of the concept were not uniform and clear-cut but uneven and equivocal.

Of course, the artists here were as convinced of its rightness as those in Europe—Charles Willson Peale as much so as his teacher Benjamin West. Peale once made a marginal notation: "Nature is very perfect, and a juditious Painter cannot finish too high." The members of his family learned that from him, and nowhere in their formative years would they have encountered any contrary conception effectively presented. It was therefore natural that among the pictures which Raphaelle Peale sent to the first Columbianum exhibition in 1795 one should be entitled *A Deception,* and that one shown by him at the Pennsylvania Academy in 1812 should be a *Catalogue for the Use of the Room—A Deception.*

These particular paintings are not now known, but a remarkable example [privately owned] with the signature of the Boston portraitist John Johnston testifies to the prevalence of illusionistic intention; its bee and caterpillar among

39. VANITY OF AN ARTIST'S DREAM   *by* CHARLES BIRD KING
Courtesy of The Fogg Museum of Art, Harvard University.

peaches and grapes shedding drops of water are a fitting pictorial succession to John Mare's fly. Henry Smith Mount, the eldest of three painting brothers, painted still-life which earned Dunlap's commendation; of two examples now known the *Fish* [c. 1830: Suffolk Museum, Stony Brook, N.Y.], though its first freshness is dimmed and cracked, shows the same striving for exactness in textures and effects of light. The praise locally recorded for the flower and fruit pieces of Asa Park in Kentucky is not specific about their imitativeness, but it is evidence of the early appearance of still-life painting on the frontier. Illusionism was very ambitiously attempted by Charles Bird King in the multiple details of his *Vanity of an Artist's Dream* [c. 1830: plate 39]; a cupboard is seen crowded with tattered books, old bread, a plaster head jaggedly broken at the neck, useless palette and brushes, and a dozen other objects—the whole giving the effect of careless disorder and at the same time revealing a care for pictorial structure. The literally spelled-out irony of the notice of a sheriff's sale and of book titles like Campbell's *Pleasures of Hope* may have helped the picture with its first audience; they now seem an unnecessary re-enforcement of the pictorially achieved emotion of bitter abandonment. Before he smiled his way to success as a mediocre portraitist in Washington, King in this picture made loveliness out of ruined things; and the thoughtfulness with which he composed a clutter of trash into the melancholy beauty of light and shadow suggests that in coming to terms with his own tragedy he experienced that one time a measure of artistic success.

There were others who sought satisfaction in depicting inanimate objects; in the first Columbianum, for example, eight painters and one worker in enamel were represented by still-life and a japanner sent "Five flower pieces, in imitation of enamel." It is even a little puzzling why so many should have painted still-life through the Federal Era when leading professionals ignored or deprecated the species. To dramatize convincingly his own catholicity of taste, Washington Allston said: "I cannot honestly turn up my nose even at a piece of still-life . . ." The elder Peale, after several years of other activities, resumed painting in 1815 with some practice work in still-life, but he thought that branch too elementary for mature minds. Fortunately this opinion did not deter his brother and his eldest son from making the most important contribution of all to the first phase of still-life painting in the United States.

Through the eighteen-twenties the brother James inscribed a series of still-lifes to point up the phenomenon of his continuing to paint as he approached his eighty-second year; one typical example is so noted in his seventy-sixth year [1825: Worcester Art Museum]. Yet he is recorded, along with his nephew, as contributing a painting of this type to the first Columbianum thirty years earlier;

and he is said to have had better luck in selling such works than other painters. Perhaps that was partly because of his success in other branches, but perhaps it was also because his still-lifes were liked for themselves. At least they seem well suited to what is known about contemporaneous taste. There is usually a first impression of much detail being present, which is rather insistent because of a uniform emphasis throughout. The arrangement is generally satisfactory, although it is never stimulating; the lighting is sometimes naturalistically inconsistent, but in almost unnoticeable ways, when it is used to minimize background darks.

He may have had illusionist intentions along with other painters at the time, but it may also be significant that there was no hint of it in any picture title he used. Nor do the pictures themselves make it certain he tried to earn that praise. His aim does seem clearly to have been a minuteness of detail which would solicit the test of "nearly looking." He maintained his drawing in steady crispness and sharpened every edge for exactitude; but in this respect the painter who takes on too many grapes is always in danger of defeat. James Peale, at least, multiplied his monotonous little ovals and fitted them out with almost microscopic high lights—even in places where they were naturalistically unlikely; in this way he busied himself with accumulating the evidences of labor for those who thought they wanted their information bit by bit. But at times he could reduce the quantity of his craft and enhance the quality of the picture; the *Fruits of Autumn* [1827: plate 40] is kept small in feeling by the hardness of treatment, but the relative simplicity of its elements makes it more winning than his usual heaps of fruit in which the design does not quite control a tendency to dispersion.

It would be easy to write about Raphaelle Peale entirely as a picturesque personality who remained likable in his worst weaknesses of character; and such a treatment could play up the jolly stories about his fondness for tricks and amusing deceptions in paint. Such things may have been almost constantly present in the conscious mind by which he made contact with others and yet be unimportant in estimating his pictures, because he, like every other significant painter, created them from out much more than his conscious mind. The relationship between Peale's frequent practical jokes and the poetry of his pictures may be interpreted as a parallel to Valentine Le Grice's perceptive words about Charles Lamb:

. . . his wit, flashing out of his melancholy, was as the summer lightning playing innocuously round the very cloud which gave it birth. And thus the overburdened spirit relieves itself; a pun may discharge a whole load of sorrow; the sharp point of a quibble or a joke may let out the long-gathered waters of bitterness. . . .

40. FRUITS OF AUTUMN *by* JAMES PEALE *Courtesy of Whitney Museum of American Art.*

A pictorial deception is a visual pun, and more than one little picture by Raphaelle Peale could be taken in that sense except for the way in which their darkened atmospheric richness suggests a burdened spirit seeking consolation.

Only a half-dozen pictures are needed to establish his supremacy in still-life painting for his time, and among the half-dozen the *Still-life with Cake* [1822: plate 41] may be cited as typical. To sum up his general merits is not in itself exciting: good drawing, an observation so close that not only textures but solidities vary in wood and apples and dishes and leaves, unusual sensitiveness to what happens when one object touches another, a tact in placing and grouping which achieves integration without so much as hinting at an imposition of design. These qualities in combination would make Raphaelle Peale remarkable in any age; yet he, so far from making parade of them, kept them all in place as no more than the professional morality of a sound craftsman. The more remarkable thing in all this is the end which he attains with his craft.

Nowhere in print are there any words of his which would allow the historian to speak with positiveness of his deeper intentions; apparently he was content to let the pictures speak for him. Therefore any interpretation must in turn be content with reading the pictures themselves. However, certain ideas out of them and about them seem valid whether or not the ideas ever rose into Raphaelle Peale's own consciousness.

These paintings embody the completest possible belief in the reality of material substance and of sensuous response to its tangible qualities. For the painter, who has to deal in appearances even if he wants to paint what does not appear, that belief may not be the act of credulity which philosophy since Peale has called it. The brooding air of the pictures comes not from subjectivity of turning inward but from a self-forgetting contemplation of the things represented. That mainly is why the pictures stay in the mind; even the uniquely large *After the Bath* [1823: Nelson Gallery, Kansas City] has its own measure of mystery, though it does not equal that of the smaller-scaled perfections. In all there is an unconscious mysticism of matter quieted into the stillness which shelters the spirit's intensest life.

In these pictures there is not only regard for the objects they depict but an equal regard for the material in which they are rendered. The painter loved pigment, its physical properties, its obedience to his mind and hand. A few before him had manifested something of this, but no American before him had manifested so complete a trust in the medium. Raphaelle Peale was able to do without the human face, without historic event and casual incident, without improving ideas and flights into fancy; he was innocent enough, or knowing enough, to go as far as was then possible in eliminating the "impurities" of associated ideas and thus allowing beautifully handled paint to exert its unmixed appeal. In the record as now known he was the first American to do that; and though he never stretched his mind on the uplands of art, he intensified it in the intimacies of still-life. There can be greatness in the small, and the completeness with which Raphaelle Peale gave his mind to humble things was an act of strong imagination.

41. STILL–LIFE WITH CAKE *by* RAPHAELLE PEALE *Courtesy of Brooklyn Museum.*

43. The summit of a useful life

Charles Willson Peale: 1741–1827

Through a long life the first of the artistic Peales exemplified the many-sidedness which was so long advantageous to the rapidly expanding nation. Dunlap's summary runs:

. . . He was a saddler; harness maker; painter in oils, crayon, and miniature; he sawed his own ivory for miniatures, moulded the glasses, and made the shagreen cases; he was a soldier; a legislator; a lecturer; a preserver of animals,—whose deficiencies he supplied by means of glass eyes and artificial limbs; he was a dentist—and he was, as his biographer truly says, "a mild, benevolent, and good man."

The tone was not openly derogatory, but Dunlap immediately added one of his beloved moralizings: ". . . life is too short to bring any one to perfection." But Dunlap's prejudice betrayed him into predicting that Peale's works, except for a few portraits done in old age, would be forgotten; he further wrote: "Now Mr. Peale appears rather to have delighted in mechanical employments; and his *genius* was devoted to making money. . . ." At that point unfairness in Dunlap became overt, for if any pragmatic censure is possible upon an admirable man who married three times and fathered seventeen children, it would be that he was too idealistic toward his means of support.

That support, through the years when there were just not enough people paying for portraits, came from his museum. It was not the first, but it was the first to be financially successful through three decades; it exhibited some things which no museum would show today, but its founder conscientiously refrained from cheapening the institution and eventually paid the price of losing out to peepshows and freaks. Much was made of a deceptive waxworks of Peale at work painting, which could fool visitors who knew him; and at one time there were even some stuffed monkeys engaged in human activities. But the natural history specimens were enlightening, and Peale was the first in this country to present birds in their normal settings, with appropriate backgrounds painted by himself. Although the progressively worsening exploitation of the museum idea through the mid-century caused Peale's idea to be long neglected, he may be said to have initiated an educational concept capable of development into an effective instrument for whatever authentically democratic culture might prove possible in this country. Probably he was so intelligent about equipping his museum because he was himself one of the most notable among many American self-educators; acquiring and installing the birds and animals, reconstructing the skeleton of the "Mastodon," painting habitat landscapes and portrait heads of prominent men—these activities not only supported his family and allayed his artisan need to do things with his hands but also satisfied his intellectual craving for knowledge.

Before the museum developed into a paying proposition, he had tried other schemes and during the museum's best years he made some inventions which may have brought in some money; but a large amount of his energy was given to philanthropic activities. The call of patriotism could stir him to exhausting efforts—devising and executing decorative adjuncts like illuminations and triumphal arches for celebrations. One of his most important undertakings was the formation of an artists' association, the Columbianum, in 1794 and assembling under its auspices the first public art exhibition held in the United States; Peale attached still more importance to an effort through this association to establish an art school which would even have a life class—and when no model could be secured, Peale himself posed in order to get things started. The whole idea outraged those who guarded the proprieties; some of the artists who joined with him to found the association then seceded, and the whole project disintegrated. But in all of his public endeavors, and in spite of those who disliked and thwarted him, Peale maintained the same attitude which earned him affection from friends and family, an attitude of benevolence which he himself put into better words than anybody else has ever used in praising his character: "I am disposed to do all I can to make others happy, and thus make myself so."

However, praise for Peale's character and philanthropy need not now carry Dunlap's implication that they were an excuse for bad pictures. It is true that he was not a great painter, and much of his work has only the narrowly historical importance of bridging two periods; it is further true that much of it was hasty. On the other hand, it should probably be remembered that, when engaged in other things, he would leave off painting for months or even years at a time—would even decline work in trying to increase patronage for his brothers and his sons. Moreover, a rule for judging invoked with Stuart should be equally applicable to lesser men, and any closing words on Peale should emphasize his best pictures. These stand out quite clearly above his own average; and though they are all ostensibly portraits, they do so stand out because they are pictorially much more than likenesses.

When at work upon his *Self-Portrait in His Museum* [1823: Pennsylvania Academy, Philadelphia], he wrote a son: ". . . I mean to make the whole piece a deception, if I can. . . ." He shows himself standing in the foreground with

42. EXHUMING THE MASTODON by CHARLES WILLSON PEALE Courtesy of Mrs.
Harry White. Photograph: Courtesy of The Metropolitan Museum of Art, New York City.

raised arm drawing aside a heavy red curtain to reveal the long museum room, its walls lined with cases of stuffed birds and animals and, high above, a row of his portraits of famous men. The perspective lines are set down, but there is no effect of the illusion Peale desired. For one thing, as the historian Isham pointed out, the background is thinly painted. For another, the important detail of the centrally placed bench is inadequately drawn; and for a third, the lighted depth at the left and the shadowed bulk of the mounted mastodon at the right are inconsistently conceived in terms of space. Yet there is considerable vigor in the figure, not overlooking the relaxed and well turned left leg; and the head is well drawn and well lighted and solidly painted. It is worth remarking that these last-named technical characteristics, had they been extended to everything else in the painting, would have given a result quite close to that which Peale intended. Indeed, the recurring words about deception, or exact imitation, or "nearly looking," or however else it may be phrased, often suggest or imply just such painting qualities; it would be fair to conclude that, among painters at least, the inadequate expression came to contain concepts which were later given greater verbal precision.

The Family Group [1773–1809: New-York Historical Society, New York] was a long time in the making, and in consequence some portions (notably the woman seated second from the right) were not allotted a sufficient amount of physical space; yet the whole is an exceptional performance in achieving an animated visual unity for the figures. Only two or three faces exhibit interesting characterization; yet everywhere can be felt a high degree of geniality—a relish for people, for things, for painting. Contemporaneous with the later stages of The Family Group was the even more animated Exhuming the Mastodon [1806: plate 42]. The animation is all in the arrangement of so many little figures under and around the strongly dominant triangle formed by the dredging apparatus and its supports. There are many inconsistencies in proportioning the figures, and the opaque pigment does not capture outdoor light; but on the level where this picture can please such things don't much matter. The curious inaccuracy of putting in friends and relations who were not there simply to let them share in the honor of the great discovery shows a pleasing willingness in Peale himself to be agreeable by taking liberties with the facts.

One of Artemus Ward's profundities was his remark: "The highest part of that mountain is the top." The top of Peale's work lay backward in time behind, as well as above, the pictures just discussed. It is the so-called Staircase Group [1795: plate 43], the portrait to which President Washington is said to have bowed. It shows two of Peale's sons; one of them who looks back into the room is well balanced in the arrested motion of ascending an enclosed stairway and the other a few steps higher up looks around from the stairway frame which partially conceals him. Its very installation in the museum emphasized its illusionistic intention; it was set flush with the wall but had its lower foreground seemingly brought farther forward by an actual step which matched the painted ones. Deception may very well have been the single conscious aim in Peale's blandly extrovert mind—a mind without half-lights. The actual result is artistically much more important.

Peale's conscious craft as a painter was responsible for the handsomeness of the design: the strong leftward-bearing diagonal of Raphaelle as he starts up the stairs is accentuated by his leaning on the maulstick. That diagonal in solid flesh and bone is beautifully relieved from overassertiveness by the countering diagonal made by a shadow that extends upward and to the right from the head. Equally thoughtful in design are the lights and darks of the partially visible younger son whose relaxed upright figure enlivens the upper portion and effectively counters the upward lines of the lower. All this constitutes a conscious mastery of design which owes nothing to happy accident except an initial suggestion.

Around intentional skill lies a border where it and unconscious fulfilment mingle beyond the possibility of disentanglement in words. Yet it is legitimate to point out how any conscious ideal of illusionism is inevitably affected by the necessity of repeated examinations and recurrent working periods. The image cannot be recorded in one fell swoop; it must be set down by a succession of efforts. The result cannot be a mechanistic copy of appearances; it must be the registration of a mental concept. And in setting that concept down there are many subtle elisions of confusing details, contracting the line here and swelling it there in rhythmic compensation. How much will be conscious and how much will be unconscious depends upon individual idiosyncrasy; in Charles Willson Peale most of it was probably unconscious in operation, but it functioned. And that is why he could intend a piece of illusionism and achieve a work of art.

43. THE STAIRCASE GROUP *by* CHARLES WILLSON PEALE
Courtesy of Philadelphia Museum of Art [*The George W. Elkins Collection*].

44. History painting

Edward Savage: 1761–1817
John Trumbull: 1756–1843
John Vanderlyn: 1776–1852
Jeremiah Paul: act. 1791–1820

Henry Sargent: 1770–1845
William Dunlap: 1766–1839
Rembrandt Peale: 1778–186c

The patriarch of the painting Peales had always believed that history painting was the highest level to which the art as a whole could attain; but when his prints after his own picture of Pitt did not sell readily, he adjusted himself to the market for portraiture. Toward the close of a long life of painting and museum-keeping, he witnessed a considerable flurry of interest in history painting by the general public and himself attempted with little success to attract part of the interest by one Revolutionary and one religious subject. Younger painters had sporadically better luck, with his own son Rembrandt securing the most profitable share of popular attention; but only Allston and Trumbull managed to do enough important work within the kind to hold their places in history as history painters.

The historical subject in its most obvious phase of recording actual and recent events was of course mixed up with the fanfare of self-conscious patrioteering which was one cultural accompaniment of political unity. The innumerable repetitions of Washington's countenance—in oil, in pastel, in miniatures of ivory and of enamel, as etchings and engravings, on glass pitchers and china plates—made his face as common, and often as unrecognizable, as the eagle infinitely repeated on wallpaper and in chintz. Washington was also the natural focus for more ambitious designs which began upon the border of straight portraiture and thence conducted him through battles and river-crossings toward his ultimate apotheosis upon the Capitol dome in the eighteen-sixties. It is somewhat curious that about the most satisfactory attempt to combine portraiture with the stateliness of history should be an early one by a portrait painter who did not even in that instance overcome his usual mediocrity in color and deficiency in drawing. In *The Washington Family* [1796: National Gallery, Washington] Edward Savage only accentuated his own inexpressive drawing when he elongated the arms toward the center in order to link the group on one side with the group on the other; yet that naturalistic distortion served a higher end, for it permitted a spaciousness which is something more than the physical area of

the canvas—a spaciousness of design by which the balanced masses are given
not only size but dignity. The picture is stiff with provincial self-consciousness
and it does not satisfy the eye in search of thorough modeling, but it is impressive in a degree which is exceedingly rare in American painting between 1790
and 1860.

Of full-fledged history painting as the record of great events, John Trumbull
remains the only important exemplar; both his own ambition and the intrinsic
merit of his achievement in its opening phase made this the determining factor
in his long life even though his actual painting ranged much more widely in
subject-matter. Besides the few landscapes, Trumbull made many experiments
with imaginative themes, religious and classical and literary; and besides many
portraits which were commissions in likeness-making, he executed a number
which were ambitiously "official" in character. Five were commissioned by the
City of New York as part of a long-continued program in accumulating a gallery
of portraits by which the City Hall has been luckily adorned with some good
and a few excellent works. The first of Trumbull's five was *George Washington*
[1790: City Hall, New York]; some rhymer, celebrating New York in the
Sentinel during September of 1790, allotted one stanza to the portrait:

> Justly admire the glowing work,
> A lasting honor to New York;
> An honor to our corporation,
> A future honor to our nation.

Impeccable in sentiment, such verses mark a declension in literary skill from the
ostentatious artificiality of those on Smibert and Wollaston, and even from the
domestically romantic praise of Peale, to a democratic jingle which must have
irritated Trumbull if he read it. For this portrait and the four succeeding ones
came out of an eighteenth-century mind and were addressed to similar minds
that retained the concept of partly idealized remoteness in semi-historical portraiture; but the formality and stateliness which were virtues then are now often
seen as the vices of frigidity and pomposity. Polar opposites to such works were
several dozen small heads on oval mahogany panels, most of which Trumbull
made as preparatory documentation for the "national history" series which he
intended as his life work. The delicately spontaneous drawing and color, in
brushwork that is frequently delicious in its technical ease, which Trumbull
concentrated into the few inches of each one, raise these near-miniatures as a
group into one of the principal successes of the Federal Era.

These studies made a technically brilliant beginning for that "national
history," but several factors combined to keep it in a state of suspended animation for almost a quarter of a century and it ended ingloriously with only four

paintings (out of the larger number proposed) installed in the Rotunda of the Capitol. They are monumental only in their dullness; even so, they are more tolerable than some of the later artistic calamities which have almost succeeded in marring the noble space beneath the dome. The dullness of Trumbull's pictures resulted from his loss of skill, the Congress having delayed too long in commissioning them; and the delay had been caused in part by opposition from cultural philistines present in every popularly elected legislature and in part by a young nation's natural cautiousness in money matters. Even the cultivated among the lawmakers did not feel any richer as a government than they did as individuals, and the cost of adequate public buildings unadorned seemed heavy enough without adding the exorbitant fees asked by sculptors and painters for mere adornments. When he encountered that attitude, touchy Trumbull felt personally aggrieved, much as he had felt about his army commission in 1777; for by temperament he lived in a state of self-righteous resentment against everything that happened to him from the time of his father's original opposition to his artistic ambitions. When, after his study abroad, he returned to this country in 1789 for his five years of accumulating the brilliant little portraits and the studies of the sites where Revolutionary events occurred, his attitude was an almost self-defeating mixture of hope and hauteur; he seems to have thought that fame and money both would be quickly awarded him by a grateful government, and he certainly came to think they should be. While Trumbull was still in Paris, Jefferson had kindly offered him the post of secretary as a form of financial help toward the great undertaking; in an elaborately self-conscious letter, which he preserved for more than fifty years to print in his autobiography, Trumbull composed a document of extreme psychological—even psychiatric— interest. A small portion of it reads as follows:

. . . The greatest motive I had or have for engaging in, or for continuing my pursuit of painting, has been the wish of commemorating the great events of our country's revolution. I am fully sensible that the profession [of painting], as it is generally practiced, is frivolous, little useful to society, and unworthy of a man who has talents for more serious pursuits. But, to preserve and diffuse the memory of the noblest series of actions which have ever presented themselves in the history of man; to give to the present and future sons of oppression and misfortune, such glorious lessons of their rights, and of the spirit with which they should assert and support them, and even transmit to their descendants, the personal resemblance of those who have been the great actors in those illustrious scenes, were objects which gave a dignity to the profession peculiar to my situation. And some superiority also arose from my having borne personally a humble part in the great events which I was to describe. No one lives with me possessing this advantage, and no one can come after me to divide the honor of truth and authenticity, however easily I may hereafter be exceeded in elegance. Vanity was thus on the side of duty, and I flattered myself that by devoting a few years of life to this object, I did not make an absolute waste of time, or squander uselessly, talents from which my country might justly demand more valuable services; and I feel some honest pride in the prospect of accomplishing a work, such as had never been done before, and in which it was not easy that I should have a rival.

Trumbull then took three more pages of print to explain why he could not give a definite answer immediately, and said he was going to the United States to secure the advance subscriptions for engraved reproductions which would enable him to paint the picture: if enough are not obtained, he concluded, he would abandon painting.

The necessary subscriptions were not obtained, and for ten years he was a diplomat and a business speculator without entirely abandoning his art. Then followed four years of professional disappointments in New York, and four more in London, where he attempted to work through the War of 1812. A last return to this country in 1816 resulted in the bitterest disappointments of all: the failure of the American Academy under his presidency and the many censures of the four paintings which Congress finally authorized for the Capitol. Before being installed there they were taken on tours of the leading cities, so that a good deal of faultfinding preceded them to Washington. In December of 1818, the antiquarian Bentley noted how Bostonians were complaining that one among them "has too much Connecticut foreground." Charles Willson Peale recorded his dissatisfaction when he saw them in Baltimore. After they were in place one legislator affirmed that though they cost the government thirty-two thousand dollars they were not worth thirty-two cents; and several years later John Randolph excoriated *The Declaration of Independence* as "the shin piece," since no such collection of legs had ever before been submitted to the eyes of men. This is an example of the excitable congressional oratory which still goes on; but on the first of January in that same year (1828), Mrs. Basil Hall had unexcitedly described Trumbull's pictures as "large, cold, flat, chalky." Mrs. Hall was an irritating but essentially harmless snob while in this country; yet even a snob can sometimes make correct observations.

Those sad failures by Trumbull, were it not for their prominent location and their wide influence on the public, could well be forgotten, along with the dreary series of quarrels and frustrations which preceded them, in turning back to his half-dozen brilliant historical compositions which he composed between his twenty-ninth and thirty-ninth years. The subject of *The Sortie from Gibraltar* involved the labor of many drawings and three attempts to attain a satisfactory design; the other five all dealt with Revolutionary themes. *The Battle of Bunker's Hill* [1786: plate 44] remains perhaps the most satisfactory as well as the earliest. For the time being he was reveling in the technical ease which came as he got rid of his colonial hardness and acquired a cosmopolitan sophisti-

44. THE BATTLE OF BUNKER'S HILL *by* JOHN TRUMBULL *Courtesy of Yale University Art Gallery.*

cation temporarily equaling that of Stuart himself. He was living through a high romanticism of spirit which flushed his color into brilliance, animated his drawing into liveliness, fired his design into wave-like restlessness, and idealized his subject-matter of war into staged heroisms and graceful deaths. By adjusting the facts to the requirements of dramatic design, Trumbull advanced from the level of record-making to that of a perfectly harmonized pictorial conception. For once a grittily cantankerous New Englander found himself painting a picture with style.

John Vanderlyn, after two stays in Europe, the second of which had lasted twelve years and brought him continental fame, came back to the United States in 1815, not long ahead of Trumbull; and the two at once became open rivals for the Capitol commission. Trumbull's friends proved to have greater political influence, and Vanderlyn was thereupon compelled to stake everything upon his already planned but ultimately disastrous venture with the panorama. The bitterness between the two painters never lapsed, although the passage of time necessarily lessened the active partisanship of others. In 1832 Congress ordered from Vanderlyn a state portrait of Washington which proved to be better in its kind than Trumbull's Rotunda paintings were in theirs; but not until after the latter's death was Vanderlyn commissioned to paint a picture for that room—the subject to be *The Landing of Columbus* [1842–1844: United States Capitol, Washington]. By then Vanderlyn had lost his skill; alongside Trumbull's his picture does present a more fluent handling of pigment, but by dependable report that was done by an assistant executing Vanderlyn's idea. Once more the government had made a bad bargain because of its delays. A fair number of portraits which occasionally approach brilliance give Vanderlyn a respectable rank in that category; but he is more interesting as a mind in the three ambitious history paintings with which he earned a European repute before 1815.

The principal merit of all three lay in draftsmanship, for Vanderlyn had sought his training in Paris rather than in London; and in consequence his line was both more positive and more sensitive than that which his fellow Americans had learned from West. The ideals then imposed upon French painting by David were more rigidly oriented toward the antique than West's had ever been; subjects, poses, and designs were all as neo-classic as women's clothes. The figure was conceived as a statue; but where West's outlines were of a uniform hardness reminiscent of plaster casts, a more delicate precision was cultivated in Paris. Vanderlyn's drawing in his academic figure-pieces is superior to that of his fellow Americans; but the relativity of his rank is made clear by simply naming his French contemporary, Ingres. *Marius Musing amid the Ruins of Carthage* [c. 1806: De Young Memorial Museum, San Francisco] is really in the ruins of Rome, where the picture was painted; as a picture it was more at home in the Paris of David. The medal it received in the Salon of 1808 was from no considered verdict of a jury of artists but from the arbitrary command of Napoleon—and probably for that very reason more effective in bringing fame to the painter. Vanderlyn's picture of the nude, *Ariadne* [1812: Pennsylvania Academy, Philadelphia] showed an advance in draftsmanship to the point where it could seem satisfactory enough as a nude even in a Salon exhibition. Its pictorial merits were not imaginative, although the theme asked for that treatment; its qualities are indeed best described in negative phrases—absence of offense against any taste except that of prudishness, absence of hardness in the edges, absence of vulgarity in color. Positive praise must be limited to saying that it is a competent exercise in linear modeling in which the technique as a whole remains rather drily conditioned by the studio. Even in relation to its time, admiration for it can be no warmer than the academic coldness of the figure. The most interesting of Vanderlyn's historical subjects is his first, *The Death of Jane McCrea* [1803: plate 45]. In correctness as then understood it falls short of the other two, and the poses are both calculated and exaggerated; but despite the static quality in each figure taken separately, there is a dominant effect of movement from one component shape into the next. There is also an attempt, though incompletely worked out, to get free from the obvious frontality of a bas-relief through expressing depth with the tomahawking gesture of the Amerind as he bears down upon the kneeling woman. The thing that most impairs the success of all three pictures is the nature of the line itself; it is not precisely sluggish, but it certainly lacks the energy of Trumbull's first sketches.

The *Ariadne,* when exhibited in New York, became an occasion for scandal which permanently injured Vanderlyn's career. Other pictures also were involved, such as his copies after Titian's *Danaë* and Correggio's *Antiope;* but in the state of American taste at the time even the inoffensive *Ariadne* could be turned against Vanderlyn by the machinations of Trumbull and his agents. Dunlap made an exception of the picture in his condemnation of nudes, and later a masterly steel engraving of it by Asher Brown Durand did something toward mitigating a prudish philistinism; but that came too late to preserve Vanderlyn from failure and poverty and a lonely death in his very birthplace. It would seem, also, that circumstances had been rendered unpropitious for the *Ariadne* by Wertmüller's *Danaë* and the circumstances under which it was shown after the painter's death. In the very year of that event [1811] Jeremiah Paul made an effort to rival it with *Venus and Cupid,* seven by nine feet, "taken from living models," which Dunlap called "a naked exhibition figure, which I was induced to look at, in Philadelphia, but looked at not long." This was mild for Dunlap, and he had stronger language for an *Adam and Eve* which he thought were better called *Venus and Adonis.* In 1818 a museum in

45. THE DEATH OF JANE McCREA   by JOHN VANDERLYN
Courtesy of The Wadsworth Atheneum, Hartford, Conn.

Philadelphia charged twenty-five cents extra for viewing a room in which were gathered statues from France, ten anatomical wax figures, "The Handsome Danaë," Wertmüller's *Venus* and *Wood Fauns,* and paintings of bathers by Otis and Bodet. Reaction against such things most easily takes the form of moral censure like Dunlap's, although that is not always effective; the best remedy is a taste which turns away from inartistic technique and vulgar treatment, and to date that has been attained only by individuals or relatively small groups.

The history paintings which produced the greatest enthusiasm through the Federal Era were those which ". . . impress us with the moral sublimity of virtue, and give us the majesty of religion in all her sweetness. . . ." Quoted by Dunlap with approval, that had been written about Henry Sargent's *Christ Entering Jerusalem,* which he sold for three thousand dollars and which then brought considerable profit to its purchaser through several years. Despite its popularity on tour, it did not please Bentley nearly as much as Sargent's *Landing of the Pilgrims;* to Bentley the religious subject seemed cluttered with too many details and confused with inconsistent emotions. The two pictures are lost, and so are the four which Dunlap himself painted and launched for exhibition one after another through five years beginning in 1822. The first one was not an original composition but was painted from a printed description of West's *Christ Rejected;* it continued in circulation until 1829, when West's son landed in New York bringing the original. When Dunlap saw this, he altered his own by painting out the figures which corresponded to West's and introducing "others of my own, worse." About 1825 he painted another after West, *Death on the Pale Horse,* this time utilizing not only the printed description but also an etched outline. Then he ventured upon an original composition, *The Bearing of the Cross,* and in 1826 all three were being exhibited in different parts of the country by as many agents. Profits greatly diminished in the winter of 1827–1828, yet he started a fourth on its way, the *Calvary,* "probably my best"; when a fifth attempt, *The Attack on the Louvre,* proved to be a failure in 1830–1831 he abandoned this type of work. He further remarks that when West's *Christ Rejected,* after a two-year circuit, was brought back to New York even it failed. ". . . Nothing but novelty attracts our people."

Dunlap regarded that observation of his as a condemnation of the American public; but from a man whose greatest love and greatest successes were in the theater, it seems naïve. This word is also the right one for the earlier picture painted immediately after his return from London—*The Dunlap Family* [1788: New-York Historical Society, New York]; he intended it as a justification for his three years of almost unused opportunity for study under West, but it simply shows him, to quote his own words, "ignorant of anatomy, perspective, drawing, and coloring." A couple of later pictures of scenes in plays he staged, with better execution, preserve some of the naïvety of the family group. His miniatures are all second-rate; most of his portraits in oil are perhaps, in their dullness, not that good. This leaves his water-color landscapes as his most attractive, as well as technically his most amateur, pictures. Painter of four types of picture, writer and producer of plays, author of a diary and of gossipy histories, earnest advocate of much he did not practise and much he could not do— Dunlap is perhaps the most illustrious American dilettante who ever engaged in painting; a dilettante in the additional meaning of experiencing delight even though he communicated little.

In contrast, no one could have been more of a professional picturemaker than Rembrandt Peale through a painting life that began about the age of twelve and continued for sixty years more. Near the outset he combined painting with trips as far as London and Paris to exhibit the skeleton of the mastodon and also with museum-keeping in Philadelphia and Baltimore; about mid-career he was for a time an enthusiastic teacher of drawing in the Philadelphia public schools, and put his ideas about it into print. He advanced the interesting thesis that children should not learn to write until after an elementary course in drawing; but he oversimplified when he claimed: "Writing is little else than drawing the forms of letters; drawing is little more than writing the forms of objects." He published a book about travels in Italy which is very wordy but factually valuable and of some psychological interest; he also contributed some unreliable reminiscences to *The Crayon*. However, portraiture was his major occupation; and there were enough good ones among his large output, especially during and just after the two visits to Paris [1808–1809] in which he learned to paint in encaustic. In this process as occasionally practised in modern times the principal vehicle for the pigment is refined beeswax, and in his excitement Rembrandt Peale wrote words that are perhaps too lyrical to deserve being smudged by the charge of smugness:

. . . I can produce the most brilliant effects—my tints surpass the fairest complexions and equal what the imagination can conceive. Beauty shall come to me for immortality, for its texture flows from my pencil as I trace its forms . . .

He was not the first painter to dream of artistic salvation through a technical process, nor was he the last to decline from a first freshness into coarse brushwork and muddy color. For a generation he capitalized upon being the only man who had painted George Washington from life; for this he resorted to the curious and delusive procedure of trying to combine into one Washington-to-end-all-Washingtons the best features of everybody else's portraits. This so-called Port Hole portrait he took on tour to illustrate a sentimental lecture, and engaged in some unpleasant pressure tactics to obtain unconvincing certificates of authenticity from men who had also seen the subject. With the aid of his wife he made replicas of this concocted "portrait-history" about eighty times!

Despite the quantity of his portraiture, this younger Peale, who once publicly tried to drop the name and become known more simply but more pretentiously as Rembrandt, is most interesting as one of those who painted history during its opening flurry of popularity. His activity in this branch may well have been instigated by his involvement with Wertmüller; at any rate in the next year he exhibited *The Roman Daughter* and successfully scotched the rumor of plagiarism started by the Russian diplomat, Svinin. In 1813 he painted a *Jupiter and Io* which he prudently kept from public exhibition, but he did exhibit several more—classic (Lysippa), secular (Napoleon), and religious (Elijah). But the climax of his historical efforts was literary—the theme of death as expounded in a poem by the English churchman Beilby Porteus. Rembrandt Peale's *The Court of Death* [1820: plate 46] contains twenty-three figures on twenty-four feet of canvas. The painter pressed family and friends into service as models; he painted the dead man in the center from an actual corpse; he worked out his lighting scheme of daylight, torchlight, and reflected light, all overarched by grisly gloom—and sent it on tour as "The Great Moral Painting" with a descriptive pamphlet to publicize it, part of which reads thus:

The picture of "The Court of Death" is an appeal to the public taste by a native artist. It is an attempt to introduce pure and natural allegory (or rather *painting by metaphor*) in the place of obsolete personification and obscure symbols. It is a demonstration of the science of painting applied to its noblest purpose,—the expression of moral sentiment. It is a discourse on "Life and Death," equally interesting to all ages and classes, delivered in the universal language of Nature—the eloquence of the painter's art—which speaks not by the slow progression of words; and is calculated to remove the misconception of prejudices and terror, and to render useful the rational contemplation of death.

It would be difficult to find a more concentrated amalgam of the cultural ideas floating about in the Federal Era: the appeal to patriotism, the claim of something modern superior to the past, the re-enforcement of morality, the suggestion of awe, words to say that words are inferior to painting, and—perhaps most characteristic of all—the plain usefulness of solemn thoughts. The picture was immensely successful; on tour for thirteen months, sometimes requiring specially constructed buildings, it attracted thirty-two thousand people and earned nine thousand dollars.

The most likely reason for success was that this picture and the others of its kind were a substitute for the theater among people made uneasy by the word. In fact, most of the history pictures are themselves best understood in terms of theatrical performance; and certainly this one by Rembrandt Peale was so conceived. On the basis of a literary program supplied by the Bishop's poem, the painter set himself to devise human figures in poses appropriate to the sentiments, to dispose them agreeably before the spectators and provide a key (pamphlet or lecture) by which they could recognize the dramatic significances. In that way an intelligible plot was unfolded, and the audience departed with a feeling that something had happened. The method could be effective with one audience and one picture; but no inanimate canvas, saying nothing new and still dependent for its meaning upon the same words, could successfully play a return engagement. Eventually, too, that early reliance upon the "inferior" art of words to supply the audience with ideas and feelings to be read into the pictures killed off the species. To look at *The Court of Death* without a knowledge of its literary source and without a scenario of proper emotions is to perceive a row of models posing, each in entire obliviousness of all the others; it might be contended that this is appropriate on the general principle that each dies his own death, but in a picture which is supposed to have narrative as well as visual unity it uncomfortably strengthens the effect of shallow artifice. Instead of joining in an intelligible single thought, they compete with one another in a series of staged gestures. By mimicking emotions they reduce the picture to visual elocution—almost. For the figures are not quite the whole picture. The painter had seen fine paintings in London and Paris and as a pupil of West he had heard much talk about chiaroscuro. His handling here of light-and-dark, originally more varied and lively than can be seen today, has some drama in itself. His mind was too prosaic to animate his actual brushwork with imagination, but the labored shadows above the still more labored figures can at least remind other minds how imagination may be caught in paint.

46. THE COURT OF DEATH *by* REMBRANDT PEALE *Courtesy of Detroit Institute of Arts.*

45. An artist of impulse

Washington Allston: 1779–1843

The romanticism which so markedly distinguished Washington Allston among the painters of his own time in this country seems to have started at birth. Born on a South Carolina plantation, he was the child of his father's second marriage; only two years after his birth his father died, and part of the legacy was a dramatized prediction that the boy would be great. In later years Allston would tell about the ghost stories he had heard from the slaves and about drawing and painting before he was six. Through the springtime of youth—boarding school in Newport, art lessons from Samuel King, more education at Harvard—the prediction of greatness was no burden to his spirit; time enough for that later on. Quicker than his classmates at college courses, he found time for painting also; when he was designated to write a Commencement poem, he chose for his subject "Energy of Character"—perhaps a natural impulse in one who had noted his own laziness and procrastination. Two months later he wrote his mother that he was

. . . determined, if resolution and perseverance will effect it, to be the first painter, at least, from America. Do not think me vain, for my boasting is only conditional. . . .

Thereupon he sold his inherited Carolina property for money with which to go abroad and in 1801, with the miniaturist Malbone as his companion, went to London for study.

His letters to friends here were full of enthusiasms, the normal reactions of an impressionable youth to that vast city's visual and human drama, to pictures and painters. Some of his verdicts were perceptive: he thought Trumbull's *Sortie from Gibraltar* (possibly the now lost version given by the painter to West) charmingly painted and said flatly that English Lawrence could not paint so well as American Stuart. Other verdicts were apparently colored by sudden personal likings: he was fascinated by Fuseli the man and ever after thought him a genius; he impulsively reversed his derogatory opinion about West's painting through being captivated by the old man's grandfatherly kindness. Most revealing of all were the youthfully brash counsels ostensibly directed to his friends but actually addressed to himself. He advised Fraser in Charleston

339

to avoid mixing art and love as incompatibles; and Fraser remained the bachelor while Allston married twice. He also urged Fraser to be ambitious, since "Confidence is the soul of genius." To a writer friend Allston penned a passage which has the accent of accustomed thoughts about himself:

. . . But you should never forget what you owe to the future fame of your country; you should never forget that the muses who nursed you and watched round your cradle are now mystically anticipating the future reputation of their favorite. . . .

A heart thus swelling with destiny would naturally dream of artistic horizons more romantic than London; and late in 1803, with Vanderlyn this time, he crossed the Channel to spend five years on the continent.

The first eighteen months or so were spent in Paris, and there he was magnetized by the Louvre, then full of all the art which Napoleon had brought back as the spoils of war. Because of the subsequent ways in which nearly all of Allston's own pictures were influenced by this or that painter among the dozen or more whom he particularly admired, it is easy to affirm that his experience of the Louvre was too much for his romantically responsive temperament; but it may be observed that, since the temperament would have been the same anywhere, a less ample environment would have resulted only in his being influenced by less admirable painters. In any event, no general prescription can possibly be written as to any young artist's dosage of tradition, and even less judicious would be any pronouncement why a particular artist should have chosen a different course of action from the one he did choose. The Louvre at least nourished Allston's mind with authentic greatness, and whatever excess of worship he may have rendered was the error of a generous nature. It was that experience which enabled him later to speak the final word upon the still prevalent misconception of the artist's education: "There is no such thing as a self-taught artist . . ." And later he made a deeply true and suggestive generalization out of his youthful hours in the Louvre:

Titian, Tintoret, and Paul Veronese absolutely enchanted me, for they took away all sense of subject. . . . It was the poetry of color which I felt, procreative in its nature, giving birth to a thousand things which the eye cannot see. . . . [The pictures] addressed themselves, not to the senses merely, as some have supposed, but rather through them to that region (if I may so speak) of the imagination which is supposed to be under the exclusive domination of music. . . .

This experience was basically the same as Copley's earlier response to Europe, upon which his inadequate sentence about the luxury of seeing threw a shaft of revelation. Allston raised the experience to the more complex level of the romantic's self-awareness, and was accordingly able to use words which com-

municated more of it; and where Copley merely noted the charm of music without uniting it with painting in his conscious thinking, Allston advanced toward
the concept of the unity of all esthetic experience. He even went so far as to
say that "I have been more affected by music than I have ever been by either
painting or poetry." All that came out of the romantic's need to break down the
barriers between the arts as part of his conscious merging of art and living into
one continuous experience.

Allston's immediate response in picture-making was completely romantic in
itself but *The Deluge* [1804: Metropolitan Museum, New York] was incompletely pictorial in its expression of that romanticism. The snakes and howl-
ing wolf now seem insufficient for shudders, and the drowned bodies are ill
drawn; as *dramatis personae* all the figures are inadequate to the stage-set effectiveness of the waste of waters. However, *The Rising of a Thunderstorm
at Sea* [1804: Museum of Fine Arts, Boston] has a wilder grace in the spaciously
curving clouds and the horizontally stretched double curve of the cresting
waves that toss the foreground boat. It is supposed that the influence upon
this first continental phase of Allston's work was from the pictures of Claude
Joseph Vernet, but in his next manner the young American emulated a greater
painter: Poussin. Apparently Allston's way of recovering from one influence
was to replace it quickly with another, and this impulsive rush from one extreme to the other looks like a sound instinctual self-recovery from emotional
excess. He had left Paris for Italy when he painted the *Classical Landscape*
[1805–1808: Addison Gallery of American Art, Andover, Mass.], in which the
derivative element is obvious enough: a static composition of trees and water,
with architecture dominating the middle distance and with dream-lit mountain
masses in the far background. Seated in the foreground is an old man in a
cloak who might be of any period, but the costumes of several women in the
two near-by groups have the picturesqueness which was then so conveniently
at hand on any professional Roman model. From among the buildings the light
picks out the upper half of a pillared portico which, in that setting, passes for
a temple but which might as well be a new private home in the neighborhood
of Philadelphia. A shadowed building in front of the portico has more of a
Renaissance look, and still others in the group—especially a bridge with towers
at both ends—are definitely medieval. In short, this was no studio exercise in
archaeological correctness; it was a design influenced by Poussin but perhaps
more deeply animated by Allston's response to Poussin's own source: Italy.
The picture, like Italy itself, is romantic even in its classicism—and all the
stronger for that.

The very atmosphere of the Rome in which Allston lived, as distinct from
the Rome of West and Copley a quarter of a century earlier, was taking on a ro-

mantic tinge even as neo-classicism continued its triumphs in Paris; the Italian city's significance for art was changing with the minds of men. When Vanderlyn finally caught up with Allston, he took up his residence in a house said to have been the home of Salvator Rosa. Washington Irving appeared in Rome about the same time as Allston; he was no Goethe seeking out the antique but a "modern" with an appetite for the picturesque. Irving, by the way, had a minuscule talent for drawing, and such was the contagiousness of Allston's impulsive persuasion that for a short while he considered becoming a painter. After Irving had gone north to Paris, Samuel Taylor Coleridge appeared, and the months which he and Allston spent together settled them into a lifelong mutual admiration; for their temperaments all Rome and all life was a spectacle and a vision full of romantic lights and darks. They could have fancied that in *The Prelude,* then fresh from London, Wordsworth had written two lines valid for them at that moment:

> Bliss was it then to be alive,
> But to be young was very Heaven!

Allston himself was of course very busy accumulating the experiences and conceptions of painting which would enable him to live up to his own and his friends' expectations of his destined greatness. Although his project was warmly romantic in character instead of coldly neo-classic, its basic weakness was the same as that which had defeated West: the idea that the way to become a master for the new time was to be an eclectic among the masters of old time. The youth who impulsively and perhaps only half seriously wished "to be the first painter, at least, from America" was now consciously preparing to become his country's Raphael-Angelo; and though his daylight mien of dedication (as shown in self-portraits and a miniature by Malbone) seems a countenance assumed by an actor, he probably continued to wear it in his sleep. While young he flourished in the role of the man of promise.

This second act ended with his return to Boston in 1808; with marriage it concluded what his new brother-in-law, the soon famous minister William Ellery Channing, called "a long and patient courtship"—its length being Allston's contribution and the patience that of his affianced. For three years he occupied Smibert's painting-room, and most of the work he did in it seems to have followed precedent in being portraiture. However, he also painted an anecdote, *The Poor Author and the Rich Bookseller* [1811: Museum of Fine Arts, Boston], lame in humor, not very good in figure construction, but very interesting in its handling of space with a complex scheme of lighting from three sides. Intrinsically a better picture, and also more indicative of what was to be Allston's most personal note, was the *Coast Scene on the Mediterranean* [1808–1811: privately owned]; it was essentially a memory-piece, though probably worked up from a sketch or a color study. Several of the figures exhibit the tightly bulbous limbs of those in his anecdotal painting of the same period; and again the main pictorial element is lighted space—only here it is sun-rayed water and clouds. In this respect it is memory not only of Europe but also of Claude, but it is nonetheless a personal discovery too—as much so as the medieval-classic compound out of Poussin. The Boston for which Allston had prepared himself seemed in actuality thin and stony to his romantic nature, and with his wholly romantic composition he dreamed himself back into Europe.

He was still conscious of his self-imposed obligation to achieve the grand style, and from Boston in 1811 it must have seemed that London was the place to do it; Copley had just made his last bid for renewed favor with an immense equestrian showpiece of the Prince of Wales with attendant officers, and West had already begun his series of religious pieces for exhibition as a means of replacing his income from royal grants. To England, therefore, the Allstons went, and with them went young Samuel Finley Breese Morse as the painter's pupil; and the next seven years, divided between London and Bristol, saw a serious and seemingly successful campaign to win the palm of greatness. Two pictures may be mentioned in passing: a coldly correct exercise in the Raphaelesque, *The Angel Releasing Peter* [1812–1815: Allston Trust], and a heroically correct exercise in the Michelangelesque, *Uriel in the Sun* [1817: Allston Trust]. The latter won first prize at the British Institution exhibit of 1818, and an additional gift of a hundred and fifty pounds. The most ambitious effort of these years, in the sense of complex design, was *The Dead Man Restored to Life by the Bones of Elijah* [1813: Pennsylvania Academy, Philadelphia], which is not only especially eclectic in its general effect but also especially embodies the strain which the colossal put upon Allston's far from colossal talent. This, too, was an artistic sensation upon its exhibition, and the Royal Academy made the painter a special present of two hundred guineas; West, then its President, said: "He has commenced where most of us leave off." Even now the triangulated monumentality of the design has some impressiveness as an academic exercise; every arm and leg is placed with care—one difficulty being, indeed, that the care is too obvious. For in the upper portion of the major triangle Allston used energetic gestures and body movements which were frozen into a painful immobility by his static concept and by a draftsmanship that made no allowance for transitoriness in the poses. The play of light-and-dark over the whole has some interest for the eye, but the only figure with life is the nobly sculpturesque man returning from death with tragic unwillingness. The fright, astonishment, and terror of the supposedly living compose a rigid monument to a dead mode of art.

About the time of painting that picture Allston had a severe illness, and in 1815 his wife died; physical and emotional strains were thus added to the burden of his painting ambition. In 1818, despite the seeming certainty of a success in England as the history painter he wanted to be, he decided to return to the United States and persisted against the wishes of his English friends; after he had left London he was elected an Associate of the Royal Academy. The only completed picture he brought back with him—the history pieces had all been sold—was one which he had conceived and executed in a spurt of only three weeks: *Elijah Fed by the Ravens* [1818: Museum of Fine Arts, Boston]. This was essentially a memory of Salvator Rosa; its significance as a work by Allston lies in the pictorial gains which came from his rapid follow-through upon the original impulse. The resulting combination of consistency in treatment and spontaneity in handling made the painting unique in his work up to that date. Perhaps the most interesting technical feature was his willingness to stop short of the degree of finish which he had previously thought necessary; in consequence the brushwork approached the expressiveness of calligraphy in its modeling of the forms. This is romanticism in subject and feeling and design and execution: a unity so successful that its derivative quality seems of little consequence in comparison to its directness and coherence. One other canvas—unfinished—Allston brought with him to this country, the *Belshazzar's Feast* which was intended to be his masterpiece and which was never completed during the twenty-five years of Act the Fifth.

Allston's friends here, as well as those in England, believed in his greatness; believing also in *Belshazzar's Feast,* they raised a fund for Allston in order that he might complete it. He had just passed his thirty-ninth birthday and, as the saying goes, "Forty is the old age of youth; fifty is the youth of old age." No doubt his personal troubles in England had already sapped his energies, but for more than thirty years both his friends and his circumstances had exceptionally favored the romantic role which he had played up to the hilt—appropriately enough in a time when Junius Brutus Booth acted off the stage even better than he did on it and Edwin Forrest boomed and ranted. Not that Allston ever indulged in such vulgarities of personal conduct, but he had all along been playing a character consciously modeled upon his boyish idea of what a great artist should be. He had been young a long time, and now "Shades of the prison-house begin to close" upon the aging youth. He was face to face with the necessity of greatness, of fulfilling expectations. That well meant financial assistance was apparently just the thing to induce a palsy of spirit in Allston; desperately anxious to paint a supremely great picture, he wavered between including or excluding this or that personage, adopting one or another lighting scheme, and he accepted advice from Gilbert Stuart about altering the

47. BELSHAZZAR'S FEAST by WASHINGTON ALLSTON Courtesy of The Washington Allston Trust. Photograph from Museum of Fine Arts, Boston.

entire perspective. More than a decade elapsed, toward the end of which Allston married again, and some of the contributors to the fund murmured against the delay; with the quixotism of a noble nature, Allston painted and sold other pictures until he had repaid the money. By then it was too late; probably it had always been, in the sense that Allston was attempting something too ambitious for his capacity. Yet even through his last decade, unproductive as it was, many people continued to expect the canvas to "justify" American painting in the art of the world. Allston had freed himself from living on financial credit, but he could not get free from others' continuing belief in his greatness: a form of unlimited credit which is always, so Hazlitt said, "as dangerous to success in art as in business." Therefore disappointment was strong when Allston died without having completed the masterpiece, and the too hasty immediate verdict of failure upon his career as a whole has long obscured his real success in ways quite different from the grandiosity of the picture which his first biographer so grandiosely called *The Handwriting on the Wall in the Palace of the Babylonian Monarch*.

Incomplete, and in part incoherent, *Belshazzar's Feast* [plate 47] is not only historically important but still interesting in its own right. One reason is no doubt the unfinished state of Belshazzar seated on his throne; for Allston would not only have worked more detail into the costume but he would also probably have modified the angularity of drawing which now has much to do with the figure's emotional expressiveness. The almost caricatured faces of the group of soothsayers, opposite the king, possess considerable narrative effectiveness within the conventions of history painting; and irrespective of all outworn conventions, the central figure of Daniel has majesty in the head and impressiveness in the gesture, which are effectively supported by the exaggerated breadth of the dark robes so handsomely scaled to the horizontal canvas. The two visible portions of the long banquet table in the background possess great beauty of painting in the still-life; the massed shadows of the crowd along the balcony at the top re-enforce the spirit of the whole by their sense of agitation. Several of the more distant columns need more exact values to make them seem strong enough to support anything, but the three principal ones supporting the heavy balcony have been brought far enough along to be visually adequate. Yet all such details are subordinate to the major source of pictorial interest— the management of extensive enclosed space; and Allston's pictorial skill is revealed by the way in which he dramatizes the space by focusing the whole upon the distant detail of what would seem to be a statue illuminated by artificial light from above. The literary and narrative elements of history painting as then understood were in this instance being infused with a genuine painter's way of conceiving the whole. Imperfect as this picture remains, it proves that among the Americans who ventured upon the physical immensities of the grand style only Allston was in the company of Copley by virtue of a partial transformation of its dead weight of unpictorial matter by a purer artistry.

Both of them had intensely and imaginatively experienced the works of past masters; the intellectual approach of Copley and the emotional approach of Allston had yielded similar results in their work. Both could at least reach out for much more than the other history painters even though they could not grasp it all. It was this fact about Allston which gave him a special importance as an example after he returned to this country. He was the first one actually painting here to embody the ideal of the complete artist in paint; as Mr. Edgar P. Richardson puts it, he was the first explorer in America of the whole range of painting. Copley had that ideal in mind before leaving here, but did not attempt its realization until after he left. Charles Willson Peale, in his heartily matter-of-fact way, would have gladly painted anything; but perhaps a little too sensibly he adjusted himself to conditions which prevented him from leading other painters away from hack work and specialism. Stuart knew from first-hand contact with fine pictures what the whole art of painting could be and emphatically rejected it as a program for himself. In the studio-home which Allston built in Cambridgeport, just across the river from Boston, when he remarried in 1830, he remained a shadowy personage for all except his intimates; but every other painter in the country knew he was there, and for every painter who could conceive of his art as comprehending the whole of experience Allston was a cloudy symbol of the possible.

The further characteristic in Allston which helped to make him into such a symbol was the spirit of fancy and imagination which in one way or another animated even his derivative and unsuccessful work. He was the first American mind to seek the poetical treatment of pigment. So far as his poetry of mind is concerned, his printed poems may be largely disregarded; though some evidences of it could be sifted out, they would have a narrowly biographical interest, of little bearing on his painting. They are rivulets of rhyme, no more literature than his prose tale of *Monaldi*, completed in 1822 but not printed until 1841; its idea is that the most dangerous form that evil takes is one not of ugliness but of beauty, an idea which never comes to life among the genteel abstractions of Maldura and Monaldi and Castelli and Alfieri and all the other Italian names which masquerade as people. The *Lectures on Art*, published after his death, have much biographical value in what he says about his European years and his judgements on a few painters; as an intellectual ordering of the esthetic world it is an elusive semi-system, seemingly out of Kant by way of Coleridge, in which Allston tries to harmonize particulars by "arguing down from the pure idea." It is perhaps more feasible to take the

48. MOONLIT LANDSCAPE *by* WASHINGTON ALLSTON *Courtesy of Museum of Fine Arts, Boston.*

cash of specific experiences of particular pictures and let go the credit of arranging them into abstractions which, being intellectual, cannot possibly take
in the fullness of any sensuous art. More valuable are some among a group
of aphorisms by which Allston showed his own responsiveness to the approach
of the Transcendentalism which was soon to dominate New England. "Originality in Art is the individualizing the Universal . . ." is orthodox doctrine,
but better is the saying that ". . . All effort at originality must end either in
the quaint or the monstrous." That is almost equal to another saying by the
Fuseli whom Allston admired: "Indiscriminate pursuit of perfection infallibly
leads to mediocrity."

But words were, after all, a side issue with Allston; he was a painter who,
despite the distractions of influences from other painters and of a too ready
acceptance of the current concept of greatness in art, in a few things achieved
a characteristic pictorial utterance. Among these few probably the finest is the
Moonlit Landscape [1819: plate 48], in which his personal synthesis of the
classic and the romantic became peculiarly intense. The picture is also about
as good an example as any of the best aspect of Allston's technical procedure,
which was briefly but belatedly described by his first biographer in 1892; the
principal point consisted in not mixing his colors with a palette knife and
thereby getting a uniform hue but in mixing them on the brush with light
dippings into the pigments and thus securing a mingled effect when put upon
the canvas. Still greater liveliness was gained by adding small touches of pure
color in greater or less degree according to the desired brilliance. In this respect
the *Moonlit Landscape* was of course restricted in range because of the night
effect, but it was that way of using paint which gave the picture its remarkable degree of luminosity. Here it is worth re-telling that Allston himself said
that William Hazlitt had in conversation described his idea of Titian's habit
as one of "twiddling" his colors; the word aptly suggests the physical motion
required in this procedure. It is a more delicate action than was possible to
Stuart in his old age, but the color-mixing with the brush was essentially the
same as Stuart's late practice. For the theme of the *Moonlit Landscape,* Allston resorted either to straight memory or to the combination of sketch and
memory which apparently served him so well in the Mediterranean coast picture of 1811; imaginative memory of this sort would seem to be the naturally
creative mood of all romantics. In spirit this lunar reverie was Allston's elegiac
farewell to Europe and to youth; but it was also his coming home not to
America but to his deepest self—the only home that any romantic can ever find.

46. An artist of forethought

Samuel Finley Breese Morse: 1791–1872

As just mentioned, when Allston went to England for the second time he took with him as pupil the twenty-year-old Samuel Finley Breese Morse. This son of a Congregational minister painted miniature portraits while still attending Yale College, and after his graduation in 1810 there were a few months of tension (without personal unpleasantness) between him and his father over his desire to become a professional painter. Some of the father's opposition was based upon the son's youthful impulsiveness and a tendency to engage in too many inconsistent activities; the father's attitude seems to have been a somewhat solemn version of that much later expressed by Artemus Ward: "Early genius is like early cabbage, don't head well." There are also plenty of stories about Morse's continued tendency to change overreadily from one thing to another even in maturity; so that the seeming paradox of calling him an artist of forethought must depend for its validity upon the indications in the most successful and characteristic pictures that he had thought them through completely before he began painting them.

At any rate, it was with parental sanction, based on Stuart's approval of their son's work, that the youth accompanied Allston to England. Perhaps it was in part from a sense of responsibility to the minister-father that Allston kept his pupil in England for the entire four years of his pupilage. The reason assigned was worded in terms of painting style, Allston saying that the English school alone could afford a thorough grounding for future work. It may be guessed that Allston was moved, however obscurely, by other considerations as well, for the word by which he characterized the French school was "corruption."

From Allston and from West, who was as generous to Morse as he had always been to young Americans, Morse absorbed a supposedly purer concept of painting than the French one; after some necessary months in routine schooling, he made his first attempt, *The Dying Hercules* [c. 1812: Yale University Art Gallery]. Just as Allston was at the time working from his own clay model for *The Dead Man Restored to Life,* so Morse made one for his Hercules, a cast of which is also now at Yale. The painting was well placed in the Royal Academy exhibition of 1813, and in that same year the clay figure received a gold medal at the Society of Artists. Of the two, the cast is the more interesting, as being more restrained in treatment; the picture exaggerates further some of the exaggerated muscularity of the Farnese *Hercules*. Only history painters wearing the dogmatic blinders of indiscriminate belief in the antique could accept that monstrosity without a qualm at its stylistic "corruption." Morse then knew it only from some cast in London, but it seems strange that he could not have rejected it on his own initiative when he was at that very time rising early in order to draw from the Parthenon marbles and writing home how they surpassed all sculpture after their time. Another historical attempt, *The Judgement of Jupiter* [1814: privately owned], might have won him a prize at the Royal Academy itself if he had been able to remain in London to receive it in person; as it was, he returned to the United States with the "ambition to be among those who shall revive the splendor of the fifteenth century; to rival the genius of a Raphael, a Michael Angelo, or a Titian. . . ."

The words were from the pen of Morse, but the idea was from the mind of Allston; but by both it was bravely affirmed in the face of earlier warnings from Morse's mother that only portrait work could support a painter here. In Boston Morse was personally well received, but he was given no commissions for historical pictures; with the idea that the necessity would be only temporary, he turned to portraiture, but even for that he had to travel about New England doing small panels at fifteen dollars each. By 1817 he had begun to find prosperity in Charleston, South Carolina—enough to let him return north that summer and bring back a bride the following winter. But early in 1821 patronage declined to the point where he had to seek work in other places. Since his portrait work continued for fifteen more years, its quantity alone became sufficient to constitute a painting career; for technique it stands out in the Federal Era with combined clarity and substantiality, and for content it was marked by a frequently strong grasp upon character. *John Bee Holmes* [1817–1820: privately owned] and *De Witt Clinton* [c. 1826: Metropolitan Museum, New York] each shows how much individuality Morse could concentrate into the features alone; *David Curtis De Forest* [1823: Yale University Art Gallery] extended this registration of personality into the pose, but the companion portrait of *Mrs. De Forest* [1823: same owner] subordinated the subject to a daring use of brilliant color which shows how much more interested Morse could be in painting than in human beings.

The strength of this interest can be discerned in a picture done while he was still at college, *The Morse Family* [1809: Division of History, National Museum, Washington], a small water color which emphasized the colors and pattern of the carpet and the architectural primness of the setting and the carefully balanced placing of three sons and the mother so as to let the father dominate the group—the whole naïvely thoughtful composition, with its effect of silhouette and its uncertainty about perspective, suggesting that a gifted amateur had been seeing the work of itinerant artisans. After his return from England more family portraits indicate the same preference for pictorialism over likeness. *Mrs. Jedediah Morse* [privately owned] is primarily a problem of candlelight; the much later portrait of *Mrs. Richard C. Morse and Children* [c. 1835: privately owned] is a much more complex problem of cross-lights by day falling over furniture and figures and marble-inlay floor of a Greek Revival interior. A commission from the city of Charleston to paint *President James Monroe* [1819–1820: City Hall, Charleston] gave him scope for a handsomely designed state portrait bordering upon the historical picture; and another from the city of New York for *Lafayette* [1825–1826: City Hall, New York] enabled him to achieve the most successful example of the kind by any American. There is a feeling of impetuosity in this large-scale splendor—the only instance of intense romantic emotional pressure in Morse's work. But in all the drama of magisterial figure and stately setting and looming clouds there is a steadiness of control from a mind that foresaw the end in the beginning. He may have actually painted other pictures with as much speed as this one, but there is here a strong sensation of rapidity in the brushwork; the few others which are as finely designed as this give an even stronger impression of deliberation. If it is necessary to account for this exceptional trait in the *Lafayette,* a biographical reason may possibly be found in the death of his wife while he was away from her for the purpose of this picture; his loss also had much to do with his being so active in the formation of the National Academy of Design in the years immediately following. Yet he was certainly much stirred by the personality of Lafayette. Whatever the reason, he succeeded in embodying a fine idea; the individual was exalted into a symbolical statesman-hero; the picture succeeded in registering both the living man and the legendary man he had become while still alive.

Morse had not only intended from the first to be more than a portraitist but he also more than once attempted to escape that specialism; though portraiture, because of unfavoring circumstances, formed the bulk of his work, it is the few other pictures that give the most adequate measure of his mind. Aware of the financial success attendant upon the traveling exhibition of Rembrandt Peale's *The Court of Death,* Morse believed he could do likewise with a large canvas of *The [Old] House of Representatives* [1821–1822: Corcoran Gallery, Washington] which would include portraits of the members, the Justices of the Supreme Court, and such other people as might be appropriate to the occasion—eighty-six in all. The likenesses are there insofar as they could be achieved under the conditions of artificial illumination throughout the large

49. EXHIBITION GALLERY OF THE LOUVRE *by* SAMUEL F. B. MORSE *Courtesy of Syracuse University.*

hall which of itself dwarfed all human beings; but only the factually curious would insist upon looking for miniature portraits in a painting which is so beautifully pictorial in its management of lighted space and the enclosing architecture. This truly artistic subordination of knowledge to vision was one reason why the painting was a failure on tour; the other was the absence from it of the moralistic subject which then could attract the public in terms of the theater. Morse misjudged what the public would pay to see, but in doing so he made a momentous artistic advance. He composed a picture which, with its factual material, seems to be only a transcript of appearances, whereas actually its visual appeal is so pure that it exerts almost no appeal except through the painting in it. The luminosity, in the shadows equally with the lights, the pattern made by the arrangement of the darkest darks, the processional columns and curtains, the daring simplicity of the surmounting straight lines and shallow curves—all exemplified the "direct attainment of a foreseen end, simply and without waste" which is the philosopher Whitehead's description of style in everything.

This is an estimate of the picture which its own time did not make; Morse lost money in exhibiting it and went on painting portraits for seven more years in order to get out of debt and even a little ahead financially. Then, backed by some commissions for both original pictures and copies, he made his first trip to the continent: Paris, the Alps, and Italy. His stay of three years did not leave his technique entirely unchanged, but at thirty-eight he made no such stylistic response to his first contact with the masterpieces of painting as Copley had made at thirty-seven. The most interesting result of his trip was a new historical picture, involving a tremendous amount of careful work, which was surprisingly successful in execution but as much of a financial failure as its predecessor. *The Exhibition Gallery of the Louvre* [1832–1833: plate 49] shows one wall and parts of two others crowded to the ceiling with paintings most of which are still considered famous examples of the masters: Leonardo, Titian, Raphael, Poussin, Claude, Correggio, Murillo, Rubens, Veronese, Van Dyck. It is not, however, an anthology of pictures as *The Oxford Book of English Verse* is one of poems; it is a painting about pictures, as George Saintsbury's *The Peace of the Augustans* is a book about books. Just as Saintsbury's book has a plan of its own, partly given by its chosen material but more importantly determined by a unifying concept in the critic's mind, so Morse's work is primarily a picture in its own right, its design partly given by the chosen point of view but more importantly determined by a unifying concept of space and tone out of Morse's own mind. Each reproduced picture's own manner of draftsmanship and color was summarily but essentially given in miniature; yet all the widely varying stylistic accents, together with the lines of gilt that enclose them, were harmonized into Morse's ordered idea of atmosphere. Like its predecessor, this picture only seemed to transcribe appearances; it actually controlled and shaped them into an architectonic unity. Even the placing of the human figures was planned to point up the interior volume which is the major theme of the painting.

Morse returned to New York in 1832, resumed his activities for the Academy, painted a few more portraits, and experienced the disappointment of seeing the last commission for a Rotunda picture in the Capitol go to another. In 1835 he was appointed Professor of the Literature of the Arts of Design at New York University and took up his residence in its building on Washington Square; there he taught some pupils in painting and took a hand in the American phase of the daguerreotype. There, too, after some near-starvation which he kept to himself, he reached the successful end of his experimentation in search of a workable telegraph; and thenceforward his connection with painting was increasingly tenuous. How much of a loss to American painting that involved remains debatable; it is possible to say that in his half-dozen best pictures he had already said about as much in design and color as his mind could say, but it seems more likely that if the kind of patronage he desired had actually been extended—and earlier—he would at least have said the same things better. And what he had to say was important for American painting as a whole. The telegraph and the National Academy are unquestionably important effects of his mind and activities, but they at once became external matters, changing strands in the impersonal workings of civilization at large. For a direct understanding of his mind as it was, the pictures are still the principal means; and among the pictures were a few landscapes which contribute a little more to what can be discerned in the history pictures.

The last in point of time was the *Allegorical Landscape* [1836: New-York Historical Society, New York], apparently done in accordance with a theory of color which Morse himself thought was based on Veronese but which probably owed more to the conversation of Allston. The historical approach to painting frequently suggests a measure of adjustability to standards as they may be modified by circumstances, but there is always some point at which such flexibility is liable to become an abandonment of all standards. This picture by Morse would seem to be one of those points; toleration for its vulgar gaudiness of color would be esthetically incapacitating. There are two versions of the *Chapel of the Virgin at Subiaco* [1830: Worcester Art Museum], and a comparison of the sketch made on the spot with the larger picture later worked up from it in the studio gives a very good insight into the kind of improvements then considered academically suitable. The changed relationship between mountains and sky, the strengthening of contrast between darks and lights, the intro-

50. VIEW FROM APPLE HILL *by* SAMUEL F. B. MORSE *Courtesy of Mr. Stephen C. Clark.*
Photograph from The Metropolitan Museum of Art.

duction of differently posed figures engaged in a more of a "story," adding tree branches and slenderizing the chapel shaft itself—all these alterations resulted in a more professionalized picture. But in the sketch there remains a reassuring freshness of touch which gives a longer lasting pleasure to the eye. Moreover, there remains one still earlier landscape, the *View from Apple Hill* [1828–1829: plate 50], which has in it all that freshness and also the quality of foreordained completeness which further enhances the freshness. This subject, like the two history pictures, has been filtered through a selective mind. The flat bulk of bridge and buildings has been tactfully contrasted with the broken masses of foliage, the transparency of water and sky with the opacity of the fields. Again the illumination was Morse's main pictorial interest—here the pellucid day, almost

> "An airy calm too bright and good
> For human nature's daily food."

It is a scene of grace so light that every touch of the brush had to fall sensitively into place in order that the whole might gleam with this spare and provincial elegance. In a way the picture is a summation of the impression left upon the mind by the age as a whole; in a fully historical sense, of course, such an impression is illusory, yet the cruder actualities of the Federal Era do tend to drop out of memory and leave an emotionally valid residue of charm. As a region of the mind for the play of fancy, the Federal Era is a *View from Apple Hill.*

47. The first effective art organizations

The building which had been erected in Richmond for an Academy of the Fine Arts in 1786 was altered to serve as a theater; Charles Willson Peale's Columbianum was disrupted after giving only one exhibition. The Redwood Library at Newport, founded in 1747, was becoming a repository for pictures along with its books; but in 1800 there was no active public organization specifically fostering the exhibition of art, and all teaching of art was still in the hands of individuals and private schools. To fill the void, a small group of business and professional men formed the New York Academy of the Fine Arts in 1802. In the winter of 1803–1804 that organization placed on exhibition in a rented building a collection of about two dozen casts from antique statues and busts chosen by Robert L. Livingston, then the American Ambassador to Paris; but the interest in them declined so quickly that they were put into storage and the organization languished. Nevertheless, it received a state charter in 1808 under the revised name of the American Academy of Arts. This beginning suggested to Joseph Hopkinson in Philadelphia the formation of a similar institution as the Pennsylvania Academy of the Fine Arts; he and his associates went further than the New York group and provided at once for a building, which was ready in 1806, the same year that the organization was chartered. The first exhibition there opened in 1807: another collection of casts, also from Paris and chosen by Nicholas Biddle. For a while this was all, but Robert Fulton, made wealthy by his inventions, had been buying pictures —among them some of the Shakespeare Gallery paintings commissioned from famous painters by Alderman Boydell in London; when Fulton placed his collection in the new institution, public interest reached a point where regular exhibitions were thought practicable; and the newly formed Society of Artists of the United States [1810] was offered the use of the galleries. From May of 1811, with the first showing of current work under the Academy's auspices, such annual exhibitions have been continuous.

Late in 1816 Governor Clinton, then president of the American Academy in New York, led in an attempt to resuscitate the institution; coincident with a new exhibition in new quarters granted by the city, Clinton delivered a discourse and resigned so that Trumbull could move up from vice president to president. All these early institutions occasioned discourses of varying elaborateness and almost uniform tedium, but this one by Clinton is historically important for embodying several concepts of the age as a whole: the separation of the arts called "fine" (a word now inserted into the Academy's title) and a renewed insistence that they are only ornamental, the previous degradation of art by criminal tyrants and vicious monarchies, to be now remedied by better conditions in this American Republic, provided the artists "respect the decencies of life, the charms of virtue, and the injunctions of morality." The flurry of prosperity from paid admissions to the new exhibition caused the new president to expose his attitude more openly than he had done hitherto. All the lay members, leading figures in city life at large, were his friends to the extent of accepting his opinions about how art and artists should be treated. Trumbull was attempting to turn the American Revolution into his private painting preserve and the Capitol Rotunda into his personal shrine; so it was not surprising that he should regard the Academy as his own property. What he did now was to persuade the directors to purchase two of his religious pictures for seven thousand dollars, together with some smaller pictures for smaller sums; the idea was that the money would come out of admission fees. Although the Academy's collection remained on view, public attendance declined, and in the end Trumbull had the pictures back on his hands; yet to the end his control was based on the assumption that the organization was essentially a stockholding device for his own support.

If that had been all there was to the American Academy, it might well have died from public indifference, but in 1824 it made a second attempt to offer art schooling—actually nothing more than allowing some to draw from the casts between six and nine in the morning. A few young men were so in earnest that they would present themselves promptly even in winter, only to be kept waiting in the cold at the whim of a doorkeeper who took it as an insult if they presumed to knock. In this he was confirmed by Trumbull, who clinched what he thought was his case against the aggrieved students by the quotation of "beggars are not to be choosers"; Dunlap was quite right in calling it "the condemnatory sentence of the American Academy of Fine Arts." Dunlap meant that in a moral sense, but it proved true in a practical sense as well, for one thing led fast into another until Morse and others became interested in the students' predicament. In the rooms of the New-York Historical Society, in the same building with the Academy, was formed the New York Drawing Association on the eighth of November, 1825. Its thirty members, more or less, began meeting in those same rooms three times a week to draw by the light of small individual lamps supplemented by a large central oilcan which smoked abominably because it had no chimney. Within less than a month the group saw an impressive intrusion from Trumbull ordering them to sign a register as pupils of his Academy; upon being ignored, he stalked out, leaving the register for the signatures which were never written. In one more month the Drawing Association, after the failure of an attempt to join the American Academy upon terms that gave them a share in its policy-making, began its self-transformation into the National Academy of the Arts of Design, under the presidency of Morse; and four months later opened its first exhibition—May 14th to July 1st, 1826.

At the time the whole affair could have been taken for a battle of personalities between Trumbull and Morse; actually it was one in which a personality was defeated by an idea. As a personality Trumbull was a fascinating psychiatric case; from the basis of the inverted pride of his letter to Jefferson, he had advanced to a morbid resentment against the world for not showering him with riches and honors commensurate with his own consciousness of conferring benefits upon it. Since no city was large enough to enclose his ego in peace with his fellows, New York made an irritatingly small domain in which to wreak his dictatorial temperament. Santayana has written: "A way foolishness has of revenging itself is to excommunicate the world"; and Trumbull's excommunication of a few young art students seems a pitifully petty act to be overtaken by so large a retribution. But the act only brought to a head the general evil that his institution, because it was his, had in it no principle of life; and it produced by reaction the idea that art and art training were not things to be doled out by favor but things which should rightly be available to all who wanted them.

It was on this point that Morse proved to be such an effective leader. He held many of the limited ideas of his time such as formed the discourse of Clinton to the older institution; but Morse had a wider knowledge of history than any other who then ventured into print about art, and he also had an intimate awareness of current conditions as they affected painters. He did not have to resort to small recriminations to make his case; he could and did rest it upon impersonal argument from historical premises, and he centered it all upon one cardinal concept: ". . . the common-sense principle that *every profession in society knows best what measures are necessary for its own improvement.*" The older institution fought the new one with intrigue, social pressure, and an increasingly ill tempered campaign of magazine articles and letters to the papers—most of the documents were reprinted in the first third of Cummings' *Historic Annals of the National Academy of Design*—and through it all Morse, as the principal spokesman of the new Academy, kept his temper while he demolished arguments and exposed twisted reasonings.

Within the organization Morse's energy and practical good sense operated in ways which remained unrecorded. He had known the workings of the Royal Academy as a school and as an exhibition forum under exceptionally favorable conditions; he had even been a leader in an earlier organization here —the South Carolina Academy of Fine Arts, which was organized in 1821, only to languish after he left Charleston. It is not necessary to claim that every sound idea originated in Morse's mind, but it seems probable that every major policy was shaped by him. Though there were practical men and even some good artists among the founding group, there was no other capable of his leadership; one of the best things to be said about the group is that they kept him in the presidency for nineteen years. Several wise decisions may have been largely due to his influence, such as the initial one to eradicate the word *fine* from all attempted classification of the arts. In consequence, those participating from the first were not only picture-painters but also scene-painters (an artisan craft) and engravers and architects and the only available sculptor, John Frazee. Hardly less important was the decision taken after the second exhibition that henceforth copies would not be shown—only "original" works. True, originality in that sense is usually but a shallow thing, yet the result of the rule in ensuring for each exhibition work that was at least fresh had much to do with keeping the institution alive even through lean years.

The central principle of self-determination by the artists gave the National Academy certain characteristics reminiscent of the earlier craft guilds. Though the full consequences did not appear immediately, they were so clearly implicit from the beginning that they may rightly be suggested at this point. The artists were themselves fortified by their group association, and in making a collective impact upon society each gained an importance in his own estimation that was more solid and valuable than self-importance. As the antagonism of Trumbull and his clique was in time discounted, the new Academy earned some confidence from the well-to-do who wished to buy pictures; the way in which it worked and the regularity with which it offered its wares made art in general appear more substantial and dependable to the members of a business society. The exhibitions further enlarged the audience for art in making possible at least part-time contact with it for a non-buying public; this was not actually a mass audience, but as an intermediate and growing one it counted increasingly in the national total. All these effects were in a sense consequences of another thing: the artists' program, though long marred by weakness and inconsistency, of establishing and improving professional standards. Where there had earlier been nothing like that on which a lay public could rely, it now became possible to discuss pictures in terms of technical merit which became better understood as the exhibitions recurred; and eventually even newspaper reviews could break the news of a vague but gradually clarifying thing called esthetic quality. Less in the public eye but still important was the equally gradual improvement of the instruction made available to art students.

In sum, the National Academy was proving that the best results for everybody came from the artists' running their own affairs. But meanwhile in Philadelphia the artists were having trouble over this very point. By 1828 the Society of Artists had accumulated such a sizable set of grievances against the Pennsylvania Academy that a group of twenty-seven presented a memorial; to this the laymen in control made a reply that caused resentment, but the artists found no way to make their feelings effective, and their organization lapsed. In Boston the Athenaeum, which had been established as a library in 1807, began giving loan exhibitions of art works in 1826; from the first they were large in size and mixed in character, but interest was well maintained for a few years. A Stuart memorial show benefited his destitute family; and in 1829 the institution allowed the exhibition of a collection of "old masters," direct from Florence, whose assigned authorship seemed even then too good to be true. Dubious works were sold weekly at New York auctions, where people were beginning to buy by ear rather than by eye. "It is naught, it is naught, saith the buyer; but when he is gone his way, then he boasteth." Young Charles Loring Elliott once saw a picture of his go for seventy-five cents at auction; afterward the auctioneer told him it was too definite and too fresh in color. "Make your pictures black and shiny, and your fortune is assured." Even the established dealers were recklessly reassuring in their sales; old Paff, in Wall Street, who put some pictures by young Cole in the shop window and thus started him to fame, sold counterfeit "old masters" and continued long in business even after some buyers began to find him out.

Yet all the activities here described concerned a relatively small public; the taste for pictures which existed on the mass level in the Federal Era was still largely fed by street signs. These were now re-enforced by many commercial museums which corrupted the original ideal of Charles Willson Peale by the addition of "curiosities" of increasingly dubious character and a sideshow element of freaks. The statuary ran more and more to waxworks, often anatomical in character, and the painting more and more emphasized sensationalism. To a certain extent Rembrandt Peale participated in this tendency; his "useful and pleasing institution" in Baltimore featured a mastodon skeleton and his own *Court of Death* [plate 46], together with

. . . an entire statue of wax, colored like life, representing a beautiful female modestly reclining on a Grecian couch; snakes, lizards, and insects; shells and petrifactions; miscellaneous curiosities; optical amusements and philosophical demonstrations; and a painting called the *Dream of Love,* representing an elegant young female reclining in a grotto, repelling the enchantments of Love.

Rembrandt's brother Rubens Peale later operated another museum in New York, and there had the enterprise to exhibit the first Egyptian mummy seen in this country. John Scudder's American Museum, in New York from 1810 until it and Peale's were both absorbed by Barnum, featured naval paintings and waxworks. Daniel Bowen started a museum in Philadelphia but eventually located it in Boston; and there the antiquarian Bentley in 1800 praised the paintings, but deprecated the poor arrangement and "the monstrous excess of wax figures." When the museum was re-opened after a fire in 1803, he censured the paintings without saying whether they were new ones. The rapid increase in the number of such institutions is reflected in newspaper advertisements and notices; when these are collated with visitors' accounts preserved in diaries and books of travel, there results a strong impression that the promoters' emphasis on cultural uplift was a fairly certain indication of shoddy stuff.

48. Artisans and amateurs of the Federal Era

Benjamin J. Severance: act. 1823
Hill: act. 1804
William Clarke: act. 1782–1799
George Rutter: act. 1782–1799
George Ropes: 1788–1819
L. Whitney: ?
John Ritto Penniman: 1783–?
John A. Woodside: 1781–1852
Thomas Hanford Wentworth: 1781–1849
Moses Morse: act. 1789
Samuel S. Rooker: act. 1821

J. Atwood: act. 1815–1820
Theorem painting
Jane Stuart: c. 1812–1888
Lydia Hosmer: act. 1812
Mary Ann Bacon: 1787–?
Eunice Pinney: 1770–1849
Cephas Thompson: 1775–1856
George Washington Parke Custis: 1781–1857
John Blake White: 1782–1859
John Stevens Cogdell: 1778–1847
Joshua Johnston: act. 1789–1825

Practically all that has been here related, beginning with Stuart, is concerned with the studio professionals; but at the same time the artisans also were enlarging their activities. The bustle of general prosperity, modest as it would seem beside today's activities, meant new business and new homes, new things to go into the homes; and it made a multitude of occasions for all-round painters to do something. Possibly the greater part of that work occurred in the more modest homes, built with little self-consciousness, straight out of handbooks, by local workmen who didn't know any better than to do an honest job. The results were often homely in the invidious sense, but perhaps more often homely in the intimate and lovely sense of plain humanity. A large proportion of the homes were soon adorned with pictures of identical spirit. Whether they were by itinerant artisans or by amateurs who lived there, the paintings had a vital relationship to place and time and people. Their cultural significance was not connected with any of the current studio formulas for beauty; it consisted in their homely adequacy of expressiveness for homely experience.

Throughout the East even the smaller places now began to support artisan-painters who sometimes claimed the old-time omnicompetence. Northfield in Massachusetts, for example, was the location in 1823 of Benjamin J. Severance, who undertook house and sign and ornamental painting, decorated carriages, composed landscapes, and offered to make views of country seats. In other places the painter sometimes combined unexpected activities, as did a certain Hill in

51. AMERICAN LANDSCAPE *by* L. WHITNEY *Courtesy of The Newark Museum.*

Hartford, Connecticut, as late as 1804. He advertised profiles in gold on glass for three dollars and in cutouts by the physiognotrace for fifty cents; he solicited orders for plain and fancy painting and also subscriptions for a vocal and instrumental music school. "From knowing the taste and generosity of the Citizens of Hartford he feels that he need only to merit their patronage to receive it."

Such sign painters as could venture beyond plain-grounds with lettering could be sure of work because the public interest in pictorialism was intensifying. One branch of decoration in which this was noticeable was on the coaches. As befitted the new democracy, private coaches quickly became much less important than public ones; the latter just as quickly spread like a network across the more settled regions. With the aim of accommodating as many people as possible, they were strikingly altered in size and shape "from dashing rococo chariots into squared-off lumbering carryalls"; and the bigger they became, the more surface there was available for bright colors and fanciful pictures. These were a form of advertising, quite as likely to attract trade as signs on shops; a great deal of thought went into devising effective ideas. There is a hint of poetry in the description of one which was doubtless exceptional for deserving to be described in writing—gilded sides, with the painting of a postboy and a couple of lines:

> He comes, the herald of the noisy world,
> News from all nations lumbering at his back.

The annals of sign painters are full of characters about whom little is known but who seem tantalizingly interesting as human beings. There was a group of temporary business associates of Matthew Pratt in the latter seventeen-nineties; among these Jeremiah Paul and his ambitious mythological picture have been mentioned, but there were also William Clarke, who left some amusing attempts at dignified portraits in Baltimore, and George Rutter, against whom Christian Gullager's challenging advertisements were directed. Lack of information may keep the personal relationships within that short-lived firm permanently unknown, but Jarvis' reminiscences at least faintly suggest psychological complications. In Salem, Massachusetts, the young deaf-mute George Ropes, by his painting, supported the family after the early death of his father and helped a younger brother on to where he could eventually paint academically uninteresting landscapes; at the time, the younger one's pictures doubtless seemed the better work by the two brothers, for the elder Ropes was always a fumbler. He got a little painting knowledge from Corné, and with that little he made a few pictures which evidence a personal feeling for decorative pattern. There is no information as to whether a certain L. Whitney was an artisan painter by profession, but the handling of paint in the *American Land-scape* [plate 51] suggests that he was. The awkwardness lies in the drawing, as if it were simply the visual image that was difficult. The vision, the concept, of the picture is direct and unified. As Mr. Holger Cahill has pointed out, this freshness occurred with greater frequency in artisan and amateur landscape than it did in portraiture, probably because a widespread demand, as in the latter, tends to produce a formula in response. Through the Federal Era the painting of landscape was still largely what it seems to have been with Smibert —an expression of personal taste in the painter; and this would of itself account for the spontaneity of touch seen in Whitney's clouds and tree patterns. It might also be the explanation for the seemingly instinctive, certainly unobvious, balance of the design. Landscapes were occasionally done by artisans whose treatment clearly indicates a semi-professionalized competence beyond that of Whitney and the elder Ropes; such an individual was John Ritto Penniman, in Roxbury, Massachusetts, who was a long-time friend of Stuart. His personal failings, infallibly noted by Dunlap, put him in the almshouse several times; but he executed a large amount of work quite varied in subject-matter. Peale's museum in Philadelphia once exhibited a "sea serpent" caught off the coast of New England, and along with it a painting by Penniman of its capture. He attempted religious and classical themes, and some landscape work done early in the nineteenth century shows an approach rather like that of Ralph Earl.

Probably the most competent artisan painter of the Federal Era in the entire country was John A. Woodside. He executed decorations for fire engines and hose carriages, and it is said that he decorated the first locomotive. By the time he made the sign for Philadelphia's new Union Hotel in 1820, which was copied or adapted from "Mr. Binn's beautiful copper-plate engraving of the Declaration of Independence," Woodside was famous enough to be called "that justly celebrated artist." As with Pratt before him, Woodside's signs remained in use after his death; a handsome one of *The Indian Queen* could be seen in place up to the Civil War.

He was much praised for his careful workmanship, the praise being that he "finished to perfection"; and it was no doubt this characteristic of his signs which allowed the association with his name of a variant on the oldest sort of admiration-story in the legendry of painting. It concerned a sign he made depicting fish and game and meats and it said that one day a dog jumped for the food, got his nose bumped, and ran off with his tail between his legs. The chronicler advisedly adds: "So it is said!"

The story has some significance for Woodside but more for the history of popular interest in painting. Those who started the story and kept it going,

52. COUNTRY FAIR *by* JOHN A. WOODSIDE *Courtesy of Mr. Harry T. Peters, Jr. Photograph from The Metropolitan Museum of Art.*

either as an expression of admiration for the sign or as amusing in its own right, were telling more about themselves than about the painter or the dog. They were reiterating one of the major notes in all American interest in painting, and they were also (probably unawares) affirming that Americans were steady in the broadly human tradition coming down from Greece through Rome and Renaissance Italy and nearer England.

On at least two occasions, in 1817 and 1821, Woodside exhibited paintings along with other men who thought themselves above making signs. Probably the pictures so shown were better than one earlier landscape of *Laurel Hill* [1807: Pennsylvania Historical Society, Philadelphia], which is uncertain in drawing and very tentative in its use of pigment. For the *Country Fair* [1824: plate 52] shows him in full possession of the minutely exact descriptive skill which not only won the approval of his own time but also exerts a considerable appeal to this time. Its present attractiveness comes from more than the fillip of quaintness exerted by a certain naïveity of perception; Woodside's particular kind of similitude combines a neat way of drawing with sensitively graduated values, and remarkably intensifies the visual sensation.

A later work, the *Merchants Exchange* [1836: privately owned], displays a still sharper definition because the principal subject is a building. Even more positively than the earlier *Country Fair* it illustrates a saying by Delacroix: "Painters who are not colorists produce illumination and not painting . . ." Yet Woodside did produce pictures, and attractive ones. In them form underwent a kind of purification and space a kind of clarification. Somewhat as Blake called on the evening star to "wash the dusk with silver," Woodside with unconscious daring washed the full light of day with gold and white. It is a singularly ingratiating sort of vision which frequently recurred in the nineteenth century simply because it so well suited a widespread state of esthetic innocence.

Woodside seems to have had no trouble making a living in one place— Philadelphia; but dozens of others took to the road. In the more thickly populated states northeast of the Potomac it was often possible for the itinerant portraitist to make a satisfactory living on a relatively limited circuit of travel. There was, for example, Thomas Hanford Wentworth, at work in Connecticut and westward into New York, who has been credited with more than three thousand portraits of all sorts before 1824, most of them quickly executed small likenesses in pencil. If that estimate be trustworthy, Wentworth depicted more people than Saint-Mémin and all the Sharples together.

Few itinerant portraitists were so prolific, and some may not have done portraits at all, being content to use semi-mechanical means of decorating walls and floors. On their journeys they carried ready-cut stencils, and with them

painted repeating patterns in variable combinations of small units. Their handiwork remains sprinkled across New England from Long Island to Maine, and
an occasional example is found in that portion of the Old West where surplus
New Englanders settled. Itinerants of greater skill or greater courage rose above
stenciling to freehand decorative panels and even to pictures which were not
the relatively small overmantels but covered all four walls of the room. In
Marlboro, Vermont, the Mather house of 1820 contains second-floor rooms
decorated in repeating designs, some of which are freehand and others stenciled;
the first-floor parlor and the halls on both floors have elaborate designs whose
technical inadequacies prevent the full pictorialism apparently intended but
emphasize an instinctive decorative ability in their maker.

The sign painters of adventurous temperament or lesser ability, or both,
ventured to the frontier. One Moses Morse is the first painter recorded as entering the Old Northwest; he went on foot from New England to Marietta, Ohio,
in 1789, and all the way along left behind him a series of Black Horse tavern
signs he had made with a stencil. In 1821, the year that Indianapolis became the
capital of Indiana, Samuel S. Rooker arrived from Tennessee; his sign for the
Eagle Tavern turned out to be a turkey, and when the upper part of his figure
of General Lafayette left insufficient room for the legs he attached the feet
directly to the knees. Those are at least good stories, and they are good history
too in that they can be stretched to illustrate the proverbial remark about the
Jack-of-all-trades being master of none. It was just such creatures whose work
or passing presence stimulated painting ambitions in Chester Harding and
Thomas Cole.

Back in the thickly settled portions of the East the traveling painter would
be better trained than venturesome Moses Morse and Samuel Rooker; in the more
populous regions many village and country amateurs now wanted lessons. Some
teaching itinerants would get their patronage by word-of-mouth recommenda-
tion passed along, and some by newspaper announcements, but some carried
with them ready-printed cards with blanks left for writing in the necessary details about locations and dates and hours. One such card left in Deerfield,
Massachusetts, specifies that J. Atwood was prepared to teach painting of two
sorts—not only from nature but also "in the new mode called the Hornfleur
System."

More than one such "System" was favored from time to time; whatever their
variations, they were all devised to by-pass that little difficulty of nature. The
pupil—student would be too ambitious a word—was relieved of the major difficulties of picturemaking. The pupil copied pictures outright or put them
together from units of prepared stencils and in this way became familiar with
a few pictorial concepts that were capable of minor variations of pattern and

somewhat greater variation of color. The conscious mind was centered almost entirely upon a process, the manipulation under controlled conditions of a particular medium. The process was sound as far as it went. Despite the degradation of techniques and the limited goals, and despite the inadequacies of transmission, it was essentially a continuation of a shop practice followed in the medieval guilds. It gave scope for a love of craft and a modest degree of originality; it enabled hundreds of cheerful people to make several thousand pleasant pictures. And in all that busyness there occasionally occurred the mystery of creation.

One widespread system had several names—Indian tint, Poonah, theorem, theoremetrical—and was a peculiar domain for girls and women, even though men sometimes taught it. The theorem was a set of stencils which reduced drawing to tracing but left some leeway for choice in combining stencil units and a larger opportunity for originality in color. However, guidance and conventions were so strong that variations remained well within the bounds of discretion; from these lady amateurs comes no story to match that of the girl in Connecticut who made her living by stenciling decorations on clocks. She up and made one horse blue because she was tired of brown: a very early instance of rebellion against industrial monotony, for this commercial stenciling with oil pigment required quantity production. The lady amateurs used colors in the form of powders which had to be mixed with tragacanth gum and water for application. If the picture was on paper, the coloring presented no unusual difficulty; but if on velvet, which was the most fashionable painting base, considerable skill was needed to control the tints on so variable a surface. The stencil method favored still-life of flowers and fruits as the most manageable subjects, but it was extended into landscape and figures. The main reason why the pictures on velvet, now usually brown with age, are so attractive is that the stencil outlines and velvet surface together imposed arbitrary pattern and non-naturalistic color upon the results; the pictures were of course not thought of as abstractions in the way of recent theorizers, but they approached that state through technical necessities.

For their subjects many ladies went to nature, as the phrase has it, but the quavering outlines and timid color washes in their little landscapes have only the charm of naïvety—a charm which may be genuine enough within narrow limits but which is likely to receive exaggerated attention from later sophisticates. The Federal Era was not an age in which to look for mature originality among women artists; even that which was attributed to one of Stuart's daughters, presumably Jane, needs discounting. In the eighteen-twenties, upon the occasion of a private view of her picture of *The Magdalen Forgiven,* the *Columbian Centinel* published some verses of praise:

There's something Raphael vainly sought
  That flows in every line,
A something that he never caught,
A something that he never taught,
  A something all divine.

A less lofty degree of originality can be made out in a little painting on glass by Lydia Hosmer of *The Fishing Party* [1812: Antiquarian Society, Concord, Mass.]; the fact that it took a premium at the Concord Cattle Show of that year may serve as a reminder of how important a part such annual events played in furnishing an audience and an incentive not only to the lady artists but also to the artisans and amateurs generally. The cattle shows were initiated by Elkanah Watson at Pittsfield, Massachusetts, in 1807, and from 1817 they were called by the more inclusive and more accurate name "fairs"; Woodside's painting [plate 52] constitutes an important record of such an event despite the obvious idealization of its static neatness.

A more modest personal stamp is visible in a couple of water-color views of Quebec by Mary Ann Bacon [Historical Society, Litchfield, Conn.]; seemingly derived from other pictures, they display a technical peculiarity of brush strokes which, consciously or unconsciously, assumed the look of embroidery. This peculiarity occurred with other pictures executed entirely in water color, but not as frequently as the combination of the two mediums in the same work—usually of a memorial nature. The personal papers left by Mary Ann Bacon from the period of her attendance at Miss Pierce's school in Litchfield make up a record of school life away from home from which are missing the unpleasant personal overtones of Nancy Shippen's experience before the Revolution; but for Mary Ann Bacon there was an intensification of religious pressure, evident in her moralizings at fifteen, which may have found fortunate relief in picture-making and in the piano lessons she didn't like at five o'clock in the morning. Mrs. Eunice Pinney, also of Connecticut, left a half-hundred little pictures wholly free from technical timidity; they all date from about her fortieth to about her fifty-fifth year, and at least one of them has an interest out of the ordinary. Where most of her pictures achieved their spirited charm as adaptations of other pictorial material which she subjected to an unusual degree of personal fancy, this one took its subject from life without in the least abandoning established habits of drawing and coloring. The formally balanced pattern of *Two Women* [c. 1815: plate 53], the attempt to indicate bulk in the figures by partially indicated shadows, the absence of perspective in the drawing even though she sees it in nature, the candle-flame doing no more than symbolize the illumination that is not there—all such contradictions are interesting details in the general problem of a painter who is beginning to perceive naturalistically

53. TWO WOMEN *by* EUNICE PINNEY *Courtesy of Jean and Howard Lipman.*

but is unable to express her perceptions through a hand which has been conditioned by a "System."

By the lady pupils and their artisan teachers almost the entire gamut of mediums was practised: water color, charcoal, pencil, pen-and-ink, india ink, chalk, pastel, oil. They called one of their ways of painting "fresco," though that was not a correct use of the word. Nor did they ever rise to the difficulties of mosaic and encaustic; but for their purposes they devised some short-lived hybrids such as pasted tinsel and water color combined with embroidery. They also found their subject-matter in every namable type: portrait, landscape, allegory, mythology, religious and secular history, anecdote, still-life, decoration, illustration—not a single label for any kind of picture but can be fitted to examples by the artisans and amateurs.

Among the itinerant portraitists of the Federal Era there was a continuation of the habit of colonial workmen in turning out canvases which are identical except for some quite minor detail or two. Cephas Thompson was a Massachusetts man who made winter tours of the more southerly regions; he is said to have been the painter who depicted three sisters in Norfolk in a costume which differs only in the ribbon or band which draws the dress together under the breasts; and his use of the idea in two more portraits outside that family suggests that he traveled with the canvases ready prepared. He had some interesting quirks of character, too, for he taught his craft to one son only and refused it to another son and a daughter, saying that one more painter was enough to wish onto the world.

With seeming inconsistency, however, he taught George Washington Parke Custis, who was Mrs. Washington's grandson and who inherited a sizable estate from the great man for whom he was named. Custis built Arlington across the Potomac from Washington, and directly on its walls he painted designs which, to judge by the fragments which remain, were as inflated in feeling as the outsized columns across the front of the house. Some plays by him, actually staged, presumably listened to, and afterward printed, were marked by a parallel inflation of language. Virginian dilettantes before him had ventured into writing and playing on musical instruments, but Custis was apparently the first to push on into painting. Where eighteenth-century Carters and Byrds practised their dilettantism for purely private pleasure, nineteenth-century Custis practised his with a considerable flourish of talk about social obligation, which was essentially just more of the cultural inflation characterizing his whole life.

The concept of the dilettante had had a somewhat longer history in Charleston, and through the Federal Era it was re-enforced by several successors to Isaac Mazyck and Alexander Gordon. John Blake White practised law for a living and yet found time to write plays and to paint pictures which constantly

repeat a few revolutionary subjects associated with South Carolina. Some instruction from West in 1803 was not enough to make a good technician out of
White, and the praise which his labored paintings received from Dunlap might
now seem to have been earned by his abilities as a lawyer. Another lawyer of
Charleston was John Stevens Cogdell, who was painting as early as 1816; following Allston's advice, he began to model as a help to his painting and found
the new process so interesting that at the age of forty-nine he turned sculptor—
all the while continuing as a lawyer and engaging also in government work:
another whose general respectability won Dunlap's approval for his art. The
actual works of these and many other dilettantes do not endure critical examination in terms of later technical and esthetic concepts; and perhaps all such works
need more indulgence than they are likely to receive in history. Yet the ideal
of a wide-spread amateurism in all the arts is an admirable one for any society
in that it increases the audience for those arts and immensely increases the resources for individual happiness.

Probably the principal reason why important works are not produced by
amateurs is that they themselves are not deeply enough engaged in the making
of them. Not only the artist of studio training but also the artisan with shop
training has a better chance of creating something significant because he is more
at ease with whatever technique he may have, and of course continuous practice
helps to imbue his work with a professionalism denied to the amateur by definition. For him art is an adjunct to living; for the professional, art is not only a
means of making a living but also living itself—sometimes the whole of it.

This general idea may help to explain why the work of Joshua Johnston, with
a technique stiffer and thinner than that of either White or Cogdell, carries
more conviction in his awkward portraiture. Johnston was a negro, probably
a freed slave, but there is no trace of racial accent in his work. As Mr. Alain
Locke has pointed out in his recent study of the whole field of negro art in
this country, until recently a negro could not succeed in art by taking his own
race for subject-matter. Despite puristic theories about painting, the subject is
the natural starting-point for developing any specific accent—personal or racial,
regional or national. Johnston could not take his own race for subject because
nobody then was buying such pictures; and in turning to the portraiture of
white people he became one among many semiskilled, semiartisan in-betweens
whose production has a moderate interest of quaintness.

An omnipresent handicap for all this work is that in the United States before
the Civil War none of the artisans and very few of the studio men were acquainted with the whole range of the craft and art they practised. Therefore
even if the amateurs had been capable of learning more than they did, the
actual knowledge available to them was sharply limited at the sources; and all

that the amateurs could do in the circumstances was to give themselves and their fellows a little guileless pleasure by means of whatever scraps of technique might be handy. The severity of this estimate is inevitable in approaching the work with awareness of the technical complexities and spiritual subtleties which are the necessary prelude to the seeming simplicities of really great painting. But if the amateur art of nineteenth century America is approached in imagination from the basis of the circumstances in which it was produced, it collectively assumes a moral beauty. It was very healthily just one among several partially mastered crafts by which people with a little leisure undertook to brighten life with some inexpensive things that were good to look at. It was a heartening affirmation that people will have art even if they have to make it for themselves. The people and the homes and the pictures were all of one piece in a cheerful simplicity that now seems Arcadian; and despite its inadequacy to greatness then and to conditions now, that spirit is still a valuable part of the American inheritance.

49. Retrospect from the year 1830

Alexander Wilson: 1766–1813
Titian Ramsay Peale: 1799–1846
Charles Robert Leslie: 1794–1859

Every period of history can be presented as transitional in one way or another, but the Federal Era exemplified the transitional with a singularly harmonious completeness. The post roads and canals had already begun the circulation of people which has ever since been so important for national unity; and, on the eve of another stage in the national development, the railroads began to take over the function and accelerate the process to a degree which seemed physically tiring and culturally dangerous to foreigners but simply exhilarating to most Americans. In politics there occurred the shift from the open-class rule of the Federalists through Jeffersonianism to the open-democratic rule embodied in Andrew Jackson. This last change, which of itself initiated the next phase of history, sounded like a thunderclap announcing chaos to the ears of the conservatives; but in retrospect it seems without the convulsiveness of later changes. The economic structure during the Federal Era was sharply modified by the increase of commerce, with the agricultural class becoming relatively less powerful even while increasing in numbers and productivity.

Since 1750, when the merchant group began to emerge with the promise of becoming the dominant group, their patronage of painting had been the factor which permitted its existence on a level above sign painting. But that patronage had also imposed on the craft a limitation to portraiture which it was long in overcoming. Accordingly, indications of a broadening taste in this group during the Federal Era have significance in a gradually improving state of things, and even more in presaging for painters still better conditions to follow. A second-generation merchant like the younger Robert Gilmor in Baltimore spent some of his youth in Europe, during which he practised amateur sketching of the picturesque and commenced the habit of buying pictures that eventually ranged from medieval manuscripts through all schools including the contemporaneous British; in the eighteen-twenties he became prophetic in his patronage of Americans by ordering landscape views painted on his country estate by Thomas Doughty. Gilmor also early bought pictures from Thomas Cole, and in this he and Daniel Wadsworth, of Hartford, competed. But such buyer support for

landscape or any other subject-matter, going to the painters in the guise of
what the language of the time termed "pecuniary emolument," had to become
fashionable in New York if it was to affect American painting as a whole. For
by 1830 the double flow of merchandise through that port, inward from Great
Britain and outward from sources using the Erie Canal, had given New York a
lead which was still further strengthened through the nineteenth century. Only
the merchants who controlled the metropolis of commerce could also set the
pattern of the cultural adornments which accompanied business success.

Through most of the Federal Era itself such patronage as there was for
pictures other than portraits occurred principally in Philadelphia; and there,
too, appeared the earliest indications of still another indirect kind of support
for picturemaking. Ever since the day of Franklin an important element in
the city's intellectual life had been scientific curiosity, and during the first phase
of the national history that interest manifested itself in illustrated publications
about plants and insects and birds. Such earlier scientific draftsmen as Mark
Catesby, in this country twice between 1712 and 1726, and Frederic A. J. de
Wangenheim, a Hessian officer fighting for the British in the Revolutionary
War, took the fruits of their investigations back to Europe as the explorers and
their artists had done long before. The drawings and books of the Federal Era
were not only concerned with American material but also addressed to the
American public. The Scotch-born Alexander Wilson was the first whose published work of this type combined a reasonable degree of scientific accuracy
and artistic skill; his subjects were birds for his *American Ornithology,* begun
in 1808; Wilson made arduous trips through the country, collecting material
and selling subscriptions, and died while getting ready his eighth volume. In
the mid-twenties Charles Lucien Bonaparte, a nephew of Napoleon then living
in Philadelphia, began the publication of his own *American Ornithology,* which
established his scientific reputation both here and in Europe; and for some of
the illustrations he sent a son of Charles Willson Peale on a sketching trip to
Florida. The son was Titian Ramsay Peale, who had already been on two
scientific expeditions and had made the drawings for Thomas Say's *American
Entomology* [1817]. A somewhat curious fact about the younger Peale is that
he was the second of that name; the first was a child of the first wife and died
at the age of eighteen; when a son was born to the second wife in the following
year, he received his dead half-brother's name. After his work for Bonaparte,
he went on two more scientific expeditions: to South America and to the South
Seas. After that his position with the Patent Office in Washington must have
seemed tame—perhaps pleasantly so. The engraver Alexander Lawson did the
plates for both Wilson and Bonaparte, and it was in defense of Wilson's accuracy that he strongly censured the water colors which were brought to Bona-

parte by John James Audubon; yet it was the later man who, with a remarkably developed instinct for design, raised scientifically intended art into greatness.

John Neal, whose rough-and-ready comments on art began to appear in print even before Dunlap commenced the composition of his history, very perceptively observed that the landscape and still-life pictures already produced before 1830 were "better than we deserve; and more than we know what to do with." Possibly the appearance of such pictures in quantity on the walls of the well-to-do was delayed somewhat by such people's liking for imported pictorial wall-papers; a framed oil would be offensive in a room where *The Voyages of Antenor* or the story of *Paul and Virginia* in elegant French designs continued all the way round. At the same time, this fashion must have helped, too; for when its vogue waned, it must have seemed positively necessary to have pictures to look at which had some subject interest apart from family likenesses. One natural answer to the need would have been anecdote, but in the United States landscape gave indications of popularity a little earlier. Charles Robert Leslie, one of the best painters of anecdote of the time, had gone to London in 1811 for his advanced training; and since he found there both a richer artistic life and a much better market, he became permanently identified with the English school. His experiment in returning to this country for a short term of teaching at West Point did not succeed; and back to London he went, to continue satisfying the English appetite for anecdote which had been expressed in the obituary of young Duché and to earn the praise of Ruskin for the fidelity of his craft.

The pictures beyond portraiture which did appear in American homes before 1830 inevitably lacked intensity. There was a great deal of intensity in the language used about the moral improvement to be got out of religious history pictures and about the patriotic pride to be felt from pictorial dramatics of the Revolutionary War, but there was in the pictures themselves no artistic intensity to match the words. Stuart felt passionately about pigment, which was immaterial to his patrons, and Raphaelle Peale felt passionately about the objects he depicted, which was almost certainly missed by the few who bought his paintings; Allston could feel passionately in himself, but his pictures were lyrical or nothing, and Morse seems never to have been profoundly moved by either subject or process. The rest of the painters were eminently of their time; the note of passionate intensity would have been as incongruous in an anecdote by Krimmel or a landscape by Ralph Earl as it would have been in the literary placidities of Washington Irving. After colonizing a new country and achieving independence, the logical material goal became comfort; after the initial intensity of Puritanism, the spiritual desire was for reassurance that comfort was itself the evidence of spiritual living. So all the pictures were pleasant.

PERIOD TWO

THE PROVINCIAL

DIVISION FIVE

The Mid-Century—

1830 to 1860

50. The reign of the genteel

Despite political indications of the strains which were to result in a calamitous Civil War, the American scene of the mid-century appeared steady enough to the casual eye. There was an immense amount of activity: new states taken into the Union, more than two million immigrants absorbed in addition to an equivalent increase among the native-born, factories spreading through the North, with ribbons of railroads lacing the whole country to distribute their products. The defeat of the conservatives by Jackson and his coalition of voters in the Midwest and the eastern cities initiated a reconstruction of society which might have been completed peacefully except for the war; but the effect of all those activities together was to shut the South into a pocket with an economy made brittle by its basis of slavery, and with a culture already dangerously retrospective in character. Its collapse was only postponed by the westward march of "manifest destiny," a war with Mexico, and the Gold Rush. The lustiness and raggedness of the mining frontier were matched by the exuberance and dirtiness of the eastern cities. When Morse returned from Europe to New York in 1833, he wrote to Fenimore Cooper in Paris that money-making and fires and scavenging continued as usual, but with different people and houses and pigs. Though no city yet ranked as cultural capital of the nation as a whole, many cities were sprawling messily into their surrounding countrysides; and it was in unconscious acknowledgment of the careless disorder accompanying the roar of progress that strong connotations of approval gathered around the word "neat." Just before the opening of the period a New York museum advertised "a neat collection of curiosities." The head of the Troy Female Academy, twelve years later, advocated water-color painting for ladies because it could "be performed with neatness and without the disagreeable smell which attends on oil painting." In a much admired piece of oratory dedicating Charleston's Magnolia Cemetery in 1850, Charles Fraser said: "There we behold a neat funeral chapel." And not long after the period closed Tuckerman, in suitable praise for one of its leading lights, Henry Inman, wrote of the "completeness and neatness of style in his landscapes."

Neatness, however, was hardly the word to fit the prosperous homes for which paintings were bought. The well established Greek Revival manner was stately throughout New England, less sophisticated in Ohio and Michigan, and palatially extravagant in its southern apotheosis. But well before the war the style began to seem unfashionably simple in comparison with somewhat more complicated Italian villas and strikingly inconsistent combinations of English and Oriental motives. The Gothic in a few masonry churches was passable, but in private houses, generally of wood, it was turreted and bracketed into steeply unstructural trivialities. The extravagant eccentricity of Barnum's show place in the country, "Iranistan," with bulbous domes and with an elephant at work on the grounds, was as frank a piece of advertising as the painted displays on the exterior of his museum in New York; but there was also ostentation in the elegant words about simplicity which accompanied the designs for villas sanctioned by the current esthetic authority, Andrew Jackson Downing. The interiors of these homes were deprived of light by heavy curtains and the furniture was beginning to swell into ponderousness. Gift books appeared on marble-topped tables and antimacassars on chairs, while roses in the carpets competed for attention with the wide gilt frames of the paintings on the walls. As a result of machine-made possessions, what had been superfluous was becoming necessary.

Machines in general commanded instant attention from Americans, and the unlimited progress which thus seemed promised received complete belief. A machine for setting type, or one for harvesting, interested Americans because it worked, because it did something useful, and because it reduced human labor. Therefore when a machine suddenly appeared for making images such as the painter had previously monopolized, enthusiasm was tremendous—even among the portraitists, for they at once accepted the daguerreotype as both a means and a guide to greater exactitude and felt themselves still professionally needed for adding the crowning touch of color. Morse, who had become a professor at New York University, played a leading part in developing and spreading the process; for some years he taught the daguerreotype process, and had for one of his pupils Mathew Brady, who afterwards made the amazing camera record of the Civil War. Upon the first exhibition of works by a pupil of Daguerre himself, in New York late in 1839, newspaper and magazine comment was verbosely ecstatic; and in the diary which Philip Hone, former mayor and life-long leader of intellectual fashion, was composing for the edification of posterity he wrote:

. . . It is nothing less than the palpable effect of light occasioning a representation of sensible objects. . . . Every object, however minute, is a perfect transcript of the thing itself. . . . How greatly ashamed of their ignorance the by-gone generations of mankind ought to be!

The genteel ease with which that last sentence disposes of history is itself historic. The painter Charles Loring Elliott was content to remark that the daguerreotype established the truth of Rembrandt's light and shade; and in the midst of the current hysteria his comment might pass for good sense even though scientific verification of Rembrandt's handling could be needed only by excessively literal minds.

It was a mind both literal and unduly optimistic that expected the daguerreotype to revolutionize "the morals of portrait painting" by eliminating the all too visible improvements with which the portraitists favored their subjects. By 1857 photographers had learned how to enlarge to the size of life; and in order to make their products more salable, they had assistants to color the prints in pastel or water color or oil. Such a portrait, as large as five by seven feet, could be sold for as high as seven hundred and fifty dollars; and the editor of the *Photographic Art Journal* claimed that no painter could equal such a picture "in truthfulness to nature." Machines were already fast shaping man's environment here into something new, and it was as natural as it was undesirable that his idea of accuracy should become so easily and so quickly conditioned by a machine's one-eyed registration of appearances. Even that did not send painting into complete eclipse; but a serious cultural damage was effected by the seeming proof that art as well as physical comfort must show continual progress and that the progress should consist in ever more minute exactness. For two generations most laymen and many painters blurred the virtues of two distinct crafts by believing that they had the same function and served the same end.

However, before the appearance of an image-making machine the mid-century merchants and their wives had begun buying paintings that were not portraits—and buying them to such an extent that the painters of landscape and anecdote and even still-life could have their modest share of material comfort. In this respect the painters actually preceded the writers a short while, probably because, under democratic conditions, a differing scale of payment enables a painter to get along with relatively few patrons while a writer must achieve mass sales. The mid-century situation was more complex and in some ways more advantageous than a lot of pictures selling on an impersonal market; many of the painters and patrons knew one another, in some cases quite well, and they agreed both upon what subject-matter was interesting, and upon how it should be treated. The painters developed techniques appropriate to their concepts; they and their businessmen friends together found in those concepts a working philosophy adequate to their common experience in life and in art. The fact that both the techniques and the philosophy proved inadequate to the experience of later generations does not impair their significance for their own time. Putting to one side the esthetic quality of the pictorial results, the success with which mid-century patrons and painters together created a common culture is a singularly cheerful historical manifestation. Among the arts painting par-

ticularly thrives upon its visible present; and though its mid-century discretion
in looking only at what was pleasant was spiritually shallow, even in this it was
being adequate to the age as a whole. Certainly the effective extension of subject-matter beyond the portrait proceeded as far as contemporaneous taste permitted and embodied great gains in geniality beyond the previous rigid utilitarianism which had prevented Americans from an adequate experience of painting.

To be sure, such gains did not do much to make the age in general more
tolerable. Whitman, for example, could speak so harshly on other occasions that,
in comparison, he seemed to be simply describing when he wrote:

. . . To prune, gather, trim, conform, and ever cram and stuff, and be genteel and
proper, is the pressure of our days. . . .

That is even milder in tone than many denunciations from Emerson and
Thoreau; and moral earnestness befitted their protests. In a more objective
manner a later historian may note that, in relation to the rapid disintegration
of established manners and taste, genteelness was itself an effort by a turbulent
society to impose some measure of order upon itself. It was just not thorough
enough or noble enough in conception for spiritual achievement. The trouble
with the genteel class was not its desire to become better but its willingness
to believe that it was better by merely maintaining the proprieties of conduct
and culture. The anxious correctness of literary and artistic opinion could be
so ludicrous that it needs no embellishment of facetiousness now; a little discreet quotation can be a sufficiently revealing indiscretion. Philip Hone, whose
welcome to the daguerreotype has been quoted, centered his existence so completely upon displaying impeccable cultivation that he never became an individual even in the pages of his voluminous diary; more effectively than the
current newspaper editorials, and in the same verbiage, his entries record everything that was proper to think in the best society. Setting down his participation
in a dinner which preceded the opening of a National Academy exhibition in
April of 1839, he reflected how much more admirable pictures are in a home
than mirrors; pictures

. . . are, indeed, the precious products of an art the tendency of which is to refine
the mind, enrich the imagination, and soften the heart of man.

Another such glimpse of the collective attitude of the time is equally unconscious but startling in its bluntness; a lady, writing a book of advice to young
ladies, defined a gentlewoman as "the daughter of a rich man."

The entire genteel phase of American civilization has sometimes been charged
against women. Certainly it was upon them that the gift books were "bestowed,"
and these still exude a sticky sentimentality from their rhymes and steel en-

gravings. But the time's ideal vacuity of expression on the female face was put there by male painters of an ideal, and it was a man who sang of Sweet Alice

> "Who wept with delight when you gave her a smile
> And trembled with fear at your frown."

The very concept of woman as a decorative adjunct, as the most comfortable feature of a comfortable household establishment, was a device of men. But this exclusiveness was not entirely feasible in a time when Sarah Josepha Hale edited *Godey's* and Harriet Beecher Stowe affected history. Yet offsetting the more admirable features of Mrs. Hale's periodical were the *Fern Leaves from Fanny Fern's Portfolio,* and the energy of a Mrs. Stowe had to contend with the emotional downward pull of Lydia Sigourney. Most girls readily enough fell in with the current pattern of female behavior and clung as gracefully as they might to the stalwart male ego; but the vapors and tears and fainting spells of some women can be interpreted as a not too subtle rebellion against masculine domination, and therefore a manifestation of incipient intelligence.

Such stirrings and other more direct modifications of manners and ideas began to lighten the oppressiveness of the genteel even before the war shattered it to bits. One notable change of immediate effect in the visual arts, and one which might well have been much longer in coming, was the admission of the nude to some degree of public respectability—not in painting as yet, but in sculpture. The health of these two arts in any climate of culture always involves the question of the nude, not for its morality or immorality, but primarily for its availability in art schools as fundamental training and secondarily for its usability as subject-matter in the works which base themselves on naturalistic vision. Not one of the few art schools in the United States in the mid-century dared to teach its students from the nude model; and the result was not merely the rarity of good figure drawing but also a scarcity of draftsmanship adequate to render the construction of objects at large.

It was natural that sculpture should be ahead of painting in achieving tolerance for the nude; without it, academic sculptors cannot learn their craft at all and would find it extremely difficult to embody many of the ideas expected of them. A number of American sculptors had appeared by the mid-century, but in the absence of training here and in the belief that marble was their only possible medium they had gone to Italy, where they stayed for cheap living and assistance from Italian marble-cutters and an almost ready-made market from traveling Englishmen and Americans. Their fame was carried back to this country, and Fenimore Cooper initiated American patronage by bringing in Horatio Greenough's bas-relief of *Chanting Cherubs,* which scandalized many by its nudity and disappointed others when the figures did not move. But it was

Hiram Powers' approximately life-size statue of *The Greek Slave* which broke the tabu; grave committees of businessmen and ministers in various cities issued certificates of chastity which permitted the most moral-minded to view the statue without inner qualms and in safety from the censure of their neighbors. Again Philip Hone gushed approval:

. . . I have no rule by which to estimate the merit, or appreciate the faultless beauty, of this statue which could guide me in placing it below the Venus de Medici. I have no personal acquaintance with Powers, nor had I with Praxiteles; but I am not willing to undervalue my countryman because he was not born so soon as the other gentleman of the chisel. I certainly never saw anything more lovely.

Two details certainly helped the statue with Americans of literal mind: the extreme "finish" of the white surface and the trick marble-cutting by which a free-swinging chain carved out of the original block manacled the wrists.

Any painter who attempted to satisfy that sort of literalism with an academic nude inevitably encountered the difficulty of at least semi-naturalistic color, and only a few instances sanctioned by literary titles, such as Sully's *Musidora* [begun 1813, completed 1835: Metropolitan Museum, New York], managed to receive public exhibition. Asher Brown Durand painted his own picture of *Musidora* and engraved it; that engraving and his engraving of Vanderlyn's *Ariadne* seemed almost as tolerable as sculpture, since they also lacked color. But when William Page, praised for his color in other pictures, ventured upon a *Venus*, he was immediately censured. At the same time, a fairly large number of imported nudes were being placed in many American cities—in gambling rooms, saloons, and bawdy houses. This was a phenomenon which reached full splendor only after the war, but before that it had become noticeable in New York, New Orleans, and San Francisco; in the latter city Mark Twain printed a seriously intended art criticism—about a saloon painting of *Samson and Delilah*—in which he stressed the anachronism of a pair of scissors on the floor. Normally such pictures would enter the country through the art dealers who were, as a group, beginning their important role in the mid-century; but for the time being, at least, that was not a traffic to be allowed prominence in the public notice. In the American institutions which housed them in the mid-century they were not really needed as enticement to vice; but once there, they became the most effective means of building up in the collective male American mind an almost ineradicable association of ideas between art and wickedness.

51. The decline of the miniature

Charles Fraser: 1782–1860 (work after 1830)
Thomas Seir Cummings: 1804–1894
Richard Morrell Staigg: 1817–1881
Ann Hall: 1792–1863
Henry Colton Shumway: 1807–1884

Some of the miniaturists already considered continued working beyond 1830, but the only one who consistently maintained and even improved his own earlier skill was Charles Fraser in Charleston. Good as his mid-century production was in relation to the work of his contemporaries, it constituted a decline from certain earlier achievements by other men—Malbone in particular. Fraser's drawing was competent but not so sensitive as Malbone's; his color was satisfactory but never so pure and brilliant. At the same time, and probably because his mind was more prosaic, he never "improved" his sitters to the extent that Malbone usually did; and that refusal put him into even sharper contrast with the most popular mid-century miniaturists of New York and other northern cities. Almost the only way Fraser joined in changing tastes was to use somewhat larger pieces of ivory than those sanctioned by the Federal Era.

Though Fraser's later work retained a dignity and restraint by which younger men were not hampered, as a beloved bachelor of seventy-five he was the center of genteel adoration into which he fitted as a period piece. In 1857 an exhibition of his work from the landscape sketchbook of his youth through three hundred miniatures—out of about five hundred then known—and well over a hundred miscellaneous other paintings to his last still-life compendiously summed up his long career. The catalog was as elaborate as the exhibition itself: complete with biography, eulogiums in the best platform manner, quotations from Fraser's own writings, and a description by "the accomplished authoress of *The Southern Matron*" of Fraser daily receiving visitors in the gallery.

. . . As no accumulation of a surplus-fund was contemplated, the admission of ladies of all ages was gratuitous—a feature of the occurrence which was regarded as peculiarly characteristic, and worthy of a refined and liberal community. . . .

This cultivated inflation of language is the same as that of *Godey's Lady's Book* every month or of Philip Hone's *Diary* every day; and though some of

Fraser's printed prose almost matched it, his portrait miniatures never displayed any corresponding high-flown artificiality.

Other professionals not only increased the dimensions of their miniatures pretentiously but also covered the large areas with finical drawing and saccharine color. Thomas Seir Cummings and Richard Morrell Staigg and even Ann Hall possessed enough technical skill for them to have continued at least the average of the earlier times; but they shared in the prevailing ostentatious sentimentality so fully that their miniatures became vulgar in the affectation of refinement.

That was deterioration from within, so to speak, but the finally destructive blow came from without, from the daguerreotype and its photographic successors. Late miniaturists like Henry Colton Shumway found their craft useless and were reduced in the end to tinting photographs for wages. For Shumway, at least, that was just misfortune; but others were deluded enough to fancy that applying color to a photographic base was by itself the ultimate exactitude, and some workmen claimed that the "portraits in little" thus produced were miniatures instead of spoiled photographs. This was to abandon painting not merely as an art but even as a craft; it was no intelligent use of a machine in ways proper to machinery but an abdication of the mind in perverting both a machine and a craft.

52. Mid-century portraiture

THE BASIC AVERAGE

Nathaniel Jocelyn: 1796–1881
Thomas Le Clear: 1818–1884
James Reid Lambdin: 1796–1863
John Beale Bordley: 1800–1882
Robert Matthew Sully: 1803–1855
James Bogle: 1817–1873
Oliver Frazer: 1808–1865
Allen Smith: 1810–1890

MECHANISTIC FINISH

Seth Wells Cheney: 1810–1856
Gennarino Persico: act. 1834
Charles Cromwell Ingham: 1796–1868
Joseph Fagnani: 1819–1873

THE COTTON SOUTH

Francisco Bernard: act. 1848–1868
Jacques Amans: 1801–1888
Jean Joseph Vaudechamp: 1790–1866
Thomas Cantwell Healy: c. 1821–?1873
George Dury: 1817–1894

THE OLD WEST

Manuel Joachim De Franca: ?–1865
Theodore Sydney Moise: 1806–1883

Thomas Trevor Fowler: act. 1830–1850
Joseph H. Bush: 1794–1865
Robert S. Duncanson: 1821–1871
Alfred Payne: c. 1815–1893
Jacob Cox: 1810–1892
Alvah Bradish: 1806–1901
Samuel Marsden Brookes: 1816–1892
Bernard Isaac Durward: 1817–1902

THE OLD SOUTH

George Cooke: 1793–1849
William Garl Browne: 1822–1894
William James Hubard: 1807–1862
James De Veaux: 1812–1844

THE EAST

Henry Inman: 1801–1846
Thomas Sully: 1783–1872 (work after 1830)
John Neagle: 1796–1865
Charles Loring Elliott: 1812–1868
Thomas Hicks: 1823–1890
Chester Harding: 1792–1866
George Peter Alexander Healy: 1812–1894

With the decline of the miniature in quality and quantity both, portraiture in oil became more important than ever. Although it was possible in the mid-century for painters to make their living in other branches, the portrait remained the major business by which they secured patronage from Americans. An increasing population and a rising level of prosperity (subject to recessions) brought about a corresponding increase in the number of portraitists. Practically all of them traveled much—for training or for work—but that became almost unnoticeable in the growth of travel as a national habit; and perhaps the most significant economic fact affecting the painting profession as a whole is that so many of its members found it possible to make their living as residents of smaller places. Naturally it is among such localized workmen that the basic average of the craft can be most clearly discerned.

Nathaniel Jocelyn is said to have retired to New Haven soon after 1830 because he found the competition in New York too strong. Comparison between his work in the twenties and in the forties shows that he improved even after his removal, and no doubt that had its bearing upon the position he made for himself in the smaller place. He wrote all the definitions of words connected with art for the 1847 revision of Webster's Dictionary. Certainly his settling in New Haven was advantageous to that community, and he may be said to have added to the national wealth along the level of popular painting by teaching George Henry Durrie. Jocelyn's work has the academically dependable prosaicism which, like the humanly dependable people whom it depicts, later times usually overlook. But on one occasion Jocelyn was moved to impart to his placidly objective manner a tragic dignity; his portrait of the slave-hero *Cinque* [1839–1840: Historical Society, New Haven], with well drawn dark head and shoulders dramatic between light background and white drapery, is visually as well as humanly haunting.

For fifteen years in Buffalo, Thomas Le Clear painted routine portraits. James Reid Lambdin, born in Pittsburgh, experimented there and in Louisville with museum-keeping, but from 1838 was identified with Philadelphia, where he had previously received his brief professional training; some strength of character occasionally emerges from his undistinguished brushwork. In Baltimore, John Beale Bordley began with a hard manner which became duller as it softened in texture and loosened in drawing. Robert Matthew Sully, son of the famous Sully's actor-brother, after four years of study in London, heavy-handedly repeated the British portrait manner in Richmond; his romantic evasiveness of temper lends irony to the unfulfilled project of his becoming portraitist and history painter to the State of Wisconsin. James Bogle lived much in New York, but most of his work was done on trips back to his home state of South Carolina; there he and a brother working as a team turned out many likenesses of little character. Oliver Frazer in Lexington, Kentucky, after one year in Europe and three more in London, intermittently painted portraits which in their derivative and repetitious character disappointingly contradict the interesting personality which appears in a photograph of himself. Allen Smith in Cleveland, Ohio, executed reasonably competent portraits before 1860, only to be a victim of the photographic tendency which infected practically all American likeness-makers of second or third rank as the nineteenth century neared its last quarter.

Although this contagion did not achieve its full effect until after 1860, it clearly commenced during the mid-century. Its earliest noticeable manifestation in portraiture was in the fashion of crayon likenesses—not the often charming pastels of earlier periods but a labored rendition of the features in the medium of charcoal. The end product of a surface from which every calligraphic trace of the operation of the human hand had been eliminated seemed to eliminate the human mind as well. It is said that the first individual to achieve a reputation and financial success in this was Seth Wells Cheney, the younger of two brothers in Massachusetts who also engraved; any example by him serves as well as any other to sample his sweetish commonplace. Commonplaceness uncompromised by the sweetishness marks the *Joseph Carrington Cabell* [Virginia State Library, Richmond] by Gennarino Persico. Their superiority in craft to the later commercial exploiters of country districts makes them exceptional, but that very superiority now calls up astonishment at so complete an abdication of eye and mind together to a mechanistic ideal.

A similar ideal of depersonalized handling was already prevalent among those who worked in oil. Several of the best known portraitists affected by this ideal—Elliott, Harding, Francis Alexander—had commenced their work on the technical level of sign painting and were therefore predisposed to accept its general hardness of effect as desirable in itself. However, among the more prominent painters who received their training here only Inman maintained this manner with complete consistency; and even he may have done so simply because of his shorter life. This characteristic mid-century hardness of treatment did not derive from the daguerreotype and its mechanical successors even though its results are often characterized as photographic; it was a continuation in a modified technique of the fondness for the definite which has been one of the steadiest traits in the American taste. During the mid-century, too, it received decided confirmation from several foreigners who brought not only the academic sophistication of Europe but also the sentimentalism which corroded every art of the time.

Charles Cromwell Ingham at twenty came here from Dublin equipped with a glazing technique particularly effective for preserving brilliant pigments and minutely drawn details under the shiny surface; through forty-five more years he commanded almost universal admiration for "the most exquisite beauty of finish and delicacy." The long-standing prominence of his *Flower Girl* [1846: Metropolitan Museum, New York] causes him to be often thought of as a painter of anecdote, but the whole meaning of his career lies in portraiture—in the popularity he won with his careful sweetening of the human countenance. With men the process was mainly negative—the omission of all the external traces of forcefulness or even positiveness in character; with ladies it was a process of costuming the expression as well as the figure—composing the features into self-conscious blandness which was the current evidence of culture. Almost precisely at the mid-century Joseph Fagnani arrived with an Italian version of the general stylism which had by then captivated Europe and the United States alike. With a large section of American society the fact that Fagnani had been patronized by the Bourbon queen-mother at Naples and by lesser royalties elsewhere in Europe was the major reason for their patronage; visual flattery completed the conquest. His capacity for this may be indicated by his success with the Marquise de Boissy, who as the Countess Guiccioli had been Byron's mistress; depicting her at sixty, he made her a discreetly plump thirty. A painter so obviously skilled—or, perhaps, skilled in such an obvious way—was able almost single-handed to bring about in his American clients the penultimate corruption of fashionable taste; worse was to come after the Civil War, and to that worse Fagnani was to contribute his full share.

One more influence direct from Europe was brought here by some Frenchmen working for the colony of still unreconstructed French in the Cotton South and by a few Creoles who also sought their training in Paris. Francisco Bernard had what would have been in Paris itself a merely average control of the school manner, and he made it serve a flattery almost as blatant as Fagnani's; not only that, but in his later work he capitulated to the camera. The drawing of Jacques Amans was both stronger and more sensitive; in portraitizing the ladies he sometimes identified elegance with a trick of elongating the torso, but with the gentlemen he did nothing so obvious. An example above his own average is the *Gentleman* [1845: Brooklyn Museum]. A better draftsman than either of these was Jean Joseph Vaudechamp; though most of his work would not be outstanding in Paris itself, in mid-century Louisiana an occasional example is a not ignoble reminder of Ingres. Perhaps it was this quality in one of his pictures which led Degas, the visiting French painter, to take it back to Paris from New Orleans in 1873.

Some of these Frenchmen worked here for a considerable time, but the narrowly regional patronage which they received prevented them from contributing anything to the rest of the country. Moreover, at the very time they were working, the Creoles in New Orleans itself were being outnumbered by the people who were creating the Cotton South; and as part of this growth from without, increasing numbers of visiting painters came and went with the steamboats. The traveling professionals also made stopovers up the river—particularly in Natchez, which saw a concentrated accumulation of spoils from everywhere: from Europe perhaps even more than from the United States. The vulgarity of all arts and crafts in the mid-century originated in what were supposed to be the very centers of good taste, and the only startling thing about its manifestation in Natchez was its thoroughness; coming into wealth so quickly, the cotton planters outfitted themselves with a completeness unusual even in America.

The homes that remain much as they were in the great days are full of objects which are like Fagnani's paintings: admirable specimens of a certain kind of craft which breach all the restraints of what had been good taste before the flamboyant Cotton South was created. Yet vulgarity itself is at times redeemed by vitality, and some of the accumulations of overdone objects in Natchez mansions have not merely a stylistic coherence but also a period aliveness which derives from the spacious scale of the containing architecture.

The paintings in Natchez homes were not exclusively portraits, for everywhere in the United States the monopoly of the human countenance over the patrons' pocketbooks was being broken up. But the paintings in the South, both New and Old, were a particularly mixed lot, and the portraits remain on the whole more interesting today; the other pictures were very often copies of well known paintings in Europe, and, less often, acquisitions owing much to chance bargaining. In February of 1835 the famous Irish actor Tyrone Power observed to John Howard Payne in Natchez that the paintings being sold there by peddlers were worse than those in the pawnbrokers' sales in London.

Twenty years later Natchez had a resident portrait painter in Thomas Cantwell Healy, younger brother of another portraitist whose fame was European as well as American in extent. The younger Healy remained a localized painter, his works being found in the homes of Natchez and Port Gibson mainly; it was the locality's good fortune to have one so sound and so restrained in a time of so much sentimentality. He was not equally at ease with every position of the figure, and his drawing would show itself provincially unfluent if put alongside his brother's. But he knew the secret of the dignity that comes from a steady spirit within, and his often darkish and sometimes palely subtle color schemes now please in contrast to the harsh glossiness preferred by the age as a whole.

To Nashville, placed between the Cotton South and the Old South, went George Dury about 1850. Like Fagnani, he wore the halo of patronage from minor royalty—in his case, King Louis I of Bavaria—and it was as advantageous to him in Nashville as it was to the Italian in Washington and New York. Possibly Dury went that far west because his quite ordinary academic skill could not compete with the greater technical virtuosity available to patrons in the eastern cities. No doubt Nashville seemed visibly raw and culturally uncouth after Munich, but the place attracted visits from such famous stars as Edwin Booth and Jenny Lind, and the entire company of the French Opera from New Orleans. Moreover, there were two female poets in residence: Clara Cole and Lucy Virginia Smith French. Young Frank Mayer, a painter from Baltimore on his way to Minnesota, wrote in his diary about a Mrs. F. who tried hard to make an impression with her prodigiously animated conversation; he attributed her poetic temperament to "the study of elegant extracts." Dury would have depicted the lady without a trace of the satire with which the visitor saw her.

A portraitist prominent in the Old West was the Portuguese-born Manuel Joachim De Franca. Although he had studied at the Lisbon Academy before coming to the United States at nineteen, he must not have been possessed of a mature technique, as Ingham was when he came; for in Philadelphia De Franca became a pupil under Thomas Sully. Echoes of Sully can be found in his drawing and placing of the figure, but his color schemes tended toward a darker tonalism than Sully used. De Franca moved through Pittsburgh into Kentucky and on to St. Louis, with a gradual increase in perfunctory handling until the end. Farther down the Mississippi, in Natchez and New Orleans, portraits can be found by other men of only average period skill who seem to have done most of their work, like De Franca, in Kentucky. Two who worked much as a team were Theodore Sydney Moise and Thomas Trevor Fowler. Native to Kentucky itself, and working there continuously except for winter trips to Natchez and New Orleans, was Joseph H. Bush. Work such as the early *Self-Portrait* [Public Library, Lexington] showed the artisan's formula for assembling the features, in which definite edges blocked in a sound foundation for face painting; but Bush was not equal to the complications of an ear or a hand. The manner was basically the same as that which earlier easterners such as Winthrop Chandler had used and with which Trumbull and Earl had begun. That manner, moreover, was then being practised all across the country from Kentucky to Maine; and nearly all who practised it had ambitions to acquire the greater fluency of the specialists. Bush studied two years with Sully, in Philadelphia, and then went back home to be for the rest of his life a parochial Sully, just as Sully was a provincial Lawrence.

During these years Cincinnati experienced its own version of localized cultural patrioteering which Boston had begun a hundred years before, which Philadelphia and Charleston had repeated, and which Creole New Orleans was even then repeating as a protest against everything which Cincinnati embodied. The latter city had not accepted the Englishwoman Mrs. Trollope at her own valuation, and no doubt the tone of the book in which she took her revenge was somewhat less than admirable; but her facts were another matter, and it was unwise for a local newspaper editor to claim that the Queen City's cultural activities had already, in 1835,

. . . given her a name, not only among the cities of the Great Valley, but of the civilized world, that will go down to the most remote posterity.

Even if the claim had been part of a Fourth of July oration, it would have needed more justification than the Beecher family's brand of Congregationalism,

a museum in which the principal attraction was a lurid waxworks of the Inferno, and the impending appearance of the first *Eclectic Reader* put together
by the president of the local college, William Holmes McGuffey. To be sure,
practically every self-conscious cultural movement beginning with the Italian
Renaissance itself has been marked by boasting; and a reasonable number of
such manifestations have been made good by positive achievements.

Painting and the associated arts widened their range for the Midwest's
general public during a few mid-century years of activity by the regional
Western Art-Union, which was modeled on the extraordinarily successful
American Art Union in New York. Exhibited under the auspices of the Cincinnati organization were Powers' statue called *The Greek Slave* and Cole's series
of paintings called *The Voyage of Life,* the artistic faults of which were noted
by Mayer in his diary. He also remarked that the local students at work in
landscape, like Sonntag and Whittredge, tended to "hardness & harshness of
drawing and color." But they were attempting that subject-matter more to
satisfy themselves than to meet any sizable local demand. Only by portraits
could Whittredge earn enough money to get away and become the landscapist
he wanted to be. As the negro Joshua Johnston in Baltimore had to paint the
portraits of white people in order to paint pictures at all, so did Robert S. Duncanson in Cincinnati for a time; but the Anti-Slavery League there made it
possible for him to go to Edinburgh for art instruction, and in England he had
some success with anecdotal paintings. On a return to Cincinnati he was able to
paint some landscapes and some decorations in the Taft House, but he found
portraiture still most in demand. Again he went to England and stayed there
except for one more visit after the Civil War. For Ohio boys who could not get
to Europe, Cincinnati continued to be a goal for instruction. Christopher Pearse
Cranch, then serving as a minister, but also an amateur artist and president of
the local art society, gave some lessons to young Alfred Payne, who painted
quiet and sincere portraits for forty years in Ohio, Wisconsin, and elsewhere.

In Indianapolis Jacob Cox became an institution in old age, but through his
working years newspapers several times reproached the community for not
buying enough of his paintings. Nevertheless, he was able to quit his trade
of tinsmith in the eighteen-fifties, and even to sell some landscapes along with
his staple stock of portraiture. He made a stay of several months in Cincinnati
soon after he had announced himself in print as a portraitist; perhaps there
mainly did he acquire his rather nondescript technique which gave mediocre results. A large exhibition of art objects in the Fireman's Hall of Detroit
in 1852 contained allegories and anecdotes along with the portraits; but the
latter predominated in local production through the mid-century at the hands
of such ordinary workmen as Alvah Bradish and a few others. The increasing

pace of life generally was perhaps the reason why Milwaukee attracted portraitists more quickly after its founding than older places had done. With an
artisan's harshness Samuel Marsden Brookes depicted people among curiously
inappropriate accessories until he moved to San Francisco after the Civil War;
Bernard Isaac Durward, with a greater degree of competence acquired in Scotland, became a permanent and rather romantic personage in Wisconsin; and
other portrait painters passed through or stayed a while without raising the
standards set by Brookes and Durward.

The Old South, in process of losing its political power in Washington and
preoccupied with maintaining its economic existence on the basis of slavery,
no longer attracted the major portraitists. Typical of the lesser talents was
George Cooke, who had been drawn into painting from a business career by
copying some pictures that he had bought at auction; turning professional relatively late, he made up for lost time. About four years in Europe were also
filled with copying, which, Dunlap commented, showed industry but not
necessarily artistic gains. Returning here in 1830, Cooke became as peripatetic
as the miniaturist Benjamin Trott had been. Landscape in the Catskills, portraits in New York, Washington, Richmond, landscape in the mountains of
Georgia, exhibitions in New Orleans and Alabama and Athens, Georgia—
cholera put an end to a very busy life. Possibly this busyness, perhaps something else, kept him from painting very well. English-born William Garl
Browne was content to range only through Virginia and the Carolinas, except
for a trip to Mexico to paint General Zachary Taylor; he was a reasonably competent technician with a prosaic mind who thought it was a portraitist's business to gloss over any signs of character in the ladies, though he might not find
them out of place in a man.

Biographically the most interesting figure in mid-century Virginia was William James Hubard, but the most interesting part of his biography occurred
before he settled there in 1836. He had been a boy wonder in Great Britain
for cutting profiles and had earned much money for his promoter both there and
here before they separated. Then Hubard had some advice about oil painting
from Stuart in Boston and more from Robert W. Weir in New York. A series
of full-lengths just before and after 1830 used an almost miniature scale of
presentation, which is fascinating in itself, and joined with that an awkwardness almost painfully sincere. A stay in Europe sent him back to Virginia with
an academically ordinary competence by which he reduced everybody's appearance to commonplaceness. One strange exception in his work, the *Painter
and Patron* [c. 1850: Valentine Museum, Richmond], raises speculation as to
whether he was an artist suppressed by portraiture. On a circular canvas, the
painter's author-patron, Mann S. Valentine, in profile turns away from the specta-

tor to contemplate a cloud-like pageant of the characters out of his own novels; at the left, with his back to all this, the strongly shadowed (and thereby pictorially subordinated) face of the painter looks full at the spectator. Only the monotonously hot reds mar this double portrait in which a usually obvious mind for once, with the aid of a literary fancy, crosses the border into the unconsciously enigmatic.

A Southern-born painter who is still interesting as a human type of the age and the region was James De Veaux from Charleston. His youthful talent interested local picture buyers to a point of sending him to Philadelphia for instruction; and later he was sent abroad with money which he redeemed by copies from Rubens and Van Dyck. On his return he began accumulating for another European trip by doing portraits which, like his earlier ones, ran along a fairly even and undistinguished average. He was not stirred at all deeply by the business of recording the human countenance; maybe he, like most others in his time, did not have a mind deep enough to be stirred to good purpose. But at least from what he knew about Allston, whom he thought next in rank after Michelangelo, he had caught the idea of getting beyond portraiture to romantic subjects which he intended to treat with imagination. De Veaux went to Italy, painted a few pictures of that type which are now known only by their titles; subjected to exposure, he died of tuberculosis and was buried in the Protestant cemetery in Rome.

In the eastern cities where he worked and in his own time Henry Inman was pronounced supreme in portraiture—a position he does not hold today. He himself chafed at the dominance of that branch of painting and spoke hopefully of "a higher and purer taste" to come; his own few departures from portrait work have the interest of contrast and also some intrinsic attractiveness despite his habit of glossy brightness and cloying sweetness. But such ventures were simply holidays from the portraits which, as one biographer put it, "almost always looked better than the originals." Any portraitist and his patron have the right to give and receive that treatment if they so desire; and it seems to have been as open a covenant between Inman and his sitters as between Blackburn and Miss Lucy a hundred years earlier. The trouble, however, always is that the understanding means not more character, which would constitute an intensification of truthfulness, but more prettiness, which is always a dilution. This flattery and the hard smoothness of his pigment combine to make Inman's portraiture now appear more trivial than the portraiture of a few longer-lived contemporaries who did not, whether from choice or inability, go so far as Inman in either respect. An occasional example which Inman himself did not bring to his usual "finish" can give more pleasure now: one such is the small *Nathaniel Hawthorne* [1835: Essex Institute, Salem, Mass.]. But his most interesting work might well prove to be the *Self-Portrait* [Pennsylvania Academy, Philadelphia]. Likeness is not the dominant theme; here Inman was, more nearly than elsewhere, an artist in paint, working only with what he saw, free of all pressure from an audience, and for once withholding the deliberate injection of sentimentalism. He made a picture out of colored forms dramatized by shadow; he pleased himself—and in the long run may please the largest number of appreciators—by a charming device of putting the brightest light and darkest shadow next to each other: the device which he himself called a "climax."

Thomas Sully accentuated the tendency to sentimentality which he had shown before 1830. The genteelness of the mid-nineteenth century was essentially a form of social and cultural timidity in which everybody strove for the protective coloration of doing only what everybody else was doing, and with such an ideal of anonymousness any individual functioning as a leader might appear anachronistic. Yet leaders there were, and in portraiture the priority in time and for a while in influence belonged to Sully. He led the way into the genteel portrait heaven where every man was romantically handsome and every woman romantically pretty; where men and women together, looking at his transmutations of their workaday selves, might well have anticipated Browning by twenty years and said:

> "What I aspired to be
> And was not, comforts me."

Nevertheless, even as the concept of unsullied female beauty became *de rigueur*, Sully's own version of it began to seem antiquated beside the high finish of such men as Ingham and Inman. This might indeed justify at least a mild resurgence of interest in Sully's later performances, for in comparison to the mid-century fashionables he did preserve a charm of fluent handling as a factor of interest to the eye. In some examples, such as the *Thomas Handasyd Perkins* [c. 1831: Athenaeum, Boston], the earlier control of space shown in the *Samuel Coates* [plate 35] was replaced by a vaporous equivalent in pigment which fully justified Leslie's remark to Sully a few years later: "Your pictures look as if you could blow them away." Yet those pictures have retained their interest, and an occasional later example such as the *Andrew Jackson* [1845: Corcoran Gallery, Washington] looks as if Sully were working with Leslie's words in mind.

In those examples, and particularly in the famous *Queen Victoria* [1838: St. George Society, Philadelphia], Sully was the most competent mid-century practitioner of the older tradition of stately elegance in official portraiture. John Neagle, who married Sully's stepdaughter, caught from him a good deal of

54. HAMILTON FISH   *by* THOMAS HICKS

Courtesy of The Art Commission of the City of New York.

that manner, as seen in the *Doctor William Potts Dewees* [1840: University of Pennsylvania, Philadelphia]; but his earlier and better known *Pat Lyon* [1826: Pennsylvania Academy, Philadelphia] had been an unsuccessful attempt to combine a discreet official romanticism with the sitter's desire for factual accuracy about his occupation of blacksmith. Neagle was always a second-flight portraitist, and is likely to show himself now more interesting in his less pretentious efforts. The relatively unknown Charles Wesley Jarvis achieved one successful official portrait in the *Henry Clay* [1854: City Hall, New York], which has been often erroneously reproduced as by his father, John Wesley Jarvis; this is about the last example that retains the older habit of elevating an individual in tone and attitude toward embodying a type or an idea.

Official portraiture continued to thrive; commissions were still given by such city corporations as New York and Charleston, and even by the national government. But about all that the later kind shared with the earlier was physical size. The spirit changed from generalization to particularizing—to the point where the subject was only an individual surrounded by a lot of space which often contained a good many objects. Upon the largest scale of all, such as Thomas Hicks' *Hamilton Fish* [1852: plate 54], there occurs considerable period interest from the sheer quantity of accessories; but their execution evidenced neither that thoroughness of construction upon which Copley concentrated his mental power nor that graceful fluency of brushwork with which Sully lulled the mind into overlooking construction. Hicks was neither thorough enough nor superficial enough for so ambitious an effort; he commenced painting too late to accept the British-school fluency, and he did not learn enough from Couture to achieve the thoroughness. Charles Loring Elliott's *Horatio Seymour* [1861: City Hall, New York], and more by him on the same scale, show how painters could stay away from Europe and yet be thoroughly imbued with the mental attitude and technical characteristics of the age as a whole. The most striking general impression from all such colossally prosaic mid-century importancies is one of a materialism unmastered by the intelligence.

Both Hicks and Elliott could produce attractive portraits on a less ambitious scale, such as Elliott's *Mrs. Thomas Goulding* [1858: National Academy of Design, New York] and Hicks' *Doctor Oliver Wendell Holmes* [1858: Athenaeum, Boston]. But other and less competent painters worked with appalling industry upon the hundreds of bust portraits which eventually reached the walls of libraries and hospitals and chambers of commerce and historical societies. During the eighteen-fifties, too, the corridors of the government departments in Washington began to fill up with the likenesses of departed officials. The effects of such collections upon taste cannot be satisfactorily documented, but their dreary wastes of dullness probably played a considerable part in bringing to pass a general state of mind into which Mark Twain could blow fresh air with his remark: "It is a gratification to me to know that I am ignorant of art."

Through the mid-century the most likeable personality and on the whole the liveliest (but very uneven) portraitist was Chester Harding. He is worth knowing in his own words; he himself wrote the account printed by Dunlap, but still better was the much later *My Egotistography,* as he called it, with his admirable capacity for being amused by himself as well as by others. His daughter in her introduction to the book wrote that Harding liked a story to the effect that a cat, disconsolate at the death of its mistress, saw Harding's portrait of her on a sofa and, straightway jumping up, tried to nestle down in its lap. It is another of those stories that tell so much more about human beings than about animals, and in the annals of American painting at least the cat is a novelty. The often repeated story which Harding himself first told, about his grandfather's telling him it was ". . . little better than swindling to charge forty dollars . . ." for the portraits he painted is worth recalling, because it shows how the Kaintuck ideas of Jouett's father were eastern ideas too where the East was rural.

As much as any predecessor Harding profited from the popular belief that he was entirely self-taught, but he did not let either the fact or the profit delude him. He saw it work to his advantage in Boston in Stuart's day, and he said all the while that Stuart was the better painter. When he left for England in 1823, a Boston lady poet wrote:

> Most wonderous gift, from nature's self derived,
> His genius of all foreign aid deprived,
> Sprung up and bloomed amid our wilds obscure,
> And won its self-taught way to glory sure.

This aura helped to make him fashionable in England, as it had helped West sixty years earlier; Harding took in twelve thousand dollars in three years— paying out the same amount for expenses. Sagaciously he brought his family back and prospered ever after at home.

In the run of his work Harding's competence was not outstanding; in order to produce an exceptional picture, he had to be confronted with the exceptional in life. He was lucky to find some women who united striking costumes and decided personalities; such was *Mrs. Daniel Webster* [privately owned]. *Anna Hardaway Bunker* [c. 1857: plate 55] may be less forceful as a personality, but she has greater individual charm; and in depicting her so well placed on the oval canvas, in full mid-century panoply of fashion, Harding recorded the most attractive aspect of this country's version of Victorian romanticism. In his own character Harding was strikingly a man's man, but that seems not to have

55. ANNA HARDAWAY BUNKER *by* CHESTER HARDING
Courtesy of The John Herron Art Institute.

helped him much in his painting of men. His male portraits show plenty of superficial variety in the faces, but no revelation of inner deeps. In making portraits both the intellectually objective and the emotionally subjective painters have an advantage over bluff and hearty natures who may make easier human contacts but are incapable of either impersonal judgement or spiritual penetration.

Tuckerman, the late-century historian of American art, praised George Peter Alexander Healy for an industry rarely excelled and described his portraits as rugged. All that can be accomplished by industry, Healy achieved; but what seemed to be ruggedness in the midst of the routine dullness of the contemporaneous average now appears as a routine academic competence. That is to say: it was a routine matter with Healy, for the technical uniformity of his large output by itself tends to obscure its equally uniform superiority to any matching quantity by any other portraitist. In portraiture Healy was as dependable as Longfellow was in poetry, and Americans liked reassurance in both arts. Moreover, such Americans as were conscious of European opinion were further reassured by the fact that both the poet and the portraitist were praised and bought across the Atlantic. It was indeed only the downfall of the French monarchy, and with it of the politicians who had been his patrons, which caused Healy to make this country his home for a second time. There were of course immense contrasts of appearances between Paris and Chicago, and Mayor Ogden, who had invited Healy there, wielded his power with less pomp than Louis Philippe. But the politicians of France and the millionaires of Chicago shared not only their common humanity but also the somewhat narrower experience and tastes of middle-class humanity; and Healy, the midcentury cosmopolitan in technique, was everywhere at home with respectable society.

It was probably his own evenness of painting temperament—or does the evenness eliminate the temperament?—which enabled Healy to be so successful with American men. In depicting the ladies he was prone to accept their own erroneous preference and make portraits of their clothes. Since Healy's handling of pigment was as solid as his own respectability, the colors and intricacies of feminine fashions frequently took on too much assertiveness. Surely there must somewhere have been a female Hamlet to cry: "O! that these too too solid clothes would melt." Healy rendered men's clothes with equal thoroughness; but they, being less voluminous, interfered less with figure construction and also, being more sober, subordinated themselves more readily to faces.

Healy's state portraits rank well up in the roster of nineteenth-century official art, and to look at many of them together, as at the Newberry Library in Chicago, suggests the verdict that he was the best among the mid-century specialists in portraiture. This large group of large works also suggests that he may not have been completely cosmopolitan by nature; at least the ponderous officialism of the *Thiers* is far less vivid than the robust energy of the *Cardinal McCloskey* [1862: plate 56]. There is, however, one human difficulty about estimating ability in so human a craft as portraiture: the painter whose competence is the sole or principal thing to admire can never quite gain an admiration that is complete. Emerson quotes someone as having said about Thoreau: "I love Henry, but I cannot like him . . ." The student confronted with Copley's portraiture may not like the technical procedure but must love the qualities of mind which used the technique to such admirable ends. Confronted with Healy's portrait work, the student is neither impelled to dislike the craft nor compelled to love the mind; but he can at least call up the respect due to a competence that is more than respectable.

Everyone who follows Dunlap in writing about American painting must not only draw morals, as he did, but reiterate some of them. Once more the moral is that portraiture as a specialty is inadequate to produce great painting. Mid-century Americans got about what they wanted in portraiture; the unfortunate thing was that they wanted only what they got and that no portraitist was great enough to insist upon giving them more than they wanted. The result is that, in their portraits, mid-century Americans appear formidably dull and stodgy. But they seem more likable when attention is turned to the other pictures they bought; and though their purchases of landscape and history and anecdote did not give them definitely great painters in their own times, the effective extensions of interest in subject-matter did make possible the later appearance of painters with minds comprehensive enough for greatness.

56. CARDINAL McCLOSKEY *by* GEORGE P. A. HEALY
Courtesy of Newberry Library, Chicago.

53. Mid-century landscape

Thomas Birch: 1779–1851
James Hamilton: 1818–1878
Robert Salmon: act. 1800–1840
Fitz Hugh Lane: 1804–1865
Martin Johnson Heade: 1814–1904
Thomas Doughty: 1793–1856
Thomas Cole: 1801–1842
Asher Brown Durand: 1796–1886
John William Casilear: 1811–1893
John Frederick Kensett: 1818–1872

Sanford Robinson Gifford: 1823–1880
Jervis McEntee: 1828–1891
David Johnson: 1827–1908
William McDougall Hart: 1823–1894
James McDougall Hart: 1828–1901
Jasper Francis Cropsey: 1828–1900
Worthington Whittredge: 1820–1910
Regis François Gignoux: 1816–1882
George Inness: 1825–1894 (work to 1865)

Mid-century picture buying of landscape subjects by a relatively small group of patrons from a smaller group of painters was on so intensive a scale, with such an intimacy of sharing, that it constituted a cultural episode of the first importance in American painting. The origin and proliferation of what later came to be called the Hudson River School display a completeness of logic which has rarely been achieved in this country. That very rarity, however, has enabled the group to come near to monopolizing the word *landscape* in a way that is unhistorical. Not only were there brave men before Agamemnon, but there were brave men around him; and so it was with the Hudson River men. They had not only predecessors long lost from sight but also contemporaries until recently ignored. And while these did not have the same degree of coherence, since they formed no group by personal association, they yet stood apart with distinctness from the Hudson River men—different in technical tradition and to a lesser extent in subject-matter.

That difference in subject-matter, in its limited validity, consisted of sea and shore. Its initiator here on the studio level of technique, following the numerous examples by artisans and print-makers, was Thomas Birch. He was for a time the assistant of his engraver-father in producing topographical views. Some of the son's early paintings of scenes in and around Philadelphia [Pennsylvania Historical Society, Philadelphia] are themselves of that general type and show the same smooth and somewhat dry handling of pigment noted in the one known oil by Barralet. During and immediately after the War of 1812 Birch painted history pictures of its early naval engagements, which constituted the only phase of the conflict that Americans could contemplate without

417

chagrin; they are reasonably competent in execution but perhaps unreasonably repetitive. Following them Birch from time to time painted inland rural scenes, particularly in winter time, which shared the homely authenticity of sentiment in country incidents that was to be spread everywhere by lithographic prints; of this phase, a representative example is the *Winter Scene in Pennsylvania* [1835: Whitney Museum of American Art, New York]. However, his technique was marked by considerably more animation, and the pictorial results were more vigorous, in various scenes of river and shore and open sea; most of them remained lyrical in their lightly running waves, but a few of them dramatized romantic storms. An Irish-born painter, James Hamilton, also worked in Philadelphia before and after going to London for training in 1850; the few works known at present, though they do not range so widely in subject as those by Birch, have a crisper brushwork and a greater transparency of light.

A third painter, arriving here in 1828 from England, was, unlike Birch and Hamilton, fully trained before he came; this man, Robert Salmon, painted theatrical scenery and signs, and also more than five hundred harbor and shore subjects in Boston and the neighborhood. An occasional example makes effective use of wind-whipped water, but his more characteristic manner used static contrasts between the horizontals and uprights of vessels docked in harbor; his pigment, too, was often opaque but with good impasto. Fitz Hugh Lane relied upon similarly static lines in composing his horizontally elongated pictures of bays and inlets along the New England coast, and the best among them have in plenitude the feeling of repose which seems most fitting for the shape itself. Lane's tendency to a minutely linear treatment is saved from undue thinness by closely rendered values in the smallest details, and the equally successful textures sometimes render surprising depths in glassy waters and lighter skies. Except for some of the pictures by Salmon, the works of these men are marked by a clarity of light which favors definiteness in the forms: a trait which makes them akin to the earlier landscapes by Trumbull and Vanderlyn. These later men, however, crossed the invisible line between neoclassicism and romanticism. Salmon crossed by means of warmth and harmony in color; in their water scenes Birch and Hamilton embodied the new spirit in consistently spirited flicks of the brush that gave a calligraphic character to the picture surface; and Lane, in almost obliterating brush strokes and in drenching his scenes with an illumination remarkably pellucid, simply intensified the romance by seeming to suspend it in a waiting quietude.

Another painter of the time shared the general liking for long and relatively narrow horizontal canvases, but most of the subjects chosen by Martin Johnson Heade were radically unlike those of other men—and they were treated with a technique even more obviously different. After some portraits in Pennsylvania, Heade went to Italy; later he made a stay in Brazil to paint hummingbirds for a book which seems never to have been published, and to them it was easy to add orchids and exotic landscape backgrounds. In the United States he was a peripatetic throughout the East, and winters in Florida added its palm-fringed rivers to his scenic effects. His handling of pigment was not always the same, and a storm over glassy water could yield him a thinly painted visual melodrama of great purity; but his usual impasto was somewhat thicker than was common in his time and its somewhat misleading impression of unevenness comes from its variable opacity more than anything else. Though he was not a first-rate painter, he was interesting in his time for becoming so quickly alert to a treatment of light which departed from its average steadiness and attempted to suggest its changeableness. His best successes in this were with light-spotted fields and commonplace haystacks. In the naturalistic terms in which he thought and worked, his landscapes of Florida are failures, but there he is in the company of hundreds of successors; it may be claimed that not even a first-rate technician in oil has yet satisfactorily solved the special problems presented by the coldly white illumination characteristic of its semi-tropical sunlight.

In their scattered locales those five painters and some others were left obscure by the concentration of both professional and popular attention upon the work of a distinct group of men who later received the nickname "Hudson River School." There seems to have been more than a trace of derision in the first use of the term, an intention to belittle the group's supposed localism of interest as well as their provincialism of technique; but it, like other art terms thus motivated, proved so useful that its emotional overtones now are as likely to be admiration. Both in numbers and in common aims, the Hudson River School did not take definite shape until the late thirties. Since their aims and procedure were anticipated a few years earlier by Thomas Doughty, he makes the natural beginning for discussion. In the United States of 1820 courage was required for quitting a leather business to paint landscapes exclusively, yet somehow that seems not the word to use about Doughty's way of doing it; all his works, and especially the early examples, give such a strong impression of easy naturalness, almost of casualness, that it is difficult to credit them with being the venturesome experiment which they actually were. In Doughty's decade of work before the mid-century opened he had become not only well known but popular, exhibiting and selling pictures from Baltimore to Boston —and painting them, too, in his travels through the intervening country. He had a particularly prosperous five years in Boston before going on his first trip to England in 1837; on his return about two years later he established himself in New York, and painted there until his death except for the interval of one more stay abroad. Despite his identification with that city, the National Academy of Design kept him in the status of honorary member, although he had become a full member of the Pennsylvania Academy in 1824. Being thus excluded from active participation in the National Academy, and experiencing a loss of popularity in his latter years, Doughty felt himself subjected to undeserved difficulties; he turned against the Art-Union also and helped to destroy the main source of his earlier prosperity.

Aside from being the first to succeed in making a career of landscape, Doughty indicated what was to happen later on in two respects, one a matter of technique and the other a matter of expression. In technique he allowed the touches of the brush to remain visible; in this way his canvases acquired an over-all texture from the pigment itself—something distinct from the rendering of differing textures of individual objects. He was of course not the first painter to do this even here, but he was different in the extent to which he relied upon it for attaining his principal painting quality. In relation to what later men did in this respect, Doughty's touch is wearisomely monotonous; but his way of working with a satisfactory impasto resulted in a picture-surface which appeared freshly animated to eyes accustomed to glossy hardness retaining no trace of the brush. The reason why Doughty's pictures remain in a relatively low rank among naturalistic paintings is that his minute touches of paint do not build up structural forms which are observed with a corresponding minuteness. Objects are not specific in character; a tree stump is recognizable enough, but it is acceptable only so long as the eye's attentiveness remains casual. Another consequence of this uniformity of touch is that in a few examples where the views are extensive, with some degree of spaciousness in the skies, the hills or fields lack volume; they are not large forms seen from a distance but are reduced to a trivially miniature scale. However, Doughty not only pointed out a direction but also accomplished his own most positive advance: he showed a dawning recognition that nature is alive in its own right. In *The Raft* [1830: plate 57] trees and rocks, despite their structural weakness, water and sky, despite the merely approximated textures—all shift and play into a visually unified episode which apparently owes nothing to the painter beyond the good luck of his chancing upon it. Essentially a naturalist in seeming to be content with transcribing appearances, Doughty subjected them neither to the severely intellectual ordering of the classicist nor to the emotional intensification of the romanticist; he was apparently watching for the moments, bright or pensive, in which nature breathed with a life that took no account of the little creatures who have almost lost their human significance in the scene. In making this only partly conscious affirmation about the visible world, he

57. THE RAFT *by* THOMAS DOUGHTY *Courtesy of Museum of Art, Rhode Island School of Design, Providence.*

began the clarification of an attitude which was to prove itself capable of nour-
ishing two generations of American painters.

Doughty initiated the American discovery of the American landscape—one
of the things not noted by the extraordinarily perceptive French traveler Tocqueville during his study-trip through the United States (1830–1832). But when
Tocqueville censured the Americans for not being aware of the natural beau-
ties of their own country, he seems to have had in mind those wilder portions
which by their dramatic difference made the strongest appeal to a European
mind. Doughty and his audience were largely content with the pastoral; and
any scenery still unsubdued to the use of man was seen not in terms of savage
grandeur but in those of gentle lyricism. Yet even while Tocqueville was here
another painter was opening the way for later Americans to do what the
Frenchman thought they ought to have done already. Tocqueville was correct
in saying that Americans were too preoccupied with admiring their own conquest of nature; but perhaps, if he had reflected upon what a powerful enemy
the wilderness still was, he would not have asked them to pause in the conquest and admire it. Not until after the worst dangers are past can a people
rise to a recognition of qualities dissociated from them—an observation verifiable
in American experience by the timing of both wild nature and the Amerind
as acceptable subjects in several American arts.

The call of the wild in American landscape painting was first sounded by
English-born Thomas Cole, and it is significant that before leaving England
at eighteen he had read a book of new-world travels which gave him the no-
tion that the wild is beautiful. It is equally significant that, though Cole had
some training as an engraver on wood before he came here, his first lessons in
painting were from an itinerant in Ohio. There he himself turned itinerant
portraitist with little success and after some independent attempts at landscape
he spent two years in Philadelphia, where he nearly starved but attended art
school, sold a few pictures, and felt humble before the work of Birch and
Doughty. Moving on to New York in 1825, he attracted the attention and
help of Trumbull and Durand and Dunlap, and became one of the group who
founded the National Academy of Design. Thereafter, though he wrote about
unsold pictures or pictures that he fancied were unsalable, he had such a good
market that most of his work was executed on commission. His major difficulties were temperamentally inescapable, and came from an increasing in-
compatibility between the ideas of his later years and his own degree of technical skill.

Cole was not a rich colorist, and when he tried for brilliance he got gaudiness; his speculations about color sensations to parallel those of music are an
intellectualized attempt to compensate for a deficiency of instinct. Cole never

mastered figure drawing—a failing quite widespread among landscape painters and with some the main reason for their turning to landscape. On the other hand, he had from the first a pen which subordinated naturalistic structure to calligraphic expressiveness; certain early drawings of tree trunks, for instance, use form and texture almost as a point of departure for a freehand exercise in rapid strokes which by their own rhythmic repeats and variations create visual excitement. In oil he retained this trait—habitually at first, recurrently later on —by agitated brush strokes which left the pigment fibrously distinct, especially in high lights; and the result was the same sort of visual appeal especially suited to a romanticism emphasizing wildness. And to offset, at least in part, his shortcomings in color, he could re-enforce that romanticism with a lively drama of light-and-dark which is almost always adequate when seen a picture at a time but is felt as a limitation when a number are brought together. These technical characteristics of chiaroscuro and calligraphy were fully developed before he paid his first return visit to England; the *Landscape with Tree Trunk* [c. 1827: Rhode Island School of Design, Providence] is not only striking in these two respects but remains one of his most satisfactorily rounded utterances.

That indeed makes it exceptional among the completed works; a fair number of sketches and studies are interesting not only as preliminaries but also intrinsically as spirited pictorial ideas, but from 1830 everything that has in it any content beyond straight landscape is flawed with serious imbalance among the complex factors he tried to harmonize—color and drawing and design, structure and space, medieval story or moral contemplation or religious consolation. After 1830 there were some changes in his technique which operated erratically, the most notable among them being an oily shine to his brighter colors; but by that year integrated development had apparently ceased, and he was continually reaching for more than he could communicate in pictures. His journal meditations received a good deal of this mental surcharge, and he may have been pressured into his ornate prose and occasional poetry by a partial consciousness of being spiritually distant from painting in many of his feelings and ideas. Perhaps the point at which Cole ceased growing as a picture-craftsman was when, late in 1829, he concluded that the subject is everything in painting, that the subject alone speaks to the feelings and affects the imagination; nor did he hold back from the corollary that chiaroscuro and color and form are wholly secondary. In going still further to affirm that they were "merely for sensual gratification, mere food for the gross eye," he renounced the painter's reason for being; the word "sensual" from Cole is his fearful epithet for the sensuousness by which painting chiefly lives. So puritanic a denial might be an unconscious self-protection against acknowledging technical inadequacy;

58. THE EXPULSION FROM THE GARDEN OF EDEN by THOMAS COLE Courtesy of Museum
of Fine Arts [M. & M. Karolik Collection], Boston.

but whatever its cause, its consequences were unfortunate in directing the major efforts of Cole's short life into *The Course of Empire* in five pictures and *The Voyage of Life* in four and the project of *The Cross and the World* in five. The first-named cosmic drama seemed great beyond parallel to Hone and Fenimore Cooper; the second was transcribed into the best known series of religious engravings ever circulated in this country.

But an earlier example of this narrative element perhaps gives the most complete account of Cole's mixed mind. *The Expulsion from the Garden of Eden* [1828: plate 58] could be dismissed as unimportant by anyone who thinks that works of art must be "original," for its close dependence upon a mezzotint illustration by the contemporaneous English painter, John Martin, would today be called plagiarism. Although Martin's illustrated edition of *Paradise Lost* was well known here, no moralistic hue and cry was raised against Cole, any more than a few years earlier against Dunlap for using an outline engraving after West's *Death on the Pale Horse;* and what the age accepted with admiration should be acceptable now as a record of its taste. Cole's use of Martin's picture is not only significant in this way; it is biographically important as documenting the major influence upon his mind toward the ideas which either lured him away from painting better or consoled him for not being able to. It is psychologically important because it illustrates something that is very likely to happen to a young artist of talent: finding in the work of another a motive almost ready-made for his own temperament not only communicates excitement but also sets him momentarily free to venture further into self-discovery. The graphic brushwork seen here had appeared in earlier pictures, but less effectively; and here, too, there is even a striking appropriateness, which may not have been conscious with Cole, in the alteration of stroke across the canvas. The idyllism of Eden is rendered with blunted touches that build up static forms; the flicks of light on the foliage themselves grow smaller with the distance until they merge into the general glow beyond. The central portal of rock at the chasm's edge hides the source of the light rays which are given a fine velocity by the length and impetuousness of the brush stroke; that is another example of strongest light juxtaposed to strongest dark which Inman called a "climax" and which here justifies the word with visual melodrama. The whole driving storm, artfully prepared for by the wind-blown water falling out of Eden, is most dramatically concentrated into the fibrous high lights of riven stump and twisting trunk; the excitement which the subject stirred in Cole's own mind gets into the handling of the pigment where it can affect the eyes of those whose minds do not respond in Cole's own way to the narrative. This part of the picture also demonstrates the kind of feeling in which Cole felt himself most intensely alive; a derivative romanticism impelling him to go beyond his source.

In an exceptionally obvious way the *Expulsion* is synthetic, attempting to combine violent emotional contrasts rather than to harmonize everything into a single effect. Yet even those pictures in which Cole was content with the latter had from the first been composites, and an early example like the *Landscape with Woodsman* [1825: Minneapolis Institute] shows how contrived the results could be. In a letter of 1825 Cole contended that composing a picture from sketches is the way by which imagination can enter into the work; and there he was on safer ground than in his assertion that imagination lives only in subject-matter. At any rate, this way of making pictures freed Cole from his time's tendency to ask for a literal delineation of a recognizable spot. Paradoxically, a few of his most interesting works are visually the most specific, and *The Oxbow* [1836: Metropolitan Museum, New York] adds to that a panoramic character which was later to be developed into popularity and fame by Cole's only pupil, Frederick E. Church. But with that extensive content Cole's brushwork is no longer the major element; with it, too, an appropriate degree of objectivity rules the scene, and even the still romantic dead tree in the immediate foreground is little more than a stage prop which sets off the distance as itself the pictorial motive. The sensuous appeal of calligraphic pigment was necessarily sacrificed to the new idea, and the emphasis was shifted from feeling to knowing; the emotions of romance, though not directly expressed in the craftsmanship, were for a considerable time associated with the idea of space transcribed by a naturalistic vision—only to fall away from it when another generation advanced to a fresh understanding of paint.

The strongest influence upon the Hudson River School's general concept of landscape came from the painter in the group who was third in point of time: Asher Brown Durand. He was almost forty when he began to think seriously of landscape; he had not even done much painting at all. In the first twenty years of his career he had become the leading engraver in the country, having attained renown at twenty-seven upon completing his plate of Trumbull's *Declaration of Independence*. Besides the commercial work which gave him his living, Durand issued a financially unsuccessful set of landscape prints; he also reproduced his own *Musidora*, then made the famous plate of Vanderlyn's *Ariadne*, with which his engraving career practically ended in 1835. Portrait commissions from the merchant Luman Reed led to commissions for landscapes; Reed's son-in-law, Jonathan Sturges, made it possible for Durand to go abroad in 1840; and upon his return, after executing some more portraits, he found his landscape subjects sufficiently popular for him to specialize in them. Three

59. KINDRED SPIRITS *by* ASHER BROWN DURAND
Courtesy of The New York Public Library.

younger men accompanied him to Europe as pupils; in part because he was president of the National Academy of Design for sixteen years, his advice was much sought, and he printed a good deal of it in *The Crayon*. All this guidance of others, together with the popularity of his own pictures, affected the younger men; and for a time they exemplified his beliefs before they went on to more individual and usually more interesting manners.

The dominant preachment from Durand was:

Go first to Nature to learn to paint landscape, and when you shall have learned to imitate her, you may then study the pictures of great artists with benefit. . . .

This of course reversed the advice of far greater men and it ignored—or was ignorant of—the shop procedure of the entire European Renaissance. The student receives his best initiation (along with practice) from pictures because they familiarize him with first things first: the problems of design—the ordering of the whole. Once he catches the spirit of that, comprehends its meaning, acquires the incentive to it, the student can develop his own principles of pictorial organization; and they, more than nature, can give him a criterion of what to include and how to treat it. Going first to nature, he may learn a lot about this or that item of nature yet never learn what to do with it. Something like that happened to Durand himself; as Isham wrote: "The composition never perfectly fits the frame, and sometimes it does not fit it at all."

Durand's success lay not in picturemaking but in accumulating landscape details depicted with hard and minute authenticity extremely congenial to contemporaneous taste—a taste which still continued the habit of "nearly looking" so firmly established a hundred years earlier. With Durand himself it was the direct consequence of his practice of engraving. In the biography by his son it is related that, in the days before the government printed paper money, a bank president gave Durand an order for a design with an eagle in it and said: ". . . give him the real steel-trap look." Durand's own grasp upon the structure and texture of a tree trunk was like that, and the results were naturally enough lauded as portraits of particular trees. His means of attaining such results were regular and logical: the form first—and by drawing, not by painting. Broadly handled sketches in color, he said, are useful only to the mature artist; but he might have been asked how else could a beginner become mature—as to color? Durand's commendation of color at any time was quite lukewarm, as his own color sense was limited. He once said: "I paint green because I see nature green," adding that other colors were present only as local tints. Unfortunately his earlier yellow-greens and his later blue-greens are harsh in themselves; but some examples with large-scale birch trees and a good deal of sky display the

silveriness which Isham praised. Further, his counsel was that all traces of execution should be eliminated, a thing made necessary by his aim of minute exactness;
the consequence was that his pictures flatly contradicted the most characteristic
ones by his friend Cole, being placid rather than restless and making their state-
ments in visual prose instead of rhetorical brushwork. Such differences, of course,
do not carry praise or blame for either man except with those who are partisans
of the one manner or the other; art has as much room as life has for contradictions. Besides, Cole and Durand had two important things in common. They
both believed that painting was justified by its benefit to men; and Durand at
first, because of Cole, attempted allegorical landscape in *The Morning of Life* and
The Evening of Life [1839: New-York Historical Society, New York]. It was
beneficial to Durand and American painting together that he soon got beyond
overt moralism of subject and relied upon unadulterated scenery to convey its
own "lessons of high and holy meaning." But to the end of his ninety years
Durand remained like Cole in seeing nature primarily as light-and-dark, with
inadequate colors added; accordingly the pictures of both as a rule gain strength
by black-and-white reproduction.

Durand's picture called *Kindred Spirits* [1849: plate 59] is in one respect un-
typical; not only are human figures present, in itself very rare in his landscapes,
but the figures are miniature portraits of William Cullen Bryant and Thomas
Cole. The intention was to record both their friendship and its special bond in
the feelings they shared toward nature. But in the age of genteelness no creature
of the age, as both of them were, could ever forget the prime duty of being
gentlemanly in every expression of emotion. Both the overarching tree branches
and the pines at the lower right show Durand's merit as a craftsman; the dry
meticulousness of his edges and textures does not here appreciably weaken his
solidity of construction. Both Kensett and Whittredge were soon to paint rockier
rocks than these, but the way in which the stream breaks white below is spiritedly
delicate. The touches by which the middle-distance foliage is built up become
tedious, but the discrimination of values in the receding mountain slopes is
sound. The picture exemplifies the craft which Durand passed on to younger
men: close imitation of detail preserved from total slavishness by what he called
"the necessity of selection," which was his rather modest version of the painter's
immemorial right to manage nature to suit the needs of his picture. And here for
once, and almost uniquely, Durand pushes "selection" to the point of achieving
a compact design; he has been raised clear of his habitual dependence on the
casual good luck of a pleasant view by the formality of his pictorial homage to
the friendship between his own two friends.

One of the younger men who accompanied Durand to Europe, Thomas Rossi-

60. RYDAL FALLS, ENGLAND *by* JOHN FREDERICK KENSETT
Courtesy of George Walter Vincent Smith Art Museum, Springfield, Mass.

ter, turned into a history painter, but the other two went on with the landscape they had commenced painting before they left. John William Casilear, however, after his return renewed the engraving that had been his first profession, as it had been Durand's; and the continuation of that into middle age reduced the amount of his painting below the output of others. Durand's third pupil on the trip, John Frederick Kensett, remained in Europe for several years to make pictures on long walking trips since he was dissatisfied with such instruction as he sought out after Durand had left. The concentrated and varied picturesqueness of the scenes through which he walked and sketched probably did most to develop his eye for good compositions. Returning to the United States in 1848, he became about the most popular and possibly the most prolific of the School; indeed, the steadiness of his technique and attitude made him its most representative figure. Whittredge painted more interesting pictures, and Inness stayed within School bounds for only a few years; but Kensett's

> ". . . sober wishes never learn'd to stray;
> Along the cool, sequester'd vale of life
> He kept the painting habit of his day."

With Kensett, the "sequester'd vale" was his painting-room, and what he never wished to stray from was his cool and even technique. In a physical sense he traveled widely through this country gathering his sketches, which he took back to his studio; there, unlike Durand, he made his final versions in relative freedom from the dictation of visual accident and with more success in ordering objects and planes within the frame. He could isolate a large tree against the sky without giving the impression that he had thought it necessary to count the leaves; he could depict a brook breaking white against the stones without a suggestion of breaking glass. Apparently he sought out his subjects for the sake of compositional variety, and his work therefore is not so monotonous in that respect as are the paintings of others in the School. But whether the scene was a mountain valley or a river valley, the coldly brilliant coast of Newport or the bloomily tinted Jersey shore, it was always placidly minor. Given a minor mind, which he could not help, and given a minor and merely descriptive technique, which was all that his era made available to him, he was wise in his contentment with a rather dry precision in drawing and a uniformly pellucid light in thin pigment. *Rydal Falls, England* [1858: plate 60] shows him already beyond his teacher in tactful treatment of pigment; specific textures of different substances and local colors of different objects are subordinated to an over-all texture appropriate to paint and an over-all tone appropriate to a painting. By the time he came back from Europe and established his studio in New York City, he was ready to paint anything he had seen so long as it was rather pale in tone, quite simple in arrangement, softly vivacious in color.

Sanford Robinson Gifford was eminently a School man, though he was perhaps the first to extend his roamings through most of the known world except the Far East. Better than any other, he shows how fallacious it would be to regard the Hudson River School as a geographical term and how necessary it is to interpret it as an attitude of mind. From Turkey and Greece to the Rocky Mountains, he put his pictures through their invariable stages of development from the first outline sketch for composition to the final version done on the spot under favorable circumstances whenever possible. He was, more than most in the School, conscious of sound technical procedure, but in his devotion to his concept of it he gave every subject a hard competence which killed all the poetry he stressed in his conversations about painting; significantly, he expressed impatience with Corot's slovenly pictures! In contrast to Gifford's efficiency was Jervis McEntee's uneven weakness. David Johnson, before his later decline in skill, painted attractive pictures. The average School product, on a lower technical level than Kensett's, can be found in the work of the Hart brothers, William and James; it is straightforward, but its lack of distinction indicates that many well-to-do middle-class families were following a fashion in picture buying without exercising any genuine discrimination as to individual examples. James Hart once genially said that his patrons wanted "something with cattle in it," and in his pictures the cows take their places very well; after all, to put a cow in her place takes a certain kind of skill, which may well be sufficient for those who like cows. Jasper Francis Cropsey was another who remained faithful to the School manner through years when others were outgrowing it, and his increasingly anachronistic contributions to the exhibitions at the National Academy through the last quarter of the century were ridiculed by younger painters and critics alike. Earlier examples, like the *View of the Kaaterskill House* [1855: plate 61], are good enough to help the school as a whole when any general verdict is attempted. Typical in its subject, it is handled more broadly than are most of the School productions. The receding planes are given with a nice variation of texture; and the spotting of whites, from the foreground rocks and the usual dead tree to the building and the floating cloud-wisps, lightens the wooded stretches with rhythmic sparkles. But its outstanding merit is the freedom of touch. This trait, in contrast to Durand's handling, gives a life to all the objects; and in contrast to Kensett's thin smoothness, it gives liveliness to the picture surface itself. The continual variety with which definite forms are interspersed through the simplified mass of paint, and especially the exactness with which the ground contours and mountain weight are conveyed underneath their

61. VIEW OF THE KAATERSKILL HOUSE *by* JASPER FRANCIS CROPSEY *Courtesy of The Minneapolis Institute of Arts.*

beautifully modulated coating of foliage—all this exhibits a high order of painterly thinking in naturalistic terms.

The best mind among those who consistently maintained School characteristics to the end was that of Worthington Whittredge. Beginning with housepainting in Cincinnati while clerking in a store, he advanced to portraiture and was thereafter drawn to landscape; in Cincinnati he saw examples by Doughty and Cole and Durand, and sold a few of his own there before he left for Europe with the backing of Nicholas Longworth and others. He was one of the first native-born to study for a while at Düsseldorf, which was the European headquarters of spit-and-polish finish at the time. *Deer, Mount Storm Park* [before 1850: plate 62] shows how little he really needed that training; and *Camp Meeting* [1874: Metropolitan Museum, New York] shows how little it actually harmed him. The earlier picture makes a great play with tree foliage, which is well distributed across the upper part, with its masses fairly well broken up for the eye to penetrate into their depths; but there is much timidity in the brushwork and the trunks are almost all flabbily drawn. More importantly, the distant town and river are lovely in their values and patient detail; and the sun-dappled foreground hill, with its dozen deer, is given as a bright discovery of beauty by a freshly perceptive mind. The later picture exhales the same feeling of discovery, but the glow is mellower and the mood is elegiac. The many tiny figures here are not drawn with the tight insistence of the more commonplace School minds; the detail is known to the painter, but he is content to suggest it. Even his edges are reticent compared to those of Durand, and he sees all his figures as spots of color in relation to the over-all color. For the spectator it is a continual surprise to find this visual tact always restraining and lightening a technique that seems calculated for the hard obviousness of Gifford; and the inescapable, but welcome, inference is that Whittredge possessed an intensity of feeling which was missing in his fellow School-men and which could poetize even the technique which their example persuaded him to adopt.

All of the Hudson River men, beginning with Doughty, might fairly be described as School-men by temperament, since even Cole's romanticism never veered once its course was set. The evenness of their minds and the uniformity of their productions make the School as a whole appear in history much like one of the broad and steady-flowing reaches of the river itself. Unlike all that, George Inness manifested an impetuous and stormy personality, having its physical basis in epilepsy; at first clearly a School-man in both technique and ideas, his intense emotions and exceptional susceptibility to influences took him fast and far from the haven of the Hudson. Good luck in friendship and marriage saved him from any psychological disaster due to his illness, and after shifts in manner and mood he experienced a time of fine stylistic coherence before the disintegration of his later years. For one month in 1846 Inness was pupil in Brooklyn to the French-born Regis François Gignoux, who had come here six years earlier in possession of a mildly glittering Parisian technique which suited the current American taste for minuteness; his usually competent landscapes indicate a craft procedure as logical and invariable as that of Gifford, and it was in all likelihood intolerable to Inness' impatient rapidity. The brevity of this formal instruction was probably the basis for the recurrence in Inness of the often repeated American claim of self-teaching; but again the painter who fancied he was self-made found his teachers in the pictures of other men. With Inness such teachers were indeed so many and so diverse that he had trouble discovering his essential self after assimilating their teachings. For the nine years following his month with Gignoux his works show fleeting influences from several sources: a temporary carefulness of detail out of Durand, a romantic medieval subject out of Cole, an attempt at a history piece that turned out to be just some figures in a landscape.

Although no single picture can be typical of this period of Inness' work, *The Old Mill* [1849: plate 63] permits a few specific observations upon his very complex mind. At first glance it gives an impression of strongly constructed forms, and the foliage in particular has a broken-up density beyond the habit of the Hudson River School and akin to the Norwich School of England. Second and subsequent looks at the picture will discover a rather thoughtless haste in high-lighting the tree trunks for an effect of solidity; the high lights are not specifically observed, but are applied out of studio knowledge, quite as arbitrarily as was Kensett's custom and with more irregularity. The brush strokes giving reflected lights on the stream establish a movement across the current rather than with it; their main interest consists in showing how Inness even in the learner's stage did not accede to Durand's dogma of eliminating all traces of execution. The foreground figures are so poorly articulated that they give the eye discomfort—Inness never learned to draw human beings; and their awkwardness raises extreme curiosity about a picture of the preceding year which is now lost: *Diana Surprised by Actaeon*. However, another quality in *The Old Mill* is more significant for his future; it is the general management of space. The immediate foreground in shadow is not interesting, and at the left there are several indications of that ubiquitous but usually unnecessary thing which Wyant was later to ridicule as "the foreground plant"; but this is only a starting-point, of course, the very portion which the eye must leave in order to experience the picture. Ignoring the flaws, the eye advances into the distance through space that is well controlled; the recession is both steady and continuous. At only one point, the depth beyond the patch of light on the hillside at the extreme right, is the eye

62. DEER, MOUNT STORM PARK *by* WORTHINGTON WHITTREDGE *Courtesy of Worcester Art Museum.*

balked by an inexact value; indeed, so successful is this major effect that the mind is reassured even as to the distance that remains unseen behind the masses of foliage.

The Old Mill was painted after Inness' first trip abroad, and by 1855 he had made two more; in the three of them he attained first-hand acquaintance with the work of Constable and Turner, Claude and Poussin, and had visited Barbizon. All these influences can be discerned in various works a little later, but their collective significance is that they took him rapidly away from the schoolish literalism at which he began. If any pictures were actually painted in Europe at this time, they remain unknown; but his gains in technical ease and unity of vision were at once embodied in *The Lackawanna Valley* [1855: National Gallery, Washington], a commercial commission which gave him some annoyance in its exactions but which marked a definite stage toward his mature self. In 1858 he painted a reminiscence of Italy with the obvious subject of an aqueduct striding the Campagna, but his elevation into the mood of a romantic classicism was far more adequately expressed in *Delaware Water Gap* [1859: Metropolitan Museum, New York]. A subject with obvious similarities to earlier Hudson River School pictures, it received from Inness what had been missing in them: a pulse of emotion in the color and an intensification of physical distance into imaginative extent which are both part of a poet's apprehension of the world. After 1864, when he moved from Massachusetts to New Jersey, Inness was to paint pictures which reduced his earlier landscapes to the status of preparation; but even in that stage he had come clear of the School. Almost coincident with the move to New Jersey, he became an adherent of the Swedenborgian religion and thereby secured an intellectual foundation for his increasingly mystical interpretation of appearances.

Inness' escape from the mental limitations of the School was unquestionably speeded by his trips to Europe, but its primary cause was the quality of his mind. All except one of the School members here named went to Europe, some at a later age than Inness and a few at an earlier age; but they did not discover what he discovered because their natures were otherwise. It was a merchant patron who made Inness' first trip possible, just as other merchants had done for Cole and Durand; and Cincinnati merchants did the same for Whittredge. These men were more than picture buyers; they were collaborators in developing the art of painting here. And their interest was not only in their painter-friends; it was also in the landscape that the painters wanted to depict. For these merchants were city men, a formative element in the inexorable change of the United States into an urban and industrial society. Yet most of them were not city-born, but country boys who had made good in the new environment. There they began to remember the country—perhaps not yet with regret, but certainly with affection. Alexandrians, with the help of Theocritus, dreamed of a pastoral Sicily; rich Venetians liked pictures with mountains in them. The latter-day merchants were not similarly poetic, and almost none of their painters had poetry in their brushes; they were mid-century Americans together, with a liking for landscapes that could leave them somewhat passive but on the whole cheerful and assured. The literalness of the visual record was determined by their desire to verify every detail, and the inherent lyricism of the dawning nostalgia was turned into prose by the paramount obligation to be genteel.

63. THE OLD MILL by GEORGE INNESS Courtesy of The Art Institute of Chicago.

54. The popularity of the panorama

Frederick Catherwood: 1799–1854
John Rowson Smith: 1810–1864
John Banvard: 1815–1891
Henry Lewis: 1819–1904

John J. Egan: ?
Thomas Coke Ruckle: 1811–1891
James F. Harris: act. 1850–1860
John Insco Williams: 1813–?

The landscapes just discussed were executed for individual owners and went into their homes as private possessions, but among the people at large (including the private picture owners) the panoramic landscape had a generation of fabulous popularity. Where Vanderlyn's cyclorama had failed in the New York of the Federal Era, a successor in the mid-century achieved the importance of big business. The lucky man was an Englishman, Frederick Catherwood, who had been trained in London by Burford, the successor there of Barker; Catherwood's opening attraction, *Jerusalem,* was artfully lit by gas and drew large crowds. He consequently imported several of Burford's own panoramas, and while one was shown in New York others were on tour through other cities in the East. All this was managed by business associates while Catherwood went to Central America to explore Mayan ruins with the American businessman, John Lloyd Stephens, whose earlier travel books Catherwood had illustrated; and when the building specially erected for Catherwood burned in 1842 it was not rebuilt. The approval which Dunlap had first voiced in this country was continued by Tuckerman:

. . . The accuracy and illusions of these experiments are sometimes marvellous. . . . As exhibition works, panoramas are very desirable. They afford satisfactory though general ideas, gratify intelligent curiosity, and appeal most vividly to the imagination. . . .

This would have been cold praise if meant for another type of panorama which was the mid-century's special development: the panorama that moved. Motion of some sort had been present in a few earlier manifestations, but in this period of popularity motion was achieved by winding long strips of canvas from one concealed roller to another before audiences listening to explanatory lectures. This was for its time an effective visual substitute for travel, and as such an important phase of mass culture. The simple mechanics involved may have meant added popularity with a public already inclined to pin too great a faith on mechanisms, and this particular mechanism took painting to the people as a form of theatrical entertainment.

447

The technique of the painting itself was in the known instances actually out of the theater. Easel pictures by the two most famous practitioners, John Banvard and Henry Lewis, conform to studio practice; but the coarse and rapid workmanship of Banvard's panorama was noted at the time, while Lewis' skill in easel painting was acquired in Europe after he had taken his panorama there. The first man to succeed outstandingly with the device was John Rowson Smith, son of the John Rubens Smith who executed topographical views; the younger Smith was primarily a scene painter, and as early as 1832 was working on panoramas in St. Louis. His great success, however, occurred seven years later in Boston, though that production was soon burned. With assistance from another painter he produced a panorama which opened at Saratoga, New York, and took in twenty thousand dollars in six weeks: enough to dwarf the success of Rembrandt Peale's *Court of Death* twenty years earlier. Smith's subject was the Mississippi River, and since it was the subject of all the most famous panoramas of the period, that phenomenon of nature may have been the real reason for their sensational impact upon public attention.

John Banvard's romanticizing of his own career is in the best frontier tradition, so that, though born in New York, he gives a strong impression of hearty westernism. His words about himself were verbosely inexpressive in any literary sense; it is the events of his life that count: going west young, clerking in a drugstore, joining other youths in a disastrous venture of exhibiting small-scale moving landscapes on a boat, recouping his fortunes by more painting, making another disastrous venture in museum ownership, and recovering himself once more by peddling wares. Having saved more money, he then addressed himself to his life-ambition; early in 1840 he spent several months in a boat descending the Mississippi from St. Louis to make four hundred sketches of the twelve hundred miles; he then settled down at Louisville and in a specially built studio enlarged and joined the sketches upon one continuous strip of canvas specially woven for him in Lowell, Massachusetts. His publicity claimed that it was three miles long; a recent estimate reduces it to somewhat less than one-quarter of a mile—about twelve hundred feet. But at that time the spirit of Barnum was great in the land, and equivalence of size and greatness was an article of faith. Longest river—longest painting: biggest country—greatest artist: the implied logic was irresistible. Nathaniel Parker Willis, even more influential than Philip Hone, was quoted as saying:

Mr. Banvard has refuted the assertions of foreigners, that America had produced no artist commensurate with the grandeur of its scenery.

When Banvard's panorama reached Boston, Longfellow was composing *Evangeline,* and he attended several performances so as to be able to write correctly about the Louisiana landscape he had never seen. In 1848 this painted spectacle was taken on to England for the visits of six hundred thousand people, and the fanfare over the command performance at Windsor for Queen Victoria obscured the fact that a few years earlier Rowson Smith had experienced the same honor at Balmoral. Banvard's money enabled him to travel widely and paint as far away as Palestine; apparently he brought some sections of his "greatest" picture back to this country, but they seem to have been lost. Banvard also wrote what he called poetry and two dramas which were produced in Boston and New York; but after settling in South Dakota in 1880 his contributions to culture dwindled into publishing a handbook for a system of shorthand.

Banvard's self-trumpetings created a long-lived legend that he owned the Mississippi pictorially, yet he was neither the first nor the last, and an immediate successor exceeded him. Where Banvard showed only the lower part, Henry Lewis included the whole of the river from St. Paul to New Orleans. This he managed in two sections, which together made a panorama twelve feet high and about three times the length of Banvard's. The first one, giving the upper stretch of the river, required nine months of work in Cincinnati by Lewis and four assistants who formed a scene-painting firm there; it involved an outlay of fifteen thousand dollars before its initial showing. The second portion was done in St. Louis with other assistants, who themselves made independent panoramas after quarreling with Lewis. Lewis also had a tremendous European success, for curiosity about this country was never more intense than then. On the proceeds of the panorama and an elaborately illustrated book drawn from it Lewis settled down in Düsseldorf, and there he learned to paint. As Vanderlyn and Catherwood had brought the old world visibly to the new, so Banvard and Lewis took the new world to the old; and it was the latter pair who earned the money and the fame. Rowson Smith alone performed both services, for in Europe he prepared for another panorama with which to report the scenes of that continent to Americans.

All the mid-century examples seem lost except one; this was painted in Philadelphia by John J. Egan, who worked from sketches prepared by a Doctor M. W. Dickson, an amateur archaeologist wishing to publicize his work. Its two sections [University of Pennsylvania Museum, Philadelphia] exhibit a fluent stage-scene technique, with all the forms quite knowingly simplified for quick appeal to hasty eyes; the archaeological portions which the Doctor wished to have emphasized are so treated without sacrificing unduly the sweep and continuity of the whole, and the prominent high lights are applied so as to maintain a liveliness through the whole. It is pure guesswork to speculate whether this one is more or less skilful than the others were; but certainly this one is no work of art with spiritual significance—it is a work of craft calculated for immediate effect:

journalism in paint. And it is a fair inference that all the others were also.

The Mississippi panoramas were only the most famous among a host of minor attempts all through the country, most of them apparently dealing with other subjects. A cosmorama, the name for a panorama of the world, was brought all the way from Europe to St. Louis. In Baltimore Thomas Coke Ruckle, son of a painter, showed a panorama of *Pilgrim's Progress* at the Temperance Temple. In Indianapolis, James F. Harris painted the first one there: *The Mirror of Intemperance,* in thirty-five scenes, which made a successful tour and was advantageously sold. It would seem as if Harris crowded his luck somewhat when he followed that with another on *The Evils of Intemperance,* but perhaps he was inventive enough not to repeat himself even on the same theme. John Insco Williams in 1849 exhibited a panorama of Bible history from the Creation to the Fall of Babylon; from Dayton it went to Cincinnati and on to Philadelphia, where it burned. Sure of public interest, Williams painted another and larger version of the same; when it reached Baltimore, a flood washed off the paint; it was then repainted and eventually sold for enough to keep the artist for the rest of his life. In all of this quantity production there must have been much work which seemed shoddy even at the time it was done, and it was from experiences with minor road-shows that a writer in the *Southern Literary Messenger* for August, 1859, felt moved to mourn:

. . . As the canvas rolls by, unfolding to our view Alps and oceans, cathedrals and battles, coronations, conflagrations, volcanic eruptions, etc., we hear, in the pauses of a cracked piano, the voice of the Showman, as of one crying in the Wilderness, who tells us all about the localities represented, with a good deal of pleasant information to be obtained in no other manner, because it is improvised for the occasion.

55. Painters of the Amerind

George Catlin: 1796–1872
Seth Eastman: 1808–1875
Alfred Jacob Miller: 1810–1874

John Mix Stanley: 1814–1872
Frank Blackwell Mayer: 1827–1899
Carl Wimar: 1828–1862

Vicarious enjoyment of scenery through the panorama was paralleled by vicarious travel among the Amerinds through easel pictures. Both were addressed to the same city audiences who would not see the real thing, and both satisfied the same kind of intellectual curiosity. The fact that painting was the means of accomplishing it was esthetically both accidental and incidental; in these two fields painting in the mid-century was a craft of reporting rather than an art for spiritual sustenance. Literature partly cultivated a popular interest in the Amerind as pictorial subject-matter, just as Bryant and Irving had partly prepared the field for the Hudson River School. Probably Freneau's occasional use of Amerinds in his poems did not count for much, but the noble savage soon became material for early plays in George Washington Parke Custis' *Pocahontas* and James Nelson Barker's *Indian Princess;* and a definitive literary embodiment of the romantic Amerind was given by Fenimore Cooper's novels.

George Catlin remains in some ways the most important painter identified with this subject-matter, and his interest was apparently not literary but incited by first-hand contact with visiting braves in Philadelphia. This was in 1829, and the impression upon him was so strong that within three years he had begun his long labor: living with tribe after tribe through the better part of each year and spending the winter months making finished pictures from his sketch material as it accumulated. In 1838 he re-appeared in the East with six hundred paintings and an accessory troupe of live Amerinds, the two factors together attracting large crowds. As a technician Catlin presents an uneven mixture; his first work in miniature has some interest, but his early portraiture in oil had earned only condescension from Dunlap, who ironically congratulated him on having no rivals among the Amerinds "and nothing to ruffle his mood in the shape of criticism." Catlin never did master the figure, but from whom in his time could he have learned it? In the bust portraiture which made up the greater part of his immense production this deficiency was little noticeable, but in the full-length groups by which he tried to give some idea of their customs it kept his work near the documentary level. Yet Catlin was in earnest, and his mind and hand were often keyed up to an excited perceptiveness. Among the hundreds of his pictures still remaining [National Museum, Washington; Museum of Natural History, New York] are a good many spirited compositions of landscapes in which the figures—humans on horseback or buffalo herds—play a subordinate role; the more successful ones show a haste in execution which, however much it may evade construction and err in proportions, succeeds in communicating the painter's quick eye for the picturesque. The visual dullness of the work when he becomes concerned mainly with exact detail may not impair its value as information of a kind. And both kinds of pictures by Catlin have together done most to shape the popular image of the Amerind; they have been almost as effective in visual myth-making as Trumbull's history pieces.

Seth Eastman's technique was hardly better than Catlin's, and it is in the main quite as static as most of Catlin's; nowhere does Eastman achieve the spiritedness in Catlin's best, but he could work up his preliminary sketches into paintings which well enough satisfied the ideas of his time as to composition. An example like the *Lacrosse Playing Among the Sioux Indians* [1851: Corcoran Galley, Washington] is less an account of Amerind life than a currently academic conception of what such an account ought to be. Alfred Jacob Miller, who sketched in water color with more uniformly attractive pictorial results than Eastman, was conditioned by the academic training of Paris, where he had lived in picturesque fashion and been the only American student of his time at the *Beaux-Arts.* He was Baltimore-born, but was seeking work in New Orleans when the Scottish traveler, Captain William Drummond Scott, invited him to go along as artist on a western trip as far as Oregon. Miller's written account is fully as interesting as his pictures, if not more so, to judge by extracts which have been printed. As unaffected illustration, his water colors are informative about topography, become more interesting as designs when rooms or courtyards of buildings make the setting, and dispose of groups with compositional effectiveness. They fall short of physiognomical authenticity, however, and in a few attempted idyllic renderings of Amerind girls spoil the effect by a prettiness as evasive as a society portrait. A third painter in the group subordinate to Catlin was John Mix Stanley who was somewhat more observant of racial characteristics, but his attempts at formal picturemaking with Amerind subjects, such as the large *Trial of Red Jacket* [Buffalo Historical Society] containing a hundred figures more or less, are tediously designed. Out in Hawaii in 1848 he executed two portraits of King Kamehameha and his Queen, which are not helped to impressiveness by their huge size because they have in them nothing but the mid-century's dullest officialism and drabbest imitation pomp. For a measure of Stanley's genuine artistry, one must look to some of his landscapes, such as the *Western Landscape* [c. 1847: Detroit Institute] wherein the crisscrossing diagonals of mountain slopes above glassy water build back into deep space: a pictorial idea which was becoming more and more important as a source of emotion for Americans looking at pictures.

Two somewhat younger men also took up the theme of the Amerind in the mid-century. Frank Blackwell Mayer, whose diary has been noted in connection with Cincinnati and Nashville, was drawn to Minnesota by his interest in the Amerind before he was a good enough technician to do much with the material. His *Treaty of Traverse des Sioux* [1851: Minnesota Historical Society, St. Paul] is almost amateur in the uncertainty of design and of drawing; but it served as good source material to another painter, Francis D. Millet, when years afterward he was commissioned to decorate a wall in the State Capitol. Mayer's sketches are frequently promising, but his best painting was in anecdote after he had gone to Paris for more adequate schooling. Carl Wimar, however, made a few pictures which put to good use the academic training he acquired in Düsseldorf. He had begun as an assistant on a panorama devised by Leon Pomarede, who had been one of the quarreling assistants under Henry Lewis for his Mississippi panorama. Wimar's preparatory material made on trips westward from St. Louis have documentary merit; when he came to organize that material into ambitious pictures, documentation quite properly was subordinated. But only once, perhaps, did Wimar achieve a really impressive design; the *Indians Approaching Fort Benton* [1859: City Art Museum, St. Louis] uses distance with emotional effectiveness.

56. *Painters into distant regions*

TEXAS

T. Jefferson Wright: 1798–1846
Herman Lungkwitz: 1813–1891
Richard Petrie: act. 1850
Mrs. Louise Heuser Wueste: 1803–1875
Mrs. Charles Lavender: 1817–1898
Theodore Gentilz: c. 1820–1906

CALIFORNIA

Alburtis De Orient Browere: 1814–1887
Norton Bush: 1833–1894
Samuel Stillman Osgood: 1808–1885
William Smith Jewett: 1812–1873
David Daloff Neal: 1838–1915
Charles Christian Nahl: 1818–1875

The painters of the Amerind engaged in cultural forays into the Great Plains and brought back pictorial spoils, but there were other regions equally remote in spirit into which painters were penetrating to stay; and those who went to Texas constitute something of a special case. American infiltration into the region began in the eighteen-twenties when it was technically still a foreign country, and the cultural aspects of that trend seem to have been impeded by the political complications. In the interim when Texas was an independent republic, a Kentucky portrait painter, T. Jefferson Wright, served as Secretary of State under President Sam Houston. Portraits by him during the 'thirties remain in his home state, to which he paid several return visits; they are moderately interesting examples of the technique already noted there as exemplified in Bush—at a stage between the artisans and the studio men. In early Texas Wright was unusual in being a painter from the States; but there are records of several others direct from Europe.

Herman Lungkwitz was a political refugee from the abortive revolution of 1848 in Germany, an event which sent other artistic talents to the Midwest. With Lungkwitz was his brother-in-law, Richard Petrie; and they worked together on commercial commissions—Petrie for figures and Lungkwitz for landscapes. Making a living there was difficult for painters; Petrie died at thirty-six, and Lungkwitz for a long period earned his way by photography alone. The paintings of both evidence a sound academic training without markedly personal accents; they are so obviously European in technique that they seem culturally homeless in the Texas of 1850. About that time, too, Mrs. Louise Heuser Wueste came to San Antonio to live with a daughter; her presence is here noted as another link with German painting, for she had been taught at

Düsseldorf and there her sisters were married to the painters Schroeder and Lessing. The simple facts about another woman, Mrs. Charles Lavender, suggest that she was a romantic figure on the southwest frontier. She was born Eugénie Etiennette Aubanel, first cousin to the famous historian and politician Guizot; she studied under Delaroche and Ary Scheffer, and was becoming known in Paris as a painter at twenty-one. With her husband and two baby girls she landed at New Orleans in 1851 on the way to Texas; the family brought a large collection of pictures and books, but had to leave them at Houston when they pushed farther on by wagon. After the birth of a son in the wilds, they settled at Waco with only six other families, and the mother resumed her painting. When she used up the paints she had brought along, she made her own out of herbs and clays; and she painted so much that she gave her pictures away. Later, when living at Corpus Christi, she had the satisfaction of seeing her work begin to function in community life when the cathedral housed her large painting of a saint. Theodore Gentilz was also born in France, and even after coming to Texas went back there for some training; he taught and painted in San Antonio for half a century, and despite what he learned in Paris his work shows the timidly scrupulous carefulness which sometimes results from isolation. All these painters only repeat a general pattern observable much earlier in eastern regions, but the connotations of geographical vastness which are still part of the total idea of Texas make these European painters appear singularly isolated from one another and especially distant from their cultural home.

To the sparse settlement of Texas, California contrasts startlingly with the effect of a swarming hive; and wherever so much happens so fast, picture-makers usually show up. Artists can be as adventurous as other people, and a few painters who were not doing so well as painters thought they could do better digging gold; so they joined the rush in which men from England and Australia, from Germany and China, and from all countries in between, converged upon San Francisco. This convulsive process telescoped the usual development of culture: a half-century into a decade, a decade into six months. The interest of the outside world was so great that artists and writers were immediately sent there for accounts of what was going on, and some men combined both functions. Bayard Taylor's El Dorado did much better with its words than with its illustrations. When he arrived, lumber was so scarce that few of the buildings scattered over the hill slopes around the harbor had walls of wood more than waist-high; the upper portions were of cloth. Seen from the water at night, the tent-shapes, lit up from within, had for him the fantasy of a magic lantern "which the motion of a hand can build or annihilate." Other men were professional illustrators, and sent back drawings to the East which were quickly turned into lithographs as a form of news; these could convey some of the thin newness and flimsy makeshifts which appear on every frontier, but so far as San Francisco was concerned they might become pictorial lies overnight, for the wooden city was burned over five times. What no picture of the time did convey was the turbulently rolling stream of humanity that churned its way through those shacks and that dust.

Alburtis De Orient Browere might be considered as an eastern painter of signs and landscape and anecdote: a personally picturesque figure but secondary in every branch of work. However, he made two trips to California and there painted a number of landscapes which are not only valuable as records but also better pictures than his usual eastern product; the large-scale visual drama of verticals in the West, so unlike the relatively low-rounded Catskills, gave to his brush an unaccustomed simplicity of form and positiveness of color. A landscape painter settling in San Francisco was Norton Bush, who had been a pupil of Cropsey; perhaps his services later on in connection with the local Art Association were of greater historical consequence than his landscapes, for these lack the pictorial clarity which Browere temporarily achieved in California. Samuel Stillman Osgood was at first identified as a portraitist with Hartford and New York; but after the death of both wife and daughter, he went to California, where he made a large fortune with a continuation of his commonplace semi-photography. But William Smith Jewett, who has been at times confused with the William Jewett who was Waldo's partner, was in his eastern years a better painter than Osgood; in California he, too, became wealthy by portraiture and investments together. His technique hardened into a glossy obviousness which may have been a conscious response to the preferences of patrons taking up where a good many easterners were leaving off. Another portraitist who was popular for some years in California before he settled permanently in Munich was David Daloff Neal; he is said to have painted anecdote also while in this country, and it was in pictures of this type that he specialized after becoming a very minor European school-man. A better than equal exchange occurred through a German-born painter's settling in California: Charles Christian Nahl. To be sure, it was advantageous only in the sense that the Far West stood to gain through having an even moderately good technician permanently around; Nahl could not fairly have been expected to change his technique into something as rough as his new environment when the whole desire of his patrons there was for him to give them European sophistication. When he painted little *Miss Annie Grant* [1857: M. H. De Young Memorial Museum, San Francisco], he gave her and all her accessories a very German air of middle-class prosperity; and when he painted *Sunday in the Mines* [Crocker Art Gallery, Sacramento], the grave readers and carousing dancers and even the horsemen rushing past have a Tyrolean look—and that despite the superficial accuracy of the roughly boarded shack and the over-hanging foliage. The beautifully kept beards on several of the miners serve to recall the fact that Alonzo Delano, both a writer and a draftsman, assured his California patrons that his fee of an ounce of gold dust for a portrait included the whiskers; but most of his writing, too, was humorous.

57. Mid-century art organizations

Dunlap, writing his history in the early eighteen-thirties, permitted himself a note of satisfaction over how much better conditions were for artists than when he himself was young.

. . . Artists know their stand in society, and are now in consequence of that conduct which flows from their knowledge of the dignity and importance of art, looked up to by the best in the land, instead of being looked down upon by those whose merits will only be recorded in their bank books.

He thought the improved situation the result of the artists' own good conduct; and no doubt he, both a painter and a man of the theater, needed his own double amount of respectability to overcome those handicaps. But the personal good qualities of individual artists would have counted for little in advancing their profession as a whole without their effective organization; and the main reason for better conditions was that the National Academy of Design was now reaching the point where it could certify to a reasonable degree of technical respectability in the regularly offered results of its members' industry. It would be putting it too crassly to say that the merchant-buyers of supposedly spiritual goods demanded a tangible guarantee of quality, but to the extent that the tendency existed the National Academy benefited by vouching for its pictorial merchandise.

As for the American Academy, one of its directors gave it another chance by erecting a building for it; but when the public found the same unchanging objects on exhibition, they left it again to its slumbers. Dunlap a little smugly recorded its habit of "letting out the rooms to adventurers and picture dealers"; but in its new quarters later on the National Academy itself resorted to the same means of recouping expenses. Meanwhile Trumbull sent all his pictures to New Haven in return for a life annuity from Yale College, and at the same time retained enough influence in the American Academy to thwart a well pre-pared attempt in 1833 to unite the two institutions. Later on the older one had the bad luck of a fire, and before Trumbull's death its collection of casts was bid in at auction by the younger one. However, before this inglorious end of the American Academy, the National Academy, as the more active organiza-tion, encountered difficulties of its own.

It was in its exhibition of 1832 that Greenough's marble, *Chanting Cherubs,* caused scandal by its nudity, and as a result of public censure the members passed a resolution "that the statues in the Antique School suffer mutilation" and "that a plaster leaf be placed in lieu thereof." But nudity in art was in double jeopardy: censured in the halls of the Academy, it had more scope in vulgar commercial ventures. As Cummings noted, "two gorgeously colored French pictures" of *The Temptation* and *The Expulsion* were making a fortune for their owner, who capitalized them as "great moral pictures"; and six years later the Academy rented its own rooms to their proprietor to show them in. Nor was that showman alone in thus anticipating Artemus Ward's advice: "Cum the moral on 'em strong." Phineas Taylor Barnum in 1842 combined the two New York museums of Rubens Peale and John Scudder, exhibiting West's *Christ Healing the Sick* but swamping all the pictures and statues with miscellaneous curiosities, many of them fakes, and dwarfing everything else by featuring General Tom Thumb. The exterior of Barnum's establishment was decorated with about a hundred paintings of things to be seen inside, and therein he featured "a new and gorgeous exhibition saloon" for performances by jugglers and acrobats and the like which anticipated the later vaudeville show.

The Boston Museum, not to be confused with the much later Museum of Fine Arts, was praised in the *Transcript* for its "innocent mirth and rational amusement" and its "purity of language and morals." The latter phrase is explained by the fact that its elaborate paraphernalia of paintings and statues and curiosities, which included half of Charles Willson Peale's museum brought up from Philadelphia, had become by 1850 quite subsidiary to its theatrical performances. As a commercial museum it had existed from 1812, and in 1841 it became the property of Moses Kimball; at that time the collection contained Sully's *Washington Crossing the Delaware* and Rembrandt Peale's *The Roman Daughter*, together with many other pictures and the usual conglomeration of objects. Kimball began offering both moving devices, such as a model of Niagara with real water, and individual entertainers, as Barnum was doing. In 1845 Kimball presented a musical drama based on Allston's poem, *The Paint King*; by that year, indeed, full-fledged theatrical performances were the principal feature, with the collections relegated to a device for cloaking with respectability what the community would not accept as an independent activity. A traveling actor in 1849 described in his journal how church members who blenched at the word "theater" attended it under the name of "museum." "Such conduct they call *religion*. I call it hypocrisy." But if any stray visitors felt like abstaining from the performances of actors, they could find plenty of moral profit in the gruesome waxworks of the upper hall, which were Boston's counterpart of the *Dante's Inferno* in wax devised by Hiram Powers in Cincinnati. In Boston the Athenaeum's art exhibitions continued with variable success, but by the 'fifties it was relying much upon paintings from out of town—Cole's *Course of Empire* series, two canvases by Rosa Bonheur, some English Pre-Raphaelites. In 1858 local opinion compelled it to withdraw Page's *Venus* from exhibition.

In New York the National Academy at first welcomed a new kind of art organization: The Apollo Association [1838], which from 1844 became better known as The American Art-Union. It was a commercial venture by James Herring, who had already had success with a set of illustrated books called *The National Portrait Gallery*. After a little uncertainty as to its proper procedure and some difficulty in the general financial crisis about 1840, it developed its tremendously successful program centered around drawings by lot. For a moderate membership fee every subscriber got a chance to win one among a number of original oils purchased by the Art-Union for that purpose, the drawings being held under conditions of public attendance and supervision by the most respectable personages. Not only did a few each year receive valuable prizes in this way but everybody received excellent engraved reproductions of paintings sure to be popular as subject-matter, such as Bingham's *Jolly Flatboatmen*. On one occasion the engravings were supplemented by a medal in honor of Allston. The Art-Union's peak membership of more than sixteen thousand was reached in 1848, but that was an increase of nearly seven thousand over the year before, and was due to the fact that among the pictures to be won were Cole's series called *The Voyage of Life*. The American Art-Union drew its memberships from all over the country, but this did not prevent the establishment of other Unions, patterned after it and regionally successful, in Philadelphia and Boston and Cincinnati. Together they quickly made the country art conscious to such an unprecedented extent that they may be credited with creating the first mass audience here for the studio professionals. Tuckerman more elegantly described this as "the era when Art, emancipated from the care of Kings and Popes, finds sustenance by alliance with commerce and the people. . . ." The original Art-Union, before it went out of business, had distributed about one hundred and fifty thousand engravings and twenty-four hundred original works by more than two hundred and fifty artists.

It and its emulators were all ended by a court decision against the whole scheme as a lottery. The legal proceedings which had that result were not initiated by the National Academy as an organization, but it had reached the point of protesting to the Union that the latter's activities were injuring attendance and sales at the Academy's exhibitions. At one point the Art-Union bought about three dozen paintings by Academicians in a lot and for a price which for the moment freed their organization from debt. The Art-Union had been buying their work all along, but some Academicians believed that favoritism was developing, and some individuals among those thus dissatisfied had a share of the responsibility for beginning the suit which eventually destroyed the Art-Union.

One of the organization's services consisted in circulating its *Transactions* and its *Bulletin* among its members, for at that time there was no periodical concerned exclusively, or even mainly, with art. These publications were not illustrated and a good proportion of their pages was filled with merely statistical information. But there were also some articles, not well enough expressed to be called essays, and apparently all of the extensive "remarks" made at the annual meetings by men prominent enough to be asked. These productions have the culturally immature verbosity of the time's political oratory, and there is entirely too much exhortation of patriotism to the rescue of art. Yet at least art was being talked about. William Cullen Bryant in 1845 declaimed: "The canvas is stretched and the pencil dipped amid the solitude of the prairies." And a certain Charles F. Briggs almost succeeded in concealing a good idea in a lot of words:

. . . It may seem paradoxical, but it is nevertheless true, that men are first led to a contemplation of nature by the blandishments of art.

To the inhabitants of cities, as nearly all of the subscribers to the Art-Union are, a painted landscape is almost essential to preserve a healthy tone to the spirits, lest they forget in the wilderness of bricks which surrounds them the pure delights of nature and a country.

. . . Such a sight must improve the digestion of the dyspeptic merchant as he sits at his pampered table. . . .

If anybody could have been reached by the argument that art has therapeutic effects, the speaker did right to advance it; but the significance which the historian extracts from his somnolent prose is that the success of the Art-Union both helped and required a really wide expansion of painting beyond portraiture. People will not buy chances on new oil paintings that are only images of somebody else's relatives; and the swift extension of subject-matter through the mid-century was in itself valuable for the maturing of American taste.

An attempt to establish a permanent gallery of art by keeping together most of the collection assembled by the patron of the landscape painters, Luman Reed, was not successful; for a while it was housed in the New-York Rotunda erected for Vanderlyn's panorama, but admission fees were insufficient for its maintenance and in 1858 its incorporators wound up its affairs and donated the collection to the New-York Historical Society. The earnestness of their original hopes was stressed in the catalog introduction:

A Gallery of Art in a city, is a source of refinement; nay, more, it is a stronghold of virtue. . . . Call it a lounge, if you please; let it catch the idle hours or arrest the weary step; yet idling and relaxation here, can hardly fail to be improvement. . . .

Moral therapy didn't work any better than physical amelioration; and when the Crystal Palace, constructed in 1853 out of iron and glass in imitation of the London original, opened its display, mainly of machinery but with some pictures, its catalog mourned:

No well-bestowed wealth has founded long galleries of sculpture and painting, and opened their doors to the gratuitous access of the public.

With the disappearance of the Art-Union, the most active promotion in New York of art for collectors fell to the dealers; the most influential of these, however, now stressed pictures from Europe rather than works by Americans, and many Academicians lamented the disappearance of the institution they had once feared. The Paris firm of Goupil opened a branch in New York and the establishment calling itself the Düsseldorf Gallery, replete with immensities by the Germans who had been teaching Americans, became the lounge of esthetic idlers and the shrine of self-improvers.

58. Mid-century history painting

John Gadsby Chapman: 1808–1889
Robert Walter Weir: 1803–1889
William Henry Powell: 1823–1879
James Walker: 1819–1889
Emanuel Leutze: 1816–1868
Junius Brutus Stearns: 1810–1885
Dennis Malone Carter: 1827–1881

Peter Frederick Rothermel: 1817–1895
Thomas Prichard Rossiter: 1818–1872
Daniel Huntington: 1816–1906 (work to 1860)
Christian Schussele: 1826–1879
Mark Robert Harrison: 1819–1894
George Caleb Bingham: 1811–1877

The condemnations of Trumbull's paintings voiced by some members of the Congress may have had something to do with the lapse of a decade before any more commissions were given; but the four spaces that remained empty in the Capitol Rotunda insistently asked to be filled. Too, the visiting public began to express approval of the whole idea of making the Capitol into a shrine of American history. The great majority of the visitors did not recognize the technical inferiority of Trumbull's four, and if they heard about any foreigners' scoffing at the pictures they would be indifferent or at best irritated. The very setting of the pictures made them impressive to the average mind, and their subjects re-enforced the aggressively patriotic emotions of the time; accordingly Trumbull's pictures not only began to affect the popular visual imagery of the Revolution but also created a popular desire for more historical works in the Capitol. Subsidiary but also effective was the continued political wirepulling for this or that painter anxious for Trumbull's fame, and in 1836 the Congress commissioned four more paintings for the Rotunda—from Vanderlyn, Inman, Weir, and Chapman.

The artistic failure of Vanderlyn's *Landing of Columbus* has been noted; Inman continued under the pressure of portraiture and soon fell into ill-health, so that he died without completing his picture. Meanwhile, like Vanderlyn, John Gadsby Chapman went abroad to paint his *Baptism of Pocahontas* but Robert Walter Weir executed his *Embarkation of the Pilgrims* here while fulfilling his duties as Professor of Drawing at West Point. Chapman's life and personality offer several features more interesting than his Capitol painting; he was a handyman in several different processes, and rested himself by change of craft rather than by not working, and he had the interesting opinion about mechanics that they were "the most original and deserving among the

463

people." Tuckerman's description of the painter's New York studio—"very artist-like," he calls it—gives a very good idea of the props considered desirable for atmosphere and for use in picturemaking. In naming some of them Tuckerman brings in associated ideas as compendiously as do the pictures of the time; a suit of armor suggests a string of medievalisms, a deer's head implies woodland freedom, and plaster casts remind of the Vatican statues. A self-portrait by Chapman made years later, in Rome, shows similar but perhaps more orderly surroundings. Before removing permanently to Rome in 1848, Chapman had drawn about fourteen hundred illustrations for Harper's *Illuminated Bible* [1846] and had published a good book on drawing. Weir, too, was more interesting as a person than as a painter; his early talent had been such that, in the New York of the eighteen-twenties, his imitation old masters had been marketed as originals. His forty years of teaching did not interfere with his painting many pictures of all subjects, but his two painter-sons did better ones. At Inman's death in 1846 manoeuvering immediately began for re-assigning his commission, and the Congressional friends of Morse lost out before the political consideration that it should go to a man from the Midwest, William Henry Powell. He was in Paris at the time and stayed there to paint his *Discovery of the Mississippi.*

With the new quartet of paintings installed in the company of Trumbull's, the Rotunda walls were not filled, since the space is so vast that all eight of the large canvases are dwarfed, but the Rotunda was at least spotted at regular intervals with history in color. The second quartet were in striking technical contrast to Trumbull's, for they were in the current academic manner of Europe; they were costume pieces full of the elocutionary heroics most at home in the annual Salon exhibitions. It was about the Salon product that Gustave Courbet was soon to remark: "Historical art is by its very nature contemporary." Unknown to him, the proof already existed on the Rotunda wall; the four mid-century additions were only exercises in the theatrical masquerades which the time thought appropriate to history. Courbet's observation does not exclude the historical subject from the painting of any age; the necessary thing is that the age, or the painters of the age, shall possess enough range of technical knowledge and enough tact to adjust the scale and execution to the setting. All of the Rotunda history pieces were conceived as easel pictures; they were merely enlarged to a size which was then thought appropriate to their setting. And even on that larger scale they were executed with a relative minuteness of detail that would satisfy the continuing popular desire for "nearly looking"—but not without error. For years the Capitol guides used to tell the tourists about an extra leg in the row of statesmen declaring independence and an extra toe on one of the Amerinds watching Pocahontas being baptized. All five painters were entirely of their time and obedient to the tradition of seeing things small in the manner of West; not one, not even those among them who had been to Italy, had any idea of the large simplicities functionally necessary for wall decoration on the scale of the Rotunda.

Powell's luck with the politicians continued a while longer. The legislature of his home state, Ohio, commissioned a painting of *Perry's Victory on Lake Erie* [State Capitol, Columbus] for five thousand dollars; he spent so much time over it that he asked fifteen, and got ten. In 1865 the Congress called upon him for an enlarged replica of it, and it was placed on the landing of the east staircase of the Senate wing, one of the outlying regions that are part of the vastness of the Capitol. On the west staircase of that wing hangs James Walker's *Battle of Chapultepec*, executed in the late 'fifties and placed in 1862. Both paintings use the conventionally heroic posings for individual figures, but much of the treatment is nearer than the Rotunda pictures to the naturalism which had already been begun in the anecdotal painting of the time. It is of course only a coincidence that both pictures should have presented similar problems in design; but the difficulties of water level in the one and the flat Mexican plain in the other were met in differing ways. Powell found no real solution at all; he resorted to gigantic close-ups. Walker simply filled the plain with a horde of gesticulating figures and left the upper part rather finely spacious with nothing but the distantly towering fortress and a cloudy sky; and he avoided the worst difficulties of design in that area by shaping the frame into an enormous shallow arch. But again these works emphasize the fact that swollen easel pictures do not decorate.

All the mid-century painters chosen to adorn the Capitol were professional mediocrities, but even in mediocrity there are degrees, and in his contribution Emanuel Leutze almost succeeded in breaking the Capitol precedents. His picture was not actually executed until the years 1861 to 1863, but the painter was of the mid-century in his career and spirit both; and in these respects he deserves some attention independently of his climactic effort. His three preliminary years of training in this country did nothing to make his painting American in character, for he had been born in Germany and when he had once decided upon painting as a career, he gravitated to Germany as naturally as English-born Sully had been attracted to England. Going to Düsseldorf, Leutze not only acquired the distinctive technique of that school but also spent most of his life there and in turn became one of its most famous teachers. His prominence there coincided with the opening of a market here for Düsseldorf pictures, and his large history pieces were easily sold here without his having to live here. He nevertheless made himself a permanent figure in the history of American painting by the impact upon the popular consciousness of his *Washington Crossing the Delaware* [Metropolitan Museum, New York]. The first version remained in Germany, and it was the second, improved by the figures being given more space around them, which made the sensation in this country. Among the Americans most impressed was Henry James, then about ten years old; in recollecting the New York of his boyhood, he made a vivid passage out of the way in which, under the flaring gaslight, details like the strands of rope stood out as insistently as the hero himself stood up. James was speaking with the affectionate derision which many Americans come to feel for their youthful environment; and in singling out those two elements in the picture he spotted the reasons why the Düsseldorf technique was received with such enthusiasm and why this painting was the first major addition to the mythology of George Washington since Stuart's Athenaeum portrait. Later, much ridicule was heaped upon Leutze's canvas because of the incongruity between the ice floes and the standees in the heavily loaded boat, but that was to miss the point not only of the picture but also of a whole age. The mid-century wanted its painting in naturalistic terms in order to marvel at the "likeness" of everything; but even more it wanted its emotions stirred.

Probably the exhibition of the *Crossing* in the Capitol in 1852 impressed the members of Congress as much as the general public, for a few years later Leutze was commissioned to place a painting on the west stairway of the House wing: *Westward the Course of Empire Takes Its Way* [plate 64]. The ambitious theme of crossing the Rocky Mountains caused Leutze to make a trip to the region in search of the literal kind of accuracy then necessary to every history picture; maybe the trip did something to reassure Leutze himself, but the composite results must be judged in terms of the theater. Action and gesture in the people are also theatrical in conformity to the current conventions of history painting; and the harsh emphasis upon all the foreground detail of pack-rolls and Kentucky rifles and rope seems to be an ultimate in the Düsseldorfian. This is more noticeable nowadays because the picture is no gigantic easel painting in oil, as the others are, but stereochromy: a process of applying water color directly to the plaster and preserving the original intensity of tints by water glass. Leutze made a special trip back to Germany to learn the method thoroughly; and James Jackson Jarves, one of the most perceptive among American nineteenth-century writers on art, soon deplored Leutze's technical success at making permanent his raw brilliance of color and confused design. Certainly the picture is decidedly of the Capitol company in its lack of simplicity, and it even has some additional faults of proportion—note the exceptionally obvious instance of the man in the coonskin cap bending forward over the seated woman near the center. Yet it is possible, without admiring the results, to admire the spirit in which the results were attained. Leutze was himself excited enough

64. THE COURSE OF EMPIRE *by* EMANUEL LEUTZE *On the west staircase, House Wing, United States Capitol.*

to infuse the whole wall with visual excitement. It may be guessed that this impression of the painter's own state of mind comes from the directness of the process he chose; in it he could not indulge in the second thoughts and repaintings that are possible in oils, which had much to do with the frigidity of the Rotunda pictures. True, Leutze didn't know when to stop; and perhaps in fear lest the human gestures would not say enough, he made the wagons and the mountains gesticulate also. It is the inevitable penalty of a lesser nature trying to pump up more emotion than he is capable of feeling; but his willingness to risk bathos is more worthy of respect than the other Capitol painters' preoccupation with the current artistic respectability. They may be left in the damnation of Joubert's verdict: "Mediocrity is excellence to the mediocre."

Plenty of painters whose pictures were not chosen for the Capitol were also busying themselves with patriotic themes. Junius Brutus Stearns idealized George Washington in roles of Soldier, Farmer, and the like. Dennis Malone Carter showed him as host at a reception, or congratulating Molly Pitcher for her cannon-fire at Monmouth. Peter Frederick Rothermel, depicting Patrick Henry's speech or the landing of the Pilgrims with equal facility, rendered them in a technique fresh from current European exhibitions. Thomas Prichard Rossiter, without the continental fluency, produced a similar quantity of prosaic groups; his awkwardness served him ill in the distantly historical subjects but better in those of his own time, such as *A Studio Reception, Paris, 1841* [Albany Institute]—a group portrait of the American painters who happened to be in Paris at the time. No doubt they were in that city then, but they were not all in the room together posing as Rossiter shows them, and his literal mind compelled him to leave them stiffly apart, as separate in the picture as they were when he made his studies for combining into the picture. This compositeness he later carried to absurd lengths, collecting likenesses of the leading New York merchants (some of them already dead) into one ornately crowded assemblage or showing twenty of his more famous acquaintances posing for dear life in an impossible outdoor picnic. Two of his religious paintings, now lost, formed "The Great Moral Exhibition" that visited Milwaukee in 1851.

However, it was the long-lived Daniel Huntington who, in the first half of his life, best embodied the mid-century's pietistic sentimentality. Half a dozen miscellaneous religious subjects met with approval, but his ambitious illustrations to *Pilgrim's Progress* gave him contemporaneous fame. He found it profitable to make replicas of *Mercy's Dream* [Pennsylvania Academy, Philadelphia: Metropolitan Museum, New York: Corcoran Gallery, Washington]—a fact as significant for the taste of the time as Powers' sculptural repetitions of *The Greek Slave*. This earlier phase of Huntington's career included plenty of portraiture; but he always regretted that the market for his religious subjects practically vanished before the Civil War. By that time, too, he had made his principal venture into the patriotic subject, an immense canvas containing sixty-four figures, *Lady Washington's Reception* [Hamilton Club, Brooklyn]; as a large-scale engraving it proved to be one of the most popular framing prints of the postwar period, but through those years Huntington's patrons for paintings insisted almost exclusively on portraits. A few German-born specialists in religious pictures found work in the Roman Catholic churches of several cities; and French-trained Christian Schussele had some success with patriotic subjects while teaching in the school of the Pennsylvania Academy. There is also the curious case of Mark Robert Harrison, working in Fond du Lac, Wisconsin, who had been able to sell pictures in England when he was a student there; to that distant market he shipped out history pictures from the Midwest. But not one of the European-trained painters achieved anything in history painting that can compare with a few by a man from Missouri who had his major training in Philadelphia: George Caleb Bingham. His best work was done before he went to Düsseldorf at forty-five; yet this needs no chauvinistic emphasis in estimating his importance, for the real reason lies in the quality of his mind.

Born in Virginia, Bingham was taken to Missouri at the impressionable age of eight; his desire to paint was apparently wakened in the following year by Chester Harding passing through on his way to paint Daniel Boone. At another meeting seven years later Harding gave him enough instruction for the youth to go ahead on his own and paint portraits which, he afterward said, were mistaken through a window for live people. The likenesses of the early eighteen-thirties show the standardized artisan hardness which prevailed among the lesser men throughout the country, but there is a degree of positiveness in the drawing which was to be Bingham's trait to the end. In 1837 he briefly attended the art school of the Pennsylvania Academy and, after several years of portrait work in Washington, went back to Missouri in the middle 'forties and commenced his series of canvases depicting what he later termed "our social and political characteristics." He was also very active in politics and held public office; his success as a painter, with the incentive to ever more ambitious works, came largely from the Art-Union and art dealers reproducing his pictures as engravings and lithographs.

Bingham's own phrase may be taken as an indication of his prevailing attitude of mind: that of a conscious social historian. His objectivity and his encyclopedic intention in his major pictures are reasons for regarding him, rather than all the other men considered in this section, as the true history painter of the mid-century. He approached his maturest works through a series of pictures which, for the seeming casualness and usualness of their subjects, are called anecdotal; but in comparison to the visual anecdotes of a painter like Mount, they have a

65. RAFTSMEN PLAYING CARDS *by* GEORGE CALEB BINGHAM *Courtesy of City Art Museum, St. Louis.*

lesser degree of intimacy and warmth. A strain of poetry in Bingham was manifested in the *Fur Traders Descending the Missouri* [1845: Metropolitan Museum, New York]; but man and boy and fox in the shallow and burdened boat remain unaware of what the painter sees beyond and above them: an immensity of misted riverbank and sky too great for human loneliness. It was the now lost first version of *The Jolly Flatboatmen* which earned Bingham his first fame by being engraved for Art-Union members in 1847; and he immediately followed out that vein with more pictures of river life. In the *Raftsmen Playing Cards* [c. 1847–1850: plate 65] the scenery begins to diminish in emotional importance and the figures to increase; and in the treatment of the figures relative lack of intimacy and warmth emerges into the positive traits of ample design and emotional remoteness. These raftsmen's absorption in their game is accentuated by the visual pyramid in which they are enclosed; their unawareness of both the river and the painter isolates them in an existence which is being impersonally observed. The river setting occurred a few more times but disappeared from the pictures in which Bingham turned to the theme of politics as the main community activity.

The Verdict of the People [1855: plate 66] is the climax of that theme, and of Bingham's painting skill as well: the last picture exhibited before going to Europe in 1856 for three years. His work during and after his stay in Düsseldorf is disregarded in this estimate; his technique was not improved, even his portraits being affected by photography, and his attitude became infected with sentimentality. If done after his return, a landscape or two may be excepted; but in any case *The Verdict of the People* remains the culmination of his career. Men and boys, again, throng the courthouse steps and pack the side street leading back into an attractive town vista; the small group of women as onlookers from a balcony constitute the only appearance of "the sex" in all his river-life and political series, but two women are prominent in the *Daniel Boone Coming Through Cumberland Gap* [1851: Washington University, St. Louis]. This subject was of course specially suited for a western painter even if the dead trees and rocks seem pretty close to the Hudson River; for one thing, it enabled him to show the pioneer party approaching, where an easterner would have naturally seen them—departing! Bingham's picture of election results, despite its objective spirit, is so intimately rendered in details of place and time that it requires an effort of the mind to realize how completely academic and traditional is his technique all through. It affords a vivid instance of how the life of art depends upon each generation's learning from the past and using that knowledge in its own way. Bingham's mind was not creative in the most important degree because he did not add to the expressive capacity of his medium itself; he did not better the instrument for those who would use it after him. But painters capable of that are very few indeed. Bingham went much beyond the other history painters of his day, for their minds were so completely absorbed in the acquisition of the craft that they had nothing left over either for discovering fresh subjects or for seeing old subjects freshly. Bingham did not command the studio fluency of Leutze, for instance, but the skill he did acquire he used in a way to enhance the human theme; his was a mind fortunately fitted to its historic moment and equipped with a technique adequate to his purpose.

It is known that Bingham built up his compositions in the studio from separately made drawings, and the self-contained definiteness of every closely-seen figure proves it; yet all the emphatic detail is successfully subordinated to the whole. He studied his scenes and his people with an eye well guided by the compositional devices of European masters; the broad triangulation of the massed lights and darks, both across the frontal plane and in depth, is as classic in spirit as a picture by Poussin. Bingham's study must of course have been with the help of engravings, and this, together with the inadequacy of his teachers, accounts for the limitations of his coloristic ideas; a few reds and greens, with transitional yellows and browns, sufficed for his usually harsh and often hot color schemes. Even there, however, he attained harmony of a sort, that and the harmony of design being strictly visual in character. Perhaps equally remarkable is the degree of narrative unity achieved out of his separate studies; the acts are all individual, but each has an appropriateness to the occasion which results in a collective life.

The foundation of everything else in Bingham's art is drawing. It was vigorous but obvious. Its greatest merit consisted in giving the larger aspects of form first, even though it neglected the finer points of modulation; it rendered the simplified mass and weight of the coarse-textured and relatively heavy clothes which, from long use and little pressing, had acquired character in their own right. The draftsmanship, like the color, suited a mind that had no patience with uncertainties and no use for subtleties. It was a mind satisfied to pronounce after fifty years of painting:

I have no hesitation in affirming that any man who does not regard imitation of nature as the great essential quality of Art will never make an artist.

True, Bingham disclaimed the effort to deceive the eye and said that imitation should derive from the image in the mind; but both the idea and the positiveness of its assertion arise from the fact that his instrument of draftsmanship was one of formula whose commonness of texture and edging was redeemed by its robustness. Its intention, adequately achieved, was documentation. It sought the obvious differences on the surface—wrinkles in costume and countenance, the hearty laugh or the vigorous gesture; it did not pause for the secrets of personality.

66. THE VERDICT OF THE PEOPLE *by* GEORGE CALEB BINGHAM *Courtesy of The Boatmen's National Bank of St. Louis.*

When the documentation was assembled, it became evident that the goal was not the individual but the type; the collection of types gave a cyclopedia of humanity then and there.

For these history pictures have no single hero, no extraordinary occurrence, for their themes. They celebrate, not Washington, but men who need no names; no rendezvous with destiny, but the recurrent rhythms of common life. Appropriately, too, there is no irregularity of emphasis in the painter's mind; the pressure of interest is uniform, equal with the fat man laughing or with the sodden drunk. Nowhere does Bingham give any hint that he could respond in his own art to the flaring imaginativeness which transformed Davy Crockett into a demi-god and synthesized a hundred flatboatmen into Mike Fink. Bingham the historian sought the typical in men, the characteristic in events, the comprehensive in rendering; he was intellectually keen and emotionally cool, hearty and straightforward and strong.

59. Mid-century anecdote

William Sidney Mount: 1807–1868
William Ranney: 1813–1857
Tompkins Harrison Matteson: 1813–
  1884

Edward Troye: 1808–1874
William Holbrook Beard: 1824–1900
James Henry Beard: 1812–1893
David Gilmor Blythe: 1815–1865

From the exaggerated patrioteering and pietistic sentimentalism which dominated the mid-century's conception of history painting, the anecdotal painting marked a refreshing change. An unaffected liking for the human situation in paint is intrinsically more admirable than the most earnest prostrations before pictorial solemnity because it is more free from the strain of cultural self-consciousness; response to the anecdote is likely to be uncomplicated by the individual's idea of what others expect him to admire. Peculiarly a pleasure to the middle-class mind, anecdotal painting was historically notable in seventeenth-century Holland; its literary counterpart, the novel, became similarly prominent in eighteenth-century England. In the mid-century here the middle class at length worked free from the cultural prison of its colonial aristocratic pretensions and its economic stringency during the Federal Era; it reached a position where it could gratify its actual tastes as never before. The initial popularity of novels was for reprinted English ones, but the anecdotal pictures were painted here; and the spread of both meant that the secular character of ordinary living was at last beginning to receive its natural expression in art. So far from marking any corruption of a taste previously more noble or refined, both forms are the permanently normal constituents of artistic experience for the middle class.

This generation of buyers were not unacquainted with pictures, but they certainly found anecdote as much of a novelty as landscape. The vocabulary of appreciation was still inadequately developed; although Edgar Allan Poe was soon to initiate a greater precision in literary criticism, and even to make some intelligent incidental remarks about the visual arts, the average commentator in the newspapers and periodicals was no better equipped with suitable words than John Adams had been for praising Copley. Therefore most of what was printed about anecdotal pictures consisted of narrating the human situations with overtones of approval or disapproval, and this usually made the pictures seem more sentimentalized than they were. Pictures by William Sidney Mount, being admirably painted and honestly felt, thus had their permanent merits slighted and even their current appeal misrepresented. The silly verses and boring prose printed about Mount's work may be passed over for one sentence by Charles Lanman, who was himself a painter and wrote periodical criticism which was later collected into *Letters from a Landscape Painter* [1845]. The praise for Mount which Lanman thought most important was this:

. . . His productions are stamped with an entirely American character, and so comically conceived that they always cause the beholder to smile, whatever may be his troubles.

In Holland nearly two hundred and fifty years earlier, another painter, Carel Van Mander, had written about Pieter Bruegel:

. . . Indeed, there are very few works from his hand that the beholder can look at seriously, without laughing. However stiff, serious, and morose one may be, one cannot help laughing, or smiling. . . .

So unchanging is the basic appeal of anecdotal painting for its own ever-changing but repetitive audience.

Mount himself apparently did not feel aggrieved at being considered an entertainer even though he knew his painting was better than his audience realized. His largest audience, indeed, did not see his originals and knew his pictures only as lithographs and engravings. But Mount was singularly at ease in his time, and sincerely said: ". . . never paint for the few, but the many." This was no cheapening of his own talent; on the contrary, he worked hard and with surprising success toward a charm of brushwork which does most to keep his pictures alive after one hundred years. His regard for the audience arose out of his respect for other people as human beings; he did not ask that they be also intellectually sophisticated and esthetically mature. In technique he started from the level of sign painting learned under his brother Henry S. Mount; and William's uninteresting portraits almost all retained some traces of his own early hardness. (The brother between these two in age, Shepard Alonzo Mount, specialized in portraiture with mediocre results.) William was among the first group of students in the newly organized school of the National Academy of Design, drawing from casts and copying paintings; and from this not extensive enlargement of his earlier training he went on to increase his freedom of handling from observation, reading, and experiment. He seems never to have looked beyond what was immediately available for his mental food, and in particular he rejected offers of trips to Europe for study. Along with Bingham and Quidor, he could be cited as proof of Emerson's idea that all a man has to do is to accept his inheritance and environment and go serenely forward in the confidence that life itself will somehow supply him all he needs as he needs it. It is doubtful if that part of Emerson's creed has the universal validity he thought it had, but these three major painters of the mid-century show how workable it was for them.

Emersonian also was the tenor of Mount's counsel written more than twenty years after his first painting lessons: ". . . Every artist should know his own powers best and act accordingly." His independent career began with an act of rejection; in its first two years he painted and exhibited several attempts at history painting, and with an abrupt change to anecdote in 1830 he never swerved thenceforward from that subject-matter, except for a few more portraits. Later on he recorded the change as a general verdict that what had been written about ideality and the grand style could make a man miss the true study of nature, which he chose for himself in truth and soberness. However, his treatment of his anecdotal material underwent much modification. For one thing, he devised a system of freehand figure-drawing and of sketching in oil for placement and for light-and-dark; even if he found his subject ideas in actual incidents he put each picture through this building-up process. In consequence every grouping, indoors or alongside a barn, was tested and retested for its compositional rightness; and it is not surprising if now and then the carefulness impaired the intended casualness. Another point on which he schooled himself through the first few years was the construction of the figure in paint without the tightness of current portraiture and without the artifice of pose in current history painting. *Bargaining for a Horse* [1835: New-York Historical Society, New York], *The Long Story* [1837: Corcoran Gallery, Washington], and *The Painter's Triumph* [1838: Pennsylvania Academy, Philadelphia] embody the first maturity of his art in its fully congenial phase. *Fortune Telling* [1838: New-York Historical Society, New York], in leaving the cheery homeliness of common life for the elegant triviality of a genteel middle class, was an error in judgement which Mount repeated only a few more times. What happened with his later characteristic pictures was a still further loosening of the brushwork, so that the stroke approached the freedom of handwriting, and a more pronounced use of a golden tone in the midst of which his more positive colors were sometimes spotted rather than harmonized. *Landscape with Figures* [1851: Pennsylvania Academy, Philadelphia] is an interesting compositional experiment and while the thin painting is not quite successful atmospherically, its lyricism of feeling makes a welcome break in a habit of rather obvious jollity. Still lovelier because more substantial in its lyricism is the later *Long Island Farmhouses* [after 1854: Metropolitan Museum, New York]; Mount's fidelity to the pale daylight illumination seems so purely objective that his own poetry of perception can be overlooked.

The picture here chosen as representative of Mount's career was done midway in his life: *Eel Spearing at Setauket* [1845: plate 67]. It has the objectivity and

67. EEL SPEARING AT SETAUKET *by* WILLIAM SIDNEY MOUNT *Courtesy of New York State Historical Association, Cooperstown, N.Y.*

the poetry of the later work, but intensified to almost a breathlessness of beauty unique with him and unique in the age. No landscape painter of the time achieved Mount's transparent perfection of tone and no figure painter of the time achieved his daring simplicity. The placing and balancing of the few forms, real and reflected, compose into a thoughtful design. What Henry James wrote about Hawthorne's *House of the Seven Gables* fits Mount's picture better than it does the book:

. . . the summer afternoon is peculiarly still and beautiful; the atmosphere has a delicious warmth, and the long daylight seems to pause and rest. . . .

Physical illumination coincides completely with spiritual perception. Life is poised on the turn of a breath. This is actuality, and it is also reverie.

Here is perhaps the main point about Mount's work: neither in his idyllism nor in his jollity did he falsify his own experience. Hawthorne found this general situation a handicap and lamented

. . . the difficulty of writing a romance about a country in which there is no shadow, no antiquity, no mystery, no picturesque and gloomy wrong, nor anything but a commonplace prosperity, in broad and simple daylight. . . .

Hawthorne found the tragedy he needed for his art, but in the Puritan past, not in his mid-century present. Mount lived in that present with simplicity and directness; his art and his mind together were unconsciously summed up in a sentence he wrote to his friend Lanman:

. . . I sometimes pick up very fine ochres along the country roads, and the grape-vine, when burnt to a coal, makes the best black I know.

It may be that, for their time, Emerson and Mount did right—Emerson in his counsel, Mount in his living. It may be wise to accept one's fate even if it happens to be a pleasant one, and some may achieve art without seeking anything different. If their art in consequence seems limited in scope, that need not impair its genuineness.

Mount, the first native-born painter to succeed in making a career of anecdote, remains so much the best among his many contemporaries that, by himself, he would leave an erroneous impression of the time. From among the others two may be taken to illustrate the average of the greater number of mid-century anecdotists: William Ranney and Tompkins Harrison Matteson. Matteson specialized in episodes from the early life of New England and Ranney, after a few paintings of events in the Revolution, turned with more success to frontier subjects. To judge only by their chosen titles, the two could be classed as painters of history, but their treatment lacked the convention of superficial stateliness that was usual among those here selected as representative painters of the formal historical subject. The more tolerable phase of Matteson's work is illustrated by *A Sculptor's Studio* [1857: Albany Institute], which has the value of recording paraphernalia and people without mawkish sentimentalizing; but he often resorted to melodramatic action in an effort to attract attention, and the insuperable mediocrity of his mind made such exaggerations ring especially hollow. Ranney's quieter casualness with his scouts and pioneers wears better; and it is significant for a kinship of temperament that after Ranney's death, Mount undertook to finish some of his canvases to make them salable.

Edward Troye practised a very specialized variant of anecdote in his portraits of pedigreed horses. Other painters sometimes tried this subject; Alvan Fisher, for example, made probably the earliest attempts and the well known French specialist, Henri de Lattre, made two tours here. But Troye's known works in this kind now number more than three hundred, and many of them are technically admirable, such as the *Self-Portrait* [1852: Yale University Art Gallery]. Portraitized animals are as anecdotal in character as pets in real life, and Troye often accentuates this trait by accessory attendants and landscape backgrounds. Animals in general formed the more comprehensive specialty of William Holbrook Beard, the younger and less capable painter of the two once famous brothers. His treatment of bears and rabbits and monkeys was never for their own sake or interpretive of their specific traits; it was always for satirizing human beings—in his own words, "to take the conceit out of people." Therefore his pictures do not have even the partial justification of literal accuracy, for an essential to his so-called humanization was to make them walk like people and sometimes wear clothes. *Bears on a Bender* [privately owned] and *The March of Silenus* [ownership unknown] were the veriest dregs of a peculiarly repulsive species of presumptive ethical teaching. He excused his incapacity for painting well with a plea that his concern was with the thought rather than with its vehicle. Jarves, in one of his few errors concerning contemporaries, wrote that this Beard's paintings were "jokes vital with merry thought and healthful absurdity"; but it must be remembered that some of them were large, that all of them were framed and hung in rooms furnished on the principle of superfluity. Owners and guests spiritually sluggish with propriety no doubt welcomed an opportunity for humorous small talk, but the supposed moralisms in the pictures now seem a singularly futile justification for such perversions of paint.

James Beard, the older brother, also added to America's store of pictorial trash with his animal subjects; he did not make them tolerable, but he mitigated his offense in two ways—by a technique of hard drawing and glossy pigment which rose above fumbling and by confining the sentimentality to the expressions. That mistreatment of domestic animals seems to have been for the most part

68. THE LONG BILL   *by* JAMES HENRY BEARD
Courtesy of Cincinnati Art Museum.

a late phase of his total work, and may be regretted as just one more of those commercializations of skill so common in all occidental art of the nineteenth century. An earlier phase of straight anecdote is represented by *The Long Bill* [plate 68], wherein a moderate technical talent as yet only partially developed was still capable of pictorial presentation of anecdote. The awkward drawing and imperfect control of illumination have their own appropriateness to the mid-century Midwest; and perhaps the content of genial humor may be taken in the philosophic sense attributed to it by the French thinker, Henri Bergson— as a sign of civilization's becoming settled. Unquestionably the settledness was a necessity for domesticating the art of painting, and whatever truth there may be in Bergson's idea as applied to the Midwest must depend upon the mildness of the humor; for the wild imaginings in the tall tales of the two generations preceding James Beard are raucously uncivilized in their untamed poetry of idea. When Harriet Martineau and her ear trumpet visited Cincinnati, the young James Beard's humorous pictures of children seemed to her almost worthy of Wilkie, although she thought the earlier portrait work very bad; and with her usual perceptiveness she noted his self-admiration and his contempt for Boston, acquired during a stay of only two weeks. Infallible indications of provincialism in mind, his opinions shed light upon his technique in *The Long Bill* and possibly also upon his later willingness to waste a better technique upon sentimentalisms. This comment may be applied also to Sir Edwin Landseer and the dear queen who admired his noble stags, for provincialism is a temporal as well as a geographical phenomenon in culture.

An Ohio-born man working in Pennsylvania, David Gilmor Blythe, was unique in his time for often striking a note of intensely felt satire. In his environment it might appear that his kinship was with the careless savagery so prominent in the tall tales from the backwoods and the great rivers. But his subjects are all obviously of town and city, and a consideration of their spirit will suggest a parallel with such eastern literary caricatures as Thomas Chandler Haliburton's Sam Slick. Sam Slick in London, engaged in an imaginary dialogue with Copley called back to life for the occasion, asks him to paint a fashionable party "as large as life, and twice as nateral," but only as a prelude to an apostrophe:

. . . paint me nateral, I beseech you; for I tell you now, as I told you before, and ever shall say, there is nothin' worth havin' or knowin', or hearin', or readin', or seein', or tastin', or smellin', or feelin', and above all and more than all, nothin' worth affectionin' but *Natur*.

The feeling in the quotation was inflated into the obvious rhythms in much the same way that Blythe depicted a braying mule in *Dry Goods and Notions*

[Duquesne Club, Pittsburgh]—a mule which backs violently away from a hoop-skirted female stepping out of the store with the exaggeration of fine manners often practised in small places where there are so few to set off one's own superiority. Both Haliburton and Blythe wanted their nature "twice as nateral."

Blythe was a picturesque personality, starting with hard portraits on the artisan level and trying his hand at a panorama on rollers offered as a theatrical entertainment; after showing in some Pennsylvania and Maryland towns, the scheme went bankrupt and the long canvas was cut up into sections to serve as theater backdrops. He carved an eight-foot wooden statue of Lafayette [1847–1848: Fort Necessity Museum, Pennsylvania] which is large in feeling as well as in size because its simplified modeling displays an instinctive recognition for the material. He wrote a lot of rhymes and had a happy marriage for one year before his wife died of typhoid. Grief and alcoholism, with frustration and misanthropy following, sharpened his perception of comic ugliness by shutting him off from others into a solitude of mind which he both hated and loved. Yet such pictures as *The Pittsburgh Horse Market* [privately owned] and *January Bills* [Garvan Collection, Yale University] are no trivial attempts to get even with the world; Blythe's subjective emotional recklessness was projected into pictorial objectiveness. *Post Office* [c. 1863: plate 69] is motivated as caricature, though it lacks the bitterness Blythe sometimes showed—and also the more precise drawing that accompanied the more intense feeling. However, this relatively genial relish of human absurdity and knavery was artistically validated by a painter's conception of light-and-dark; and the rather slapdash technique maintained a consistency of rapid emphasis which came from a mind using nature only as a point of departure. Blythe liked to ridicule human beings by distortion, but his distortion was controlled by pictorial unity.

69. POST OFFICE   *by* DAVID GILMOR BLYTHE
Courtesy of Department of Fine Arts, Carnegie Institute.

60. The mid-century concept of imagination

Henry Peters Gray: 1819–1877
William Page: 1811–1885
Thomas Chambers: act. 1835–1855
John Quidor: 1801–1881

In the eighteen-thirties neither Tocqueville nor Harriet Martineau could discover any imagination in American literature and art; the Frenchman thought that it would not be developed in a democracy, but the Englishwoman thought that it already existed in our commerce and our politics, and that it would extend into art when the state of society allowed the artists to become as distinct a group as the merchants and the politicians. In 1839, after the two travelers' books had appeared in their respective countries, there took place in Boston a retrospective exhibition of forty-seven pictures by Allston. Because the event made cultivated New Englanders think about the "problem" of imagination, a good many people throughout the rest of the country soon became aware of it, for those particular New Englanders habitually did their thinking in print. No doubt it was advantageous to have the question considered at all in a situation where most people were intent upon more concrete things, but the difficulty was that the people who thought most about Allston's pictures found it easiest to soar away from all pictures into intellectual abstractions. They were actually uncomfortable with paintings because they could not regard sensuous experience as good in itself and were always seeking to transcend it into the pure idea. Other intelligent Americans might not feel the transcendental urge, but they were equally inexperienced in the language of pigment; and those who had been to Europe, presuming that they had the greater right to pronounce judgement, were most likely to admire pictures here which reminded them of pictures there.

To be sure, reminiscent pictures were exactly what many painters intended to paint; and it was through reminiscence that Henry Peters Gray acquired his reputation for doing imaginative work—the "sweet autumnal spell" praised by Tuckerman. *Greek Lovers* [1846: Metropolitan Museum, New York] or *The Judgement of Paris* [1861; Corcoran Gallery, Washington] could make almost anybody think of Titian, perhaps even of what had been merely written about Titian; Gray and his admirers together thought that, since Titian had in general opinion supremely exemplified imaginative color, an effort after Titianesque color would of itself achieve imaginativeness. It was somewhat like Longfellow's use of European material for his early poetry; to him and his admirers together, the old-world stories seemed warranted as eighteen-carat culture simply by their point of origin. Thoreau might have been describing that phase of Longfellow, and equally Gray's whole production, when he wrote: "Much of our poetry has the very best manners, but no character." However, artistic good manners, even though artificially assumed, then had a temporary value as practised in this country. Unfortunately, those who assumed the manners assumed further that the manners were culture itself, whereas they were only a stage on the way to culture, like the social good manners of the first privileged colonials. The transplanted themes of Longfellow and the transplanted designs of Gray were elements in a cultural mulch enriching the soil for more vital poems and pictures.

In the personality of William Page there seems to have been a strain of imagination, but the degree to which it infused his art remains difficult to assess. Much of it has been lost through peeling and fading colors. Most of the examples that do remain in the museums are portraits; though they have traces of poetry beyond the habit of his contemporaries, they are insufficient to validate imaginativeness. Along with his experiments in technical procedure, Page tried several styles, ranging from a Flemish exactness of detail to a Venetian glow of tone. His professional variability was matched by his actions. After an early and brief episode in a lawyer's office, he turned to art long enough to learn from Morse and the drawing-school of the National Academy, where he received a silver medal in the first anniversary exhibit. There followed a two-year interlude of ministerial study at Andover Theological Seminary before he returned permanently to painting. In religion he changed from Presbyterianism to Swedenborgianism, and was the instrument through whom Inness was stabilized in the latter belief. And lastly, to anticipate a little more, he divorced two wives before he found lasting happiness with a third.

All this may be adequate proof of imagination in the man, but justifies a closer look at the sources for the praise of his painting. The most quotable bit consists of two lines from Lowell's A Fable for Critics: two lines out of the many in which Apollo counsels Americans:

> Be true to yourselves and this new nineteenth age,
> As a statue by Powers, or a picture by Page.

Lowell's citation of Powers practically obliterates the value of his intended praise of Page; the couplet is just one more instance of the professional writer's usual failure to comprehend any language except that of words. Henry James,

70. THE YOUNG MERCHANTS *by* WILLIAM PAGE
Courtesy of The Pennsylvania Academy of the Fine Arts.

whose greatness draws so much from his altogether exceptional understanding of painting and architecture, has testified to the desiccated intellectualism of Emerson's response to painting; and Emerson thought Page a great painter. There must be some significance in the fact that those who most admired Page were least able to judge painting. If they praised the pictures because they read into the work the qualities they discerned in the man, that would be an easy mistake for a literary mind.

The minor portrait sculptor, William R. O'Donovan, undertook to defend Page's *Venus* by admitting it was sensuous but claiming that the sensuousness was "arrived at through the intellect rather than through the feelings." As an attempted critical discrimination the statement raises psychological difficulties by its loose phrasing, and it is quoted merely because it seems to be unconscious testimony from a practising artist that the impression of Page's quality was actually made more by his mind than by his work. Jarves, a competent witness, said straight out that as a painter Page theorized too much. The figure emerging from the evidence is of a fluent and highly theoretical talker, capable of reaching the minds of writers with ideas about art and giving them the illusion that they could understand painting without paying too much attention to either the material or the process. In his effect upon others Page seems to have gone even beyond Allston, and it might be fairly said that Page assumed or was handed the mantle of "greatness" which Allston had worn.

As with Allston, too, some of his less ambitious work does most to make him worth knowing as a painter. *The Young Merchants* [before 1844: plate 70] was done before his first trip to Europe; it has several serious flaws, but it can also still give pleasure by its use of pigment. The spontaneity of the brushwork is attractive enough at important points to outweigh its carelessness at others. The picture also in places offers a nice equivalent in paint for light; it is not light in the naturalistic sense, but it is a complicated play of high lights across a variety of shapes which makes an active pattern for the eyes. There is a striking defect of figure construction in the girl's right arm as it disappears behind the boy's head and re-appears on the other side. Yet the several forms entering into the design are interestingly composed. Perhaps most noticeable of all is the variety of the textures here given. Like the light, they lack naturalistic verisimilitude; Page seems to be using pigment for its own sake, as many later painters have done, and exploring a succession of textural transitions from one contrast to another—something like a *collage* restrained within the range of pigment. It would be rash to say that Page could not do better; but, if he were capable of manifesting an imaginativeness that could endure, it would be by some development from this basis of handling paint. It is indeed the rarity of this technical virtue among the mid-century men of the studio that perhaps justifies so much attention to a picture which was a very minor item in relation to Page's total effort and his own time's estimate of his quality.

For the cultural elite of that age would not have considered that the foregoing description of Page's picture had any bearing upon the high mission of art. Nor would they have accepted a criticism which could turn aside from the noble subject of the academic men and find pleasure in what they deprecated as coarse handling. For them Thomas Chambers was just a sign painter; and if he ever tried to get into their exhibitions he apparently did not succeed. His record at present consists only of the appearance of his name in New York and Boston directories through about fifteen years and about two dozen pictures so far identified. These are river landscapes, harbor views, and marines; and a few of them are either certainly or probably adapted from prints. But the designs go much beyond any prints in energy of conception and impetuousness of execution; they also possess a remarkable brilliance of color achieved through a bold reliance upon contrasts in hues instead of harmonies of tone. *Looking North to Kingston* [plate 71] is one of the quieter designs, yet even in it there is plenty of activity for the eyes. There is a positive and compelling rhythm to everything; the spotting of the darks as well as of the lights, the repetition of converging diagonals, the recession of similar shapes—all steadied by the high-keyed diminishing form of the steeple rising in front of foliage and mountainside. The rhythmic working of his mind extended even into the brush strokes, which repeat and repeat with little or no regard for naturalistic surfaces but with an evident pleasure in the way their large dottings and blunt curvings activate large areas of the picture surface. This mental stylization is the only element of control over a tendency to lavishness; and the stylization would seem to be as clearly derived from sign painting as that of Edward Hicks.

With John Quidor, as well as with Chambers, the brush stroke is the principal means by which the picture is constructed, and it has equally little reference to the currently prevailing concept of appearances. And if the National Academy as the embodiment of the time's official concept may have simply not known about Chambers, there are indications that the organization intentionally snubbed Quidor because of the unorthodox character of his art. It may have started back when Inman and he were fellow workers in the studio of Jarvis; but in 1828, when Quidor was showing three pictures at the National Academy, John H. I. Browere, a maker of masks in plaster who had not been taken into the Academy as a sculptor, made a public attack on Morse, Ingham, and Inman for their control of the organization; in the course of his letter, Browere pitted Quidor against Inman as the better painter. Nine years then passed without Quidor's being represented in an Academy show. Cummings, in his *Annals,* makes a later reference to Quidor's renting a room in the Academy

71. LOOKING NORTH TO KINGSTON *by* THOMAS CHAMBERS *Courtesy of Smith College Museum of Art.*

building for the separate exhibition of some large religious paintings; and even this item in his chronicle seems shadowed by some distaste. Quidor lived a long life by means of his painting, but it mostly took the form of shop work: parade banners, fire-engine decorations, and the like. Sixteen paintings now lost are documented as to title; and eighteen are in existence which fall into two chronological groups on either side of a sixteen-year interval without dated pictures.

The last three are uncharacteristic and unimportant in themselves; one takes a New Testament subject and one is from *Don Quixote;* one subject concerns Cooper's character Leatherstocking and twelve are from Irving's stories of Dutch New York. The pictures were not executed as direct illustrations of the books, as were the designs of Darley; and while a knowledge of the narrated incidents helps in the factual comprehension of what is going on in the pictures, it is importantly true that Quidor was not an illustrator. At least a half-dozen among the known works have a life of their own so strong that they do not even need titles to be enjoyed, and another half-dozen are re-creations of the words in independent pictorial terms. Quidor's mind was so emphatically that of a painter that it made little difference where he found his material. For him books were only a starting-point for a subjective play of mind in which each set of images gradually or suddenly assumed a pictorial character infused by a mood sufficiently definite to give every successful picture its own degree of individuality. The Irving who wrote the tales and the Knickerbocker *History* was consistently himself in all his early writing; such changes of mood from the comedy of burlesque to the eeriness of the supernatural are kept within the limits of a bland style about equidistant from the full romanticism of De Quincey and the neo-classicism of Addison. But Quidor's transformation of Irving's material embodies each mood with much more intensity, with the consequence that the emotional range and power of the pictures surpasses their source. *The Wall Street Gate* [1833: privately owned] has a rococo play of slender forms but lightly accented in the rich over-all texture of diffused pigment; *Peter Stuyvesant's Journey up the Hudson River* [1866: privately owned], with its shapes of boat and sails making the design out of fewer and larger forms, pushes the world of fancy still closer to dreamland. *Anthony Van Corlear and Peter Stuyvesant* [1839: The Brook, New York] gives a wild gyration of forms anchored to the two principal figures drawn with such exaggerated solidity that they become a burlesque of solidity itself. *The Money Diggers* [1832: privately owned] unites burlesque and fright into a melodramatic strength of light-and-dark which leaves Irving behind and rushes upon the self-induced shudder of Poe.

Wolfert's Will [1856: plate 72] is in mood betwixt and between, at one moment seeming unmixed burlesque and at another the beginning of terror. In its treatment of form and space it comes perhaps nearest of all to appearances; its approximation to bed curtains and Wolfert's burly body and other physical details is so much closer than Quidor's other work that in comparison it might almost be called naturalistic. But the optical naturalism is only seeming, after all, because the slanting straight lines and the flowing curved lines and the artfully managed lights and darks together form one vision of a mind freed from the necessity of referring the sight back to actual things and capable of communicating its vision by a brush stroke working at all points at once. The mind conceived and the vision appeared. It has been suggested that Quidor's fancy and imagination—which are probably different degrees of the same thing, both of which he had—were nurtured on prints; but prints cannot teach brushwork, and brushwork is the sole instrument of realization for Quidor's ideas. A more likely source for Quidor's handling, though one that is perhaps forever beyond convincing documentation, is the scene painting of his time. The calligraphic stroke is not the only means in painting of conveying imagination, but it is especially well suited to expressing an imaginativeness which is effected less by solid forms than by empty space.

72. WOLFERT'S WILL *by* JOHN QUIDOR *Courtesy of Brooklyn Museum.*

61. Mid-century still-life

Anna Claypoole Peale: 1791–1878
Margaretta Angelica Peale: 1795–1882
Sarah Miriam Peale: 1800–1885
Rubens Peale: 1784–1865
John F. Francis: 1810–1885

One way of imagination in paint strongly contrasting to the way of Quidor had been that of Raphaelle Peale in still-life—almost hiding the imaginativeness within a special kind of optical exactitude. No later Peale ever made such a deep response to the visible world or ever said anything so important. His uncle James Peale had a dryer kind of exactness which could never be suspected of covering any spiritual depths, and this more accessible manner was continued into mid-century still-life by James' three daughters. Though two of them also painted many portraits in miniature and oil, the historical significance of all three consists in their maintaining the continuity of still-life as a species through the mid-century. Separate stylistic analysis is less important than notice of the fact that, although a few examples may manifest a mild charm of semi-naïvety, their technique is in decadence, not in improvement, from their father's. Actually they were improved upon by an older member of the family, their cousin Rubens Peale, who was born exactly midway in the chain of Charles Willson Peale's seventeen children. After retiring from museum work, Rubens passed his life in the mountains of Pennsylvania on property belonging to another member of the family; there, between his seventy-second and his eighty-first year, he painted a few still-lifes which are a stronger re-affirmation of his uncle's concept than were those by James' own daughters. Rubens Peale's fruit is well painted in a literal way, but a painting of *Two Grouse in Underbrush of Laurel* [1864: Detroit Institute] both renews the family link with such subjects exemplified so long before by Titian Peale and gives a more attractive impression of the aged Rubens' mind.

A number of painters helped to keep still-life painting alive during the mid-century; some were routine practitioners in other forms who may have turned to fruit and flowers as a sort of recreation, and some were so obscure that a still-life or two constitutes all that is known about them now. The only one who is known to have made an important personal contribution to this special form in both quantity and quality is John F. Francis. No doubt this was made possible largely because his pictures were popular with the Art-Union, and its purchase of these still-lifes is another credit to it in the striking enlargement of taste for which it did so much. Francis seems never to have practised the dry linearism of James Peale [plate 40] and most of his pictures are marked by an intimacy with the subject which approaches that of Raphaelle Peale [plate 41]. Here also there is a difference, and it is an important one. Raphaelle Peale's emphasis on textures was all for the sake of the textures as he saw them in the objects; Francis' picture of *Still-Life* [1866: plate 73] differentiates textures recognizably enough between glass and biscuit, cheese and cloth, but they are kept within a uniform texture of pigment which constitutes his main interest. This shift of interest gives any painter more freedom of touch. It did not give Francis any deeper perceptiveness into his subject than Raphaelle Peale's; no technique can do that for anybody. But it did enable him to rely more openly upon the physical nature of paint for appealing to the eye; and since the painter's explorations are sometimes followed by the comprehension of the public, this advance in painterliness was important as pointing the way to more general gains later on. It was also even more important because by means of it Francis himself made some pictures of a modest permanent charm.

73. STILL–LIFE *by* JOHN F. FRANCIS *Courtesy of The Art Museum, Princeton University.*

62. Painters working for reproduction

Robert Havell: 1793–1878
John William Hill: 1812–1879
William James Bennett: 1787–1844 (work after 1830)
Nicolino V. Calyo: 1799–1884
George Harvey: c. 1800–c. 1878
William Henry Bartlett: 1809–1854

John James Audubon: 1785–1851
Felix Octavius Carr Darley: 1822–1888
Thomas Addison Richards: 1820–1901
Lilly Martin Spencer: 1824–1902
Arthur Fitzwilliam Tait: 1819–1905
George Henry Durrie: 1820–1863

The immense increase of popular interest in painting by the studio professionals which has been stressed all through this account of the mid-century was intimately dependent upon the multiplication and spread of reproductions. Practically every painter whose originals were much sought after by collectors owed most of his general fame to the popularity of reproductions. These might be prints after individual pictures issued by the Art-Union to members or by commercial firms to the general public; they might also be magazine or book illustrations. In any event the money paid either as straight fees or as royalties was almost as important to many painters as their sales to patrons. In such a comprehensive sense almost every painter of the period might be treated as working for reproduction. However, there were many painters whose main or entire endeavor was specifically directed to illustration and print-making. Comparatively few among them actually practised any reproductive process, and a vastly greater part of the work was done by technicians copying the originals. But the originals were technically conditioned by the reproductive process in view, and not all of them are interesting in their own right as paintings. Though the subject of this section is the paintings, and not the reproductions, the most convenient basis for it is given by the reproductive processes, considered largely in terms of the audience which they reached.

All print-making on copper entered into a period of neglect because the soft metal would not yield enough prints for the new mass audience. No longer did the magazines have for frontispieces the timid little landscape etchings of the early Federal Era; and the mezzotint process continued in use largely because its workmen took to using it on steel. Even so, the number of impressions needed for a single issue of a magazine was so great that sometimes four plates from the same painting had to be made; and it was the use of the steel which permitted the large framing prints after Bingham and Huntington and the other history and portrait painters. Better as craft than the mezzotints were the line engravings which featured anecdotal pictures in addition to the other kinds. Both mezzotint and line engraving on steel were likely to find their source material in the oil paintings which formed a part of public and private collections; indeed, one evidence of being a connoisseur of art was to have a collection of such prints for study. Accordingly, the painters most popular in these methods of reproduction are considered where their subject-matter places them in other sections of this book.

With aquatint, however, there occurred a prolongation of the landscape views noted in the Federal Era, and with them more painters who did practically nothing else. Since aquatint uses copper, the number of satisfactory prints from a single plate is limited, though the limits vary with technical factors of biting and printing; in this respect aquatint in the mid-century began to seem, in comparison to the quantity production in the other mediums, aristocratic—an air only re-enforced by increased skill and attractiveness in the work itself. The landscape and city views which were the staple product in aquatint were no longer so dryly topographical as they had been earlier in the century; better craftsmen could get more subtle effects of light and more varied compositions, as well as use larger sizes, and the whole situation was helped by the fact that some among them were painters as well as engravers. One was Robert Havell, whose work in landscape here was done after 1839, when he completed the engraving of Audubon's birds in England; Havell not only continued aquatint here, but painted landscape in both oil and water color. Combining water color and aquatint was John William Hill, son of John Hill the engraver; the second Hill remained largely a man of formula in his water colors, but his aquatints are more pleasing in craft. Hill's specially beautiful aquatint, *New York from Brooklyn Heights* [1837], probably owes much to the reproductive skill of William James Bennett, who continued to paint and also to engrave some of the outstanding plates of this later time. Another among the many from whose originals he worked was Nicolino V. Calyo, a scene painter from Italy, who left many views in gouache and pastel which sometimes charm despite their hastiness of execution and repetitiveness of composition. The most attractive originals from which Bennett made aquatints were by George Harvey; English-born, he made a half-dozen trips back to England after first coming here in 1820, but the subject-matter of his landscape pictures was predominantly American without much modification of his English technique. Such change as did occur was a conscious increase in clarity of light after his realization in the mid-thirties that the atmospheric effects here were markedly different from those in England. Harvey's intention was to have a series of typical effects reproduced in aquatint, but on account of the cost a quartet of the seasons [1841] by Bennett proved all that was feasible. About forty water colors for this project are known [several in the New-York Historical Society, New York], and it would seem that he gained confidence as he went along. Later examples not connected with his mid-century scheme show that he responded to technical developments by which a greater range of contrast was achieved through letting the white paper count for more in high lights. Another Englishman who made four trips here to paint American landscapes was William Henry Bartlett; since his original work was specifically for London publishers, its relevance to American painting remains doubtful; yet the resulting series of plates [1839–1842], with text by the internationally popular American writer, Nathaniel Parker Willis, not only were fine in themselves but also became a source book for pictures painted here by other men.

Bartlett himself is quoted as saying that in the United States "the artist's labour is not *as in Europe,* to embellish and idealize the reality; he finds it difficult *to come up to it."* Most Americans then naturally liked such praise for their landscape, for they felt that praise of American scenery was praise of the people who owned it. They were deluded in the assumption; Europeans at all times have admired American scenery, and it was only to the American people that they condescended. For later Americans who love the English landscape as much as their own, Bartlett's words take a bit of thinking to understand. When he uttered them, Constable had just died and Peter Dewint was still working in water color; such faithful-minded painters did not intend to "embellish and idealize the reality" of the English landscape. Perhaps Bartlett was thinking of Turner's coloristic flamboyance—embellishment indeed: so much so that argument about it among American painters continued for fifty years. But a Turner is simply a Turner; it is not England any more than it is Switzerland, it is not the actuality of Venice any more than is a painting by Claude, whom Turner emulated. However, Bartlett, like the other workers for aquatint, used water color; and ever since the formation in 1805 of a professional association among English water-colorists the tendency among them had been toward brightening and purifying their medium. So the chances are that Bartlett, even though sharing in the tendency, found the sharp clarity of the American atmosphere difficult to cope with after the cloudy skies and misty air of England. But none among the many English-trained water-colorists practising here made a response of adequate technical brilliance—nor any American, either; for none as yet had become aware of the possibilities in the medium.

But in water-color designs for aquatint reproductions there was one innovator, John James Audubon, whose great bird pictures were issued in parts from 1827 through 1838. As a person he was one of the most romantic figures in American history: a birth kept mysterious with overtones of the Lost Dauphin, lonely wanderings through the wilds, passionate pursuit of an idea against difficulties and delays, and eventual success in the best American manner. He put much of this romanticism into his dress and conduct; in England he used it more advantageously than here, for there the seemingly primeval still fascinated the sophisticates. In the years of bird hunting from Pennsylvania to Kentucky and down the Great Valley, Audubon partly supported himself by any kind of painting he could get paid for; the drawings and oil portraits and landscapes thus far attributed to him with a fair degree of certainty may be only a small part of the total. But no such work yet assigned to him by any competent investigator is good enough to give him importance apart from his main endeavor. Even the early bird pictures are awkward and constricted, and the artistic drama of Audubon's career would be a detailed account of his technical and mental development out of such beginnings into the magnificence of his maturity. More than four hundred of his originals [New-York Historical Society, New York], with some of the background plants and landscapes by known assistants, constitute the autobiography of the artist, as his journals are the autobiography of the man; and though the journals give many clues to the artist, the artist gives clues to the still more important theme of artistic creation.

The task which Audubon set himself was to depict every species of North American bird with scientific accuracy and so far as possible on the scale of life. This last determined the size of his water colors and of the book-pages for the first edition in elephant folio; the aim of accuracy determined the technique. The necessity of conveying information in detail about plumage, claws, and the like, took precedence over naturalistic treatment. The light in particular always had to be arbitrary and almost unshadowed; with the *Snowy Owl* this necessity led to an inconsistency between the birds and the night background which is so handsomely handled that the result is artistically dramatic. In pictures of the smaller species, where the greater amount of habitat detail was needed to fill out the sheet, the light on bush or vine had to stay close to arbitrary simplification; but a few low-lying landscapes by assistants have a more specific illumination, with their remoteness usually minimizing the unavoidable contradiction. The larger birds often presented complex problems of design, and in this most of all Audubon showed his power. For he almost never compromised his major aim of information, and often achieved a placing which has artistic finality; in the famous first plate, of the male *Wild Turkey*, the massive shape ascends from left to right with force enough to break the predetermined bounds; the threatened disaster of design is avoided by the sudden turn of the bird's head back into the picture, both intensifying its wildness and retaining the dynamism of its feathered pattern within the arbitrary space. Audubon was one of those in whom external constraints like dry exactitude and uniformity of presentation only intensified the impulse to artistry; in the intended scientific impersonality of his visual encyclopedia he often discovered, as if by the way, the exotic strangeness of romantic art.

Audubon's birds in four volumes of aquatint plates were a costly collector's item; the fact that only about two hundred copies were printed left them inaccessible to the majority. And prosperous Americans were now so numerous that even the harsher and tougher material of steel could not hold up under the wear and tear of quantity production; the illustrations that adorned the magazines of the period were frequently pale and blurred from too much printing from the plates. *Godey's* and *Graham's* were more careful than others; the former even had some of its inserted prints colored by hand, and the latter paid particular attention to painting, with one series after old masters and another after Americans. A few periodicals devoted exclusively to art used some reproductions; but their subscribers were too few to keep them going long. The influence of *The Crayon* was exerted entirely through the printed word. The engraver James Barton Longacre and the portrait painter James Herring united to re-issue an earlier venture with additional plates; their publication of portraits in stipple and line was called *The National Portrait Gallery* [1834–1839]. This combined reproductions of portraits already in existence with others of works specially executed for the series, and though the plates were uneven enough to contain some good pictures, notably one in stipple by Longacre himself and several in line by John Durand, the total effect was dull; it was almost intolerably dull in the later issue of 1856, with still more plates. Durand's experiment *The American Landscape* [1830] was more interesting but not successful enough to be continued. Aside from Audubon's, the most important artistic career achieved by means of reproductions was that of Felix Octavius Carr Darley; his designs for all reproductive mediums and all types of publications, to a total possibly approaching three thousand, give him first place among all American illustrators—for versatility as well as for productivity, and most of all for the illustrator's supreme skill: visualizing appropriately both the physical setting and the psychological situation as described in the author's words. The surviving originals by Darley—in pencil, wash, water color, and oil—display the fluency implied by his quantity production; but when they are not preparatory to specific illustrations, they are likely to be no more than pleasant souvenirs of a great career. The loveliest works to be reproduced were in lithography from his outline drawings for Washington Irving [1848–1849] and for Sylvester Judd's *Margaret* [1856], but his mainstay came from steel engravings which, combined with stereotype plates for the text, formed standard sets of standard authors such as Cooper and Dickens.

Darley's illustrations were among the pictures worthy of being made permanent by steel plates; equally permanent in a material sense but especially temporary in quality were the line engravings and mezzotints that interleaved the
tinkling verse and edifying prose of the gift books. That is a general verdict
not to be upset by any citation of exceptional contributors of poetry like Emerson or even more exceptional pictorial sources like Mount. In the Books of
Beauty, Thomas Buchanan Read and Bayard Taylor and Henry Tuckerman
dwell in genteel communion with Thomas Prichard Rossiter and Daniel Huntington and Henry Inman. It was the plates after these painters, and two
dozen more among their peers, to which the gift annuals mainly owed their
existence. What the poetess Lydia Sigourney called the "luxurious literature"
in these publications was often specially commissioned to be written around
some plates the publisher had already ordered or had got hold of from another
who was through with them. A high proportion of the printed matter came
from newly prominent authoresses like Mrs. Sigourney; Hawthorne, himself a
frequent contributor to the annuals, railed against "a dammed mob of scrib-
bling women." The main audience for *The Token* and *Affection's Gift* and
The Diadem was also composed of women; for them such books were almanacs
of culture, foretelling in rhyme the weather of proper emotions and giving a
pictorial calendar of "die-away" behavior in the simpering of ringleted damsels
and the gestures of maidens gazing afar from turret-tops.

Such silliness seems to have been far less important in the coarsely executed
wood engravings which reached a wider audience through *Gleason's Pictorial,*
published at Boston, and *Frank Leslie's Illustrated Newspaper* and *Harper's
Weekly,* at New York. Topical interest naturally came to dominate the latter
two; but *Harper's,* the monthly, fostered illustrations for historical and travel
material which eventually re-appeared, with additions, in book form. The best
artist making such work a career was Thomas Addison Richards, who wrote his
own text as well as drew his pictures on the wood blocks for the engravers to
cut. The best book from him was *The Romance of American Scenery* [1854];
he also was active as a teacher and an official of the National Academy. The
craft of engraving on wood was improved so rapidly that before the Civil War
an occasional book was produced which is still attractive for the thoughtful
relationship between type and illustration on the same page; but their pictorial
contributions were from painters like Kensett and Matteson who were there
turning aside from their main work.

The vastest audience for reproductive pictures was reached by lithographic
prints—so cheap, even when color was added by hand, that they sold by the million. The business supported a dozen firms, and among them Currier & Ives
retained the service of a half-dozen painters to supply their needs. One painter

not connected with that firm seems to demand more amazement than can well be spared for even a mid-century phenomenon. She was Lilly Martin Spencer, born in England of French parents but living in Ohio by the time she was ten; since her father drew, the little tutelage that was needed by the prodigy probably came from him. More formal instruction was obtained in Cincinnati, where she declined an offer from Nicholas Longworth of a stay in Europe if she would copy old masters for him; after marrying, she lived in New York, then Newark, and finally at Crum Elbow up the Hudson a way, and at this last home a picture gallery was filled with her work. Six children did not keep her from painting pictures and portraits estimated at five hundred; and Parisian-made lithographs from some of the anecdotal paintings sold to the estimated number of a million copies. Her work was popular as reproduced in *Godey's* too; and the explanation is: sentiment in subject, brightness in color, definiteness in drawing—and in each picture a lot of everything. Even the lithographs have all that, and the paintings have it even more intensely. *This Little Pig Went to Market* [1857: Campus Martius Museum, Marietta, Ohio] shows a mother and baby being ostentatiously happy in the midst of an amount of detail which would quickly produce boredom except for the fact that the painter herself was fascinated with it and with her own knack of making it stand out with an extra degree of sharpness. The shiny brilliance of all textures, and in particular the sugary glossiness of what is supposed to be flesh, are amazing. This is that very rare and self-contradictory thing: genteelness that has vitality. It is not the vitality of art—hard drawing and vulgar colors prevent that; but it is a vitality able to do without art in making pictures. The craft alone is filled full with simple human joy.

Currier & Ives, publishing about three subjects a week for fifty years, or more than seven thousand with sales running into uncounted millions, wrote a long and complicated chapter of basic importance in the history of American taste. The prints have received an independent treatment of monumental scope, and discussion here must be confined to their collective significance and their use of the original material supplied by the painter. As subjects the prints included every phase of American life; esthetically they do not in themselves constitute a liberal education, but historically they can contribute a great deal to it. The rapid extension of subject was of course a mark of alertness in the men who controlled the business but even more a convincing documentation of the romantic expansion of curiosity in Americans generally; vicarious experience from this flood of prints did a great deal toward making all the people aware of their country as a whole and of the variety of its activities. The simpering insipidities of moon-faced females or the elegent tailoring of gentlemen loungers might testify to a cheap ideal of existence, and raucous comics out of Darktown and Shantytown might display an equally cheap ideal of comedy; but a rail-road laid ruler-straight toward a remote horizon or a clipper ship battling a tempest like a human hero was an imaginative enlargement of life. Quite as important was the capacity of other subjects to waken recognition of more homely and accessible pleasures: the visual geometry of the new game of base-ball or the interval of strangeness imposed upon the most familiar landscape by new-fallen snow. All this was socially creative by making pictorial experi-ence common in the admirable sense of being shared, yet it must also be noted that the chromolithographic process as then practised was itself technically common; and a technique thus limited can carry taste only a little way toward discrimination.

The nineteenth-century commercial lithograph was among the earliest mani-festations of machine-age art; this, in every phase of its mass beginnings, was impaired by a temporary misunderstanding of the new instrument. The machine itself, since it was not thought of as a piece of art, was often constructed with a cleanness of form determined by efficient functioning; but for the time being everything made by the machine and put out as an artistic production was vul-garized. This was most noticeable in crafts like furniture and silver, in which the long traditions of handicraft were too quickly nullified. Painting was still a craft as well as an art, and its quality was still primarily determined by the minds of the painters and the taste of a comparatively small group of patrons. But the commercial lithograph was in itself a pictorially new thing—as new as machinery itself; and its audience, too, was new to pictorial experience. That is why the millions of cheap prints involved no cheapening of taste; it was not a debasement of something that had been fine, but the appearance of some-thing new which was capable of betterment. Because of its technical limita-tions, the cultural usefulness of the process ended in almost a single genera-tion; but in that short time it brought about immense mass gains toward the comprehension of painting. The retrospect of history only imparts a deeper meaning to a simple statement in one of the later advertisements of Currier & Ives: "Pictures have become a necessity." It may be contended that these par-ticular pictures worked harm by becoming a cheap and passive substitute for the making of pictures by artisans and amateurs; but the change-over to in-dustrialism would have occurred even had there been no lithographs, and it would appear that it was this larger development which temporarily minimized popular painting. The prints did not cause it, but perhaps helped it to happen more quickly.

In no respect did the firm of Currier & Ives more clearly show itself a part of industrialism than in the way it used the products and skills of painters. Those who worked in the establishment itself, the most notable one being Mrs.

Frances Palmer, modified or changed or recombined incoming material wherever that was thought necessary to adapt it for the lithographic stone or to render the subject more salable. In extreme cases the adaptation might involve several hands and sources, so that the end product was assembled rather than created. Most of the artists who sent in material were specialists in subject-matter—Thomas Worth for comics, James E. Butterworth for clipper ships, Scott Leighton for horses. Existing published material was much raided for synthetic designs, such as books on the West and its Amerinds illustrated by Karl Bodmer or George Catlin. In the topical prints—events of immediate news interest, such as the explosion of some well known Mississippi steamboat—still another procedure often occurred: from a verbal account the pictorial one would be put together in the shop out of documentary material on hand adjustable to the subject—and in this way pictures would be composed in the same way as a Virginian portrait executed in England from a written description.

Not all of the pictures purchased by Currier & Ives had to be manipulated before being put on the stone. Some of the painters knew enough about what was needed to make their work right to begin with, and the work of a few had such intrinsic attractiveness for the print buyers that the firm was as faithful to their originals as the process permitted. Arthur Fitzwilliam Tait was nevertheless frequently dissatisfied with the reproductions of his paintings and fancied that the prints interfered with the sale of his original paintings; however, the real trouble may have been the formula which enabled him to depict far-western subjects, dog-and-gun episodes, and fishing catastrophes with the impartial fluency of the studio. The human and animal figures were rendered with considerable positiveness, and the brushwork of the surrounding foliage or grass was feathered out into a vagueness which forced the eye back upon the main forms. It was a mild modification of the current formula for sporting pictures in England, whence Tait had come. The American provincial, George Henry Durrie, seems to be technically quite as repetitious as Tait, but his pictures also give the impression that he had to think out the repetition each time afresh. His landscapes were done only after ten years of portraits which by themselves would have left him a quite ordinary figure; but in turning to the country subject Durrie opened a vein of interest singularly fitted to the age. It approached as near to poetry as an essentially prosaic mind could get, and in doing so it stayed within the emotional range of the average American. Its note was different from that of the Hudson River School. The near-poetry in their work was that of Bryant; its equivalent in Durrie's was akin to Whittier. A typical School picture was Arcadian in effect; Durrie was content to be rustic. His very drawing was more countrified, more blunt; his light was different—less pellucid, more dense; the edges of everything were less sharp and all forms

were a little muffled in somewhat thicker pigment. Most striking fact of all:
it was Durrie, and not the Hudson River men, who discovered the cozy strangeness of farms under snow. It was probably this romanticizing of the familiar
which made the extra-large prints from a few of Durrie's pictures extra-popular
with the public. And the intenser attraction still exerted by these among all the
Currier & Ives prints suggests that even an industrialized art can be most successful if it allows the individuality of the artist to continue strongly into the
product of the machine.

63. Mid-century artisans and amateurs

Sign painting
Ship portraits
Sebastian Heine: act. 1839–1864
T. H. O. P. Burnham: act. 1830–1840
Lewis Miller: 1795–1882
Shaker texts
J. S. Hathaway: act. 1839–1848
William Swain: 1803–1847
Louis Joseph Bahin: act. 1850
Mrs. Stephen Rumble: act. 1850
Monochromatic drawings
Mourning pieces

James Sanford Ellsworth: 1802–1873
Josiah Brown King: 1831–1888
Joseph H. Davis: act. 1835–1840
I. Bradley: act. 1830–1840
Joseph H. Hidley: 1830–1872
Anon.: *The Quilting Party*, 1840–1850
  The Runaway Horse, c. 1850
Edward Hicks: 1780–1849
Joseph W. Stock: 1815–1855
James Bard: 1815–1897
William Matthew Prior: 1806–1873
Rufus Porter: 1792–1884

Despite the impending disaster which was to be facilitated by the industrialized picturemaking of commercial lithography, artisan and amateur painting during the mid-century attained its most important expression in both quantity and quality. The quantity was much greater than at any earlier time and although the instances of quality may not have become more numerous in proportion, they do seem to have risen higher above the average than the better work of the Federal Era had done. Once more the most important thing was the directness with which this picturemaking came out of and fed back into the daily living of the largest audience in the period.

The execution of pictorial signs decreased markedly in the larger cities. The directly operative cause was restrictive legislation, which was in turn ostensibly based upon supposed dangers for pedestrians; but what did most to allow such a trend was increased literacy. As early as 1830 at least one pictorial sign was kept inside a tobacco shop and could be seen only through a window; it was of three men who were explained by a subjoined rhyme:

> We three brothers be
>   In one cause;
> Tom puffs, Bill snuffs,
>   And I chaws.

Perhaps an attempt to get around the difficulty of signs that projected too far can be inferred from the notation by a local antiquarian in Philadelphia that signs which read perpendicularly were a novelty in 1856.

But if sign-making itself decreased, the sign painters' general business in other ways increased greatly. For a long time in cities fire companies were private undertakings and did all they could to attract business in the form of subscriptions to their services. One of the most effective ways was to maintain their outfits spick-and-span, to dress their engines with bright colors and striking pictorial decorations, usually having some direct connection of idea or symbol with the name of the engine or the company. Woodside working into this period devised some of them, and for years, it was said, Quidor's living came mainly from such productions.

Horse-drawn public coaches were fast replaced by railroads in the mid-century, but for the painters the change meant only more business of the same sort. It was indeed a very natural transition, for at first a coach body was sometimes mounted on a flatcar as the handiest means of giving the passengers seats, and perhaps so gradual a change reassured those who were fearful of the new monster of speed. At any rate, the earliest railroad coaches were built in direct imitation of the driving-coach form; and with the form the habit of decoration continued. As the shape and size of the railroad coaches were altered to make room for more people, the painters moved inside for their most complex work; and the brilliance of the exterior decoration was concentrated upon the engine.

The canal boats made some play with decoration, too, but such limited and crowded conveyances seem not to have given adequate opportunity for picture-making in the splurging and flamboyant way which Americans liked. The most striking use of pictorial decoration on the water occurred on the Hudson River boats and the Mississippi paddle-wheels. But for Americans all methods of travel were associated with bright colors and gay pictures; these had a pulling power then just as streamlining does now. Pictorialism was not yet definitely associated with ocean travel, whether by sail or by steam; but there was a tremendous amount of making portraits of commercial sailing ships and whalers —for owners and captains and families who lived in the home ports. The pictures were painted in every important harbor around the world where the vessels called; and wherever they were done, the results showed considerable degree of technical similarity. It was not thought of as a widespread and coherent style because the pictures themselves did not come within the purview of the formal art criticism of the day; but it actually was an international artisan manner—so much so that even the Chinese working for the Americans trading in their ports consciously adapted an oriental technique to the occidental habit of seeing. Everywhere the manner was essentially the artisan's way of satisfying a taste for cheapness and exactness; the sailor demanded accuracy about what he knew, and for him accuracy also meant finding the detail by "nearly looking."

74. SOUTHWEST PORTION OF THE PUBLIC SQUARE, CLEVELAND *by* SEBASTIAN HEINE *Courtesy of The Western Reserve Historical Society, Cleveland. Photograph from The Frick Art Reference Library.*

Making pictures became possible wherever commercial prosperity became notable. In Cleveland, Ohio, Sebastian Heine, who advertised a repertory of painting skills as complete as any late colonial workman's, depicted the *Southwest Portion of the Public Square* [1839: plate 74]; his ruler-straight attempt at linear perspective was maintained with such arbitrary thoroughness that it seems inconsistent to eyes looking for atmospherically treated edges, but the total absence of aerial perspective only emphasizes a bright gayety beyond reach of optical naturalism. A less arbitrary handling, with some satirical intent, is seen in another such localized subject, the *Scene on the Campus Martius* [Detroit Institute] by T. H. O. P. Burnham, whose initials give rise to the amusing nickname of "Alphabet" Burnham. In the less settled portions of the Midwest itinerants continued the precedents of the earlier time; of that, no less a personage than Charles Dickens left evidence as vivid as a caricature. He made an excursion from St. Louis into rawer country; he noted that some houses at Belleville, Illinois, had been painted by a traveler who got along by "eating his way." Stopping next at the hotel in Lebanon, Dickens further noted:

. . . In the best room were two oil portraits of the kit-cat size, representing the landlord and his infant son; both looking as bold as lions, and staring out of the canvas with an intensity that would be cheap at any price. They were painted, I believe, by the artist who had touched up the Belleville doors with red and gold; for I seemed to recognize his style immediately.

On that trip Dickens was seeing everything outside New England with a jaundiced eye, but his opinion of the portraits would have been echoed by every American painter who had been to Europe.

An even stronger unfavorable verdict would have been rendered by such minds upon the work of a carpenter in York, Pennsylvania; this man, Lewis Miller, wrote poems in the regional dialect and kept an almost lifelong pictorial diary. Local characters and accidents, episodes and scenes on his trips away, carefully identified by attached inscriptions, make up a *Chronicle* [Historical Society, York] of considerable usefulness to historians of manners and probably even to a story-writer in search of homely but lively material. As pictures the colored sketches document the amateur who had no technical qualms whatever and who was therefore singularly self-sufficient; Dunlap would have cared nothing for these spirited scrawls but might have generously recognized a kindred spirit in the inscription which Miller in old age appended to the lot:

All of this Pictures, Containing in this Book I Search and Examine them. They are true Sketches, I myself being there upon the places and Spot and put down what hapened. I SEE ALL IS VANITY IN THIS KNOWING WORLD.

Thus both in spirit and in technique Miller's work was an attractively natural product of a regional society in which the semi-pictorial craft of fractur had been practised since before he was born.

Perhaps, also, it was the indirect influence of fractur which suggested in the Shaker settlements the decorative treatment of inspirational texts. These appear as an admirable though very minor act of inconsistency in the members of a sect who lived according to a rule which runs:

. . . No maps, Charts, and no pictures and paintings, shall ever be hung up in Your dwelling rooms, shops, or Office. And no pictures or paintings set in frames, with glass before them, shall ever be among you. But modest advertisements may be put in the Trustees Office when necessary.

It is true that this deprivation, which reads so painfully to the worldly-minded, was mitigated by the spiritual functionalism of the Shaker life and its setting; and if it be also true that

"Euclid alone
Has looked on Beauty bare,"

the Shakers may be credited with a Euclidian moral beauty which had compensations for certain natures. But the appearance of a semi-pictorial craft even among the Shakers is proof enough that for less rigorous people a pictureless world would be an impossible mutilation of spirit.

The people of Nantucket Island, prosperous from the whaling ships, began to pay out money for portraits at a satisfactory rate—portraits which vigorously perpetuated the artisan tradition of the mainland. The most notable mid-century names were J. S. Hathaway and William Swain. Swain, for all his early hardness of manner, showed some grasp upon personality. He was at a loss before even a halfway pretty girl, but more adequate to older women who revealed positiveness of character. Attracted elsewhere by other patronage, Swain undertook to master the current studio practice, and in doing so he sacrificed his blunt half-mastery of individuality. On Nantucket he and Hathaway made an interesting parochial reiteration of a manner that had been provincial to begin with; and Swain, by ironing out his initial angularities, blurred himself into the tedious academic average of the time.

In Natchez, Mississippi, besides the professional portraitists coming and going every winter, there occurred some interesting local activities still further emphasizing the ways in which the Cotton Kingdom culture was linked with remote places. Louis Joseph Bahin came there from France, bringing with him family portraits and home scenes done abroad; in Natchez he was active as a portrait painter and also worked for his own pleasure at history and anecdote;

75. THE 'CELLIST   *by* I. BRADLEY
Courtesy of Phillips Gallery, Washington, D.C.

in one picture he put a great deal of sunset red over a large and very mixed crowd on hand to watch a steamboat at the landing. Mrs. Stephen Rumble, the mistress of "Rosalie," filled that mansion with landscapes in the fashionable Hudson River manner which she had learned while at boarding school in New York.

She was exceptional among the lady amateurs of the time in choosing to emulate the studio professionals, in treating her subjects naturalistically, and in using oil paint. A mid-century novelty in technique of minimum difficulty in execution could for that specific reason appeal to the most timid as a feasible ornamental occupation. It was a process of using charcoal or black crayon on pre-pared boards, to which some crayon tinting was added if desired; but any such added color could be nothing more than a sickly flush over the dominant fuzzy blacks, and a landscape or an anecdote in this eye-repellent medium was inevi-tably a depressing affair. Yet no novelty of either subject or process was really needed to increase the number of female amateurs in the mid-century; the increase occurred quite naturally simply because there were more of them with more time on their hands. Price, the biographer of the Kentucky painters, tells a story about a German painter fresh from Munich who went from house to house in Cincinnati trying to get work but gave up, saying: "No good; I found a lady artist in every family. . . ."

In the East the ladies apparently were content to maintain a continuity with the Federal Era by making more and more theorem paintings. All of the char-acteristic subjects increased greatly in quantity, but there seems to have been a special increase in both the number and variety of the mourning pieces. The pictorial elements of this type were as arbitrary as any other stenciled pattern: tombstone or memorial urn, with or without mourning people around, but prac-tically always accompanied by a weeping willow tree. Although put together in the same way as the still-lifes and the landscapes, the mourning pieces were strikingly different in one respect; everything in them, beyond an occasional attempt at rendering a particular person as a mourner, was symbolical, and each picture was a collection of details which by association called up the lachry-mose emotions. However, the combination of standardized procedure and stand-ardized elements must have helped very much in conventionalizing the emo-tions themselves, and the "psychic distance" thus attained permitted the same pleasure in craft as was experienced in other theorem pictures.

For this prominence of mourning pictures sufficient reason was given in life by the appalling frequency of death. Half of all children died before the age of five, and then half of all adolescents died of tuberculosis; and of those who died of that disease between twenty and thirty-five, the number who painted pictures itself constituted a phenomenon. The mourning piece was a pictorial euphemism in which the willow served as a visual cliché to match the hifalutin language of Mrs. Sigourney, "The Sweet Singer of Hartford," who rivaled even *Godey's* magazine as a genteel influence. On Mrs. Sigourney's level of refinement the word "cat" was too vulgar for use; she called it "a quadruped member of our establishment." She was also capable of rhyming "Lafayette" with "tears are wet," and an extraordinarily high proportion of her rhymes dealt with death in the decorous conventionalism of the pictures.

Itinerant portraitists were as active as ever throughout the East, and the still increasing density of the public wanting cheap work can be inferred from the increasing restriction of the painters' routes. James Sanford Ellsworth made one trip as far as St. Louis and eventually died in Pittsburgh; but his numerous small profile portraits were practically confined to Connecticut. He gave the fillip of some oddity through a mannerism of dark clover-leaf shapes behind and above rather literalistic features. The slightly later Josiah Brown King adopted a similar mannerism of scalloped cloud-like shapes, but escaped from Ellsworth's severe flatness into bas-relief effects of modeling. A much more care-less but also more dashing formula was used in New Hampshire by Joseph H. Davis, who signed himself "Left Hand Painter." He was especially fond of placing a man and a woman seated in balanced profile on either side of a table in front of a wall, with a picture centered on it; and he drew the strongly em-phasized carpet pattern without perspective so that it does not recede but ascends. The color is always pleasing and sometimes subtle, just as the effect is always naïve and sometimes dignified. The *James and Sarah Tuttle* [1836: New-York Historical Society, New York] is as good an example as any of Davis' calligraphic spontaneity: a quality which he achieved by letting the predetermined formula take care of the larger relationships of balance and reserving only minor details of pattern for the stimulation of novelty.

Spontaneity is certainly absent from a group of portraits found in Kent, Con-necticut, which were prepared in advance with identical poses, leaving the faces and a few minor details for later insertion. Each man sits erectly centered in the canvas, and sometimes holds a carefully dated newspaper; each woman leans sharply off-center toward the upper left corner in a pose probably intended to be graceful elegance. There is no repetitiveness in the faces, and the flattery of dig-nified bearing for the men, of slim waists and soft hands for the women, is re-duced to a disarming formula for inexpensive vanity. Four other portraits using the same formula but found in other places are signed with the name of J. H. Bradley; and I. Bradley also appears on a much more attractive and individualized work: *The 'Cellist* [1832: plate 75]. Here a restricted range of color is sub-ordinated to a draftsmanship which, for all its inaccuracies, is remarkably delicate; and both color and drawing yield the place of honor to an exceptionally success-

76. THE QUILTING PARTY *by* UNKNOWN PAINTER *Courtesy of The Museum of Modern Art.*

ful design in which even the bit of curtain at the upper right corner proves its
visual necessity by effectively countering the sharply tapering diagonal formed
by a small oblong piano and the musician with his well-drawn 'cello seated alongside. Quite as vividly as the *Mrs. Freake and Baby Mary* a century and a half
earlier, the occurrence of such a picture as this among the mass of work called
artisan and amateur accentuates the fact that such classifications can be nothing
more than historical conveniences; they simply group large masses of work according to fairly constant identifiable characteristics. An occasional example like *The
'Cellist* may retain those external traits and at the same time rise above the class
with the unpredictable inner grace of esthetic creation.

A landscape parallel in quality to that figure-piece is Joseph H. Hidley's
Poestenkill—Winter [prob. 1848: privately owned], showing a village street of
subtly varied houses and a church spire, painted as from some high point. The
acute angle of vision gives the elevated horizon, which is handled with remarkable sensitiveness; the fields and hillsides beyond the village, which is given
such definite unity by the dramatic clump of evergreens stopping the street, are
beautifully suggested by subtle values and tactful brushwork. Even the edges of
the reiterated house-shapes are kept from over-assertiveness by the painter's preference for carefully graduated values.

A less well painted picture attractive in a contrasting way is an unknown painter's *Quilting Party* [1840–1850: plate 76]. In this an emphatic linear perspective
indicates an intention of pronounced depth, but the figures do not diminish in
scale at the same rate and their shadowless silhouettes contribute a piquant contradiction. The exceptionally spirited and complex contrasts of light and dark,
humorously pushed as far as the way in which the dark hair of some of the men
is broken out against the light background, are mainly responsible for the effect
of festive animation; but this is strongly re-enforced by the narrative interest of
such details as the contrasting profiles of the two old women seated at the center
and the foot-and-hand flirtation engaged in by the couple at the right. The
gayety is fully felt in terms of incident, but its effectiveness consists of the way
in which it is embodied in paint.

A few other anonymous examples are outstanding, such as the dashingly
romantic *Runaway Horse* [c. 1850: Whitney Museum of American Art, New
York]; but in the main the mid-century artisan and amateur work of exceptional
quality is associated with workmen about whom some facts are known. Edward
Hicks was among the first to become biographically definite at the very beginning
of the twentieth-century interest in this hitherto neglected phase of painting in
the United States. A Quaker preacher and sign painter, in his later years he executed a number of pictures most of which were variations upon his favorite
theme, *The Peaceable Kingdom*. Trusting babes and demure sheep and placid

cows are joined by lions and leopards whose round eyes seem to wonder at their own self-restraint in such defenceless company; and at a distance to one side William Penn is usually effecting his treaty with the Amerinds. This last episode is derived directly from Benjamin West's painting in Philadelphia; and a possible source in the pictures by Charles Cotton has already been suggested for the wilder members of Hicks' menagerie. A source for the farm animals in *The Residence of David Twining* [plate 77] might have been such a picture as Woodside's *Country Fair* [plate 52]. This suggested documentation of other pictures drawn upon by Hicks has no bearing upon the intrinsic charm of his adaptations; but it has considerable relevance to the general idea that the artisans as a whole, together with the amateurs whom they coached, in their endeavors to achieve paintings of pictorial interest above the utilitarian level of signs, owed much of their thematic material to the works of men whose training had from the first familiarized them with picturemaking as an independent activity. Hicks was preserved from pictorial slavery to other men's work by his Quaker innocence, which can sometimes be as effective in esthetic matters as it perhaps more rarely is in those of conduct. But in art innocence of mind is not genius, nor can it be a substitute for genius, however ingratiating it may be in its own limited way.

With Hicks, at least, innocence was a positive quality which determined the pictorial result in its technique and spirit both; with other men the simplicity and repetitiveness of their works came from the largely negative trait of their matter-of-fact contentment within craft habits which they made little or no effort to transcend. Of this type are the full-length of a few young boys and pantaletted girls by Joseph W. Stock in Springfield, Massachusetts, and the many river-boats by James Bard in New York City. The nature of this man's main business is to be seen in the lettering that is so prominent on the sides of the boats themselves: *Sylvan Dell, Sylvan Shore, Sylvan Glen, Sylvan Stream, Sylvan Grove* [New-York Historical Society, New York]. Only an antiquarian of boats could be concerned to note whether differences of detail extend beyond the single word; one in search of intrinsic pictorial interest would note rather that the execution of boat rails and water ripples and all their minute accompaniments indicates a mind for which mechanical procedure was an ideal in itself. And out of picturemaking practised in a way to avoid thinking, only a period quaintness can come.

William Matthew Prior is like a good many other American workmen in being more interesting as a person than as a painter. His activity was for the most part in Maine and Massachusetts, but he also made trips in search of work; he became one of the Millerites who experienced two disappointments when the world did not end as their prophet twice predicted; and he specialized in consoling parents with spirit portraits of children who had died in infancy. The incon-

77. THE RESIDENCE OF DAVID TWINING by EDWARD HICKS Courtesy of The Museum of Modern Art.

sistency of his known work finds a logical explanation in the fact, documented by a newspaper advertisement and his shop label, that he worked in different manners according to the price paid—the cheaper manner being "without shade or shadow." Another indication of the approaching subsidence of shop craft in painting generally may be found in some articles in the initial volume of *The Scientific American* [1845]. Its founder and first editor, Rufus Porter, ran a series embodying detailed directions for executing practically every branch of painting on the artisan level: signs, banners, portraits, and even landscape wall decorations composed with stencils. Some actual examples of the last-named in several Massachusetts houses are by Porter himself; they are pleasant enough when first seen but have nothing in reserve with which to satisfy the twice-seeing eye. In other hands the results of his printed directions were likely to be good only by accident; every craft requires the personal relationship between master and pupil for any widespread and waxing vitality. In other ages and for crafts more important than sign painting, written codifications of procedure have signalized the waning of their sustaining impulse and the shift of interest to some other form of fulfilling man's need to make things in the image of his own spirit.

64. Mid-century dilettantes

Francis William Edmonds: 1806–1863   Christopher Pearse Cranch: 1813–1892
Walter M. Oddie: 1808–1865   John Landis: 1805–after 1851
Thomas Buchanan Read: 1822–1872   Sylvester Genin: 1822–1850
Bayard Taylor: 1825–1878

The relationships between painting and life in this country have required the mention of many amateurs, the word being used to designate inadequate technical equipment; in that sense, too, some who passed as professionals in their day were actually amateurs, such as John Watson and Jane Stuart. The word "dilettante" also has connotations of amateurism in technique, but for lack of a better word it has here been used with some disregard of such connotations. Throughout this book, the dilettante has been regarded as marked by one negative and one positive characteristic: a failure to achieve personal expressiveness in painting and a union of painting with some other activity which is performed as well or better. In these terms the dilettante may be technically competent or incompetent; the dilettantism of the work consists in the absence of expressive individuality. For example, T. Addison Richards was professionally skilled in his painting, Francis Hopkinson was neither skilled nor clumsy, and George Washington Parke Custis was, in the wall decorations remaining at "Arlington," definitely incompetent. Richards wrote at least as well as he painted, and the others definitely wrote better. The occasion for being more precise with this partly arbitrary definition is the recurrence of the type through the mid-century on a scale sufficient to modify the general public's attitude; it was an effective preparation for the doctors and lawyers and business-men who nowadays find recreation in painting.

Francis William Edmonds was listed as a professional painter upon being elected to membership in the National Academy because he had sold pictures; but the Academy's secretary, T. S. Cummings, when compiling its *Annals,* attempted to re-classify Edmonds as an amateur because he worked in a bank for a salary. Tuckerman later praised Edmonds for not allowing the "spirit of trade" to infect his painting! Edmonds was occasionally as good a technician as some other Academy members who made their living from anecdotal painting, but he was not sufficiently consistent in either good or indifferent technique to be recognizable as an individual in paint. The same lack is observable in the landscape work of Walter M. Oddie, although Dunlap called it "distinguished."

Oddie, a businessman, was only an honorary Academician, and even that limited compliment was apparently conferred mainly as a recognition for his rather extensive purchases of the real Academicians' canvases. The friend of Oddie who composed the notice used by Dunlap made it unnecessary to indulge in any burlesque of genteel taste, for his wrote that Oddie's themes

. . . were cottages and purling streams, with some gentle swain and his true love strolling through the meadows, or seated beneath the shade of some wide-spreading tree. . . .

Oddie sometimes appropriately fitted such subjects into the horizontally oval shapes so widely used for sentimental steel engravings in the gift books; but even his sentimentality seems to have dried up with the surfaces of his pictures, with their brittle and monotonous brushwork, their dull browns hardly enlivened by acid greens. Nevertheless, Oddie and Edmonds should be noted with some approval, like the Charleston lawyers White and Cogdell, because in the existing state of American culture it was advantageous for painting to be known as the avocation of men who had a more generally recognized professional standing in society.

However, those who combined business with painting seem to have done less toward securing additional public esteem for painting than three men who combined painting with authorship. Two of the three—Thomas Buchanan Read and Bayard Taylor—were so prominent in their time and their painting was so well publicized as an important part of their total accomplishment that anybody who knew about the one activity could hardly escape knowing about the other. Taylor drew the illustrations for some of his early books of travel like *El Dorado;* as they were filtered through the commercial engraving of the time, they exhibit nothing more than topographical mediocrity. But his drawings ceased to be used in this way and his picturemaking increased during his extensive travels: sketches in letters home and water colors in most of the countries from Russia to Japan the long way round. At home in the intervals of travel he would work up some of the material into oil landscapes. His poems were better than his pictures, and his translation of Goethe's *Faust* still better; but every historical anthology of American literature is likely to include something by him: the "Bedouin Love Song" or one of the idylls of rural life in Pennsylvania. The same is true of Read, with "Drifting" a usual choice and "Sheridan's Ride" an almost certain one. Read quit rhyming after the middle of the century and attempted to become much more of a painter than Taylor in the sense of participating in exhibitions and selling his pictures; the latter are now in fact somewhat better known than the poems, but his repetitious versions (follow-ups in paint for his poem) of a bouncing Sheridan on a cavorting horse were comic in their technical badness.

Christopher Pearse Cranch painted better than his two fellow rhymers, but sometimes only one of his poems gets into the anthologies: "Gnosis," eight stanzas in which a too regular lilt almost spoils an idea still attractive to those susceptible to the hopeful ultimates of transcendentalism. Cranch began painting as an amateur, but in the end his landscapes became more interesting than his older brother's professional portraits. As a Unitarian minister in Cincinnati, the younger Cranch also helped local painters; and upon marriage his wife encouraged him to leave the ministry and make painting and poetry his principal interests. Several stays abroad modified his technique into an international average which prevented it from ever becoming memorable in any individual instance; he was capable of absorbing and practising the best teaching he could find among the academic painters and pictures of his day, but he remained always the dilettante in the sense here defined of never having anything to say that was distinctively personal. He could follow all the rules; though a transcendentalist by temperament, he could never transcend them.

All three of these rhyming painters cut a fairly wide swath in the nineteenth-century popularization of a romanticism which was largely derived from Europe, and the tendency of later criticism is to trim them down considerably from their importance while they were alive. The inevitability of this process with all cultural second-raters does not alter their serviceability in their time. The very existence of culture under democratic conditions requires a large number of successful second-raters in all the arts; and since their only chance must be with their immediate audience, they are entitled to the largest audience they can captivate. These three, for their time, successfully embodied an idea which is valuable for any time: the mixture of artistic interests and the practice of more than one art which, even though it fall short of creativeness in any, maintains the possibility of a rounded experience.

The two businessmen-painters succeeded in this in the stronghold of mercantilism, and the three writer-painters on an international stage. Others attempted it in far more constricted environments and from a basis of self-help so inadequate that their self-confidence approached the sublime in futility. Two in particular—John Landis and Sylvester Genin—who tried to be poets and painters without success are fascinating in their outlandish eccentricity and significant in what they reveal of the total cultural situation in this country.

Because middle Pennsylvania was settled by stubborn religious splinter-groups, most of its individual eccentrics have been religious in their freakishness; but the quirkiness of John Landis involved much more. As an excessively vain and dressy youth he worked on a newspaper, studied medicine, and made a nice sum of money in a lottery that he himself conducted. A traveling painter persuaded him that to take painting lessons would be a sure way to permanent affluence;

and to judge by the titles of pictures now unknown, Landis' goal must have been history painting. Following upon some religious subjects, he devised a *Battle of New Orleans*, fourteen by twenty-two feet in dimensions; this immensity he took to England for exhibition, where it failed in popularity because the foreground held too many British redcoats—all dead. Landis brought the picture back to this country and got it placed in the Rotunda of the Capitol for inspection as a possible governmental purchase. The Senators apparently liked the foreground details, for they were making ready to pay him thirty thousand dollars for the picture when someone discovered that a horse in it had five legs; the error was easily corrected, but the Senate would not complete the purchase. During an attack of smallpox a religious vision called him to preach; he then composed many hymns, some longer poems, and a prose work of 1839 entitled *Discourses on the Depravity of the Human Family, Particularly Applied to These Times.* He once addressed himself in these words:

> Landis! great Poet Painter 'f the time
> By Pencil touches and in Rhyme;
> Thy Poetic fire is displayed;
> In Heaven's glory arrayed!

After that it needed only a disappointment in love to unbalance his mind for a time. But he went traveling in the Holy Land and was found by Arabs wandering feverish in the desert several days away from Jerusalem. From Alexandria he was sent back to this country a permanently crazed man.

Tuckerman remarked that the memoir of Sylvester Genin "adds a curious chapter to the anomalous artist-experiences of the West"—certainly no overstatement. The whole affair, in both its ridiculousness and its tragedy, started with the father, but he pushed both characteristics to a climax in the son. In the Ohio of the eighteen-twenties the father was apparently akin to the scholars whom Harriet Martineau had noted on the frontier: men who knew so much more than their neighbors that they were permanently warped into a private infallibility which had lost touch with the realities of culture elsewhere. A lawyer father who could himself write an epic poem entitled *The Napolead* would naturally enough be watchful for signs of similar genius in his children; and he chose to educate his two sons at home in a strenuous regimen of English, French, and Latin, with some Greek and German. When Sylvester showed interest in drawing at the age of twelve, the father pushed him energetically and very soon urged history painting upon him as the road to fame. By the time the son was sixteen he had composed the preparatory design for *The Passage of the Granicus* showing some eighty figures participating in Alexander's victory over the Persians.

. . . There was difficulty in procuring well-formed persons who were willing to denude, and maintain a given posture a sufficient length of time. . . .

An engraver, Hugh Anderson, appeared on the scene; and after some instruction and much conversation, Sylvester Genin remodeled the study and executed it in oil.

. . . His father did not wish him to go among artists, and conoiseurs, until he had accomplished so much on the score of design, that his genius would not be likely to be dwarfed by their affectation and pedantry. . . . the father was solicitous, that the son should prolong his study of painting in Ohio, in nature's school, which he held superior to any in the Atlantic cities, or Rome itself, until a certain confidence in his capacity, and maturity of judgement, should enable him to distinguish between the true and the false in criticism and taste: that when he should hear of impossibilities, he might consider them as merely difficulties.

Yet the father could have read in Reynolds' *Discourses*: ". . . he who begins by presuming on his own sense, has ended his studies as soon as he has commenced them. . . ."

From the spring of 1840 Sylvester Genin spent about nine months in the East seeing collections and exhibitions, showing his drawings and the first painting to the principal painters, and frequently encountering the belief that he had only adapted them from some prints. He visited relatives on Long Island, painted some portraits, and at last reached New Haven, whence his long letters echo all the discouraging opinions that elderly Trumbull expressed to him about art in the United States. Then suddenly, although he had a letter to Allston, he turned back home, became a lawyer in double-quick time, continued to sketch or draw ambitious designs, engaged in flowery political oratory, and wrote rhymes. Tuberculosis appeared in both sons, and they tried curatives that sound violent; the brother died, and Sylvester sought out Jamaica in the hope of healing, and died within a week of landing at Kingston.

Most of the prose fragments printed in the memoir consist of the empty rhetoric of the day; there are some childish speculations about the mind and the brain, phrenological in tendency, and the idea that vindictive feelings are the result of "lateral pulsations" of the blood while reverential feelings logically arise from "vertical pulsation." Among the rhymes "A Bachelor's Musings" speculates on the mystery of a woman's bustle and a poem of thirty-six lines entitled "Stooping to Conquer Undignified, But Perhaps Excusable" concludes with:

> If sources of power
> Lie deep in the mud,
> One cannot high tower,
> If reach them he would.

One illustration in the memoir is from an original etching, and there are fifteen more reproduced as plates by his engraver-teacher. It would be unwise to feel certain from this evidence alone, but it seems possible that not all of the awkward figure-drawing was the work of Genin. In any event all he could do in Ohio was to make some drawings and a very few paintings whose degree of originality was of no consequence because they all looked like bad copies from inferior prints. Poems, prose, and pictures point the moral that the frontier experience becomes artistically valuable only after it has been left behind.

65. Retrospect from the year 1860

William Edward West: 1788–1857
Miner K. Kellogg: 1814–1889
Richard Caton Woodville: 1825–1855
Edward Harrison May: 1824–1887
George Loring Brown: 1814–1889

Cephas Giovanni Thompson: 1809–1888
William Stanley Haseltine: 1835–1900
John Rollin Tilton: 1828–1888
Francis Alexander: 1800–1880

A considerable part of America, geographically speaking, had already effectively transcended the frontier, yet without having become culturally mature. One thing that still delayed this result was the rapidity of change itself, now accelerating beyond what was noted of the Federal Era. The railroads had achieved control of all travel except on the rivers; the telegraph, the steam engine, and the daguerreotype had become for Americans generally not merely the symbols but the experienced actualities of civilization. There had been a war with Mexico, and in only four years the nation had expanded to the Pacific Ocean. In 1856 an old-timer in Philadelphia regretted the change from quiet and moderation to excitement and extravagance, lamented the replacement of "natural" music by opera, and deplored the indecent exposure of the polka—all quite as if he were in the Boston of 1734 and waxing indignant against Peter Pelham. The mid-century was the time when the phrase "a man of competence" came to mean simply a man with money, and the implication that money was the only evidence of personal ability may give a roughly accurate measure of the culture.

It was the general condition suggested by this which repelled some painters who had for a time known better things. William Edward West was born in Kentucky, then still a frontier, and painted there before becoming a student of Sully in Philadelphia; he then painted portraits for several years in Natchez, whence a friendly patron sent him to Europe in 1820. He remained there almost twenty years and painted not only the usual touring Americans but also some famous writers. With the latter his range extended from Mrs. Hemans to Lord Byron, the range from excessive respectability to excessive impropriety; yet West reported that they both liked him and his work. West was a temporary member of the Byron-Shelley group in the neighborhood of Pisa, and from that experience contributed some anecdotes to Moore's biography of Byron. He returned to this country in 1839 on what proved to be an ill judged attempt to make a fortune in some friend's business venture, and he found both Baltimore and New York raw and repulsive; he "lived chiefly in himself and the past." In relation to his average portraits and his mediocre "fancy" pictures with high "finish," it seems ironical that he kept always by him Sir Joshua Reynolds' *Discourses;* but for an American who in America felt himself exiled from Europe, the book may have had some talismanic connection with the lost paradise of a cultivated tourist.

The long stays of some painters in Europe have already been noted in passing, but still others became long-time or permanent refugees from the United States. Miner K. Kellogg fled Cincinnati, but eventually returned to live in Cleveland. Richard Caton Woodville was helped by Robert Gilmor, Jr., to flee Baltimore; he made a couple of return trips in the interest of painting American anecdote with his Düsseldorf technique. Edward Harrison May was born in England and brought here so young that his early work as an engineer and his first training as a painter occurred in this country; his permanent identification with Paris ought to relieve the United States of responsibility for his Salon story-pictures that were praised by Théophile Gautier. However, not Paris but Italy was heaven for most of the refugee American painters of the mid-century. Rome and Florence were the permanent headquarters of the time's American-born sculptors, and the more fluctuating group of painters who joined them formed a very large artistic family brimming over with genial friendships and bitter animosities. George Loring Brown, a landscape man, and Cephas Giovanni Thompson, a portrait man who tried to become a history man, were long-term expatriates. Hawthorne's journals have passages about the beauty of Thompson's works—beauty of a kind so well suited to the time, Hawthorne wrote, that he preferred it to all but one or two of the old masters, names unspecified. William Stanley Haseltine, whose real career was not so much painting as being rich and handsome, and John Rollin Tilton, who painted many Venetian sunset-lighted sails while living in Rome, were permanent expatriates. An older man, Francis Alexander, was unique in one respect. He had been quite successful in New England as a portraitist, especially after a trip to Italy for improving his technique; but ten years of Boston proved to be all he cared to take and all that was necessary for him to acquire enough money to go back to Italy. His uniqueness was that in Italy he stopped painting, whereas the others lived there because they thought they could paint better there.

However, those men were no longer students; so their idea may have had reference to subject-matter. Certainly they were everywhere surrounded by the obviously picturesque scenes which some wanted in contemporaneous subjects and by the masterpieces on which others wished to model their uncontemporaneous subjects. Or perhaps they had also in mind the cheapness and the freedom of living in a foreign land, the visual and emotional richness of being so closely surrounded with the past. As one of them wrote in a letter to *The New York Times* in 1841,

> . . . One day in the city of the Medici is worth more than a hundred within the walls of Gotham; it is better to be the janitor of the Grand Duke than the inmate, for the whole of one's natural life, of the White House.

If they were simply in search of personal happiness, they were doubly lucky in being able to live where they wished and to sell their pictures too. They were mighty fine fellows, but about all they did as people was to acquire an extra depth of tourist patina.

In thinking they were fine artists, they were mistaken. Not because they lived where they did, but because they were what they were. Horatio Greenough could live in Italy and turn out sculpture which was indeed mediocre; but it is also possible that his residence in Florence was exactly what gave him perspective on this country and stimulated his intelligence to develop the seminal concept of functionalism, which was to be a later catchword for many who would never have recognized its source. To achieve important art in a foreign land requires exceptional talent or genius—just as it does at home. Henry James or James McNeill Whistler required a foreign residence for his art; Herman Melville and Thomas Eakins had to come home for theirs. It may have been some loss to this country not to have the mid-century refugees living here, but the pictures they painted were no gain for Europe. Though many of them were sincerely praised by the Europeans themselves, and were for that reason brought here, they did no more for Americans than bed down the cultural soil. Bayard Taylor, dramatizing himself as "The Ancient" in his amusing *Diversions of the Echo Club,* predicted that the nineteenth century would surpass the Middle Ages as a graveyard for poems; he might as well have included pictures, and among those which the historian of American painting has to resurrect for examination none look any deader than the average production of the cultural refugees.

Back in America at the time a good many Americans were beginning to work free not only from the stuffiness which the refugees had left but also from the substitute which the refugees had devised for themselves. The main instrument of this new freedom was humor. The Reverend Mrs. Sniffles was as imaginary as the pictures she admired, but the miasma she helped to blow away was real enough; she is telling about her visit to Mr. Bungle, the local portrait painter, and a picture she saw in the shop:

> . . . an elegant lady a lyin' asleep by a river, and ther was a little angel a hoverin' in the air over her head, jest a gwine to shoot at her with a bow and arrer. I axed Mr. Bungle what 'twas sent to his shop for, and he said how't Miss Billins wa'n't

quite satisfied with it on account o' the angel's legs bein' bare, and she wanted to have him paint some pantalettes on 'em. . . . Them Scripter pieces that Sister Myers has got hangin' strikes me as wonderful interestin', especially the one that represents Pharoh's daughter a findin' Moses in the bulrushes. Her parasol and the artificials in her bunnit are jest as natral as life. And Moses, he looks so cunnin' a lying there asleep, with his little coral necklace and bracelets on. O it's a sweet picter. And I like that other one, tew, that represents Pharoh a drivin' full tilt into the Red Sea after the Israelites. How natral his coat-tails flies out. . . .

PERIOD TWO
THE PROVINCIAL

DIVISION SIX
Aftermath of the Civil War—

1860 to 1880

66. The age of plunder

The Civil War was more than a war; it was a struggle won by industrialism, whose victory enabled it to reshape the nation in a very few years. The industrialists and financiers controlled the politicians, and they were all in league for loot. The mendacity of Jay Cooke and Jay Gould, the thievery of Jim Fisk and Daniel Drew, the venality of Grant's officials and friends, the corruption of Tammany and Tweed—these things marked the brutalization of politics and business. The South was plundered economically through carpetbag government; in the North the plunder consisted of banks and stocks and railroads; in the West it consisted of metals and land. Whatever its source, the plunder produced a generation of pushing plutocrats who flaunted their colossal fortunes in the purchase of colossal things. Their spending, in its amount and rapidity, affected the arts and crafts more quickly than that by any preceding generation of newly privileged Americans, and the immediate aberrations of taste were so violent that, whatever they may have revealed about the state of art, they certainly indicated vitality in the people.

Building became a chaos of misused Gothic and Byzantine, Mansard roofs and Egyptian wall-slopes, with frequent indescribable monstrosities hailed for their originality. The exteriors were a riot of ornament: jigsaw filigree for the wooden buildings, stone superfluities for those of masonry. Stores boasted the chic of cast-iron fronts, and the lawns of suburban villas featured cast-iron maidens in sweeping robes made classic with white paint. Intensifying the tendencies of the mid-century, the interiors were large and gloomy, darkened by double hangings at the windows, filled with massive black walnut suites upholstered in red plush and planted upon flowered carpets of livelier colors than the maroon pattern in the wallpaper. A plush album of photographs on the marble-topped table, a square piano smothered in a "throw," a brown-varnished plaster group by John Rogers of *Weighing the Baby,* and a whatnot in the corner bearing souvenirs of travel—these objects would effectively compete with the broad and heavy gilt frames around the hand-painted oils on the walls. The popular Harriet Prescott Spofford, who wrote about romantic artists in dangerous Paris, turned away from her fiction to publish a book of advice about making interiors beautiful:

. . . Provided there is space to move about without knocking over the furniture, there is hardly likely to be too much in the room.

The idea probably came from her experience of artists' studios in this country, which were full of even more brass and ruby glass and armor than was needed as material for their paintings. The artists' old junk and the new-rich's new adiposities gave all the interiors their primary aspect of plunder.

Most of the people were adipose with overeating; if they were not, they seemed so in the time's superfluity of clothes. This was especially true of the women; beginning with lofty coiffures, descending through leg-of-mutton sleeves and bustles to ruffles and trains, they were walking monuments to the ideal of adding art to nature. All these complications of personal adornment and possessions contributed to the artistic satisfactions of monumentally simple souls. Only their entire esthetic inexperience—and servants—protected them from the oppressiveness of things. People liked the multiplicity of things because it was the evidence of their own wealth, and they liked what now seems to be the ugliness of things because it was the evidence of machine manufacture. It was this which accounted for the bulbous swellings in furniture legs suddenly pinched into spindly insecurity—indeed, for the nightmare of turns and twists in brackets and finials, of scoops and bulges in newel posts and stair rails. All this tortured wood violated the character of the material in order to express a mastery over it by the machine, and the esthetic corruption of the machine came from the designers' irresponsibility toward materials which they mistook for creative freedom. It was exploitation as rampant as any in business or finance.

This cultural situation was concentrated into the new building of the National Academy of Design opened for use in 1865. In its prominent location on one corner at Twenty-third Street and Fourth Avenue it afforded an inappropriate reminiscence of the Palace of the Doges at Venice, and upon a scale that seemed painfully pinched to eyes acquainted with the original. It was not in itself architecturally chaotic; rather the reverse in its careful choice and re-arrangement of derivative elements. It did, however, add another manner to the prevailing stylistic confusion out of which a little later Henry Hobson Richardson's version of Romanesque was to rise with massive coherence. The Academy building was marred not only by its triviality but also by mechanical multiplication of detail. The elevated main story, approached by a not very grand staircase, was assertively repetitious in the patterns around its fourteen windows on the two street sides. And the full effect of the machine's deadening of decoration was to be seen both in the elaborate cast-iron railings on the street level and in the "arcaded cornice of white marble" and its surmounting crested parapet at the top. As for the exhibitions which were given here, some people had begun to question whether they were not lowering taste instead of raising it; certainly the hanging of the pictures on those occasions fulfilled the Harriet Spofford idea so far as walls were concerned, for paintings were ranked in four rows from floor to ceiling. The closeness of the frames to one another—they almost touched—seemed to justify their width, since otherwise the painted canvases would have been insufficiently separated; but such an excess of gilt gave a certain advantage to gaudy colors in catching the average person's attention. In this connection, it may be significant that Inness liked to paint on a canvas already framed, so as to gauge the effect of gilt on his picture. As for subject-matter, a visitor from today would be struck by the absence of nudes, for they were still housed elsewhere—from the bar of the Grand Hotel in San Francisco to the bar of the Hoffman House in New York.

However, on the lower floor the Academy had provided room for a life class in its school, and that was an important advance in the training of would-be painters. The drawback was that it and all the other activities of the organization were controlled by a small group of members who tended toward an ever-tighter intolerance of younger talents. This is recurrent in every long-lived academic institution, and in those concerned with art it is usually met by rebellion. So it happened with the National Academy of Design. When a fresh generation of postwar students returned from Europe with better techniques, only to have their pictures badly hung or refused altogether by the Academy juries, they formed another association; and in this they were helped and joined by a few members of the Academy who knew that the younger men deserved attention. Since they had in mind no institutional prestige and were aiming only at gaining respectful attention from the public for their work, they were content to call themselves the Society of American Artists [1877]. From their first exhibition in 1878, through their succeeding ones at changing locations, they surpassed the Academy in seriousness of work, in brilliance and variety of technique, in freshness of subject-matter. As an organization they did most to initiate and shape the Cosmopolitan Period of American painting, which is usually taken as lasting from 1880 to about 1915; and after this had been accomplished by the Society, both it and the Academy found it mutually advantageous to merge in 1906.

The Society of American Artists was by no means alone in rejecting the postwar combination of vulgarity and stodginess and in working to replace it with something better. What is now the American Water Color Society was started in 1866, and the New York Etching Club was founded in 1877; these were of course not in rebellion against the Academy, but their significance as specialist groups in the world of art was considerable. In 1872 the Metropolitan Museum had opened in temporary quarters, and in 1880 it entered the original building at its present location. In Boston the Athenaeum held its fiftieth and last exhibition in 1873; for a few more years it allowed its rooms to be used for exhibitions by the newly formed Museum of Fine Arts, which was housed in a lively Victorian Gothic home of its own by 1878. Meanwhile the Pennsylvania Academy, whose exhibitions had been continuous since 1811, moved into the most heavily Gothic of all American museum buildings. That was in 1876, the year of the Centennial Exposition in Philadelphia, and the hundreds of thousands who visited its art collections carried away a very good idea of what American painting had been—principally in its phase of Hudson River landscape, but also in portraiture and anecdote. The European paintings sent over emphasized current production, and the French group in particular upset a good many Americans by their lack of decorum; but within a few years the nude was tolerated on gallery walls so long as it was French, and the way was open for French-trained Americans to exhibit nudes without ruining their careers. The once famous actress, Fanny Kemble, visited the Exposition at the age of sixty-seven; her long familiarity with the cultures of both Europe and the United States made it impossible for the art exhibits to enlarge her experience by a sudden revelation, and she wrote about the hideous buildings, the statues made out of butter, the water dripping on terra-cotta umbrellas protecting little terra-cotta boys and girls. But the majority of Americans were seeing machinery and art in a significant way for the first time; and where *Appleton's Journal* in 1875 had bluntly affirmed, "As a means of culture, art is over-rated," the *American Art Review* in 1880 could attribute great gains in the appreciation of art to the stimulation of the Exposition's art collections upon the crowds of visitors.

Yet the unfavorable symptoms affecting art that appeared among the new-rich extended very much further than their homes. For the wealth of many among them came from owning the machines that made things for the masses, and in these the ugliness seemed to increase in proportion to their quantity. The people accepted the ugliness, not because they preferred it to beauty, but because their instincts were on the side of cheapness. This esthetic misuse of the machine was for the time being less important than its extension of cheap comforts to the many. Samuel Eliot Morison has recently described the times in a sentence: "The clank of machinery and the clink of dollars silenced religion, letters, and the arts." However, for so complex an age, epigrammatic characterizations can rarely do more than summarize one aspect; and it is well to recall a sentence by the most intelligent art critic of the time itself, James Jackson Jarves, who wrote: "Machine-work is the one great idealism of our prosaic civilization." And it was no less a person than the Chinese scholar, Dr. Hu Shih, who said that American materialism is in many ways simply effective spirituality. At any rate, the postwar period achieved an almost miraculous spread of material well-being; and if the things in which that well-being consisted were artistically vulgar, they yet served a common good. Moreover, vulgarity on so grand a scale indicated, by its mere release of energy, the possibility of artistic creativeness.

67. Painting in the remoter regions

THE SOUTH

   Fisher: act. 1867

   Louis Mathieu Didier Guillaume: 1816–1892

   John A. Elder: 1833–1895

   William L. Sheppard: ?–?

   Conrad Wise Chapman: 1842–1910

TEXAS

   H. A. McArdle: 1836–1908

   "Trader Horn" (Alfred Aloysius Smith): c. 1854–1927

CALIFORNIA

   Fortunato Ariola: ?–1871

   Ivan Buckingham Wandersforde: 1817–1872

   De Francheville Erneste Narjot: 1826–1868

   Jules Tavernier: 1844–1889

The intensification of industrialism following the Civil War determined the center of power for the country as a whole; that was the broad strip north of the Potomac from the Atlantic into the Old Northwest—in other words, the region which had won the war. The eastern cities were still the main art market, and most painters worked in or near them.

The defeat of the South opened up the region to brutal exploitation and thereby temporarily accentuated its emotional and intellectual remoteness from the species of civilization by which it had been defeated. A people ruined economically and decimated in man power might show little inclination to art, yet a few southerners were moved to some elegiac poems more admirable as literature than anything ever written there before. For actually the prewar South had never felt deeply about art of any kind; the music of Gottschalk and the early poems of Timrod are a rather inadequate best to show for two hundred and fifty years of living. This established habit of shallowness in art determined the manner of most southerners' emotional compensation for defeat: a literary romanticizing of the past in which heroes and heroines were visible only by moonlight and sustained only by the fragrance of roses and magnolias. The twentieth century recovery from that was a natural and perhaps necessary pendulum-swing into the lurid violence of recent novels.

The prewar South had produced much portraiture by patronizing localized painters; but painting limited to that branch will rise no higher in the scale of esthetic worth than literature confined to political oratory. After the war portraiture could of course continue to exert its perennial appeal even upon those who had seen much better days, but an inability to pay for it sharply reduced the amount. Almost the only kind of portrait painting which continued at all strong in the South was intended to glorify, or at least to commemorate, the leaders in the war. The actual portraits and history pieces of the period collected at various points from Richmond to New Orleans require a heavier veil of retrospective romance than even a southern-born historian of art can supply; when they are examined for esthetic intensity or artistic feeling or even for technical competency, they represent a parallel in paint to the economic devastation which reduced the region to a low subsistence level.

This extreme subsidence in talent in the postwar South had also its natural accompaniment of unjustified claims. In *The Whig* newspaper for May 10th, 1867, there was a letter from Lynchburg in praise of one Fisher. He is the best painter in the country, north or south; his works are ". . . more like life itself, more characteristic, more completely individualized . . ."; he is as good as Reynolds nor Kneller or Lely. (No higher praise could occur to anyone brought up in reverence for the portraiture of colonial Virginia.) Fisher, the letter continued, is now taking up the painting of both history and landscape, and doing work as fine as any in the country; and there is no better lithographer anywhere. "He is indeed an artist—open-minded, frank, industrious, self-denying man. What is better still, he is a good fellow and a thorough Virginian." Yet it still remains to be shown how being a thorough Virginian, or Californian, or New Englander can make a man artistically creative.

One type of portraitist is reasonably sure of patronage wherever there is any at all to be had: the one who catches the gleam of jewelry and silk, who draws so minutely that every slightest detail can be examined closely, who confers upon all the ladies soft hair and rose-petal complexions and regular features—without making them unrecognizable. That explains the frequency in the upper South of pastels by Louis Mathieu Didier Guillaume. From France by way of New York, he arrived in Richmond as early as 1857 and apparently worked there until after the war; removal to Washington must have enlarged his opportunities for commissions, but patronage came to him from as far away as Atlanta with the reappearance there of business activity. The sort of flattery that Guillaume practised was not intrinsically worse than that to be found everywhere else in the country at one time or another; it was very like that given to ladies farther north by Fagnani, whose own European birth and training had given him a similar success.

The painter best equipped for the more ambitious efforts of history painting was John A. Elder, whose *Battle of the Crater* [Westmoreland Club, Richmond] is the most adequate southern counterpart to northern stage-set pictorializations of Gettysburg. Elder had been readied for making this kind of picture by some study under Daniel Huntington and more under Leutze in Düsseldorf; he had also painted many portraits which share in the dreary mediocrity prevailing throughout the country as a whole. William L. Sheppard had supplied illustrations for northern periodicals before the war; he left a series of water colors dealing with army life [Confederate Museum, Richmond] which are as pitiful in their technical inadequacy as the last of the series is in subject—*A Confederate's Homecoming*. But in that Richmond museum there is also a remarkable group of thirty-one paintings of war scenes in and around Charleston harbor by Conrad Wise Chapman, a son of the historical painter mentioned earlier. The South's share in this exception to the rule of its late-century painting was the accidental one of providing subject-matter, for Chapman had received his general cultivation of mind as well as his technical training in Europe; his presence in Charleston was the result of his private romantic response to the call of sectional patriotism. His postwar reaction led to exile in Mexico, and further stays in Europe, and an eventual return to this country. In Mexico he achieved more painting of great charm, as can be seen in various landscape studies now in the Valentine Museum at Richmond.

Two or three painters of French descent continued painting in New Orleans, and two or three from other parts of the South sought careers in Texas by means not only of the portraiture that can serve almost anywhere but also of ambitious renditions of Texas history appealing to the sharply localized patriotism. Notably there was H. A. McArdle, who had come from Ireland to art study and teaching in Baltimore, then entered the Confederate army, and eventually went to Texas by way of the West Indies. The State offered him eight thousand dollars for *Lee in the Wilderness*, which was unfortunately burned before payment; he then essayed a *Battle of San Jacinto* and a *Dawn at the Alamo,* both of which hung in the Senate chamber for thirty-five years before the state got around to paying his heirs three thousand five hundred dollars. The last-named picture alone contains any money's worth of melodramatic incident—enough to have occupied the painter for thirty years, as his inscription indicates. It was during those years that Trader Horn journeyed through Texas and found art, as he reported a half-century later,

at the lowest ebb. They'll give their hearts for a picture there. I taught the rudiments of painting to the daughters of A— and B—. Wealthy fellers, those, but pitiful in their ignorance. Hungry to see the children do what life had denied to themselves. Piano, oil painting, et cetera and so forth. Education, so-called.

The traveler's own contribution to the culture of Texas was only "painting—so-called," but the feeling of the "wealthy fellers" for their daughters which he notes is a warmingly human touch in the historically impersonal process by which Texas was repeating the cultural pattern of older regions.

Although San Francisco was linked to the East by telegraph in 1861 and by railroad in 1869, the full artistic consequences of closer ties were postponed until after 1880. For the travel involved, California was as remote as Egypt, and going there still implied the temperament of an adventurer or a drifter. The Far West in general, from the Rockies to the Pacific, was pictorially raided, so to speak, by the painters of grandiloquent landscape, and two of them eventually settled in California; but the American portraitists who sought out the market after the war were all indifferent technicians. A more interesting circumstance is the way in which the region continued to attract painters of foreign birth and training. Fortunato Ariola, a painter of romantic landscape from Mexico, worked there for a few years. After reaching California, the Englishman, Ivan Buckingham Wandersforde, belied part of his name and stayed the rest of his life there, becoming first president of the San Francisco Art Association in 1872. The technical likeness of his landscape style to that of the Hudson River School was natural enough, since England and the United States were still effectively interchanging minor landscapists. A Frenchman, De Francheville Erneste Narjot, painted pictures of the mining camps which are said to be indifferent; and Jules Tavernier, another Frenchman, painted much better ones of Amerind life and of landscape. Some western subjects by him were reproduced by Currier & Ives, and the lithographs indicate in the originals a competent European academic technique with little personal accent. Although *tavernier* means "innkeeper," the French painter was no such steady character; he moved on from San Francisco to Hawaii and died there only because the island law would not let him leave until he paid his debts.

68. *Postwar portraiture*

Alonzo Chappell: 1828–1887
Francis Bicknell Carpenter: 1830–1900
Daniel Huntington: 1816–1906 (work after 1860)

The decline in the average of technique which followed upon the war was not in the South alone but in the North as well, and there it can be easily demonstrated in the work of those who were considered portrait specialists. Painting in general was still extending its range beyond previous limitations; much more often than earlier in the century, individual painters with sufficient mental reach were painting any subject that happened to interest them sufficiently. With this way of escape from a narrow specialism becoming more and more feasible, it was natural that the best portraits should now be done by painters who were both more interested and more interesting in other types of work. For American culture as a whole this was a gain—so much so that even the enormous quantity of poor specialist portraiture can be historically disposed of by a generalization or two and documented by a very few painters chosen to typify the many.

The work of Alonzo Chappell reached the widest public of the time through the now deteriorating medium of the steel plate. Under the stimulus of the war and its generals, there appeared still another set of books with the title *National Portrait Gallery* [1862]; and for this Chappell prepared the so-called originals from which the engravings were made. The implication of lack of originality is necessary because Chappell's practice was to rifle every possible source—other engravings, portraits by other painters, and photographs; this material he reduced to a decided uniformity of aspect by means of a commercial facility surprising in its capacity for quantity but not surprising in its inability to cope with individuality. His slick superficiality passed muster with the uncritical, but his haste occasionally laid him open to ridicule. The engraving of *General George S. Meade,* for instance, is adapted from some picture, presumably a photograph, which showed him leaning back relaxed in a chair; in depicting him in camp before a tent, Chappell moved him from chair to campstool, and the general trustingly relaxes on air.

From among the mediocrities who worked from life with what they thought was faithfulness it would be unfair to pillory only one; their work can be found in many public libraries, almost every historical society, the corridors of state and national Capitols, the anterooms and offices of government departments. But one significant thing emerges from this postwar level of portraiture: what the painters did to Lincoln. His nomination raised such widespread curiosity that many portraitists journeyed out to Illinois at once, thinking to profit independently from the general interest or being sent there by publications whose business it was to keep their readers pictorially informed. All through his presidency other painters made portraits of him, and after his death images of him became an industry bigger than that which followed Washington's. Those effigies caused someone to remark that Lincoln was assassinated many times before his death, and it was no less unfortunate that the deed was so often repeated after the event. There may once have been an oil portrait adequate to the subject, that by William Morris Hunt which was burned in the great Boston fire of 1872; a sketch that remains is worth more than all the hundreds of finished works by other hands. Walt Whitman saw Lincoln close enough to comprehend his spiritual greatness; and almost two years before the end, on August 12th, 1863, Whitman wrote: "None of the artists or pictures has caught the deep though subtle and indirect expression of this man's face. . . . One of the great portrait painters of two or three centuries ago is needed." After Lincoln's death, Whitman noted again: "The current portraits are all failures—most of them caricatures." The caricaturing was unconscious, of course, and originated in the painters' own incapacity to equal their subject. Lincoln's spiritual grandeur was inseparable from a countenance which his time in general, and its portraitists in particular, thought was ugly; the painters knew no better than to sleek down the furrows and smooth out the wrinkles. Inevitably they produced characterless masks. Since the run of painters could never rise to the height of this great man, they were even less able to do justice to ordinary people. A poor painter may occasionally surpass himself by his own exceptional response to greatness in the sitter; but where there is no such greatness in the subject, the painter must supply some distinguishing quality if a fine picture is to be attained.

The painter who had the best opportunities to depict Lincoln made no better use of them than the others who had to do without them. Francis Bicknell Carpenter was allowed to live for several weeks in the White House in the course of preparing *The Reading of the Emancipation Proclamation* [1864–1865: Capitol, Washington]. This moment of history was reconstructed with all possible literal exactitude, and it was necessarily a collection of portraits; in a fair enough composition eight men have turned from the business in hand to assume self-conscious poses at the direction of the painter. The faces have the same accuracy as the trouser legs and table, and everything is artistically untruthful. The principal reason is even narrower in scope than the inartistic prosaicism of mind which Carpenter shared with his fellow specialists in portraiture; it lies in the way in which he and many others subordinated human vision to that of the camera. It is possible for painters to use photographic source material without compromising the qualities proper to paint, but it involves a process of translating one kind of visualism into another. The principal change is from monocular vision into binocular vision, and there are a whole series of further adjustments required by the fact that in painting the pigment is applied with a brush wielded by the human hand obeying mental directives. Carpenter and his generation accepted the camera's record as the ultimate of accuracy, copying not only its immobility of line but also its uniform texture and even reducing color to a neutral scale of values. How far Carpenter himself went in that respect is seen in *The Lincoln Family in 1861* [New-York Historical Society, New York], which was kept unusually close to photography by being executed in grisaille.

The miniaturist Thomas Seir Cummings was also the Secretary of the National Academy of Design and its historian; recording the fact that a photographer in 1863 offered to make free portraits of all the Academicians, he commented:

Here, certainly, is one of the wonderful effects—one of the advantages of the art. Instantaneous portraiture, &c., &c.,—by it may be handed down to futurity, in compact and undeniable truthfulness, the portraits of all. The battlefields—nay, almost the battles—have been given by Brady; and the very doings in the streets, by Anthony's instantaneous views—everything that may be interesting to future generations.

Waiving the question of whether futurity will want that much, the characteristically incoherent emotion dramatizes what amounted almost to mass delusion among the lesser painters. It was their share in the general American willingness to accept everything mechanical as something good in itself, and to regard every mechanical improvement as cultural progress. And to the unskilled painter photography seemed to promise an escape from the uncertainties of human eyesight and the strain of mental perceptiveness; it seemed to make available to all an unassailably objective perfection. If it were possible for a painter to go the whole way toward rendering a mechanistic vision, it would be philosophically difficult to determine whether his success were superhuman or subhuman in character.

The man who was then President of the National Academy, Daniel Huntington, recognized the painter's inability to equal the camera and suggested that he do something else.

. . . For example, in painting a lady's portrait wouldn't it be just to subdue minor infelicities of profile or complexion, to present the best of her appearance, and so to

make amends for our lack of ability thoroughly to reproduce a human face?
That painting, it seems to me, is of a higher order which discerns the germs of truth
in the sitter's character, and brings them out. . . .

The test of a man's words is his acts, and Huntington's portraits, to which he was
now almost exclusively devoted after the earlier history painting, show that his
conception of idealization was to eliminate character in favor of bland com-
placency. His several Lincolns were as bad as other men's, but he succeeded well
with people who, whether or not they were historically important, were self-
important. Upon them he had a monopoly earned by his personal popularity, his
presidency at the Academy, and his long life. Most of the public buildings of
New York and the eastern museums contain some portraits by him, and the
larger ones are either more interesting or more boring, depending upon the
visitor's own degree of interest in the intricate costumes and accessories which
surround the bright blankness of the countenances.

69. Postwar history painting

Constantino Brumidi: 1805–1880
William De La Montagne Cary: 1840–1922
Henry F. Farny: 1847–1916
John Mulvaney: 1844–1906

In the decoration of the Capitol, history painting underwent a change which might not have been expected at the time, but which in retrospect seems fitting enough. The great dome over the Rotunda was now completed, and the elaborately patterned ceiling rising to the central canopy made a pictorial treatment of the canopy seem architecturally necessary. Even the most prosaic mind could hardly demand that a factually accurate scene be installed more than two hundred feet above the floor. Since the emotional pressure toward George Washington the hero was still increasing, the logical answer seemed to be an *Apotheosis of Washington* [1863]; and for allegory, with a complete late-Renaissance equipment of personifications and restless pagan deities, all rendered in the most admired foreshortening, the right man was right at hand. For five years Constantino Brumidi had been at work in the Capitol building itself, covering its halls and committee rooms with decorations in the true fresco process of Raphael's *loggie* in the Vatican. Brumidi had in fact been freshening and repairing those very decorations when the French, capturing Rome in 1849, put him in prison. Upon his release he sought a free country; he became an American citizen in 1854, and began decorating the Capitol the following year. When Whitman was in Washington during the war, he examined this earlier work and wrote to his brother about

. . . The incredible gorgeousness. . . . Costly frescoes of the style of Taylor's saloon in Broadway, only really the best and choicest of their sort. . . . (Imagine the work you see on the fine china vases in Tiffany's, the paintings of Cupids and goddesses, etc., spread recklessly over the arched ceiling and broad panels of a big room . . .) . . . by far the richest and gayest, and most un-American and inappropriate ornamenting and finest interior workmanship I ever conceived possible. . . . the style is without grandeur, and without simplicity.

The *Apotheosis* is a different matter, and its difference made it more important. The intent was to create a spiritually useful idea; but serviceableness in picture-

559

making is directly depenaent upon its imaginative intensity. Not surprisingly, Brumidi and his Congressional employers thought this grandiose reminder of Italian ceilings was imaginative; for it has some technical merits which would have been surprising at the time even in Italy itself. Coloristically it is well adjusted to the great room over which it presides, and it extends real space into imaginary space with fair skill. The most serious defect is that Brumidi miscalculated the scale of his figures, making many of them too small for full effectiveness; on the other hand, this is a merit provided the mind can rest content with the general impression of distant animation. And that might be the best way to take a collection of hackneyed symbols. The popular idealization of Washington had indeed endowed him with Jove-like qualities, but the visitors from Olympus by way of Rome were not acclimatized here by being placed around the country gentleman from near-by Mount Vernon. As a means of emotionally linking the present with the remoter past, it was no more effective than endowing a small group of frame buildings with the name of Syracuse or Cairo.

Even more promptly than after the Revolutionary War, painters began translating the Civil War into theatrical easel pictures, but in them no one succeeded in freshening up the old compositional recipes. For the majority in this generation who wanted an exactitude which they could praise in calling it "photographic," subjects were best rendered in the large-scale circular panoramas introduced by Vanderlyn almost a half-century earlier. One novelty of this later phase was the frequent attempt to accentuate illusionistic perspective by placing in the immediate foreground an actual object—a dead tree prone or a few feet of railroad track—which was made to seem continuous with the painted scene by tricks of drawing. But the authentic visual history of the war had already been made, as its events occurred, by Mathew Brady with his camera. Persisting against great technical difficulties and at some personal risk, Brady had photographed every accessible phase of the war. Such artistry as his prints display seems an almost unconscious by-product of his conscious care for thoroughness. Their success in reporting how things happened made the compositional contrivances of both the easel pictures and the cycloramas ineffective in their artifice. The photographs made it desperately necessary for history painting to be infused with a quality which the painters did not know they lacked: imagination.

In painting, as in other arts, subject-matter of established popularity is often purveyed after the life has begun to go out of it, by workmen who do not manifest the feeling of discovery which may have marked their predecessors. For example, both William De La Montagne Cary and Henry F. Farny had points of technical superiority over Catlin, but their pictures of Amerind life have not the earlier man's rough vigor. The Amerind subject, however, had a short flare-up of prominence from the frontier episode in which Custer and all his men were killed (1876). In the following decade a half-dozen painters caught popular interest with versions of *Custer's Last Fight,* or *Charge,* or *Stand,* or *Rally* [all surviving originals privately owned]. The *Fight* was a fairly competent Düsseldorfian composition by Elder, at work in the South; the *Stand* was one of the latest, the one reproduced in the hundreds of thousands of lithographs spread through the country's saloons and barbershops to increase the sales of a well known beer. The *Rally* was by John Mulvaney, who made a trip to the locality for information which he thought would make his picture more authentic. Better than its authenticity was the genuine do-*and*-die spirit with which he infused this example of history painting conceived as factual reporting. In a narrative picture the emotions were properly embodied first of all in expressions and gestures, but the emotional effectiveness of such details would be dissipated if it were not for the compactness and density of design.

Despite its academic competence, Mulvaney's picture is cited here less for its own sake than for the impression it made upon Walt Whitman. Certain ideas and key phrases in his published remarks may be mentioned for the light they throw on the supposedly literate segment of current taste. He approved the painter's two-year stay "on the spot"; he himself remained more than an hour "completely absorb'd" in the "vast canvas, I should say twenty-two feet by twelve." It seemed so vivid and colorful that he needed time; "it is all at first painfully real, overwhelming, needs good nerves to look at it." His account of his contemplation was mainly a description of the incidents, in the course of which recurred the patriotic note of his own poem on the subject five years earlier. The event was "autochthonic"—"nothing in the books like it, nothing in Homer, nothing in Shakespere; more grim and sublime than either, all native, all our own, and all a fact." That is aggressive enough, surely; but it is significant that he falls back on books for his comparisons. As for the artistic character of Mulvaney's painting, "There is an almost entire absence of the stock traits of European war pictures." No doubt Whitman had seen plenty of them, but he was so absorbed by his subject that he did not note how every technical trait was entirely European. Of course, the source of technique is much less important than the use made of it; and in this, again, Whitman's reading of the picture was exclusively literary. When he advised the painter to take it to Paris so that Frenchmen might be compelled to admit that America was as good as France in art, he did not suspect that anywhere in Europe the *Rally* would be technically as much at home as in New York. Still nearer to universality was the picture's subject appeal and Whitman's own response. His ability to express his response in words in no way differentiates it from that of a backwoodsman or a cowboy. The patrioteering was itself a characteristic element in all such responses to pictorial narrative, and that is the basic level of all mass appreciation in every generation. Humanly permanent, it cannot be ousted from the experience of even the most sophisticated except by a proportionate dehumanization of their artistic appreciation.

78. THE VILLAGE POST OFFICE *by* THOMAS WATERMAN WOOD *Courtesy of New York State Historical Association, Cooperstown, N.Y.*

70. Postwar anecdote

Johannes Adam Oertle: 1823–1909
Archibald M. Willard: 1836–1918
John George Brown: 1831–1913
Thomas Waterman Wood: 1823–1903
Edward Lamson Henry: 1841–1919

In history painting the product of mediocre minds was melodrama, since emotions were forced beyond the natural capacity of such minds; in the quieter reaches of anecdotal painting such minds lapsed easily into sentimentality. Johannes Adam Oertle, a political refugee from the thwarted German revolution of 1848, first practised here his craft of engraving as a means to painting. His earlier pictures were anecdotes of patriotic and topical subjects, some of which caught on with the larger public in lithographic reproduction. Later in life he became a minister, and his religious interests were embodied in some large-scale subjects of which *The Walk to Gethsemane* [National Museum, Washington] is typical. Other pictures were placed in various churches, but it was reproduction royalties from his *Rock of Ages* [1866] which proved how well his soft draftsmanship and saccharine color suited the current religiosity. A sentimentality entirely secular formed the content of Archibald M. Willard's pictures; and again lithographic reproduction was the means to popularity and the test of temporary fame. Two paintings which dealt with child subjects preceded the great success of his career, *The Spirit of '76* [Abbott Hall, Marblehead, Mass.]. From the first roughly humorous idea it was developed into seriously intended patrioteering in time for the Philadelphia Centennial of 1876; thereafter it toured the country from Boston to San Francisco. Possibly the thousands of people who viewed the original were in the end outnumbered by those who purchased reproductions, placing Willard among the very few who have made a lasting contribution to the popular iconography of American patriotism.

Where thousands of homes contained such reproductions, only a few dozen homes of rich men could house the original paintings of bootblacks by John George Brown; but there could be no disputing about tastes so nearly the same. Brown was as much aware as the others of the advantages of reproduction; from one of his paintings a lithograph was made for giving away with packages of tea, royalties on which brought him twenty-five thousand dollars. The subject was not one of his bootblacks or newsboys, but he made a habit of inscribing the originals of these with the prominent word "copyright"; and toward the end of his life originals and reproductions together gave him an income of better than forty thousand dollars a year. The street-urchin phase of Brown's work was quite ordinary as painting, but it had more than ordinary significance for a new phase of American taste. Among the painters thus far considered, some, since they did not succeed in hitting the taste of their times, turned to other ways of making their livings; and some were even careless in their work in defiance of their patrons. But in no case does the available biographical information or the indications discernible in the work suggest that the painter seriously compromised his attitude or technique for the sake of sales he could not otherwise make. Even Pratt, although he turned to sign painting when portraiture failed to yield him a living, continued to paint the best he could, with the result that younger painters found stimulation in his signs. It seems to have been generally true that the painters were like Pratt in that respect, and when their work turned out to be inferior as art or cheap in feeling it was because they were themselves at one with the people who liked such pictures. With Brown, however, there appeared a buying public which brought definite pressure upon the painter to give them both subjects and technique which he knew to be below his own capacity. There were patrons who wanted the better things, such as *The Music Lesson* [1870: Metropolitan Museum, New York], with its extra degree of definiteness in details. The human situation of the girl blowing into her young man's flute has sentiment enough for anybody, but it does not display the repulsive sentimentality which Brown injected into his visually falsified boys. In *The Music Lesson* the hardness and wearisome uniformity of emphasis on clothes and flowers and pictures and harp make it a painting to be read rather than contemplated; but as craft it embodied the severest effort of eye and hand that Brown was capable of; it expressed the kind of mind Brown had, and what he did in his picture was good in that mode of rendering appearances. The success of the buying public in persuading a painter to lower his own standards was an ominous development in American culture; artistic inferiority unaware of anything better by which to judge itself is capable of growth, but an art which knows the good and chooses the inferior is corrupt.

Other painters of postwar anecdote continued the precedent of personal genuineness in their work even though they were not capable of great things. Thomas Waterman Wood began as a pupil of Harding and, after some training in Paris, traveled through Kentucky and Tennessee as a portrait painter; his portraits commenced on a technical level close to artisan craft and went on

79. THE 9:45 ACCOMMODATION by EDWARD LAMSON HENRY *Courtesy of The Metropolitan Museum of Art.*

into the semi-photographic dullness of so much other portraiture of the time. Wood's anecdotal pictures, too, were at first labored in execution and unsatisfactory in design; but he made gains in pictorialism which can be studied in the Gallery which bears his name at Montpelier, Vermont. An occasional example like *The Village Post Office* [1873: plate 78] remains a veracious record, attractive in spirit despite its technical clumsiness. Here is none of the roughly satirical intention of Blythe's *Post Office* [plate 69]; this is unforced sentiment, content with quiet observation. The contrast between the lighted foreground figures and the relative dimness of the rest is insisted upon a little arbitrarily, but all through the area of shadow there is a patient notation of detail which, lacking intensity, is managed with discretion. Rural subject and provincial technique are appropriately united. A subject equally rural and a technique not quite so provincial are joined in an out-of-door scene by Edward Lamson Henry: *The 9:45 Accommodation* [1867: plate 79]. With no trace of the technically radical impressionism soon to be introduced from France, the illumination has in it enough naturalistic accuracy to free it from the bondage of the studio even though the execution of the picture required Henry to work there. Its overcast but pearly lucidity permitted the painter to indulge his love of multitudinous detail without an uncomfortable degree of inconsistency; and the skill with which the slight atmospheric veil is maintained is notable. A general impression of distant animation was apparently the major pictorial intention in the anecdote. Henry almost never equaled this picture again, and long before his death his works began to seem technically anachronistic in the current exhibitions. But his modest and sincere conception of the story-telling picture, necessarily unfashionable in times of intellectual and stylistic complexities, can never be humanly anachronistic to those who like sincerity; it may be neglected because it is spiritually innocent, but that is actually a reason for remembering it.

71. Postwar artisans and amateurs

Anon.: act. 1880
Joseph Becker: 1841–1910
A. Persac: act. 1860
Hunt P. Wilson: act. 1885

James Whitcomb Riley: 1853–1916
Lew Wallace: 1827–1905
Ernest Wadsworth Longfellow: 1845–1921
Erastus Salisbury Field: 1805–1900

Artisan and amateur painting perhaps never dies so long as communities function, but the evidence of actual pictures indicates that after the Civil War its quantity diminished. Possibly the spread of a taste affected by machine-made things induced more people to neglect or destroy such postwar pictures, for there are records of more having been done than are now known. About 1880 Robert Louis Stevenson sympathetically observed an isolated lighthouse keeper near Monterey, California, who kept himself busy, and maybe sane, with playing the piano, making ship models, and painting oils of dawn and sunrise. An oil of *The First Transcontinental Train* [1869: privately owned], by Joseph Becker of Sacramento, has been preserved. A certain A. Persac drew wash and water-color pictures of Louisiana plantations with an almost microscopic vision which made his world diminutive. A few more pictures are documented as coming from Colorado or Pennsylvania or Maine. Hunt P. Wilson, of St. Louis, made a sign painter's version of several Civil War scenes [Confederate Museum, Richmond]. Even more amusing than most of the pictures are some anecdotes about the men who made them. James Whitcomb Riley for a time painted signs in Indiana, and introduced the novelty of being led about under the pretense that he was blind; his quick change-over to playing the banjo in a medicine show suggests meager returns from the attempted stunt. As Riley turned to rhyming, so Lew Wallace turned to the army and novel writing, but not without making a try at painting as his boyhood ambition. He had ground colors for Jacob Cox and taken some home to his garret, where he tried to use them in combination with castor oil and brushes of dog's hair; several days were spent on a portrait of Black Hawk, but his pigments dried out on his tin palette and his father bullied him for being so foolish. A Civil War subject by him was exhibited in 1878, and a little earlier a purple-winged cupid derived rather literally from the scene in *Paradise Lost* where Love "waves his purple wings." All his life Wallace envied painters, as indeed others do—even some who write about paintings.

The incurable amateurism of skill which inheres in timid minds despite all favoring circumstances was typified in the work of Ernest Wadsworth Long-fellow, son of the poet. This son, like the son of Robert Browning, preferred painting to writing; and it may be guessed that the fame of the two fathers may not only have played a part in the original choice of a different activity but also have exerted a certain oppressiveness even after it was made. Both fathers were fondly solicitous for their painter sons; instead of interposing difficulties they rather played the part of Benjamin Jowett at Oxford and "overwhelmed them with feasibilities." With every advantage of instruction and conditions of work, both the younger Longfellow and the younger Browning manifested the academic amateurism of possessing more technique than ideas to put into it.

The good pictorial qualities expressed in amateurish painting usually come in different ways: through a mind experiencing feelings too intense for its technical equipment or conceiving ideas too ambitious for it. Often the feeling or idea breaks through with an effect of struggle which enables the appreciator to participate by perceiving an intention larger or more complex than its tangible embodiment. Or a workman in possession of a technique adequate for his ordinary purposes may venture into unfamiliar territory of the mind with a bland unawareness that he needs a different technique. He may be ignorant of what he needs, but his self-forgetful confidence in what he wants to say transforms his ignorance into an innocence fresh enough to bring him easily through.

This seems to have been the case with Erastus Salisbury Field, who had studied briefly with Morse and had been painting portraits through a portion of New England for thirty years. They were very soundly done in the manner that was fundamental in every region, neither wholly of the shop nor wholly of the studio, but uniting the studio's ruddiness of color with the shop's hard simplification of form. Within the general manner Field manifested enough individuality for him to have deserved comment in the section on the mid-century; but his good portraiture is less interesting than his later departure from it. For during and after the war he turned to imaginative works, the largest of which was nine by thirteen feet: an architectural fantasy entitled *Historical Monument of the American Republic* [before 1876: privately owned]. Ten gigantic circular towers, built with receding stories and united on their top level by suspension bridges, rear into the sky from a continuous architectural base which of itself dwarfs the people in the foreground; on every tower repeating columns, many of them standing free, form a forest of perpendiculars. Probably all of this impossible detail came out of current architectural handbooks of historic styles, but in the process it was mastered by one mind and thus given a somewhat grotesque unity. The impression is of multiplied masses of Sumerian ziggurats rounded into dwindling Tombs of Hadrian and walled with

Romanesque arched galleries so maze-like that the total effect approaches the Gothic. This cannot be described as a work of true imagination because it possesses no emotional drive or spiritual meaning; but the dryly multitudinous detail comes near to the "high fantastical." It is no nightmare, but a waking dream of exorbitant architectural logic.

In a few other pictures of Biblical and mythological subjects Field approached closer to imaginativeness—perhaps so close that it would be ungracious quibbling to deny that quality to *The Garden of Eden* [1860–1870: plate 80]. For it has the inward grace which not only pleases those who are likewise simple but also can persuade even sophisticates to be at least momentarily so. Field's brushwork here is by intention as precise as in the *Historical Monument,* but the general effect is freer because the blockish forms are not forced into his idea of architectural exactness. Trees and beasts seem to have been taken from some natural history book, but they have been ordered into an original conception of space which is indeed Edenic. The rigid perspective of the central valley receding between mountains makes it quaintly garden-like instead of naturalistically wild; the miles of meandering stream only emphasize the purposed orderliness of the scene. Eve plucks two apples, but surely no disaster can follow in a garden where there is so little need of shadow. Dunlap wrote about William Jewett: ". . . as a boy he was delighted with the bright . . ." Field was even luckier; he found delight in brightness when he was old. The brightness he discovered was in the timeless light of the mind where the innocent in heart have their home.

80. THE GARDEN OF EDEN *by* ERASTUS SALISBURY FIELD *Courtesy of Museum of Fine Arts [M. & M. Karolik Collection], Boston.*

72. Postwar still-life

Andrew John Henry Way: 1826–1888   Filippo Costaggini: 1837–1907
Severin Roesen: act. 1860–1870   William Michael Harnett: ?1848–1892
George Henry Hall: 1825–1913   Jefferson David Chalfant: 1856–1931
Walter M. Brackett: 1823–1917   John Frederick Peto: 1854–1907
Constantino Brumidi: 1805–1880   John Haberle: 1856–1933

The five sections immediately preceding have been concerned mainly with the distinct lowering of the average technical skill. By way of contrast, the average technique in still-life was easily maintained about as it had been or maybe a little improved; and in work even along this level there was a considerable spread of interest. Andrew John Henry Way, after portraiture in Baltimore, turned to still-life with success; his somewhat sober literalism retained a freshness of execution which made him the best of the few who continued the semi-scientific objectivity of James Peale. A dramatic incursion of flamboyance into still-life was made by a certain Severin Roesen, said to have been a German, established in Williamsport, Pennsylvania, from 1860. *Nature's Bounty* [Whitney Museum of American Art, New York] contains a mountainous surfeit of detail, but it is perhaps preserved from vulgarity by a texture which approaches pastel in its dry brilliance. George Henry Hall sentimentalized still-life with soft drawing and obvious color; he, if anyone, vulgarized what Tuckerman called "the trophies of Pomona," and he obtained his immediate reward in twelve thousand dollars from his auction of seventy-five small pictures. The praise for Walter M. Brackett as "a painter of piscatorial treasures," which have not as yet been brought forward by resurrectors of the quaint, would indicate that he satisfied some sportsmen's unaffected desire to be reminded of holiday exploits.

Equally unaffected as a taste in pictures was the continuous American (which is only a qualified way of saying: the permanently human) desire for a maximum exactitude of visual imitation. Coincident with the postwar intensification of materialism, this desire was satisfied as never before by a group of remarkable technicians. In the last few years William Michael Harnett and a few more with similar aims have received much critical and popular attention; and since their works were easel pictures, many of them have been extensively exhibited. They were paralleled, and even slightly preceded in time, by a decorative undertaking in the Rotunda of the national Capitol which was also important as an expression of the same taste. After Brumidi had finished the ceiling of the Rotunda, he commenced the project of a frieze around the three hundred feet of wall at the height of seventy-five feet above the floor. After three years Brumidi died and the work was carried on by his assistant, Filippo Costaggini, until the whole was about two-thirds done, when he too died. Continuous as a piece of painting, nine feet in height, it was to consist of a series of episodes commencing with the landing of Columbus and covering the entire history of this continent. The painting was to be in *grisaille* in exact imitation of high relief carving in stone, and the completed portion is still praised by the official guides for its merit as illusionism. Its technical success in this respect, however, depends to some extent upon its illumination, the even daylight that prevails, and to a much greater extent upon fixed conditions in angle of vision and irreducible distance. The easel paintings now to be discussed constitute a much more complicated experience.

Harnett was born in Ireland and brought here as a child; the accident of settling in Philadelphia would seem to have been a determining factor in his career, for his beginnings as a painter of still-life indicate a knowledge of work by the Peales and by Francis. The pictures of Harnett's first period, from 1874 to 1880, show some of the awkwardness that is unavoidable at the beginning of all painting which sets out to embody any variety of naturalistic vision; but they also show an immediate concentration of interest upon what was to be Harnett's lifelong concern: textures. For a while, indeed, this went to the naïve extreme of rendering such minute details as match heads by building out the pigment itself from the rest of the surface; in depicting a beer mug Harnett would thicken the pigment and then roughen it in a quite tangible approximation to actuality. He soon turned away from such tricks to a technically severer effort to compass everything by brushwork alone; but it was a brushwork eliminating as far as possible all evidence of separate strokes for the sake of a uniform handling which tried to persuade the eye that it was looking not at paint but at actual textures. Within the National Academy itself the technique was becoming old-fashioned by the late 'seventies, and it is therefore not surprising that the art critic of the *New York Tribune* in 1879 belittled Harnett's imitativeness as relatively easy to do and of low worth when done. The objects which Harnett used at that time were quite ordinary—a pipe or a bottle of milk, a pile of bargain books; in later years he said quite simply that cheap objects had been all he could then afford. But there was one striking exception in the *Still-life* [1878: Fogg Museum, Harvard University] which a well-to-do Philadelphian commissioned. The odd thing was that the picture was made from objects which the patron owned: vases, candlesticks, a scimitar, a large old book, and the like—trivial but costly-seeming symbols of culture. Harnett responded with a design which, forsaking the intimacies of his own homely materials, attempted a more removed stateliness of a complex pyramid; he also emphasized the obvious luster of metal and china kept in ornamental brightness.

This may be the origin of one change in Harnett's taste which became visible in his pictures after he went to Europe in 1880. He began to use in his still-life a miscellany of old objects from which he could extract richer colors and mellower tone, and also, from the nicks and cracks and indentations of long use, technical complications of detail giving more variety to the surfaces. He changed from the obviously ordinary to the obviously exotic, and with his collection of curios—he brought them back to this country and used them the rest of his life—he tried for the profuse and studied designs which he had seen in late Dutch work. In Europe he also commenced using a more individual pictorial motive: a green door against which a variety of objects stand out in minutely exact relief. A very large example, almost six feet high, was shown in the Paris Salon: *After the Hunt* [1885: California Palace of the Legion of Honor, San Francisco]. In this a dead rabbit and three dead game birds contrast their soft textures to those of metals and cloth and horn and wood in a dozen objects—hanging one on top of another upon an ornately hinged door. This was praised by an unorthodox critic in Paris, and when Harnett brought it back and sold it, with other pictures, to a well known saloon in New York, the saloon and the picture and himself became famous among great numbers of people who were unaware of the more self-conscious cultivation of the Academicians and their public. And among the larger public there were plenty of fairly wealthy men who, not yet snared into fashionable buying, were willing to back their own untutored tastes with their own money; and within five years of his return Harnett could get ten thousand dollars for *Emblems of Peace* [1890: Springfield Museum, Springfield, Mass.]. This was one of the best of the elaborate compositions out of his European souvenirs, but about the same time he was combining the door motive with homely detail in *The Faithful Colt* [1890: Wadsworth Atheneum, Hartford]; and the bold diagonal of the revolver was balanced with daring simplicity by only a small piece of microscopically painted newspaper print below. These feats by Harnett were quickly emulated by a painter of Wilmington, Delaware: Jefferson David Chalfant. Within three years he adapted the idea of hunting trophies on a door, the first in a series by several painters coming down as recently as 1927; soon after his first emulation of Harnett, Chalfant featured a painted newspaper clipping on a small piece of enameled copper where he had pasted a real two-cent stamp next to his painted imitation of one, with the challenging title: *Which Is Which?* [c. 1890: privately owned]. Another way in which Chalfant followed

Harnett was in painting paper money, and a story is told about his having painted a gold coin on a bar so deceptively that men did not need even a beer to try to pick it up.

John Frederick Peto used the same type of homely material—mugs and candlesticks and old books—found in the early phase of Harnett, but he was also very fond of a special type of illusionistic subject, which Harnett had also previously used, in which boards have on them cloth strips holding cards and letters and torn clippings and old photographs; the extremely shallow visual depth which this permits makes illusionistic exactitude easier to achieve than with objects of greater volume. A recent study using recorded facts and stylistic analysis and laboratory examination with shadowgraphs has assigned to Peto a fair-sized group of paintings all bearing the added signatures of Harnett. It should be said that Peto himself had nothing to do with these "adaptations" for the higher prices that Harnett's pictures bring. All types of evidence converge to establish a convincing case, and in particular the evidence of technique seems now so clear that the wonder is how the contradiction of style proved acceptable to begin with. For the two men's skills were not only different but consistently different, and different to such a degree that the two ways of using color and rendering form could hardly have come from the same mind. Where Harnett was exceptionally precise with edges and almost invariably depicted the right amount of space for the full volume of his objects, Peto left edges blunter, sometimes inexact, and failed to maintain physical space to a depth sufficient for his objects to stand free. Peto's pigment also retained much more of a painty character, was never pushed as far in differentiating textures as was Harnett's; and where Harnett habitually attained transparency in color, Peto was content to be opaque. Among the group re-attributed, the *Discarded Treasures* [Smith College Museum, Northampton, Mass.] can serve as well as any to illustrate the differences here generalized, together with further differences of detail peculiar to the two men's handling of books: Harnett being much more minute in his treatment of lettering and bindings and leaf-edges. Peto's personal qualities of more sharply contrasted light-and-dark and greater carrying power for the design as a whole are sufficient to keep him in history as a interesting minor figure of his age.

Peto often refused to be definite in details and manifested more interest in a peculiar veil of silvery tone obtained by mixing white with other colors; and in these respects he stayed nearer to the current conception of painting pictures rather than fooling anybody's eyes. But with John Haberle the latter intention is further developed with an individual quirk which sets him somewhat apart in his own time. He did not begin to exhibit until 1887, but his painting in this kind was finished before 1900, as apparently the strain of it gave him eye trouble. He began with paper money, and did it so marvelously well that his product resulted in more than an admonitory visit from secret-service men. An art critic of a Chicago newspaper brought the charge that Haberle's picture in the 1889 exhibition at the Art Institute was not painted but was actual money pasted on canvas; Haberle took the train to Chicago and forced a public retraction, upon which it came out that the accusing critic had relied upon the assurances of Eastman Johnson. In short, Haberle had fooled the eye of one of the leading painters of the time! Haberle's pictures followed precedent by making certain saloons famous for housing them; and one such owner in Detroit commissioned him to paint a picture which necessitated a departure from his usual shallow depth in an attempt to secure full three-dimensionality: *Grandma's Hearthstone* [1890: privately owned]. Haberle's two years of work on this earned him not only good money but a recurrence of the illusionist's final praise: the fire in the picture fooled a cat, and people repeatedly tried to brush the flies off. This is of course a robust revival of the stories told about Raphaelle Peale; but in Haberle's work there is not the slightest indication of the secret poetry that sometimes exhaled from the humblest of Peale's still-lifes. Since this streak of pawky humor is so prominent in the total American experience, it is altogether fitting that it should make its special contribution to painting. It may even have been so intended as early as its first appearance with John Mare, but it is certain that then the illusion of the fly was whole-heartedly admired by the best judges; Haberle's flies, too, were wholeheartedly admired. His most remarkable success with his special aim was *Torn in Transit* [privately owned], in which the illusionism of string and torn paper wrappings depends for its effectiveness upon the fact that the exposed portion of the picture supposedly wrapped for shipment is painted in the current non-illusionistic manner of the studios. Mr. Alfred Frankenstein, who writes with most authority about this phase of American painting, has effectively pointed out the ultimate involved in this establishment of illusionism by means of its opposite technique being juxtaposed.

This particular painting, and perhaps the whole of Haberle's career, involves an element of burlesque which is not inappropriate to the aim itself in relation to the whole of painting; yet the American pursuit of "nearly looking" has been in a way more significant than its usually trivial expression in paint. Here Harnett is so clearly supreme in the postwar group that the interpreter must return to his work for one of the rare appearances of deeper meaning in a search which has been mostly concerned with superficial things. This is no more paradoxical than the claim of spirituality made by some thinkers for American materialism, and that is no more of a paradox than the all-inclusive one of body and mind which is the inescapable condition of human existence. Starting out as he did with ordinary objects in arrangements that were far from subtle, Harnett subtilized his design and shifted to exotic pictorial material. Before the end, some of his pictures became endowed with a mysteriousness by which they haunt the memory. Unquestionably the improvement in design had much to do with this, but the change in the character of the objects did not; for the mystery is perhaps most intensely felt in a canvas of the third period where he reverts in part to the homeliness of the earlier things: *The Old Violin* [1886: plate 81]. Like his Salon picture, this one also exerted considerable influence on other painters; a chromolithograph of it was made, skilful enough in itself to sell extensively but falling short of Harnett's skill and containing some minor errors. From this reproduction several painters made oils which attempted to rival the original in exactitude, and they all repeated the minute errors in the notes of music for which the lithographer was responsible. Almost needless to say, this popularity and influence occurred on the level of mass taste which had not yet been effectively reached by the ideas and performances of the painters engaged in supporting or revolting against the National Academy of Design.

To the casual eye *The Old Violin* seems rather obvious in design; but further acquaintance will gradually reveal the subtleties of placing and illumination by which the strong horizontals and uprights are counterpointed with diagonals and curves. The greatest gain over certain others of his pictures lies in the small number of objects involved: only five standing out in shallow relief against a heavy-hinged door. In other works the very multiplicity of things, with their different textures, minimizes the appeal of the whole by dispersing interest among too many competing details; here, tact in design is re-enforced by restraint in content which allows a far stronger appeal to be exerted by a tactility of startling verisimilitude. Better than in the more ostentatious examples, Harnett's search for exactness in tactile qualities can be seen for what it was—a passionate pursuit of a certain kind of perfection. It was a perfection of surfaces particularly congenial to the pragmatic American temper because the attainment of it seemed to be entirely a matter of craft, and therefore feasible. Like other absolutes, it proved to be illusory; but like all other searches for an absolute, it proved to be worth making. For it at least came near to an ultimate of tangibility; as Mr. Frankenstein has said, these surfaces asked to be touched. At the same time, the knowledge that it is a painting checks the impulse; and the mind is left in the puzzling situation where, in an effectively heightened manner, one sense functions in place of another. Not only for average people in ordinary life but for everybody in all conditions, such a near-dislocation of experience is tantalizing, and the meaning of it is elusive. Painter and audience together desire complete convincingness for the mind, and assume that it requires a purification of physical qualities, a clearer light and a sharper differentiation of textures than actually exists—if that be possible. Belief in materialism at this intensity is a form of idealism: therein lies the mystery.

81. THE OLD VIOLIN *by* WILLIAM MICHAEL HARNETT
Courtesy of Mr. and Mrs. Charles Finn Williams. Photograph from Cincinnati Art Museum.

73. Grandiloquent landscape

Frederick Edwin Church: 1826–1900
Albert Bierstadt: 1830–1902
Thomas Hill: 1829–1913
Thomas Moran: 1837–1926

The landscapes of the Hudson River men were sometimes large; and when they were, they usually seemed to be mistakes in judgement because the meticulous handling characteristic of the School resulted in monotony through the larger stretches of scenery. It is rarely possible to say that a School-man succeeded in giving space itself a directly pictorial significance, for he was too preoccupied with whatever things happened to exist in the space. Cole, however, did advance toward the general concept; his only pupil, Frederick Edwin Church, developed that lead in a way of his own, thereby taking the popular interest in landscape painting on to a new phase. Church was a pupil during only the last four years of Cole's life; therefore his work starts with one characteristic which had come relatively late with his teacher—the reduction of brushwork to an almost unnoticeable role in painting. How great an advantage it was in furthering the principal aim of all Church's work can be seen in the *Scene in the Catskill Mountains* [1852: plate 82], for with Church the unobtrusive brush stroke was the means to an exceptionally minute and exact notation of values. This gave him his complete control over naturalistic distance and caused Tuckerman later to admire his work for "the most photographic imitation of the natural objects and effects." Intended as praise, it would have been more accurate if the key adjective had been *stereoscopic,* but it did specify well enough what the age thought was the supreme merit in the canvases of Church. Tuckerman was of course entirely correct in remarking how the earlier Catskill subjects exemplify the "authenticity of executive skill." The precision in values, remarkable though it would be at any time, nevertheless now seems both less important and less interesting than the unobtrusive skill in composition. This consists of a series of repeating and overlapping triangles across the picture surface: first the foreground log cabin with its lean-tos, next the middle-distance mountain, then the far-distant mountain the line of which continues across the nearer mountain to that of the water's edge still nearer, and last the sky-piled clouds which combine the two triangles of the mountains into a third and larger triangle controlling the whole. Mainly because of the accurate values, the building and the mountains are substantial enough in mass to count as pyramids with slopes down the unseen sides; and this gives a special importance to the close repetition of shape discernible on comparing the sunlit walls of the building with the shadowed form of rocky height and wooded slopes beyond. At twenty-six Church was manifesting a skill in arranging objects and in managing light which was adequate to keep the eye interested through panoramic stretches of nature.

In the following year, 1853, he undertook the first of his many journeys outside the United States: to South and Central America, Mexico, the West Indies, Labrador, and eventually Greece and Palestine. He had an idea derived from a reading of *Kosmos,* by the German traveler and scientist Alexander Von Humboldt, that landscape should be studied and presented with scientific exactitude; for him it was good fortune because it sanctioned his already meticulous execution and supplied a motivation to a mind already irrevocably committed to the craft of pictorial description as distinguished from the art of pictorial creation. However, Church believed that he was creating because the tremendous travelogues he showed the public were no humdrum views of just what could be seen from one particular spot but composite summations of whole regions out of many sketches and studies; in this way, he thought, he got clear of the tedium of the actual and achieved the higher truth of an ideal. Such was the famous painting which he composed after his second trip, *Heart of the Andes* [1859: Metropolitan Museum, New York]; exhibited by artificial light—apt illumination's artful aid—it attracted crowds who paid to marvel. They were excited by the subject, remote and splendid; by admiration for the painter, that he went so far and worked so hard and did so much; amazement at the size of the canvas as well as the extent of the view; and by pleasure in "nearly looking"—when Mark Twain visited the picture in St. Louis, he admiringly counted leaves through an opera glass. For both the painter and the people believed that the large area of the canvas could be validated by the minuteness of the detail; more people wanted to look into the picture than were content to look at it. The inclusion of so much information made atmospheric unity impossible and required the harsh glare of uniformity, which affects a later audience as being exploitation rather than interpretation. That is why all the excitement was about the pictures and not in them; but there was money enough in exhibition and copyright and sales of the originals for what another writer about Church called "other ventures in the same line of business." The painter continued his search for still greater—that is to say, merely larger—wonders.

Church commissioned himself to paint the world, but on one important occa-

82. SCENE IN THE CATSKILL MOUNTAINS *by* FREDERICK EDWIN CHURCH *Courtesy of Walker Art Center, Minneapolis.*

sion he gave his audience an additional thrill of patrioteering subject-matter. In painting *Niagara* [1857: Corcoran Gallery, Washington], he chose an angle of vision which allowed him to fill the foreground with a rush of water, and here his "scientific" observation produced an effect which can be admired even today. In its day it wakened enthusiasm, earned the approval of Ruskin, and received a medal at the Paris exposition of 1867. Albert Bierstadt, however, was a professional Americaneer in paint, and his four years of training at Düsseldorf equipped him to meet the current taste in landscape as well as Leutze did in melodramatic history. He necessarily followed the same procedure as Church, accumulating sketches and studies on his journeys and from them composing the big exhibition canvases in the studio. The first of many trips was to the Rockies in 1858, and later he visited California and Oregon with equally grandiose results. A painting like *The Rocky Mountains* [Metropolitan Museum, New York] astonished the public by its scale and its detail both; but Bierstadt was not so good a draftsman as Church, and his Düsseldorfian handling of pigment was oilier and less crisp. For the time being that did not matter, and Bierstadt obtained his thousands for a canvas just as Church did; his European contacts, further, placed his pictures from England to Petrograd and earned him several decorations. *The Last of the Buffalo* [plate 83] is unusual among the larger productions in the one respect of attempting to depict a few figures in vigorous movement—not very successfully; otherwise the painting exhibits their characteristic immobility. The scene is effectively staged, but the illumination was not thought out thoroughly enough to minimize studio inconsistencies. It is a little like the conception of research which was then being brought back by American students from German universities, wherein the accumulation of accurate details tends to impair the scholar's capacity to synthesize them into a more important general truth. Bierstadt was heavy-handed and the pigment on the canvases which won him most acclaim while alive is repellent in its dull monotony.

Thomas Hill and Thomas Moran, both born in England and both brought here as children, both receiving their first art instruction here and both remaking their techniques in later European study—these two in maturity practised a looser brushwork and a better unified colorism than Church and Bierstadt, but they accentuated the vice of the gigantic. Hill's largest works remain in the Far West itself, with which he became identified by residence, but some of them were exhibited in the East, where they received official honors and earned him satisfactory fame. However, the panoramic extensiveness seems compositionally hollow: a visual emptiness which parallels the hollow ring of Joaquin Miller's reams of rhymes. After viewing some of the western scenery, Oscar Wilde questioned its serviceableness to painting and poetry because it seemed to him that man was not its master. No uncertainty about his own mastery of such subject-matter ever entered the mind of Thomas Moran, who had the most effervescent temperament and the most fluent and variable technique of all those addicted to grandiloquent landscape. Everything considered, it was a sound instinct which sent him to Turner's work even though he was so impressionable that he never fully recovered and could modify that influence only by almost equally strong influences from other sources. Probably nothing could have made him into a major painter, least of all insulation from the work of others; and for all of his Colorado and Yellowstone immensities he reverted openly to the Turneresque. He accompanied two government exploring expeditions, to the canyons of the Yellowstone and the Colorado, and it is not surprising that explorers and scientists remarked in understatement that he "never stuck to local limitations"; out of the two trips came the two enormous pictures purchased for ten thousand dollars each by the Government for the Capitol— *The Grand Canyon of the Yellowstone* and *The Chasm of the Colorado*. The latter wakened dismay in an art critic writing in *The Atlantic Monthly* for September, 1874; only in the sky could he discover the peace and rest which art should properly give: otherwise the canvas was but a demoralized land from which the true lover of nature must turn aside until the tantrum was over. "The only aim of art is to feed the sense of beauty; it has no right to meddle with horrors and desolations." A later writer would be likely to find nature not so horrible, after all, and to lament the desolation of raw paint. The scenery of the West was pictorially more manageable on a smaller scale, as when Moran himself succeeded in concentrating so much into his *Western Landscape* [1864: plate 84]. In comparison with Church and Bierstadt, the pigment is thinly handled and the modeling of form bears every evidence of haste; but it is a better picture for its spirited composition, its crisp brushwork, and most of all its animated illumination. Some weaknesses in construction are more than offset by the quick coherence of all the pictorial elements.

Almost any among the smaller pictures in Moran's huge output will be found intrinsically more interesting than the panoramic enormities which had most to do with his fame while alive; but the smaller things are also unpredictable in manner, giving evidence variously of Turner and Ziem and Corot and the Dutch, together with occasional treatments which ally him momentarily with this or that Hudson River man. Hill's smaller pictures are more likely to be shoddy than not, since he painted hundreds out of his head to a formula for the tourist trade. Bierstadt and Church are much more interesting in their sketches and preparatory studies—the material out of which their exhibition pictures were constructed, for it was only the latter which they subjected to the dead evenness of "finish" so uninteresting now, whereas the smaller things frequently have

83. THE LAST OF THE BUFFALO *by* ALBERT BIERSTADT *Courtesy of Corcoran Gallery of Art, Washington, D.C.*

interesting brushwork and almost always more vivacity of color. [Sketches by Church at Cooper Union, New York; small paintings by Bierstadt in the Brooklyn Museum, New York, and in the M. & M. Karolik Collection at the Museum of Fine Arts, Boston.]

As for the immensities which made these men important while alive and therefore did most to determine the nature of their treatment in history, they came out of an idea that is fallacious in easel painting: the idea of equating physical size with epic character. More importantly, the mistake was made by minds that had an incorrect conception of how imagination could be released into pictures. Whatever intensity they possessed was channeled into minutiae of execution, and the inconsistency between this and their chosen scale gave not grandeur but bombast. As Dryden wrote, "Bombast is commonly the delight of that audience which loves Poetry, but understands it not."

74. Lesser landscape

James David Smillie: 1833–1909
George Henry Smillie: 1840–1921
Robert Swain Gifford: 1840–1905
Samuel Colman: 1832–1920

Alfred Thompson Bricher: 1837–1908
Albert Fitch Bellows: 1830–1883
William Rickaby Miller: 1818–1893
William Trost Richards: 1833–1905

The ideals of the Hudson River School were continued in a more direct line than that represented by the grandiloquent landscapists who attracted most attention; but those who remained somewhat faithful to the School habit soon seemed anachronistic. Among those who came into prominence after the war the Smillie brothers were typical. They came of a family of engravers, and the elder, James David Smillie, practised that craft until about 1864; the work of the younger, George Henry Smillie, does not show any evidence of the dry minuteness with which his brother commenced painting. Both were moderately responsive to what their contemporaries were doing, and made their brushwork and impasto a little more personal than the practice of the School had been; but both were in every technical respect secondary, and the younger Smillie developed a brightness in color which insists too much upon the smiling aspects of nature. Robert Swain Gifford, a distant cousin of the earlier Sanford Robinson Gifford, traveled widely before settling down in New York to painting and teaching; he was better aware than the Smillies of the trend away from the monotonous "finish" of the School, and he exerted an important influence toward a technique of emotional expressiveness. His own pictures were surpassed in that respect by those of intenser minds. Samuel Colman was at first an almost indistinguishable School man and he also made pictures of European subjects which are only dullish versions of Turner; but some postwar American subjects of eastern pastures and westward-traveling emigrant wagons are quite broadly handled and interestingly composed.

Colman holds his place in painting by those oils, but he also led in the movement which at that time brought water color into special prominence; he became the first president of the organization which, starting in 1866, soon adopted the name The American Water Color Society. Although they worked principally in oils, Swain Gifford and others contributed to the Society's exhibitions water colors which at least pointed the way toward the spontaneity of handling which is the most rewarding as well as the most demanding characteristic of the medium;

84. WESTERN LANDSCAPE *by* THOMAS MORAN *Courtesy of The Art Museum of the New Britain Institute.*

but the mass of earlier work sponsored by the Society was in technique essentially a transfer into water color of the habits already established in oil. This meant that even the semi-transparent washes and simplified shapes of the earlier men who prepared water colors for aquatint reproduction had been supplanted by a multitude of minute touches completely covering the paper in an effort to build up the textures and forms more appropriate to oils; the result was complete opacity. Typical of this variant in landscape was Alfred Thompson Bricher; and Albert Fitch Bellows, from a close study of English work, used a blurry softness of color which made woodland bits of New England seem like Old England. He reversed the technical change by which George Harvey had responded to this country's climate and he lagged far behind such a transplanted Englishman as William Rickaby Miller [New-York Historical Society, New York], whose postwar landscapes in water color evidenced a marked alertness to the technique then developing in belated rendition of the brilliant light characterizing the northerly portion of the United States.

Some of the water-colorists were among those who tried to develop an American version of Pre-Raphaelism as preached in England by Ruskin. Ruskin's writings had been extensively reprinted in *The Crayon* during its three years of existence in the 'fifties, but hardly anyone who read them had a first-hand knowledge of the buildings and the pictures he wrote about; nor did many have it when, the Civil War being still in progress, a small group of architects and painters in New York founded *The New Path* to re-preach the doctrine. The painters among them announced that they would exemplify it in their pictures, but it is remarkable how the works they offered the public were censured in terms equally applicable to Durand and Kensett, although the American Pre-Raphaelites denounced Hudson River School work in general. With a reverence caught from Ruskin's moral fervor his followers here sought to give each natural object its greatest precision of form and its greatest intensity of local color. On this account the writer Jarves reproached them for literalism and neglect of spiritual characterization; the portraitist Elliott resorted to humor, claiming that a Pre-Raphaelite would distinguish the east and the west sides of a hair—"But there isn't much expression, after all, in a single hair." He might have been speaking of some English work, but again he might not, for he never left America. Actual examples by the men directly associated with the magazine are scarce in the public collections at present, but museums frequently possess pictures by William Trost Richards, who consciously practised the Pre-Raphaelite aim in oil painting after his return from Europe in 1858. What Durand had striven for in tree bark and foliage, Trost Richards also aimed at, and then tried to achieve an even more minute exactitude in the wild flowers beneath. His defenders, like the critic Sheldon, were indignant because younger painters said he was no artist—younger men who dared to exhibit "simply studio-studies" as complete pictures. Trost Richards did his best work in his later years, when he turned to the sea for his subjects; but none of his expanses of water or stretches of breaking wave was more successful in texture or color than Church's *Niagara*, done the year before Richards' return from Europe.

The currents of technique and feeling in landscape painting were setting definitely away from the tightness and hardness which the American Pre-Raphaelites tried to re-validate by their Society for the Advancement of Truth in Art. Their relatively few pictures could not do it, nor could the preachments in *The New Path* against Inness and Homer Martin. Of the latter's *Adirondack Mountains*, shown in the Academy exhibit in its new building in 1865, one writer remarked: "Indeed, it is difficult to recall any canvas covered with such a thickness of dirty paint, and absolutely without form and void." The individual picture may have been poor enough, but it was their rejection of the entire tendency of which Martin was only a part that defeated the Pre-Raphaelites in the end. Denunciations in *The New Path* of certain painters who were entrenched in official positions and in public favor doubtless had their effect in clearing some minds for better things. If the *New-Path* writers could surprisingly find a manly sincerity in what they recognized as the uncouthness of Carpenter's *Emancipation*, they could in compensation condemn Huntington's *Lady Washington's Reception* as a feeble compilation, its color worse than usual but its drawing not worse than usual. They could puncture the puffery by which Bierstadt's reputation was being maintained, they could expose the vulgarity of J. G. Brown and call the turn on the artistic indecency by which W. H. Beard degraded animals into cheap moralisms for humans.

75. Poetic landscape

George Inness: 1825–1894 (work after 1865)
Alexander Helwig Wyant: 1836–1892
Homer Dodge Martin: 1836–1897
Ralph Albert Blakelock: 1847–1919

A few painters of landscape were not content to continue a weakening repetition of the Hudson River School formula, neither were they willing to adopt the literalness practised by those who invoked the name of Ruskin. Their idea was that even the most accurate recording of the visible world afforded insufficient satisfaction in the doing and insufficient mental nourishment after it was done. After all, painting as an art was needlessly hampering its own communicativeness if it stayed too close to factual information. Accordingly, their tendency was from the objective to the subjective and their study was to modify technique into communicating emotion directly. Not only did they vary and intensify color and tone for the sake of mood; they also stressed the handling for its own sake, lengthening or shortening the brush stroke, thinning or thickening the pigment, jabbing it with the brush handle or laying it on with the palette knife, combining any or all of these processes and more into one picture if doing so would express their feelings. To be sure, this early group of emotional landscapists used their technical freedom with a restraint that was thrown off by later generations; but the handling which in retrospect seems full of sobriety was in its own time an important adjustment of painting into a more expressive instrument. For the time being, restraint in its use was natural to temperaments whose own moods did not range widely.

In his own time George Inness was thought adventurous in emotion, and his pictures did encompass both joy and gloom, with cheeriness and sadness in between. The limitation that must be noted in his work was in the degree of convincingness with which he could present one or another mood; and it is inextricably involved with the technical mannerism of his later years. By 1855 he had come clear of the Hudson River School; and after a decade more of veering impulses combining into a general growth, he painted one of his most ambitious pictures, *Peace and Plenty* [1865: Metropolitan Museum, New York], canonizing the American feeling for autumnal fulfilment. Here "meadow, grove, and stream" are indeed "apparell'd in celestial light" from a cloud-aureoled sunset.

It is the glow of light which keeps so much space from being panoramic, for it warms into intimacy a middle distance not too large for the call of a human voice. With Wordsworth in his thirties such a vision as this had been supplanted by "the light of common day"; for Inness at forty this was not common, and it was also an experience possible in maturity, which he did not have to call up from a distant boyhood. It was as if Inness were attempting to change a line in Wordsworth's own poem, to make it read: "That there shall pass away no glory from the earth." As Inness' latest interpreter has pointed out, *Peace and Plenty* is part of the American consciousness.

Beginning in 1870, and because his dealer thought that foreign subjects would sell better, Inness passed four years in another European stay, most of it in Italy, with a stop in France on the way back to this country. Other pictures besides *Peace and Plenty* done before this trip suggest that he need not have made it in order to improve his painting or to clarify his composition into classic spaciousness. He may not have needed the trip even for subject-matter, for before he went he painted *Lake Albano* [1869: Phillips Gallery, Washington] from memories of an earlier stay. Yet the Italian pictures of this later time do make a specially handsome group in Inness' total work, and *The Tiber Below Perugia* [c. 1871: Toledo Museum] is all the more effective in its antique nobility of spirit for having in it none of the neo-classic trappings of temples and bed-sheeted statues acting out emotions loftier than common people are supposed to have. Back home, Inness painted *Autumn Oaks* [c. 1875: plate 85] in unconscious valediction to this, his best, decade. Comparison with *The Old Mill* [1849: plate 63] shows how much surer in hand and greater in spirit he had become. With a subject in which the major masses are about the same distance from the eye, his world seems bigger because he has learned to manage space with more freedom and subtlety, steadier because he can now simplify his masses, stronger because he constructs his forms without exaggeration, and richer because he sounds his color in one harmonized chord instead of striking it insistently note by note. But there is also a Tennysonian "lin-lan-lone of evening bells" which marks a softening toward the structural disintegration of the latter years.

Of course, not every picture of his best decade was up to his own mark at the time; his nature was too impulsive for him to avoid sudden sags at almost any moment. The same characteristic was to work to his advantage through the years of declining ability, for equally sudden spurts would temporarily renew his architectonic control of design. In such times particularly he was helped by his developed ability to paint rapidly and well, re-enforced by use of a quickly drying medium which would allow his freshness of feeling to achieve its effect before being exhausted. But more and more his do-or-die spontaneity changed into hit-or-miss picturemaking. There was a parallel manifestation in his writings of this

85. AUTUMN OAKS *by* GEORGE INNESS *Courtesy of The Metropolitan Museum of Art.*

period. Some semi-theological prose makes heavy going; some emotional *vers libre* is very *libre;* and some opinions about painting exhibit a frenetic violence beyond Ruskin—Turner's *The Slave Ship* is "the most infernal piece of claptrap ever painted" and impressionism is "the original pancake of visual imbecility . . . from the lie of intent to the lie of ignorance." He had earlier evolved a more balanced statement for his guiding idea:

. . . A work of art does not appeal to the intellect. It does not appeal to the moral sense. Its aim is not to instruct, not to edify, but to awaken an emotion.

But his habit of spasmodic emotion was ultimately disintegrating to his expression of it in art, especially when it was accompanied by a further stage of semi-pantheistic thinking about nature as the Garment of God. This idea was not the cause but only the accompaniment of Inness' willingness to cover overlarge canvases with a film of pigment under which shapes of tree and shrub glimmer submerged. The earlier poetry of feeling was now rationalized into conscious poeticism; and it is to the earlier works that one must turn for whatever evidence there may be to substantiate Tuckerman's neat verdict of ". . . unequal . . . sometimes unequalled . . ."

Ohio-born Alexander Helwig Wyant, during an apprenticeship to a harness maker, painted signs out of hours and drew leaves and trees from nature. Seeking further training and portrait work in Cincinnati, he there saw a picture or two by Inness in 1857; this led him to make the eastern trip for a meeting, after which he returned to Cincinnati with a determination to break away from signs and portraits. His desire to paint landscape met with some favor, and quite soon he painted one of his most interesting works, *Falls of the Ohio and Louisville* [1863: plate 86], a picture commissioned with the intention of helping him in his ambition. Never again did he dare so marked a degree of asymmetry in composition, and the contrast of scale between large trees and little figures is another factor in the superiority of this picture over many later examples. The stretch of riverbank and distant city is meticulously delicate in detail, without the usual Hudson River School hardness of touch; and the illumination suggests that he may have seen Inness' *Lackawanna Valley* of 1855. Wyant went to Düsseldorf in 1865, only to be dissatisfied with the school's emphasis upon unselective detail; yet the phase of his work which most clearly shows the influence of its method has a merit of its own. *Winona Falls* [City Art Museum, St. Louis] is an important example of this stage in his development; it is not Düsseldorf in the school's full insistence on the obvious, but it is Düsseldorfian in the linear character of its design. The mitigating and refining element here is Wyant's instinctive poetry, by which he was led to subordinate what is less important than the strong and lively diagonal of light which both divides and composes the picture. By the end of the 'sixties he had begun loading his canvas with paint. In hope of new subjects and more of improved health, he went with a government expedition of 1873 into Arizona and New Mexico; but illness ensued, and he underwent a paralysis which necessitated his learning to paint with his left hand. Apparently the change did not impair his ability to say what he wanted to say in paint, but what he said was repetitive. He adopted the habit of working in the studio from memory; the pictures which Wyant produced in that way have the merits of good tree construction and, rather surprisingly, a close rendering of light as it filters through foliage. Yet however he shifted the positions of the trees, his composition tended to one of two results: two-thirds sky and one-third bush and tree, or the reverse. This, as the main element of variety in an art staying within the narrow range from elegy to somberness, resulted in an uncomfortable degree of monotony.

Homer Dodge Martin could be elegiac, and once or twice his somberness was intensified into the tragic. But Martin had other moods as well, so that his work as a whole can give a more rounded emotional experience: which is by no means to say he was successful in all he attempted. His earliest work was poor even within the limits of the Hudson River School, but a study of Kensett's pictures enabled him to paint somewhat better than with the little instruction he had received from James M. Hart. After fifteen years of professionalism he visited Europe and absorbed the ideas of Barbizon toward which he had already felt drawn; but it was during another stay from 1881 to 1886 that he changed most markedly. Yet before the first trip in 1876 he had painted *Lake Sandford* [1870: The Century Association, New York], wherein relatively simple horizontals and perpendiculars express a desolation more quieting than it is disturbing. *The Westchester Hills* [c. 1887: privately owned], less linear, with the richer facture from the Barbizon influence, conveys a milder loneliness. Some of the Normandy subjects are sharply localized in observation, with recognizable bits of architecture and the characteristically heavy soil. One French subject is Martin's most famous picture, *The Harp of the Winds* [1895: Metropolitan Museum, New York]; here the otherwhere heavier touch was lightened and the somber color was brightened into an attractive kind of lyricism. His habitual melancholy is too thoughtful to be charged off to mere low spirits, and the robust wit which at times flashed out in his conversation should free him from any suspicion of morbidity. The purchaser of one of his woodland interiors asked him for a poetic title to go with the picture, and Martin replied: "The home of the telegraph pole." That has as much poetry as is due anyone who insists upon something over and above what a painter puts into his picture. The personal tragedy of Martin's latter years was that he lost the sight of one eye and the other clouded with cataract.

86. FALLS OF THE OHIO AND LOUISVILLE *by* ALEXANDER HELWIG WYANT *Courtesy of The J. B. Speed Art Museum.*

The foregoing trio of landscapists, in their development of pigment for its direct emotional expressiveness, maintained a degree of likeness to appearances which the average picture buyer soon began to comprehend; but the modification to which Ralph Albert Blakelock subjected appearances presented greater difficulties. In woodland sunsets and moonlit waters his intentionally limited color schemes and his reliance upon silhouette were at first condemned before they were tolerated and at last enjoyed for their own sake as he had hoped. By then it was too late to do him any good, for even the dealers and collectors who had sense enough to buy his pictures had mistreated and cheated him so continuously that he became permanently deranged in 1899 and was kept in an asylum for about twenty years before his death. Insane, Blakelock created no more art; but he painted little landscapes having the size and superficial appearance of paper money and at least once in 1916 he gave three of them to a visitor as money. Almost as soon as his asylum life began, his fame commenced to grow; yet the increasing prices at which his pictures changed hands brought no benefit to the painter in confinement or to his wife and nine children living in abject poverty. Within a very few years after Blakelock lost his mind the forgers were at work, and now the forgeries much outnumber the originals. The final turn of the screw came when his eldest daughter Marian began to gain some of the support for the family by painting pictures and later found that a dishonest dealer was altering her signature and selling her work as her father's; in 1915 she, too, was confined to a sanitarium. The Blakelock story is the bitterest known tragedy in the history of American painting—so appalling, indeed, that it is now difficult to see the pictures clear of the cruelties out of which they came.

The pictures themselves, despite their burnished moonlight and glooming darks, are not tragic. Some early mountain scenes in fact exhibit a technique fairly close to the Hudson River School inheritance, and one little canvas of New York shanties evidences the beginning of his later preoccupation with a very personal texture in pigment. A long trip roaming the Far West stored his mind with memories of the forests and of Amerind life with which his imagination later nourished itself. The poorness of a specific picture is no proof that Blakelock did not paint it; he did some in haste, some with misjudged pigments, and some in indifferent repetition of designs that had once been fresh. In color, however, there was considerable variety from picture to picture: chords confined to gray-blue, glissandos from silver to black or from gold to darkest brown. As to his methods, the only point upon which several accounts agree is that they had in them no discernible consistency, but in the finer examples the results were unusually consistent. One remark by Blakelock which tells nothing specific about procedure yet says a great deal about the way his mind worked ran to the effect that the artist, equipped with knowledge, must trust his emotions to use it; and after all is done, he will discover that the work corresponds to nature. Others have described his building up a heavy impasto, followed by long drying and often by grinding down with pumice stone before "floating" the final integument of paint over the base. What he spoke from within and what others described from without combine to depict an artist who worked by instinct and who completely trusted the materials with which he worked.

Brook by Moonlight [c. 1890: plate 87], which Blakelock had to sell for so little that it brought on his initial breakdown, is among his most characteristic works in what seems at first glance an excessive patterning of form. But somehow the leaves have substance in their silhouette and the now overdark tree trunk and stream bank at the right have weight and thickness and strength. To examine the texture of these portions of the canvas, and thus share in the process of applying the paint, is to understand how in every touch Blakelock was feeling and thinking about these physical properties in the objects he was rendering; but his feeling and thinking were for the purpose not of imitating the surface appearances of nature in these respects but of making these tangible qualities come into existence within the pigment itself. The middle distance and the sky recede sufficiently to give depth; but again the sense of space is attained not by naturalistic imitation but by an entirely arbitrary choice of simplified values as determined in relation to the dark intensities of the foreground. What Blakelock most characteristically did, then, was not to depict any actual scene but to start with a pictorial idea and keep working his pigment until he had produced an imaginatively satisfying parallel or equivalent to nature. His method is partially documented for this particular picture in an amusing way; he got his idea from the pattern made by worn-off white paint in a zinc bathtub; after showing his wife what he had seen, he began the painting. Visually and psychologically, Blakelock was practising what Leonardo advised: to study cracks and stains in walls as suggestions for design. The pictorialism which resulted with Blakelock also seems to have been connected with his habit of musical improvisation and his frequent resort to music for achieving the mood in which he wished to paint. The mood, moreover, was limited in range. However bitterly he felt at times about the world's mistreatment of him, his pictures are singularly pure in their simple romanticism, with no more sadness in them than is unavoidable upon finding that the world of dreams is more desirable than the world of actuality.

87. BROOK BY MOONLIGHT   *by* RALPH ALBERT BLAKELOCK
Courtesy of The Toledo Museum of Art.

76. *Poetic figure painting*

Jonathan Eastman Johnson: 1824–1906
George Fuller: 1822–1884
Robert Loftin Newman: 1827–1912
William Morris Hunt: 1824–1879

For more than a generation prevailing opinion considered that in landscape the United States had made its most individual contribution to painting; the opinion was much favored, and perhaps originated, by Europeans. Without denying what may seem self-evident to those who live in immediate awareness of the European inheritance of art, it is advisable for Americans to realize that the figure is the major element in painting as an art of complete spiritual significance. It is so vitally the center of all thorough training that the long reluctance of public opinion to sanction the nude model in art schools has by just so long delayed that full mastery of the craft which is necessary to the maturity of the art. To be sure, not all painters make their careers in figure painting; but a thorough grounding in figure construction is the secret of sound construction for everything else, from a vase of flowers to shifting clouds. Although the mid-century developed no master of the figure in the academic sense, four painters—Bingham, Mount, Blythe, and Quidor—used the figure with significant effect; and the tiresomeness in most of the landscapes in the mid-century is due mainly to the fact that the landscapists did not feel free or compelled to go beyond literalism as those figure painters did. Perhaps the greatest service of the figure to painters is its paradoxical demand upon them that accuracy must be transcended by expressiveness. For this reason a scrutiny of figure painting in its strength or weakness yields specially important evidence for every attempt to estimate the state of painting as a whole.

Besides variability of success in communicating poetic feeling, there are also degrees of intensity in the emotion itself; and in using the adjective for much of the painting of Eastman Johnson it is necessary to note the relatively limited way in which feeling enters into it. His baptismal first name, Jonathan, which he never used, indicates his Yankee origin; and such poetry as the Yankee mind has manifested has always necessitated special care in defining its characteristics. Johnson's partial poetry did not lie in any transforming apprehension of life or personality. In reaching out for emotionalism of incident he could be guilty of the gross sentimentality of *Old Kentucky Home* [1859: New-York Historical Society, New York]; the portraiture to which he confined himself in his latter years (from about 1890) is marked by a superficial and semi-photographic slickness. Both that earlier anecdotal picture and the later portraiture are marked by an indiscriminate meticulousness of handling which he acquired while sharing the studio of Leutze in Düsseldorf from 1849 to 1851. But the paintings which bring him beyond the postwar average of portraiture and anecdote are all so clearly marked by a broader technique that his particular kind of poetic feeling can be in the main attributed to his handling of pigment. This is demonstrable by comparisons which are possible between preparatory sketches and finished works—even as early as the 'sixties, when he made the sketch [privately owned] for the final version of *The Stage Coach* [1871: Layton Art Gallery, Milwaukee]. The final version makes a slight compositional gain by the addition of some space and two more figures, but the over-all loss of freshness in the change to meticulous handling shows the difference between the poetry of a rapidly modeled impression of volumes and the careful prose statement of detail still deemed necessary to "complete" painting. How spirited his brushwork could occasionally be is shown by a sketch, somewhat incompletely thought out, done during the decade of the visits to Nantucket: *In the Fields* [1870–1880: Detroit Institute]. When and where Johnson came by this free use of loaded high lights remains mysterious. For freedom of brushwork he could have absorbed plenty of hints during his stay in The Hague before returning to this country in 1855; but as a fact he not only practised the Düsseldorf tightness after his return but also reverted to it now and then after he had begun to loosen his treatment with such admirable results. It has been conjectured that he took a hint from some early pictures by Winslow Homer, but if so he went beyond Homer's habitual dryness at that time into a mild lusciousness of pigment which constitutes his particular accent.

Another type of picture in which Johnson achieved two notable successes is the conversation piece, which partakes of both anecdote and portraiture. The earlier *Family Group* [1871: Metropolitan Museum, New York] revived to some extent his Düsseldorfian precision, no doubt in obedience to the clearly defined preferences among practically all patrons of the time; but the very successful interior light is painted so as to save it from the repellent texture of *Old Kentucky Home*. In the *Family Group* fifteen persons, from grandparents to a weeks-old baby, are arranged in an acceptable human situation, though with a degree of pictorial studiedness that departs from the eighteenth-century ideal of informality. This, however, is a remarkable record of the later century's middle-class grandeur, which was never sufficiently easy to be casual about anything. A

88. TWO MEN *by* EASTMAN JOHNSON *Courtesy of The Metropolitan Museum of Art.*

similar degree of pictorial formalism animates the later *Two Men* [1881: plate 88], but this has a depth of feeling and a distinction of design beyond the rest of Johnson's work. In the crossed legs the drawing of the leg that goes under is inadequate, but everything else is well realized in an interacting unity of spaces and volumes. The specific moment of intellectual interchange between the two sitters is superbly rendered, and the outstretched hand of the man who is talking says as much as his facial expression. No doubt the living man had the nobility of head here given; but the painter's response to it was equally noble. The occurrence of the trait of mind in the painter on this occasion is best discerned in the way he has used shadow to sustain the weight of the high seriousness in which the design was conceived and executed. Possibly, even probably, this element in the picture was suggested to him by the work of Rembrandt; but it is not carried out in Rembrandt's manner. With the Dutch master in his most personal phase, shadow is pushed far beyond its naturalistic appearance into an independent emotional expressiveness; shadow as given by Johnson stays close enough to visual actuality to be acceptable to the average eye. For once Johnson's feeling penetrated much deeper than the handling of pigment; he used light and shadow, but principally shadow, to make out of ugly objects a beauty to match the distinction of the heads.

The intensity of the picture remains unique in Johnson's work, and he may not have been wholly aware of what he was doing; George Fuller consciously and consistently sought a very personal but only gradually discovered ideal of beauty through a great deal of fumbled pigment and uncertain drawing. It was not so in the beginning, but that was only because he had not then commenced his seeking. After overcoming parental objections and obtaining some slight training, he became an itinerant portrait painter in the early 'forties in western Massachusetts and central New York. From 1847 he maintained a studio for a decade in New York City, with professional trips into the South; and all his portrait work of that time showed a sincere carefulness which promised nothing better than a routine competence for his future. In 1859 both a brother and his father died, and he decided to take their place on the home farm at Deerfield, Massachusetts; in preparation for what he knew would be isolation to a painter, he spent several months of travel in Europe—a courtesy call on the old masters. His letters are a record of admirably unconfused reactions to what he saw; and if he could have maintained the same directness in his painting process thereafter, a very different body of work would have resulted. But in the intervals of farm-work his painting became a search for something which proved elusive, and his search itself developed an oblique character. It would be highly speculative to guess that fifteen years of prolonged labor in inescapable routine gave him a sense of luxuriating in the uncertainties of getting his pictures to "come right." He sought a broad handling by means of a multitude of small touches and identified mysteriousness with crepuscular effects; in some pictures, where solitary figures hesitate to assert themselves in distinctness from stretches of field or hill, it is the painter who seems lost. Yet at times he found something, too; and though it was always essentially the same thing, each time he also caught and kept his sense of discovery. In *The Quadroon* [plate 89] the seated figure gives a more interesting design than his more usual standing solitaries, and the fact that she fills the greater part of the canvas minimizes his frequent difficulty in relating figure and background with satisfactory minor transitions of tone. The difficulty was not entirely overcome even here, and the intentional vagueness of foreground detail is more of an evasion than a solution. There is also some impairment of the pigment surface in skirt and face which is attributable to Fuller's own lack of technical sureness; and it serves as a reminder of how he himself once said that the painter's materials irritated him. The dark fall of hair and the repeating V-lines of necklace and low-cut dress concentrate into the face a sadness which, wavering between resentment and resignation, sinks into hopelessness. That is the "story" reading of the picture, the more obvious aspect of a conception which can also be read in the handling of the paint. The very tentativeness of the touch embodied the delicacy of Fuller's own human feeling for the subject; the subtlety of modulation within the narrow range of tone established the pathos of human separation. The painter's preference for suggestion rather than assertion yielded him the reward of his picture's being remembered as a vision. There lies the positive aspect of such successes as his tentativeness achieved, and that is what makes Fuller so admirable as a human being. Through the years of isolation and labor at other tasks he was content to do without the applause of others for his painting; seemingly he did not even concern himself with any possible vindication by a posterity he would never know; he had his self-sufficient happiness in making the pictures. Because of the failure of his tobacco crop in 1875, he placed some of his pictures on sale in Boston, sold them all, got out of debt, and was able thereafter to maintain the family by painting more pictures.

Robert Loftin Newman, too, was a seeker; and after his second and final return from Europe he maintained even in New York that degree of solitude necessary to all in search of a city of the mind. He had gone to Europe in 1850 with the intention of studying at Düsseldorf, but he stayed in Paris for instruction from Thomas Couture. On a second trip in 1854 he met Jean François Millet at Barbizon and thenceforth painted in the belief that the important thing was to make pigment directly responsive to the emotions. So worded, it reads like the aim of Inness, but the results were very different. Newman was perhaps little more sensitive to pigment than Inness, but he cared less about visual appearances; and his imperfect control of the medium prevented him from attaining the degree

89. THE QUADROON *by* GEORGE FULLER
Courtesy of The Metropolitan Museum of Art.

of consistency needed for entire convincingness in so subjective an art. *The Good Samaritan* [1886: privately owned] was remarkable at its date for an effective use of distortion to convey the dead weight and the strained effort of the two figures involved; in them the brushwork is so direct that its unconsidered character toward the edges of the small canvas becomes puzzling. Often, too, Newman was content to dramatize a tiny area of brilliance by filling out the rest with paint of little meaning; and in such cases the color combinations themselves were usually so obvious that they exaggerated satisfaction into satiation. He rarely needed the whole of even his habitually small canvas to express his idea; he would begin with largely felt simplicities of form at the focal point, but from them he never radiated a design with emotional pressure sustained to the picture's edges.

The stronger and much more varied talent of William Morris Hunt also had difficulty in developing all the qualities desirable in painting to a point where they were consistent with one another. His admiration for spontaneity increased as he grew older, and for its sake he was ready to slight or ignore other factors equally necessary to make a particular picture intrinsically great. Yet Hunt's mind was great in its comprehension of greatness; and although his ideas were met by much incomprehension in his New England, the sanity and wit around which his seemingly disconnected utterances cohered might be profitably presented anew for today. That, however, would necessarily emphasize Hunt the thinker and teacher, whereas it is Hunt the painter who is important for his use of the figure in advancing the art of painting in the United States a stage nearer to maturity.

Significantly, his first art studies, of the early eighteen-forties, were in sculpture; when he turned to painting, he was repelled by the mechanical training at Düsseldorf but attracted to the more sculpturesque modeling in light-and-dark taught by Couture in Paris. How strange that way of painting seemed to Americans about 1850 is indicated by the fact that a picture by Hunt which had been praised in Paris and requested for an exhibition of the National Academy occasioned the remark that it showed "what could be done with a trowel." So far as Hunt was concerned, all the pictures of his five years under Couture were derivative in feeling as well as technique; the softness of handling in *The Hurdy-Gurdy Boy* [1851: Museum of Fine Arts, Boston] is not inappropriate to its sentimentalism. The worshipful friendship which Hunt established with Millet at Barbizon strengthened both his painting and his emotion; in *The Belated Kid* [1854–1857: Museum of Fine Arts, Boston], even more clearly out of Millet than the other is out of Couture, the drawing is firmer and simpler, and the sentimentalism has been purified to sentiment. The influence of Millet the man apparently went deeper still, into Hunt's character; for it was Millet's question about what he was going to do with his painting that saved Hunt from the tourist patina of other Americans in Europe through his return to his country in 1855 after twelve years' absence.

He was made to realize at once that New Englanders were still imprisoned in the personal egotism of the portrait; but his willingness to paint portraits, if that was all they wanted, did not make him abandon the figure as a vehicle for more painter-like concepts. He married a Miss Perkins in Boston, and for six or seven years lived partly in Vermont but mostly at Newport, where he had for pupils William and Henry James and John La Farge. In preparation for settling in Boston he painted one of his most important portraits, *Chief-Justice Lemuel Shaw* [c. 1860: Court House, Salem, Mass.], in which he did not wince at the local homeliness of the few accessories and fully accepted the provincial character of the subject, but transcended both limitations with massive design and impressive interpretation. Fashionable Bostonians did not perceive that Hunt had both preserved and enlarged something more authentic than they themselves were, but they did respond to Hunt's personal charm and commission portraits. Most of these were of women, and in perceptiveness for the refinement of some among them Hunt surpassed all his American predecessors except Stuart. The women art students of Boston also came to Hunt for guidance, and to his various classes through the years he would talk aphoristically about painting, with asides about life and literature and death; much of this was preserved in the two series of *Talks on Art* set down by his pupil and biographer, Helen M. Knowlton. In the great Boston fire of 1872 Hunt lost most of his own pictures and some by Millet; after that disaster his fresh start at painting was with lighter color and looser brushwork. In one afternoon he executed the *Gloucester Harbor* [1877: Museum of Fine Arts, Boston] and said: "I believe I have painted a picture with light in it!" In the same year while on a country jaunt he saw two boys swimming and was so struck by the sight that he went straight back to the studio to paint the brilliant *Bathers* [1877: Worcester Art Museum]. He was always urging his pupils to rely upon memory because then "so much is forgotten"! In a way, his theory worked even for the short time that elapsed in this instance, for errors of anatomy exist which count as nothing in comparison to the freshness of the impression. Later he made a larger replica [privately owned] and thought that his intention to retain his original freshness required him to repeat the original misjudgements of construction; the errors he had no trouble in repeating, but the freshness he did not recapture.

In 1878 the architects of the new State Capitol at Albany, New York, asked Hunt to paint two large lunettes for the Assembly chamber—each one sixteen by forty feet, in which the figures were finally adjusted with a height of ten feet. Both had to be completed within six months, a condition which would have balked any man less impetuous than Hunt, but which was for him an attraction in itself. For the project he revived two ideas on which he had been at work before the Boston fire: *The Discoverer* and *The Flight of Night* (also called *Anahita*). The latter subject had occasioned several preparatory studies and a final version either completed or almost so, all of which had been burned; accordingly, Hunt's problem for the State Capitol was not to devise wholly new concepts but to reconstitute two which he had previously meditated. No doubt this was important in making the quick execution seem possible to him. Both subjects were again prepared in preliminary studies and in full-scale cartoons within four months; then, with the aid of assistants, they were painted on the walls in a little less than two months. The painting was done in oil directly on walls of a light colored stone, an experiment which of itself doomed the pictures from the first, although that was not known until too late. In addition, structural defects in the building soon showed up; because the contractor had skimped on his materials, rain seeped through and damaged the decorations beyond repair. The only basis for any opinion about them, therefore, consists of the praise of some who liked them and the studies that were made during the first four months. One of *The Discoverer* [Museum of Fine Arts, Boston] is unsatisfactory in itself; but in one version *The Flight of Night* [plate 90] can be considered as a picture in its own right. Since the time of his association with Millet, Hunt had known and taught that art is found inside the artist himself rather than outside him in the subject; and through the years that had immediately preceded this picture Hunt had taught further that the artist communicates primarily by his treatment. In this version of *The Flight of Night,* however, artist and theme and handling are inseparable and constitute a seemingly instantaneous act of the imagination. As with the bathing boys, so here in the horses there are errors of anatomical detail; but perhaps even they contribute to the wave-like forward plunge by which the horses invigorate "this insubstantial pageant" of the gray and rose of a coming dawn. Years earlier, when working on the burned picture, Hunt had modeled the horses in clay; and now, when he renewed the concept under emotional pressure, the memory of them returned with enough forgotten to let him model them with rash simplifications of form. Along the line of their heads the main curve of the design dips forward sharply and then recedes almost languorously into the slumbering mother and child before it rises to Anahita seated in the new moon's crescent.

With this vision communicated, why should Hunt be looked upon as the victim of unfavorable circumstances here? There is, of course, his own remark that seems to sanction that interpretation: "In another country I could have been a painter." It is true that he was not powerful enough either in mind or in art to be a creative force acting upon a whole nation's art; yet he maintained an admirable balance through years of talking persuasively about art to people who knew far less about it than he did—and in Boston! No ordeal of culture could be more difficult. When his great opportunity came, he exhausted himself physically, but in doing so he achieved a finely imaginative thing. Soon after the Albany decorations were completed, Hunt held an exhibition of his work in Boston; its reception by the local public was cold. On the eighth of the following September he was found drowned in a pool to which he had gone alone. Years earlier he had spoken a few words to his art class about eternity, and ended with: "A ripple closes over us."

90. THE FLIGHT OF NIGHT   by WILLIAM MORRIS HUNT   Courtesy of The Pennsylvania Academy of the Fine Arts.

PERIOD TWO
THE PROVINCIAL

DIVISION SEVEN

National Culmination

91. THE DEAD BIRD *by* ALBERT PINKHAM RYDER *Courtesy of Phillips Gallery, Washington, D.C.*

77. The transformation of nature

Albert Pinkham Ryder: 1847–1917

Any of the great pictures by Albert Pinkham Ryder can be cited as exemplifying a transformation of appearances remote from the painted facts of contemporaneous academic landscape. While yet a boy Ryder showed an interest in drawing and painting, and the family indulged him in it because his health had been injured by an ill judged vaccination which permanently affected his eyes; when his local drawing teacher put him to work copying engravings as the first step in becoming a painter, he soon rebelled and tried to paint by himself. Eye trouble may have been the origin of a way of painting which so markedly departed from the usual; but eventually the important thing was to be the emotional expressiveness which incited and controlled the glooming shadow and gleaming light of Ryder's transformations. And according to his own account that, too, commenced quite early; in trying for accuracy he got lost in detail and became more and more discouraged until one day he happened to see his subject framed between two trees as three masses of sky and foliage and earth, blue and green and brown, harmonized in luminous golden light. He threw aside his brushes and worked his pigments on canvas with a palette knife. "It was better than nature, for it was vibrating with the thrill of a new creation. Exultantly I painted until the sun sank below the horizon, then I raced around the fields like a colt let loose, and literally bellowed for joy." Johannes Brahms was about fifteen years older, but he began composing later than Ryder began painting; so it may well have been about the same time that he raced and bellowed in the fields above Vienna. What Ryder discovered was also melody and harmony.

He followed a brother to New York in 1867 or 1868, and until 1880 lived with the family while he painted. For a while he sought instruction from a portraitist who had studied with Couture; then, at a second try, he was admitted to the National Academy school, but when he was put to drawing from casts, he soon quit and thereafter worked in his own way and alone. His brother prospered with a hotel and supported him, but Ryder never felt rich enough to use expensive pigments; so he early had trouble with keeping his colors in the relationships he intended. Further, he always used an excessive amount of varnish without waiting for thorough drying, and at times he risked ruining his pictures with alcohol as a solvent. All that can be said now is to regret his lack of sound technical knowledge and to deplore the consequent deprivations of later times. Ryder had one trait in common with the Master of the Freakes two hundred years earlier. Both men showed no awareness that there were more facile ways of using paint; both were concentrated entirely upon overcoming their personal difficulties of drawing and design. But the anonymous master had obtained such sound training that his work may well last another couple of centuries, where it is doubtful how long Ryder's will. Ryder kept his pictures by him for years before he was sufficiently satisfied with their depth of impasto and jeweled color to let them go; in later years he would sometimes get them back from their owners in order to work on them further, and after 1900 he was as likely to injure them as to improve them. The paintings he exhibited at the National Academy and the Society of American Artists sold for modest prices to a few buyers; and Daniel Cottier, a dealer friend, was able to sell enough more for Ryder's simple living needs. In later years he did not even spend all the money he took in, and kept checks lying around indefinitely; but this was not success as the world counts it—only a singularly ascetic life.

When he set up in a studio of his own in 1880 he entered upon the most productive time, extending for almost twenty years. It was a time notable for relative solitude as well. He had friends, and some of them visited the studio; he kept his family contacts, and he made trips uptown to see pictures and hear music. He even went on a journey through Europe with Cottier and the sculptor, Olin Warner, and a couple of voyages to London and back with a sea captain friend; on these voyages he would stay on deck all night to study moonlight and water. In the latter years a few art students would get occasional access to him. But through all his years of creation he delicately but decisively guarded his aloneness for the reason that his pictures came out of not merely laborious trial and error of technique but out of long-brooded visual memories modified to imaginative ends. Perhaps the most precise way of describing him would be to say he kept himself to himself, for that has the implication that it was his own active mental life which made much association with others unnecessary. People like Ryder are so complex, whatever may be their simplicity in worldly terms, that they experience a continuous companionship within themselves. Ryder lived alone, but he was not lonely.

Toward the middle of the 'nineties he made one more remove, to some rooms on Fifteenth Street, and there he became really peculiar, accumulating so much trash in fifteen years that he left himself only a path through it from door to stove and easel and chair. Ashes were piled around the stove, empty cereal boxes rose to meet the streamers of wallpaper hanging from the ceiling; newspapers

92. PASTORAL STUDY *by* ALBERT PINKHAM RYDER *Courtesy of National Collection of Fine Arts, Smithsonian Institution, Washington, D.C.*

and magazines, empty milk bottles and unwashed dishes were stacked about. To a visitor he said: "I never see all this unless someone comes to see me." He made friends with a couple who lived long on the floor below him; and after his dangerous illness in 1915 they took him to where they were then living on Long Island and looked after him until he died. Well before his death the forgers were at work, as they had been with Blakelock; and now, Mr. Lloyd Goodrich estimates, there exist eight to ten times as many forgeries as the approximately one hundred and fifty originals. Ryder's erratic working habits have made an accurate chronology of his paintings impossible, and it is therefore not only permissible but advantageous to consider a few of his pictures in an order of emotional crescendo.

The Dead Bird [plate 91] is marked by unusual emotional intimacy, but in Ryder's work it is unique for an additional visual immediacy. Others among his pictures possess immediacy, but theirs is mental; here the impression is of Ryder painting with a passion of tenderness in the actual presence of the tiny death. It is an almost startling instance of that "nearly looking" which Americans had so long been conceiving in illusionistic terms; it gets as close to the object as Raphaelle Peale did [plate 41], but with the profound difference that Ryder was not trying to efface his medium but was rather emphasizing pigment for its own emotional expressiveness. The brush and the palette knife speak their own language of modeling, and small ridges of pigment distribute pictorial emphasis across the whole. And because of this, the intense and sorrowful perception of Ryder's heart is not left to inference but is written directly into the pigment. Even the exceptionally restrained color—just browns and grays and a pale yellow—contributes its note of elegy.

It was the capacity for handling his medium emotionally which had most to do with Ryder's high proportion of creative successes despite his technical mistakes and misjudgements. In the Pastoral Study [plate 92] field and trees, cows and sky were made pictorially coherent not alone by their relationships in the design but also by the consistent treatment they received in pigment. Probably Ryder's defective eyesight had much to do with this; he might examine a tree or a cow with intentness and store up in his memory a precise knowledge of how it looked near at hand. In the studio, and taking his time to build up his heavy impasto, he could base himself on such memories and feel himself, so to speak, into the pigment equivalents of the objects; thus, neglecting the more or less imitative textures of the naturalistic painter, he would replace them with an over-all texture arising in the medium itself. He could make every form in the picture equally plastic, and in so doing replace nature with what he early found to be "better than nature"—better, that is to say, for a painter's purpose. Accordingly, although the tree trunks and their foliage frankly consist of paint, they are alive because Ryder felt their vitality while he painted. The cows, too, are solid—not because of any superficial accuracy of texture but because of his modeling their solidity in the pigment. Ryder was drawing upon strong physical sensations stored up in memory, and transforming them into equally strong sensations within the limits of a relatively narrow physical medium of expression. To the cows might be applied Ryder's own words which he once used about an unnamed painting: "Perhaps you wouldn't say it had much drawing, but I think it has what you might call an air of drawing." And because he was so undividedly working to translate every visual and tactile experience into a language whose only aim was to be consistent with itself, because he was transforming nature into paint, that "air" was all he needed for everything he chose to include.

It was his concentration of his mental life into the medium that enabled Ryder to go beyond even memories of naturalistic sensation and communicate sensations which are wholly of the imagination. *Pegasus* [Worcester Art Museum] vibrates with a precipitancy bringing into the picture a tremor from the vast sky beyond. *Siegfried and the Rhine Maidens* [plate 93] startlingly transforms an experience of sound into an experience of sight; the agitated arabesques of dark a-gleam with coruscating lights swirl into the mind with the wild wind that wrenches the resisting trees. In *Macbeth and the Witches* [Phillips Gallery, Washington] the drama consists of a ladder of lights ascending between massed darks, causing the design to advance with a slower tread. A number of years after the picture had been started a friend asked him how it was coming along; Ryder said: "I think the sky is getting interesting." The humor in his answer is as modest and as delightfully sly as that in his remark about his drawing; and the long meditation upon his medium which it implies does much to account for his ability to take ostensible subjects from literature and from music and transform them as completely as he transformed the appearances of nature. No retelling of the stories themselves and no criticism of them in their original art forms will do more than give a parallel to what Ryder did with them in paint.

For the additional fact is that Ryder's meditation upon his medium was imaginative in character. His own words, perhaps the most quoted of all he said, describe this:

Have you ever seen an inch worm crawl up a leaf or twig, and there clinging to the very end, revolve in the air, feeling for something to reach something? That's like me. I am trying to find something out there beyond the place in which I have a footing.

Hobbes called imagination "nothing but decaying sense" and identified it with memory; and a further depreciation of the imagination came from Havelock Ellis

93. SIEGFRIED AND THE RHINE MAIDENS *by* ALBERT PINKHAM
RYDER
Courtesy of National Gallery of Art [Mellon Collection], Washington, D.C.

when he wrote, "Imagination is a poor substitute for experience." Certainly Ryder started his imaginative reaching-out with a stock of memories, and certainly he made imagination into a substitute for experience in Ellis' meaning. But what becomes of those belittling descriptions in the face of the fact that Ryder made imagination into experience itself and thereby created things otherwise not to be experienced? With *The Flying Dutchman* [National Collection of Fine Arts, Washington] and the *Jonah* [plate 94] Ryder transformed paint into epic grandeur, and replaced one kind of experience by another.

Of the *Jonah* he wrote: "I am in ecstasies over my Jonah; such a lovely turmoil of boiling water and everything." His reference to ecstasies echoes the racing and bellowing of his youth; his being so specific about the water reiterates how his mind had its life in pigment. In the *Jonah* the pigment is also water—with oceanic weight and a turmoil so powerful that it bends the boat itself into a terror of near destruction. The dark ocean monster curves ever so slightly away from the boat toward the human sacrifice that has been thrown him. The image of the Almighty above the rhythmic convolutions of the waves controls them with a pyramidal tip of calm; but upon the doomed agony of Jonah is gathered all the complex turmoil of the mighty design. There is the pictorial miracle; it commands belief because Ryder could transform the sensuous experience of material things into imaginative experience of hallucinatory intenseness. At another time, and in seeming contradiction to the Almighty's gesture of benediction over Jonah, Ryder wrote:

> Who knows what God knows?
> His hand He never shows,
> Yet miracles with less are wrought,
> Even with a thought.

78. The transcription of nature

Winslow Homer: 1836–1910

The use of the word "transcription" for the art of Winslow Homer points to the fact that in painting his pictures he modified nature; but the psychologically curious thing is that he denied doing so. In a conversation he stressed the necessity of selecting the point of view, waiting for the right atmospheric conditions, and then painting the scene "exactly as it appears." That was the conscious procedure of Homer's predecessor, Durand, and also of Homer's impressionist contemporary, Claude Monet; yet the results in the pictures of all three were technically incompatible. Homer was quite as sure as the others that the painter's principal concern should be with external conditions. Apparently he never realized that for every painter the appearances of nature become conditioned by his own mind and by the technique he practices. Homer's unawareness of the subjective was an advantage to him; indeed, it had most to do with the particular character of his achievement and with its general popularity then and since. Unplagued by either introspection or by doubts about what was real, Homer forgot himself in what he did, kept a sharp eye upon the external world, and by a continually refreshened brush stroke increased the element of unconscious transcription which altered appearances into pictorial unities.

The transcribing was so acceptable to the average eye that its development from his original level of illustration into full pictorialism was followed without much difficulty by most people who looked at pictures then. At first Homer scandalized the conservative painters by his academically unorthodox technique, and there was some early faultfinding in print for his hard drawing and eccentric composition. But even those painters and the critics in time could not avoid recognizing the vigor of the results; and with the lay public his popularity was cumulative as his pictures were installed in public collections and assembled for special occasions like expositions. The very accessibility of his broadly handled naturalism has all along made it easy to overlook that this brilliant approximation to ordinary vision actually required an extraordinary mind.

At the beginning the mind itself seemed ordinary. His mother painted for her own pleasure, and his childhood habit of drawing became a desire to be an artist; this was channeled, not into any art-school or studio training, but into

636

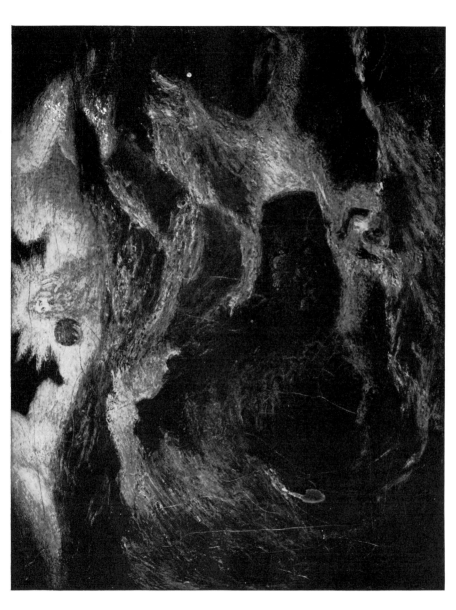

94. JONAH *by* ALBERT PINKHAM RYDER *Courtesy of National Collection of Fine Arts, Smithsonian Institution, Washington, D.C.*

a practical apprenticeship to the well known lithographic firm of Bufford in Boston. Within three years his drawings of contemporary scenes began to find a reproductive market in *Ballou's Pictorial* and *Harper's Weekly*; his work was so satisfactory that he was soon able to support himself as a free lance and he moved to New York in the autumn of 1859 because his work sold there to best advantage. For a while he attended a drawing school in Brooklyn and put in some time in the night school of the National Academy of Design; but then, as always, his effective training consisted in doing marketable work. In this earliest phase of subject-matter he actually was what he later inaccurately called himself: "just a reporter." Newport bathing beaches and West Point dances, skating and shoveling snow—he concentrated upon visual journalism, training himself into the virtues so often missing from journalism, quickness and simplicity; he learned to make the everyday subject effective by his workmanlike concern for direct presentation. *Harper's Weekly* asked him to report the Civil War, and from his various trips to the front he sent or brought back material which, though concerned with war, preserved the essential character of his previous subject-matter: casual, even marginal, but for that very reason more actual: bivouacs and supply trains, and only an occasional battle scene. From this phase of his career the sketchbooks and rather numerous miscellaneous drawings remain much more interesting than any of the woodcuts that appeared.

It was by way of war subjects that he began to use oil paint. In this medium, too, he characteristically relied more upon learning by doing than upon formal instruction; his few lessons from the painter Frederick Rondel could hardly have done more than show him how to use brush and pigment. At first all he did was to get acquainted with the medium, retaining in it his established habits of composition and subject-matter; and this alone was enough to make him startlingly different at the time. For the current academic painters were fighting shy of the everyday subject; only some of the landscapists were using what was right around them, while the anecdotists were predominantly busy with studio costume pieces. *Prisoners from the Front* [1866: Metropolitan Museum, New York], which did most to make him known at this time, was not his first war picture; but it was a sensation in its refusal to be sensational, in its retention of reportorial virtues in painting so soundly direct that they and it together made the academic average appear anemic. In becoming a painter Homer was retaining his habit of regarding his subject as more important than himself. If he did this in conscious rejection of his own generation's preference for making the painter more important than his subject, Homer is to be admired for his long-term wisdom; if he unconsciously continued an established trait of mind, he is to be envied for the good luck of his temperament. However, the continuation of his reportorial knack into a habit of relying upon appearances meant

that he would be unlikely either to transform them as Ryder did or to comprehend what lay underneath them as Eakins did; his mature achievements were
thus conditioned by his youthful aptitudes.

Animation strongly pervades a large group of anecdotal oils from 1866 to
1880 in which he used that medium to re-explore the same type of subject-
matter with which he had begun as an illustrator. His illustrations were still
being used by periodicals, but his own mind was more and more engrossed by
his rapidly increasing mastery of oil. Most of the year 1877 was spent in France,
but just what he did there is not clear; he seems to have ignored the studios and
the schools, and he did none of the once customary copying in the Louvre. It is
not beyond possibility that he visited the museum only briefly or not at all; as a
youth at Bufford's he had said to a fellow apprentice: "An artist must never
look at pictures." That is worth remembering as a point of view; but its significance may be simply that as an apprentice in a reproductive business Homer
had to work most of the time from what were probably a despicable lot of
originals devised by others for commercial purposes. His mind was certainly
alert enough to perceive the shortcomings of the academic productions he found
in New York. As a verdict on the mass of current work, Homer's seeming
philistinism was largely justified; if in Paris he continued to feel that he could
get along without other men's pictures, even those of the masters of past time,
he may have been just following his Yankee instinct. It remains generally true
that painters begin from the pictures of other men; and so may Homer himself
have begun, if only by way of quick and conscious rejection. Upon his return
from France, at any rate, the distinguishing characteristic of his work was still
that he painted, as Mr. Lloyd Goodrich puts it, "by eye." Upon full-skirted
ladies playing the newly fashionable game of croquet, upon children playing in
fields or studying in country schoolhouses, upon Virginia negroes and their cabin
life Homer looked with an eye of remarkable directness. *The Bridle Path* [1868:
Whitney Museum of American Art, New York] is light and high in feeling, as
appropriate to the mountaintop; the piquant silhouette of the girl on horseback
is given along with her swinging weight and the slow straining of the horse.
A Fair Wind [1876: National Gallery of Art, Washington] gives the movement of the boat and the compensating pressure being exerted by all three boys
against the pull of the bellying sail. It would be superficial for criticism to suggest that Homer was unduly dependent upon appearances when in his search
for pictorial material he proved to be so delightful and perceptive a discoverer of
things new to American painting.

It would also be critically unjust to Homer because he discovered much more
than subject-matter; he discovered light, which is purely pictorial, and developed
its use in a way that made it an original contribution to American painting of

95. LONG BRANCH, NEW JERSEY *by* WINSLOW HOMER *Courtesy of Museum of Fine Arts, Boston.*

the first importance. Before 1880 he was beginning to use it in water color as no one had done before; but his major contribution in water color was not achieved until later. The subject-matter alone of these years is too varied for them to be successfully typified in a single picture; but *Long Branch, New Jersey* [1869: plate 95] dramatizes both light and wind in a way characteristic of the entire period of radiance in Homer's work. The crisp brushwork plays animatedly through a highly unconventional design—logical in itself, once it has been set down, but perceivable in the first place only by an unjaded mind. No figure is a person; even the two nearest of these fashionably dressed women are only component elements in the design; they are like almost all the other people in Homer's pictures—figures in landscape. From the first Homer had directed his mind to a pictorial rendering of life in which people possess meaning only in a particular setting; and whatever they might be doing, human beings were for Homer primarily forms which stopped the light and moulded shadow. In this picture all the liveliness of touch and oddity of design seem the easy result of instinct. It apparently confirms something he said to an interviewer eleven years later, in advocating that painters always work outdoors: "The thing is done without your knowing it."

A stay in England during 1881 and 1882 was to have consequences in his technique which enabled him to grow in stature as an artist, but for the time being the effects were doubtful. With one so dependent upon what he could see, the change in climate was probably sufficient to induce some change in technique; the moister air and grayer light eliminated from his oils his previous dry crispness of touch and sharp brightness of color. His new subject-matter of girls from the fisher-families softened his story content into sentimentalism. But climate and subject together freed his draftsmanship from a tendency to brittleness and taught him how rounded and thick the human body is. In water color the effects were perhaps even more noticeable; and he seems also to have experienced his first emotional stirrings from the sea. Yet all these modifications together, extricating him from the danger of formularizing his previous manner, were good only for the future; nothing actually executed during the English stay is intrinsically valuable alongside his American work.

Upon returning to the United States he fixed his permanent residence on a rocky point at Prout's Neck, in Maine, where he could be companioned by the sea with sound and motion, with the restlessness which he relished in proportion to its violence, with the ever-changing patterns made by the crash and fall of waves upon the rocks. Almost at once, too, he began to alternate his stays in Maine with trips to the bright-hued islands from Bermuda southward into the Caribbean; traveling light, he carried with him on these journeys only water colors and paper and brought back pictures of sun-spotted waters and the vast, bright calms that follow upon the sudden tragedies of the tropics. In both oil and water color Homer's perceptiveness intensified from his old-time keen observation into about as much emotionalism as any Yankee can ever permit himself, and his continued restraint of it almost within the limits of objective reporting only added to the impact of the pictures on the eye. In both oil and water color Homer increased his technical freedom; the oils became remarkable, and the water colors supremely so.

It might seem that this judgement on the water colors is in effect a sweeping confirmation of Homer's own prediction that by them he would live on in art; but the matter is more complex. It does mean that he re-made the craft; no one since has added to its technical resources, and it is even unlikely that anyone can. He did not develop his economical exuberance in the medium until he began to visit regions where nature itself challenged him to it; but the fact that water-color painting as a whole had to wait for him to do it leaves him undisputedly a creative force in art. He invented the handling where everything depends upon a trained spontaneity capable of its own kind of completeness without subsequent changes. However, that technique requires the omission of more naturalistic detail than it includes in order to attain Homer's own kind of naturalistic vision; and even Homer did not achieve perfection in his own method. The inventors in art rarely do. For example, in *After the Tornado, Bahamas* [plate 96] the boat fragment is not heavy enough to match the rendering of other qualities quite as physical throughout the rest of the picture; yet Homer unified everything by open reliance upon the texture of paper and water color. Within that unity the broad sweeps of the brush differentiate sand and sky and water not only in texture but in structure: the bright solidity of sand, the energy of the nearer water and the depth of the water farther away, the slow dissipation of threatening cloud. The necessarily smaller strokes by which the recumbent figure is constructed preserve the largeness of feeling even as they discriminate the textures of skin and trousers, the differing amounts of light that they reflect; and in the figure, at least, there is no failure in conveying motionless weight. Homer's success with this new way of finding a visual equivalent for nature was such that from perhaps three dozen water colors any one would serve as well as any other to typify its boldness and its luminosity. And among these would be some of northern scenes into which he carried the sense of release which the tropics first gave him in this medium. Guides and woodsmen, Canadian Amerind camps and canoeists in river rapids were occasions for his swift notations of a light quite different from that of the Caribbean but made almost as interesting by the painter's vigor and simplicity. Taking into consideration the general tendency of this method toward replacing statement by suggestion, it is possible to cite as one of Homer's most remarkable

96. AFTER THE TORNADO, BAHAMAS *by* WINSLOW HOMER   *Courtesy of The Art Institute of Chicago.*

achievements a picture which omits so much that some might claim it is no picture. *Rowing Home* [1890: Phillips Gallery, Washington] gives one strip of oncoming darkness that lowers over a strip of ominously quiet water gleaming with the last vestige of reflected light, upon which the vague, low-lying boat seems much too far from home; almost at the point of saying nothing, the picture haunts the mind with implications.

Even if Homer should prove to have been right in his estimate of the historical importance of his water colors, individual examples of the later oils contain more complex satisfactions for the mind. In 1884, just a little more than a year after his return from England, he voyaged with a New England fishing fleet and thereby acquired ideas for a series of pictures over a period of several years; he used his eyes to good effect in catching some oddities of design offered him by the action of small boats on deeply rolling waves, but in several of them a literalism almost photographic marred his handling of the medium. The climax of the theme of life at sea came much later, with *All's Well* [1896: Museum of Fine Arts, Boston]. Here is no stretch of restless water with men rowing or hauling in the nets; here is only the head of the watchman calling, his hand raised with a gesture to emphasize the unheard sound, and above him the massive bell in relief against a moonlit sky. Yet with the vision concentrated upon this small fragment of an unseen whole, the slanting lines of ropes and rail, the angle of the partially seen shoulder, convey that boat's roll upon the water and the watchman's stance of adjustment to the roll. Quite as important is what Professor Mather has termed "its exquisite frostiness of lunar blues"; and if nature gave Homer this much of his picture, as it gave him the blinding brilliance of the tropic sea, there was in both cases the artifice of man by which he alters nature into the art that gives its own different kind of experience.

Another strand of subject-matter in the later oils uses somewhat dramatic human situations at the sea's edge, often so well painted that to refuse the painting because of the story could be only a self-spiting esthetic snobbery. But the later Homer was most impressively embodied in other pictures whose only story is the conflict of the surf with the rocks which concentrates and symbolizes the vast and tireless energies in the midst of which man is precariously balanced. As with the water colors, more than one example might well enough typify the group. *Winter Coast* [1890: plate 97] has one quality in common with the earlier *All's Well*: a design well adjusted to the canvas which also extends the mind beyond the picture itself. The solitary hunter is emotionally appropriate, but it is doubtful that his business there is to humanize the scene; it is more likely that his pictorial function is simply to give the eye a scale of measurement for the only partially seen gigantic stretch of coast. To a student Homer once said: "Paint figures, my boy, leave the rocks for your old age—they're easy." Here both the figure and the rocks look easy because the painter was then at that peak of his artistry where eye and hand were a fused instrument for registering a conception which came from a mind's habitual absorption in an experience drained of egotism. The dark zigzag of the exposed rocks mounts to resist the crash of mountainous waters; and underneath the lightly brushed snow the rock waits on—to resist.

In this later Winslow Homer there had developed a personal streak of resistance to human associations. It is said to have originated in a disappointment in love, but for a mind that removed itself from most human contacts in order to set down so powerful an experience as that of the stormy shore scenes, a thwarted love would seem to have been no cause but only an occasion for the removal. As he grew more famous in age, people intruded upon his shore-edge refuge; when evasion proved insufficient, he was rude, and in their resentment they gave him a reputation for misanthropy. But he still had more important things to do than to talk with the idly curious; and while anybody had as much right to do trivial things as Homer had to do important ones, there was also plenty of margin to be trivial without going to the length of asking autographs. Homer was equipped with a rubber stamp. No doubt by the time he was famous enough to be thus pestered he had come to like his aloneness for its own sake. The day before he was fifty-nine he wrote to his brother:

The life that I have chosen gives me my full hours of enjoyment for the balance of my life. The sun will not rise, or set, without my notice, and thanks.

97. WINTER COAST   *by* WINSLOW HOMER
Courtesy of The John G. Johnson Art Collection, Philadelphia.

79. The renewal of nature

Thomas Cowperthwait Eakins: 1844–1916

Thomas Eakins observed appearances as closely as Homer did, but he wanted to understand why appearances assumed their form. Eakins also lived himself into the medium as completely as Ryder did, but he wanted to make it a dependable instrument for attaining foreseen ends. In short, Eakins had an intellectual curiosity which other painters got along without and which made painting much more difficult for himself; among all his American predecessors only Copley had manifested a similarly penetrative mind, and the cultural climate of Eakins' day complicated his problems far beyond the experience of Copley. Where Homer painted what he saw, Eakins studied anatomy to the point of taking medical courses and dissecting bodies; where Ryder, knowing his goal of design and mood, had to reach it by circuitous experiments with pigment and varnish, Eakins made elaborate studies of perspective and light in order that the direct action of the loaded brush could at once render form and location in space and atmosphere. The range and thoroughness of his investigative intellect made Eakins unique in American painting, and to characterize him as this country's supreme intellectual painter is accurate enough; but it cannot be taken as a complete description of his complex nature or as an adequate definition of the total experience afforded by his pictures. They yield a diversity of significance according to the perceptiveness of the audience because they came out of a mind which, staking its effectiveness upon rationality, yet functioned as a whole. Eakins' intellect was itself ingrainedly passionate; the fire of his emotion burned so deep that many never knew it was there, but it maintained the pressure of his art. The operation of his mind did not seem imaginative to others because it did not obviously transform appearances; yet his way of rendering appearances relied primarily upon acquired knowledge of what lay beneath them, and the complete thing was re-constituted in the mind in the act of being painted. In that process the imagination is used to validate the researches of the intellect, and it constitutes the renewal of nature in terms of paint.

Eakins had decided to become a painter before he was through high school; he knew so well what he was about that simultaneously with working in the art classes at the Pennsylvania Academy he was learning anatomy at the Jefferson Medical College. His art teacher Schussele had been trained in Paris, and it was to Paris that Eakins went at twenty-two; he overcame the difficulties of getting admitted to the governmental *École des Beaux-Arts* in order to secure instruction from Jean Léon Gérôme, the famous exponent of exact painting of local color over careful academic drawing. In addition to the discipline there Eakins began independently to train himself in memory drawing; he also took lessons from the portraitist Léon Bonnat, and from the equally academic sculptor Augustin Alexandre Dumont. The work in sculpture was essentially a continuation of a search for three-dimensional form and anatomical structure; and though it was undertaken simply for a better comprehension of the painter's problems, it made possible some admirable modeling by Eakins himself in later years—especially of horses. Late in 1869 he went to Spain for a stay of about six months, during which he was markedly affected by Velazquez and Ribera and attempted a picture in the open air "to strengthen my color and to study light." *Street Scene in Seville* [1870: privately owned] was no masterpiece —Eakins himself wrote at the time that "a painter can see in it at least earnest clumsiness"—but it came surprisingly close to success in what the young man of twenty-five attempted. Letters home showed that he was already thinking out a painter's working philosophy, and the remarkable thing is that it was definitely broader and more organic in conception than what he got from his Parisian teachers. It was essentially one in which the painter studies nature, not to copy, but to re-create within the limits of painting:

. . . He learns what she [Nature] does with light, the big tool, and then color, then form, and appropriates them to his own use. Then he's got a canoe of his own, smaller than Nature's but big enough for every purpose. . . . With this canoe he can sail parallel to Nature's sailing. . . .

In its wording as well as its idea this has the stamp of individual thinking, and from a young American art student in Europe it shows an unexpected maturity in getting free from the official dogmas and enlarging the official techniques. During the time Eakins was in Paris, impressionism was beginning; but already he was clear in his own mind that the figure was the major factor in great painting, and the broken color of impressionism would have made it plain to him at once that the figure and all other solid form would lose their cohesion in scintillations of light.

Soon after the middle of 1870 he was back in Philadelphia, to spend the rest of his life where he had been born, despite the censure and indifference which were to be his fate there. Eakins stood up to it, morally and artistically; and while it undoubtedly crippled his creativity before the end, it did not prevent him from leaving an impressive legacy of work. The real significance of his seeing things through in Philadelphia was that he unreservedly accepted his inheritance and environment both as a man and as a painter; he did not find it necessary to seek out a place less bleak, culturally speaking, where painters of a slighter sort were making little oases of mutual understanding as refuges from a philistine world. In his opinion art needed no such protective nursing; it produced nothing but artistic respectability, and he said: "Respectability in art is appalling." Of a picture by Whistler he said: "It is a very cowardly way to paint." For Eakins' temperament, the mastery of one's own experience as given was the only way to sound and lasting work; and it so happened that for him the experience given by a small geographical area was sufficient. He had no thought of preaching similar limitations for others, and looked upon the gadabout Winslow Homer as the best American painter of the day. For Eakins one house was space enough to live and die in; the people who came to that house and the life that could be observed within the radius of a few miles were good enough for art.

Upon his return from abroad he began at once to make pictures out of the members of his own family in their usual indoor setting. They were pictures rather than portraits; that is to say, the factor of individual likeness was distinctly subordinated to design and modeling and lighting which constituted a visual structure transcending the everyday materials out of which it was made. One of his sisters playing the piano, or watching a child on the floor, or playing with a cat in her lap: the subject-matter was all of the type called anecdotal; but with Eakins the word took on a larger and graver sense than is appropriate to other American practitioners. This was not because Eakins anywhere exaggerated the casually intimate subjects into a portentous and self-conscious solemnity; it was simply because his fundamental and pervasive seriousness infused all his pictures with a sense of ritual by thoughtful composition and by a use of strong shadow in sculpturesque modeling. The gravity of Eakins' productions came from the self-forgetting and essentially tragic quality of his mind.

The predominance of shadow in the paintings of interior scenes came from its predominance in actuality; Eakins was never a man to contradict what he observed—he never copied the retinal image, but in reconstructing the mental image in paint he remained faithful to appearances even while emphasizing what lay beneath them. A few outdoor subjects of the time also make considerable use of shadow in dramatic contrast to areas of light, but the most successful ones in this kind dramatize the light itself as the main pictorial theme. One that does is the *Max Schmitt in a Single Scull* [1871: plate 98], in which the human incident is only a subordinate device for a painting of the level light of a late afternoon sun conferring a timeless majesty upon this familiar space of river and sky. The long diagonals of light-struck scull and oars project their lines across the water to the banks on both sides, where spots of feathery foliage are united through the middle distance by the complex curves of two bridges; overhead is poised the shallow and broken curve of a thin line of cloud. It is one of those hours when nature itself prolongs the light into a promise of time-lessness, and gives the most analytical eye opportunity to discern the deep trans-parencies and subtle solidities which spiritualize the world of matter. Choosing this particular illumination, the painter maintained the conditions in which his visual logic of deep space and his perception of structure in solids could unite into one of his finest and most spacious designs.

A short while before the Centennial Exposition in Philadelphia Eakins com-pleted what was to remain among his most significant pictures, *The Gross Clinic* [1875: Jefferson Medical College, Philadelphia], partly as a challenge to him-self in the complex design suggested by a hospital operation theater and partly as an act of homage to both a type of man and an individual whom he admired. In the course of an operation Doctor Gross straightens up momentarily, while assistants continue their work, to make some remarks to the assembled medical students; this act gives Eakins the strongly lit head of the surgeon as the highest point along the sharply rising curve made by the group of foreground figures. The rules of charity cases then required that a relative of the patient sit in the operating well, and this gives Eakins the reason for the agonized gesture of the seated woman. But it was the patient's cut leg and the bloody hands of Doctor Gross and his assistant which caused denunciation of the picture as a "degrada-tion of art" and denial of its admission to the art section of the exposition. Its being shown in the medical section of the Centennial made it all the more easy for the general public to miss seeing the impersonal mastery of the art in it: the monumental design, the semi-abstract atmospheric upper portion in which the tiers of students make a background of shadowy beauty for the strong light upon the heroic head of the surgeon. Eakins at thirty-one was aware as no other painter in the United States of how the artist must in the end go direct to life in order to give the deepest meaning to his art. Yet in this very subject Eakins was also renewing in American terms a painting tradition which reached back as far as Rembrandt, whose *Anatomy Lesson* is better painted but less well composed in a scheme of light-and-dark; the fact that Doctor Tulp was dissecting a dead body enabled Rembrandt to arrange the Doctor's professional audience as a series of portraits satisfactory to individual egos, but Eakins' choice of an actual operation gave him a ritualistic drama of intense significance which he conveyed both by the complete absorption of its participants and by the bold and Grail-like light in the midst of the mystery of shadow.

98. MAX SCHMITT IN A SINGLE SCULL *by* THOMAS EAKINS *Courtesy of the Metropolitan Museum of Art.*

In 1876 Eakins began teaching the life class at the Pennsylvania Academy, and during the ten years he held that position he not only renovated the instruction in the Academy but introduced a thoroughness of technical training which in due time affected the teaching of art in the country as a whole. In the end he was forced out over a point which, minor in itself, involved a compromise of his ideal of probity in teaching; he insisted that the nude male model be posed before girl students. Some of the girls were the daughters of Directors of the Academy, who themselves were examples of the ubiquitous American businessman allowed by long-established custom and money-power to interfere in matters where prejudices can override professional judgement. When they made Eakins' position untenable, they destroyed the direct effectiveness of a creative teacher.

A strand of irony in the whole situation was that Eakins was as far as any painter could be from fostering the production of academic nudes for exhibition under the conventional titles of *Hope* and *Memory* and *The Genius of America Presiding over the Marriage of the Atlantic and the Pacific*—the kind of painting that would soon begin to deaden all the art shows and expositions of the age. For Eakins the study of the nude was simply the painter's severest discipline, the way to the fullest mastery of his necessary professional skill; its use in picturemaking, he thought, should be limited to occasions and conceptions where it had some expressive fitness. While still a student in Paris he had written home:

. . . I can conceive of few circumstances wherein I would have to paint a woman naked, but if I did I would not mutilate her for double the money. She is the most beautiful thing there is—except a naked man. . . .

He twice made pictures of the male nude. One was *The Crucifixion* [1880: Philadelphia Museum of Art], which is a powerful presentation of the last faint twitches of physical agony; and one was *The Swimming Hole* [1883: Fort Worth Art Association], which raises the anecdotal subject to his characteristic height of seriousness. In a setting of fresh green foliage and rocky platform some men are bathing in the water and the sun. Without in any way impairing the casualness of the event, Eakins has ordered the poses and gestures of light-sculptured bodies into a triangle which gives pictorial permanence to the accidental. The only flaw is that the slanting dive of one man involves a speed of motion to which Eakins' draftsmanship was unsuited. His one completed picture of a feminine nude, *William Rush Carving His Allegorical Figure of the Schuylkill River* [1877: Philadelphia Museum of Art], is a masterpiece of firm construction and delicately tapestried color with which a mind of Quaker restraint might parallel the richer sensuousness of the Venetians. The model is seen from the back as she faces into the studio toward the sculptor at work beyond, while the same slanting light that eloquently reveals the structural subtleties of flesh and bone delineates with equal eloquence the dress folds on the woman seated alongside and the exquisite disorder of discarded clothes piled upon the foreground chair. In textures of flesh and cloth, in a tone where shadow is only a little less luminous than light, Eakins set down with a final beauty the austere sensuousness which vitalized his lofty intelligence.

Yet he did not need the nude in order to demonstrate his knowledge of the figure or his perceptiveness of atmosphere and texture. *The Pathetic Song* [1881: plate 99] shows that it was his knowledge of bodily structure which determined his rendering of the breaks and folds of a heavy dress, of the postures of bodies obscured by shadow. Again it was his control of atmosphere which enriched the picture depth, and it was his management of relations between the forms which imparted nobility to the design. A further trait here manifested which was characteristic of Eakins in many of the pictures which he extracted and reconstructed out of the life around him, a trait rare among painters in general, is the unconsciousness of the people that they are being painted. This of course came from the sharp watch which Eakins maintained upon everything and further upon a strong memory for effects that are in their own nature fleeting; but the original realization of this difference between studio art and life itself, the conscious decision for greater authenticity, were emotionally allied to Eakins' own care to eliminate himself so far as possible from his pictures. Friendships and a happy marriage made a personal life which had its satisfactions apart from his professional difficulties, but both the happiness and the difficulties he chose to keep to himself. When once asked for information about himself, he replied in about seventy-five words which concluded: "For the public I believe my life is all in my work."

Thus the contagion of his example as well as the effectiveness of his instruction gave him his influence over the young so long as he was allowed to teach; and although words of advice taken out of their original context of workshop practice in the arts are especially liable to give only partial insight, some of Eakins' own words so spoken not only tell what he taught but also strengthen the total impression of his mental strength. In the year when he took charge of the life class he gave an interview explaining the fundamentals of his method to the critic, William C. Brownell. The general idea of first things first was given concrete application to painting by the practical proposition that, since the painter's knowledge of the figure would have to be used in painting with the brush, he might most efficiently acquire that knowledge itself by using the brush from the first. This was a most radical idea at the time, because it eliminated the laborious approach to painting through black-and-white drawing,

99. THE PATHETIC SONG *by* THOMAS EAKINS
Courtesy of Corcoran Gallery of Art, Washington, D.C.

usually in charcoal, and this in turn compelled the student to study and render the figure not in terms of line and edge but in terms of mass and weight. Furthermore, the component masses which articulate the body had to be seen in an over-all unity which preserved the organic capacity for movement discernible even in sustained quiescence. Charles Bregler, a specially devoted pupil, noted down from time to time various brief remarks occasioned by the accidents of classroom events. Eakins seems to have used the words "think" and "feel" almost interchangeably, saying: think of the third dimension or of the weight; feel the swing or the slant. What Eakins did in all these intermittent and repeated bits of advice was to tell his pupils not how to paint in this or that manner but how to think in paint, as he did, how to make the mind come alive in the act of painting. The sum of his counsel, as of his practice, was more than the mastery of anatomy or perspective or light; it was the intellectual comprehension and imaginative application of the vitalizing forces of nature itself. This is what the academic teaching of art should always be and almost never is, for the reason that academic organizations sink by force of gravity toward an inertia in which the modification needed for keeping tradition itself alive is forgotten in the repetition of a semi-mechanical teaching formula.

After the Pennsylvania Academy excluded Eakins, he devoted the major portion of his effort to portraiture—but notably without the co-operation of those who were willing to pay for portraits. Their position, conscious or unconscious, was: no flattery, no pay. Consequently, Eakins' portraits were mostly of people whose personalities interested him to the point of his asking them to sit; not being commissions, the pictures accumulated in Eakins' house to the point of making portions of it take on the look of a warehouse of unwanted canvases. The penetrative perception which Eakins had hitherto applied mainly to the impersonal problems of structure and light and design was now concentrated upon the interpretive problems of personality; and even among those whom Eakins thought worthy of his study there were some who did not like what his study brought forth. For even as he had first turned to medical dissection in order to comprehend physical structure, so now he engaged in psychological dissection in order to understand human individuality; and anybody might reasonably decline to be subjected to either treatment. But the profundity and nobility which Eakins could discover—or contribute: for portraiture is an inextricable blend of painter and sitter—were a new note in American painting. The solidly modeled but lightly brushed blue-blacks and yellows in the voluminous dress of *Signora D'Arza* [1902: Metropolitan Museum, New York] make a visually rich foundation for her face of almost tranquilized tragedy. Where Eakins chose to give the whole figure in a portrait, he could make the whole figure as expressive of character as the face; *The Thinker* [1900: Metropolitan Museum, New York] stands solidly and, crowding hands into pockets, becomes solitary in the concentration of his thought.

During this last phase of his career Eakins turned once more to the theme of surgery for perhaps the most ambitious work of all: *The Agnew Clinic* [1889: plate 100]. The operation is still dramatic, but no longer with the accentuated drama of shadow; medicine had by this time begun to adopt the techniques of asepsis, and the surgeon's robe of ritual is clinical white. This keys up the whole lighting scheme, and allows more light to pervade the mass of student observers. Accordingly the design by which everything in the large canvas is made to serve the foreground group consists of complicated converging lines which come into existence through the naturalistic movements among four rows of men in their efforts to get a direct view of what is happening. Once more Eakins dramatized an act of collective life carrying semi-religious implications of modern civilization's hope in science. As the engineers of his day created structures then called ugly because they were bare of copybook stylism, so Eakins created pictures then called ugly because they did without the discretions of subject-matter and the suavity of technique used by derivative minds. It is well to enlarge the concept of beauty to include such vitality, for then it can be perceived how heroically consistent Eakins' whole life and art were from beginning to end. As a youth in Spain he had written home:

. . . O, what a satisfaction it gave me to see the good Spanish work, so good, so strong, so reasonable, so free from every affectation. . . .

Beginning with such admirations, he made a life and an art free from affectation, reasonable and strong. In his art he penetrated to the secret springs of energy, physical and spiritual; his art is therefore durable. As a person and as a painter he embodied integrity. For greatness of personality there can be no greater quality; for an artist in the United States there can be no higher praise.

100. THE AGNEW CLINIC by THOMAS EAKINS   Courtesy of University of Pennsylvania.   Photograph
from The Metropolitan Museum of Art.

80. Conclusion

Copley had bad luck in choosing for his traveling-companion of 1774 from London to Rome an artist by the name of Carter who made elaborate notations in his journal of various episodes which annoyed him, but Carter's persistent intention to ridicule Copley now makes him appear satisfactorily ridiculous himself. Toward the end of their trip Carter wrote:

My companion is solacing himself, that if they go on in America for a hundred years to come, as they have for a hundred and fifty years past, they shall have an independent government: the woods will be cleared, and, lying in the same latitude, they shall have the same air as in the south of France; art would then be encouraged there, and great artists would arise.

In a physical sense Copley's American experience was regional, and his American pictures were a regional manifestation; but just as his work developed a grasp upon actuality which was to become prominent in American painting as a whole, so his mind transcended his locality to dream, like Nathaniel Ames, of a national future.

Just eight years and about two months after Carter wrote that entry in his journal, Copley and his American friend Elkanah Watson together witnessed the occasion on which the king made public acknowledgement of the independence of the United States, and together they returned to Copley's studio and its portrait of Watson. This was not the Watson whose loss of a leg in Havana harbor Copley had celebrated in one of his best paintings; this Watson was a patriotic merchant of Massachusetts who, in commissioning Copley to paint his portrait, planned for it to show in the background the ship that would take to the new nation the first direct news of the king's act. Watson's own journal records how

immediately after our return from the House of Lords, he invited me into his studio; and then with a bold hand, a master's touch, and I believe, an American heart, he attached to the ship the Stars and Stripes. This was, I imagine, the first American flag hoisted in Old England.

It is doubtful that in 1774 Copley had thought independence so near; his conjecture about a change in the American climate may be left to the meteorologists, but his third one about the appearance of artists seems almost miraculously precise. By 1874 Ryder had exhibited his first picture at the National Academy of Design, Homer had been ten years an exhibiting member, and Eakins was completing the four years of significant work which followed his return from Europe.

These three painters appeared at a time when painting was encouraged here with a quantitative patronage inconceivable to Copley. Not much of the encouragement, however, was expended upon the three themselves. To be sure, Homer's accessible art brought him a relatively satisfactory financial return, but the "pecuniary emolument" which the other two received certainly did not constitute what Americans in general would consider worldly success. It may be that, in any democratic culture, contemporaneous acclaim and fortune are inevitably missed by the greatest artists, since artistic greatness itself seems to require a degree of difference from the average which the average at first prefer to ignore or to dislike. In the very approximate justice which is all that some can discern in human affairs, neglect or antagonism has been in recent centuries the usual lifetime reward for artistic originality; but it would be rash for any individual artist to assume that his own experience of either constitutes a proof of his originality. At any rate, two painters among these postwar three worked away without the good fortune that came to lesser men; and in a historical perspective stretching back to this country's cultural beginnings, it seems fairly certain that the prosperity of the lesser men was itself an essential part of the conditions which permitted the more significant minds to develop at all.

Irrespective of their material rewards, the postwar trio became in their achievements representatively American to a degree which had probably been impossible before their time. For a fully typical American painting necessitated first the appearance in quantity of people characteristically American; one hundred and fifty years were required before the point of the national unity and cultural effectiveness was reached. A second necessity as affecting painting was that, from among the characteristically American minds, some of intrinsic superiority should master the art sufficiently to make it expressive of both their character and their superiority; it is not surprising that another hundred years were required. Certainly by that time, if not earlier, American experience and American character had become so complex that no individual could embody it all. In a country where the Yankee and the Planter, the Backwoodsman and the Forty-niner, the Cowboy and the Tycoon had all achieved a valid Americanism of character, no single person could be *the* American. A country so dramatically pluralistic in human terms had to be also pluralistic in culture; and in the art of painting, a lofty imaginative and an objective recorder and a profound intellectual were all needed to embody the full extent of American experience. The work of Homer, less imaginative than that of Ryder and less intellectual than that of Eakins, lies between but also extends part way up both the other peaks; and the work of all together still forms the highest range so far discovered in the exploration of America by American painters.

The first painters commenced their journey from Europe, and in their baggage they naturally brought with them European techniques; but as their successors explored America, techniques began to lose the European fluency and assume an awkwardness as provincial as the people themselves. Ryder's father was a petty customs official and sold coal; Homer's father dealt in hardware; Eakins' father was a Quaker writing master. The three sons were as direct in their attitude toward painting as their fathers were toward their ways of making a living. In becoming painters they remained as untroubled by the academic conventions of their time as their fathers were by the social pretensions of the plutocrats. In the laborious naïvety of his technique Ryder developed his localized memories into timeless imaginations; with his brusque technique Homer recorded human episodes of outdoor life and then passed on to uninhabited stretches of stormy coast; with a technique which seemed rude to others, Eakins re-created organic structures so vital that they could do without superficial attractiveness. All three painters had the power to expand to the spiritual dimension of greatness; thereby they did more than transmit a craft—they accomplished painting's share in creating a culture. They added to its range and its intensity, permanently enriching it for times to follow.

The enrichment they conferred came from the reality they discovered. All art of consequence is a search for reality: that is the simplest way of defining its major significance. By transforming nature into his small pictures, Ryder imaginatively communicated the immensities of life and death. By transcribing appearances in oil and water color, Homer veraciously communicated the actualities and some of the implications of things seen. By renewing the structure of things and people in paint, Eakins communicated a comprehension of them by the intellect which was itself an imaginative act. The subjective mood, the visual fact, the inner organization which shapes the visual fact—all three are phases of reality.

The reality which Ryder, Homer, and Eakins created came directly out of their own experience; their maturity as artists was achieved in the unavoidably provincial terms of their time and place. Their American accent makes them especially valuable for Americans in achieving and maintaining a sense of identity, and that will increase with every generation's acceptance and confirmation. The provincialism will of course affect their value as technical sources for painters, but the maturity of their attitude will keep them central in any tradition which may be possible in this country. A vital tradition is essentially an increasing spiritual coherence; and in the art of painting Ryder and Homer and Eakins have created a core of reality from which Americans can draw much of the power that will be needed to resist and adapt and transmute a different experience into a more complex reality.

Notes

The following lists give the sources which have been drawn upon in the writing of this book. Since many books and articles were examined without being used, these lists cannot be taken as a complete bibliography of the subject. Students who may wish more discursive annotations upon the text will find them in type-written form at the Frick Art Reference Library, New York City.

A FEW BOOKS HAVE BEEN CONSULTED CONTINUOUSLY:

A History of the Rise and Progress of the Arts of Design in the United States, by William Dunlap. 2 vols. New York, 1834. Edited with additions by F. W. Bayley and G. E. Goodspeed. 3 vols. Boston, 1918.

Historic Annals of the National Academy of Design . . . , by Thomas S. Cummings. Philadelphia, 1865.

Book of the Artists: American Artist Life . . . , by Henry T. Tuckerman. New York, 1867 (fifth impression, 1870).

A History of American Art, by Sadakichi Hartman. 2 vols. Boston, 1902.

A History of American Painting, by Samuel Isham. New York, 1905. Reprinted with additional chapters by Royal Cortissoz. New York, 1927.

The American Spirit in Art, by Frank Jewett Mather, Jr., Charles Rufus Morey, and William James Henderson. New Haven, 1927 (Vol. XII in *The Pageant of America* series).

Art in America, by Suzanne La Follette. New York, 1929.

American Folk Art: The Art of the Common Man in America, by Holger Cahill. New York, 1932 (catalog of an exhibition at the Museum of Modern Art).

THREE BOOKS HAVE BEEN SPECIALLY SUGGESTIVE FOR THE SPIRIT IN WHICH THEY APPROACH AMERICAN CULTURE:

The Golden Day: A Study in American Experience and Culture, by Lewis Mumford. New York, 1926.

American Humor: A Study of the National Character, by Constance Rourke. New York, 1931.

Estimates in Art, Series II: Sixteen Essays on American Painters of the Nineteenth Century, by Frank Jewett Mather, Jr. New York, 1931.

THE FOLLOWING BOOKS HAVE SUPPLIED VALUABLE BACKGROUND MATERIAL:

The History of American Sculpture, by Lorado Taft. New York, 1905. New edition revised and with new matter. New York, 1924.

The American Spirit in Architecture, by Talbot Faulkner Hamlin. New Haven, 1926 (Vol. XIII in *The Pageant of America* series).

A History of American Graphic Humor, by William Murrell. 2 vols. New York, 1933, 1938.

A History of Travel in America, by Seymour Dunbar. New edition in one volume. New York, 1937.

The Saga of American Society: A Record of Social Aspiration, 1607–1937, by Dixon Wecter. New York, 1937.

Treasury of American Drawings, by Charles E. Slatkin and Regina Shoolman. New York, 1947.

THE STUDENT MAY ADVANTAGEOUSLY CONSULT:

Dictionary of American Biography, ed. Allen Johnson, Dumas Malone, and Harris E. Starr. 21 vols. New York, 1921–1944.

Limners and Likenesses: Three Centuries of American Painting, by Alan Burroughs. Cambridge, 1936.

Life in America. New York, 1939 (catalog of an exhibition at the Metropolitan Museum of Art).

A History of American Watercolor Painting. New York, 1942 (catalog of an exhibition at the Whitney Museum of American Art).

Art in America for Oct., 1945. A special number devoted to research problems in American art, with contributions by several authors, ed., Lloyd Goodrich.

Magazine of Art for Nov., 1946. A special number given over to American art, with contributions by several authors and a bibliography by Elizabeth McCausland.

CERTAIN VOLUMES OF MISCELLANEOUS ESSAYS DEAL WITH INDIVIDUAL PAINTERS AC-
CORDING TO THE TASTES OF THE WRITERS AND MAY BE READ WITH PLEASURE ACCORD-
ING TO THE TASTES OF THE READERS:

American Masters of Painting, by Charles Henry Caffin. New York, 1913.

Landscape and Figure Painters of America, by Frederic Fairchild Sherman. New York, 1917.

American Painters of Yesterday and Today, by Frederic Fairchild Sherman. New York, 1919.

American Painting and Its Tradition, by John C. Van Dyke. New York, 1919.

Adventures in the Arts, by Marsden Hartley. New York, 1921.

American Artists, by Royal Cortissoz. New York, 1923.

Personalities in Art, by Royal Cortissoz. New York, 1925.

Early American Portrait Painters, by Cuthbert Lee. New Haven, 1929.

America's Old Masters, by James Thomas Flexner. New York, 1939.

PERIOD ONE: THE COLONIAL

A GOOD PANORAMIC VIEW OF THE PERIOD AS A WHOLE IS SUPPLIED BY THE FIRST FOUR
VOLUMES IN THE SERIES A HISTORY OF AMERICAN LIFE:

The Coming of the White Man, 1492–1848, by Herbert I. Priestley. New York, 1929.

The First Americans, 1607–1690, by Thomas Jefferson Wertenbaker. New York, 1927.

Provincial Society, 1690–1763, by James Truslow Adams. New York, 1927.

The Revolutionary Generation, 1763–1790, by Evarts Boutell Greene. New York, 1943.

FOUR OTHER BOOKS HAVE BEEN ESPECIALLY HELPFUL:

The Roots of American Civilization, by Curtis P. Nettels. New York, 1938.
Cities in the Wilderness, by Carl Bridenbaugh. New York, 1938.
The Middle Colonies, by Thomas Jefferson Wertenbaker. New York, 1938.
The Old South, by Thomas Jefferson Wertenbaker. New York, 1942.

FOR COLONIAL PAINTING AS A WHOLE, THREE BOOKS SHOULD BE CONSULTED:

Seventeenth Century Painting in New England, ed. Louisa Dresser. Worcester,
  1935. Based upon a single exhibition of regional work before 1700, this book
  is invaluable in charting a correct course for the entire period; not until scholarship of this quality has been applied to the beginnings of painting in other regions
  can the general historian find a sure footing there.
The Birth of the American Tradition in Art, by Oskar Hagen. New York, 1940.
First Flowers of Our Wilderness, by James Thomas Flexner. Boston, 1947.

DIVISION ONE: Colonial Beginnings—to 1725

§ 1. EXPLORATION, CONQUEST, AND SETTLEMENT.

For pictures by California Amerinds: *The Mission Trail.* Los Angeles, 1940 (cata-
  log of an exhibition at the Los Angeles Country Museum).
For retablos: *Santos, the Religious Folk Art of New Mexico,* by Mitchell A. Wilder
  with Edgar Breitenbach. Colorado Springs, 1943.
For French Canada: "The Arts of French Canada," by Marius Barbeau, in *Art
  Quarterly* for autumn, 1946.
Quotation from Duquesne as given in *The English and French in North America,
  1689–1783,* by Andrew McFarland Davis. Boston, 1887 (pp. 62–63) (Vol. V in
  Narrative and Critical History of America, ed. Justin Winsor).

§ 2. PROTESTANTISM AND ART.

The Religious Background of American Culture, by Thomas C. Hall. Boston, 1930.
For heterodoxy in the Middle Ages: *Medieval Panorama,* by G. G. Coulton. New
  York, 1938 (Chaps. XXV–XXVII incl.).

§ 3. EARLY VIRGINIA.

For Kneller's studio: *Artists and Their Friends in England, 1700–1799,* by William T.
  Whitley. 2 vols. London, 1928 (Vol. I, pp. 4–5).
For the present state of family legend in Virginia, see information supplied for the
  earlier portraits in *Virginia Historical Portraiture, 1585–1830,* ed. Alexander Wilbourne Weddell. Richmond, Va., 1930.

§ 4. THE FIRST CENTURY IN MASSACHUSETTS.

Quotation about New England from *Description of New England, 1616,* by Capt.
  John Smith, as reprinted in *Old South Leaflet,* No. 121.
For the Plymouth settlement: *Saints and Strangers,* by George F. Willison. New
  York, 1945.
For the Boston settlement: *Builders of the Bay Colony,* by Samuel Eliot Morison.
  Boston, 1930.

Quotation about John Winthrop from *Nehemias Americanus, the Life of John Winthrop,* by Cotton Mather. A portion of his *Magnalia* reprinted in *Old South Leaflet,* No. 72.

Cotton Mather's description of Reverend John Wilson's refusal to let his portrait be painted is not quoted because it has been so often used to convey an erroneous impression of the period as a whole; it is easily accessible in Dresser, *op. cit.* (p. 126).

§ 5. THE ARTISAN PAINTER.

For Child: Dresser, *op. cit.* (principally pp. 114–115).

Child's sign is reproduced in "Painters Arms Signs in the Society's Collections," by G. R. Marvin, in *Proceedings of the Bostonian Society* for Jan., 1934.

For Child's paint mill: "Old Red Paint Colored with Burnt Ochre," by Marion Nicholl Rawson, in *New York Sun* for Aug. 7, 1937.

For funeral customs: *Gravestones of Early New England,* by Harriette Merrifield Forbes. Boston, 1927. "Colonial Hatchments," by Howard M. Chapin, in *Antiques* for Oct., 1929. Additional details in Flexner, *op. cit.* (pp. 283–284).

§ 6. THE AMATEUR PAINTER.

Quotation about Allen as given in Dresser, *op. cit.* (p. 19).

Quotation about common art from "The Economic Laws of Art Production," by Sir Herbert Llewellyn Smith, as given in *Artifex,* by John Gloag. New York, 1927.

§ 7. THE SIGNS.

Annals of Philadelphia, by John F. Watson (enlarged by Willis P. Hazard). 3 vols. Philadelphia, 1881 (Vol. I, pp. 463–471; Vol. III, pp. 344–369).

History of Philadelphia, 1609–1884, by J. Thomas Scharf and Thompson Westcott. 3 vols. Philadelphia, 1884 (Vol. II, pp. 984–990). Kindly lent by Mr. Hervey Allen.

Early American Signboards, by Howard M. Chapin. Providence, 1926.

"Early Sign Painters," by Mabel M. Swan, in *Antiques* for May, 1928.

For itinerants in general: *Hawkers and Walkers in Early America,* by Richardson Wright. Philadelphia, 1927. Most of the facts are later than 1725, but the presentation as a whole has retrospective implications.

§ 8. PORTRAITS BY ARTISANS AND AMATEURS.

All of these portraits except *Mrs. Anne Pollard* are discussed in Dresser, *op. cit.*

Quotations about the *John Endecott* from *Diary,* by William Bentley. 4 vols. Salem, Mass., 1905–1914 (Vol. II, pp. 198, 400).

Quotation about Boston in 1654 from *Wonder-working Providence,* by Edward Johnson, as given in Dresser, *op. cit.* (p. 14).

Quotation about Boston in 1670 from *An Account of Two Voyages to New England,* by John Josselyn (London, 1674), as given in *Jeremiah Dummer,* by Hermann Frederick Clarke and Henry Wilder Foote. Boston, 1935.

§ 9. THE MASTER OF THE FREAKES.

Dresser, *op. cit.* (pp. 81–83).

§ 10. PORTRAITS OF CHILDREN.

Dresser, *op. cit.* (pp. 84–89, 98–103).

For English background: *English Painting of the Sixteenth and Seventeenth Centuries,* by C. H. Collins Baker and W. G. Constable. New York, *ca.* 1930.

§ 11. ANTICIPATIONS OF STUDIO TECHNIQUE.

Quotation about Boston from *Diary,* by Jasper Danckaerts, as given in *The Puritans,* by Perry Miller and Thomas H. Johnson. New York, 1938.

For the *John Woodbridge:* Dresser, *op. cit.* (pp. 159–161).

For Thomas Smith: Dresser, *op. cit.* (pp. 62–66, 130–140).

For Cooper: "J. Cooper, an Early New England Portrait Painter," by Bartlett Cowdrey, in *Panorama* for Nov., 1945.

§ 12. THE CENTRAL COLONIES.

"New York Painting Before 1800," by George C. Groce, Jr., in *New York History* for Jan., 1938. Conversations with Mr. Groce in 1937 were exceedingly helpful.

For inventories: *Dutch New York,* by Esther Singleton. New York, 1909 (Chap. V). Additional details in *John Watson,* by John Hill Morgan. Worcester, 1941. See § 19.

For Evert Duyckinck the First: *Early American Glass,* by Rhea Mansfield Knittle. New York, 1927 (pp. 72–74).

Gerardus Duyckinck advertisement: *The Arts and Crafts in New York, 1726–1776,* compiled by Rita S. Gottesman. New York, 1938.

The workman here called the Hudson Valley Master was once confused with Pieter Vanderlyn. James Thomas Flexner (*op. cit.,* Chap. 3) designates him as "Aetatis Sue Manner," from the often repeated inscription on the portraits; but it is possible that he painted portraits not so inscribed.

For Christopher Witt: *Catalogue . . . of the Paintings . . . in the Historical Society of Pennsylvania,* by William Sawitzky. Philadelphia, 1942.

§ 13. THE SOUTH.

For Kühn: *Justus Engelhardt Kühn,* by J. Hall Pleasants. Worcester, 1937 (reprinted from *Proceedings of the American Antiquarian Society* for Oct., 1936).

For Henrietta Johnston: "Art and Artists in Provincial South Carolina," in *Half-Forgotten Byways of the Old South,* by Robert Wilson. Charleston, 1925 (reprinted from *Charleston Year Book* for 1899). "Who Was Henrietta Johnston?" by Anna Wells Rutledge, in *Antiques* for March, 1947.

§ 14. INDICATIONS OF A BROADENING TASTE.

For Burgis: *American Graphic Art,* by Frank Weitenkampf. New edition, New York, 1924 (p. 46). *American Historical Prints,* compiled by Douglas Haskell. New York, 1927 (reprinted from *Bulletin of the New York Public Library* for Dec., 1927).

For the Clark-Frankland House decorations: *Early American Wall Paintings,* by Edward B. Allen. New Haven, 1926. The suggestion there made that the workman was one Robinson in London seems hazardous.

Partridge advertisement: *The Arts and Crafts in New England,* by George Francis Dow. Topsfield, Mass., 1927 (p. 302).

The two mythological paintings by Gustavus Hesselius were once assigned to *ca.* 1742, a stylistic improbability. This early placing is suggested by Mr. E. P. Richardson, who also suggests the new title for the one now owned by the Detroit Institute; this had been called *Pluto and Persephone.* An existing picture of *The Last Supper* has been attributed to Hesselius, but there are difficulties about accepting it. See "Doubts about Hesselius," by Homer Eaton Keyes, in *Antiques* for Sept., 1939.

§ 15. RETROSPECT FROM THE YEAR 1725.

"Old and New England," by E. P. Richardson, in *Art Quarterly* for winter, 1945.
"The Americanism of New England Painting," by James Thomas Flexner, in *Magazine of Art* for April, 1945.

DIVISION TWO: Colonial Culmination—1725 to 1775

§ 16. THE EMERGENCE OF AN UPPER CLASS.

Murasaki quotation: *The Tale of Genji,* by Lady Murasaki. Translated by Arthur Waley. 2 vols. Boston, 1935 (Vol. I, p. 311).

An interesting discrimination between arts and crafts of the seventeenth and eighteenth centuries is "A Parallel of American Styles," by John Fabian Kienitz, in *Art in America* for April, 1946.

§ 17. A CONSCIOUS TASTE IN PAINTING.

Emmons obituary: *The Arts and Crafts in New England,* compiled by George Francis Dow. Topsfield, Mass., 1927 (pp. 1–2).

Quotation about Copley portrait: *Copley-Pelham Letters* (p. 30). See § 24. Ainslee is actually quoting the words of his own father-in-law.

§ 18. SPECIALISTS INTO NEW ENGLAND.

Dunlap does not discuss Peter Pelham, but Bayley and Goodspeed give extensive notes. See also *Notes Concerning Peter Pelham,* by William H. Whitmore. Cambridge, 1867. Letters against his "assemblies": Dow, *op. cit.,* § 17 (pp. 9–11). For his engraving: Weitenkampf, *op. cit.,* § 14 (pp. 87–88). *The Month at Goodspeed's* for Nov., 1935. *The Portfolio* for Feb., 1942.

For the son as musician: *Our American Music,* by John Tasker Howard. Third ed., New York, 1946 (pp. 22–23).

For Smibert: "Smibert-Moffatt letters," in *Massachusetts Historical Society Proceedings* for 1915. "John Smibert, Notes and a Catalogue," by Theodore Bolton, in *Fine Arts* (formerly *Antiquarian*) for March, 1935. For the poem: "Mr. Smibert Shows His Pictures," by Henry Wilder Foote, in *New England Quarterly* for March, 1935. "Notes on Smibert's development," by Alan Burroughs, in *Art in America* for April, 1942. Obituary: Dow, *op. cit.,* § 17 (p. 4).

§ 19. SPECIALISTS INTO THE CENTRAL COLONIES.

For the child portraits: "Some Hudson Valley Portraits," by Helen Comstock, in *Antiques* for Sept., 1944.

Kilburn advertisement: Gottesman, *op. cit.* § 12 (p. 3).

For Watson: *John Watson, Painter, Merchant and Capitalist of New Jersey,* by John Hill Morgan. Worcester, 1941 (reprinted from *Proceedings of the American Antiquarian Society* for Oct., 1940). *Further Notes on John Watson,* by John Hill Morgan. Worcester, 1943 (reprinted from *ibid.,* for April, 1942).

For Gustavus Hesselius: *Gustavus Hesselius,* by Christian Brinton. Philadelphia, 1938 (catalog of an exhibition at the Philadelphia Museum).

For Williams: "William Williams, First Instructor of Benjamin West," by William Sawitsky, in *Antiques* for May, 1937. "The Amazing William Williams, Painter, Author, Teacher, Musician, Stage Designer, Castaway," by James Thomas Flexner, in *Magazine of Art* for Nov., 1944.

§ 20. SPECIALISTS INTO THE SOUTH.

Quotation about Robert Carter: *Journal and Letters,* by Philip Vickers Fithian, ed. John Rogers Williams. Princeton, 1900 (pp. 67, 83).

Letter about Bridges: "The Letters of Col. William Byrd 2d," in *Virginia Historical Magazine* for Jan., 1902.

For Theüs: Robert Wilson, *op. cit.,* § 13. Phrase about "pouter-pigeon pose" used in an exhibition review by Mr. James W. Lane.

About the portrait here reproduced as *Mann Page the Second* by Charles Bridges (plate 14) there exists a difference of opinion. Subject and painter here correspond to those assigned when the picture was included in an exhibition at Virginia House in 1929, out of which exhibition came the volume *Virginia Historical Portraiture* (cited in § 3). Examination then and on two subsequent visits to Williamsburg has not suggested that revision is necessary. However, Dr. Thomas Thorne, Chairman of the Fine Arts Department at the College of William and Mary, writes that the portrait is now considered to be possibly of *Mann Page the First* and possibly by Gustavus Hesselius.

§ 21. THE SPREAD OF FOREIGN FASHION.

For Blackburn: *Joseph Blackburn, a Colonial Portrait Painter,* by Lawrence Park. Worcester, 1928. "An American Artist of Formula, Joseph Blackburn," by Theodore Bolton and Harry Lorin Binsse, in *Antiquarian* for Nov., 1930.

An Extension of Lawrence Park's Descriptive List . . . by John Hill Morgan and Henry Wilder Foote. Worcester, 1937 (reprinted from *American Antiquarian Society Proceedings* for April, 1936). Letter quoted as given in this monograph.

For Wollaston: "Notes on John Wollaston . . ." by John Hill Morgan, in *Brooklyn Museum Quarterly* for Jan., 1923. "Wollaston, an Early American portrait manufacturer," by Theodore Bolton and Harry Lorin Binsse, in *Antiquarian* for June, 1931.

For Cosmo Alexander: John Hill Morgan's biography of Stuart in Lawrence Park's work on Stuart. See § 37.

§ 22. A NATIVE-BORN TALENT.

Robert Feke, Colonial Portrait Painter, by Henry Wilder Foote. Cambridge, 1930.

"Robert Feke, First Painter to the Colonial Aristocracy," by Theodore Bolton and Harry Lorin Binsse, in *Antiquarian* for Oct., 1930.

Robert Feke, by Lloyd Goodrich. New York, 1946 (catalog of an exhibition at the Whitney Museum of American Art).

Quotation about Feke from *Itinerarium,* by Alexander Hamilton. St. Louis, 1907 (pp. 123–124).

Such marked differences of interpretation exist that special note should be taken of the treatments in Burroughs' *Limners and Likenesses* and Hagen's *Birth of the American Tradition.* Flexner's *First Flowers* gives still a third, which attempts to upset previously accepted biographical details. To this there was an elaborate reply by Mr. W. Phenix Belknap in *The Art Bulletin* for Sept., 1947.

§ 23. MORE NATIVE-BORN.

For Badger: *Joseph Badger,* by Lawrence Park. Boston, 1918 (reprinted from *Massachusetts Historical Society Proceedings* for Dec., 1917).

For Greenwood: *John Greenwood in America,* by Alan Burroughs. Andover, Mass., 1943.

Nathaniel Smibert obituary: photostat in Frick Art Reference Library. "Paintings by Nathaniel Smibert," by Alan Burroughs, in *Art in America* for April, 1943.

For John Hesselius: "John Hesselius: An Account of His Life and the First Catalogue of His Portraits," by Theodore Bolton and George C. Groce, Jr., in *Art Quarterly* for winter, 1939.

§ 24. A NATIVE-BORN GENIUS.

The Domestic and Artistic Life of John Singleton Copley, by Martha Babcock Amory. Boston, 1882.

Letters and Papers of John Singleton Copley and Henry Pelham, 1739–1776, ed. Guernsey Jones. Boston, 1914 (Vol. 71 of the *Massachusetts Historical Society Collections*).

John Singleton Copley: American Portraits, by Barbara Nelville Parker and Anne Bolling Wheeler. Boston, 1938.

"Henry Pelham," by Denison R. Slade, in *Colonial Society of Massachusetts Proceedings* for Feb., 1908.

§ 25. IMPORTANT STYLISTIC BEGINNINGS.

For bibliography of C. W. Peale, see § 43; of Trumbull, § 44; of Ralph Earl, § 42; of Stuart, § 37; of Pratt, § 33.

"The American Work of Benjamin West," by William Sawitzky, in *Pennsylvania Magazine of History and Biography* for Oct., 1938. For additional bibliography, see § 31.

§ 26. MORE ARTISANS AND AMATEURS.

For Faris: "William Faris, Annapolis Clock Maker," by Lockwood Barr, in *Antiques* for April, 1940.

For Blyth: Bentley, *op. cit.,* § 8 (Vol. III, p. 470).

For Medici: A. W. Weddell, ed., *op. cit.,* § 3.

For George Mason: Bayley and Goodspeed's edition of Dunlap (Vol. III, p. 316).

For Gordon: Robert Wilson, *op. cit.,* § 13.

For Francis Hopkinson as a musician: John Tasker Howard, *op. cit.,* § 17 (pp. 41–42).

For Precour advertisement: *The Huguenots of South Carolina*, by Arthur Henry Hirsch. Durham, 1928 (p. 157, note 18).

For J. & H. Stevenson advertisement: *The Arts and Crafts in Philadelphia, Maryland, and South Carolina*, collected by Alfred Coxe Prime. Topsfield, Mass., 1929.

For Smither's advertisement: Prime, *op. cit.* For Smither's engraving: *Colonial Craftsmen of Pennsylvania*. Philadelphia, 1925 (cover design).

Quotations about Nancy Shippen: *Nancy Shippen, Her Journal Book*, compiled and edited by Ethel Armes. Philadelphia, 1935 (pp. 41–42).

On girls' schools: "Amateur Art in Early New England," by Grace B. Peck, in *Harper's Magazine* for May, 1902.

§ 27. THE FURTHER BROADENING OF TASTE.

For Warren advertisement: Bayley and Goodspeed's edition of Dunlap (Vol. III, p. 340).

For Hamilton drawings: "A Humorous Artist in Colonial Maryland," by Anna Wells Rutledge, in *Art in America* for Feb., 1947.

For Greenwood painting: "The Other Side of Colonial Painting," by Alan Burroughs, in *Magazine of Art* for Nov., 1942.

For still-life advertisement: *Everyday Life in the Massachusetts Bay Colony*, by George Francis Dow. Boston, 1935 (p. 6).

For J. Durand advertisement: Bayley and Goodspeed's edition of Dunlap (Vol. I, p. 169).

For history prints: Douglas Haskell, compiler, *op. cit.*, § 14.

Quotation from Henry Pelham: *Copley-Pelham Letters*, cited in § 24 (p. 83).

For *Conference of Ministers*: "An Early Overmantel," by Alan Burroughs, in *Art in America* for Oct., 1941.

For Haidt: "John Valentine Haidt," by Garth A. Howland, in *Pennsylvania History* for Oct., 1941.

For Remick: *Christian Remick, an Early Boston Artist*, by H. W. Cunningham. Boston, 1904.

For Albertina Ten Broeck: *Home Life in Colonial Days*, by Alice Morse Earl. New York, 1923.

For Chandler, see § 33.

For Holliman: Forbes, *op. cit.*, § 5. Bentley, *op. cit.*, § 8 (Vol. IV, p. 392).

For Rusbatch and Warwell advertisements: Prime, *op. cit.*, § 26.

For "Marmion" and Warner House: Allen, *op. cit.*, § 14 (pp. 9–12, 21–25).

§ 28. THE BEGINNING OF WEST'S INFLUENCE.

For bibliography of Pratt, see § 33; of C. W. Peale, § 43.

For Benbridge: "Henry Benbridge, American Portrait Painter," by Anna Wells Rutledge, in *American Collector* for Oct., Nov., 1948.

§ 29. RETROSPECT FROM THE YEAR 1775.

For Gains advertisement: *Notes on American Artists, 1754–1820*, compiled by William Kelby. New York, 1922.

For Winter advertisement: Prime, *op. cit.*, § 26.

Division Three: Revolutionary Transition—1775 to 1790

§ 30. THE DISRUPTION OF THE UPPER CLASS.

For Duché obituary: *Anecdotes of Painting in England,* collected by Horace Walpole, ed. Frederick W. Hillis and Philip B. Daghlian. New Haven, 1937.

For Mather Brown: "Mather Brown," by F. W. Coburn, in *Art in America* for April, 1932.

§ 31. BENJAMIN WEST IN LONDON.

The Life, Studies, and Works of Benjamin West, Esq. . . . , composed from materials furnished by himself, by John Galt. London, 1820.

"Benjamin West in His Historical Significance," by Fiske Kimball, in *Benjamin West, 1738–1820.* Philadelphia, 1938 (catalog of an exhibition at the Philadelphia Museum).

Quotation from West: *Copley-Pelham Letters,* § 24 (pp. 194–196).

Quotation from Farington: *The Farington Diary,* ed. James Greig. 8 vols. London, 1921–1928 (Vol. IV, p. 227; Dec. 1, 1807).

Quotation from Mrs. Hall: *The Aristocratic Journey,* by Mrs. Basil Hall, ed. Una Pope-Hennessy. New York, 1931 (p. 145).

§ 32. JOHN SINGLETON COPLEY IN LONDON.

For bibliography, see § 24.

Quotation from Hoppner: Whitley, *op. cit.,* § 3 (Vol. II, p. 49).

§ 33. TRANSITION ARTISANS AND AMATEURS.

For Pratt: "Pratt, Painter of Colonial Portraits and Sign-Boards," by Theodore Bolton and Harry Lorin Binsse, in *Antiquarian* for Sept., 1931. *Matthew Pratt: A Study of His Work,* by William Sawitzky. New York, 1942. Newspaper anecdote: Kelby, *op. cit.,* § 29.

For Chandler: "Winthrop Chandler," by James Thomas Flexner, in *Magazine of Art* for Nov., 1947. "Winthrop Chandler," by Nina Fletcher Little, in *Art in America* for April, 1948. Obituary: *The Chandler Family* . . ., Worcester, 1885 (pp. 277–278).

§ 34. FRACTUR.

"The Survival of the Medieval Art of Illuminative Writing Among Pennsylvania Germans," by Henry S. Mercer, in *Proceedings of the American Philosophical Society,* Philadelphia, 1897.

Pennsylvania German Illuminated Manuscripts, by Henry S. Borneman. Norristown, Pa., 1937.

Folk Art of Rural Pennsylvania, by Frances Lichter. New York, 1946.

§ 35. ANTICIPATIONS OF LATER DEVELOPMENTS.

For bibliography of miniature painting, see § 39.

For Mack advertisement: Prime, *op. cit.,* § 26.

For Ramage: *John Ramage,* by Frederic Fairchild Sherman. New York, 1929.

For Fulton: "Robert Fulton as an Artist," by Eleanore J. Fulton, in *Papers of the Lancaster County Historical Society*, Lancaster, Pa., 1938.

For the Eidophusikon: *Tidewater Virginia*, by Paul Wilstach. New York, 1925 (p. 178).

For Quesnay: "Richmond's First Academy," by Richard H. Gaines, in *Proceedings of the Virginia Historical Society*, Richmond, Va., 1892. Advertisement: Kelby, *op. cit.*, § 29.

PERIOD TWO: THE PROVINCIAL

A GOOD PANORAMIC VIEW OF THE PERIOD AS A WHOLE IS SUPPLIED BY THE SECOND GROUP OF FOUR VOLUMES IN THE SERIES A HISTORY OF AMERICAN LIFE:

The Completion of Independence, 1790–1830, by John Allen Krout and Dixon Ryan Fox. New York, 1944.

The Rise of the Common Man, 1830–1850, by Carl Russell Fish. New York, 1927.

The Irrepressible Conflict, 1850–1865, by Arthur Charles Cole. New York, 1934.

The Emergence of Modern America, 1865–1878, by Allan Nevins. New York, 1927.

ONE OTHER BOOK HAS BEEN ESPECIALLY HELPFUL:

Democracy in America, by Alexis De Tocqueville, ed. Phillips Bradley. 2 vols. New York, 1945.

FOUR BOOKS GIVE A GOOD IDEA OF THE CHANGES IN ATTITUDE TOWARD PAINTING WHICH OCCURRED WITHIN THE PERIOD:

The Artists of America, by C. Edwards Lester. New York, 1846.

The Art Idea, by James Jackson Jarves. New York, 1864.

Art Thoughts, by James Jackson Jarves. New York, 1869.

Art in America: A Critical and Historical Sketch, by Samuel Greene Wheeler Benjamin. New York, 1880.

THREE BOOKS SURVEY THE PERIOD FROM THE STANDPOINT OF THE PRESENT:

The Way of Western Art, 1776–1914, by Edgar P. Richardson. Cambridge, 1939.

Romantic Painting in America, by James Thrall Soby and Dorothy Miller. New York, 1943 (catalog of an exhibition at the Museum of Modern Art).

American Romantic Painting, by Edgar P. Richardson, ed. Robert Freund. New York, 1944.

Division Four: The Federal Era—1790 to 1830

§ 36. THE NEW NATION.

For architecture: *Greek Revival Architecture in America*, by Talbot Hamlin. New York, 1944.

Quotation from Svinin: *Picturesque United States of America, 1811–1813*, by Avrahm Yarmolinsky. New York, 1930.

Quotation from Freneau: *That Rascal Freneau: A Study in Literary Failure*, by Lewis Leary. New Brunswick, N. J., 1941 (p. 263).

§ 37. A RETURNING MASTER.

Gilbert Stuart: An Illustrated Descriptive List of His Works, by Lawrence Park. 4 vols. New York, 1926.

Gilbert Stuart, by William T. Whitley. Cambridge, 1932. The description of Stuart painting in old age is from this book, p. 177.

Gilbert Stuart and His Pupils, by John Hill Morgan. New York, 1939. This contains the full text of Jouett's notes.

Quotation from Mather: *Estimates in Art, Series II*, by Frank Jewett Mather, Jr. New York, 1931 (p. 4).

§ 38. AN INFLUX OF FOREIGNERS.

America and French Culture, 1750–1843, by Howard Mumford Jones. Chapel Hill, 1927.

Perovani & Cocchi advertisement: *The Arts and Crafts in Philadelphia, Maryland, and South Carolina, 1786–1800*, Series II, collected by Alfred Coxe Prime. Topsfield, Mass., 1932.

Robertson advertisement: Whitley, *op. cit.*, § 37 (pp. 90–91).

For Sharples: *The Sharples*, by Katharine McCook Knox. New Haven, 1930.

For Saint-Mémin: *Sketch of the Life of . . . Saint-Mémin*, by Frank Weitenkampf. New York, 1899 (for an exhibition at the Grolier Club). "The work of Saint-Mémin," by John Hill Morgan, in *Brooklyn Museum Quarterly* for Jan., 1918. "C. B. J. F. de Saint-Mémin," by Stephen Decatur, in *American Collector* for June, 1944.

Early American Portrait Draughtsmen in Crayon, by Theodore Bolton. New York, 1923.

§ 39. THE POPULARITY OF THE MINIATURE.

For the miniature in general, see: *Early American Portrait Painters in Miniature*, by Theodore Bolton. New York, 1921. *American Miniatures, 1730–1850*, by Harry B. Wehle and Theodore Bolton. Garden City, 1927.

For anonymous advertisement: Prime, *op. cit.*, § 38.

For Field: *Robert Field*, by Harry Piers. New York, 1927.

For Trott: "Benjamin Trott: An Account of His Life and Work," by Theodore Bolton, with a catalog by Theodore Bolton and Ruel Pardee Tolman, in *Art Quarterly* for autumn, 1944.

For Fraser, see § 51.

For Malbone: "Malbone and His Miniatures," by R. T. H. Halsey, in *Scribner's Magazine* for May, 1910. "Malbone the American Miniature Painter," by Ruel Pardee Tolman, with check list in supplement, in *Art Quarterly* for spring, 1939. "Edward Greene Malbone's Self-Portraits," by Ruel Pardee Tolman, in *Antiques* for Dec., 1942.

§ 40. PORTRAITURE IN THE OIL MEDIUM.

For Gullager: "Christian Gullager," by Louisa Dresser, in *Art in America* for July, 1949.

For Ralph Earl, see § 42.

For Jarvis: "John Wesley Jarvis," by Theodore Bolton and George C. Groce, Jr., in *Art Quarterly* for autumn, 1938. "John Wesley Jarvis," by H. E. Dickson, in *New-York Historical Society Quarterly Bulletin* for April, 1940.

John Eckstein is not indexed in Bayley and Goodspeed's edition of Dunlap, but he is treated in Dunlap's text, Vol. II, p. 292.

For C. W. Peale, see § 43.

For Eichholtz: *Jacob Eichholtz*, by William Uhler Hensel. Lancaster, Pa., 1912.

For Thomas Sully, see § 52.

For Negus: *Nathan Negus, an American Painter*, by Mary W. Fuller. Manuscript kindly made available by Mrs. Fuller.

For French cultural life in New Orleans: *Les Écrits de langue française en Louisiane au XIXᵉ siècle: essais biographiques et bibliographiques*, by Edward Laroque Tinker. Paris, 1922 (Vol. 85, *Bibliothèque de la revue de littérature comparée*). This book discusses several interesting amateur and newspaper artists.

For Salazar: Sawitzky, *op. cit.*, § 12.

For Kentucky painters as a group: *The Old Masters of the Bluegrass*, by Samuel Woodson Price. Louisville, 1902.

For Jouett: *Matthew Harris Jouett*, by E. A. Jonas. Louisville, 1938.

§ 41. FORMS STRENGTHENED BY THE FOREIGN-BORN.

For Wertmüller: "La Peintre suédois Wertmüller en France," by Arthur Laës, in *Actes du congrès d'histoire de l'art, 1921.* Paris, 1924 (Vol. II, Pt. I, pp. 378–390).

For Krimmel: "Krimmel, the American Hogarth," by Joseph Jackson, in *International Studio* for June, 1929.

For topographical prints: Weitenkampf, *op. cit.*, § 14; Haskell, *op. cit.*, § 14. "John Hill and American Landscapes in Aquatint," by Frank Weitenkampf, in *American Collector* for July, 1948.

For Corné: Allen, *op. cit.*, § 14 (pp. 26–45).

For Beck, Groombridge, Guy, and Winstanley: *Four Late Eighteenth Century Anglo-American Landscape Painters*, by J. Hall Pleasants. Worcester, 1943 (reprinted from *Proceedings of the American Antiquarian Society* for Oct., 1942).

§ 42. FORMS DEVELOPED BY THE NATIVE-BORN.

For anecdote in general: *American Genre: The Social Scene in Paintings and Prints, 1800–1935.* New York, 1935 (catalog of an exhibition at the Whitney Museum of American Art). *New England Genre.* Cambridge, 1939 (catalog of an exhibition at the Fogg Art Museum).

For landscape in general: *A Century of Landscape Painting, 1800 to 1900.* New York, 1938 (catalog of an exhibition at the Whitney Museum of American Art). *The Hudson River School and the Early American Landscape Tradition*, by Frederick A. Sweet. Chicago, 1945 (catalog of an exhibition at the Art Institute of Chicago). *American Landscape Painting, an Interpretation*, by Wolfgang Born. New Haven, 1948.

For still-life in general: *Still-Life Painting in America*, by Wolfgang Born. New York, 1947.

For Otis: "Pictures in the Old State House," by Anthony J. Philpot, in *Proceedings of the Bostonian Society*, Boston, 1934.

For Fraser, see § 51.

For Ralph Earl: *Connecticut Portraits by Ralph Earl.* New Haven, 1935 (catalog of an exhibition at the Yale University Art Gallery). "Ralph Earl's Historical Painting . . .," by William Sawitzky, in *Antiques* for Sept., 1935. "The Painting of Ralph Earl," by Frederic Fairchild Sherman, in *Art in America* for Oct., 1939. *Ralph Earl,* Worcester, 1945 (catalog of an exhibition at the Worcester Art Museum). "Ralph Earl," by Lloyd Goodrich, in *Magazine of Art* for Jan., 1946. "A New Landscape by Ralph Earl," by Albert Reese, in *Art in America* for Jan., 1948.

For Fisher: "A Letter from Alvan Fisher," by Alan Burroughs, in *Art in America* for July, 1944.

For Dunlap and Trumbull, see § 44.

For newspaper comment on Vanderlyn: Kelby, *op. cit.,* § 29 (p. 54).

For H. S. Mount: *The Mount Brothers.* Stony Brook, L. I., 1947 (catalog of an exhibition at the Suffolk Museum).

For Raphaelle Peale: Sellers, *op. cit.,* § 43. "Raphaelle Peale, Miniature Painter," by Edmund Bury, in *American Collector* for Aug., 1948.

§ 43. THE SUMMIT OF A USEFUL LIFE.

"The Peale Portraits of Washington," by Theodore Bolton and Harry Lorin Binsse, in *Antiquarian* for Feb., 1931.

"Charles Willson Peale," by Theodore Bolton, in *Art Quarterly* for autumn 1939 (with a catalog of the portraits in supplement).

Charles Willson Peale, by Charles Coleman Sellers. 2 vols. Philadelphia, 1947.

§ 44. HISTORY PAINTING.

For Trumbull: *Autobiography, Reminiscences, and Letters,* by John Trumbull. New York, 1841. "Early Landscape Drawings by John Trumbull," by Jean Lambert Brockway, in *American Magazine of Art* for Jan., 1933. "Trumbull's *Sortie*," by Jean Lambert Brockway, in *Art Bulletin* for March, 1934. "A Tentative 'Short-Title' Check List . . . ," by Theodore Sizer, in *Art Bulletin* for Sept., 1948; Dec., 1948; and March, 1949. The reissue of this in book form will discuss the way in which Trumbull's paintings determined the visualization of the Revolution for the nation at large.

For Vanderlyn: "Recollections of Vanderlyn," by William Ingraham Kip, in *Atlantic Monthly* for Feb., 1867.

For Paul: "A Note on Jeremiah Paul," by H. E. Dickson, in *Antiques* for June, 1947.

For Dunlap: *William Dunlap,* by Oral Sumner Coad. New York, 1917. *William Dunlap, Painter and Critic.* Andover, Mass., 1939 (catalog of an exhibition at the Addison Gallery).

For Rembrandt Peale: *An Exhibition of Paintings by Rembrandt Peale.* Baltimore, 1937 (at the Municipal Museum: now the Peale Museum). The quotation from Rembrandt Peale is taken from Mr. Macgill James' introduction to this catalog. The quotation about *The Court of Death* is from Scharf and Westcott, *op. cit.,* § 7 (Vol. II, p. 1038).

For the pictures in the Capitol Rotunda: *Art and Artists of the Capitol,* by Charles E. Fairman. Washington, 1927. Quotations about the Trumbull paintings: Mrs. Basil Hall, *op. cit.,* § 31 (p. 166); Bentley, *op. cit.,* 48 (Vol. IV, p. 565).

§ 45. AN ARTIST OF IMPULSE.

Lectures on Art and Poems, by Washington Allston, ed. Richard Henry Dana, Jr. New York, 1850.

The Life and Letters of Washington Allston, by Jared B. Flagg. New York, 1892.

"Allston and the Development of Romantic Color," by Edgar P. Richardson, in *Art Quarterly* for winter, 1944.

Washington Allston. Detroit, 1947 (catalog of an exhibition at the Detroit Institute).

"Allston, the History of a Reputation," by Edgar P. Richardson, in *Art News* for Aug., 1947. This was part of a biography, *Washington Allston,* by Edgar P. Richardson. Chicago, 1948. That book appeared after § 45 of this book was written.

§ 46. AN ARTIST OF FORETHOUGHT.

The Life of Samuel F. B. Morse, by Samuel Irenaeus Prime. New York, 1875.

Letters and Journals, by Samuel F. B. Morse, ed. Edward Lind Morse. 2 vols. Boston, 1914.

Samuel F. B. Morse, American Painter, by Harry B. Wehle. New York, 1932 (catalog of an exhibition at the Metropolitan Museum).

The American Leonardo, by Carleton Mabee. New York, 1943.

§ 47. THE FIRST EFFECTIVE ART ORGANIZATIONS.

A History of the Metropolitan Museum of Art, by Winifred Howe. New York, 1913.

The Athenaeum Gallery, 1827–1873, by Mabel Manson Swan. Boston, 1940.

National Academy of Design Exhibition Record, 1826–1860, compiled by Bartlett Cowdrey. 2 vols. New York, 1943.

"The Artist's Profession in the Early Republic," by H. E. Dickson, in *Art Quarterly* for autumn, 1945.

Quotation from Rembrandt Peale as given by Macgill James in catalog, cited in § 44.

Quotation about Bowen's Museum: Bentley, *op. cit.,* § 8 (Vol. III, pp. 3, 51).

§ 48. ARTISANS AND AMATEURS OF THE FEDERAL ERA.

On this type of art throughout the nineteenth century: *American Primitives,* by Holger Cahill. Newark, 1930 (catalog of an exhibition at the Newark Museum). *American Pioneer Art and Artists,* by Carl William Drepperd. Springfield, Mass., 1942. *American Primitive Painting,* by Jean Lipman. New York, 1942.

For Severance: "Connecticut Valley Painters," by Agnes M. Dods, in *Antiques* for Oct., 1944.

For Clarke: *Two Hundred Fifty Years of Painting in Maryland.* Baltimore, 1945 (catalog of an exhibition at the Baltimore Museum of Art).

For George Ropes: "Early Marine Painters of Salem," by Mabel M. Swan and Louise Karr, in *Antiques* for Aug., 1940.

For Penniman: "John Ritto Penniman," by Mabel M. Swan, in *Antiques* for May, 1941.

For Woodside: Watson, *op. cit.,* § 7; Scharf and Westcott, *op. cit.,* § 7; Sawitzky, *op. cit.,* § 12.

For Wentworth: Notices in *Antiques* for Jan., June, and July, 1937.

For Moses Morse: *Early Ohio Taverns, Tavern-Sign . . . Painters,* by Rhea Mansfield Knittle. Ashland, O., 1937.

For Rooker: *Art and Artists of Indiana,* by Mary Q. Burnet. New York, 1921.

For Atwood: professional card in possession of Mrs. Mary W. Fuller, Deerfield, Mass.

For Theorem Painting: "Theorem Painting," by Louise Karr, in *Antiques* for April, 1936.

For Jane Stuart: Whitley, *op. cit.,* § 37 (p. 173).

For Mary Ann Bacon: *Chronicles of a Pioneer School from 1782 to 1833,* by Emily Noyes Vanderpoel. Cambridge, 1903.

For Eunice Pinney: "Eunice Pinney, an Early Connecticut Water-Colorist," by Jean Lipman, in *Art Quarterly* for summer, 1943.

For Cogdell: "Cogdell and Mills, Charleston Sculptors," by Anna Wells Rutledge, in *Antiques* for March, 1942.

For Joshua Johnston: *Joshua Johnston, the First American Negro Portrait Painter,* by J. Hall Pleasants. Baltimore, 1942. *The Negro in Art,* by Alain Locke. Washington, 1940.

§ 49.   RETROSPECT FROM THE YEAR 1830.

For Robert Gilmor: "One Early American's Precocious Taste," by Anna Wells Rutledge, in *Art News* for March, 1949.

For Titian Peale: "Titian Peale," by Albert C. Peale, in *Philosophical Society of Washington Bulletin* for Dec., 1905. Information concerning this Peale was kindly given by Mr. Donald Culross Peattie.

For Neal: *Observations on American Art,* by John Neal, ed. H. E. Dickson. State College, Pa., 1943 (No. 12 in *Pennsylvania State College Studies*).

DIVISION FIVE: The Mid-Century—1830 to 1860

§ 50.   THE REIGN OF THE GENTEEL.

For this division as a whole: *The Sentimental Years, 1836–1860,* by E. Douglas Branch. New York, 1934.

For the daguerreotype and its successors: *Photography and the American Scene,* by Robert Taft. New York, 1938.

Diary, by Philip Hone, ed. Bayard Tuckerman. 2 vols. New York, 1889. (Quotation about the daguerreotype, Vol. I, pp. 391–392; about paintings, Vol. I, p. 353; about *The Greek Slave,* Vol. II, p. 322.)

§ 51.   THE DECLINE OF THE MINIATURE.

See Wehle-Bolton, *op. cit.,* § 39.

For Fraser: *Catalogue of the Miniature Portraits, Landscapes and Other Pieces Executed by Charles Fraser.* Charleston, 1857. *Charles Fraser,* by Alice R. Huger Smith and D. E. Huger Smith. New York, 1924. *A Charleston Sketchbook, 1796–1806,* by Charles Fraser. Introduction and notes by Alice R. Huger Smith. Charleston, 1940.

§ 52.   MID-CENTURY PORTRAITURE.

For Jocelyn: "Nathaniel Jocelyn," by Foster Wild Rice, in *Art in America* for Dec., 1947.

For Robert Sully: *Art in Wisconsin*, by Porter Butts. Madison, Wis., 1936 (pp. 88–94).

For Cheney: *Memoir of Seth Wells Cheney, Artist*, by Edna Dow Cheney. Boston, 1881.

For Fagnani: *The Art Life of a Nineteenth Century Portrait Painter, Joseph Fagnani*, by Emma Fagnani. Privately printed, 1930.

For Cincinnati: *With Pen and Pencil on the Frontier, 1851*, by F. B. Mayer. St. Paul, 1932. Alain Locke, *op. cit.*, § 48. Quotation from the Cincinnati newspaper as given in *Henry Ward Beecher: An American Portrait*, by Paxton Hibben. New York, 1927 (p. 73). Information about Alfred Payne kindly given by Mr. Donald Culross Peattie.

For Cox: *Paintings by Jacob Cox*. Introduction by Wilbur D. Peat. Indianapolis, 1941 (catalog of an exhibition at the John Herron Art Institute).

For Michigan: "Painting and Sculpture in Michigan," by Clyde H. Burroughs, in *Michigan Historical Magazine* for autumn, 1936.

For Wisconsin: Butts, *op. cit.*

For Hubard: *William James Hubard*. Introduction by Helen G. McCormack. Richmond, Va., 1948 (catalog of an exhibition at the Valentine Museum and the Virginia Museum of Fine Arts).

For Thomas Sully: "Thomas Sully's Register of Portraits, 1783–1872," ed. Charles Henry Hart, in *Pennsylvania Magazine of History and Biography* for Oct., 1908, Jan., 1909, April, 1909. *The Life and Works of Thomas Sully*, by Edward Biddle and Mantle Fielding. Philadelphia, 1921. *Catalogue of . . . Portraits by Thomas Sully*. Philadelphia, 1922 (an exhibition at the Pennsylvania Academy). "Journal," by Thomas Sully, in *New York Times Magazine* for July 2, 9, and 16, 1922 (extracts concerning his painting the portrait of Queen Victoria).

For Neagle: *Catalogue of . . . the Works of John Neagle*. Philadelphia, 1925 (an exhibition at the Pennsylvania Academy). "John Neagle's Diary," by Marguerite Lynch, in *Art in America* for April, 1949.

For Elliott: *Reminiscences of Charles Loring Elliott*, by Thomas Bangs Thorpe. New York, 1886 (reprinted from *New York Evening Post*). "Charles L. Elliott, an Account of His Life and Work," by Theodore Bolton, in *Art Quarterly* for winter, 1942.

For Harding: *A Sketch of Chester Harding, Artist*, ed. Margaret E. White. New edition with annotations by his grandson, W. P. G. Harding. Boston, 1929.

For Healy: *Reminiscences of a Portrait Painter*, by George P. A. Healy. Chicago, 1894. *Life of George P. A. Healy*, by Madeline Charles Bigot. Chicago, 1913.

§ 53. MID-CENTURY LANDSCAPE.

See general works cited in § 42. "American Art, a Geographical Interpretation," by Frederick A. Gutheim, in *American Magazine of Art* for May, 1925. "The Coast and the Sea," by John I. H. Baur, in *Art News* for Nov., 1948.

For Heade: "Martin Johnson Heade," by Elizabeth McCausland, in *Panorama*, Vol. I, No. 1, 1945.

For Cole: *The Course of Empire, Voyage of Life, and Other Pictures of Thomas Cole*, by Louis L. Noble. New York, 1853. "Thomas Cole and the Romantic Landscape," by Walter L. Nathan, in *Romanticism in America*, ed. George Boas. Baltimore, 1940. *Thomas Cole One Hundred Years Later*. Introduction by Esther Isabel Seaver.

Hartford, 1948 (catalog of an exhibition at the Wadsworth Atheneum). "Some Clues to Thomas Cole," by Everett P. Lesley, Jr., in *Magazine of Art* for Jan., 1949.

For Durand: *The Life and Works of Asher Brown Durand,* by John Durand. New York, 1894.

For Inness, see § 75.

§ 54. THE POPULARITY OF THE PANORAMA.

See Butts, *op. cit.,* § 52 (Chap. IV), and Born, *op. cit.,* § 42, Landscape. "Newsreel— Old Style, or Four Miles of Canvas," by John Francis McDermott, in *Antiques* for July, 1943.

For Catherwood: "Mr. Catherwood's Panorama," by Victor W. Von Hagen, in *Magazine of Art* for April, 1947.

For Banvard: *Banvard, or the Adventures of an Artist.* Boston and London, *ca.* 1848 (a pamphlet printed for visitors to his panorama).

For Lewis: *Making a Motion Picture in 1848,* by Bertha J. Heilbron. St. Paul, 1936.

For Ruckle: *Two Hundred Fifty Years of Painting in Maryland, op. cit.,* § 48.

For Harris: Burnet, *op. cit.,* § 48.

For Williams: *Ohio Art and Artists,* by Edna Maria Clark. Richmond, Va., 1932.

Quotation about panorama: *A History of American Magazines,* by Frank Luther Mott. 3 vols. Cambridge, 1930–1938 (Vol. II, p. 190).

§ 55. PAINTERS OF THE AMERIND.

See Butts, *op. cit.,* § 52 (Chap. III).

For Catlin: "The George Catlin Indian Gallery," by Thomas Donaldson, in *Smithsonian Institution Report.* Washington, 1885.

For Miller: "Exhibition review," by Sara Wilson, in *Baltimore Evening Sun* for Oct. 21, 1941.

For Stanley: "John Mix Stanley, Pioneer Painter," by Benjamin Paff Draper, in *Antiques* for March, 1942.

For Wimar: *Carl Wimar,* by W. R. Hodges. Galveston, 1908. *Carl Wimar,* by Perry T. Rathbone. St. Louis, 1946 (catalog of an exhibition at the City Art Museum).

For Mayer: Mayer, *op. cit.,* § 52.

§ 56. PAINTERS INTO DISTANT REGIONS.

For Texas: *Art and Artists of Texas,* by Mrs. Esse Forrester O'Brien. Dallas, 1925.

For California: *The History and Ideals of American Art,* by Eugen Neuhaus. Stanford, 1931. Richardson and Freund, *op. cit.,* for Provincial period.

For William Smith Jewett: "The Jewetts, William and William S.," by Helen C. Nelson, in *International Studio* for Jan., 1926. "A Case of Confused Identity: Two Jewetts Named William," by Helen C. Nelson, in *Antiques* for Nov., 1942.

§ 57. MID-CENTURY ART ORGANIZATIONS.

See Howe, Swan, and Cowdrey, *op. cit.,* § 47.

For the Boston Museum: *The First Decade of the Boston Museum,* by Clair McGlinchee. *One Man in His Time: The Adventures of H. Watkins, Strolling Player,* ed. Maud and Otis Skinner. Philadelphia, 1938.

For the Art-Union: *American Art-Union Transactions.* New York, 1839–1849. *American Art-Union Bulletin.* New York, 1847–1853.

§ 58. MID-CENTURY HISTORY PAINTING.

For the Capitol: Fairman, *op. cit.,* § 44.

For Bingham: *George Caleb Bingham, the Missouri Artist,* by Fern Helen Rusk. Jefferson City, Mo., 1917. *George Caleb Bingham.* New York, 1935 (catalog of an exhibition at the Museum of Modern Art). *George Caleb Bingham of Missouri,* by Albert Christ-Janer. New York, 1940.

§ 59. MID-CENTURY ANECDOTE.

See general works cited in § 42.

For Mount: *William Sidney Mount, an American Painter,* by Bartlett Cowdrey and Hermann W. Williams, Jr. New York, 1944. "Mount and the Golden Day," by Elizabeth McCausland, in *American Collector* for March, 1945. Catalog of Mount Brothers exhibition at Suffolk Museum, *op. cit.,* § 42.

For the Beard brothers: Clark, *op. cit.,* § 54.

For Blythe: "David G. Blythe, American Painter and Wood-Carver," by Evelyn Abraham, in *Antiques* for May, 1935. *Paintings by David G. Blythe: Drawings by Joseph Boggs Beale.* New York, 1936 (catalog of an exhibition at the Whitney Museum of American Art).

Quotation from *The Attaché, or Sam Slick in England,* by Thomas C. Halliburton, as given in: *Native American Humor,* by Walter Blair. New York, 1937.

§ 60. THE MID-CENTURY CONCEPT OF IMAGINATION.

For Page: "Two Portraits by William Page," by E. P. Richardson, in *Art Quarterly* for spring, 1938.

For Chambers: "Thomas Chambers, Man or Myth?" by Nina Fletcher Little, in *Antiques* for March, 1948.

For Quidor: *John Quidor,* by John I. H. Baur. Brooklyn, 1942 (catalog of an exhibition at the Brooklyn Museum).

§ 61. MID-CENTURY STILL-LIFE.

See Born: *op. cit.,* § 42, Still-life.

§ 62. PAINTERS WORKING FOR REPRODUCTION.

For Harvey: "George Harvey, English Painter of Atmospheric Landscape in America," by Donald A. Shelley, in *American Collector* for April, 1948.

For Bartlett: *William Henry Bartlett and the American Scene,* by Bartlett Cowdrey. New York, 1941 (reprinted from *New York History*).

For Audubon: *Audubon the Naturalist,* by Francis Hobart Herrick. 2 vols. New York, 1917. *Audubon,* by Constance Rourke. New York, 1936. *Audubon, an Intimate Life . . .* by Stanley Clisby Arthur. New Orleans, 1937. *Audubon's America,* ed. Donald Culross Peattie. Boston, 1940. "John James Audubon, Artist," by Donald A. Shelley, in *Magazine of Art* for May, 1946.

For steel engraving: "The Steel Plate in American Art," by *Frank Weitenkampf*, in *Art in America* for Sept., 1947. *American Literary Annuals and Gift Books*, by Ralph Thompson. New York, 1936 (especially Chap. IV).

For Lilly Spencer: "Lilly Martin Spencer, Painter of the American Sentimental Scene," by Bartlett Cowdrey, in *American Collector* for Aug., 1944.

For Currier & Ives: *Currier and Ives, Printmakers to the American People,* by Harry T. Peters. 2 vols. Garden City, 1929 and 1931.

For Tait: "Arthur F. Tait in Painting and Lithography," by Homer Eaton Keyes, in *Antiques* for July, 1933. "Arthur Fitzwilliam Tait, Master of the American Sporting Scene," by Bartlett Cowdrey, in *American Collector* for Jan., 1945.

For Durrie: "George Henry Durrie, Artist," by Mary Clarissa Durrie, in *Antiques* for July, 1937. *George Henry Durrie, Connecticut Painter of American Life.* Hartford, 1947 (catalog of an exhibition at the Wadsworth Atheneum).

§ 63. MID-CENTURY ARTISANS AND AMATEURS.

See general works cited, § 48.

Information about Sebastian Heine kindly supplied by Mr. Russell H. Anderson director, Western Reserve Historical Society, Cleveland, Ohio.

For Miller: "A Pennsylvania Artist in Old New York," by J. Bennett Nolan, in *Antiques* for Oct., 1935.

For Shaker texts: "Shaker Inspirational Drawings," by Edward D. Andrews, in *Antiques* for Dec., 1945.

For drawings in charcoal and crayon: "Monochromatic Drawing, a Forgotten Branch of American Art," by James Thomas Flexner, in *Magazine of Art* for Feb., 1945.

For Ellsworth: *James Sanford Ellsworth, an Early New England Miniaturist,* by Frederic Fairchild Sherman. New York, 1926.

For King: "Josiah Brown King," by Julia D. S. Snow, in *Antiques* for March, 1932.

For Davis: "Joseph H. Davis, New Hampshire Artist of the 1830's," by Frank O. Spinney, in *Antiques* for Oct., 1943 and May, 1944.

For Bradley: "Portraits in Kent, Connecticut," by Mrs. H. C. Nelson, in *International Studio* for March, 1925. These portraits have been since identified as by Bradley. "J. H. Bradley, Portrait Painter," by Jean Lipman, in *Art in America* for July, 1945. "Another Signed Bradley Portrait," by Wolfgang Stechow, in *Art in America* for Jan., 1946.

For Hidley: "Joseph H. Hidley," by Jean Lipman, in *Art in America* for June, 1947.

For Edward Hicks and Stock: Cahill, *op. cit.,* general list.

For Bard: "James and John Bard, Painters of Steamboat Portraits," by Harold S. Sniffen and Alexander C. Brown, in *Art in America* for April, 1949.

For Prior: "The 'Painting Garret' Artist," by Grace Adams Lyman, in *Antiques* for Nov., 1934. "William M. Prior, Traveling Artist and His In-laws, the Painting Hamblens," by Nina Fletcher Little, in *Antiques* for Jan., 1948.

For Rufus Porter: see Lipman, *op. cit.,* § 48.

§ 64. MID-CENTURY DILETTANTES.

For Read and Taylor: *Yesterdays in Chester County Art.* Philadelphia, 1936.

For C. P. Cranch: *Life and Letters of Christopher Pearse Cranch,* by Leonora Cranch Scots. Boston, 1917. A new biography by Professor F. DeWolfe Miller, of the

University of Tennessee, will soon appear; this will give due importance to the painting.

For Landis: "John Landis, Painter," by Mrs. Mary N. Robinson, in *Lancaster County Papers*, Lancaster, Pa., 1912.

For Genin: *Selections from the Works of the Late Sylvester Genin, Esq., in Poetry, Prose, and Historical Design.* New York, 1855.

§ 65. RETROSPECT FROM THE YEAR 1860.

For Woodville: "Richard Caton Woodville, an American Genre Painter," by Bartlett Cowdrey, in *American Collector* for April, 1944.

For Greenough's ideas: *Form and Function*, ed. Harold A. Small. Berkeley, 1947.

Quotation from *The Widow Bedott Papers*, by Frances M. Whitcher, as given in *Native American Humor*, by Walter Blair. New York, 1937.

DIVISION SIX: Aftermath of the Civil War—1860 to 1880

§ 66. THE AGE OF PLUNDER.

American Painters, by George William Sheldon. New York, 1879. Valuable for first-hand reports of the ideas of the painters themselves.

The Brown Decades: A Study of the Arts in America, by Lewis Mumford. New York, 1931.

Quotation about furniture: *Art Decoration Applied to Furniture*, by Harriet Prescott Spofford, as given in *Oscar Wilde Discovers America*, by Lloyd Lewis and Henry Justin Smith. New York, 1936.

For American painting in the Centennial: "The Painters of the Hudson River School in the Philadelphia Centennial of 1876," by Mildred Byars Matthews, in *Art in America* for July, 1946.

§ 67. PAINTING IN THE REMOTER REGIONS.

For Fisher: *Manuscript Notes*, by Helen G. McCormack, at Frick Art Reference Library.

For Guillaume and Elder: *Portraiture in the Virginia Historical Society*, by Alexander Wilbourne Weddell. Richmond, Va., 1945.

For C. W. Chapman: "Conrad Wise Chapman's Valley of Mexico," by James B. Ford, in *Gazette des beaux-arts* for Oct., 1942.

Quotation about Texas from *Trader Horn* (by Alfred Aloysius Smith). 3 vols. New York, 1928 (Vol. 2, p. 267).

For California: Neuhaus, *op. cit.*, § 56.

§ 68. POSTWAR PORTRAITURE.

Lincoln in Portraiture, by Rufus W. Wilson. New York, 1935.

"A Rare New Find of Lincoln Material," by Stefan Lorant, in *Saturday Evening Post* for July 19, 1947.

§ 69. POSTWAR HISTORY PAINTING.

For Brumidi: Fairman, *op. cit.*, § 44.

For various pictures of the Custer episode: *Life* for June 21, 1948.

§ 70. POSTWAR ANECDOTE.

For Oertle: *A Vision Realized: A Life Story of Rev. J. A. Oertle*, by J. F. Oertle. Milwaukee, 1912.

For Willard: *The Spirit of '76: Some Recollections of the Artist and the Painting*, by Henry K. Devereux. Cleveland, 1926. "The Spirit of '76," by Alberta Thorne Daywalt, in *Antiques* for July, 1941.

For Henry: *Edward Lamson Henry*, by Elizabeth McCausland. Albany, 1945. "Edward Lamson Henry, an American Genre Painter," by Bartlett Cowdrey, in *American Collector* for July, 1945.

§ 71. POSTWAR ARTISANS AND AMATEURS.

For Riley: Wright, *op. cit.*, § 7.

For Wallace: Burnet, *op. cit.*, § 48.

For Field: "Erastus Salisbury Field," by Frederick B. Robinson, in *Art in America* for Oct., 1942. "A Check List . . ." by Agnes M. Dods, in *Art in America* for June, 1944.

§ 72. POSTWAR STILL-LIFE.

See Born: *op. cit.*, § 42, Still-life.

For Brumidi and Costaggini: Fairman, *op. cit.*, § 44.

For Harnett: "Notes on William H. Harnett," by Hermann W. Williams, Jr., in *Antiques* for June, 1943. "Harnett, One Century," by Alfred Frankenstein, in *Art News* for Sept., 1948.

For Harnett and Peto: "Harnett True and False," by Alfred Frankenstein, in *Art Bulletin* for March, 1949. "Harnett and Peto, a Note on Style," by Lloyd Goodrich, *loc. cit.*

For Haberle: "Haberle, or the Illusion of the Real," by Alfred Frankenstein, in *Magazine of Art* for Oct., 1948.

For this group as a whole: "Entirely with the Brush and the Naked Eye," by Alfred Frankenstein, in *Illusionism and trompe l'oeil*, San Francisco, 1949 (catalog of an exhibition at the California Palace of the Legion of Honor).

§ 73. GRANDILOQUENT LANDSCAPE.

See general bibliography, § 42.

For Church: *Paintings by Frederick Edwin Church*. Introduction by Charles Dudley Warner. New York, 1900 (catalog of an exhibition at the Metropolitan Museum of Art). "Scientific Sources of the Full-Length Landscape, 1850," by Albert Ten Eyck Gardner, in *Metropolitan Museum Bulletin* for Oct., 1945.

For Thomas Moran: "Thomas Moran, Dean of Our Painters," by Harriet R. Gillespie, in *International Studio* for May, 1924. "The Watercolors of Thomas Moran," by Robert Allerton Parker, in *International Studio* for March, 1941.

§ 74. LESSER LANDSCAPE.

For Miller: "William Rickaby Miller," by Donald A. Shelley, in *Art in America* for Nov., 1947.

For American Pre-Raphaelites: "Comment," by Elizabeth Luther Cary, in *New York*

Times for Jan. 31, 1932. "The American Pre-Raphaelites," by D. H. Dickson, in *Art in America* for July, 1942.

For W. T. Richards: *William Trost Richards: A Brief Outline of His Life and Art,* by Harrison S. Morris. Philadelphia, 1912.

§ 75. POETIC LANDSCAPE.

For Inness: *George Inness: The Man and His Art,* by Elliott Daingerfield. New York, 1911. *Life, Art, and Letters of George Inness,* by George Inness, Jr. New York, 1917. "Half-Forgotten Poet," by John Cournos, in *Art News* for July, 1944. *George Inness, an American Landscape Painter,* by Elizabeth McCausland. New York, 1946.

For Wyant: *Alexander Wyant,* by Eliot Clark. New York, 1916.

For Martin: *Homer Dodge Martin: A Reminiscence,* by Elizabeth Gilbert Martin. New York, 1904. *Homer Martin, Poet in Landscape,* by Frank Jewett Mather, Jr. New York, 1912.

For Blakelock: *Ralph Albert Blakelock,* by Lloyd Goodrich. New York, 1947 (catalog of an exhibition at the Whitney Museum of American Art). See notes there given for bibliography of earlier material.

§ 76. POETIC FIGURE PAINTING.

For Johnson: *Eastman Johnson, an American Genre Painter,* by John I. H. Baur. Brooklyn, 1940 (catalog of an exhibition at the Brooklyn Museum). See notes there given for bibliography of earlier material.

For Fuller: *The Life and Works of George Fuller,* by J. B. Millet and others. Boston, 1882. "George Fuller's Pictures," by William Howe Downes, in *International Studio* for July, 1922. *George Fuller.* Introduction by Augustus Vincent Tack. New York, 1923 (catalog of an exhibition at the Metropolitan Museum of Art).

For Newman: "Robert Loftin Newman," by Marshal E. Lundgren, in *American Magazine of Art* for March, 1935.

For Hunt: *Art Talks by William Morris Hunt,* compiled by Helen M. Knowlton. Two series. Boston, 1875 and 1876. *The Art-Life of William Morris Hunt,* by Helen M. Knowlton. Boston, 1899. *Boston Days of William Morris Hunt,* by Martha A. S. Shannon. Boston, 1923. "William Morris Hurt," by Lloyd Goodrich, in *The Arts* for May, 1924.

DIVISION SEVEN: National Culmination

§ 77. THE TRANSFORMATION OF NATURE.

"The Art of Albert P. Ryder," by Roger Fry, in *Burlington Magazine* for April, 1908.

"On Albert P. Ryder," by Walter Pach, in *Scribner's Magazine* for Jan., 1911.

"Albert Ryder," by Duncan Phillips, in *American Magazine of Art* for Aug., 1916.

"The Romantic Spirit in American Art," by Frank Jewett Mather, Jr., in *Nation* for April 12, 1917.

Albert Pinkham Ryder, by Frederic Fairchild Sherman. New York, 1920.

"Albert Ryder As I Knew Him," by William H. Hyde, in *The Arts* for May, 1930.

Men of Art, by Thomas Craven. New York, 1931 (Chap. XIV).

Albert Pinkham Ryder, by Lloyd Goodrich. New York, 1947 (catalog of an exhibition at the Whitney Museum of American Art).

§ 78. THE TRANSCRIPTION OF NATURE.

Winslow Homer, by Lloyd Goodrich. New York, 1945. See notes there given for bibliography of earlier material.

§ 79. THE RENEWAL OF NATURE.

Thomas Eakins, by Lloyd Goodrich. New York, 1933. See notes there given for bibliography of earlier material.

"An Estimate of Thomas Eakins," by Bryson Burroughs, in *Magazine of Art* for July, 1937.

Thomas Eakins. Philadelphia, 1944 (catalog of an exhibition at the Philadelphia Museum).

"Thomas Eakins Today," by Lloyd Goodrich, in *Magazine of Art* for May, 1944.

Thomas Eakins Centennial. New York, 1944 (catalog of an exhibition at M. Knoedler and Company).

§ 80. CONCLUSION.

Homer, Ryder, Eakins. New York, 1930 (catalog of an exhibition at the Museum of Modern Art).

"The Art of Eakins, Homer, and Ryder: A Social Revaluation," by Wallace S. Baldinger, in *Art Quarterly* for summer, 1946.

Index

The more important discussions of painters and ideas are indicated by figures in italics. All pictures cited are listed under the painters' names, with those of unknown authorship collected under Anon.

OWNERS OF THE PAINTINGS MENTIONED IN THIS BOOK

Private owners are named only in cases where the pictures are illustrated.